Britain in the early nineteenth century, then the most advanced bourgeois society, saw the emergence of a new type of landscape painting, distinguished by its modern imagery and innovative naturalism.

However, the development of this new art was not straightforward, since it was difficult to represent the modern within a landscape genre which traditionally centred on the pastoral and the picturesque. It is the various methods by which artists negotiated this problem that provides the focus for this study.

Andrew Hemingway interprets landscape painting of this period as an essentially urban phenomenon. Works by Turner, Constable and Crome, as well as many lesser-known painters, are placed within the context of the London exhibition scene and the social world of the metropolis. Different class attitudes towards art and towards landscape painting in particular are explored through an analysis of contemporary aesthetics, art theory and criticism. The author draws upon the topographical literature of the period, as well as on poetry and social history, to illustrate an extensive account of landscape imagery, which focusses particularly on the representation of rivers and seaside resorts.

This book differs from most studies of British Romantic landscape painting in concentrating neither on individual artists nor on the relationship between landscape painting and rural life. Instead, it examines the ways in which the imagery of landscape functioned in the modern urban milieu of Georgian London.

Landscape imagery and urban culture in early nineteenth-century Britain

Landscape imagery and urban culture in early nineteenth-century Britain

ANDREW HEMINGWAY

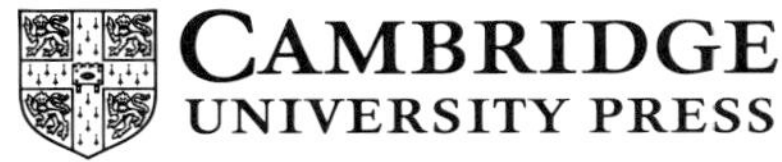
CAMBRIDGE
UNIVERSITY PRESS

Published by the Press Syndicate of the University of Cambridge
The Pitt Building, Trumpington Street, Cambridge CB2 1RP
40 West 20th Street, New York, NY 10011–4211, USA
10 Stamford Road, Oakleigh, Victoria 3166, Australia

First published 1992

Printed in Great Britain at the University Press, Cambridge

A catalogue record for this book is available from the British Library

Library of Congress cataloguing in publication data

Hemingway, Andrew.
Landscape imagery and urban culture in early nineteenth-century Britain / Andrew Hemingway.
p. cm.
Based on the author's thesis.
ISBN 0–521–39118–0 (hardback)
1. Landscape painting, British. 2. Landscape painting – 19th century – Great Britain. 3. Naturalism in art – Great Britain. 4. City and town life in art. I. Title.
ND1354.5.H46 1992
758′.1′41094109034 – dc20 91–28963 CIP

ISBN 0 521 39118 0 hardback

CE

Contents

Plates

Following page 300

Maps

Preface

When I first conceived the plan of this book (or of one something like it) in the late 1970s, both the project of a social history of art and its connection with a radical politics seemed much clearer than they do today. Developments in the history and analysis of culture together with changes in the world order have made the certainties of that moment seem far less certain in many instances. My files of abandoned and altered drafts of these chapters record my responses to the events of the 1980s, whatever else they may record. The reader must decide for her or himself whether or not I changed enough. However, I want to be absolutely clear on one point. There is no value-free history, and this book rests on the presupposition that one of the primary functions of history is as cultural critique. It is also only right to acknowledge that what I have written is the product of a collective enterprise of historical writing. The book partly represents a debate with other scholars committed to a radical art history, and with many more who are not. My debts to, and disagreements from, the work of some particular individuals are recorded in the endnotes and in a few cases in the main text. But there are others whose ideas I can no longer distinguish from my own, either because I have absorbed their work at some subliminal level, or because we have simply arrived at the same conclusions. My hope is that this book will contribute to the type of dialogue on the nature of bourgeois society which can inform a renewed socialist politics. At this moment in time, it seems more necessary than ever to say this.

Acknowledgements

This book has grown out of a doctoral thesis which I began at University College London in 1977. I was fortunate to have as my supervisor Will Vaughan, and it was his continued encouragement and critical stimulus which made the protracted task of completing a part-time doctorate possible. The thesis was typed by David Baughan, who put up with my endless changes with a degree of patience far beyond that I should have expected of him. Much of the book was worked out while I was on the staff of Ealing College of Higher Education. I am grateful to my friends and former colleagues: Barry King, Frank McMahon, Peter Smith, and the late Roger Andersen, all of whom either read early versions of some chapters, or discussed ideas with me at length. The thesis was read in its entirety by David Bindman, John Gage, Dian K. Kriz, Michael Kitson, and Alex Potts, and I have benefited greatly from their advice, even when I haven't followed it. In writing a book of this kind one is inevitably dependent on the assistance of many museum curators and librarians. I can only express my thanks to them here in general terms, but I would like to record my particular appreciation of the help of Norma Watt at Norwich Castle Museum, and Brian Allen, Assistant Director of the Paul Mellon Centre in London. Parts of chapters 8 and 9 were written during a short-term fellowship at the Yale Center for British Art. I am grateful to the staff there for making my stay in New Haven so pleasant, and my use of the Center so productive. My editor, John Trevitt, was not only unfailingly enthusiastic about this project, but also responded sympathetically to my quaint notions of book design. Finally, the process of transforming the thesis into a book could not have been anything like as enjoyable and rewarding as it was without the conversation and friendship of Carol Duncan.

Quotations from the Dawson Turner Correspondence are by permission of the Masters and Fellows of Trinity College, Cambridge.

Photographic acknowledgements can be found at the end of the plate section.

1 Art as seen

Let us imagine the experience of visiting an early nineteenth-century art exhibition. This did not start in the gallery, it started in the city. And most characteristically, of course, in London – that London which Southey described so evocatively through the eyes of his fictional Don Manuel Alvarez Espriella in *Letters from England* (1807). The prospect of Southey's London, seen from St Paul's, although it had nothing individually sublime in it, was sublime from scale alone. 'In every direction the lines of houses ran out as far as the eye could follow them', with 'patches of green more frequently interspersed towards the extremity of the prospect'. The streets nearest the cathedral were 'blackened with moving swarms of men, and lines of carriages'. At ground level, in the West End, the streets had 'the most monotonous appearance imaginable', stretching in strict parallels, the regularity of which was reinforced by the uniform brick walls, windows, and doors of the houses.[1] Some of Southey's contemporaries found the many new public buildings of the metropolis had an almost temporary look – as if they were built just for profit, and not for permanent fame.[2] The extent of London made it unknowable, 'an endless labyrinth of streets'. And in the heart of that labyrinth, as at Cheapside, the crowd was remarkable, both for its numbers, and the determined and regular ways individuals moved about their business. 'Nobody was loitering to look at the beautiful things in the shop windows', windows which were notable for their large plate glass frontage. Displays were ever-changing, as 'the ingenuity of trade, and the ingenuity of fashion are ever producing something new'. Posters and advertisements abounded, and pedestrians had handbills continually thrust upon them.[3]

The interiors of the houses of the better off matched the regularity and newness of their exteriors. Furniture had become an article of fashion too, and the development of veneers made it often seem other than it was. The rapidity of changes of fashion in English dress was notorious, and while it seemed to Southey that women were 'more extravagant than the men', male fashions too were 'followed with avidity in proportion as they are extravagant and indecorous'. In short:

> luxury here fills every head with caprice, from the servant-maid to the peeress, and shops are become exhibitions of fashion.

This urban milieu was thus one which everywhere bore the imprint of what Southey and his contemporaries called 'commerce' and 'luxury', and what is defined in my terms of analysis as 'capital'. Its mark was stamped on persons as much as on buildings.[4]

I do not refer to Southey's account of London as an impartial description. We may understand it as the judgements of a conservative male intellectual, recently settled in the Lakes, who conceived the countryside as the realm of social and moral health. However, what it does offer us is a vivid image of the experience of the city, sharpened by the author's critical distance from what he described.

In the absence of a public gallery devoted to modern British art, the exhibition was the place in which art was given its most public definition.[5] When Southey's *Letters from England* was first published, there were already three institutions which held regular annual exhibitions in the metropolis, and for much of the period covered by this book there were four. In addition, a growing number of individual artists financed shows of their own. By 1822, one critic could observe (doubtless with some exaggeration) that:

> So great is the sensation excited over the Metropolis at this season by the multitude of Exhibitions, that, in the present state of things, the Arts may very truly be said to occupy the public attention next to food and dress.[6]

Exhibitions were certainly one of the most frequented types of 'public amusement', and featured prominently in guide books, such as the successful *Picture of London*, which went through numerous editions over the years from 1800 to 1828. Visitors to any of the major exhibitions went to those parts where crowds were less thick than in the City of London itself, and where trade was less in evidence. They went to Somerset House on the Strand, to the British Institution at 52, Pall Mall, to the Society of British Artists in Suffolk Street (off Pall Mall), or the Water-Colour Societies' exhibitions, which moved around various venues on or off Pall Mall, in Piccadilly and Old Bond Street. The major exhibitions thus took place among or near the capital's major public buildings in the City of Westminster.

In attempting to evoke the experience of these exhibitions, my main resource is the representations of them in the contemporary press.[7] These representations are necessarily interested views. The periodical press was a textual space in which several types of discourse came together: political commentary, reports of accidents and bankruptcies, fashionable news, and reviews of the theatre, literature, and the arts. Although the text of the periodicals is somewhat heterogeneous, these different discourses inform one another in varying degrees. Art criticism was framed by political statements, and frequently functioned as a mode of cultural critique. It provided both entertainment, and a variety of fashionable knowledge – varying in its aims and functions with the character of the periodical concerned. I am not suggesting, therefore, that the reviews give us any direct access to the experience of the exhibitions. But they are an effect of that experience, and the most extensive contemporary account of it to survive.

To judge from this evidence, it seems the different exhibition spaces varied somewhat in social tone. While it was a common criticism at the time that the Royal Academy was not a properly public institution, it was housed from 1780 in the major public building of George III's reign, along with other academic bodies and government offices. Whatever the limitations of Somerset House in terms of the rhetoric of public architecture, the situation of the Academy linked it with the authority of the state.[8] But, run by mere artists, the status of the Academy was somewhat ambiguous, despite its royal charter. The British Institution situated near the royal palaces also offered opulent surroundings, and explicitly excluded artists from its management. With royal patronage, and a substantial number of the nobility in its Directorate, it could hardly fail to become 'the favourite morning lounge of our fashionable amateurs', as the *Morning Post* described it in 1807.[9] The Institution was seen by some as a rival to the Academy, and indeed came to represent a critique of the limitations of that body.

The Water-Colour Societies and Society of British Artists inevitably attempted to dignify their wares through lavish decor, and by private views and dinners. But it was impossible for them to compete in social tone with the Academy and the Institution. Not only were they run by artists, they were artists who were by definition not academicians and who operated them like a stock company. Landscape and genre painters tended to dominate in their management. Water-colour was widely described as a 'humble' branch of art (despite the claims made for it in some periodicals), and it was indissolubly linked with the practice of amateurs, some of whom were also active in the Society of British Artists. The Society of Painters in Water-Colours even acknowledged its commercial function by listing the prices of works in its catalogue.

By 1806, the Academy's exhibitions contained more than nine hundred exhibits, and in the 1820s there were generally more than a thousand objects on show. Works were so crowded, that one critic complained the gilt frames 'notch into one another like the dissected maps for children'.[10] Many commentators described the total effect as overwhelming. The number of visitors was correspondingly large, and in the 1820s an older critic complained of being jostled by the throng. It was difficult to see popular works because of the masses in front of them, and the bonnets of women visitors he found particularly troublesome.[11] To judge from the Academy's accounts, admissions rose somewhat unevenly from 54,853 in 1805 to between a high of 91,827 and a low of 70,036 in the 1820s (figures from 1822 and 1824 respectively).[12] A further indication of the scale of the occasion and the social complexity of the crowd is that a regular entry under exhibition expenses was for the attendance of Bow Street constables, to 'Keep the Peace' as the 1820 accounts put it. By comparison, the attendance at the British Institution seems to have been far less, but even so at times the rooms were so crowded that visitors were turned away.[13] The exhibition itself was smaller, partly because it excluded the portraits which frequently made up almost a half of the Academy's display, and sometimes more. The Institution had a smaller exhibition space than the Academy, and up until 1830 its shows fluctuated between a quarter and rather less than a half the size of that body's. More than 10,000 tickets were sold for its first exhibition in 1806, and the figure fluctuated a little above this for the next two decades.[14]

To put these attendance figures in some perspective: the population of London in 1801 was 900,000, among which it has been estimated there were 4,500 gentry families; 10–15,000 of the wealthy bourgeoisie; and some 30,000 families of tradesmen, businessmen, and professional people of middling wealth. In Britain as a whole there were rather more than 300 aristocratic families.[15] Given the sheer scale of the figures, visitors necessarily came from a range of social groups. In 1822, the *Literary Gazette* observed that to judge from the crowd at the Academy 'all Cockney-land was peopled with connoisseurs', while some years before the *Edinburgh Review* referred to the 'motley multitude' which flocked to exhibitions.[16] Comparing visitors to the British Institution's 'Old Masters' exhibition of 1816 with those of the spring show of contemporary art, the *New Monthly Magazine* observed:

> when the same rooms were filled with portraits, gewgaws, and indifferent battle pieces, they were the morning lounge of military fops from St James Street, and the idle gaping of *all classes*, but the persons who now visit them are of a more refined cast, and seem in some degree to partake of the superiority of the pictures they behold.[17]

Of course the term 'all classes' should not be taken literally, but it does indicate that aristocracy, gentry and different ranks of the bourgeoisie came together in the crowds. This was one of the implications of the status of exhibitions as urban entertainments – they could not depend on an exclusive audience alone if they were to be profitable.

One consistent feature of reviews in newspapers and magazines is comments on the fashionable presence at exhibitions. Whether or not this presence was viewed with approval depended on the political stance of the periodical concerned. Conservative periodicals, those which were most satisfied with the contemporary social order, tended to represent exhibitions and their audiences most favourably. To give some instances, in 1806 the *Oracle* newspaper observed of the Academy show:

> The EXHIBITION ROOMS were crowded during the whole of yesterday. About three o'clock the blaze of beauty was at its meridian, and admirable as are the exertions of our most esteemed Artists, the promenading groupes of Fair Originals seemed to afford certain Connoisseurs more pleasure in the examination, than all the glowing efforts of the pencil.[18]

Such statements appeared frequently in the *Morning Post*, a consistently conservative paper directed at an aristocratic readership. In 1807, it commented on the 'great number of fashionable visitors' at the British Institution, and continued:

> It has been often observed, that female charms are never seen to more advantage than in the Exhibition at Somerset House: the remark may be justly extended to the British Gallery[19]

Such comments not only neatly illustrate assumptions about the gender of the newspaper reader, they also suggest that for this imagined reader, part of the pleasure of the exhibition experience may have been of the same sort as that provided by any other fashionable occasion.

Periodicals which were more critical of the social and political establishment found both the display of wares and the rituals of the audience in front of them less pleasing. Indeed the two were seen as mutually expressive – as Hazlitt observed caustically of the Academy show in 1814:

> Is it at all wonderful, that for such a succession of connoisseurs such a collection of works of art should be provided[20]

Hazlitt's comment appeared in the *Morning Chronicle*, the leading opposition daily paper of the period, and within the liberal press generally, the fashionable presence was much criticized as an improper distraction from the serious contemplation real art demanded. In 1816, the *Champion* described the Academy as 'one of the gay spring-amusements of the metropolis', which was 'at present' only 'a little eclipsed by the Bazaars'.[21]

Complaints that the exhibitions encouraged mediocrity, flashy meretricious effects, and banal subjects were frequent. They were likened to a battle between artists, in which pictures were 'pitted against one another like champions in a ring'.[22] In 1818, the *Annals of the Fine Arts*, one of a new genre of specialist art magazines, observed that the academicians sought to outdo each other, and dashed off their works:

> giving birth to pictures hurried up like new pantomimes at the theatre, and with no other object than that of the theatre, of producing a temporary effect.[23]

To find success, it was claimed, paintings had to make no intellectual demands on the audience, and what the audience sought was primarily novelty – the vicarious thrill of the new and the eye-catching, rather than an art founded on solid principles. Here is Hazlitt again, writing this time in the liberal Sunday paper, the *Examiner*:

> The artists have not time to finish their pictures, or if they have, the effect would be lost in the superficial glare of that hot room, where nothing but rouged cheeks, naked shoulders, and Ackermann's dresses for May, can catch the eye in the crowd and bustle and rapid succession of meretricious attractions, as they do in another hot room of the same equivocal description.[24]

Hazlitt is comparing the exhibition room to a brothel, and this of course reveals that there was a distinctly gendered element to the critique of fashion. The ideal spectator was the intellectual male.[25]

Even when the audience was described as attentive, the quality of its attention was often found lacking. The figure of the ignorant visitor became a stereotype of criticism, and one necessary to license its functions. Such visitors always flocked to the most popular works. The *London Magazine*, probably the most intellectual general magazine of the period, described them in 1821 surrounding Martin's *Belshazzar's Feast* (Yale Center for British Art) at the British Institution 'three deep' – it was necessary to wait an hour to see the picture. The year before, the same critic had evoked 'a parcel of chuckleheaded Papas, doting Mammas, and chalk-and-charcoal-faced misses' 'riding upon one another's backs' to see Wilkie's *Reading of the Will* (Munich, Bayerische Staatsgemaldesammlungen), not to study the expressions of the faces, but to wonder at the 'brass clasps of the strong box'.[26] Such statements invited the reader to identify with a select group among an audience, the majority of which were incapable of 'refined judgement in art' because of the 'obtuseness of vulgar perception'.[27]

In this period, comments on the deficiencies of the growing public for art and literature were made by commentators from across the political spectrum – from conservatives such as Payne Knight and Coleridge, to the Benthamite Radicals – the avant-garde of bourgeois ideology. Although their solutions to what they perceived as the problem differed, they were agreed that its cause lay largely in the commercialization of literature and of art. The aspect of the exhibition display in which this commercialization was most clearly signified was the predominance of portraits at the Academy. In 1820, John Scott, writing in the *London Magazine*, described the impact of the exhibition room as follows:

> we must confess, that, on getting to the top of the Academy stair, and coming full in the way of that flood of brilliancy which streams from the frames and colours of so many whole lengths ... it seemed as if we were committing an unjustifiable intrusion on a number of ladies and gentlemen, whose gowns and coats, wigs, ringlets, and rosy cheeks, concern themselves very much, but have very little relation to Fine Art.[28]

It should be noted that whatever the intellectual grounds of Scott's critique here, it can also be read as manifesting an effect of exclusion. The portraits of fashionables which lined the best places on the Academy's walls spoke to an ideal spectator, a select group among those assembled in front of it. Those who did not belong to the same class as that ideal spectator would presumably have been made to feel the inferiority of their rank. For liberal critics, such paintings were not representations of individuals, rather they were 'portraits of velvet robes, satin gowns, dandy coats and gaudy regimentals' – that is they were representations of the display of rank through dress, and thus displays of rank in their own right with no redeeming aesthetic aspect.[29]

In 1817, a review in the *Champion* asserted:

> The walls of Somerset House are now deplorably stocked with insulted canvass: – It is in this precious temple of art that painters hang out the banners of Mammon; – and it is here that the creatures of *high-life* crowd to gaze at flashes of red and yellow, and to compliment each other on their own gaudy countenances.[30]

Somerset House is like a market or a shop, and it is a fitting setting for the creatures a commercial society produces, and who throng there to disport themselves. But if fashion was generally represented as an effect of commercial societies in contemporary political discourse, the connection was not an unbreakable one. For the bourgeois radicals, fashion was produced by the idleness of aristocratic life, and those who led industrious lives were less likely to succumb to its lure. However, for critics who took such a position there remained the problem that the outlook generated by commercial societies was inherently materialistic – that they generated a preoccupation with gain above all qualitative values. Exhibitions could thus signify the commercial character of British society in another way than through the image of a corrupt landed elite. They could signify it through the dominance of mundane subjects and what was perceived as the absence of imaginative power. This response is exemplified by the effect of the Academy's display of portraits as reported by the Benthamite *London Magazine* in 1828:

> The loyal and domestic character of the English nation eminently stares one in the face on the walls of Somerset House; – the sense of property and self-respect is everywhere inculcated[31]

The 'routine' art of the Academy 'smacks somewhat of the city; is steeped a little in the mud of the Thames'.

The variety of the responses I have been describing can be attributed partly to the interests of the critics. But criticism must work to a large extent with commonplace notions, and most critics presumed that the exhibition would signify the same ideas for a section of the audience, which was also their ideal readers. This readership was offered images of the exhibitions which ranged from gracious scenes of high life in a setting dignified by images of the great and good, to crowded jostling scenes in which pictures were crammed together like wares in a bazaar – where reflection and contemplation were impossible, and the display of personal wealth and status was the main concern of most visitors. Such evidence suggests that if we are to reconstitute the effects of early nineteenth-century pictures on their original audience, we should imagine this as mediated through an overall display of glittering frames containing a wide range of types of work of varying quality, and experienced by visitors whose sense of identity was immediately formed both by the space of the exhibition rooms, and by their passage through the city to reach them.[32]

2 Ideology and naturalism

(i) Aims and approach

I have begun with the city and the exhibition partly to indicate something of the scope and character of my inquiry. This book is centred around what has come to be called the naturalistic landscape painting produced in Britain *c.* 1805–30. Whereas some studies have assumed that the key to interpreting British landscape painting lies in the countryside, I approach it primarily as an urban phenomenon.[1] From this perspective, Constable's adventitious connection with the Vale of Dedham is less significant than his life as an artist in the metropolis, and his real field of campaign becomes the exhibition room and not the fields of Suffolk. Further, landscape painting is understood as part of a larger art system, which means that it cannot be adequately interpreted in isolation from other types of painting, and debates and struggles around the functions and value of art. Landscape paintings were produced for use primarily within urban spaces, and what we can know of their meanings comes mainly from texts produced by urban intellectuals.

I shall start from the premise that the art status we accord to paintings is not the result of some quality inherent in the objects concerned, but was, and continues to be, conferred on them by their functions within a particular set of social relations. In what follows, art is understood as a category of experience, which takes different forms in different social orders. And that experience is understood to have been shaped through historically specific patterns of relations, institutions, and ideologies. The fact that the same objects continue to have an art function in our own society is another matter – those functions are different if genealogically related.[2] It is for this reason that the book does not follow the standard pattern of art historical analysis, in as much as I do not start out from the artists and the objects they made; instead, my inquiry works towards the objects through an analysis of social relations and texts. There are two key theoretical presuppositions which underpin this approach.

Firstly, societies are conceived here as complex structured totalities, which are organized fundamentally around relations of power, whether these are entered into knowingly or unknowingly, willingly or unwillingly. The structure of these multifarious relations we describe by terms such as the family, the economy, state, empire and so on. The position predicated here is that relations of production, reproduction, and exchange offer a primary organizing principle for historical inquiry, since the relations humans enter into in their exploitation of the natural environment and the reproduction of their material existence have a fundamental determining influence on the others. These relations are conceived as structuring society into a hierarchy of classes, and class relations are understood as expropriative and antagonistic in their larger aspects. However, while the basic structural antagonism of capitalist society is that between capital and labour, societies can rarely be characterized in terms of a single mode of production, and almost invariably need to be conceived in terms of complex interrelations between different exploitative relationships. I thus assume that the propertied classes in early nineteenth-century Britain (whatever their common interests) are best understood as a complex of class fractions, divided by the interests particular to various types of expropriation, and also by important regional differences. Differences of gender and ethnicity are seen as embedded in the system of class relations, on which they exert a determining influence, and of which they are inextricably a part.[3]

While class is defined in the first place through an individual's position within the structure of relations of production, reproduction, and exchange, class identity and status are also affected by personal style, family history, education, and taste.[4] Given that class is taken to be a principle of social ontology, it seems reasonable to speak of different class cultures, in the sense that particular class positions predispose individuals to live in different ways, and encounter types of experience which give them a sense of identity with other individuals of the same category, and a sense of difference from those who belong to other categories. However, the varieties of lived experience associated with class categories are not so much my concern here, as the various types of discourse through which class identity was partly formed.

Secondly, communication between individuals depends on systems of signs which are necessarily social and collective. Of these the primary system is language. While language can not convey some of the meanings communicable through other sign systems such as pictorial imagery, it is coterminous with the realm of communicable thought. In Vološinov's words, all non-verbal signs are 'bathed by, suspended in, and cannot be entirely segregated or divorced from the elements of speech'.[5] But while language is understood to exert a determining influence on non-verbal systems, they in turn are understood to influence it. Despite their dependence on language, pictorial sign systems are not taken to function in precisely the same way as language systems.[6] Signs in themselves are treated as essentially neutral material entities. However, they become the focus for conflicts of interest between different social groups, which take the form of struggles over meaning and use. To draw on Vološinov again:

> various different classes will use one and the same language. As a result, differently oriented accents intersect in every ideological sign. Sign becomes an arena of class struggle.[7]

The same argument can be applied to visual signs, and this book is partly concerned with the ways in which naturalistic landscape paintings functioned in relation to the larger struggle over the meanings of artistic signs in the early nineteenth century.

I start off with a brief account of the social relations within which art functioned and artists worked (chapter 3), and proceed to an extended analysis of the specialized discourses through which artists thought their practices, and the meanings of pictures were construed by their audiences (chapters 4 to 7). This part of the book provides the ground on which the analysis of imagery in chapters 8 and 9 is based. Writings on art in the eighteenth and early nineteenth centuries served a variety of functions, and vary in form and content according to the materials from which they were built, the different interests and concerns of their authors, and the practices and institutions to which they were oriented. Looked at in this way, such writings can be understood as falling into three basic categories:

(i) *aesthetics*, that is general theories of the arts in the form of systematic treatises, which were then known as 'philosophical criticism'. These were produced mainly by Scottish university professors or well-to-do amateurs – that is to say by members of the dominant social groups or their professional ideologues.

(ii) *art theory*, that is accounts of the practices and principles of painting produced by professional artists, usually backed by the authority of the Royal Academy, and usually taking the form of lectures designed for art students and a wider audience. Although there was inevitably some overlap with philosophical criticism, academic theory was concerned with a different and narrower range of problems, and was based on different premises in some important respects.

(iii) *art criticism*, that is occasional writings on art in the newspaper and periodical press, primarily in the form of exhibition reviews, and mainly produced by journalists. This kind of writing drew on both aesthetics and art theory, but it was decisively determined by the particular forms demanded by the economics of the press. It is through analysis of this more vernacular category of writing that I shall seek to illustrate the play of class interests in the cultural field, and the contemporary functions of naturalistic landscape painting.

Put crudely then, philosophical criticism may be regarded as representing attitudes to art among the educated element in a dominant patrician culture, academic theory may be regarded as representing the outlook of practising artists, and criticism may be regarded as attempts to interpret art for various sectors of a growing art public, many of whom were outside patrician culture, and some of whom were antagonistic to it.

The discussion of art writing in the early chapters may seem an unduly extended preliminary to the subsequent analysis of imagery, but I regard it as essential at this point in time. To date, the ideological functions of philosophical criticism have not been the subject of sustained investigation, and its implications for the visual arts have received little attention from historians – with the exception of some notable studies of picturesque theory. While the theory of painting has been the subject of a major book, this works within a different conceptual framework from that used here.[8] The criticism of the periodical press has only been mined to discover comments on individual works, and no general analysis of it has been published. Whatever the limitations of exhibition reviews as a record of contemporary attitudes to art and responses to individual works, they are almost the only evidence we have in this area. To interpret them effectively, they must be seen in relation to the more systematic discourses around art, on which they were conceptually dependent. Finally, I should stress that this book is concerned with a particular category of art, and not with a category of material objects. From this perspective, the analysis of texts is as important as the analysis of the objects to which they gave an art status – indeed, the two are inseparable.

The analysis of landscape imagery in chapters 8 and 9 is limited to representations of seaside resorts and rivers. These particular themes were selected because the sheer volume of imagery indicated they were subjects of major importance. While the same approach could have been extended to other landscape types such as urban and agricultural scenes (and to some extent both these types overlap with those I have considered), to establish the meanings of resort and river images involved discussion of such a large quantity of evidence that further chapters were precluded.

While this book is concerned primarily with larger ideological structures and systems of imagery, it also gives certain images more sustained consideration than others. Underyling this distinction is a concept of value which appraises art objects in terms of their cognitive effects. Value is measured in terms both of the acuity and depth with which objects engage with the historical development of the forms of representation involved, and with contemporary beliefs and social phenomena. These kinds of engagement are almost necessarily interrelated. The theory of history underlying this inquiry, and the character of the historical phase I am examining, require that *modernity* be the basic criterion with which I operate.[9] It is a truism that in the years around 1800 Britain was the society in which capital was at its most advanced stage of development, where urban forms most clearly displayed its effects, and where the state was rapidly being forced to adapt to the growing pressures of new capitalist interests. In the previous half-century a new kind of 'scientific' social theory had been developed by Scottish thinkers, a central concern of which was the effects of an unprecedented type of 'commercial society' on psychology and manners, and on the character of public life. This was developed and partially superseded in the first decades of the nineteenth century by the Utilitarians and other radical thinkers, who remorselessly measured established institutions according to their value in some future stage of human development. Concurrently, a self-consciously modern literary genre had emerged in the novel, which was widely understood at the time as a form adapted to the 'middling ranks', which undermined traditional cultural values.[10] In short, there are many kinds of statement produced in this period which indicate that tradition, as we may understand that term in relation to a whole range of aspects of culture, was almost everywhere threatened by 'progress' – for better or worse.

Visual culture was necessarily affected by this sense of immanent historical change among those sections of society which were active, or aspired to be active, in the public sphere. While that relentless questioning of traditional forms which characterizes Modernism had not yet appeared, there was a strand in aesthetic discourse which placed a new emphasis on innovation, and which contributed to a self-consciously progressive position taken in some art criticism. Linked with this were certain new developments in the practice of landscape painting, which I refer to as naturalism. Thus if there was not yet Modernism, theoretical and critical statements in favour of a kind of modernity in visual culture were produced, and these were associated with innovations in pictorial practice. This struggle towards an art of modernity, and the social interests which underlay it, is the ultimate focus of this book.[11]

To avoid ambiguity, I must now explain briefly the specific senses in which I use the terms ideology and naturalism.

(ii) Ideology

The concept of ideology derives from a concern with the analysis of ideas which legitimate the domination of ruling groups, and the distortions of knowledge such legitimation involves. The most extensive and useful elaboration of the concept has been within the Marxist tradition, and in much Marxist theory 'ideology' designates a species of 'false consciousness' which results from the social forms of class societies, and which is to be contrasted with the true knowledge of science. In my usage ideology does not refer to specific forms of miscognition, but rather to the general principle of the social formation of ideas.[12] What matters in socio-historical analysis is how human actions are determined by ideas – whether those ideas are true or false is a secondary consideration. Having said this, the truth value of ideologies may have some bearing on the success or non-success of the practices they tend to promote.

Following the Swedish social theorist Göran Therborn, I take ideology to refer to:

> that aspect of the human condition under which human beings live their lives as conscious actors in a world that makes sense to them in varying degrees.

To consider a 'text or an utterance of ideology' is to examine how it functions in the making and remaking of social identities. It incorporates both institutionalized systems of thought and everyday notions or common sense. Ideologies are seen not as bodies of ideas possessed, but as complex 'processes' of address speaking to the individual: processes which are diverse and often contradictory, and which constantly interact, reinforcing, competing and clashing with one another.[13]

Ideologies are generally not simple expressions of class interests, and neither are relations between them usually directly determined by such interests. They have their own effectivity, and they operate through a complex range of institutions, which in many instances represent sectional as much as class interests. To further their particular interests, different class groups utilize different non-class ideologies, or use the same ones for different ends. Ultimately, the prevailing pattern of social relations structures ideological interrelationships and determines ideological change. Like all aspects of social life, artistic production is framed by ideology, and indeed the very category of art is defined in ideology. This model allows for the fact that ideologies do not have uniform effects but contribute to the formation of very different subjectivities, and that individuals almost invariably hold contradictory positions. Further it reintroduces a dialectical dimension into the understanding of ideology by insisting that individuals are not only subject to a particular definition of their role through ideology, but are also thereby qualified for conscious action. While this book is concerned primarily with the larger structures which inform individuals' sense of their identity and influence their actions, some of the historical evidence it addresses could only be effectively explained through reference to specific people with unique life histories making conscious decisions among a range of alternatives.[14]

The term discourse has already appeared a number of times, and I must say briefly what I mean by it. The term is not used here with reference to the specialized models of linguistic analysis, but instead in a loosely Foucauldian sense, to refer to the 'body of anonymous historical rules' which governs what can be said within a particular category of knowledge within a specific historical context.[15] Philosophical criticism, academic theory, and art criticism are here considered as distinct discourses, in as much as they were governed by somewhat different rules, were enunciated within different institutional frameworks, and were related to different power interests. However, the general approach to the social functions of knowledge here is predicated on the concept of ideology, and not on Foucault's discourse model.[16]

Thus the theory which underpins my inquiry allows considerable autonomy to ideologies and the institutions which sustain them. At a basic level the emergence of a distinct fraction of ideologues in modern societies is seen as causing a double determination of ideological production. This has been well put by Pierre Bourdieu:

> The dominant fractions, whose power is based on economic and political capital, seek to impose the legitimacy of their domination either through their own symbolic production ... or through the intermediary of conservative ideologists who only ever serve the interests of the dominant fractions incidentally, i.e. only to the extent they thereby serve their specific interests as professional producers, and who always threaten to divert to their own advantage the power of defining the social world which they hold by delegation.[17]

The fraction of professional ideologues always tends to make cultural capital pre-eminent in the hierarchy of social distinctions, since it is to this it owes its own authority. Thus ideologies are determined crucially by the functions they serve for both specialist and non-specialist groups. This is undoubtedly a formulation which is more apposite in relation to the technocratic societies of the late twentieth century than it is to British society of the eighteenth and early nineteenth centuries, but it does have an explanatory value in relation to some aspects of art writing of the latter period.

If the formation of ideas is not determined in any simple and direct way by the interests of the ruling class, the production of ideas is always shaped within the overall pattern of class relations. But while ideologies are used to further particular group interests, they are not to be explained by simply allotting them a necessary role in the reproduction of the social order as in Althusser's theory. The actual diversity of ideologies and of ideological conflicts can not be explained if ideologies always function just to secure the incorporation of the dominated.[18]

It is sometimes assumed that art objects function to confirm the central beliefs of a class, presumably because such beliefs need to be manifested in all aspects of its lifestyle. However, while paintings can serve important cognitive functions in some circumstances, they also serve kinds of decorative, entertainment and status functions, which can only be comprehended in relation to a less cognitive theory of use. Such a theory is offered by Bourdieu's concept of the 'habitus': a term which describes the processes of environmental conditioning whereby individuals learn the manners and attitudes appropriate to their social position through their physical environment and personal relationships. Bourdieu defines the habitus as a kind of social unconscious, a 'knowledge without concepts', because it is completely internalized and applied unknowingly. This '*practical* mastery of classifications' is supremely non-reflexive, and is precisely described by the metaphor of taste. While Bourdieu's theory does not give sufficient weight to the cognitive functions of art, it does remind us that we should be prepared to recognize a range of levels of use from the critical and informed to the essentially unreflective, casual, and snobbish – as our own observations might suggest.[19]

In this book the concept of ideology has two main applications: firstly, in relation to the types of statement about art analysed in chapters 4 to 7; and secondly, in relation to the effects of the images discussed in chapters 8 and 9. Philosophical criticism, academic theory, and art criticism are taken to be the specialized discourses most relevant to the interpretation of art images in the period under study, but it is a presupposition here that the meanings of such images were also formed through a range of ideologies which were not understood as having any special relationship with art. Given the range of ideologies which might be drawn on in any act of interpretation (according to the social position of the individual subject), and the different interests they could serve, it follows that images have no single meaning, meaning is always contested in some degree, and the same image can be appropriated by different groups and serve different ideological functions.

(iii) Naturalism and style

Whereas the concept of ideology has been defined primarily within the discipline of sociology, that of naturalism, in the relevant usages, has been defined only within art history. As an art-historical term naturalism has two common applications. Firstly, it is used in a general sense, as Gombrich employs it in *Art and Illusion*, to refer to the dominant paradigm of representation in the art of Ancient Greece and Rome, and in European art from the Renaissance to the late nineteenth century. Secondly, it is used to refer to a specific nineteenth-century aesthetic.

In Gombrich's work naturalism is a kind of epistemological principle, according to which western art developed through a process akin to that of scientific progress, conceived on the model of Karl Popper's philosophy of science. Effectively this is an attempt to rest a conservative defence of Eurocentric humanist values on a now discredited theory of knowledge, and Gombrich's naturalism can not possibly support the massive historical hypothesis he rests on it. (Which is not to deny that it has some explanatory value in relation to the development of representational codes at certain times.) Whether or not one accepts Gombrich's notion that perspective and related devices have a unique and privileged relationship with processes of perception, or prefers the more thorough-going conventionalism of his critics,[20] painting remains fundamentally an art of visual signs, governed by a changing framework of rules, which constitute both the conventions of denotation and the rhetoric of connotation. Thus the principle which underlies my analysis of imagery is a semiotic one, and I use 'naturalism' to refer to a style concept for reasons I shall now explain.

It should be noted to begin with that the term 'naturalism' was not in common currency in relation to the visual arts in the early nineteenth century (although it had some currency in relation to philosophy), and it seems to have been seldom used in connection with painting prior to Ruskin. In his *Elements of Art* of 1809, Shee distinguishes between two great sects in the history of art, who he describes as 'idealists' and 'naturalists', using Michelangelo to epitomize the former, and Rembrandt the latter.[21] The possible meaning of the term to refer to 'a style of accurate external representation' is already evident here, but such usage was uncommon. In France, later in the century, 'naturalism' seems to have been imported into literary theory from the art criticism of Castagnary et al., and came to be associated with the new Realism of Zola and his followers, which involved an 'attempt to apply to literature the discoveries and methods of nineteenth-century science'. Both the literary and pictorial aesthetics of French Naturalism demanded an art which eschewed the picturesque, the historical, and the supernatural, and which concentrated on the representation of the average and the quotidian – on objects which did not conform to conventional aesthetic standards.[22] In its current usage in relation to British landscape art in the early nineteenth century, the term has some of these connotations, but is closer to Gombrich's sense.

The main text which established this usage was John Gage's 1969 exhibition catalogue *A Decade of English Naturalism 1810–1820*, an erudite if brief essay, without theoretical pretensions. The exhibition brought together works by a wide range of artists which were said to belong to a distinct tendency characterized by 'a thirst for objectivity' and 'the innocent eye'. The 'philosophy of naturalism' entailed:

> a conception of landscape painting as essentially a scientific activity, or, at least, as an activity involving a scientific commitment to research.

Effectively this meant a commitment to recording the observable variety of nature, to researching the particular, and 'above all', a concern with the changing effects of light. At the level of practice naturalism involved numerous studies of atmospheric effects, and an 'attempt to close the gap between outdoor sketch and finished picture'.[23]

Many of the landscape paintings included in *A Decade of English Naturalism* are representations of social life as well as of atmospheric phenomena and specific places, but although Gage linked naturalism to a pre-occupation with English subject matter, he gave little attention to iconology. This omission suggests that naturalism is to be seen as an approach to representation, without any strong implications for what was represented – a usage which relates to what I shall describe, somewhat tongue-in-cheek, as the Gombrichism of the essay.[24]

Gombrich's argument that in the western tradition painting had been 'pursued as a science' through a process of 'ceaseless experimentation' contributed to an over-emphasis on science and observational procedures. As Gage acknowledged in a lecture at the Polytechnic of Central London in 1976, the term science did not have the same connotations in the early nineteenth century as it does today, and referred to a range of different practices and institutions.[25] Raymond Williams has argued that by this time the contrast between science and art implied a distinction between a knowledge which depended on theoretical principles and experimental demonstration, as opposed to one which depended on practical skills and experience.[26]

Thus Constable's famous assertion in his Fourth Lecture at the Royal Institution that:

> Painting is a science, and should be pursued as an inquiry into the laws of nature. Why, then, may not landscapes be considered as a branch of natural philosophy, of which pictures are but the experiments?[27]

needs to be seen as a statement that painting was not merely a mechanical skill, but depended on principles and theoretical knowledge, rather than as a statement of the need for a disinterested observation of natural phenomena. As Gage noted in 1976, the application of the term experiment in relation to painting was not new – and neither was that of the term science. Constable's idol, Reynolds, used the term on at least three occasions in his *Discourses*: to distinguish painting as a liberal art from a 'mechanical *trade*', to distinguish it as a practice requiring a 'profound knowledge of ends and means', and to compare it with 'experimental philosophy'. However, more directly comparable is John Opie's recommendation that to develop an understanding of chiaroscuro, the young artist should 'practice a scientific observation of the more enlarged phenomena of nature, and a thorough investigation of the works of those masters who have excelled in this important branch of the art'. Opie is careful to insist that the artist does not need to be 'profoundly versed in optics' to achieve this.[28]

By the time Constable delivered his lectures, late in life, his work was far more overtly symbolic than it had been in 1810–20. In his Second Lecture he was explicit that the route to excellence was not through 'servile' imitation of nature, and it is reported that when he delivered the lecture in Worcester he gave a eulogy on the landscapes of the 'ancient masters', and condemned those who merely copied nature 'without a sense of her grandeur or her real beauty'. He then went on:

> The works of the truly great men who have shone in art were not mere copies of the productions of Nature, which can never be more than servile imitations. Yet, it should be remembered that the study of Nature in her most minute details is indispensable and can never be made in vain.[29]

The second of these sentences can be interpreted as an attempt to redress the influence of what Constable regarded as an overemphasis on generalization in the theory of Reynolds and other academic authorities, yet he himself follows academic theory exactly in his attachment to the principle of selection. According to him, English landscape painting must become a 'General Landscape' and a 'classical art'.[30] Constable's concern with observation and details always needs to be set in relation to his overall conception of landscape painting as a didactic genre, which conveyed significant moral truths through unity of effect and the association of ideas.

I am thus suggesting that the concept of 'science' which underpinned the practice of Constable and other landscape painters of his period can not be adequately registered through the transhistorical category of Gombrich's naturalism, and that it was a concept which was as much oriented to expression as it was to observation and description. Gage's debt to Gombrich is given away partly by the fact that naturalism is described mainly in terms of method, procedure, and attitude. This led to an undue emphasis on sketching practices, and allowed works very different in their formal characteristics to be brought together under the same label, without explanation or qualification.

Despite the conceptual problems which *A Decade of English Naturalism* raises, it remains valuable as a serious attempt to define and explain a major trend in early nineteenth-century landscape painting. However, it seems to me unacceptable to define naturalism primarily in terms of procedure and artistic attitudes, because these do not in themselves constitute the semantic functions of objects which I believe should be art history's primary concern. Indeed, the preoccupation with procedures reflects the folklore so endemic in bourgeois art history that the individual maker confers meaning on art objects. Admittedly, if the idea that some types of work are produced through direct observation has widespread currency, it may stimulate a particular response to them as a result of the value accorded to such practices in discourses about art – but ultimately, it is the presence in the work of features which signify either direct observation or the accurate description of natural phenomena which matter. Such features can be produced with or without the observational procedures they supposedly imply. At a semantic level, it is the finished work and the discourses in relation to which it is situated which produce meanings. Thus, if naturalism is to have value as an interpretative category, it needs to be reconstituted in terms of a definition as style.

If the analysis of style is not to become a pursuit of formal typologies which segregates art objects from the historical process as a whole, and if the material characteristics of art objects are to be accorded a proper effectivity as signifiers, no firm distinctions can be drawn between style and subject, or form and content. Nelson Goodman has made this point with characteristic pithiness:

> Style comprises certain characteristic features both of what is said and how it is said, both of subject and of wording, both of content and of form.

It is a complex property which involves a range of features. Indeed, Goodman has made the interesting suggestion that most works are in several styles, which are present in varying degrees, and which intersect in various ways. It comprises the features of the symbolic functioning of a work that characterize it as belonging to an author, a period, or a school.[31]

In this book, therefore, I use naturalistic landscape painting as a period style concept, which embraces types of painting in both oil and water-colour, which were understood as accurate representations of real places in their contemporary appearance, as if seen at particular times of day, in specific seasonal moments, in specific atmospheric conditions. Historical and poetic landscape paintings are excluded from this category, which was partly defined in contemporary critical discourse in terms of differences from them. Crucial to this naturalistic painting was the new importance accorded to topography in its different forms, which was itself regarded as a 'science' in this period,[32] and beliefs about the significance of the British landscape, which derived from such discourses as association aesthetics and nature poetry. This kind of painting could involve procedures of the kind Gage identified, and some others he did not discuss, but my definition does not entail procedures except in so far as they were signified by certain formal characteristics. None the less, I do acknowledge that outdoor sketching procedures can have a determining effect on the appearance of paintings, and that some of the most exciting images of the period were partly produced through them. Further, it is accepted that a new emphasis on direct observation from the motiv contributed to formal innovation in landscape painting, and it will be argued that it also helped to bring about an engagement with new types of modern subject matter. As in late nineteenth-century France, naturalism and Naturalism were interrelated.

(iv) Naturalism and the picturesque

The emergence of naturalism may be conceived partly as a critique of the category of the picturesque, a critique articulated through both theory and practice. While the picturesque aesthetic had certainly been a key feature in the process through which the British landscape came to be conceived as an aesthetic object, I will argue that it had to be transformed or even denied in the formation of naturalism.[33] Naturalism involved a radical shift in the imagery of rustic labour, together with a new concern with painting *sur le motif* and a quite different approach to technique and colour. What I am pointing to here, is the marked distinction between the 'elegant' forms used to represent the labouring population in Gainsborough's *Cottage Door* (Huntington Art Gallery, San Marino) of 1780 or Westall's *Harvesters in a Storm* (Private Collection) of 1796, and the circumstantial description of dress and actions in Linnell's *Kensington Gravel Pits* (Tate Gallery, *Plate 4*) of 1813 or Lewis's *Harvest Scene* (Tate Gallery, *Plate 5*) of 1816. I would equally wish to stress the distinction between the generalized signs for trees and locale in the former, and the topographical character of the latter. As I shall show, these differences were seen as highly significant at the time.

The picturesque aesthetic, as first defined by Gilpin, was founded fundamentally on a distinction between the rules of selection derivable from painting, and the overwhelming variety of natural phenomena which presented themselves to the amateur artist and traveller. In the first of his published tours, the *Observations on the River Wye* of 1782, Gilpin described his aim as that of:

> not barely examining the face of a country; but of examining by the rules of picturesque beauty: that of not merely describing; but of adapting the description of natural scenery to the principles of artificial landscape; and of opening the sources of those pleasures, which are derived from the comparison.[34]

The pursuit of the picturesque traveller is described similarly in his most considered pronouncement, the *Three Essays: On Picturesque Beauty; On Picturesque Travel; and On Sketching Landscape*, which appeared a decade later: that is to examine the 'face of nature' by the '*rules of painting*'.[35] While it is true that Gilpin always emphasizes that nature is superior to art, this was a truism of philosophical criticism, and an inescapable consequence of the current natural theology. Gilpin describes the traveller's application of the rules of the picturesque as a 'scientific employment', which he recommends as a 'rational and agreeable amusement' preferable to the licentious pleasures of the age. The 'chief pleasure' of travel does not lie in this, but rather in a kind of Shaftesburyan trance affected by the spectacle of nature in the large:

> We are most delighted, when some grand scene, tho perhaps of incorrect composition, rising before the eye, strikes us beyond the power of thought – when the *vox faucibus haeret*; and every mental operation is suspended. In this pause of intellect; in this deliquium of the soul, an enthusiastic sensation of pleasure overspreads it, *previous to any examination by the rules of art*.[36]

This 'enthusiastic sensation of pleasure' we experience when we 'feel the landscape as a whole' – that is when we apprehend the divine order which underlies it.[37] It is not produced by the details of ordinary nature which Gilpin found offensive to taste, and consequently inappropriate to art.

Gilpin's picturesque was to be found only in the wilder kinds of natural scenery, and he took as his model the works of Salvator Rosa:

> the wild and rough parts of nature produce the strongest effects on the imagination; and we may add, they are the only objects in landscape, which please the picturesque eye.

His preference was for the 'Grand Style' in landscape painting, and he was insistent that the painter must not simply copy nature. It was a convention of contemporary tourist literature on the Lakes to emphasize that landscape is infinitely varied according to the changes of light and shade, and Gilpin says that there are few landscapes which do not have their 'happy moments', and advises the traveller that 'he who does not attend to the variations of the atmosphere, loses half the beauty of the views'. In a premonition of Constable, he described light and shade as the 'Life & Soul' of landscape painting, and the sky as 'an endless study for the painter'. But Gilpin did not approve of unselective representation of natural phenomena, and in contrast to Constable, he insisted that painting had no room for exact observation.[38]

Gilpin accepted the common notion that imitation is in itself a source of pleasure, but agreed with Reynolds and so many other theorists, that it is a pleasure which even the ignorant enjoy, while the sophisticated picturesque spectator looks for beauty in objects themselves and in their combination. However, Gilpin recognized that his type of picturesque landscape was unappealing even to many in the dominant classes, a fact which he attributed to the gloomy associations that the sublime scenes of nature tended to evoke in the average spectator:

> There are few, who do not prefer the busy scenes of cultivation to the grandest scenes of nature's productions. In general indeed, when we meet with a description of a pleasing country, we hear of hay-cocks, or waving corn-fields, or labourers at their plough, or other circumstances and objects, which the picturesque eye always wishes to exclude.

Most people it seems prefer a cultivated landscape, but Gilpin consistently insists that utility and the picturesque are incompatible. He wrote of the 'picturesque eye':

> It is not its business, to consider matters of utility. It has nothing to do with the affairs of the plough, and the spade; but merely examines the face of nature as a beautiful object.[39]

It is clear that Gilpin's usage of the term 'picturesque' represented a considerable narrowing of its meaning in comparison say with the way that Arthur Young had used it to describe cultivated landscape in the early 1770s, or in relation to its use in tourist literature, which generally emphasized the pleasures to be derived from variety and the evidences of agricultural prosperity.[40] Gilpin himself admitted a pleasure to be derived from 'the works of tillage' and allowed them a place in pastoral poetry, but he denied that they had qualities suitable for pictorial representation and they were thus not picturesque. Man deforms nature, and all his distinctions of property are a nuisance to the 'picturesque eye'. Gilpin could not tolerate the cottage as a subject in painting, and as to figures, the picturesque conflicted with utility again, for 'the industrious mechanic' might be pleasing from a moral point of view, but he detracted from the dignity of the picture.[41] It is ironic that Reynolds found Gilpin's picturesque more characteristic of the lower than the higher schools, for Gilpin quite simply did not like the works of the seventeenth-century Dutch painters, whose 'colouring does not compensate for their subjects'.[42]

It is clear from the several satires it provoked, such as William Combe's *Dr Syntax in Search of the Picturesque* (1812) and Thomas Love Peacock's *Headlong Hall*, that Gilpin's concept of the picturesque was far from representing a general attitude. Agricultural prosperity was of compelling interest to the gentry in the late eighteenth century, and the majority of that class would probably have found the idea of taking pleasure in desolate scenery as artificial as Jane Austen's Edward Ferrars does in *Sense and Sensibility* (1811). The existence of a dual standard by which natural landscape could be assessed has been shown by John Barrell in his analysis of the writings of John Clark, Arthur Young, Thomas Ruggles and others for the *Annals of Agriculture*. In this publication the writer's commitment was inevitably first and foremost to agricultural improvement as an economic desideratum. But although the associations of 'improved' landscapes made them a source of pleasure, they were also felt to conflict in some degree with an influential norm of taste which was virtually inimical to the appearance of cultivation.[43] Naturalistic painting would take up precisely the kind of improved landscape which Gilpin's picturesque had so firmly excluded.

As is well known, whereas Gilpin's definition of the picturesque was oriented primarily to the experience of travel for pleasure and amateur sketching, the codification of the picturesque in the 1790s by Uvedale Price and Richard Payne Knight was oriented primarily to the gentleman 'improver' making a leisure park out of his estate. Gilpin regarded gardens as 'but paltry imitations of the genuine works of nature'. Price also believed that the garden was but an imitation, and maintained that the closer it seemed to nature unadorned the better it was.[44] However Price's picturesque was not the sublime scenery which epitomized Gilpin's category, and it was modelled on the paintings of his friend Gainsborough and of the seventeenth-century Dutch artists for whom Gilpin had so little time.

Rather than rocks, mountains and castles, Price enthuses over such subjects as 'old neglected bye roads' and 'hollow ways', banks overhung with trees, cart tracks, pollards, old quarries and chalk pits, hovels, cottages, mills, and barns.[45] These are the subjects which have attracted all 'painters who have imitated the more confined scenes of nature', and they should also provide models for the gardener. Although Price did allot associations of utility a role in aesthetic pleasure, he did not specifically do so with regard to agriculture, and thus agricultural landscape seems to offer only a rational and moral satisfaction.[46] As we shall see, Knight's concept of the picturesque was broader and more flexible than Price's, but he also found it exemplified in Dutch art.

The theory of the picturesque certainly had considerable influence on British landscape painting, and particularly water-colour drawing in the late eighteenth and early nineteenth centuries. The tourist routes in the Lake District and North Wales provided a staple subject for artists seeking that combination of the sublime and picturesque Gilpin had recommended,[47] while the tumble-down cottages and overgrown roads of the Pricean variant featured in numerous publications of prints.[48] In his essay on the picturesque of 1797, *Remarks on Rural Scenery*, Constable's early friend and mentor John Thomas Smith drew on the theory of Price and Knight, transforming their recommendations on the landscape garden into prescriptions for the painter. Referring to Knight's 'image of a rustic habitation' in his didactic poem *The Landscape*, Smith emphasized the possibilities of the cottage as a subject for painting, while stressing that he recommended 'rural and cottage scenery' as no more than 'a sort of low-comedy landscape'. Poets such as Thomson, Shenstone, Cooper and others were praised for their 'spirited sketches' of cottages, and the works of Gainsborough were held up as offering 'profound and accurate observations of Nature'. Smith emphasized the non-utilitarian character of the picturesque, decaying ruinous cottages being more picturesque than neat and regular ones, and he recommended scenes in the 'inmost recesses of forests, and most obscure unfrequented villages', 'on the remote wild common – on the straggling undetermined borders of the forest – or in the silent sequestered dell'. In the pursuit of picturesque irregularity and harmonious colour, the artist is free to take liberties of a kind quite unacceptable in topography. But although Smith followed Gilpin in finding 'white' unpicturesque, he did emphasize the importance of studying green, in contrast with the preference for colours of autumnal decay in earlier picturesque theory.[49]

Smith's precepts relate not only to the twenty etchings of cottages published with his essay, they also match with a large body of imagery of similar subjects produced in the years *c.* 1798–1810. Works such as Girtin's *An Overshot Mill in Devon* (*c.* 1798, Leeds City Art Gallery, *Plate 1*), Cotman's *Cottage in Guildford Churchyard* (1800, Nottingham Art Gallery), Crome's *Blacksmith's Shop* (*c.* 1807, Philadelphia Museum of Art) illustrate this category. However, this period also saw the production of a growing volume of images (often by the same artists), which the picturesque aesthetic, as it had been formulated by Gilpin and developed by Price, could not accommodate. Works of this type include Girtin's *White House at Chelsea* (1800, Tate Gallery), Cotman's *Ploughed Field* (1808, Leeds Art Gallery, *Plate 2*), Constable's *Vale of Dedham* (1815, Museum of Fine Arts, Boston, *Plate 3*), the works of Linnell and Lewis (*Plates 4 and 5*) I referred to earlier, and many more. All of these contain representations of modern utilitarian activities, and depart from picturesque precepts in colour or composition or both: Girtin's image with its barge, its expansive foreground without picturesque incident and its striking white house; Cotman's expanse of enclosed, flat, ploughed land and its tidy-looking labourer; Constable's dung-heap, his busy agricultural activity, and his fresh colouring; and Linnell's foreground of mundane toiling figures, and his sharp, bright, colours and hard technique.[50]

What appears to happen in the early nineteenth century is that landscape painters became increasingly restive with academic categorization of their genre and increasingly interested in adapting the topographical mode and Dutch models as a vehicle for serious expression. Linked with this was a more critical attitude to earlier pictorial conventions, and a commitment to improvisation and experiment *sur le motif*, which may have some connection with the authority of the natural sciences, and their increasing popularization. This new approach inevitably led to a critical attitude towards the restrictive landscape aesthetic of the eighteenth-century picturesque. Further this category was tainted by its connection with amateurism at a time when artists generally were increasingly concerned with establishing the specialist nature of their practices. In 1806 the *Edinburgh Review* referred dismissively to 'mere artists, and the picturesque men of Mr Gilpin's school', who circumscribed drawing with 'narrowness and pedantry' because they were unable to surmount the difficulties of representing many aspects of nature. The *London Magazine* in 1825 was even more scathing, referring to 'the vile and contemptible daubs' of Gilpin, which were upheld only by the ignorant, and 'utterly unlike' either nature or art. They were 'worthy of the writings of this feeble and miserable quack'.[51] Both Gilpin's aesthetic and his approach to sketching looked unacceptably *unscientific* in

the early nineteenth century. I shall also argue that it conflicted with a powerful aesthetic of originality which influenced both artists and critics in the period.

By 1800 the term 'picturesque' was used to cover a far wider range of phenomena than those which Gilpin or even Price had incorporated in their categories, but it still implied certain variegated effects of contrasted light and shade which were regarded as the central principle of pictorial organization by those committed to the theory. Further, there was a distinction between the picturesque and the 'natural', although the boundary between them was not sharply defined. Thus in the 'fragment' 'On the Picturesque and the Ideal', published in his *Table Talk* (1821–2), Hazlitt defines the 'natural in visible objects' as that which is 'ordinarily presented to the senses', while the picturesque 'is that which stands out, and catches the attention by some striking peculiarity'. I don't want to suggest that Hazlitt's definition was standard, but there is much in it which ties in with more general features of the concept. Thus he exemplifies the picturesque through the work of Rembrandt (as did Payne Knight), and he uses 'an old stump of a tree with ragged bark' and 'a little stunted hedge-row line' to illustrate it in landscape.[52] In the essay 'On Imitation' in *The Round Table*, he defined the picturesque as a pursuit of the 'principles of art' carried to excess.[53]

While those who developed naturalistic landscape painting would probably not have agreed with Hazlitt that Van Dyck's portraits represented the 'purely natural' in art, they would have recognized his distinction. In 1802, Constable's friend and fellow-student in the Academy schools, Andrew Robertson, wrote to his brother recommending direct study from nature and painting on the spot. The letter specifically emphasizes the value of the 'exact copy of nature', even when nature seems 'unpicturesque':

> Often what is least picturesque to the eye, becomes full of character when on paper. Draw and copy the colouring of rocks, stumps, foregrounds, plants, etc. and when you introduce them in landscape, you will be astonished at the originality of them. Clouds, if sketched as they pass, will always carry something to distinguish them from ideal conceptions.
>
> As to colouring let a man look at the camera . . .

The letter proceeds to recommend 'finishing' 'in the field', as opposed to just sketching there. It is this which makes 'the great artist'.[54] Robertson's statement suggests that some artists saw the picturesque as an elastic and extendable category – a conclusion which was also to be drawn by the theorist Payne Knight.

The whole premise of picturesque theory had been that there were a limited range of effects which were suited to pictorial representation, and that these could be effectively discovered from the study of earlier art. This premise was dramatically contradicted in the only developed statement of the naturalistic aesthetic to be produced, that is Henry Richter's short book *Daylight: A Recent Discovery in the Art of Painting* (1817). Richter (1772–1857) was an engraver and water-colour painter active in the Associated Artists in Water-Colours, who made a considerable reputation in the second and third decades of the century by his innovative genre subjects. The text of *Daylight* is based on the fancy that the author, examining an exhibition of Dutch and Flemish pictures at the British Institution, suddenly finds himself surrounded by the ghosts of their authors. He overhears a conversation between them, a young amateur, and a portrait painter, in which the amateur takes the ghosts to task for having only achieved crepuscular tones and colours and never having achieved the representation of ordinary daylight. Speaking to Van Dyck, the amateur argues:

> I am . . . of the opinion, that the effect which the evening sun and a purple sky produce upon objects is infinitely more delightful and affecting to the imagination, than any artificial combination of tints which the most elegant fancy could arrange, or the most fortunate hope to discover in the accidental blottings on the palette.

It is notable that Richter had rejected the academic view, still being reiterated by Thomas Phillips in a lecture of 1829, that the Dutch School had attained 'the most entirely perfect imitation of nature, as seen in her ordinary productions'. In Richter's fantasy Cuyp and Rembrandt are made to see the 'IN-DOOR GLOOM' of their productions, and Cuyp proposes the project that the Directors of the British Institution should:

> form a COLLECTION of genuine studies of light and colour, taken faithfully from Nature itself, out of doors, under all its various aspects

which would provide a school for the study of colouring amongst artists and public. Rembrandt suggests that this would free the Arts from:

> their long and dark imprisonment, and set free the genius of the age from the restraints of AFFECTATION and PREJUDICE

and provide new space for originality.[55]

The main text of *Daylight* is a mere thirteen pages, while the fifty-three pages of notes are the real substance of the book. Apart from a long note on Kant, which is irrelevant to my discussion here, the most important of these is note 4 (pp. 16–60), which is an outspoken attack on the imitation and idolatry of Ancient Art and the 'Old Masters' as irrelevant to the conditions of modern society. The elevation of the study of the 'Old Masters' over the direct study of Nature is:

> the natural consequence of an ignorant and frequently affected admiration of the remains of a LOST ART, so different from the genuine interest which the true master would take in the simple and modest progress of an Art originally springing up from the pure fountain of nature . . .

This 'absurd process' is not the fault of the artists themselves, but is caused by 'the laws which custom and fashion impose upon them', and is the 'great obstacle' in the path of modern art.[56]

As we shall see, this was a position which could have certain political connotations, and Richter himself was a radical democrat, as *Daylight* makes clear.[57] I do not wish to suggest that his radical rejection of earlier artistic models represented the general attitude of those who developed naturalism, but I do regard it as symptomatic of a wider impatience with what were regarded as cramping connoisseurial standards, and a concern with modern techniques and subjects which affected many landscape and genre painters in this period. It was this concern with novelty and modernity which forced a transformation or even a denial of the picturesque. I do not claim that this was entirely clear-cut, but that a rather hazily defined distinction between the natural and picturesque prompted some of the most innovative landscape painting of the period is borne out both by the painting itself and by some of the criticism I shall discuss later.

(v) Naturalism and meaning

The reconceptualization of naturalism as style allows the category to encompass works from a wider time span than the 1810–20 decade. It is evident that from about 1800 a number of artists were exhibiting paintings of English scenes in both water-colours and oil, which were innovative in some of their formal devices, and in the aesthetic pretensions which they gave to images of ordinary objects. Among these, Callcott, Girtin and Turner are pre-eminent, and Turner's paintings of the Thames valley from 1805 onwards are a major focus for the argument of chapter 9. From that year or earlier, a whole range of artists were experimenting with sketching outdoors in oil or water-colour including Constable, Cotman, Delamotte, W. H. Hunt and Linnell. (The vogue for outdoor sketching in water-colour may have been stimulated by Girtin's example.[58]) While some of the major exponents of naturalism in the 1810–20 decade, such as De Wint, Mulready, and G. R. Lewis, seem to have given up landscape painting in oil by 1820, and Turner's work began to take a new direction around that time, works such as Linnell's *Southampton from the River* (1825, Private Collection) and Joseph Stannard's *Buckenham Ferry* (1826, Yale Center for British Art) or *Boats on the Yare, Bramerton* (1828, Fitzwilliam Museum) all come within the reconstituted category. Equally, while there are certainly important changes in Constable's output in the 1820s, I see no reason not to regard much of it as naturalistic, whether produced in the field or not. There are no absolute criteria which would exclude from the category some works of the 1830s and 1840s by F. W. Watts, Frederick Lee, David Roberts, Clarkson Stanfield and others, but it seems to me that their work lacked both the experimental vigour and willingness to go beyond the conventional picturesque which characterized the best painting of the pre-1830 period.

There remains the issue of the very considerable variety of techniques and formal properties utilized within naturalistic painting as redefined. I treat these as semantic variants of period style, and as markers of individual styles. Thus while a range of works by Constable, Danby, Linnell, and Turner might be selected which all represent the same type of object, each would draw differently from the wide repertoire of stylistic patterns and formal variants which made up the legacy of European painting. Formal properties which were understood to refer to the precedents of say Early Flemish painting, or the works of Claude, Cuyp, Rembrandt, Rubens, Ruisdael, or Titian, all had distinctive semantic values which gave different representations of the same kinds of object subtle nuances of meaning. Thus naturalistic painting could draw on a whole range of formal techniques which could perform the same denotative functions, but which differed significantly in their connotations. Particular uses of technique, and particular choices of subject came to be seen as characteristic of individual artists, and in so far as the character of these individuals was constructed as an interpretative category in critical discourse, these properties acquired another semantic function as markers of the personal style of a 'Constable' or 'Turner' as discursive entities.

Finally, there is the question of naturalism as a representation of social life. I shall argue subsequently that early nineteenth-century naturalistic landscape painting was indeed understood as an art of 'accurate external representation', which had achieved unprecedented degrees of verisimilitude, but also that conviction of its verisimilitude functioned as a guarantee of its truth as social representation. While the late nineteenth-century theory of naturalism rested on an essentially secular conception of both nature and society, many prominent landscape painters of *c.* 1800–30, such as Constable and Linnell, had a profoundly theological ontology. For them the natural order was ordained according to divine plan, and proper representation of it had to suggest the power, majesty, and benevolence of the creator among other things. None the less their understanding of the workings of the natural order was not an animistic one, and these painters, far more than their eighteenth-century predecessors, were expected to produce images which could be read as truthful representations of natural phenomena, and which suggested an understanding of their workings as defined by the natural sciences. (In the early nineteenth century science and theology were still hand in hand.) While it was claimed that Wilkie and some other genre painters had achieved a new truth to human character, there is nothing in the 1800–30 period resembling the late nineteenth-century aesthetic of naturalism as it bore on the truthful and scientific representation of social life. However, representations of the quotidian in both genre and landscape painting were interpreted in relation to norms of what constituted truth to behaviour and social role in visual images of contemporary figure types. Thus there was a sense in which early nineteenth-century landscapes were interpreted as a kind of *realism*, although that term had no currency in relation to art during the period in question.

Beyond the level of denotation, and the multiple references to other images characteristic of the European pictorial tradition as practised in the early nineteenth century, interpretation may draw on the complex of discourses and the whole mass of notions engendered through an individual's environment and personal history. While the category of pictures as aesthetic signs is constituted through the discourses of aesthetics, art theory, and criticism, together with the habituation of everyday experience, all of which contribute to make the spectator recognize (usually unconsciously) that looking at a picture properly involves a special attitude, that which the spectator sees in the work, that which it properly denotes, inevitably refers to a wide range of discourses and notions which are not defined as aesthetic. As I shall show, this transformation of a whole individual repertoire of associations in the experience of taste was well-understood in the aesthetic theory of the period.

The problem which besets the analysis of what has been described as the informational aspect of pictorial signs[59] is that of the notorious ambiguity of images, their capacity for multiple interpretation – in short their polysemic character. Denoted objects in their multiple forms have a wide range of possible meanings depending on context and their syntagmatic place in combination with other objects.[60] (The shifting of values associated with particular symbols and motivs, and the total reconstitution of their meanings in some instances is notorious in the history of art.) To establish the ideologies to which an image may have been related by contemporary spectators of different types draws the analyst into a realm of possibilities and probabilities in which she or he can only refer to those which *seem* the most relevant. The limitations of the contemporary press responses to early nineteenth-century paintings are such that it would be impossible to distinguish between the effects of vastly different works on the basis of them. In any case it is the licence of historical inquiry to situate objects in relation to structures and relations of a period which contemporaries may have only dimly grasped, and to find causes and meanings which may have eluded most of them. In short, at the point where empirical sociology comes to its limit, one is forced to adopt a more speculative and hermeneutic method in interpreting art objects.

3 Artists in British society 1800–1830

The aim of this chapter is to sketch the class formations of British society in the early nineteenth century, and to consider the place of artists within them. It offers a model of the relationship between class and political discourse on which the analysis of ideologies in the next three chapters is based, and a characterization of the artist as a social agent which informs the later discussion of individuals.[1]

(i) Politics and class consciousness

It is a commonplace that after the seventeenth-century revolutions Britain no longer had an aristocracy in the continental sense of the term, but in the early nineteenth century there remained a fairly tight oligarchy of landowning families, the most powerful of which commanded vast wealth and considerable political power. Partly because of the economic effects of the Anglo-French Wars, by 1800 landed society was richer than ever before, and the political influence of the titled families was undiminished if not actually increasing.[2] While the term 'aristocracy' was often used to describe the object of criticism in political polemics, the target for reformers in the early nineteenth century was rather what E. P. Thompson has described as 'a secondary complex of predatory interests', comprising a faction of 'great agrarian magnates, privileged merchant capitalists and their hangers-on', which dominated the political machinery of the state and used it to further its own narrow interests – Cobbett's 'Old Corruption'. To some degree this faction did indeed represent the gentry as a class, but its corruption, nepotism, and abuse of privilege led to it being seen as a parasitic and wasteful growth by some of the great magnates themselves, and by some of the middle and lesser gentry. The charges of corruption made against this faction were fuelled by the wanton display of luxury and vice of some of its members, particularly under the Regency, when George III's sons set an example in this respect. The preoccupation of the radical movement of the early nineteenth century with dissipation and corruption provided the fuel for the extraordinary political heat generated by Queen Caroline's Trial in 1820, and it also had considerable influence on the cultural commentaries of the period.[3]

Thompson has argued that the uneasy relationship between gentry and 'plebs', the rough match of paternalism and deference which characterized class struggle for much of the eighteenth century, was ceasing to work even before the 1790s – a development exemplified by the Wilkesite radicalism of the 1760s and 1770s. By 1789, middle-class radicals had already developed an intellectual challenge to paternalism,[4] in the form of Painite ideas which were taken up by urban artisans and transmitted from them to a wider plebeian culture. The late eighteenth century saw the beginnings of a crisis of paternalism which was to become acute in the early nineteenth. This is the phase of *The Making of the English Working Class* – of the formation of a new kind of class consciousness through struggles over new conditions of labour, new experiences of poverty, and new forms of political repression.[5]

The White Terror of the 1790s temporarily broke the back of middle-class radicalism, and, it has been argued, tended to drive many radical Dissenters into political quietism.[6] Part of the middle class realized its desires to participate in the public sphere in a patriotic activism, which in itself seemed threatening to the landed oligarchy.[7] But if the French Revolution and the twenty years of wars with France ultimately served to mobilize the propertied classes into support of the nation's rulers, tensions between the different factions of capital remained. Northern industrial capital emerged as a distinct influence in the early nineteenth century,[8] and there appears to be a consensus that the war years saw the emergence of an identifiable middle-class interest in the political arena, however fragmented and divided it was.[9] The formation of this interest can inevitably be traced back earlier through the campaign for the repeal of the Test and Corporation Acts in 1787–90, the economical and administrative reform movements of the 1780s, and the wave of provincial associations and societies of various sorts which began to appear in these years. However, the economic and political repercussions of the Wars gave it a new militancy. Elements in the middle class formed an anti-war movement, which voiced 'principled' opposition to the government's economic policies, moral outrage over what was seen as an interventionist war with a sovereign state, and savage criticism of the corruption and inefficiency of the dominant oligarchy. The movement's extensive provincial base drew partly upon the grievances of middle-class groups with little or no political representation, who were bitterly opposed to the dominance of Tory and High Church interests at a local level. The resolution of these opposition groups was hardened by loyalist persecution of Dissenters and reformers in the 1790s as a threat to the national interest.[10] While the middle classes were not united in their attitude towards government policies, and had no class-based organization in the political arena, if only a minority of them were actively anti-war and pro-reform, it was an articulate and vocal minority in the years leading up to Waterloo.

Those who sought to represent the middle class to itself as a class were mainly liberal intellectuals who wrote for the growing number of newspapers and magazines, in the latter of which liberal influence predominated.[11] Such writers identified a 'war faction' which enforced an inequitable taxation system, ignored key interests within the state, and depressed the middle class. War was seen as providing economic opportunities for a few wealthy men to exploit, while forcing unnecessary burdens and suffering on other sections of society. The general 'progressivism' and rational Christianity of the opposition movement led it to represent war as a kind of social disease or malaise. This tied in with attacks on the moral laxity and indulgence of the aristocracy, which were part of the strategy by which middle-class identity was established – an identity grounded in a different life experience. The anti-war liberals took from Scottish social theory the idea that the middle class was the backbone of liberty: the main bulwark against aristocratic oppression and corruption. Their ideology was essentially meritocratic, and directly critical of aristocratic privilege. It was a liberalism which was also overtly capitalistic, taking its principles from Smithian economics, and which made little use of arguments concerning the condition of the poor to advance its case. This ideological stance was precisely matched by the distance it took from artisan radicalism and popular agitation.[12]

At the same time as the increase of indirect taxes on the propertied classes led to pressure for 'economic reform' and a widening sensitivity on the issue of corruption, deeper depravation fuelled demands for peace and a more radical reformation among working-class groups. The end of the wars produced an increase in working-class discontent, as many discharged servicemen returned to their homes to find themselves without employment. Thompson has described the years 1815–20 as the heroic age of popular radicalism, a phase which came to an end with the naked class war at Peterloo, and the suppression of the Cato Street conspiracy. These years saw the formation of a new kind of radical movement characterized by a large proletarian following, which bourgeois radicals found increasingly difficult to control, and which reinforced the sense of a distinct middle-class interest.[13]

In the post-war period, bourgeois ideologues found a political focus in opposition to the Corn Laws, as a transparent expression of the interests of the landed classes, and in parliamentary reform as a way of achieving both a more just economic order, and of giving all forms of property their proper political voice. Partisanship of the bourgeoisie took its most pungent and overt form in the 1820s in the output of the group of intellectuals who took Bentham's Utilitarianism as their basic creed: the Philosophic Radicals. The chief organ of this group was the *Westminster Review*, founded in 1824, but Benthamite ideas also influenced established liberal periodicals, such as the *Examiner* and the *London Magazine*.[14] The antipathy of these magazines to the culture of 'aristocracy', to its manners, lifestyle, and tastes (that is to all that could be encapsulated under the head of *fashion*), was intense.[15] The *Westminster* was critical of Whigs and Tories alike, it attacked the clergy and the law, and was unremitting in its hostility to the hereditary nobility. Equally, it was ardent in its identification of the middle class as 'the strength of the community':

> It contains, beyond all comparison, the greatest proportion of the intelligence, industry, and wealth of the state. In it are the heads that invent, and the hands that execute; the enterprise that projects, and the capital by which these projects are carried into operation. The merchant, the manufacturer, the mechanist, the chemist, the artist, those who discover new arts, those who perfect old arts, those who extend science; the men in fact who think for the rest of the world, and who really do the business of the world, are the men of this class.[16]

Yet as this passage suggests, that which the *Westminster* really sought to promote was the influence of intellect and not of property, and the same number of the magazine contained an extended lament on the mercenary character of this 'calculating age'.[17] In this respect it resembled other liberal periodicals which consistently attacked the intellectual bankruptcy of reaction, and identified with what they saw as the progress of mind – the principle of human 'improvement' in general.[18]

The *Westminster* advocated universal male suffrage as a basic principle of justice, it advocated popular education, and argued for all kinds of religious toleration including respect for Judaism and Islam, and was vehemently opposed to slavery. In short, it stood for an embracing progressivism which was far in advance of most middle-class opinion. This is nowhere clearer than in its position on the Woman Question. Although some articles in the magazine placed the activity of women primarily in the domestic sphere, the second number contained a critique of the pervasive idea of 'female character' by the young J. S. Mill, and this was followed in 1826 by an attack on 'gallantry', which called on women to 'discountenance every kind of treatment and behaviour' which presupposed them to be 'helpless, dependent, and frivolous', and to approve only 'those men who regard and treat them as equal to themselves in their capacity for knowledge and usefulness'.[19] This position may be contrasted with the increasing hold of the doctrine of separate spheres, and the general antipathy of middle-class Evangelicalism to public activity by women.[20]

Given the depth of its radicalism, it is not surprising that the *Westminster* found the actual political behaviour of the middle class a disappointment, so that at times it seems to have expected more from the effects of popular education than middle-class action. In 1827 one reviewer asked:

> Will the middle classes ever learn respect for themselves – will they ever learn to vindicate their rank in the Commonwealth? . . . While the predominance of rank yet endures, are they contented to be classed among its humblest adorers – when that falls, are they resolved to have deserved no share in the confidence and affection of the people?

Because it had not acted, the middle class had lost its 'beneficial and natural influence', and, as an article of 1830 made clear, in the *Westminster*'s view this was because of an ungrounded fear that radical reform was a threat to the security of property.[21] In retrospect, it would appear from the popular reading of the provincial middle class that Evangelical religion and the ideal of a traditional order dominated by a modest living, socially responsible gentry, made more sense of their life experience than the grand secularized visions of the *Westminster*.[22] What this illustrates is the distance between a small circle of metropolitan intellectuals and the class they looked to as the agent of political change – a distance which the general theses about ideology set out in chapter 2 would lead us to expect. As we shall see, the positions which liberal intellectuals took on the visual arts were also probably more radical than those of the bulk of the middle class.

As is well known, from the late seventeenth century onwards, new kinds of literary, musical, theatrical, and pictorial production developed which were directed partly, and in some cases primarily, at a bourgeois audience.[23] In relation to the visual arts this development was manifested particularly in the growth of the print market, public exhibitions, and the art trade.[24] This new kind of culture was inseparable from the changing forms of urban society as provincial towns and cities became the focus for a new kind of leisure life – although London remained the nexus of high culture and fashion. The arts, like dress, furniture and a whole range of domestic objects, assumed a new importance as a field for capital investment, and they became the subject of an unprecedented level of public discussion due to their coverage as polite amusements within a rapidly expanding press.

In some degree, landed society benefited from, but did not unequivocally welcome, what was understood as the increasingly *commercial* character of British society. One of the key effects of the growing prosperity of Britain from the 1740s was the increasing pace in changes of fashion, which affected dress and domestic interiors alike. From before the mid-century the tendency of the bourgeoisie and petty-bourgeoisie to imitate the dress and manners of the gentry led to widely voiced fears that fashion was destroying the necessary markers of social distinction.[25] The ideologues of the gentry were also aware that the increasing influence of fashion and commerce in the realm of high culture conflicted with the hierarchical order of subordination, on which social stability and their own power and influence depended.

In a commercial society, the traditional models of civic and public virtue derived from an aristocratic warrior ethic appeared of diminishing relevance, and attempts were made by thinkers such as Adam Smith to resituate virtue in the private sphere as a quality of character. At a lower intellectual level, this was a fundamental belief of many middle-class dissenters. One implication of the decline of what has been called the civic humanist model of the public man was that the conception of art as a mode of inculcating standards of public virtue in society's leaders seemed increasingly problematic, and many theorists of art around 1800 were deeply concerned by the lack of demand for an elevated art in the Grand Style. They generally attributed this improper preference for a privatized art, epitomized in the predominance of portraits in the exhibitions (although it could also be identified in the popularity of genre and landscapes), to the failure of the aristocracy to manifest true public virtues as patrons – an almost inevitable consequence of the luxury and selfishness commercial societies generated. Middle-class radicals, contributing to the heated political discourse of the early nineteenth century through art reviews, went even further, and used this failure to chastise what they saw as the larger shortcomings of the landed classes, and in some cases to claim that the middle class was intrinsically more public-spirited.

(ii) Artistic 'autonomy', patronage, and the market

The issue of the functions of art in a commercial society was linked with the issue of the role of the artist. In a well-known essay Bourdieu has suggested that an 'intellectual field', characteristic of modern societies, was formed at specified historical conjunctures in the development of particular nation states – emerging at rather different moments in France and Britain in the sixteenth and seventeenth centuries. The formation of this relatively autonomous field was the precondition for the emergence of an independent fraction of intellectuals, who do not wish to recognize any obligations other than to the intrinsic demands of their individual 'creative projects'. Such insistence on the independence of intellectual production is characteristic of the intelligentsia. It is linked with the increasingly closed and sectarian character of the artistic community, and with the increasing importance of critics and other cultural authorities such as museum directors and art dealers. Bourdieu links this insistence on the autonomy of the intellectual field (which is ultimately illusory) with the refusal of artists to accept popular taste, to formalism, to art for art's sale, and to the importance of conviction as a criterion of artistic performance.[26]

This vast generalization is marked by Bourdieu's concern with contemporary social analysis, but none the less it is possible to see tendencies which relate to the intellectual field as he defines it in the early nineteenth century, particularly in phenomena associated with that nebulous historical entity: the Romantic Movement. However, an independent fraction of intellectuals is easier to identify among the literary intelligentsia than it is among pictorial artists, and it was writers who articulated more clearly the idea of an autonomous art, which was not answerable to the taste of the 'public'. This was presumably because writers already worked in a post-artisanal mode, and literature was well-established as a capitalist commodity.[27]

While the printed book is a fundamentally reproducible form which lends itself to mass production and capital investment, this is obviously not true of paintings. Pictures remained unique hand-crafted objects, the value of which depended to an important extent on what were perceived as irreducible individual qualities. At the level of production, they could not provide a field for capital investment except in so far as they were conceived for multiple reproduction through the print media. Certainly these media were of growing importance in this period and the implications of the print industry for the practices of painting require more extensive consideration, but none the less the bulk of pictorial production remained artisanal, geared in the first place to direct sale or exhibition of the individual work. Pictorial production also remained primarily artisanal at the level of distribution, since artists seem to have made little use of art dealers as distributive intermediaries in the early nineteenth century. Generally they seem to have regarded dealers with considerable distaste and maintained control of their own distribution through the institution of the public exhibition. However, there may have been important variations between different genres and media: for instance some water-colourists appear to have made significant use of dealers and provincial printsellers, and indeed to have distinguished between drawings for exhibition and drawings for dealers.[28]

The whole complex of relations between artists and the class fractions they served needs careful definition. In this era of the market, patronage relations still survived through which artists were attached to a court or aristocratic family and secured thereby a particular kudos as well as more tangible rewards: for example Lawrence was Painter in Ordinary to George III; Wilkie was Limner to the King of Scotland and then successively to George IV, William IV, and Queen Victoria; Hayter was Painter of Miniatures and Portraits to Princess Charlotte and Prince Leopold Saxe-Coburg, and so on. However, despite frequent paeans to George III's stature as a protector of the arts in the press, apart from his backing for the Royal Academy and his patronage of West he had done little to justify such tributes. (George IV, a much more improbable model of royal virtue, may have been a more important patron.) The major early nineteenth-century patrons from the aristocracy and gentry, such as Leicester, Stafford, Egremont and Walter Fawkes, were widely seen as notable exceptions to a general pattern of indifference. Further, that kind of paternalistic relationship whereby artists secured backing in the formative stage of their career for training and particularly for a visit to Italy seems to have been of diminishing importance. In contrast to France, the British state supplied virtually no support for painting from public funds in the early nineteenth century, although there was some for sculpture.[29] There were premiums, purchases, and commissions from a private institution of the public corporation type in the form of the British Institution, but these were on a scale which could hardly compare with the system of state support in the nation's main continental rival. In sum, the bulk of the English landed classes does not seem to have felt that their wealth and political power placed on them an individual duty to support the visual arts, or a public responsibility to raise state revenues to do so.

In as much as the notion of patronage implied a relationship of subservience to rank, the development of the intellectual field meant that artists must tend to welcome the decline of traditional patronal forms.[30] That this was the implication of ideas of artistic identity in the period is confirmed by a critique of Prince Hoare's *Epochs of the Arts* published in 1814:

> True patronage consists rather in facilitating the productions of meritorious works by encouraging the purchase of them, than in taking their authors under the protection of royal and noble personages, which is, at the very best, but little more than a splendid state of servitude.

The author of this argued that 'commerce' gave artists and writers a kind of independence, so that they could pursue their own inclinations 'without being shackled by the arbitrary dictates of a great man', and praised picture dealers for having raised the prices of art.[31] Numerous statements by artists describe the 'connoisseur', or more broadly 'men of rank', as being in 'extreme ignorance' of the Fine Arts.[32] However, the freedom of the market brought its own forms of servitude, and the early nineteenth century was a period in which many artists seem to have felt disoriented by increasing competition, and the contradictions of their social role.

As indicated earlier, artists had their most direct contact with capitalist relations through the print industry. However, no single relationship prevailed in print production, partly because of the marked hierarchization of the artistic profession, and partly because of the differences in status of different types of image in the art market. The use of the sale of engravings to finance the production of types of ambitious picture for which there was little market was well-established in the eighteenth century. West and Copley both made large sums from their novel modern history paintings, either by selling them to print-publishers, or by entering into some form of partnership with the engraver and publisher. In the early nineteenth century, profits from engravings continued greatly to enhance the income which successful artists could realize from their pictures. The publishers Hurst and Robinson entered into an agreement with Lawrence in 1822, by which he received £3,000 per year for the exclusive right of engraving from his work – and Lawrence seems to have received additional sums to the figure of £10,000. Wilkie received £1,200 from the firm of Moon, Boys, and Graves for the privilege of engraving the *Chelsea Pensioners*, a picture which he had already sold for 1,200 guineas. It is hardly surprising therefore that artists guarded their copyright jealously.[33]

Of course, the most notable use of engraving to finance history painting was Alderman Boydell's Shakespeare Gallery, and large claims were made for its importance. Yet it is significant that Reynolds is reported to have disliked the scheme initially, because he thought it beneath the dignity of art to serve speculation in such a way.[34] Early nineteenth-century partisans of engraving, such as John Landseer and John Pye, were critical of Boydell for what they regarded as his unscrupulous commercial practices, and Landseer's lecture series at the Royal Institution in 1806 was terminated as a result of his attack on Boydell in the sixth lecture.[35] The complaints of these engravers tend to be couched in rather general terms, but it is clear that they regarded the print-publishers as pre-occupied with profit rather than quality, and felt they tended to promote a shallow and meretricious kind of art by pandering to public demand – what Landseer called the 'mischievous tendency of unprincipled Novelty.'[36]

While very large sums were realized by artists such as Wilkie and Lawrence from engravings made after their work, the landscape painters who were employed by publishers to produce drawings for topographical publications certainly did not come into the big money. This partly reflects the very large differential between the prices for oil and water-colour paintings in the early nineteenth century, which may have been justified by the much greater outlay in time, labour, and materials demanded by the former. It may also be connected with the essentially piece-work relationship topographical artists frequently established with publishers. Artists who sold a finished work, or the copyright on such a work, to a publisher for a fixed sum or a share of the profits were in a quite different position to those who produced on commission for an agreed sum. Such drawings were understood to be different from finished exhibition drawings and consequently they were smaller – although they did not necessarily pay less. Thus Hearne and Smith were paid 5 guineas per drawing (6 ins by 8 ins) by the engraver William Byrne for a series of views of Berkshire and Buckinghamshire in 1801.[37] One might have expected Turner to do far better than this, but in fact W. B. Cooke paid him £7 10s each initially for the drawings for the *Southern Coast* (5 ins by 8 ins), although this was subsequently raised to ten guineas plus a share of the profits. In the 1820s Charles Heath paid Turner thirty guineas each for the slightly larger drawings for the *England and Wales* (6 ins by 9 ins) and was immediately offered fifty guineas for them by several collectors.[38] But Turner's prices were probably exceptional, and to give a contemporary example of similar work: in 1825 G. F. Robson received only seven guineas each for his thirty-two drawings for *Picturesque Views of English Cities*, together with some copies of the work.[39] There must have been advantages for water-colourists in doing work for topographical publications in the form of a reasonably secure income, and also the publicity which engravings brought. However, this kind of piece-work did not bring very large rewards, and Turner seems to have hired his drawings to the Cookes in the 1820s – an arrangement which was presumably only open to an artist with a well-established reputation.

Relations between painters and patrons took somewhat different forms according to genre. Thus while a portrait was almost invariably a commissioned work during the production of which artist and patron would be in direct contact, landscapes would usually have been produced in this way only when a patron commissioned a topographical view or a country house portrait. There were circumstances when genre and landscape painters were commissioned to produce works of particular subjects on a particular scale as a result of a patron having been satisfied with a previous purchase, wanting a work akin to (or even a repetition of) one seen in an exhibition, or wanting a pendant to a work already in his or her collection.[40] One of the functions of the artist's studio was to serve as a shop, and there is evidence in the case of both Wilkie and Collins of patrons visiting the studio to select a subject from among the artists' sketches, which would then be worked up into a finished painting.[41] However, the exhibition, at which artists either exhibited unsold works 'on spec', or commissioned works as a form of advertisement (clearly one of the primary motives for the showing of portraits) was surely the crucial economic site in relation to picture retailing.

I have already discussed the proliferation of exhibition bodies in the metropolis in chapter 1. The essential aim of these new institutions was to extend the opportunities for the sale of contemporary art and remedy some of the perceived deficiencies of the Academy. There was also an increasing number of exhibition bodies in the provinces, many of them short-lived.[42] Depending on the role of artists and amateurs in their running, these functioned in varying degrees to confirm artists' sense of professional identity, and to project the proper public role of the middle class through support of the arts. In economic terms, provincial exhibitions served as a mart for local artists whose work would either not find a place in the big metropolitan shows or would be lost within them, and placed their wares before a potential market which local pride and networks of acquaintanceship might make sympathetic. Provincial exhibitions also offered a less demanding display case for artists with a London base.

The importance attached to exhibitions in the artists' pursuit of a livelihood is indicated by the heated debates over their organization and control. With the exception of the British Institution, the exhibition bodies essentially represented factions in the artistic community, divided less over questions of aesthetic principle than over the organization of sales display. The increasing number of artists who resorted to the 'one-man' show thereby gained all the revenue from admission charges, ensured publicity, and controlled the environment in which their work was seen. They also carried the whole risk of failure.

While artists were not separated from the public by a distributive intermediary such as a publisher, they were in a situation in which they frequently painted for an anonymous public – for the diverse body of persons who could afford to select one of their works from among the wares on show, and needed to be attracted to do so. There is some evidence of artists deliberately producing works for a particular kind of exhibition market, such as a letter from Thomas Uwins to Joseph Severn of 1838, referring to the output of Havell:

> He goes on selling his pictures at country exhibitions, at five, ten, and fifteen guineas a piece. His principle is to meet and not to force the market. Cheap art is the order of the day.[43]

If this meant that artists were working in a situation where they were not subject to direct patronal interference and control, it also meant they could find themselves at the mercy of what seemed an impersonal market mechanism.

It was in the nature of the direct selling of pictures, even through an exhibition, that usually a painter would eventually come into direct contact with his or her patron, who might indeed require some alterations to the purchase. The artist/patron relations thus established could then lead to more enduring kinds of relationship. It seems important to discriminate between the significant interplay between artist and patron, such as that between Turner and Richard Colt Hoare, Walter Fawkes, and Egremont; Wilkie and Beaumont; or Cotman and Dawson Turner; and those passing contacts which were marked by no particular sympathy or result. In the case of the former, it is possible to see an affinity with old-style patronal relationships, even if the artist could lay claim to a new degree of independence and did not follow old norms of deference. In that of the latter, the market was comprised of essentially depersonalized buyers.

The belief that the artist was performing for an uninformed and naive mass, which seemed to respond best to facile novelties and showy effects, could foster a disdain towards the 'public' of a kind comparable to that expressed by some Romantic writers. Constable's observation in 1836 is a good case in point:

> I have truly turned out one of my best bits of Heath . . . for a very old friend – an amateur who well knows how to appreciate it, for I now see that I shall never be able to paint down to ignorance. Almost all the world is ignorant and vulgar.[44]

A rich mine of similar statements is found in the letters of Thomas Uwins from the 1830s, which refer repeatedly to the 'tyranny' of public taste. Art, he wrote in 1833, had become a 'petty trade', and so little money was spent on it that:

> the scrambling to get a share of that little leads men into things of which they would otherwise be ashamed.

In 1839 he was complaining that because of his success with genre paintings of Italian scenes, the public had 'chalked out a course' for him and would accept nothing else. Uwins resented bitterly the 'advice' and interference of amateurs and connoisseurs, who he felt knew nothing of the art, but on whom he depended for his livelihood. In 1828 he wrote to his friend and fellow-artist Joseph Severn:

> An artist ought to be on his guard against the influence of a class of people who are really of no value to him except for the money that they bring.[45]

It must be acknowledged that not all artists responded so negatively to the character of contemporary taste. Wilkie, by contrast, was full of praise for the sensitivity of British patrons, and was convinced that great art was popular art. But then Wilkie had a string of wealthy aristocratic patrons and was generally fêted in the press.[46]

Painting had attained the status of a 'liberal Art' in Britain far later than literature, and its position as such was far less secure. This can partly be attributed to the inescapable craft element in pictorial production: it was impossible to evade the fact that painters worked with their hands. Further, painters served a more obviously utilitarian function than writers, in that they made decorative objects, which were purchased as such – in 1799 Farington noted in his diary:

> It is certain that the vulgar notion of the fine arts goes no farther than to consider them as elegant amusement purchased at a considerable expense.[47]

Outside the gallery, in the modish domestic interiors of the period, pictures functioned partly as markers of status within a hierarchy of furnishings – as one element in what Veblen called 'a code of accredited canons of consumption'.[48] As Farington's remark suggests, this was no mystery of ideology. In 1805, Shee virtually conceded that painters were 'mere ministers of elegant pleasures', and hinted that pictures were generally considered as 'furniture'.[49] Humphry Repton, who had less at stake in such an admission, observed that paintings and sculptures had become detached from their original (and presumably didactic) purpose:

> for whatever might be the original uses of pictures or statues, they are now only considered as ornaments, which, by their number and excellence, distinguish the taste, the wealth, and dignity of their possessors.[50]

It was essential both for painters' sense of their social identity and for their pretensions to status that they should claim a higher function for their products.

Although it was argued that some kinds of painting fulfilled significant cognitive and moral functions, this was far less self-evident than it was in relation to literature. Such claims tended to look rather flimsy in a context in which exhibitions were dominated by endless run-of-the-mill portraits, whose authors also controlled the leading art institution. The practice of portraiture was very clearly a trade, in which the studio was in many cases run like a manufactory with assistants painting different parts of the work, and for which style was clearly related to the requirement of quick working methods and the demands of fashion.[51] Further, the trade aspect of pictorial production was demonstrated in the negotiations of exchange between artist and patron, negotiations of a type writers simply did not have to undertake with their readers.

Painters attempted to raise their social status, to rise above their class origins and to achieve a kind of prestige which neither their mode of employment nor their income would otherwise have brought them, by arrogating to themselves a similar kind of cultural capital to that claimed by writers. The main strategy in advancing their claims was professionalization, and in this the Royal Academy played a key role. Linked with professionalization was a new assertiveness as to the competence of artists to judge on matters of art over and above their patrons. This was why a body as apparently devoted to the interests of artists as the British Institution could arouse the opposition of some, since it was seen (correctly) as an assertion of patronal control in artistic affairs. The rejection of a painting by Havell, *Wallnut Gathering at Petersham near Richmond*, in 1815, on the grounds of its novel departures in the representation of natural effects, incensed many. Uwins's response sums up their view:

> The Institution know, that combining within their own body all the rank and opulence of the kingdom, they have it in their power to kill and to make alive;

> they know that artists are needy men, and that sooner or later they must submit. It is against this contemptible tyranny, set up by self-constituted judges, that I would inveigh with all the power of language, and oh! that I had a voice that could be heard![52]

It is significant in this respect that one of the leading figures in the Institution, Richard Payne Knight, publicly challenged the claims of artists as arbiters of morals, and became a particular focus of artists' hostilities. As the debate around Knight demonstrates, there was also a new willingness to enter into print and engage in polemic in defence of the profession – the writings of Barry, Shee, and Haydon, and a number of short-lived art magazines all exemplify this trend.[53] Such artists certainly wished to assert the value of cultural attainments, and to force recognition of a new degree of autonomy for artistic practices, but the autonomy they sought was far less radical than that which Bourdieu has defined in relation to contemporary society. Artists generally had no desire to deny the social functions of art, and in economic and social terms they had far more direct relations with the public than the beneficiaries of the modern gallery system.

So far I have been discussing the situation of 'the artist' in fairly general terms, but it is obviously important to recognize the hierarchization of the artistic profession and the frictions and factionalization this produced. The situation in the early nineteenth century was one in which the fortunes of an artist could range from those of Sir Thomas Lawrence, who, for all his notorious financial problems, was charging 700 guineas for a full-length portrait at the end of his life, and who mixed at the highest levels of society in the different European capitals, down to the professional drawing-master cum artist such as Cotman or Crome, who teetered along from one financial crisis to the next. The stakes in terms of fashionable success and professional dignity were thus very great. Those such as Collins or Wilkie, who were fortunate enough to attract the attention of wealthy aristocratic patrons, could suddenly find their work became fashionable and enjoy a career 'take-off'. This was Wilkie's experience after the sale of the *Village Politicians* to the Earl of Mansfield in 1806, and equally that of Collins from the sale of *A Scene on the Coast of Norfolk* to the Prince Regent in 1818.[54] However, the majority of artists were not so fortunate, and this helps to explain why the divisions within the artistic profession around the distinctions and privileges of the academicians were so bitter. The numerical restriction on membership of the Academy together with the notoriety of its internal politics, and the widespread belief that some of the artists elected were not of a high calibre while some of those kept outside it were, caused real grievances. In his evidence to the Parliamentary Select Committee on the Fine Arts in 1836, Hofland, one of the outsiders, observed that a large body of artists in the same situation as himself felt degraded by the rank given to the academicians but denied them, and there is ample evidence to support this statement.[55] Landscape painters had particular cause to be aggrieved that exhibitions were arranged to suit practitioners of portrait-painters – a branch of the art which, with few exceptions, seemed entirely lacking in the magic ingredient of imagination which was held to be essential to their own practice.

The income of artists depended partly on the volume of their output, in the sense that the sale of more pictures meant more money, and some highly productive water-colourists such as John Varley and Copley Fielding seem to have charged fairly low prices and relied on the volume of their sales. It also depended on the prices they could command. Price depended on the value accorded to the skill of the artist, and although there were some objective measures of this, the market was notoriously fickle and many artists with considerable skills made a poor living. Artists whose type of skill was in considerable demand such as the fashionable portrait painters, or the still-life painter James Hewlett who enjoyed a vogue around 1808, could realize very large profits. Those who did not attract public attention could fare very ill and secure only meagre prices. This should help to explain why the means of raising prices through markers of status such as the title 'R.A.', a good place in an exhibition, or the prizes of the British Institution were so eagerly sought after.[56]

The enormous differentiation within the profession in relation to landscape painters can be gauged from comparing the price of 350 guineas which Turner received for his *Sun Rising Through Vapour* (National Gallery, London) in 1818, with the prices recorded for John Crome's work in his 1809 receipt to Reverend John Homfray of Yarmouth of £10 for *Hunstanton Cottage*, £18 for *Blacksmith's Shop*, and £7 for *Thorp Cottage*. Neither did Cotman do any better, receiving ten guineas plus the cost of materials for his *Dutch Boats at Yarmouth* (Norwich Castle Museum) in 1825.[57] Even acknowledging the differential in the scale and importance of these works, the differential in terms of price is huge. Crome and Cotman simply did not produce oils on the scale of Turner's major works, probably because they could not command prices which would secure them a return on the expense in time and materials involved – even if they could make a sale. To some extent this is partly a question of the difference between what a provincial painter could expect from a provincial buyer, and what a London-based painter of reputation could expect from a major patron. Thus after William Collins made his market breakthrough around 1812–13, he would regularly receive prices of 100, 120, and 150 guineas.[58] By 1819, Crome's pupil Vincent could sell *On the River Yare, Afternoon* from the British Institution for 120 guineas which was probably more than Crome ever received for a picture.[59]

The vaunted pride in the title of 'artist', the assertions of status, the disdain for the public were all very well, but when it came down to it less successful artists were forced to resort to a wide range of expedients to make ends meet. As well as working as a drawing-master, John Crome was also a painter of transparencies, picture-dealer, and picture-restorer, and many provincial artists were forced to resort to these and similar activities such as frame-making, scene-painting, and print-making.[60] But such a diversity of work practices was not confined to artists based in the provinces. Uwins, Linnell, Constable, and Haydon, are only some from among a wide range of artists who turned from their chosen genre to supplement their income by producing portraits. Another expedient was the production of copies. The position of many artists was thus financially insecure, and it is not surprising that a solid member of the rural bourgeoisie such as Constable's father should have believed his son was 'pursuing a Shadow' in wanting to become an artist.[61] This constant struggle to scrape together a living in the market-place made it difficult to sustain the claims for elevated professional status. Many artists seem to have disliked the character of businessman and thought it beneath them, even if some such as Turner, Wilkie, and Linnell appear to have been financially astute. The problem of status was particularly acute for landscape painters, since although their art was increasing in popularity with the public in the early nineteenth century, many were forced to seek a regular income by teaching drawing, in which role they were apt to be treated as a kind of superior domestic servant. It was a position which was widely regarded as ignominious, partly perhaps because it was seen as a form of wage-labour and was obviously non-creative. Although some amateurs achieved a very high standard, most drawing-masters found themselves fostering a polite accomplishment in 'young ladies', rather than inculcating any real skill.[62]

In considering the structure of the artistic profession, it is necessary to note that in addition to the hierarchy of various categories of practice (history painter, landscape painter, portrait painter &c.), there is another category which intersects with these in complex ways: that of the woman artist. While women artists might be acknowledged as capable of attaining a high level as flower painters or portrait painters in pastels, it was widely felt that they were incapable of great achievement in the 'higher walks' of the art. As Parker and Pollock have demonstrated, the development of bourgeois conceptions of gender roles together with the increasing importance of academic institutions in the eighteenth century tended to worsen the position of women artists.[63] Although Angelica Kauffmann and Mary Moser were founder members of the Royal Academy, they were represented in Zoffany's group portrait of *The Academicians of the Royal Academy* (1772) only as portraits on the walls, and women were not admitted to the crucial sphere of the life school until after 1860.[64] However, the early nineteenth century was a period of considerable debate around the position of women, when radicals called for a fundamental shift in attitudes and a reformation of female education, and it is thus not surprising that there was no single view of their capacity as artists.

Academic theory had nothing explicit to say on the character of women artists, but its lack of references to them is symptomatic, and it always presupposed a male audience for the arts and a male category of artistic genius. Again, it is only in the newspaper and periodical press that I have been able to discover any direct evidence of attitudes. The figure who might seem best to illustrate the ability of women as history painters in this period was Kauffmann, and in 1806 *The Times* described her as 'among the first artists of the present day'. However, the elevated conception of artistic genius current among liberal intellectuals, being essentially a transposition of the ideal of the warrior hero, was so heavily masculinized that it made it impossible to acknowledge female achievement in the great struggle of High Art. Thus Robert Hunt's obituary of Kauffmann in the *Examiner* was largely dismissive:

> The grandeur of epic painting has never been conceived by female genius. In poetry, painting and musical composition, its best strength has been adequate only to display the gentler feelings of the human heart.

While complaining that Kauffmann's male figures were anatomically inaccurate and looked hermaphrodite (without noting the obstacles to her studying from the nude), Hunt does praise her female ones:

> This exquisite feminine delicacy is altogether her own, and unattained by the bolder hand of the rougher sex.

But he also quotes Fuseli's contemptuous description of her works as 'a bundle of rag', and the view that there were certain 'faults' 'inseparable from a female artist' was widespread.[65]

Not all appraisals of the capacities of women were so negative. In 1822 the *Literary Chronicle* was most enthusiastic about Mary Linwood's exhibition of tapestry pictures observing:

> Woman is certainly capable of extraordinary efforts – when she chuses to exert herself; but the system of education which prevails amongst most classes of society, tends so much to degrade her faculties, that it becomes at last an absolute exertion to make use of those talents which fashion or folly have bound down with infrangible chains.[66]

A review of her exhibition in the following year noted that Reynolds and West had both praised her work, and that it attracted thousands of visitors every season. While these comments indicate that the *Literary Chronicle* had a relatively enlightened view of the potential of women, and understood gender attributes partly as the product of social conditioning, it was clearly easier to give a favourable appraisal of a woman's output in tapestry or flower painting than it was in most other branches of the visual arts, the idea being widespread that women's creative abilities had a distinctly feminine character. Thus if a woman artist exhibited historical subjects, as a Mrs Ansley did in 1818 and 1821, this attracted special attention.[67]

While sketching landscape had an important place in the education of middle-class women, this was certainly not intended to foster an interest in an artistic career. It also developed skills in water-colour rather than oil, and in topography and not historical and poetic subjects. The only woman who seems to have made any mark as a professional landscape painter in the early nineteenth century was Harriet Gouldsmith (1787–1863), a pupil of Mulready, who worked in the naturalistic mode of what Marcia Pointon has called the 'Kensington School'. From about 1810 her works were regularly praised for their 'truth of natural effect', and by 1820 she could be described as one:

> who has reached a celebrity in this line of art, equalled by few of her sex ...[68]

Even allowing for the customary 'gallantry' of reviewers to women exhibitors, Gouldsmith seems to have impressed critics as a significant talent. The disappearance of most of her work, and the silence of nineteenth-century histories of British art on her contribution, would seem to confirm the deteriorating position of women artists as the century moved on.[69]

These small fragments suggest that there was a range of attitudes to women as artists, ranging from straightforward insistence on their intellectual and imaginative inferiority, to attribution of what were seen as special aptitudes. These different positions parallel the more extended discussion of the talents of women authors within the literary reviews. While there was a space for women artists, it was definitely a secondary and inferior one. The situation was one which permitted Mary Linwood to achieve considerable acclaim with tapestry pictures, but effectively prevented any woman achieving major success as a painter of history, genre, or landscape.[70] The economic implications of attitudes to women artists for their place in the market is a subject which awaits further research, but it is clear that their work would always be interpreted as that of women artists rather than of artists.

So far I have tried to indicate that the relations of production and exchange into which artists entered were various and complex, and that their engagement in the market-place was significantly different from that of writers. To fill out the rough typology sketched here, more research would be needed as to who bought the different categories of art object and the various relations between producer and consumer which were entailed. To date, the main attempt to advance general conclusions about the character of patronage in the late eighteenth and early nineteenth centuries is a doctoral thesis by Josephine Gear, the basic argument of which is that the period 1760–1840 was a phase of aristocratic monopoly in patronage of the arts, which came to an end (symbolically) with the Houses of Parliament commissions in the 1840s. This seems to me broadly correct, in as much as the early nineteenth century did see a small number of aristocrats and large landowners seeking to exercise cultural leadership in the visual arts, partly through the British Institution and partly through individual initiative: Sir John Leicester and the Marquis of Stafford being major examples, with Sir George Beaumont, Lord Egremont, Lord Mulgrave, and Walter Fawkes among the lesser figures.[71] The prominence of landscape and genre paintings in these collections helped contribute to a new definition of the 'English School', very different from that which Reynolds had envisaged.

The importance of bourgeois patrons in the early nineteenth century is hard to quantify. Some major bourgeois collectors such as Angerstein and Samuel Rogers seem indistinguishable from the aristocracy in their tastes; others such as Samuel Whitbread seem to have taken a more independent line.[72] Although the British Institution was dominated by representatives of the landed classes, the banker Thomas Hope was one of the Directors, and another banker, Alexander Davison, a major subscriber. Davison's collection in his house in St James's Square seems to have been a single-handed attempt to promote British history painting.[73] There was certainly a growing number of provincial bourgeois patrons who helped to sustain provincial art, cases in point being: the Norfolk patrons Thomas Harvey, Daniel Coppin, and Dawson Turner; the Bristol patrons D. W. Acraman, G. W. Braikenridge, John Gibbons, and Charles Hare; and William Roscoe of Liverpool.[74] Further, there is considerable evidence to suggest that water-colour paintings, which were far more modestly priced than oils, found a large market among bourgeois collectors.[75] However, the big names in the patronage of contemporary art remained aristocratic ones up until 1830.

There can be no doubt that British artists of this time generally regarded the landed classes as the 'natural leaders' of British society and looked to the aristocracy for cultural leadership. This helps to explain the widespread political conservatism among them. Although there are indications that a few artists such as Girtin, Linnell, and Cox had democratic sympathies, there is abundant evidence of the conservatism of many more such as Constable, Collins, Farington, Uwins, and Wilkie.[76] But hostility to radicalism does not equate with an uncritical admiration for the contemporary order, and many of those who feared constitutional change may have been almost equally hostile to the fashionable culture of London high society.

Artists generally identified with the class outlook of their patrons, and this is as true of the swaggering Haydon, as it is of the more deferential Wilkie.[77] The space for political radicalism in artistic practice was small indeed, and very few artists in this period produced works which were interpreted as expressions of it. The issue which mobilized artists to distinguish their interests from those of patrons seems to have been precisely the one of autonomy of artistic practice, which is central to Bourdieu's thesis. The stakes involved here were the right of artists to make decisions over matters of finish and form, to pursue subjects which were not trivial, and to execute on a large scale – and yet still find buyers. That which artists sought was the realization of the status academic theory said they should have, and this entailed primarily the respect of patrons. Writing of Leicester's patronage in the *Examiner* in 1818, Robert Hunt wrote:

> To the pecuniary remuneration of the artist, it adds the more deserved and better reward of deference.[78]

As I shall show in chapter 7, because of the perceived failings of the landed classes in politics, morality, and taste, there was potential for the general issue of patronage to be politicized. The form this politicization took was that the claim for artistic autonomy and 'true patronage' became linked with political critique in the radical press. In fact there was no logical connection between the two, except in so far as there was a continuum between the artists' release from subservience to patronage, and the larger attack on paternalistic relationships in the name of bourgeois norms of equal citizenship. This was a connection most artists missed, and the vast majority seem to have accepted the oligarchy of the landed classes. Those who did not made no evident connection between political belief and the style or subject of their artistic product.

In a phase when the language of middle-class identity was still in the process of formation, and middle-class interests were only beginning to find a voice in the political sphere, it is not surprising that no clear demarcation between aristocratic and middle-class taste was articulated. But below the level of very wealthy bourgeois such as Angerstein or Whitbread, who could mix with landed society, and even occasionally enter Parliament, there was a whole middle-class culture which was antithetical in important respects to the fashionable lifestyle of the 'great'. It is likely that the taste of this culture in the visual arts could not easily accommodate the exclusive art of fashionable display, which the reviews discussed in chapter 1 identified. This middle-class taste probably met with the taste of many of the landed classes in the popular genre and landscape painting of the period, even if what it found in this art may have been rather different. Landscape painting, in all its variety, probably did not have the badge of class taste clearly stamped in its iconography – except in so far as we may associate the country-house view with the landed classes. Modest-sized pictures are likely to have suited better the pockets and domestic surroundings of modest bourgeois patrons, although this did not exclude the gentry from buying them too. Conversely, the galleries of town mansions and country houses could better accommodate large works. Scale, finish, and colour may be more the markers of class tastes than iconography. The aspirations of landscape painters to make major statements on a large scale meant that either they must, like Turner, tend to look to the landed classes for patronage, or they must seek to finance their works through one-man shows and engravings as John Martin did. At any rate, the ambition to make large-scale public works for the exhibition space could be hard to reconcile with the actual demand for furnishings for the domestic interior.

4 Philosophical criticism's man of taste

The eighteenth century saw the appearance of a new type of literature on the arts, which was known in Britain as philosophical criticism. Most earlier art writings were treatises on the individual arts ordered around rules and technical precepts. By contrast, the new literature was conceived as a branch of that inquiry into the natural functions of the human mind which had emerged as the central concern of European philosophy in the previous century. It was thus an early form of aesthetics, although in Britain that term was not used widely in its current sense until around 1850.[1] The aspect of mental life which was isolated by philosophical criticism was known as 'taste', and the essay on the nature and principles of taste was its standard form. It was thus distinguished from the established pattern of treatises on the arts in focussing on the analysis of spectator responses, rather than setting out the principles which should guide art making – although it was understood to have definite implications for the latter.

By the early nineteenth century there was a tradition of British aesthetic speculation stretching back almost a century, which encompassed such writers as Burke, Gerard, Kames, Alison and Payne Knight.[2] Their writings, together with those of some lesser figures, provided the common currency of literary criticism, and also offered principles which could be applied to the visual arts, as they were in debates around the category of the picturesque in the 1790s. For Romantic writers such as Coleridge, Hazlitt, and Wordsworth, philosophical criticism represented the current orthodoxy: to some extent they were critical of it, but it also left a profound influence on their conceptions.

It seems reasonable to assume that the development of a form of systematic inquiry into taste was linked with the growing importance of the arts in an increasingly urbanized society with large concentrations of liquid capital. However, while we may connect concern with the nature of proper taste to the growth of the arts as a species of urban entertainment, philosophical criticism also registered the vast expenditures of landed oligarchs on the aestheticization of their estates, which is such a notable feature of the period. Eighteenth-century commentators argued that commercial societies generated luxury and refined taste and manners. However, because of the corrupting effects of luxury and the dangers of an emasculating over-refinement, it was necessary to rescue taste from the trivializing effects of fashion and place it on sound principles. This was the task of philosophical criticism.

Fortified with that philosophy of the mind which had been developed in conjunction with seventeenth-century paradigm shifts in the natural sciences, the theorists of taste attended to the systematization of the arts with a zeal for extending the progress of knowledge into new fields.[3] The logic of this position is revealed in Archibald Alison's *Essays on the Nature and Principles of Taste* (1790), in which he laments the cyclical decline of the arts in earlier cultures, and blames it partly on the lack of philosophy among artists. Philosophical criticism claimed to establish the 'genuine principles' of taste, which should guide both artists and their audience. Through it the arts would be grounded in an 'experimental' science, analogous to that which had produced the 'great discoveries' of the physical sciences.[4] Their class allegiances and the relative dignity of their social position predisposed its authors to assume an authority to legislate on the arts. They represented a group which saw itself as the 'natural' leaders of society in the arts as in politics, and who were not predisposed to acknowledge the automony which artists increasingly claimed for themselves.

What has this general theory of the arts got to do with the responses of the exhibition audience with which I began? Most of the influential essays on taste were a product of the previous century, a period in which the hegemony of the landed classes was complete, and it was therefore inevitable that the dominant norm of taste should be personified in the country gentleman. But the subject of philosophical criticism was not modelled on the real figures of London's aristocratic society. Rather *he* was an ideal type of the virtuous gentleman, living in retirement in the country, and contemplating the urban world from a distance.[5] This subject could hardly be found in the exhibition crowd. Thus philosophical criticism partly offers us a patrician norm of taste, which we may set against an emerging bourgeois ideal which took form in art criticism.

We noted earlier the gap which separated an increasingly professionalized artistic body from the class groups it served, and that this informed that body's self-representation through art theory. There was also some distance (both literally and metaphorically) between most authors of the philosophical criticism and English landed society, in as much as many of the major essays were written by Scottish intellectuals, who had passed through the universities of Edinburgh and Glasgow, or taught at one or other of them. Hutcheson, Hume, Gerard, Kames, Blair, Reid, and Alison were all products of the Scottish social and political environment, although Hutcheson was born in Ireland, and taught in Dublin before becoming Professor of Moral Philosophy at Glasgow. Payne Knight, the only author who actually belonged to English landed society, based his *Analytical Inquiry into the Principles of Taste* on Scottish models. Thus the main corpus of philosophical criticism was a product of the Scottish Enlightenment. For all the major thinkers, their system of criticism was integrated with larger projects, and those theorists who did not write on other issues rested their arguments on general propositions about the mind and society which had been worked out in the Scottish context. To explain philosophical criticism's man of taste, we must set him within the general problematic of Scottish social theory.[6]

The primary contribution of the Scottish School lies in its development of a secular and totalizing theory of society: a 'natural history' of social relations which took its methodological cue from the physical sciences, and worked out the implications of Locke's environmentalism for the understanding of historical development.[7] It has been argued by a succession of scholars that the key factor which produced this phase of intellectual vitality and gave it its distinctive character was the provincial nature of Scottish society.[8]

The Scottish intelligentsia was closely interwoven with the fraction of less well-off aristocracy which made Edinburgh the main focus of its social life after the Union of 1707. In the absence of any local legislative institution, this oligarchy distinguished itself as the heir of the old governing class through a commitment to agricultural improvement and economic modernization. It was because the intelligentsia was closely tied to a progressive elite in a society undergoing a rapid process of modernization, that their social theory was so concerned with the effects of modern commercial societies on manners, morals, and traditional norms of citizenship.[9] This has been conceptualized in terms of a tendency to replace the civic humanist model of active citizenship, derived from the warrior ethic of aristocratic groups, with a more private conception of civic virtue, exemplified by Adam Smith's *Theory of Moral Sentiments*.[10]

The new naturalistic approach to historical studies, which assumed the primacy of economic and cultural variables in the formation of human consciousness, emerged in a succession of works by Smith, Kames, Ferguson and Millar published in the 1760s and 1770s. Their method of inquiry represented the individual as a social being determined as much by the division of property and organization of labour as by political forms – indeed the former had primacy over the latter. History was conceived as a stadial progress, usually divided into four modes of subsistence: hunting, pasturage, agriculture, and commerce; to which there corresponded different kinds of institutions and 'manners'.[11] While they tended to argue that commercial societies had some unfortunate effects on morals and collective psychology, the Scottish School generally found them preferable to the earlier stages of human development. In the *Wealth of Nations*, Smith sought to show that free market economies provided a better standard of living for the poor as well as enormous luxury for the upper classes:

> The progressive state is in reality the cheerful and the hearty state to all the different orders of the society.[12]

The Scots' appraisal of feudal society was a negative one in nearly all respects, and they did not conceive of landed classes as the locus of political virtue. Hume and

Smith were agreed that the progress of commerce had brought liberty and good government, although there was no simple relation between the two, and neither thinker could be regarded as a propagandist for an urban middle class. However, unlike thinkers working within the civic humanist paradigm, the Scottish theorists (with the exception of Adam Ferguson) saw a natural division of interests between town and country, and did not regard the growth of towns as a source of corruption.[13]

From Hutcheson onwards, Scottish thought was generally Whiggish and progressivist. However, Duncan Forbes has stressed the differences between Smith's conception of progress and the naïve optimism of Hartley, Priestley, and Godwin. Smith was relatively sanguine about the future of commercial societies, but he did not believe in human perfectibility and saw certain real disadvantages in the commercial stage. Kames, although he was a strong Whig and committed advocate of Scottish economic development, maintained a cyclical view of the rise and decline of societies. The negative pole of the Scottish inquiry is most clearly illustrated in Adam Ferguson's *An Essay on the History of Civil Society* (1767), which eloquently articulates the anxiety that specialization and commercialization threatened essential qualities in human nature, and that modernization and refinement had extinguished classical ideals of citizenship.[14] But even those thinkers firmly committed to progress shared some of Ferguson's doubts. Thus John Millar, the most politically radical of the Scottish thinkers, argued that the progress of commerce diffused a 'Spirit of Liberty and Independence', while at the same time it produced a class of urban 'mechanics' inferior in 'real intelligence and skills' to the 'peasant'. Millar welcomed the decline of martial virtues characteristic of pasturage societies, but found that the 'accumulation of wealth' in the commercial stage led to arts which catered to a debilitating 'luxury and extravagance'.[15] Thus if they were relatively sympathetic to nascent bourgeois interests, the Scottish School were not apologists of the bourgeoisie, and unlike that of nineteenth-century liberalism, their idea of progress was scientific rather than propagandistic.

The importance Scottish social theory gave to refinement, manners, and the arts, as among the main advantages of commercial societies (and related to their characteristic forms of virtue) helps to explain the major contribution of its exponents to the development of philosophical criticism. Because it rejected *a priori* rules and established authorities in favour of principles 'discovered' by empirical investigation; and, because it centred on an 'experimental' inquiry into taste, a notoriously diverse disposition, philosophical criticism led to some questioning of traditional artistic values. The authority of aesthetic norms was linked with that of prevalent moral and political beliefs, and it is therefore not surprising that its exponents also attempted to define and justify a standard of taste. But such an enterprise had to be reconciled with the actual diversity, which observation of history and contemporary societies inevitably revealed.

The Scottish inquiry assumed that individuals were formed through their environment, a presupposition well illustrated by Millar's assertion:

> That the dispositions and behaviour of man are liable to be influenced by the circumstances in which he is placed, and by his peculiar education and habits of life, is a proposition which few persons will be inclined to controvert.[16]

Armed with this analytical premise, by 1800, Scottish thinkers had produced a body of sophisticated reflections on the social bases of aesthetic norms. These really begin with Hume's 'Of the Rise and Progress of the Arts and Sciences' and 'Of Refinement in the Arts', in his *Essays Moral and Political* (1742), which relate the arts to more general theses on the connections between modes of subsistence, political institutions and manners. Kames took up Hume's ideas in chapter 25 of his *Elements of Criticism* (1762), but some of the most interesting of subsequent reflections on the 'sociology' of taste appeared in works of conjectural history, such as Kames's *Sketches of the History of Man* (1774) and in more straightforward historical analyses such as Millar's *Historical View of the English Government* (1803).[17] In such texts, the arts were inserted into a narrative of social progress as a reflection of the manners and psychology generated by economic and political institutions. In philosophical criticism, the general project was rather to establish a universal psychology of the aesthetic.

While there was a consensus that taste was formed through an individual's environment and education, there was also a concern to justify the reputation of generally accepted models of artistic excellence, while allowing the possibility of innovation and change. Indeed, as philosophical criticism came to base itself on an increasingly sophisticated association psychology, its exponents concluded that traditional exemplars of beauty did not represent a set of fixed norms, but rather that they exemplified types of object with a common significatory function. Given the changeability of human cultures, it was possible that quite different types of object would have the same function in the future. In effect, the standard of taste was defended with less and less dogmatism, until in Payne Knight's *Analytical Inquiry into the Principles of Taste* (1805) it has become thoroughly etiolated in what he described as a 'sceptical view' of the subject. According to Knight:

> The pleasures of imagination ... have been varied and augmented in every succeeding age of civilised society; and we know not how much further they may yet be varied and augmented.[18]

Since the general thrust of Scottish social thought was to historicize all values, including aesthetic ones, the norms of contemporary taste had to be justified (if they were to be justified at all) through its predominantly 'progressive' tendency. But because of the sceptical character of Scottish Whiggism – its consistent acknowledgement that commercial societies had disadvantages, as well as advantages – Scottish historical theory did not offer any single view of the character and prospects of contemporary culture. This is well illustrated in the writings of Kames.

In the *Elements of Criticism* Kames had emphasized the social advantages of the exercise of taste among the proper ranks of society:

> no discipline is more suitable to man, nor more *congruous* to the dignity of his nature, than that which refines his taste, and leads him to distinguish in every subject, what is regular, what is orderly, what is suitable, and what is fit and proper.[19]

Ever complacent about the divine ordering of things, Kames situates the pleasures of taste midway between those of the senses and those of the intellect, as a preparation for higher things. They also promote benevolence, and by 'cherishing the love of order enforce submission to government' and strengthen the 'bond of society'.[20] But in commercial societies the arts have a special value in that they can prevent the fruits of commerce being wasted in vice and wanton pleasures. In the Dedication to the *Elements of Criticism*, which was addressed to George III, Kames asserts that the Fine Arts are necessary to British greatness because they can save the nation from the 'Selfishness' which opulence and luxury generate, and 'excite both public and private virtue'.[21]

But if Kames was confident that the Fine Arts would save Britain from the dangers of luxury at the beginnings of George III's reign, he seems to have felt less secure in this belief after a decade of his rule. In *Sketches of the History of Man* (1774), Kames set out the larger historical framework of his system, and developed his views on the relationship between the arts and social progress – views which owed much to the reflections of Hume. While Kames acknowledged that each age tends to regard its own taste as correct, and to disparage that of its immediate predecessors, this did not lead him to relativism: the arts are progressive, and modern authors have improved on Greek and Roman literature.[22] However, like most Scottish thinkers Kames worked with a cyclical model of the history of cultures. For him, as for others, progress in the arts results from a human propensity to find pleasure in novelty – an assumption which may be connected, at least by analogy, with the recurrent idea that progress in agriculture and maufactures is driven on by the 'endless' capacity of human desire.[23] But while the desire for novelty improves the arts in the early stages of development, it leads to retrogression when the arts are 'in perfection'.[24]

At one point, Kames says that the Fine Arts are not yet threatened by opulence in Britain because they are too far from 'perfection'.[25] Yet in his Sketches of the 'Progress and Effects of Luxury' and the 'Rise and Fall of Patriotism', Kames offers gloomy prognoses for the future. For him commerce has antinomous effects. On the one hand it is necessary to support patriotism, but on the other 'a continual influx of wealth into the capital' generates luxury and selfishness which destroy it. 'Indulgence in corporeal pleasure' has reduced the 'military spirit' of the English nobility, and their minds have been rendered 'effeminate' by indolence. Indeed, nobleman, merchant, and manufacturer all suffer from the 'gradual decay of manhood'. Although the Fine Arts humanize the mind, they can come to occupy the mind too much, and distract the nobility from more important duties. The prospects are not good:

> It grieves me, that the epidemic distempers of luxury and selfishness are spreading wide in Britain.[26]

Kames's desire to justify the pursuits of taste sat uneasily with the norm of active citizenship and martial virtue which was so central to the ideology of the landed society from which he came. This points to a tension which lay unresolved within much Scottish social thought.[27] We can find both of Kames's models in the art criticism of the early nineteenth century: the earlier type of the landed gentleman who could combine refinement of taste with a proper commitment to public service, and the dissipated aristocrat weakly indulging in a selfish taste. But in its more radical forms, art criticism would find both its civic ideal and its norm of refinement in different social types: the enlightened bourgeois and the independent urban intellectual.

It is now time to look a little more closely at philosophical criticism's man of taste. Working on the basis of Locke's epistemology, the Scottish thinkers regarded the nature of things as unknowable, and insisted that beauty and sublimity were not qualities perceived in material objects, but ideas in the mind produced by our emotional response to certain types of external stimuli. However, after Hutcheson they rejected Locke's negative estimate of the association of ideas and used it instead as the unifying principle of the mind. By the early nineteenth century the dominant theory in British aesthetic speculation was based on an associationist psychology, derived partly from Hume, but more usually from David Hartley's *Observations on Man* (1749). Association psychology rested on the assumptions that the mind could be best studied by the same kinds of observational procedures that scientists such as Boyle had developed to study the natural world, and that this study would reveal regular principles in its workings akin to natural laws. These principles were preordained by the creator of the universe (usually conceived as the God of Christianity), and thus had a teleological significance – that is to say they were informed by the dominant natural theology of the period. Basically, association theory offered an explanation of aesthetic pleasure as a particular function of the imagination, a disinterested pleasure produced by certain trains of associated ideas, stimulated either by objects in the world or by their representations in works of art that act as signs for these ideas. No object has any intrinsic aesthetic quality. Despite its teleological underpinnings and problematic concept of progress, association aesthetics offered the nearest thing to 'science' in the explanation of works of art then available, being a kind of proto-semiology framed within a theory of cultural relativism.[28]

Kames's *Elements of Criticism* may be regarded as the first treatise to make associationism its central principle. But although it was still widely read in the early nineteenth century, the most influential, consistent, and sophisticated expositions of the theory were Alison's *Essays on Taste* (republished in 1811, 1812, 1815, 1817, and 1825), and Knight's *Analytical Inquiry into the Principles of Taste* (in its fourth edition in 1808). Both books were widely and favourably reviewed, and Alison's popularity after 1811 does not seem to have been affected by the hostility to Scottish 'metaphysics' which sometimes surfaced in the periodical press.[29] Indeed, the success of the second edition probably owed something to Jeffrey's favourable appraisal in the *Edinburgh Review*, probably the most respected of the major literary magazines published from the 'Athens of the North'.

Although Alison was particularly insistent that matter had no intrinsic aesthetic quality, and that all emotions of taste derive from trains of association characterized by a single pervading emotion, this did not lead him to accept a diversity of tastes of equal value. He described the aim of his *Essays on Taste* as to establish the 'LAW OF MIND' which governs imagination, so that an artist will know:

> whether the Beauty he creates is temporary or permanent, whether adapted to the accidental prejudices of his Age, or to the uniform constitution of the human Mind[30]

The *Essays* restate the conventional cyclical model of artistic progress, but recast it in associationist terms. Having reached the apogee of their development, the Fine Arts have always degenerated since the 'nature of these Arts themselves' afford 'no permanent principles of judging'. Artists tend to give 'undue preference' to skill and 'display of Design', which are particular to the period when a work is produced, and insufficient attention to the superior beauty of character and expression, which arises from 'certain invariable principles of our Nature'.[31] It is because both artist and public generally lack the sensitivity and science to understand the permanent principles of art, that Alison asserts the importance of philosophy and criticism, which may, perhaps, in the modern world arrest this tendency to cultural decline, if only the arts can be rescued from 'the sole dominion of the Artists' and set on 'more just and philosophical principles'.[32]

The work of art, to earn the admiration of all ages, must depend upon permanent norms of expression which are derived from the 'uniform constitution of Man and of Nature'. In all the arts which concern the beauty of form (the essential beauty of material objects for Alison), the artist must try to disengage his mind from:

> the accidental Associations of his age, as well as the common prejudices of his Art; to labour to distinguish his productions by that pure and permanent expression, which may be felt in every age[33]

While in Alison's system judgement plays no part in aesthetic pleasure, it is central to criticism, which functions to distinguish true taste from fashion. Yet if art must be measured against the permanent principles of human nature, there are no fixed forms which will produce the relevant effect. The beauty of all forms arises from their function as signs, expressive of fitness, or expressive of emotion. This means that potentially there is no limit to the objects of taste. If there were an original and primitive beauty, there could be no progress, whereas a benevolent creator has organized nature for human improvement.[34]

Just as Alison recognized historical variation but asserted supra-historical values, so he also reconciled a diversity of individual tastes with a fixed contemporary norm. This is done, of course, by making normative an hierarchical order of society which enables a few persons to develop their faculties but disqualifies the majority from doing so. Alison acknowledged the common humanity of the 'lower orders' but found that their 'vulgar and degrading occupations' disfigured their minds and bodies alike.[35] As a consequence:

> The generality of mankind live in the world, without receiving any kind of delight from the various scenes of beauty which its order displays.[36]

To an important extent the capacity for taste seems to depend upon education and leisure. The state of the mind in which emotions of taste are possible is generally limited to those who do not labour for their livelihood, or are not pre-occupied with commerce, learning or personal advancement:

> It is only in the higher station . . . or in the liberal professions of life, that we expect to find men either of delicate or comprehensive taste. The inferior situations of life, by contracting the knowledge and the affections of men within very narrow limits, produce insensibly a similar contraction in their notions of the beautiful or the sublime.[37]

The 'finest natural taste' can rarely withstand the effects of constant attention to the 'minute and uninteresting details of the mechanical arts'. Those who are 'doomed' to spend their early years in 'populous and commercial cities', where 'narrow and selfish pursuits' prevail will have their sensibilities blunted, particularly since they will lack contact with nature. Sharing the sceptical attitude to commercial society general among the Scottish intelligentsia, Alison restricts taste to a leisured landed class and a few in the liberal professions.

Alison described the state of mind 'most favourable to the emotions of taste' as one in which 'the imagination is free and unembarrassed', in which it is not distracted by 'any private or particular object of thought'.[38] By contrast with this reflective aesthete, in 1816 the *Repository of Arts* described the visitors to the Academy's rooms as a 'gay scene', and the show itself as one of 'the amusements which support the listless existence of the lounger', and the '*industrious* curiosity of the *idle*'.[39] In such a social setting Alison's ideal must have been a rarity indeed.

Like Alison, Payne Knight was emphatic that artists were not qualified to regulate their own practices, and he was more explicit still about the social group which should define taste.[40] Knight begins his *Analytical Inquiry* by observing that since the organs of perception and feeling are basically the same in all humanity, whatever variations there are in individual sensibilities, one might expect that there would be mutual agreement on matters of taste, but in fact on the contrary:

> there is scarcely any subject, upon which men differ more concerning the objects of their pleasure and amusements: and this difference subsists, not only among individuals, but among ages and nations[41]

He proceeds to emphasize the variety of fashions which have prevailed at different times and the different norms of beauty which prevail amongst different races. While there have been disagreements in religion and philosophy in the course of history, these areas are matters of belief and reason which can be settled by argument and demonstration; taste, however, is simply a matter of feeling. None the less, Knight maintains that it is the universal principles of human nature, and not 'fluctuating modes and fashions' which should guide poet, painter and sculptor in 'serious compositions' when strong passions are expressed:

> for, not only the passions and affections of the human mind, but the natural modes of expressing them, are the same in all ages, and all countries; and the less these natural modes are connected with those of local and temporary habit, the more strong and general will be the sympathies excited by them.[42]

A position which provides the basis for discriminating between true taste and fashion, and between those qualified to judge, and those who should follow them.

Knight's use of association to justify an hierarchical distribution of taste resembles Alison's, and ultimately derives its rationale from Hartley's *Observations on Man*.[43] However, unlike Alison, Knight argued that there are immediate pleasures of sense which underlie the pleasures of imagination. These pleasures of sense are strongest in the young, and in adults they are overlaid by associated ideas. All the pleasures of the intellect, of the imagination and of judgement, derive from association, and the relative importance which Knight accords to these pleasures is indicated by the fact that he devotes two hundred and twenty pages of his treatise to analysing them, while the pleasures of the senses are dealt with in eighty. None the less, Knight does emphasize that if there is any discord in the purely sensual effect of the object of aesthetic contemplation, it destroys the intellectual pleasures.[44]

As individuals pass through life, their sensual tastes are refined by education and practice, and experience multiplies the range of pleasures association may provide, and so 'recollection enhances enjoyment, and enjoyment brightens recollection'. Works of art are never 'thoroughly enjoyed', except by people whose minds are:

> enriched by a variety of kindred and corresponding imagery; the extent and compass of which, allowing for different degrees of sensibility, and habits of attention, will form the scale of such enjoyment.[45]

The judgement which is exercised in matters of taste is simply a product of the 'good breeding', whether natural or acquired, which prevails in social life generally. It is a judgement which must be improved by extensive study and meditation. Knight thus makes taste the prerogative of an elite minority, a view which he asserted still more explicitly in his anonymous review of Northcote's *Life of Reynolds* of 1814 where he expressed his disdain for modern literary forms, 'histories of private and domestic life, whether real or fictitious', novels or biographies, and connected them with readers who had 'moderate wealth and superficial education' and who read merely to fill vacant leisure.[46] For him, this new kind of literature can only 'vitiate and enervate' the public taste; under the name of study it promotes a 'passive and solitary dissipation' which destroys and debases the intellect. The leaders of taste in advanced societies inevitably form a small caste, while the bulk of the public are largely incapable of thinking for themselves:

> What is called public opinion in matters of this kind, is rather impulse than opinion; and that impulse is always given by the authority of a few. The mass repeat with increased violence the expressions of wonder and admiration which they hear from the few who pretend to direct them, till grown familiar with the object; when their admiration suddenly ceases, and all of wonder that remains is, that they ever could have admired.[47]

Meanwhile, the few have made new discoveries, and thus art is kept in a state of perpetual experiment, while successive generations of artists find their work outmoded before they have had time to mature their talents. For these reasons, no single school or country maintains excellence for long.

By contrast with most contemporary theorists, Knight regarded the moral utility of art as extremely limited, and he attacked the pretensions of painters and poets to correct manners and improve social virtues. Morality is to be regulated by abstract reason, and not by the passions and sentiments on which art must rely for its effects. The only good which arises from the arts is that they turn the mind from violent to peaceful pastimes. Yet despite his controversial views on the moral value of art, Knight's notion of the final cause of its pleasures is ultimately conventional, for his faculty of taste is implanted throughout the human species by a divine creator. He saw a passion for novelty as making change and variety necessary to the enjoyment of all sensual and intellectual pleasures. While taste is corrupted by this passion, it is also the cause of improving it, and hence has a benevolent result – a fundamentally Hartleyan view. If there was no passion for novelty 'all would be dead inaction, or action without motive or effect'. Thus while there are principles of taste implicit in human nature, perfection is never to be attained, and novelty is justified by a continuous striving for it.[48]

Knight was a consistent sceptic, and he frequently emphasizes the importance of sentiment, and the necessity of deriving all principles from experience alone[49] – a position which underpins his vehement dislike of rules, academies and critics. The political temperature of the early nineteenth century encouraged awareness of the connections between taste and politics, and Knight makes the self-consciously Burkean statement that:

> in all matters of taste and criticism, general rules appear to me to be like general theories in government and politics, never safe but where they are useless; that is, in cases previously proved by experience.[50]

Art is a product of feeling and genius, and can not be bound by rules, which tend to vitiate taste, just as dogmas vitiate morals. This antipathy to abstract system is homologous with Knight's aversion to 'wild reforms and systems vain' in politics.

The critique of rules is linked to a critique of academies, which tend to cramp all individuality, and attempt to teach by rules that which can only be achieved by feeling and observation. However, Britain's Royal Academy is excused from this general condemnation, for it has escaped 'the contagion of system' – a concession which may have been tactical rather than authentic.[51]

For Knight the highest forms of visual pleasure are represented by an approach to light and colour first developed by Giorgione and Titian, and perfected by Dutch artists in the seventeenth century. This quality of 'irregular masses of light and shade' blended in 'harmonious combinations', he defined as 'picturesque'.[52] Knight rejected the doctrine of ideal form, so central to academic theory, and he recognized that the Grand Manner was not compatible with his aesthetic. He was extremely critical of works by Reynolds' hero, Michelangelo, and he claimed that Salvator Rosa's *Saul and the Witch of Endor* was preferable to the Sistine Chapel.[53] Knight avowed great admiration for Reynolds, and praised the *Discourses* as:

> on the whole . . . containing the soundest and best body of critical instruction that have ever been produced on the subject

but he refused to accept Reynolds' sharp distinction between the Grand and Ornamental Styles, and maintained that his advocacy of fresco was misguided. This argument rests on a clear separation between the provinces of sculpture and painting, which have quite distinct 'principles of excellence'. Sculpture is concerned with form, while the pleasures of painting can only arise from colour, or the variation of light and shadow. Since painting demands 'a more complete imitation of its objects', it 'requires a stricter adherence to their individual peculiarities', and Reynolds' conception of general form was thus misguided – a view which Knight shared with Haydon and Hazlitt.[54]

As a 'mere painter, whose object was to please the eye', Rembrandt was right to reject study of antique sculpture, and he understood abstract visual beauty more perfectly than any other modern artist. However, elsewhere in the *Analytical Inquiry* Knight compares Rembrandt unfavourably with Raphael:

> Raphael raises us in our own estimation by showing us images of men, such as we think might exist; and Rembrandt degrades us by showing us such as we know do exist

This comment is not inconsistent, for, as we have seen, the purely sensual sources of aesthetic pleasure, which Rembrandt manipulated with supreme skill, were for Knight less important than the pleasures of the imagination. They are innate, and are not developed by feeling, taste, and reason. Only Correggio combined the excellences of painting and expression, and thereby 'approached nearer to general abstract perfection, than any other artist of modern times'.[55]

It might seem that Knight had finally followed academic doctrine in allowing the Dutch School great technical merit, while seeing the Italian painters of the sixteenth and seventeenth centuries as the acme of the higher excellence of expression.

However, if Knight accepted the doctrine in some degree, he put it on a completely different intellectual foundation which permitted a more flexible judgement across the schools. Further, he gave the Dutch a new status, since academic theorists disapproved of the style of Dutch painting, and for this Knight had nothing but praise. His willingness to question the conventions of the Grand Manner is equally apparent from his attitude to subject matter. He found that pictures of events in modern dress, with details of common life, such as West's *Death of Wolfe* and Westall's *Harvesters in a Storm* (which he owned), were 'some of the most interesting and affecting pictures, that the art has ever produced'.[56] It was consistent with Knight's idea that the pleasures of association were infinitely extendible, that he claimed British landscape should provide the subjects for an original native school. In his didactic poem *The Landscape* of 1794 he contrasted the health and fecundity of British scenery with the impoverished Roman Campagna which had inspired Claude, recommending the landscape painter to study the former rather than visit Italy.[57]

Knight's system, more than that of any other thinker who worked within the discourse of philosophical criticism, illustrates the corrosive effects of its particular brand of psychological inquiry on the painters' professional creed of academic theory. As his opponents in the artistic community recognized, Knight offered essentially a connoisseur's aesthetic. His man of taste was not the artists' ideal of a landed patrician, who manifested virtue by promoting a monumental and patriotic public art, rather he was an aesthete delectating over the finer points of cabinet pictures in rural retirement. This model was to prove quite unacceptable to radical critics of patrician culture in the early nineteenth century in its refusal to see taste as a legitimate concern within a wider public sphere.

While Alison was an Anglican clergyman based in Edinburgh, Knight was very much part of the English landed class to which he addressed his writings. He was thus in a position to act the man of taste his *Analytical Inquiry* presented. For all his Burkean pessimism about the contemporary order, Knight himself sought to set an example of discernment through his positions as a member of the Committee of Taste and as a Director of the British Institution. Both his published work as a theorist and his public role combined to make him the foremost butt of artists' resentments in the period.[58]

Consonant with Knight's ideal aesthete, the British Institution had women as subscribers, but not as Directors. The *Analytical Inquiry* offered no model of the woman of taste, and indeed within the discourse of philosophical criticism she would almost have been an oxymoron. This may seem superficially contradictory, for after all the Fine Arts were said to call into play those feelings of 'humanity' and 'exquisite fellow-feeling', that 'peculiar delicacy and sensibility' said to be particularly characteristic of women.[59] Kames had claimed that women had both 'more sensibility' and 'more imagination' than men; and Hume had even asserted that 'women of sense and education' are 'much better judges of all polite writing than men of the same degree of understanding' – excepting books of devotion and gallantry.[60] But the term 'taste' in itself had connotations of the irrational and the feminine, and it had to be securely grounded in the realm of masculine judgement to make it a proper pursuit of the virtuous gentleman. Women's 'judgement' was always held to be less 'solid' than that of men, and it was only judgement which could distinguish the permanent in art from the whims of fashion – a social disease to which women were especially susceptible. Further, the office of critic was a public function from which women were excluded by nature as they were from all other 'public affairs'.[61] Although radical art criticism in the early nineteenth century was to challenge the class definition of the man of taste, it was to leave him just as securely masculinized as in philosophical criticism.

5 Philosophical criticism and the science of landscape

(i) The man of taste in the country – a universe of signs

If philosophical criticism's man of taste could find little to please him in the city, he was in his element in the country. Since British aestheticians sought explanations from fundamental psychological principles, they looked for aesthetic responses to properties of both nature and art. Indeed they began their analyses with responses to nature, which for most was superior to any imitation.

In Antiquity and the Renaissance beauty had been the sole aesthetic category, but the new inquiry into the psychological principles of taste forced recognition of a variety of aesthetic emotions which could hardly be classified under a single term. Eighteenth-century thinkers generally defined those emotions which could not be classified as beauty under the term sublime.[1] We may understand the enlargement of aesthetic experience represented by the sublime as an effect of changing attitudes to the natural world. The discoveries and hypotheses of seventeenth-century astronomy broke traditional notions of an animate circumscribed universe and a hierarchy of celestial spheres, and led to the conception of an infinity of worlds in absolute space. The aesthetic of the sublime was intimately linked with the strenuous efforts of advocates of the new science, such as the Boyle Lecturers, to demonstrate that it was not incompatible with the truths of revelation as these were discovered in the scriptures, and indeed that the new image of the universe actually added to the glory and majesty of the creator. In the late seventeenth and early eighteenth centuries the truths of natural philosophy were fought over by freethinkers and different factions of the orthodox, each using forms of natural theology to support their moral, social, and political views. While they differed over the weight to be given to reason and the evidence of nature, and that to be attributed to the scriptures, the argument for the existence of God from the design of the cosmos became increasingly commonplace.[2]

Marjorie Hope Nicolson has argued that Thomas Burnet's controversial attempt to reconcile scientific theory with theology in *The Sacred Theory of the Earth* (published in Latin in 1681, and in translation in 1684) marks the beginnings of a new view of mountains and other vast natural phenomena with major aesthetic implications. At any rate, given the imaginative appeal of the new science and the fierce controversy Burnet's work provoked, it is not surprising that early eighteenth-century critics such as John Dennis and Addison gave a new value to 'Vastness and Immensity', qualities which were entirely excluded by traditional norms of beauty.[3] Indeed, Addison found nature superior to art for precisely the reason that art had no vastness about it, making this factor the basis for distinguishing between the pleasures of the 'beautiful' and the 'great', using the latter term to designate what would come to be called the sublime.[4] Addison maintained that the emotions of the sublime and the beautiful could be excited by the same object, as did Kames later in the century. However, a firm separation between the two categories was made by Gerard in his *Essay on Taste*, and Burke, in his *Philosophical Enquiry*, made them mutually exclusive emotions which were excited by opposite kinds of objects. Burke's sublime was not only incompatible with traditional norms of beauty, it was also productive of a more powerful emotion – in his words 'of the strongest emotion which the mind is capable of feeling'.

Burke's account of the effect of the sublime echoes that of Addison: the mind is so entirely filled with its object that it can not 'entertain' any other and is thrown into a state of astonishment, that is a state in which 'all its motions are suspended'. While Burke does not make the infinite the sole source of the sublime, he does claim that:

> The ideas of eternity, and infinity, are among the most affecting we have

When explaining how 'Vastness' is a 'powerful' cause of the sublime, he remarks that this observation has become 'too common, to need any illustration'.[5] We may reasonably assume that Burke would not have defined the sublime in the way he did, had not a new kind of descriptive nature poetry begun to appear in the first half of the eighteenth century which was directly influenced by the new science. James Thomson's enormously successful poem *The Seasons* (published in parts 1726–30, final version 1740), marks the beginning of an era in which poets devoted even more attention to nature in this world than in the cosmos. Thomson described the aim of the poem as to demonstrate 'How exquisitely the individual Mind ... to the external World is fitted: – and how exquisitely, too – The external world is fitted to the mind ...'[6] This matching of a beneficent divine order with the mind so that nature functions like an educational scheme for human betterment was the central premise of natural theology.

In natural theology the inequalities of the social order were justified by asserting that they, like differences between species in the natural order, were divinely ordered according to the 'Government' of the deity. Bishop Butler stressed that the social and natural orders appeared by analogy:

> to be a Scheme, System, or Constitution, whose Parts correspond to each other, and to a Whole; as neatly as any Work of Art, or as any particular Model of a

> civil Constitution and Government. In this great Scheme of the natural World, individuals have various peculiar Relations to other individuals of their own Species. And whole Species are, we find, variously related to other Species, upon this Earth.[7]

Quite why this should be so was part of the great mystery of the creation, and hence, conveniently unfathomable. The same idea was being expressed in an even more explicit form, clearly related to contemporary conservative politics, in William Paley's hugely successful *Natural Theology* of 1802.[8] The connection between the argument from design and a conservative model of social order indicates that the sublime aestheticized a hierarchical and patriarchal cosmos – a cosmos which presented a model of government analogous to that which prevailed in eighteenth-century society, as this appeared from the perspective of the dominant social groups.

The idea that the cosmos manifested a 'design' which was also the model of the aesthetic was given a completely new emphasis, from the writings of Shaftesbury onwards.[9] The frequent references to the argument from design in philosophical criticism and assertions that the highest aesthetic experience is provided by the contemplation of the natural order suggest that natural theology and philosophical criticism functioned as mutually reinforcing discourses with the same kind of reassuring and integrative ideological effects. Thus Alison's man of taste is both able to experience the highest pleasures of the natural order through the advantages his education and lifestyle have conferred, and confirmed in his station by the knowledge which those pleasures can give to persons with a developed sensibility.

One of the radical features of Alison's system is his insistence that there is no single emotion of taste. In the introduction to his *Essays on Taste*, he tells us that the imagination is not to be considered as a separate and peculiar faculty, but the effects attributed to it should rather be resolved into the more general principles of our mental constitution. What goes under the name of taste is *always* a complex emotion, and the trains of association which arouse it are distinguished by an over-riding principle of connection, a single pervading emotion. The intensity of our aesthetic response depends upon a unity of effect, which derives from the principle of resemblance. Ordinary trains of thought lack this general relation, and such advantages as art works have over nature depend upon the artist's capacity to achieve unity of effect.

Alison consistently emphasizes that matter can not be beautiful or sublime in itself. As we have seen, this was a fundamental premise in philosophical criticism, and one which had been equally asserted by Kames.[10] However, where Alison differs from Kames is in asserting that matter in itself is also incapable of producing any aesthetic emotion. Taking up an idea from Thomas Reid's essay 'Of Taste', Alison argues that matter can only produce emotions by acting as 'SIGNS or EXPRESSIONS' of qualities which produce emotions. Confusion has arisen between material objects themselves and the qualities they signify because:

> the constant connection we discover between the sign and the thing signified, between the material quality and the quality productive of emotion, renders at last the one expressive to us of the other, and very often disposes us to attribute to the sign, that effect which is produced only by the quality signified.[11]

This effectively identifies the phenomenon which Roland Barthes describes as the naturalization of second-order discourse, and we may reasonably describe the theory of Reid and Alison as a proto-semiology. In modern formalist criticism 'associations' are treated as a distraction from true aesthetic experience, but in Alison's system it follows logically that the intensity of the aesthetic reverie, of aesthetic experience itself, must depend on the range of associations aroused by the art work – the more extensive the range the more powerful the effect.[12]

Alison describes a 'sensibility to the beauties of the country' as the most 'natural' sensibility of all, and this matches precisely with his views on the social bases of taste which we considered in the last chapter.[13] Consistent with this patrician ideal, that exclusive leisure preserve and status symbol of the large landowner, the landscape garden attached to the country house, is made to serve the end of a high moral order. The power which the landowner has physically to order his property means that he can exclude those mundane objects which would remind him of the real world of labour and the competition of his social inferiors and disturb the aesthetic reverie. In the wider landscape, the most beautiful scenes are frequently disturbed by 'unaccording circumstances' such as:

> the signs of cultivation, – the regularity of enclosures, – the traces of manufactures, and, what is worse than all, by the presumptuous embellishments of fantastic Taste.[14]

In the garden, however, it is possible to assert the general character of the scene without such distracting interruptions, and thus achieve an harmonious moral order.

However, Alison's theory has implications for landscape painters as well as for patrician hobbies. The painter can create even greater unity of effect than the gardener, by leaving out all distracting details and choosing the appropriate atmospheric effect to draw out a single unifying mood:

> He may select from a thousand scenes, the circumstances which are to characterize a single composition, and may unite into one expression, the scattered features with which Nature has feebly marked a thousand situations. The momentary effects of light or shade, the fortunate incidents which chance sometimes throws in, to improve the expression of real scenery, and which can never again be excelled, he has it in his power to perpetuate upon his canvas: Above all, the occupations of men, so important in determining, or in heightening the characters of Nature, and which are seldom compatible with the scenes of gardening, fall easily within the reach of his imitation, and afford him the means of producing both greater strength, and greater unity of

> expression, than is found either in the rude, or in the embellished state of real scenery.[15]

This passage seems to anticipate a basic premise of Constable's *English Landscape Scenery*, and the artist is known to have admired Alison's book.[16] Further, Alison's theory offered general principles for the organization of landscape imagery which arguably informed some of the most inventive painting of the period, and were demonstrably taken up by art critics, including some who would have rejected his model of the patrician aesthete.

For Alison, through the contemplation of the material universe our moral feelings are awakened, and our moral sensibility is developed: the universe is a 'scene of moral discipline'. (To understand the kind of feelings Alison is referring to, we may note that he attributes great importance to Thomson's *Seasons* in directing taste towards the 'natural Expression of Scenery'.)[17] Art directly serves the end of religion:

> In ages of civilization and refinement, [the] union of devotional sentiment with sensibility to the beauties of natural scenery, forms one of the most characteristic marks of human improvement, and may be traced to every art which professes to give delight to the imagination.[18]

The emotions of the sublime produced for an educated sensibility through contemplation of the benevolent plan of the natural order are the highest aesthetic pleasure, and the *Essays on the Nature and Principles of Taste* conclude with a rapturous invocation of 'the temple of the Living God', which Constable particularly liked. But these pleasures are strictly limited to the upper echelons of society, for the 'vulgar pursuits of life' have a 'melancholy tendency' to 'diminish if not altogether destroy' our sensibility to the natural order: they prevent us from reading the universe of signs which everywhere signifies the patriarchal hand of the deity.[19]

Association aesthetics thus made 'sublime emotion' before the scenes of wild nature dependent on a particular class culture. In his review of Alison's *Essays on Taste* in 1811, Jeffrey claimed:

> There is scarcely any one who does not feel and understand the beauty of smiling fields and comfortable cottages; but the beauty of lakes and mountains is not so universally distinguishable. It requires some knowledge of our species – some habits of reflection, – some play of fancy, – some exercise of affection, to interpret the lofty characters in which Nature here speaks to the heart and the imagination; and reflects, from the broken aspects of the desert, the most powerful images of the feelings and the fortunes of man.[20]

It is clear that the capacity to 'appreciate' sublime scenery functioned as a sign of cultural distinction, and this may help to explain why the 'common' English scenes of Constable et al. did not find much immediate success with art patrons in the early nineteenth century. However, the growing popularity of travelling to view sublime scenery inevitably rendered the sublime as an aesthetic emotion increasingly commonplace. That the sublime could not be a 'popular' emotion, and that it was incompatible with the modern as represented by crowds of 'artisans, labourers, and the humbler classes of shopkeeper', or broad highways and railways, was the basic argument of Wordsworth's letters to the *Morning Post* in 1844.[21]

(ii) Seeing the picturesque

Anyone familiar with the discourses surrounding landscape in the late eighteenth and early nineteenth centuries knows that the term 'picturesque' is ubiquitous within them. The publications of *Picturesque Views of* ... are legion, and the term infests travel literature and appears frequently in novels and periodicals. The systematizing tendency of philosophical criticism made it inevitable that its exponents would attempt to define a term which clearly related to a widespread norm of taste. It was also logical that an aesthetics which was essentially psychologistic would produce attempts to define the characteristic mental functions to which the term referred, and establish them as an aesthetic category.

The evolution of the picturesque aesthetic was intimately connected with particular attitudes to the countryside engendered by the lifestyle of a capitalistic landed class, which lived on its property part of the year and was predisposed to take a keen interest in its management and exploitation, and which saw itself as the leaders and protectors of a hierarchical rural society within which its predominance had to be theatrically displayed. While narrowly economic interests stimulated a positive attitude to the national landscape, the patrician self-image of the class stimulated ways of viewing it which were non-utilitarian, distanced, and profoundly symbolic. These attitudes were manifested most clearly in the arrangement of the gentleman's estate as a landscape garden, a practice which was central to the culture of the landed elite, until the economic conditions brought about by the Anglo-French Wars started to make the pursuit of agricultural profits an even more attractive activity.

It was the vogue for landscape gardening among the aristocracy and gentry, and the various forms of social vision this involved, which made the definition of the picturesque a sufficiently loaded issue for it to become the subject of a public controversy around the turn of the century.[22] It is symptomatic of the social dimensions of the picturesque that Uvedale Price and Payne Knight, the two thinkers who took on the task of defining the category in more systematic terms, should be directly critical of the Brownist landscape garden because of the social model implicit in it. However, it is equally symptomatic of the authority of philosophical criticism as a discourse that their defence of their conceptions should take on increasingly philosophical form, and that they should ultimately fall out, not over practical recommendations, but over the psychological basis of these recommendations.

In the Introduction to the 1810 edition of his works, Price described Burke as 'a very superior mind', and in his 1794 *Essay on the Picturesque* he described Burke's aesthetic system as 'the foundation of my own'.[23] Nigel Everett has argued that not only was Price indebted to Burke's aesthetic writings, but there are also profound connections between Price's concept of the garden and Burke's political theory. Like Burke's wise statesman, Price's wise improver creates a balanced and consistent composition; while the tyrant levels and destroys like the Brownist professional gardener. As we saw in chapter 2, Price's picturesque was not the wild scenery of Gilpin's tourist vision, but a homely model of rustic decay founded on the imagery of seventeenth-century Dutch painters such as Adrian van Ostade. The role of the improver calls only for sensitive and discreet intervention, and as much as possible he should let nature take its course:

> Picturesque composition seeks to reconcile the virtues of variety and imaginative freedom with a frame of order, in a fit image of the perfect constitution.[24]

Where Price differed from Burke was that as a Foxite Whig writing in the mid 1790s, he saw the main threat to the British political order not as that of anarchy but rather as that of despotism. For Price, the Brownist garden represented a divisive model of society, since by isolating the country house it emphasized distinctions of property; by contrast, he advocated a more 'natural' garden which would represent the organic gradation of ranks and the principle of social cohesion.

In his first contributions to the picturesque controversy, the privately printed *Letter to Uvedale Price, Esq.* and the *Sketches and Hints on Landscape Gardening* (1795), the professional gardener Humphry Repton sought to defend the work of Capability Brown against Price and Knight, by controverting their political analogy, and accusing them (unfairly) of recommending a system of improving 'by neglect and accident', which would turn the whole of England into one huge forest. Repton opposed the subordination of gardening to pictorial principles explicit in the theories of Price and Knight, and described the 'leading feature' of good taste in modern gardening as 'GENERAL UTILITY' – by which he meant the convenience of the landed proprietor, and not 'utility' in a Humean sense. He allowed no independent character to the picturesque, and frequently used the term 'picturesque beauty', in a sense close to Gilpin's usage. This quality was incompatible with agriculture, for:

> The shape and colour of corn-fields, and the straight lines of fences, are ... totally at variance with all ideas of picturesque beauty[25]

Price, for whom the gentleman with a sound knowledge of pictures is qualified to be his own improver, is less implacable on this issue. Although neglect and decay, the main sources of his picturesque, are often incompatible with the progress of agriculture he did not find the two necessarily incompatible, and he identified the picturesque in scenes which clearly bore the imprint of human use. The gentleman improver, humanized by the study of Gainsborough and the seventeenth-century Dutch painters, concentrates his attention on the embellishment of villages, which provides both aesthetic and humanitarian satisfactions:

> there is no way in which wealth can produce such unaffected variety, and such interest, as by adorning a real village, and promoting the comforts and enjoyments of its inhabitants.[26]

While this again illustrates how closely the picturesque was intertwined with a particular view of the model social order in Price's theory, it also demonstrates the limitation of its underlying framework, since Price's Burkean aesthetic gave only a minor role to the association of ideas,[27] and the idea of moral sympathy was fundamentally extraneous to his system.

Price's basic argument was that many pleasing objects could not be accommodated by either the sublime or the beautiful of Burke's system, and it is these which made up the category of the picturesque. Its causes were the 'two opposite qualities of roughness, and of sudden variation, joined by that of irregularity'. While picturesque objects are:

> the peculiar property of the painter and his art, being by them first illustrated, and brought into notice and general observation

it is important to note that for Price, unlike Gilpin, it is not association with painting which makes the picturesque a source of aesthetic pleasure. The pleasures of the picturesque depend on an innate propensity of the mind when it responds to physiological stimuli produced by a particular class of objects. Although Price recognized the importance of association, and he did not bear it the same hostility as Burke had, he was not concerned to investigate the role of the association principle in aesthetic experience.[28]

A great admirer of Reynolds, Price followed academic theory in many respects.[29] His statements that 'light and shadow' and landscape were the aspects of painting in which the Moderns had surpassed the Ancients, and that the Venetian school had brought landscape painting to its 'highest perfection' derive from that discourse. (Titian, in particular, through his rejection of 'minute detail' and principle of selection, had shown what comprised 'grandeur' in landscape.) However, for Price the Dutch had been equally selective, and he specifically criticizes Burke for implying an absence of selection in their work emphasizing the point, with particular reference to the cottage subjects of Ostade. In this respect Price's argument foreshadows the position that Constable (a great admirer of Ostade) would take in his lectures of the 1830s. It is true that such rustic subjects lack 'elegance' and 'grandeur', but the painter's treatment of them compensates for this. Price says of Rembrandt that through:

> his peculiar management of light and shade, ... he contrived to raise the character of vulgar objects, and to disguise that of such as were raw and disgusting.

The idea that 'breadth' of light and shadow could be used to give dignity to humble subjects is again academic, although Price gave it much greater weight than it had in the academic system, devoting a whole chapter of his 1794 *Essay on the Picturesque* to the concept.[30] What we see being formulated here, as in Knight's writings, is a connoisseur's aesthetic according to which what seems to be a nostalgic vision of an earlier rustic order embodied in small cabinet pictures is valorized as an appropriate object of contemplation for the virtuous gentleman.

Knight was undoubtedly a more systematic thinker than Price, and his *Analytical Inquiry* is far closer to a general aesthetic than the latter's various essays, which really concern only the picturesque and gardening. Knight's treatise is based on a clearly defined psychology, and he criticized Price for his dependence on Burke, for whom Knight expressed personal admiration, but contempt as an aesthetician.[31] He rejected Price's attempt to establish the picturesque as a separate category, on the basis that he sought to found distinctions in objects themselves rather than in the mode of viewing them.

For Knight, the picturesque defines pleasures produced by visual sensations in themselves, and it is not distinct from beauty as such. It is the pleasure which occurs when the sense of sight responds to certain effects of light and colour, due to an innate propensity. As far as sight affords this purely sensual pleasure it depends upon a particular 'moderate and varied irritation of the organic nerves'.[32] But although we may derive a purely sensual pleasure from the effects of light on objects without any prior knowledge of painting, association will enormously enhance our pleasure if we do acquire such knowledge. Further, as the character and range of pictorial imitation develops, the boundaries of the picturesque will necessarily be extended.[33]

This would seem to be a licence for some aspects of naturalistic landscape painting, and of all the theorists of the picturesque Payne Knight was the most able to see picturesque qualities in agricultural landscape in the raw. In *The Landscape* he contrasts the virtues of rural life with the 'delusive joys' of political ambition, and he emphasizes that the 'happy scenes of meditative ease' to which he is referring are a real landscape and not a pastoral fiction. They are such as:

> nature's common charms produce
> For social man's delight and common use

In a long footnote to the poem, Knight says that some little sacrifices may be necessary to achieve the picturesque, but these should be small and are usually limited to the grounds immediately around the house. In general, the picturesque and agriculture are not incompatible, and he criticizes modern improvers for treating them as if they were:

> The usual features of a cultivated country are the accidental mixtures of meadows, woods, pastures, and cornfields: interspersed with farm houses, cottages, mills, &c.; and I do not know that in this country better materials for middle grounds and distances can be obtained, or are to be wished for[34]

Of all the picturesque theorists, Knight comes closest to accepting the scenery as it is, both in gardening and in painting. In another footnote to *The Landscape* he writes:

> Mr Repton has observed that there are a thousand scenes in nature to delight the eye, beside those which may be copied as pictures; and that one of the keenest observers of picturesque scenery (Mr Gilpin) has often regretted that few are capable of being so represented, without considerable license and alteration (. . .) I have heard many landscape painters express the same regret; but I must add, that it has always been in an inverse proportion to their merit.[35]

Although his system theoretically allowed the picturesque to embrace the common landscape of agriculture, and despite his hostility to the 'cramping' rules of art, Knight did not emerge as a supporter of naturalistic landscape painting, and indeed was implicated in the British Institution's notorious rejection of Havell's *Wallnut Gathering at Petersham near Richmond* in 1815. None the less, his system did contribute to the science of landscape in that it offered a developed hypothesis about the pleasures produced by the formal aspects of painting, which was not there in earlier philosophical criticism.

The concept of pleasures of sight, independent of any larger frame of meaning, aroused significant debate, which touched directly on the scope of landscape painting. As Knight understood, Price's Burkean hypothesis of distinct categories of object which affected the mind in particular fixed ways as a result of physiological predispositions, simply looked *retardaire* in relation to the more sophisticated conceptions of aesthetic pleasure which association theory offered. But even Knight's idea of an innate propensity to find pleasure in certain effects of light and colour was hard to sustain in the context. A review of Knight's *Analytical Inquiry* in the *British Critic* in 1807, suggested that it was not possible for an individual to distinguish between that part of the pleasure in his/her response to a picture which was produced by the simple experience of sight from that produced by association:

> A plain man of delicate taste, but not conversant with the fine arts, if brought to view a well-painted picture of a dung-hill on a large scale, without being told that it was a picture, would instantly turn away with disgust; and his disgust could be greater in proportion to the excellence of the picture; because the more faithful the imitation, as perceptible to the eye, the more vivid would be the idea of stink and rottenness associated in his mind with such a combination of colours.[36]

However, the informed spectator would find pleasure in the picture from the 'justness' of the imitation, and the associated idea of the 'ingenuity of the artist'. In his critique of Knight's theory, Francis Jeffrey went even further, and again based his argument on a hypothetical painting of a dung-hill. Not only could such a picture show the painter's 'art and power', but the dung-hill was a useful object, and one 'associated with many pleasing images of rustic toil and occupation, and of the simplicity, and comfort, and innocence of agricultural life'. A picture of one had none of the 'odours' or 'effusions' which could make the real object offensive, and while there seemed nothing intrinsically disagreeable in the sight of a dung-hill 'in plain reality':

> we really do not see that it was at all necessary to impute any mysterious or ultimate beauty to its complexion, in order to account for the satisfaction with which we then bear to behold it.[37]

If Jeffrey attended the Royal Academy exhibition in 1815, he might have found precise confirmation of his theory in Constable's *Vale of Dedham* (*Plate 3*) exhibited in that year, in which a 'run-over dungle' is the main foreground object.[38]

Jeffrey may not have recommended the manure heap as a pictorial subject, but the fact that he could conceive it as one indicates the corrosive effect of associationism on the painter's conventional hierarchy of subjects. Further, while advocates of association aesthetics advised artists to produce works which conformed to the permanent principles of taste, there could be disagreement about what constituted these. Reaffirming the beauty of utility against Burke's rejection of the principle, Dugald Stewart claimed that:

> I am persuaded that I speak in perfect conformity to the common feelings and common language of mankind, when I say, that nothing is more beautiful than a highly dressed field.[39]

Further, associationist criticism did acknowledge that more local and particular associations could produce a legitimate species of pleasure, even if an inferior one. Thus Stewart again:

> How powerful the charm is which may be thus [i.e. by association] communicated to things of little intrinsic interest, may be judged of from the fond partiality which we continue, through the whole of life, to contrast the banks and streams of our infancy and youth, with other banks and other streams.

This demonstrates how very much Constable's famous comment on the banks of the Stour having made him a painter fell within a well-established pattern of discourse. Stewart, of course, saw such associations as particular to individuals, and they had a low place in a system which abjures the man of taste to purge his individual associations and concentrate on refining his universal ones.[40] But to individuals whose interests made patrician norms of taste less attractive, and whose taste was formed not by a classical education, but by contemporary novels of romance and manners, by a poetry which centred on English rural life, and by local topography and antiquarianism, such systems might offer a useful science of taste when purged of their universalist imperatives. As such, associationist aesthetics had a particular application to subjects of industry, labour, and historical sites in the national landscape.

(iii) The pleasures of the city – an inversion

Despite the Whiggish orientation of the social theory on which it was premised, philosophical criticism tended to assume that taste was most likely to be cultivated by those who possessed landed property. However, this was the result of certain residual assumptions from civic humanist discourse, rather than the inherent logic of association psychology. Indeed, in the late eighteenth and early nineteenth centuries forms of the association theory were adopted by progressivist thinkers including Priestley (who popularized Hartley's work), Wollstonecraft, Godwin, J. S. Mill, and the young Hazlitt, and it provided the psychological groundwork of Utilitarianism.[41] Because it made faith and morality matters of reason, what Coleridge called the 'mechanical philosophy' led easily to a questioning of received authorities and indeed to scepticism – hence his critique of associationism in *Biographia Literaria*.

A thinker who took a more sanguine view of urban society than Alison and Knight might reasonably use association theory to posit pleasures of taste which were not centred so exclusively on a rural lifestyle, or indeed to claim that the urban scene had superior pleasures to offer.[42] This possibility was realized in an essay entitled the 'Outlines of a Discourse on the History and Theory of Prospect-Painting' by the Norwich intellectual William Taylor, published as a long three-part article in the *Monthly Magazine* in 1814. Taylor was one of the leading figures in disseminating knowledge of German literature in the late eighteenth and early nineteenth centuries, and an extraordinarily prolific contributor to the periodical press in this period.[43] He came from a bourgeois Dissenting background, and although he was not interested in trade himself, he identified closely with commercial wealth, and was a liberal in politics. The 'Discourse on ... Prospect-Painting' was originally a paper read at the Norwich Philosophical Society, of which both John Crome and his son J. B. Crome were members.

In the first part of his discourse, Taylor discusses the history of landscape painting, and divides it into a progress through four stages, which is said to be characteristic of every school. These stages are the rustic, the sublime, the beautiful, and the artificial – the final and highest stage. All schools begin with the rustic because:

> The ignoble is of easier attainment than the beautiful, its very essence consisting in impropriety of outline, which may err in either direction. A degraded nature is imitated with less trouble than the entire – if a cottage is drawn out of perspective, the jagged thatch hides the undue convergence of the lines – down fally buildings, pollard trees conceal imprecision of the outline.[44]

This is a transparent jibe at the picturesque, and may have been inspired by some of the images of ruined cottages and rows of pollards, which Crome and others had been exhibiting with the Norwich Society of Artists. For Taylor, the highest kind of landscape painting is the precise contrary of the rural picturesque – it is the landscape of architecture and cities, which requires the greatest precision of outline and knowledge of perspective. The course of landscape painting is like the course of the Rhine, it begins among mountains and cataracts, and ends among cities and ports. This 'progress' from the most rugged and unyielding scenes of nature to the most artificial landscapes created by humanity, is evidence of 'the natural progress of the human mind', and analogous to its development in other fields.[45]

In his second article, Taylor asserts that a 'painted prospect' pleases either: 'directly, as an imitation of nature', or 'indirectly, as a nucleus of association'. Imitation has a less powerful effect than association, and in the third article Taylor informs us that it is by his greater command over associated ideas through selection, that the landscape painter can sometimes create stronger effects than nature itself. After discussing two paintings by Claude in association terms, Taylor returns to his attack on the rustic, which being 'the imitation of low, common, ignoble objects', would always be an inferior 'department', since 'it can only produce the direct pleasures of art'. Taylor also denounced the sublime, suggesting that there was 'something barbarous and irrational' in the enthusiasm for mountain scenery among devotees of the picturesque. In their 'fairest stage' of 'sensibility', in the most advanced stage of civilization, 'men' preferred the beautiful in landscape as exemplified by the views from Tivoli or Richmond Hill:

> which may probably excite, more completely than any other sort of scenery, the luxurious and agreeable ideas – of opulence, refinement, elegance, and enjoyment, being harboured in every dwelling, or scattered in every grove

However, Taylor found in himself a tendency to reject such 'soft associations' for some 'more stimulant'. Others can keep the joys of Alpine scenery; he prefers navigable rivers and the views of large cities, and these represent the 'highest destination' of art.[46] If he could command the 'Genius of Prospect' to place him anywhere, it would be on the balustrade of Blackfriars Bridge:

> There I can behold an immeasurably wider extent of builded space than elsewhere; houses rising above houses, streets stretching beyond streets, palaces, theatres, temples climbing from the endless mass of edifice further than the eye can trace in any direction, and beyond the majestic Thames, with the idea of world-encompassing commerce and empire, which that winding forest of masts is adapted to excite; and all this, my countrymen, our own.[47]

Not only do these model views run counter to the aesthetic of the picturesque and the standard repertoire of rural associations, they also demand a refusal of the associations of corruption conventionally connected with the urban scene.

As we shall see, Taylor's enthusiasm for the prospect from Richmond Hill and the spectacle of the Port of London were entirely commonplace. However, his elevation of townscape is unusual, if not entirely surprising in the context of the growing vogue for urban topography. It is hard to see that such a statement could have been made by someone less removed from patrician culture than Taylor, and it may stand as a notably bourgeois recasting of the association theory of the pleasures of landscape. It is a statement which needs to be borne in mind in relation to the large output of townscapes by landscape painters after *c.* 1815, such as those by John Crome, James Stark, George Vincent, and, of course, Turner and Constable.

None the less Taylor's model of the pleasures of the urban scene was not the bourgeois norm. Publications of urban topography and panoramas of city scenes indicate that there was a market for images of the urban spectacle, but the modern city did not supplant the rustic as the central subject of landscape painting. While the grand view of the city could summon up ideas of progress and the nation's providential destiny, it could also remind the spectator of the cruel struggles characteristic of commercial society, which condemned many to poverty and misery. These contradictory responses are well illustrated by a report on a panorama of London, shown at the Colosseum in Regent's Park in 1829. This stresses the ideas of the 'turmoil of commerce', 'incessant toil for the support of individual respectability and luxury', and 'the desperate energy of commercial adventure, associated with Ludgate-Hill, Cheapside, and the Thames' – but these places also bring to mind the many who are 'naked, and starving, and utterly forsaken of man'. The author judged the 'din' of 'barter and brokerage' preferable to that of feudal warfare, and claimed it was the providence of the nation 'to subdue the earth by an interchange of benefits', through trade carrying 'the seeds of knowledge' to distant regions. Even the 'freaks of fashion' had beneficial effects in that they helped to redistribute wealth. But to resolve the contradiction of simultaneous poverty and luxury, the author could only refer lamely to the duty of the rich to ameliorate the 'frightful inequalities' of society.[48]

The tendency of the middle classes in the early nineteenth century was to move away from dangers of the city centres, and to seek a lifestyle in the suburbs which combined closeness to urban amenities with a semi-rural environment. Effectively there was a growing segregation of class cultures. As the class antagonisms of the city intensified, the myth of a stable harmonious rural society which had been developed by eighteenth-century poets such as Cowper, became intensely appealing to the middle class.[49] Within middle-class culture generally, the defence of city pleasures was aberrant and more the ideal of the metropolitan intellectual – only he had the necessary distance, the disinterestedness, which could render the urban an experience of taste.

(iv) The landscape painter's science of signs

As we have seen, within the framework of philosophical criticism some of the fundamental shibboleths of academic theory received critical scrutiny. In this respect, its most subversive conclusion was that there was no intrinsic beauty of form. Such an argument was quite intolerable to artists strongly committed to academic principles, since it seemed to undercut central assumptions about the significance of the human figure on which their practice was based. The argument was particularly intolerable when it was presented with the outright disdain for the judgements of artists which both Alison and Knight manifested. It was the threat to standards of bodily perfection which those artists who attacked association aesthetics in the early nineteenth century sought to counter.[50]

By contrast, academic theory could accord only a low status to landscape painters interested in modern subjects, whereas association aesthetics could both valorize their practice and offer a body of principles for interpreting it. I shall show in chapter 7 that some of the most coherent and sensitive art criticism of the period was based on associationist premises; in this section I want to look at evidence which indicates that at least some artists understood associationism as a science of signs.

Neither of the most innovative landscape painters of the period produced significant statements on the association principle which have come down to us. Any rethinking of the academic construction of landscape painting which Turner made did not surface in his Lectures on Perspective at the Academy,[51] and although Constable did modify academic discourse in important respects and is known to have admired Alison's *Essays on Taste*, he gave no attention to association theory in his various lecture series. (On the other hand, Constable's whole project of making English 'Rural Scenery' the basis for major pictorial statements, which he set out in his *English Landscape* text, depends fundamentally on the idea that it had a particularly potent range of associations for the educated English person.)[52] As it is, the main documentary evidence for my argument here is made up of John Varley's *A Treatise on the Principles of Landscape Design* (1816–17), and the 'Scientific and Explanatory Notices' which Richard Ramsay Reinagle provided for W. B. Cooke's engravings after Turner's *Views in Sussex, Consisting of the Most Interesting Landscape and Marine Scenery in the Rape of Hastings* (1819).

John Varley was certainly one of the leading innovators in the water-colour medium in the years around 1805–20, although subsequently his reputation seems to have suffered from his large output of cheap works. Varley was also a prime mover in the Society of Painters in Water-Colours, and the teacher of many professional and amateur pupils. That he should have made the association principle central to his published landscape doctrine thus seems extremely significant. In the Introduction, Varley makes the now familiar distinction between universal and culturally specific or individual associations, which was so central to the associationist aesthetic, and advises the artist to 'carefully distinguish' between the two, so that he may 'delight mankind in general', instead of merely pleasing 'himself or a partial circle of his acquaintance'. The association principle is integrated with Varley's precepts on the practice of landscape painting by emphasizing the need for the 'fullest display of variety' controlled by unity of effect. This unity of effect seems continuous with the 'unity of subject' which he makes the key criterion of quality:

> A Painter must rest his pretensions to fame on an early and natural perception of the beauty of classification, and in the unity of subject; without which the greatest efforts are unavailing, and the grandest objects, instead of raising admiration, exhibit only specimens of extravagance or imbecility; yet this

> faculty, so rare, and so difficult of acquirement, far from being obvious, owes its power to its concealment, under the garb of simple and faithful imitation of nature, each object and its accompaniments answering to the ideas instantly raised by the mention of such scenes as those in which they occur; but surpassing them by the greater perfection of those associations which rendered those ideas estimable.[53]

This statement is clearly premised on the aesthetic principle as it had been formulated with minor variations by Kames, Alison, and Knight: that the pleasures of taste derived from trains of association united by a single pervading emotion. The 'simple and faithful imitation of nature' which Varley referred to here, sits a little uncomfortably with his emphasis on the artist's obligation to concentrate on subjects with universal associations, and in his own practice Varley moved between naturalistic topography and generalized views which referred to the ideal landscape tradition. But Varley was the teacher of some of the most original exponents of naturalistic painting, including David Cox, William Henry Hunt, and John Linnell, and if his theory was not a precise recipe for their work, it certainly offered principles which could validate some of it.

While it makes no explicit reference to the association principle, R. R. Reinagle's letterpress to Turner's *Views in Sussex* certainly depends on it. As a detailed exegesis of topographical landscapes by a practising artist, this is a text of considerable importance. Reinagle gives much attention to the ways in which the images direct the eye to points of special significance, stressing the 'science' which lies behind their apparently natural effect. Describing the engraving of the *Vale of Heathfield* he emphasized how the 'contrivance of the sky' drew attention to the 'chief object', the house, 'as by a magic spell':

> Science alone, aided by genius, can do this. These are the high qualities that can enslave and enchant the eye. It is the science of the art so little known, though never failing in the works of those who have been crowned by the praise of the world, and successive ages, that is constantly overlooked and mistaken for art only. The art is imitative: science produces choice; and entangles and entwines itself within the former so carefully, as to be unperceived.

Here we meet again with the notion introduced in chapter 2, that the science of landscape in the early nineteenth century was a science of expression (or more accurately of *signification*), rather than a science of imitation. Indeed, for Reinagle imitation is merely 'art', in the sense of craft. That the principles of science are those of mental association is most clear in his account of the engraving after *Battle Abbey, the Spot where Harold Fell* (*Plate 6*). Reinagle argued that the location represented in this image offered very little in 'materials' for the artist, and was therefore a particular test of his 'knowledge and skill'. Without a 'correct poetical feeling', he would only produce a 'common' and 'truly topographical representation' of the place. Turner has avoided this in the following way:

> The direction of the lines of the clouds in their convolutions, calls attention to the spot the Artist has to depict: the decline of the day, expressed by a low light, and long sloping shadows, together with the beautiful circumstances of a fallen tree, add an unexpected strength to the conception. The decay of the few straggling yet standing firs, united with the above circumstances, give a powerful impression of melancholy and sadness to the scene. To add to all this admirable feeling and exquisite sensibility of combination, both in form and effect, Mr Turner has given as an episode, a hare just on the point of being run down by a greyhound, which fills the mind of the observor with one only sentiment, that of Death; as no other living objects interpose to divert the mind from it.[54]

This description clearly identifies a grouping of signs which harmonized to produce a unified emotional effect, in the way association aesthetics argued all successful art should. To borrow Varley's phrase, 'under the garb of simple and faithful imitation of nature' Turner's image made topography signify what contemporaries could understand as *poetic* emotion, that species of 'bewitching reverie' which Alison defined as the experience of the pleasures of taste.

If the evidence of these two texts, together with examples of art criticism discussed in chapter 7, is insufficient to show that association theory provided the common science of landscape signs, it certainly shows that its value as such was understood by some artists and critics. This is hardly surprising since the language of associationism pervaded topographical literature, and the principle was part of the general corpus of received ideas. Whereas the association principle could seem threatening to figure painters, whose identity was constructed primarily through academic theory, it had far more to offer landscape painters to whom that theory gave a subordinate identity and little which could validate pictures of ordinary British scenery.

6 Naturalism and the academic ideal

If philosophical criticism defined the ideal type of the man of taste, the dominant ideal of the artist was set out in academic theory. But as is well known, within that theory the central model was the painter of historical subjects in the Grand Manner, and it gave landscape painting, and by extension the landscape painter, a low status. Academic theory could only validate the new naturalistic painting if some of its basic precepts were reformulated. In this chapter I want to begin by establishing the dominant terms of academic discourse in the period *c*. 1769–1840, and then suggest how artists such as Haydon and Constable altered the meaning of those terms to support novel aspects of their art. (Although Haydon was always concerned primarily with historical painting, his critique of Reynoldsian theory had implications for other genres.)[1] As we saw earlier, naturalism emerged within the public space of the new exhibition facilities of the early nineteenth century, and could be read as one strand in a deviation from academic norms of public art. Proponents of naturalism, in turn, might well argue that those norms of public art required modification to match the changed conditions of modern society.

(i) Academic theory and philosophical criticism

There is no doubt that Reynolds was the most widely read and respected English theorist of the period. The social and intellectual status he had achieved made him a key symbol of academic aspirations, and there seems to have been a virtual cult of Reynolds in the Academy in the early nineteenth century, at least among its higher officers.[2] Those who opposed Reynolds' principles, such as Haydon and Hazlitt, thereby paid tribute to his influence. Prominent aestheticians such as Alison, Price and Knight, whose theory had a fundamentally different orientation, expressed admiration for him, and the continuing authority of the *Discourses* in the mid-nineteenth century is indicated by Ruskin's frequent reference to them in *Modern Painters*. For these reasons I shall base my discussion of academic theory on

Reynolds' exposition of it, while referring to the works of other academicians to indicate that many of his views belonged to a general consensus.

Academic theory was the dominant discourse about painting in this period. Not only was this theory intended to be a guide to the practice of painters, but as it had originally been enunciated by de Piles and Richardson, it was also intended to guide the judgement of their audience, even if in some measure it failed to do either.[3] The Academy itself had been the subject of contention since before its foundation. It was born out of factional disputes, and although its status as the leading teaching institution was never really questioned, its exhibitions were certainly not the unchallenged showcase for the best of British art, partly because it simply could not cater for the enormous growth of the artistic population and the increasing variety of its output. The new exhibition organizations of the metropolis and a growing number of provincial bodies all offered facilities to those who were dissatisfied with the exclusiveness and pretensions of this 'closest of corporations', and to others who, for one reason or another, could not find a space on its walls.[4] In the early nineteenth century, a large volume of criticism was directed against the Academy as an institution, and its principles also came in for attack.

The Academy's role as a professional body was to inculcate: (a) craft skills, (b) a set of theoretical dogma which justified and hierarchized those skills, and (c) a model of the artist as a practitioner of a liberal art which should accord 'him' a high social status because of its elevated intellectual and moral character. Academic theory took the form of speeches to art students delivered at annual prize-givings, and of regular courses of lectures on the theory of painting for the same audience, repeated annually. While 'people of fashion and dilettanti' did attend the lectures, which were quite widely reported in the press, their mode of address assumed the listener or reader was a budding professional. Academic theory was thus a production-oriented account of a specific art, and did not offer any general theory of reception. It was not investigative or speculative: it was essentially the reiteration of received truths by older officers to young recruits who were not encouraged to question their commands.

In format, lectures on painting tended to follow the pattern of earlier treatises such as Richardson's *Theory of Painting*. That is to say the practice of the art was said to consist of a number of aspects which were discussed in separate chapters or lectures – Invention, Expression, Composition, Design, Colour and Chiaroscuro were common themes chosen. The Academicians generally gave some attention to the history of painting, although the extent to which they did so varied, Fuseli and Phillips giving far more consideration to it than say Opie. Because of the different nature of the occasions on which they were delivered, Reynolds' *Discourses* have a somewhat different arrangement from the lectures of the Professors of Painting, but they assume that painting can be comprehended under the same concepts.

Unlike philosophical criticism, academic theory did not set out from psychological principles or a consideration of the emotional responses of the spectator. Rather, it began from well-established precepts, codified by the late seventeenth-century theorists Félibien, du Fresnoy and de Piles, and developed by more recent writers such as Richardson and Count Algarotti. De Piles comments in the preface to his translation of du Fresnoy's latin poem *De Arte Graphica* that:

> It is sufficient that Painting be acknowledged for an Art; for that being granted, it follows without Dispute, that no Arts are without their Precepts.

Dryden, in his preface to the English translation, reiterates the point, saying that painting and tragedy: 'as they are Arts, they must have Rules'. As we have seen it was precisely this rule-oriented approach to the arts that philosophical criticism called into question, and such statements exemplify the other major strand in Enlightenment aesthetics besides the Empirical tradition – that of Cartesian rationalism. The rationalist approach rested on the belief that the arts have certain *a priori* principles which are justified through concepts of Nature and Reason, and Reynolds' *Discourses* have frequently been cited as its epitome.[5]

However, Reynolds' position on rules, as on other key issues, is notoriously ambiguous. He might claim that students give implicit obedience to the rules, and that:

> It must of necessity be, that even works of Genius, like every other effect, as they must have their cause, must likewise have their rules: it cannot be by chance, that excellencies are produced with any constancy or any certainty, for this is not the nature of chance[6]

But he also seems to admit that the rules which underlie the greatest excellence are beyond the reach of language to express, an observation he probably took from du Fresnoy. Reynolds followed such authorities as de Piles in saying that genius could not be taught, but as President of a teaching institution, he had to emphasize the value of study and the authority of examples. Rules, he says, are not fetters to genius, but they can only possibly be dispensed with once technique has reached a high level.[7]

This ambivalence towards rules and authorities is perhaps evidence of the influence of psychological criticism on Reynolds' thought. However, in *Discourse XI*, he also made a passing reference to Edward Young's *Conjectures on Original Composition* (1759), that remarkable foretaste of Romantic theory, in which he would have read that:

> Rules, like Crutches, are a needful Aid to the Lame, tho' an impediment to the strong.

Writing in *The Idler* in the same year that Young's essay appeared, Reynolds had attacked critics who judged by narrow rules:

> for whatever part of an art can be executed or criticized by rules, that part is no longer the work of Genius, which implies excellence out of the reach of rules.

He himself preferred to base his judgements on immediate perceptions 'without much fatigue of thinking'. Undoubtedly this was too heady stuff for young students at the Royal Academy.[8]

Reynolds' ambiguous attitude towards rules is matched by his qualification of the authority of reason in the arts. The idea that reason was the final arbiter in judgements on painting was well established,[9] and Reynolds' statement in *Discourse XIII* that reason 'must ultimately determine every thing and even must tell us when we should give way to feeling' (lines 88–90) seems clear enough – but it comes after a passage in which he has warned against the 'unfounded distrust' of imagination and feeling in preference for 'narrow, partial' theories. In the same *Discourse*, he says that in art imagination is the 'residence of truth', and the end of all the arts is to affect the imagination and feelings (line 41 and lines 384–5). Although it appears from an earlier passage in this *Discourse* that some aspects of taste, notably imitation and harmony, are governed by the same reason that 'relishes a demonstration in geometry' (lines 160–80), it is clear that Reynolds means something special by reason, and this is confirmed by *Discourse VII* in which he warns that the truths of art are not the same as those of mathematics. For Reynolds, Locke's calculating reason has a limited relevance in the field of art, which is governed by another faculty or sense:

> It is the sense of nature or truth which ought more particularly to be cultivated by the professors of art ... and we may add that the acquisition of this knowledge requires as much circumspection and sagacity, as is necessary to attain those truths which are more capable of demonstration.[10]

Reynolds was certainly familiar with Shaftesbury's writings, and by this time the use of the term 'sense' with regard to aesthetic judgement was commonplace – although criticized by Burke. Generally, however, Reynolds refers to this 'sense of nature or truth' by the term reason, and it is this double use of the term which causes confusion.[11]

The other key concept in rationalist aesthetics was 'nature'. As the term for an aesthetic norm, 'nature' is notoriously multivalent, and it is generally recognized that Reynolds used it in three if not more ways. Michael Macklem has identified the following meanings of it in Reynolds' writings:

1 as the normal, usual and general
2 as the Idea which informs but transcends the normal facts of experience
3 as what is natural for the imagination to find pleasure in.

Usages 1 and 2 are connected with Reynolds' concept of ideal beauty, which is central to his aesthetic, and 'the great leading principle by which works of genius are conducted'. However, this has been analysed often enough, and does not concern me here.[12] Reynolds' use of 'nature' in the third sense (as in *Discourse VII*, lines 330–2) is obviously correlated to his concept of imaginative truth, discussed above, and it also relates to the concept of a universal human psychology central to philosophical criticism. Indeed, *Discourse VII* can be interpreted as marking a shift of emphasis in the *Discourses*, away from the rule-bound orientation of the first six of the series towards a more psychologistic approach. The rules of art, such as they are, are now said to be founded on the known capacity of certain effects to please, and it is significant that Reynolds emphasizes:

> The search and study of the history of the mind ought not to be confined to one art only.
>
> (lines 523–4)

Discourse VII is in effect an essay on the Standard of Taste, which begins by telling students that there is a higher principle than the authority of previous practice in the arts, and that it is the 'operations of intellectual nature' to which those who wish to 'enlarge the boundaries' of art must refer (lines 15–20). This was the very programme of philosophical criticism.[13]

This sensitivity to recent philosophical developments in Reynolds' thought can further be demonstrated from his references to association. These are most striking in the third *Idler* paper of 1759, in which he criticizes Hogarth's notion of a criterion of beauty based on a particular type of line or form, and emphasizes that preference for the form of one species above those of another depends solely on 'custom' or 'some association of ideas', although within each species beauty is found in a central form.[14] Reynolds makes a small number of references to the principle of association in the *Discourses*, but it sits uneasily with his fundamental equation of Reason, Beauty, Truth and Nature. While he makes the pleasures of association a 'truth of nature', they are a 'secondary' or 'apparent' 'truth', not invariably established in the nature of things.[15]

The same kind of limited accommodation which Reynolds had made between traditional definitions of beauty and the new type of psychological definition can be found in the lectures of successive professors of painting. Although Barry's theory (like that of Fuseli later) gave more importance to expression and the variety of figure types than that of Reynolds, he equally regarded beauty as an eternal norm founded on selection and proportion. While he was aware of association theory, it has no substantial role in his writings.[16] John Opie seems to have been more receptive to the theory and in his First Lecture he wrote that:

> Conceptions of beauty or perfection take place involuntarily in the mind, through the medium of that wonderful and powerful principle, the association of ideas

But while Opie voiced distrust of the term 'ideal', when it comes down to it his definition of beauty is little different from that of Reynolds, being the perfection of each thing in its kind:

> nature in its purest and most essential form, unimpaired by disease, unmutilated by accident, and unsophisticated by local habits and temporary fashions

Like Reynolds, Opie emphasizes that the truth of painting and poetry is an imaginative truth. The ideal is justified because the mind is not satisfied with things as they are in common life, and aspires to a higher excellence. This essentially conventional conclusion re-inforces an essentially conventional account of the parts of painting.[17]

In the introduction to his Lectures, Fuseli directed the students to the sources of his theory, among them Félibien, de Piles, Reynolds and Mengs. From these traditional authorities come traditional definitions of Nature as the 'collective idea' or 'essence' of different species of 'visible objects' in perfection, and Beauty as 'that harmonious whole of the human frame, that unison of parts to an end, which enchants us'. It results from the standard set by the Ancients and confirmed by the imitation of the Moderns, and therefore seems unchanging. In a passage in *Lecture XII* Fuseli says that a 'genuine perception of Beauty' represents the 'highest degree of education', but at the same time describes this perception as an 'inward sense', and indeed the 'inner sense' theory seems to match most readily with the idea of a lasting standard, distinct from the transitory beauties of fashion.[18] Both of Fuseli's successors in the professorship of painting, Thomas Phillips (Professor 1825–32) and Henry Howard (Professor 1833–47), noted the influence of associationist theories of beauty, but proceeded to conservative conclusions.[19]

At this point it is useful to remember that at the core of academic education was the Life School, that the drawing of the human figure was the central skill which it sought to inculcate, and remained for it the fundamental basis of great art. (This is neatly exemplified by Benjamin West's claim in his first Discourse of 1792, that 'the great alphabet of our art is the human figure', and that through the character and grouping of figures the painter can make 'words' and 'sentences', 'by which the painter's tablet speaks a universal language'.)[20] No institution for which the figure represented the central mechanism of expression was likely to see any gain in remodelling the discourse through which it represented itself to accommodate an aesthetic which was concerned with the relations between the whole range of natural phenomena and sentiments, and tended to treat representation of the figure as an inefficient way of denoting emotions – an aesthetic for which form in itself produced relatively weak pleasures. Philosophical criticism remained centrally concerned with literature, and treated narrative and poetic imagery as the most potent aesthetic stimuli apart from the grand scenes of nature. The relative value of the pleasures of forms and the nature of their cause were the issues which inevitably came to the forefront for those who criticized association aesthetics from the standpoint of academic theory in the early nineteenth century.[21]

The limited accommodation which academic theory made with the development of aesthetics can also be shown from its response to the new categories of the sublime and picturesque. The term sublime is quite common in academic writings, but its meaning advanced little beyond the Longinian sense in which de Piles had used it in *The Idea of a Perfect Painter* to refer to the quality of style he called 'the

Grand Gusto'. Reynolds probably got his ideas on the sublime from the chapter on that subject in the second edition of Richardson's *Theory of Painting* (1725), although he replaced Raphael with Michelangelo as the model for the sublime style.[22] Despite Reynolds' friendship with Burke, and his favourable reference to Burke's *Philosophical Inquiry* in *Discourse VIII*, he did not make the radical distinction between the beautiful and sublime which was central to Burke's theory. The sublime is simply the highest excellence of expression, and the kind of definition of the sublime in terms of a psychological response excited by particular material phenomena, which philosophical criticism sought to provide, found no place in the theory of painting. In academic theory heroic male imagery was the source of the highest pleasure, and central to the painter's craft. While this could be valorized by the theory of the sublime, the implication of that theory was that it offered an inferior effect to the vastness of natural phenomena.

Academic theory found it equally hard to incorporate the picturesque. Reynolds was unwilling to recognize the picturesque as a distinct aesthetic category and wished to restrict it to natural objects only. Although he was aware of Gilpin's ideas from 1776 onwards, he made no reference to them in the *Discourses*,[23] and none of the Professors of Painting before Howard discuss the concept in their lectures. In his Third Lecture Howard referred to the connection which Price and Knight had established between the picturesque and the effects of chiaroscuro, and defined the principle as:

> the gradual discovery or perception, that light, dark, and colour are not only valuable as the necessary instruments of imitation ... but they have in themselves properties so agreeable, that when skilfully adapted, they are capable of communicating interest to the most ordinary objects and circumstances, and of making a picture ... out of the most trivial, and even repulsive materials

Howard recognized clearly that the picturesque matched ill with traditional academic values, and connected it with the Romantic style in continental art, which he described as 'a sort of chartered libertine' which abhorring the Classical, preferred the wild and capricious, and was proud of a 'bravura of execution', hardly compatible with correctness. Howard had no doubt that the Classical style is superior, and is 'calculated to excite our best feelings', although the picturesque, 'which may be considered the most attractive quality of our art' deserves to be studied very carefully.[24] These comments reveal again how difficult it was to reconcile traditional academic values with the ordering of the pleasures of taste in picturesque theory.

In conclusion then, while the theory of painting in this period undoubtedly registered the larger developments of aesthetics, it remained an essentially conservative doctrine, the ideology of a professional group unwilling to make adjustments to traditional beliefs, which seemed essential to justify its claims to status. Recognition that academic theory was ill-adapted to the practice of contemporary painters came more from those who were outside the Academy and made fewer pretensions to the higher walks of art than would-be history painters such as Reynolds and Opie, or more committed practitioners such as Barry, Fuseli, and Howard.

(ii) Landscape painting in academic theory

The status which academic theory accorded to landscape painting was intrinsically connected with the idea it represented of art as a social practice. Reynolds states clearly that beauty leads to virtue, and bestows public benefits through the refinement of taste.[25] The painter must aim to 'address' the mind and, *ut pictura poesis*, the way in which he does so is primarily through narrative, the representation of subjects from the bible, history or literature – although the contemplation of ideal forms is also improving.[26] For Reynolds, kinds of painting other than history painting had their merits and indeed: 'no part of this excellent art, so much the ornament of polished life, is destitute of value and use'. But he also maintained that the lesser genres would never earn the painter 'a permanent reputation' because they had less intellectual and moral content.[27]

Reynolds' insistence on the pre-eminence of history painting in the Grand Style was justified by two systems of classification: viz. the classification of different subjects into the hierarchy of genres on which he elaborates in *Discourse III*,[28] and the classification of styles of painting according to different schools, each with its respective merits. In *Discourse IV* he makes his famous division between the Grand and Ornamental styles: the former was history painting as practised by the Roman, Florentine, and Bolognese Schools, and the latter as it was practised by the Venetian and Flemish. The Grand Style could not be improved by any attempt to mix it with the characteristics of the Ornamental, and Reynolds rejected the idea that their different excellencies could be unified in the same work. For Reynolds, the Grand Style consisted in a 'firm and determined outline' which related to the priority of form over light, shade and colour, and this primacy of form was to be asserted even more vigorously by later theorists.[29] The Venetian School might be more natural, and its colouring more splendid, but too much attention to colour was an obstacle to the highest aims of art.

The painter in the Grand Style had to give dignity to his subject, and he did this by painting an idealized nature which he arrived at from a laborious investigation of nature and the study of the best examples of earlier art. Just as selection is necessary in representation of the figure, it is equally necessary in the other parts of a painting and especially in landscape. For this reason, Reynolds recommended the example of the Franco-Italian School in preference to that of the Dutch, in a well-known passage in *Discourse IV* (lines 385–402). However, Reynolds professes himself uncertain as to how far landscape painters have a licence to represent 'Accidents of Nature' (transitory effects of atmosphere and light), while remarking that Claude had seldom done so. Reynolds certainly believed it possible to paint landscape in the Grand Style, but it is worth noting that for him even the landscapes of Claude were insufficiently ideal to contain historical figures, and only Poussin seems to have achieved authentic historical landscape. He was also highly enthusiastic about the background to Titian's *St Peter Martyr*, a picture which was widely regarded as the perfection of landscape painting. All the Professors of Painting in the period 1800–30 stressed the insignificant value of a non-selective approach to landscape painting with reference to the Dutch School.[30]

Turner's comments on landscape painting in his 'Backgrounds' Lecture, first delivered in 1811 as the conclusion to his course of six lectures as Professor of Perspective, indicate how much Reynolds' model of academic theory dominated instruction on landscape at the Academy. As Jerrold Ziff has noted, Reynolds was pre-eminent among the authorities to whom Turner referred, and Turner's conception of the fundamental aim of landscape painting reiterates the Reynoldsian conception of the ideal:

> To select, combine and concentrate that which is beautiful in nature and admirable in art is as much the business of the landscape painter in his line as in the other departments of art.

His assessment of previous examples was absolutely traditional: Titian had produced the greatest achievements in the landscape field, and Claude, Poussin, Domenichino, and Mola were also praised. Conversely, the Dutch were criticized for their concern with 'individual nature', and only Rubens and Rembrandt: 'ever dared to raise her [ie. 'nature'] above commonality'. Cuyp, Potter, and Adriaen van der Velde:

> sought for simplicity below commonality which too often regulated their choice and alas their introductions . . .

Gainsborough, by contrast, was praised above the Dutch because he:

> rais'd their Beauties by avoiding their defects, the mean vulgarisms of common low life and disgusting incidents of common nature.

Such statements indicate why literary and classical subjects remained so central to Turner's output, and also help to explain some features of his British landscapes which will be discussed in chapters 8 and 9. None the less, they do sit a little uncomfortably with his large output of pictures of modern scenes in the period *c.* 1805–13, which overlaps directly with the years in which he delivered the 'Backgrounds' Lecture. This suggests that while the form of statements of academic theory remained the same, for some of its exponents they meant new things. It also suggests that the continuing authority of that discourse demanded that new departures be justified within the framework of its typical statements – at least for those with a prominent place in the Academy.[31]

Academic theorists spoke of selection not just in the sense of the combination of the best from different examples of nature, but also in connection with what was termed 'breadth' of light and shadow, a concept we have already encountered in picturesque theory. This quality was desirable in all subjects, but it had particular importance for landscape where selection in 'form' played a smaller role than in the human figure, and where light and shade had a correspondingly larger one. Titian, who represented both the perfection of landscape and the perfection of colour, was said to have particularly excelled in 'breadth'.[32]

The concept of 'breadth' had been present in seventeenth-century theory and also appears in the writings of Hogarth, Richardson and Reynolds.[33] However, the academic authority who made the clearest statement on its importance for landscape was James Barry in his Lecture on Chiaroscuro. The 'indisputable necessity of selection' in all parts of a picture, said Barry, was particularly evident in the distribution of light and dark for on this depended:

> whether objects shall present themselves with that disgusting confusion and embarrassment which distract our sight, or with that unity and harmony which we can never behold without pleasure. There are times when the scenes about Hyde Park, Richmond, Windsor, and Blackheath, appear very little interesting. The difference between a meridian and evening light, the reposes of extensive shadow, the half lights and catching splendours that these scenes sometimes exhibit, compared with their ordinary appearance do abundantly show how much is gained by seizing upon those transitory moments of fascination, when nature appears with such accumulated advantage.[34]

According to Barry, the 'deservedly esteemed' pictures of unbeautiful subjects by Dutch and Flemish artists would be found 'intolerable and disgusting' but for their 'lights and darks'. The idea that the Dutch School were saved by their virtuosity in such effects was repeated by many later writers, and it was given a new authority by picturesque theory. By the early nineteenth century, English painters were beginning to see the manipulation of chiaroscuro and colour as the national forte, and the development of breadth acquired certain nationalistic connotations.[35] That light and shade had come to be seen as a key part of the 'science' of painting is indicated both by Constable's writings, and by John Burnet's treatises of the 1820s: *Practical Hints on Composition in Painting* (1822), and *Practical Hints on Light and Shade* (1826).

However, it needs to be stressed that the concept of breadth, as it was employed by academic theorists, did not license the kind of naturalistic style practised by Constable, Havell, Linnell, and others in the 1810–20 period. This is clear from Barry's preference for evening light over that of midday, and also from a comment made by Opie in an article 'On Composition in Painting', published in the academician's journal *The Artist* in 1809. In this Opie asserts that:

> The imagination is chiefly struck by comparison; that which has many equals cannot be grand; and where we are presented with a multiplicity of objects of like importance – as, for instance, scattered cottages, numerous fields and

> hedges, a succession of little hills and detached houses – , though the perspective be extended to the skies, in regard to the picturesque we find it little better than a weary waste; the eye soon becomes tired with the endless catalogue, which, however, affords to the descriptive poet, and the painter, only what Boileau calls 'a sterile abundance'.[36]

Breadth was a key concept for both Crome and Constable,[37] but while Opie's concept of breadth here would license say Constable's Lakes water-colours of 1806, or Crome's oils from around 1805 such as the Tate Gallery's *Scene in Cumberland*, it could not accommodate the former's *Vale of Dedham* (1815, *Plate 3*) or the latter's *Back of New Mills* (Norwich Castle Museum, *c.* 1815, *Plate 95*). Since academic discourse could not accord a high status to works like these, which were essentially topographical representations closest in their formal properties to Dutch prototypes, to give them a new importance (and thereby raise the importance of their producers) required a modification either of academic theory or the semantic references of such pictorial forms. The years 1800–30 saw attempts to do both, by (a) rewriting the concepts of the ideal, the natural, and breadth, and by arguing that the academic hierarchies were too rigid and restrictive, and (b) by connecting paintings of English landscape with a wide range of potent mythologies already established in nature poetry, topographies, and local histories, and justified within an associationist semiotics.

(iii) Society and the artist in academic theory

The conclusions of academic theorists on the social distribution of taste were predictably similar to those of philosophical criticism. As a body with (specious) pretensions to be a national institution, one would expect the Academy's dignitaries to represent the contemporary social order as a model of how the social order should be. This is I believe the case in Reynolds' theory, and the democratic Barry confined his adverse comments on public taste and British political culture to his publications as a private individual: *An Inquiry into the Real and Imaginary Obstructions to the Acquisition of the Arts in England* (1774) and *A Letter to the Dilettante Society* (1793).[38] Although Barry's known democratic opinions contributed to his expulsion from the Academy in 1799, they received no significant expression in the Lectures he delivered between 1784 and 1798, at least in their published form. It is striking evidence of the extent to which class antagonisms were intensified in the period of the Anglo-French Wars, and of the changing character of art practices, that the Academy's Professors should begin to make public pronouncements on the condition of contemporary culture in the early nineteenth century. Fuseli (first lecture course 1801) and Opie (first lecture course 1807) had contacts in radical political circles, and the tone of their critical observations derives from a wider mood of discontent among bourgeois intellectuals. It is particularly clear from

Fuseli's Twelfth Lecture, 'On the Present State of the Art and the Causes which Check its Progress', that the models of public art advocated by Reynolds and Barry had come to seem manifestly at odds with the character and functions of painting in an increasingly privatized social order.

Since academic theorists held that a norm of beauty existed in nature, and that the human mind was formed to perceive it, they found it easier to assert the standard of taste than authors in the tradition of philosophical criticism, who tried to explain the emotion of beauty in terms of a more complex psychology.

Reynolds' norm of taste is fixed to a concept of universal human nature, but for all its claims to universality, this is the 'nature' of a particular class. Like the aestheticians discussed earlier, Reynolds allowed the lower orders a capacity for aesthetic enjoyment, but disqualified them from exercising it. He is quite explicit about this in *Discourse IX* where he writes that:

> when society is divided into different ranks, and some are appointed to labour for the support of others, those whom their superiority sets free from labour begin to look for intellectual entertainments.
>
> (lines 28–31)

These 'intellectual entertainments' are necessary for the happiness and security of society, for through them human nature is 'uplifted', and the leisured man is diverted from pursuing the gratification of the senses to excess. In fact the Academy not only disqualified the 'common people' theoretically from the enjoyment of painting, it also physically excluded them from its exhibitions by an entrance fee. Further, Reynolds specifically warned the aspiring painter against trying to please 'indiscriminately' 'the mixed multitude of people' who attended them.[39]

The Grand Style in art can only be appreciated by those with taste, and taste for Reynolds is the product of a general education and culture, available only to the higher ranks:

> This refined taste is the consequence of education and habit: we are born only with a capacity of entertaining this refinement, as we are born with a disposition to receive and obey all the rules and regulations of society: and so far it may be said to be natural to us, and no further.[40]

Thus Reynolds' strictures on the Dutch School partly imply a kind of class judgement, because their exact imitations of ordinary nature can appeal to the 'common people, ignorant of the principles of art'.[41] All the successive Professors of Painting in this period warned against the vulgarity of the Dutch School and the dangers of imitating its example, while conscientiously praising its technical merits. All implied that to cater to such vulgarity would lower the painter's status in society.[42]

Since taste is reserved for those with the education and leisure to acquire it, it follows that the artist rose above the 'common people' to a kind of equality with those whose wealth and ancestry placed them in the dominant social class. One of the basic purposes of academies was to enhance the dignity of artists and thus Reynolds was consistently at pains to stress that painting was an activity of the mind rather than a craft:

> The value and rank of every art is in proportion to the mental labour employed in it, or the mental pleasure produced by it . . . In the hands of one man, it [i.e. painting] makes the highest pretensions, as it is addressed to the noblest faculties: in those of another, it is reduced to a mere matter of ornament; and the painter has but the humble province of furnishing our apartments with elegance.[43]

This is why the imitation of nature in itself can not possibly provide the sole aim of painting. If it were painting would remain a mechanical activity and would not be a liberal art. Thus the Dutch School which did not convey elevated moral ideas was painting at its most mechanical, furthest from its true purpose.

Concomitant with the assertion of painting as a liberal art was the insistence that the profession was emphatically not a trade. In his first *Discourse* to the Academy, Reynolds describes that institution only as an 'ornament' suitable to the progress and greatness of the British Empire, and goes on to deny that it should be organized on the basis of commercial principles.[44] Artists can only contribute to taste in manufactures by aiming at a higher perfection – they should aspire after glory, but never gain.

The idea that genius could raise the artist far above his normal class position, and make him equal, if not superior to the great and wealthy had obvious attractions. The Academy sought to foster these pretensions through its ceremonies and titles, and through the Annual Dinners, where artists rubbed shoulders with persons of the highest rank. Artists were highly conscious of the status which had according to report been given to painters in the Ancient World and Renaissance Italy, and theorists from William Aglionby onwards referred to the favours bestowed by monarchs and popes on great artists: the examples of Alexander and Apelles, Francis I and Leonardo, Leo X and Raphael were trotted out with monotonous regularity.[45]

Reynolds' theory thus acknowledged that the class structure of eighteenth-century society reserved art for the consumption of an elite, and regarded this situation as natural and inevitable. In my view, Reynolds was not critical of modern commercial societies in the way that John Barrell has argued, and there is no evidence to indicate that he disapproved of the mutually beneficial relationship between landed and commercial wealth in his period, whatever he may have felt about corruption, the National Debt, and the undue influence of particular factional interests.[46] However, the unpublished *Ironical Discourse* of 1790 suggests that he did disapprove of the efforts of bourgeois interests to increase their political influence in the 1780s and 1790s, and in the introduction to this he remarked:

> It was acknowledged that more people could read and write and cast accounts than in any former age, and that more people read newspapers, magazines, &c.

> But it was not to be inferred from thence that this smattering of knowledge capacitated them to set up for legislators[47]

Equally, this extension of superficial knowledge had not made a refined taste more widespread or led to the formation of more artistic genius, and it seems unlikely that Reynolds believed the 'progress' of society would fundamentally alter the hierarchical order of aesthetic sensibility. Just as political economy naturalized the conditions of production and exchange in capitalist society, so Reynolds naturalized the conditions of artistic production of his time. 'The laws of commerce are the laws of Nature, and therefore the laws of God', wrote Burke, and he equally elevated the eighteenth-century constitution to 'the pattern of nature', and the model for all good government. Parallels between Burke's thought and that of Reynolds have been drawn often enough; suffice it to say here that both were equally conservative defenders of an 'entailed inheritance' of received wisdom, and both see an inequitable distribution of wealth and privilege as being 'natural', rather than artificial or social. For Reynolds, art is as much the preserve of an élite as government is for Burke, and although these two élites do not quite coincide, they are overlapping and mutually supportive.[48]

In his attempt to achieve a new kind of status for the painter in Britain Reynolds had taken over virtually unmodified the theoretical principles codified by the French Academy. These principles were, in effect, a development of the humanist theory of painting, formulated in fifteenth and sixteenth-century Italy by writers who, in the absence of any classical authorities on the visual arts, had developed a whole aesthetic from a few remarks by Aristotle, Horace and Simonides on the relationship between painting and poetry.[49] But the humanistic theory of painting and the dogma of the hierarchy of genres had developed in very different social conditions from those of eighteenth-century Britain, where, as was frequently observed, there was very little royal patronage of the arts, and painting was barely used at all for the decoration of public buildings and churches. Reynolds' theory not only did not match the prevailing conditions of painting in Britain, but he would have been hard-pressed to square it with his own practice.

The establishment of the Academy not only contributed to the output of art theory, but also institutionalized its precepts. As the number of artists grew in the eighteenth century, so did their ambitions, and the absence of any real encouragement for history painting became a continuing cause for complaint. Barry summed up the theoretical position as follows:

> History painting and sculpture should be the main views of every people desirous of gaining honour by the arts. These are the tests by which the national character will be tried in after ages[50]

If this was the case, then the continuing dearth of patronage for history painting in Britain must be a sad reflection on its national culture, and the idea that the nation's growing wealth and power was not matched by its artistic output runs through writings on art across this period. In a text of 1809, Shee lamented:

> There is perhaps, no similar instance of a great nation, in which, civil culture has been attended with so little of this species of refinement: in which the Arts have excited so little public interest and obtained so little public estimation.[51]

However, it could be argued that as much as, or even rather than, the 'public' failing in its duty to patronize High Art, artists were failing in their duty to produce it, lured by the greater rewards and easier life of the portraitist. If such a view was taken, many of the leading academicians were singularly culpable, and their practice stood in manifest contradiction to the creed the institution disseminated. A few artists like Barry and Haydon were induced to set themselves in opposition to the prevailing realities of patronage, and to become what Shee called 'a kind of intellectual desperadoes' (sic). Such artists represented themselves as figures of heroic self-sacrifice, and created a martyrology around their endeavours. But this martyrology contained no female saints, and the emphasis on heroic struggle indicates how patriarchal this concept of genius was – a kind of artistic machismo, precisely illustrated in Haydon's swaggering pretensions.[52]

The inadequacy of the construction of the artist in academic theory was increasingly evident in the early nineteenth century as a result of the growing prestige of landscape, genre, and water-colour painting, and their prominence in public exhibitions. However, given the inertia of established institutions and the entrenched interests involved, it is not surprising that the Academy's theorists were slow to adapt. In so far as an alternative model of the artist emerged in this period, it was shaped within the periodical press by critics who refused to accept the rules of the academic hierarchy. Such critics argued for a model of the artist genius whose power did not depend so much on traditional criteria of the Grand Style, but rather on signs of originality and a capacity to capture the attention of the public such as Wilkie and John Martin displayed. Whereas the great artist of academic theory was a man of virtue within a patrician society, the genius of radical criticism was one of the intellectual benefactors of humanity, whose efforts, like those of great scientists and thinkers, contributed to the inexorable progress of the species towards democracy and knowledge.[53] However, given the image of intellectual power on which this model rested, this new artist type was as safely male as the old one.

(iv) Modifications in academic discourse

Although the Academy's professors made no significant modifications to academic principles in this period, a few artists speaking outside the institution made statements which significantly modified them, while thinking within the same discursive framework. The status of such statements was inevitably different from that of the

Academy Lectures. Haydon's Lecture Series was initially prepared for the London Mechanics Institute in 1835, and delivered in a number of provincial cities thereafter; Constable's Lectures were first delivered at the Hampstead Literary and Scientific Society in 1835, but were also read to the Worcester Literary and Scientific Institution, and the Royal Institution. Although these Lectures were written in the 1830s (and the 1840s in Haydon's case) – there is ample evidence that the views of both artists had been formulated and achieved currency earlier.[54] The modifications I shall discuss here relate to the following issues: (a) the ideal, (b) the hierarchy of genres and the hierarchy of styles, (c) rules and originality, and (d) the public functions of art.

At the beginning of this chapter, I noted that Reynolds was the object of a virtual cult in the Academy in the 1800–30 period, and it is not to be expected that academicians would openly attack his theory. Constable's Lectures implicitly and explicitly refer to Reynolds' authority at a number of points, and his only direct criticisms of it concern the over-generalizing character of Reynolds' foregrounds – elsewhere he uses Reynolds' 'finest pieces' to exemplify the advantages of direct study from the model.[55] By contrast, Haydon's posture as the scourge of the Academy meant he was less inclined to be gentle with the institution's foremost celebrity. For him, Reynolds was a great man but a 'light' thinker, and while he recommended Reynolds' art as an example for the mature student (only), he argued that his doctrine of the ideal had been the ruin of English art. He began his First Lecture by emphasizing the contradictory character of the *Discourses* and rejecting what he took to be Reynolds' position on the relationship between genius and industry. For Haydon, genius is a natural and not an acquired power:

> a gift which sits on a possessor like a night-mare; haunts him when a lisping child, a restless growth, or in confirmed manhood.

Reynolds' 'genius' would surely have been less tormented and more urbane than Haydon's overtly Romantic model, who must feel that which he expresses.[56]

(a) The ideal

One of Haydon's basic objections to Reynolds' theory concerned his formulation of ideal form. In his discussion of this concept in his Third Lecture he argued that:

> So far from the omission of details of every kind being the basis of grand art, there is not a grand work of art on the earth where any essential detail is omitted. Grandeur of style does not consist in the omission of all details, but in the judicious selection of the leading ones.

The pretensions of Michelangelo and the 'Grand Style' had been exposed by the arrival of the Elgin Marbles, which for Haydon represented the *ne plus ultra* of 'truth to nature'. (This position is comparable to that of Hazlitt, whose criticism offers a number of parallels with Haydon's theory.)[57] For Haydon, the Greeks had attained 'the only perfect period of art' because they were closest to nature, and *contra* Reynolds he argued that the artist must not begin from the general idea, but from particulars if 'he' was to achieve excellence. He advised young artists (in this case his audience at the Mechanics Institute):

> Finally, consult Nature for everything, let your flights be ever so practical; remember, your engine is man; never wish, never try to be independent of Nature as it is the first step to incurable mannerism.

Haydon seems to envisage an art without style here, and commenting on the experience of comparing the great works of different schools in the Musée Napoléon he stressed that: 'he suffered most whose works had most peculiarity'. Yet despite his emphasis on direct observation of natural form, Haydon only reconstitutes the academic doctrine of the ideal, he does not abandon it. While 'the power of representing things exactly as they are, constitutes the painter in domestic art', in high art it is that of 'restoring them to what they were at creation'. Form is 'the basis of all art' and the perfect human figure remains central to its highest achievements.[58]

As mentioned earlier, in his First Lecture Constable took issue with Reynolds for 'over-generalizing' his foregrounds, so that when examined closely the 'rich masses' of colour and light and shade 'mean nothing'.[59] In a letter to his friend George Constable in 1835, Constable remarked that the 'ideal' in landscape was sheer nonsense: 'Even Sir Joshua is not quite clear on this.'[60] This was an understatement, since Reynolds and successive Professors of Painting had been explicit that the ideal should be the aim of landscape painting as it was that of figure painting. However, Constable's rejection of the ideal should not mislead us into imagining that he abandoned the academic principle of selection.

Constable's aversion to 'manner' is well-known, and he counterposed mannerism to an art founded on direct observation. Manner was:

> more or less an imitation of what has been done already – therefore always plausible. It promises the short road, the near cut to present fame and emolument, by availing ourselves of the labours of others.

and:

> Nothing but a close and continual observance of nature can protect them (ie. painters) from the danger of becoming mannerists.[61]

This relates both to Constable's conception of original genius, and to his conception of his own struggle – but as the earlier quotation from Haydon indicates, Constable was not alone in using the term manner in this sense.[62] Such statements need to be set against Constable's repeated insistence on the need for selection, which we noted in chapter 2. At the same time as saying that 'pictures have been over-valued' and mistakenly held up as 'ideal things' by which nature is to be judged, Constable quoted Lawrence:

> We can never hope to compete with nature in the beauty and delicacy of her separate forms or colours – our only chance lies in selection and combination.[63]

In a draft for *English Landscape Scenery*, Constable spoke of his aim as to make English scenery the basis of 'General Landscape' and classical art. Thus while he rejected 'the vacant fields of idealism', he still maintained a principle of selection derived from academic theory. It needs to be remembered that Claude remained Constable's perfect landscape painter, and he stressed the role of studio work in his practice:

> He lived in the fields all day, and drew at the Academy at night, for after all art is a plant of the conservatory, not of the desert.[64]

Yet, when all is said and done, Constable's continuing stress on the 'fields' as the 'chief place of study' does distinguish his statements from the standard dicta of academic discourse, and indicates affinities between his views and those of others who gave new importance and status to direct study from nature, be it for landscape or figure. Further, Constable effectively denied that only certain objects are worthy subjects for serious art, and considering his enthusiasm for Alison's theory he may have rejected the idea that forms are inherently ugly or beautiful, a position antithetical to academic stalwarts.[65]

(b) The hierarchy of genres and the hierarchy of styles

Although he made some qualifications to the doctrine of *ut pictura poesis*, Haydon remained fundamentally committed to a public art which illustrated literary and historical themes, and thus to the conventional hierarchy of genres.[66] By contrast, one of Constable's public aims was to raise the standing of landscape painting, and particularly of landscapes of everyday British scenes. There was really no space within the Academy for him to do this, and he made a number of bitter private comments on the pretensions of exponents of High Art in that institution.[67] He described the purpose of his Lectures as to show how landscape had evolved from history painting, securing an independent status in its own right:

> Considering, as I do, that landscape has hitherto escaped a distinction to which it is entitled.

Landscape was no longer just the 'humble attendant' of history painting, and was now qualified to 'stand side by side with it on the same eminence'.[68] Essentially Constable attempted to modify the status which academic theory accorded landscape painting, by associating it with the moral pretensions of British nature poetry, and by giving a new importance to chiaroscuro and colour as a means of art.[69]

It was a concomitant of critique of the hierarchy of genres that there should also be a critique of the hierarchy of styles, since the two were inter-related. The Roman and Bolognese Schools provided the model style for grand scale history painting;

the Ornamental style of the Venetian and Flemish Schools was more appropriate for portraiture and some types of smaller historical painting; and everyday landscapes and figure scenes were particularly associated with the 'minute' style of the Dutch School. Such were the basic correlations.

In his early *Discourses*, Reynolds had argued that the excellencies of the Grand and Ornamental styles were incompatible, although the Professors of Painting seem to have had somewhat different positions.[70] Haydon explicitly contradicted Reynolds in asserting that the excellencies of colour and design are compatible, and hoped to see them united in Britain on the model of his own work. As I have indicated, Haydon's standard for judging the various schools is a different version of the 'ideal' from that of earlier theory. 'Nature' is a term with far stronger connotations of direct observation in his system, and he argued that the disadvantage of fresco was that it did not permit painting from the model. Thus the works which Haydon believed almost represented perfection in painting, Raphael's *Transfiguration*, Titian's *Saint Peter Martyr* and Sebastiano del Piombo's *Raising of Lazarus* are significantly different from the models of High Art offered by Reynolds.[71]

Considering his practices and interests, it is to be expected that Constable would be more radical in his approach to the valuation of the different styles. The relative inferiority ascribed to the Venetian School hitherto had hinged on the idea that its contribution lay in colour, an ornamental and secondary quality. In his First Lecture, Constable was emphatic that colour was not only ornamental, but was also intellectual, and he seems to distinguish the basis of practice in the different schools without hierarchizing them:

> The 'solemn tones' of Titian have a power and poetry and sentiment, that as few have acquired as of Expression, and of form. It has a sublimity and pathos peculiarly its own, and of infinite difficulty of acquirement.

The works which Constable chose to mark 'four memorable points in the history of landscape' in his Third Lecture, represented the Venetian, French, Flemish and Dutch Schools, and he concluded by emphasizing the originality and value of Dutch Art:

> Whatever story the best painters of Holland and Flanders undertook to tell, is told with an unaffected truth of expression that may afford useful lessons in the treatment of the most sublime subjects; and those who would deny them poetic feeling, forget that chiaroscuro, colour, and composition, are all poetic qualities.

Although Constable continued to place Claude above all other landscape painters, his estimation of Ruisdael seems almost equal, and he particularly praised the 'grandeur' of his work.[72] In connection with the re-conceptualization of 'breadth', it is important to note that for Constable, Rembrandt had used chiaroscuro to 'an extreme', and although he refused to find fault with his 'exaggerated' effects, he warned that the example of *The Mill* had misled succeeding painters into imagining that they should leave out details in broad daylight scenes. In fact: 'The most perfect of all masters of real chiaroscuro are Claude and Ostade.' (A viewpoint which seems to match better with his works of the second decade than with those of the 1830s.) If Claude's and Ostade's works exemplify perfection of breadth, then a brilliant daylight scene like Constable's *Boat-Building at Flatford Mill* could also possess this quality – it would not have done so for Barry – or at least not to the degree of connoting a poetic quality.[73] That Ostade and Claude can be classed together in this way also indicates Constable's disdain for the hierarchy of styles. Only by modifying what he referred to as the 'too confined rules of art', could he make 'strictly copied' landscapes of 'real scenes' into 'classical art', and:

> place English Scenery on the same footing in respect to Landscape as that on which it has long stood with regard to Poetry.[74]

(c) Rules and originality

It is a commonplace that a key feature of Romantic aesthetics is the expressive theory of art.[75] While in Britain this is most easily identified in the criticism and theory of the Romantic poets, some of its features can be discerned in the new stress on originality and individuality in some art theory and criticism. If Reynolds, and the theorists he drew on, stressed the limitations of rules, they still saw them as providing a code of pictorial practice. The idea of there being a sharp distinction in the value of what could be learnt, and what came from some innate capacity was stated with a new force in Young's *Conjectures on Original Composition*, which distinguished firmly between two types of Imitation, one of nature and the other of earlier works of art. The first type led to Originals, the second only to Imitation, and Young was categorical as to the superiority of the former:

> Originals are and ought to be, great Favourites, for they are great Benefactors: they extend the Republic of letters, and add a new province to its dominion: Imitators only give us a sort of Duplicates of what we had possibly much better, before . . .[76]

Originality was the result of Genius, and was to be distinguished sharply from Learning which was only the result of a good Understanding. The 'unprescribed Beauties, and unexampled Excellence', characteristic of Genius are beyond the restrictions of Learning's 'Laws'. Learning is borrowed Knowledge, Genius is innate. As I indicated earlier, Reynolds referred to Young in the *Discourses*, but the emphasis of his statements on the relationship between rules, imitation, and genius is less uncompromising. Some early nineteenth-century writers such as Haydon, Hazlitt, and Constable, were far closer to Young in their heavy emphasis on originality and direct recource to nature. Hazlitt in his essay on the concept asserted that:

> ORIGINALITY is any conception of things taken immediately from nature, and neither borrowed from, nor common to others.[77]

and he concluded that the value of any work of art or science depended on the 'quantity of originality' it contained. In his first Lecture, Constable emphasized that even 'the greatest masters' had based their art on that of their predecessors, but also stressed that each was: 'distinguished from all the rest by some perfection which is to be found with himself only'. In Lecture IV, Wilson is said to have 'looked at nature entirely for himself', and the fault of mannerism derives from the 'absurdity of imitation'. The imitation of earlier styles is 'a blight on art', which can only 'reproduce a body without a soul' – it is symptomatic of the decline of painting. This distinction between 'original' and 'imitative' or 'Eclectic' art was even more emphatic in the unpublished Introduction to *English Landscape Scenery*.[78] Such emphasis on discovery of new aspects of nature through original intuitive insights is something simply not present in the concept of genius in eighteenth-century theories of painting, and it was crucial to the naturalistic phase.

(d) The public functions of art

In *English Landscape Scenery* Constable referred to: 'the almost universal esteem in which the Arts are now held'. This statement stands in stark contrast to the disdainful comments on the tastelessness of the public which he made in his letters.[79] In the Lectures, Constable denied that patronage could produce great art, and claimed that when artists did not follow true principles, patronage only hastened artistic decline. He observed a lamentable tendency towards mannerism in contemporary art and advised young artists to become 'patient pupil(s) of nature'. For Constable, artistic achievement depends on the calibre of artists, because the public is too ignorant to make effective judgements.[80] It would be interesting to know how Constable's views on the character of contemporary taste were linked with his jaundiced outlook on social and political developments in the early 1830s, but unfortunately he left no extended statement on the state of taste.

It seems symptomatic of the increasing strains which early nineteenth-century conditions put on the project of public art, that prominent academicians should begin to make more extended and critical comments on the relationship between contemporary taste and the social order. This is exemplified by Martin Archer Shee's *Rhymes on Art* (1805) and *Elements of Art* (1809), and his *Letter to the President and Directors of the British Institution* (1809), which, although not emanating from the Academy as such, were written emphatically from the position of artists as a social fraction. Both books were frequently quoted, and were recognized as a major statement of artistic discontents.[81] Inevitably Shee claimed that the reputation of a nation in posterity depended on its prowess in the arts, and that there was a 'patriotism of the pencil and the lyre, as well as of the sword'. Men of genius were seldom mercenary and their qualities were above price – they needed a nobler recompense than mere money: the respect of their contemporaries.[82]

The principle of *laissez-faire* is not applicable to the arts, and referring to the model of France, Shee called for intervention by the state to make the arts truly public. *Rhymes on Art* is critical both of nascent Utilitarianism and of radical social theory, which Shee saw as interconnected. He complained of those 'to whom this world is but as one vast market – a saleshop of sordid interests and selfish gratifications', and who judged everything according to the principles of Adam Smith, and were guilty of a commercial Jacobinism, which produced a 'levelling' of principles and feelings. One of the other reasons why the age is unfavourable to the art lies in the 'visionary speculations of modern philosophy' and 'Utopian enthusiasm'. In a profoundly Burkean passage, Shee attacked those who spread contempt for the 'gathered wisdom of ages' and offered 'visions' of 'unattainable perfection'. Society is a grand machine, characterized by 'innumerable complications of civil interest and social dependence', and attempts to simplify it would be injurious. The pervasive rationalism, which Shee finds so distasteful, is also the cause of the popularity of amateur science, politics and rural economy with the public, and this 'rage for scientific amusement' has distracted attention from the arts.[83]

Shee's strategy was thus to link the cause of state support for High Art with the discourse of political conservatism and anti-radicalism. Yet there are Whiggish elements in his texts, and particularly in the *Elements of Art* which contains a savage attack on placemen as 'commonly as devoid of sensibility as of science'.[84] It is significant that this statement appeared in a work published in 1809 since, in 1808, Major Hogan had published charges of corruption in the army, implicating the Duke of York, and in January 1809 a Committee of Inquiry was set up leading to the resignation of the Duke as Commander in Chief in March. In connecting state neglect of the arts with political corruption, Shee took the same line as that established in Leigh Hunt's *Examiner* in 1808 – although his politics were far to the right of this.

While attacking the 'political man of business', Shee, rather surprisingly, appealed to the 'Liberality' of the 'commercial man of business'. In his *Letter to the President and Directors of the British Institution*, he observed that the apathy of politicians towards the arts was particularly blameworthy, while commercial groups had the beginnings of an interest (hitherto misdirected) which could become the source of significant patronage. Thus despite his dismal and commonplace observations on commercial societies, Shee expressed the apparently contradictory hope that the 'fifth great epocha of the civilized world' would be dominated by 'Great Britain', and that it would show that the 'purest system of civil freedom' was also conducive to the 'noblest powers of intellectual excellence'.[85]

The view of the prospects of British culture which Fuseli set out in his Twelfth Lecture was yet more pessimistic, because its determinism was more profound.

Unlike Shee, and like Barry, Fuseli emphasized that religion and liberty were the principal factors conducive to the arts, which depended on:

> a general cause, founded on the bent, the manners, habits, modes of a nation, – and not of one nation alone, but of all who at present pretend to culture.

The reason why the present age provides so little opportunity for great public works is that:

> the ambition, activity, and spirit of public life is shrunk to the minute detail of domestic arrangements – every thing that surrounds us tends to show us in private, is becoming snug, less, narrow, pretty, insignificant. We are not, perhaps, the less happy on account of all this; but from such selfish trifling to expect a system of Art built on grandeur, without a total revolution, would only be less presumptuous than insane.

When the arts become only 'the hirelings of Vanity and Wealth', they fall into decline. Luxury can maintain the executive level of art in 'times of taste' but at the same time it saps its 'dignity and moral principle'. This explains the decline of portraiture into 'a kind of family calendar', and the increasing popularity of topographical views, which are merely a type of 'map-work'. Contemporary exhibitions are nothing but a 'gorgeous display of varied powers' exercised at the 'dictates of fashion and vanity'. Genuine works of art are produced only for their own sake, and it is fruitless to attempt to encourage them if the 'age' is not sympathetic. In the circumstances, theory and criticism can only endeavour to spread 'the genuine elements of taste, and check the present torrent of affectation and insipidity'.[86]

It seems remarkable that a prominent academician could use the occasion of public Lectures on Painting to denounce the general character of the Academy's exhibitions, and offer such an essentially bleak view of the prospects of the national culture. At any rate, Fuseli's successor, Thomas Phillips, noticed some of the same developments in his Tenth Lecture but represented them in a more sanguine light. Phillips observed that perpetual change was a fundamental characteristic of human history, and while the principles of the mind are immutable, changing circumstances cause them to operate in new forms. It is unlikely that individual efforts can check such changes. The great achievements of painting in Ancient Greece and Renaissance Italy had been the product of the efforts of religious institutions to control the mind. Painting is no longer used for the decoration of churches, but rather for that of the drawing or dining room:

> The increase of general knowledge and the extent of scientific acquirements, and the new ties of social life, have made the influence of the fine arts less attractive, and deprive them of their due attention. Although it is for the artist a tragic loss that no avenues of public patronage are likely to open for him, there also has been an advantage in that he has also been released from a species of thraldom

> which kept him within well-beaten tracks. For the gallery and the dining room the artist can employ the principles of art in a new manner. He can now no longer satisfy his employers with dark and sombre effects. The demand for a more ornamental class of painting has developed the picture of a lighter hue, with greater harmony of colouring and beauty in the arrangement of light and shade. To gratify men, the painter must adapt his efforts to their comprehension – this was the principle on which Italian Art was developed. The only difference for the modern painter is that he is compelled to give less to the grand and the sublime.[87]

Despite his eulogy of Reynolds, which made up most of this Lecture, Phillips seems here to be giving up the project of public art which had been so central to Reynolds' doctrine. It was perhaps more than coincidence that this tailoring of the suit of art to cover a more modest bourgeois figure should occur in a Lecture first delivered in 1832.

Clearly the extent to which the 'confinement of painting' within the domestic sphere was regarded as an acceptable development depended partly on the theorist's degree of attachment to the central principles of the academic creed. Outside the Academy, but thinking within the same discursive framework, Haydon was propounding a theory in the 1830s which, like the contemporary lectures of Howard at the Academy, asserted the enduring validity of Greek form and High Art and emphatically denied that any radical departure from tradition was necessary or desirable. But Haydon linked his conception of High Art with a different conception of the public from that of Reynolds or Barry. It was a conception of 'the people' as public, which derived from the contemporary discourse of bourgeois radicalism.[88] Equally his arguments for state support of public art were related to the radicals' campaign for popular education and free libraries, galleries, and museums. Like Shee, Haydon took elements from current political discourse and attached them to the structure of academic theory in an endeavour to use it to advance his own interests.

In his Lecture on Invention, Haydon made a strong attack on unspecified landscape painters in water-colour who asserted that the 'Old Masters' were no longer relevant to the practice of modern art: 'men who do not know the shape of a toe, and whose views of the beauties of landscape are limited to the splendid scenery on the Paddington Canal or Kensington Gravel Pits'.[89] Although it was more than twenty years old by the time Haydon wrote this lecture, he may have been referring to Henry Richter's *Daylight: A Recent Discovery in the Art of Painting*. At any rate, it is the only major statement of radical naturalism by an artist I have come across, and one which denied the whole orientation of academic theory in its rejection of the authority of Ancient Art and the 'Old Masters' and call for a new art adapted to modern society. Richter's text was partly an attack on connoisseurial standards, but also an attack on the patrician presuppositions of current theories of taste. Like so many of his contemporaries, Richter stressed the connection between the Greek achievement and religion and patriotism, but he injected a new caustic note into his account of this relationship:

> It is perfectly clear, that the Fine Arts have never hitherto prospered, but when addressed to the general mass of mankind, and used as instruments of the policy of either the state or the priesthood, resting on the grossness of superstition in the remote area of their origin, or on national vanity in the period of their greater splendour and refinement.

This clearly indicates a rationalist and democratic position, and Richter concludes that:

> the Arts, in order to prosper, must once more address themselves, not to the learned antiquary, not to the curious amateur, nor to the technical admiration of mere professors, but to the general sense, to the feelings and understandings of THE COMMON PEOPLE.

He argued that the utility of such a conception of painting was demonstrated by the work of Hogarth, whom he likened to Apelles – and who was clearly a relevant model for his own work as a genre painter.[90] Considering that within academic theory it was assumed that imitations of ordinary nature were adapted to the comprehension of the 'common people, ignorant of the principles of art' Richter's correlation between naturalism and democracy was a logical one, and one Reynolds himself had made in his *Ironical Discourse*.[91] However, while there is some evidence in art criticism that others reached the same conclusion, it was a connection which was consistent rather than necessary, as the example of Constable illustrates.

In conclusion then, academic theory was essentially unaccommodating to the naturalist aesthetic. Rather than valorizing the topographical and particular, it only valorized the ideal and the general, and effectively dismissed the former as unpoetic. However, its doctrines of selection and breadth were part of the science of painting in this period, and had considerable attraction for artists such as Constable, Crome and Turner. If we take paintings such as Linnell's *Kensington Gravel Pits*, Constable's *View of Dedham*, or G. R. Lewis's *Hereford from the Haywood Lodge* as representative of radical naturalism in the second decade, then Turner's Thames Series of 1805–12, or Constable's large Stour scenes of the 1820s look correspondingly academic in their greater degree of conventional breadth and corresponding reduction of detail. Within both academic and picturesque theory tight surfaces and brightly lit details did not have the connotations of the poetic and individual which accrued to looser brushwork and breadth of shadows.[92] (Although the latter qualities can be produced just as mechanically as the former.) To combine his 'strictly copied' images of 'real scenes' with a poetic looseness of application and a more 'old masterish' approach to chiaroscuro became Constable's project in the 1820s. But in doing so he frequently missed the intensity which he had achieved in works of the second decade, and, as his critics noted, sometimes fell into the defect of manner of which he was so censorious. Other artists such as J. B. Crome and George Vincent pursued a comparable aesthetic. We may assume from this that despite criticisms of academic theory current in this period, its definition of artistic identity was so attractive and authoritative, and carried such institutional weight, that it proved hard to abandon it as an ideology. Despite the tension between academic theory and naturalism, it remains essential to understanding both the practice of landscape painting in this period and responses to it.

7 Art criticism and the politics of landscape

(i) The metropolitan press

The main record we have of contemporary responses to early nineteenth-century paintings, as of the experience of exhibitions, lies in art criticism. To make adequate sense of the comments on individual pictures which are cited in the chapters which follow, we must establish the larger context within which they were produced, and from which they acquired their specific meanings. Thus the aim of this chapter is to illustrate the types of statement which were made about landscape paintings, and to explore their ideological functions. I am not suggesting that this can tell us what varieties of experience were available to the early nineteenth-century spectator of pictures *per se* – to do so would be to make a slippage from discourse to consciousness. Art reviews tended to be constructed from a limited range of types of statement, and often do not contain any fresh phenomenal observations. Most statements applied to any one picture could as well have been applied to many others. It could also be argued that art reviews relate primarily to the outlook of a limited social category, and not necessarily to that of the wider audience. However, at least they must have contributed to form the interpretations of the wider audience, and audience and critics necessarily drew on a common stock of received ideas. Although press criticism depended on concepts derived from academic theory and philosophical criticism, it was a different form and type of writing, determined partly by particular constraints of context which made it of limited length and generally broke it up into a sequence of separate pronouncements, and which also demanded that it be topical, political, and even fashionable or amusing according to the precise organ in which it appeared.[1]

The huge growth of art criticism in the early nineteenth century was partly the result of the growing importance of the press as a field of investment. The first decade of the nineteenth century saw the appearance on average of approximately forty new periodicals per year, many of them short-lived. This figure rose to fifty-five in the following decade and to one hundred and ten in the eighteen-twenties. In 1821, London alone had fourteen morning and evening daily papers, four tri-weeklies, nine bi-weeklies, and fourteen weeklies. By 1811, government estimates suggested seven papers had a sale of nearly three thousand or upwards, and by 1830 *The Times* had a circulation of almost eleven thousand. Although such figures seem small today, newspapers were more widely read than the circulation figures suggest because of their availability to a communal readership in coffee houses and taverns. The circulation of some of the successful magazines was apparently far bigger than that of the daily press – for example it was claimed that in 1819 the circulation of the *Quarterly Review* was between thirteen and fourteen thousand, while that of the *Edinburgh Review* was about fifteen thousand.

By this period, the amount of capital needed to start a newspaper was beyond the scale of most individuals, and they were financed by syndicates. Their staffs were becoming larger, better paid, and more professionalized. Since proprietors were concerned primarily with a return on their investment, advertising was a basic need of the 'respectable' press, and one which tended to lead to conservative or cautious journalism so as not to offend any section of the public. The commercial possibilities of newspaper publishing led to the appearance of a new kind of fashionable paper, of which the prototype was the *World and Fashionable Advertiser*, launched in 1787. Some papers were still set up for directly political purposes in the late eighteenth century, and the use of public funds to subsidize pro-government papers continued after 1800, but the practice was in decline.[2]

The growth of a readership amongst the unpropertied sections of society was much feared by conservative interests, and hence the stamp duties on papers were increased in 1789, 1797, and again in 1819. The principle of no pre-publication censorship was long established, but the second and third decades of the nineteenth century saw a protracted campaign to silence the radical press through prosecutions for seditious and blasphemous libels. The right to use the press for the whole range of political criticism was secured in these years mainly through the efforts of publishers and journalists whose work was directed at an artisan and working-class audience.[3] Freedom of the press was won in these decades. The growth of the press was one of the most significant aspects of the enlargement of the public sphere – that is of the range of persons who were sufficiently informed to be able to participate in political debate, and who felt the agencies of the state should be ultimately answerable to them as a collective body.[4] This public sphere also incorporated debates around art and literature, which in the newspapers were placed adjacent to considerations of political issues. The latter bled into the former, and helped give art criticism a kind of politics which it will be one of the aims of this chapter to explore.

The size of newspaper circulation figures suggests that press criticism had considerable influence in framing the reception of works of art, and there was certainly widespread concern that it did. Growth of the press was understood to have introduced a new factor in the consumption of art and literature in the critic, and the power of critics was a cause for manifest complaint and concern.[5] Like writers, many artists felt their livelihoods could be jeopardized by the irresponsible judgements of unqualified commentators, and within the space of the specialist art magazines, artists and their representatives objected to the pretensions of critics as much as they did to those of connoisseurs and philosophers – partly because of the blatant partiality of some critics. In 1828, a reviewer in the *Repository of Arts* aptly described 'the department of the arts' as 'a scene of conflicting interests, in which missiles are continually flying'.[6] However, the tone of art criticism generally implied that it had a responsible social role, and within the space of the newspapers and magazines it was attributed some importance, being allotted regular columns in many magazines and being allowed considerable space in most of the main newspapers during the exhibition period, except when the volume of political news forced it out.

Much criticism was anonymous, and I have been unable to identify the authors of some of the most interesting statements of the period. Among the named critics about whom something is known are John Britton, William Carey, James Elmes, Hazlitt, Robert Hunt, John Landseer, William Henry Pyne, John Scott, John Thewall, and Thomas Griffith Wainewright. With the exception of Britton, Scott, and Thelwall, all of these had some practical training in the arts, although the extent to which they identified with artists as a group varied. There seems to be a distinction between those who moved primarily in artists' circles and spoke in more technical terms of the values of paintings, and those like Hazlitt and Scott who belonged to the literary subculture of London and spoke more as independent urban intellectuals, with a kind of philosophical perspective which permitted them to take a general view. (Hazlitt explicitly denied that painters were the best judges of art, claiming that they gave too much weight to 'academic skill' and 'knowledge of the received rules of composition'.)[7]

More important than their actual identity as individuals was the voice such critics assumed, and the reader they implicitly addressed. Most assumed that their readership was a small section of society of refined sensibilities, and that the mass of exhibition-goers was incapable of making the subtle distinctions and informed judgements they offered. While there are significant variations in the political sympathies criticism assumed in its readership, much of it at the least addressed a male, who not only had a certain level of education in matters of taste, but was also 'street-wise'. I say this not because of what is said in reviews as such, but because of the reports of urban entertainments which framed them, and of which they were a part. In addition to notices on musical events and the theatre, there are also articles on the general pleasures of the city. Thus in 1822 the *Literary Gazette* began a series of 'Sketches of Society', which along with articles on such diversions as Bullock's Museum and the new Café Royal, included rapportage of London low-life described with a combination of fascination and fastidious distaste.[8] Two years later, some comparable articles appeared in the *Examiner*, one of which expressed an emphatic preference for the noise and push of the city over the monotonous regularity of the suburbs.[9] The author of this does not display quite that enthusiastic preference for the urban which we expect from the true *flâneur*, but we can find this in an article in the *New Monthly Magazine* of 1824. This 'Sketch' of 'Life in London', enthuses over the 'novelty and variety' of London, which make it a scene of amusement and instruction to *he* who can see it right. Such an individual can be neither an 'élégante' or a 'débauché', but is the 'man who studies his fellow-creatures, and whose active mind finds employment in all classes of life'. He must be able to 'pass from the senate to the ... toil and bustle of trade and commerce'. All parts of the city, all levels of life are his study. He is a pedestrian, who has quitted his 'spring pony, or dennet' to mingle with the crowd: 'Shops, countenances – but above all, manners, will all pass him by like the magic lanthorn.' To one without 'a ray of genius' such a scene produces no 'effect', but 'blest with observation, life itself seems compressed ... into the abridgement of a morning walk'.[10] Such pleasures are of course unavailable to the woman of the period, and this stroller is as masculine as his Parisian counterpart.[11] And neither are they those of the average middle-class male, who probably lives in the suburbs the stroller despises, but rather those of the urban intellectual. This article, together with the frequent reports of new buildings in the metropolis, which appeared in the *New Monthly Magazine* and its competitors, suggests that criticism's man of taste, who savours landscape, does so with a consciousness formed in the modern urban world.

Because of the huge volume of press and periodical criticism produced in the early nineteenth century, the survey on which the following account is based was necessarily a limited and selective one. Art criticism appeared in various categories of publication, and the form of these categories had some implications for the character of criticism, since they had somewhat different readerships and roles. I define these categories as follows:

(a) The specialist art press, which comprised four short-lived publications: the *Review of Publications of Art* (1 vol., 1808); *The Artist* (2 vols., 1807 and 1809); the *Annals of the Fine Arts* (5 vols., 1816–20); and the *Magazine of the Fine Arts* (1 vol., 1821).

(b) Monthly magazines, which can be divided into two types: (i) the fashionable magazines which were usually shorter and directed primarily at a female readership – these carried little coverage of contemporary political affairs and reviews were generally confined to belles-lettres; and (ii) periodicals which gave more attention to politics, carried chronicles of events, and reviewed a wide range of literature. For the purpose of a survey of art criticism, the obvious example of the former type was Ackermann's *Repository of Arts* (1809–28), both because of Ackermann's role in the art business and the quality of its reviews. The most important of the second type were the liberal *Monthly Magazine* (1796–1826), and its conservative rival the *New Monthly Magazine* (1814–36). However, although it was not as successful as either, the

London Magazine (1820–29) carried criticism which is more relevant to my argument here. For reasons of space, general comments on the two former are confined to the following note.[12]

(c) Weekly literary magazines, for which the *Literary Gazette* (1817–62) was the prototype.[13] Among these, the *Literary Chronicle and Weekly Review* (1819–29) has the material most relevant to my argument, and is the only example discussed at length. In addition, two short-lived weekly magazines which gave particular attention to the Fine Arts are referred to: the *Somerset House Gazette* (1823–4), and *The Parthenon* (1825–6).

(d) The analysis of daily papers was based on a twenty-five-year run of three papers, widely regarded as among the most important of their day: the *Morning Post*, *Morning Chronicle*, and *Morning Herald*. Some other papers including the *Sun*, *Oracle*, *Guardian* and *Times* were sampled in a few years. Two Sunday papers, the *Champion* (1813–22)[14] and the *Examiner* (1808–81), which gave wide and regular coverage of the Fine Arts, were surveyed comprehensively. For reasons of space, the *Morning Post* and the *Examiner* are used as paradigms of conservative and liberal criticism in the period. In these papers the correlations between the larger political orientation of the paper and critical values are particularly clear – most other papers were less consistent and the relationship was more ambiguous.[15]

In the remainder of this chapter, I shall show, firstly, how political discourse and aesthetic judgement intermingled in early nineteenth-century criticism, effectively producing a form of cultural critique based in varying degrees on a kind of middle-class consciousness. At the same time I shall explore the ideological functions of naturalistic landscape paintings within the range of critical systems involved, and finally indicate what art reviews suggest about the general semiotics of naturalism.

(ii) Art criticism as cultural critique

The 'Morning Post'

Art criticism in the daily newspaper press does not generally compare in quality and scale with that in the reviews and magazines. Reports usually appeared only in the exhibition season (late January to July), and they were frequently suspended or cut short if space was needed for parliamentary reports or foreign news. Some magazines carried a regular column on the 'Fine Arts', no daily paper did so.

Although Whig influence in the press was actually weak, the most powerful organs of the newspaper and periodical press were critical of the successive administrations, and in most cases gave the Whigs some kind of support. The paper most consistently connected with the Foxite Whigs was the *Morning Chronicle*, edited by James Perry, which has been seen as the leading opposition journal up until Perry's death in 1821.[16] However, while the *Chronicle* published some statements on contemporary art, patronage, and institutions which could not have appeared in the reactionary press, it did not develop a predictable critical stance, and its exhibition reviews suggest a number of 'voices'.[17]

By contrast, criticism in the leading fashionable paper of the period, the *Morning Post*, was remarkably consistent in the way it used comments on art to bolster its larger picture of British society. The paper was implacably hostile to all reformist tendencies and relied on voluble conservatism, fashionable news, and snobbery to give it a West End readership (in 1801 it had a circulation of only 1,000). Its columns were regularly filled with details of who had attended the royal levées and of what they were wearing, and it displayed a stomach-churning sycophancy to royalty and the dominant elite.[18]

For the *Morning Post* the state of British art was almost invariably a cause for satisfaction because it reflected the virtues and refinements of the aristocracy. Like the opposition papers, the *Post* represented the arts as vehicles of moral improvement, but since, unlike them, it regarded the dominant élite as virtuous, it considered the present condition of the arts as a flourishing one. It was only rarely that the *Post* complained about the superficiality of the 'public taste'. For the *Post*, the Fine Arts were accompaniments of national progress, and British society was eminently progressive. Reviewing the British Institution exhibition of 1809 it offered the 'gratifying reflection' that:

> at a moment when the ruthless hand of war is devastating the Continent, the polite and tranquil arts have found a happy asylum in this country, and are rapidly attaining maturity. Our Nobility and wealthy amateurs have nobly stood forth and rescued neglected genius from the Shade.

In 1811 it claimed that the rapid progress of the arts had become 'a favourite subject of conversation and inquiry' in the 'circles of taste and polite learning', while ten years later, it asserted that the nation now had an original and sophisticated School, which enabled it to rank with other nations:

> The nursling of an accomplished Court, and of polished society, it [i.e. Art] displays here all those blandishments, charms, and graces, which belong, not to its infancy, but to its utmost refinement.

This position reverses almost exactly the position of the *Examiner*, which even compared the situation of the arts in Britain unfavourably with that in France under Napoleon.[19]

The *Post* looked with particular favour on the British Institution as an organ of the aristocracy, which enjoyed the patronage of George III and the Prince of Wales. It was more prepared to be critical of the Academy, presumably because it was run by mere artists, although it did not regularly object to the prevalence of portraits in the way that some of the liberal and radical press did. In 1806 the British Institution was described as a 'laudable undertaking' set afoot by 'generous and virtuous characters', whose names would be transmitted to posterity as benefactors of their country. As the paper proudly affirmed;

> we have uniformly and sedulously endeavoured to give the people of these realms a due sense of those inestimable benefits they enjoy, under the administration of him who reigns uncontrolled in the hearts of his subjects ... our AUGUST SOVEREIGN.

Thereafter, it seems almost impossible for the *Post* to discuss the Institution without offering some little paean of praise to the wisdom and benevolence of its Directors and Patrons. The comments in 1816 that: 'No country in the world can boast of an Institution like this', and that the 'Old Master' exhibition was 'glorious for this country' and an 'honour to human nature' are characteristic. The British Institution thus proved the benevolence of the ruling elite, and in 1806 the *Post* even claimed, rather oddly, that those who occupied themselves with:

> collecting wretched Copies of Copies of Pictures which are daily imported into this country as originals of great painters, and damaged and impaired Works of Art

were 'as inferior in rank and fortune, as in talent and patronage'.[20]

In 1810 the *Post* praised the British Institution exhibition for its 'selectness of merit'. The small number of pictures by academicians was no drawback, and the Institution had not followed the 'erroneous practice' of the Academy in admitting an 'abundance of trash' simply to cover the wall space. It asked rhetorically of the public: had it ever seen such 'a constellation of legitimate art?'; a question which had clear implications for the standing of the Academy. Twelve years later it stated the matter even more boldly by asserting that the British Institution exhibitions had excited an interest far beyond those of the Academy in recent years, because they were not overwhelmed with mundane portraits. However, perhaps partly because of the way in which the liberal press was using criticism of the Academy as a vehicle for criticizing the political establishment, the *Post* was moderate in its criticisms of a body which also had royal patronage. In 1815 it was describing the Academy as 'this excellent Institution', and in 1821 its exhibition was the proof of the maturity and originality of the British School.[21]

The *Post* represented the foundation of the Society of British Artists as simply a legitimate response by artists who could not find an exhibition space at Somerset House. When it reported the opening dinner of the Society's exhibition in 1825 it gave great prominence to Hofland's speech in which he stated that there was 'nothing hostile' to the Royal Academy in the spirit of the Society. Although Hofland's speech was widely reported in other newspapers and periodicals, some of these also managed to point out the differences between the Academy and the Society, and the grievances of some of its founders. Oppositional papers like the *Examiner* regularly claimed the Society was a superior body, uncorrupted by invidious privileges and distinctions.[22]

Since the *Post* consistently represented the aristocracy as paragons of intelligence and taste, rather than bemoaning that Britain lacked a national gallery comparable to the Louvre, it extolled the 'Old Master' exhibitions of the British Institution as a worthier kind of model, claiming of that of 1816:

> no country could produce a collection of pictures from the stores of individuals, so entirely worthy of the patriotic design which knits together this truly national union.

That there might be other, less public-spirited, motives behind this display of conspicuous wealth did not escape the notice of some contemporary critics, who pointed out that the exhibitions seemed to be intended more as a fashionable diversion of the season than as a school for artists.[23]

The optimistic view of British culture which is the leitmotiv of the *Morning Post* is also characteristic of other Tory papers such as the *Sun* and *Oracle* in the years 1806–9. Thus the *Sun* too found the establishment of the British Institution a favourable omen for the future of British art, while the *Oracle* suggested that a new era had dawned due to the access of patronage, and that the arts were 'now advancing with an unexpected rapidity to perfection'. To prove the benevolence of British patrons, in 1808 the *Oracle* published a list of works sold from the gallery with the names of the 'Exalted and Distinguished Personages' who had bought them – a practice also followed in the *Morning Post*. In 1809 it suggested that British artists no longer had any reason to complain of lack of patronage.[24] As we saw in chapter 1, such papers were given to effusions on the fashionable presence in the exhibitions, which to the liberal press was a symptom of the corruption of aristocratic culture.

Since the *Morning Post* was predisposed to find evidence of the nation's felicity in the condition of British art, it regarded the varieties of artistic production with fairly uniform satisfaction. Thus, the *Post* looked with favour on the history paintings of Reynolds, West, and Haydon alike, but especially the two former. The exhibition of Reynolds' pictures at the British Institution in 1813 sent it into virtual paroxysms of patriotic ecstacy, and it gave the exhibition unparalleled coverage:

> But that which will unquestionably be the ultimate and triumphant feeling of every generous and patriotic breast, is exaltation, that England has given birth to a painter of such exalted genius, and of such refined taste

Along with 'kindred spirits' such as Shakespeare, Newton, and Chatham (sic), he had contributed to give Britain the character of a 'civilized' and 'intellectual' country. The exhibition was said to prove beyond any doubt that Reynolds was a great history painter, contrary to the slanders on his talents. While only a few of his works rose to the ranks of the sublime, those few were among:

> the noblest, the most touching, the sweetest, yet the most terrific productions, that ever sprang from the hand of a painter.

In the following year, the exhibition of the British Institution was said to demonstrate the benefits from his example – a position which is in striking contrast to that of say the *Examiner*, which represented Reynolds' influence as pernicious. The *Post*'s enthusiasm for West's *Our Saviour Healing the Sick in the Temple* was equal to that it expressed for Reynolds. The picture was 'by far the finest work ever painted in this country', and it would have done honour to Raphael. It was proof that Britain was not falling into an 'abyss of infidelity and corruption' as some claimed, and it was further evidence of the benevolence of the British Institution and royal family:

> It is a triumph in the arts, which like a triumph in arms, we glory in, and hail with a national feeling of pre-eminence, and congratulate the public, while we rejoice that the talents and abilities of the artist have met with corresponding liberality and patronage.

The picture would help to combat the torrent of infidelity which threatened to overwhelm the Christian world, and the *Morning Post* warmly supported the plan for its purchase by the British Institution. The posthumous sale of West's works in 1829 provided the occasion for a sequence of seven articles, some of them of considerable length. The *Post* claimed it had produced enormous interest among the Nobility and upper ranks of society, and that this showed the 'deceased Masters of our native School' were justly appreciated and that:

> taste is so universally diffused, that judgment has taken the seat (for long occupied by prejudice) and merit is honoured and rewarded according to desert.[25]

Haydon, the critic of both Reynolds and West, was not treated with the same degree of favour. I have found no notice of his *Judgement of Solomon* (Private Collection) in the *Post*; and *Christ's Entry into Jerusalem* (St Gregory's Seminary, Cincinnatti) received a fairly moderate response from it in 1820. However, in that year the paper remarked that Haydon had been 'continually honoured by the approbation of those of the highest rank and judgment', and that the private view of *Christ's Entry into Jerusalem*:

> was perhaps the most splendidly attended of any private day, to view any picture which has hitherto been exhibited in this country

The *Post* would certainly not print anything which might offend those who attended the King's Morning Levée or his birthday celebration, but while it acknowledged Haydon's success it did not make of him an idol as did sections of the liberal press – he was too controversial and independent a figure for that.[26]

While the *Post* was a supporter of history painting ('that walk of the art which we wish to see encouraged'), it was also prepared to find a positive value in the portrait industry, often providing lists of the principal portraits in Academy exhibitions – a practice which demonstrates its fashionable orientation. In contrast to the liberal press, which regularly denounced the display of portraits of 'undistinguished' and 'uninteresting' persons, it claimed with reference to those in the Academy exhibition of 1815:

> we witness with feelings of reverence, admiration, and national pride, the most perfect resemblances that art can produce, of many of those illustrious and distinguished characters, to whose firmness, talents, and valour, our country is mainly indebted for the pre-eminent advantages she enjoys.

While some in the liberal press regarded Lawrence's election as President of the Academy as a disgrace, the *Post* described him in its obituary as 'the greatest painter' of Europe, and proceeded to dilate on his polished manners and the ease with which he had adjusted to high life.[27]

For the *Post*, the lack of notable historical paintings in the exhibitions could be a cause for regret, but it was compensated in some degree by the 'perfection' to which the British School had brought 'comic painting'. As early as 1807, the *Blind Fiddler* (Tate Gallery) led it to claim of Wilkie that if his technique was not yet equal to Teniers, he excelled the Dutch painters in the 'accurate observation of life'. Wilkie's type of subject was sanctioned by a quotation from Crabbe, and it was claimed that the picture could not fail to interest strongly:

> every mind not so desperately fastidious, as to refuse to enter into the feelings and amusements of the inferior classes of society.

The *Post* subsequently claimed that Bird and Richter surpassed Wilkie in some respects, and it was also favourable to the work of Mulready. The paper's comments on two genre pictures, which might be expected to have produced uncomfortable reflections, reveal clearly that the representation of distress and poverty was not expected to promote more than a pleasing sentimental sensation among exhibition-goers. In 1816 it reported of Wilkie's *Distraining for Rent* (National Gallery of Scotland, Edinburgh):

> The disposition of its figures, the nature of their appearance, which comes home to every observer, the varied and perfectly just expression of the countenances, and the general skilfulness displayed by the Artist, almost force us to lose in admiration of his talent the sense of pain excited by so poignant a scene of distress.

Landseer's *The Stone Breaker* (Victoria & Albert Museum), exhibited in 1830, was described as one of his many 'sweet and natural compositions', and the contrast between the 'rustic beauty' of the girl and 'the care-worn visage of her father' was specifically praised. Given the predominant conservative attitude that distress and poverty were very sad but fixed in the nature of things, it could evidently be seen as both elevating and pleasurable to contemplate and sympathize with the plight of the less fortunate – and to do so via artistic representations removed the possibility of any embarrassing and disagreeable encounters with their real persons and real wants.[28]

Partly because of the constraints of space, but also perhaps because of the nature of its readership, the *Post*'s criticism offered little in the way of extended statements of principle, and its judgements on landscape and other types of paintings tended to be relatively brief. The *Post* drew the common distinctions between what was 'natural' and 'unnatural', and included statements such as that the 'master-merit' of a landscape painter was 'a constant reference to the harmony and freshness of nature'. Although it gave very scant coverage to the exhibitions of Water-Colour Societies, it responded favourably to some of the naturalistic landscapes on show in the other exhibitions. Thus Linnell's *Kensington Gravel Pits* (*Plate 4*) was singled out in 1813 as 'an excellent picture' which showed the artist fulfilling the promise of his early talent, and De Wint's *A Cornfield* (Victoria & Albert Museum) was praised in 1816 as 'a work of no small merit', although its colouring and grouping were not up to his usual standard. On a number of occasions the *Post* gave high praise to the work of Hofland and Callcott, but it noticed Constable only in brief favourable remarks until the mid 1820s, and even then made commonplace objections to his facture and colour. Somewhat surprisingly, the landscape painter who did best in the *Post*'s criticism was Turner, to whom it was extremely favourable until the late 1820s. Even in *Ulysses Deriding Polyphemus* (National Gallery, London, 1829) it recognized 'extraordinary merits in execution', and a grandeur of design which escaped many other critics.[29] Yet overall, the paper gave landscape painting a relatively low priority in its art reviews, and in 1827 it observed that it was strange that the nation which had 'invented' landscape gardening should produce so few 'great' landscape painters.[30]

Unlike some other newspapers and periodicals, the *Morning Post* did not identify with the position of artists, who it represented as the grateful recipients of enlightened patronage: its main concern was with the role of art for fashionable society. Its criticism, largely made up of cursory and often trite judgements, was no doubt well adapted for a readership which would not have been interested in any extended expositions of critical principles. This straightforward orientation to the world of fashion was not paralleled in magazines, even in those with a generally conservative orientation, such as the *New Monthly Magazine* (in its first series) and the *Literary Gazette*.

The 'Examiner'

Since magazines and reviews offered more space to literature and the arts, it is not surprising that criticism was more developed as a form of political critique within such publications. It is also significant that this part of the press was dominated by broadly speaking 'liberal' organs, for reasons which may be connected as much with the social composition of the intelligentsia as with the composition of its readership – many literary intellectuals being drawn from the non-conformist middle class. My argument in the remainder of this section is as follows. Firstly, I will indicate the way that the discourse of political radicalism in the period up to *c.* 1820 utilized cultural criticism through the example of the *Examiner*. I shall then compare its politics with those of the *London Magazine* and *Literary Chronicle*, using the latter to exemplify what I take to be a more class-conscious position on culture which evolved in the 1820s, partly as a result of the growing influence of Philosophic Radicalism. Finally, I examine criticism particularly favourable to naturalistic landscape which appeared in the *Repository of Arts* and some of the specialist art magazines.

Under Leigh Hunt's editorship the *Examiner* printed some of the most brilliant and effective political journalism of the early nineteenth century. Begun in January 1808 as a sixteen-page Sunday paper, it was published by Hunt's elder brother, John Hunt, but edited by him until his departure for Italy in November 1821. A non-party organ, the *Examiner* was an ardent partisan of Parliamentary Reform and of liberal causes. However, although Hunt was accused of republicanism and jacobinism, he professed an adherence to constitutional monarchy, and it has been suggested that he had no consistent political philosophy, but rather attached himself to certain causes.[31] The Hunts and the *Examiner* achieved celebrity partly through the series of libel prosecutions brought against them, the most notorious of which was caused by Hunt's scathing critique of the *Morning Post*'s fulsome panegyric of Prinney published in March 1812.[32] It was as a result of this that John and Leigh Hunt were imprisoned for two years in 1813–15. Just before his release, Hunt issued a new prospectus for the paper, which became increasingly bitter in its attacks on corruption thereafter, and Hunt was driven to new heights of indignation by popular distress, increasing political repression, and the Peterloo Massacre. In 1821 the paper was sold to Dr Fellowes, but up until 1830 it was probably edited by Hunt's nephew Henry Leigh Hunt, who had joined it in 1819. Under Leigh Hunt the *Examiner* had for a while achieved remarkable success. By November 1808 it already had a circulation of 2,200 and if Bentham's report is accurate, by 1812 it had reached between 7,000 and 8,000. However, by 1817–18 it had dropped to 4,000 and declined further thereafter.[33] In the era of the *Westminster Review*, the *Examiner*'s type of political critique perhaps began to look dated (although it too showed signs of Utilitarian influence), but the paper may also have suffered from the relative quiescence of radicalism in the 1820s.

From its commencement in January 1808 up until the end of 1828, the vast majority of the *Examiner*'s art notices were signed 'R.H.', the initials of Hunt's brother Robert, who had some early aspirations to be an artist. In 1829–30 the critic seems to have changed and the standard of the reviews distinctly declined. Over twenty years, Hunt maintained a fairly consistent position, although there was a slight shift in 1818. The *Examiner* was generally more willing than some other liberal organs to praise the British School *en masse*, and in his first article for the paper, 'State of the Arts in Great Britain' of January 1808, Hunt claimed:

> a constellation of British genius in painting has arisen with a splendour which cheers, enlightens and invigorates the regions of understanding and fancy.

The continental countries acknowledged the excellence of a School which now rivalled theirs in history painting. In a review of 1811 he even asserted that the talents of West, Stothard, Fuseli, Northcote, and Flaxman would do honour to any period of the arts (!), while Haydon, Hilton, and others all promised future excellence.[34]

One notable difference between the *Examiner* and less liberal papers lies in its attitude to French art and artistic institutions. It seems significant that radical organs like the *Examiner* and the *London Magazine* were generally more prepared to take an unprejudiced view of French art, at a time when conservative critics made ferocious attacks on it as a kind of loyalty oath. (In this respect they differ from the less consistently liberal *Champion*, which under John Scott's editorship was determinedly hostile both to French art and the principle of public patronage it was seen to embody.)[35] We may relate this attitude quite directly to the larger politics of the paper, since while Leigh Hunt increasingly came to see Napoleon as a tyrant, he regarded the Bourbons as even worse and detested the Holy Alliance. Comparably, although the *Examiner* emphasized the shortcomings of the French School taken as a whole, and Hunt had found David far inferior to West in his first 'State of the Arts' notice, he attributed to him 'talents of the first order' on the basis of the three portraits of Napoleon, exhibited in London in 1815. Many contemporary critics described the artist as a political monster without talent. Hunt made a favourable assessment of Lethière's *Brutus* in 1816, and gave ecstatic praise to Géricault's *Raft of the Medusa* (Louvre) in 1820. He was equally generous about Delacroix's *Marino Faliero* (Wallace Collection, London) when it was shown at the British Institution in 1828.[36]

Consistent with its larger demands for a rationalization and modernization of the British state, the *Examiner* was also a proponent of state support for the arts. In 1808 Hunt had hailed George III as the chief patron of history painting, and had referred to his reign as a 'glorious era' for the arts in which the failure of the aristocracy to follow his example was 'astonishing and disgraceful'. However, in the following year an article far more stringent in tone appeared under the title 'Patronage of the Arts the Policy of Governments', which asserted vigorously that the promotion of the arts was a duty of the state, and that the arts contributed both to public morality and commercial advantage. The policies of the British government were compared most unfavourably with those of France, and it emphasized that not only had Napoleon honoured French savants, but that Joseph Banks and Humphrey Davy had both been elected to the Institut:

> So enlarged and complete a patronage has not, with the exception of the Medicean Ages, been exhibited since the renowned eras of Greece

It was implied that George III's attachment to the arts, as represented by the Royal Academy, was purely nominal, since he 'suffers whole years to pass in succession without aiding them a single guinea'. Further in Britain, political and military advancement are achieved through wealth and influence, while in France, merit and talent receive their just deserts. A later notice of 1811 reiterates the point: although Napoleon's 'ferocious disposition and sanguinary love of conquest' are hard to reconcile with his (illusory) 'partiality for the Arts', he is the 'only modern Prince' 'sufficiently sensible of the value and dignity of the Fine Arts' to honour and remunerate artists on a proper scale. Again this position needs to be seen in the context of a publication which had been prosecuted for libel in 1811 for pointing out that the French army did not have the punishment of flogging, and contrasting it with the barbarous practices of the British army.[37]

At one point in 1811 the *Examiner* seems to have cherished hopes that the Prince of Wales was concerned with the arts in their proper functions, just as it cherished hopes that he was sympathetic to reform – presumably its hopes *vis à vis* his patronage evaporated along with its hopes for his political virtue. However, if, in the early years, the *Examiner* could see the monarchy as a virtuous family ill-advised by corrupt ministers, its view of the political establishment, and of the landed aristocracy as a whole, was increasingly critical. Apart from 'a few liberal and tasteful individuals', the aristocracy had no taste for 'refined Art', instead:

> Their relish is chiefly confined to the comparatively tinsel splendour of dazzling equipages, sumptuous household establishments, feastings, and similar expensive and grovelling pursuits.

The attitude of Pitt and his Tory successors to the arts was precisely congruent with their 'narrow, selfish, and ruinous' system of government. The corruption of the state was matched by the corruption of aristocratic taste, and thus the *Examiner* consistently linked the cause of High Art and state patronage with parliamentary reform. If Reform was brought about, the government would not waste 'thousands on lazy minions', and could spend a fraction of what it now squandered thereby on the encouragement of the arts. The paper regularly tried to stir up concern for this issue by contrasting the profligacy and injustices of the government with accounts of the penury of worthy artists and the neglect of genius.[38]

In the *Examiner*'s view of the world, the Royal Academy was just another branch of this web of corrupt public institutions which were parasitic on the body politic. The Academy was dominated by a cabal of self-seeking and untalented artists, who organized tasteless exhibitions which were notoriously unjust in arrangement, and the profits from which were used in secretive and perhaps dubious ways. When it received a truly major work like Haydon's *Dentatus* (Marquess of Normanby) it hung it in the ante-room, 'little more than a mere vestibule to the large room', because the best places belonged to the members, and particularly to portrait painters. A body of self-elected artists thus took the leading honours in the arts and ignored the genuine talent of Haydon and others because it would show up their own deficiencies. In 1808 the *Examiner* was incensed by the appointment of Sir Anthony Carlisle as the new Professor of Anatomy, when it regarded Charles Bell, author of the *Anatomy of Expression*, as the obvious candidate for the post. As a result it published a 'Letter addressed to the majority of the Royal Academicians', in which it claimed that patrons were beginning to give their support, with some exceptions, to 'untitled Professors', because the behaviour of many of the Academicians was making manifest how unworthy they were of their honours:

> They begin to perceive that in the Arts, as in our Army, and our enormously encreased Nobility, merit must not be estimated by a high sounding title, which is very often a perpetual irony; that an Ass is still a very dull beast though his *rider may call him Bucephalus*; that a noble lord is often a very ignoble person; that a Commander in Chief may be a dead and disgustful weight on the shoulders of a nation, and that a Royal Academician and an Associate may look very important in Capital Letters in an Exhibition Catalogue while his insignificancy is exhibited in the colours on spoiled canvas in the Exhibition Rooms. Such men are excrescences in the Royal Academy and worse.

The obvious reference to the Duke of York in this passage again illustrates how closely political and cultural critique were linked in the *Examiner*, for in October 1808 the paper had supported Major Hogan's charges of corruption against the Commander in Chief, and the Hunts would have been prosecuted for libel had not the investigation of a House of Commons Committee led to the Duke's resignation in March 1809. Carlisle himself was compared with the Duke in a hostile report of his Second Lecture, and the assertion of a common web of corruption was repeated in a later notice.[39]

The *Examiner*'s general view of the deficencies of the aristocracy inevitably predisposed it to look on the British Institution with a jaundiced eye, and this disposition was probably re-inforced by the way in which the Tory press wheeled out the example of that body as yet another proof of the taste, wisdom, and munificence of the ruling class. Hunt's basic position on the Institution, as set out in February 1808, was that although its aims were commendable, the taste of its patrons scarcely rose above 'prettyness', and consequently they tended to encourage 'pictures of *pleasing* subjects' rather than 'subjects of grandeur', and thus departed from their ostensible object:

> It is much to be lamented that in a society established by the riches and *professed taste* of Britain, the higher excellence of the arts should be the least encouraged, especially as there exists such a fund of elevated talent.

He had not changed his opinion by 1816, when he claimed that every succeeding exhibition had testified to the Institution's manifest failure. Indeed, it was afflicted by the prevailing corruption. Its Directors, and particularly Lord Mulgrave, demonstrated political bias by refusing to hang Cooke's painting of *King William and Queen Mary receiving the Bill of Rights* in 1809, while in a notice in June 1812, signed with the indicator motiv of Leigh Hunt, they are described as a set of 'intriguing amateurs' for not awarding a premium to Haydon's *Macbeth.* The issue was taken up again in the next number, which openly accused the Institution of bias: the merit of Haydon's performance had not been rewarded as it should have been because of his attack on Payne Knight, and in this dispute Haydon was eminently in the right. In 1815 the *Examiner* took up arms again in favour of Havell, whose *Wallnut Gathering at Petersham near Richmond* had been rejected for the exhibition. Outraged at what it saw as the intolerance of experiment demonstrated by this action, the paper claimed that the Directors' encouragement of art was secondary to 'the propagation of their own individual notions and the maintenance of a certain fashionable importance'.[40]

From 1818, the *Examiner* did begin to include some more favourable comments on the Institution, which had given a 'manifest stimulus' to established artists, while nurturing younger ones – examples of such younger artists including Collins, Haydon, Hilton, Hofland, Stark, and Vincent. This new attitude was perhaps partly prompted by the success of Martin, an artist who to Hunt seemed to confirm British capacities in High Art, and who was particularly associated with the Institution. It also owed something to the Institution's exhibition of the Raphael Cartoons, from which Haydon's pupils made well-publicized studies. In 1821, the Directors were invoked as examples of aristocratic virtue to contrast with those whose corruption was now made glaringly obvious by their persecution of Queen Caroline. However, no doubt they were always liable to slip from the path, and in 1825 the *Examiner* was again criticizing them for losing sight of the original purposes of the Institution.[41]

The reappraisal of the British Institution was matched by a more generous assessment of the Academy's exhibition in 1819. The reviewer described it as 'a large and genius-gifted assemblage', and referred those who complained of the preponderance of portraits to Wilkie's *Penny Wedding* (Royal Collection) and the works of Stothard, Allston, Leslie, Westall, Turner, Collins, Constable, Hofland, Rippingille, Mulready, and others. Although in 1824, Hunt accused the Academy of 'going back' in relation to its proper role, his attitude towards it tended to be less critical and more optimistic in the 1820s, so that, for instance, his hopes for historical painting were revived by the exhibition of Etty's *Combat* (Royal Academy of Scotland) and Hilton's *Christ Crowned with Thorns* (Royal Academy) in 1825, at an exhibition that 'eclipsed' several preceding ones. However, the *Examiner* was consistent in finding the Society of British Artists an organization more to its taste than either the Academy or British Institution. The formation of the Society in 1823 was hailed as that of a body 'which may be truly named the genuine Republic of Arts', a view elaborated in 1827, when it was stated:

> EVERY friend to the refined development of mind in the Fine Arts must be pleased to find that a Society like this is prospering, for it is established, as we are informed, on just and wholesome principles, having no invidious preferences, no

> favouritism, no bowing and scraping ordinations, no aristocratical assumptions, but a perfect equality of rights and benefits

This view of the relative merits of the different artistic institutions is very comparable to that of other liberal organs of the 1820s.[42]

While the *Examiner* modified the tone of its comments on the British Institution and Royal Academy in the 1820s, and the taint of these bodies by aristocratic corruption ceased to be a prominent theme, the paper's basic point of view did not change: reform of the political system and a reform of the arts were seen as intrinsically connected:

> a Reform of Parliament would be essentially beneficial to the Fine Arts, for then the taste and wishes respecting them would, with other tastes and wishes, scientific and political, be consulted, instead of those of the hungry and low-thoughted holders of and struggles for places, pensions, and sinecures.

However, while there was some logic in seeing the taste of the British aristocracy as an expression of its character as a class, and in the thesis that patronage of the arts and sciences would be promoted in a more rational and less corrupt order, the equation between Reform in politics and reform in painting led to the mistaken conclusion that the tribulations of Haydon were the result of his being a reformer in the arts, whose outspoken voicing of unwelcome truths was offensive to 'aristocratic prejudice and pride'. Haydon undoubtedly liked to see himself as a reformer, but his reform consisted in a purging of the mistaken principles of Reynolds from the body of the academic tradition, which was to be achieved by returning to the eternal verities of Greek art and Raphael, and was quite unconnected with a reform of the system of government, except by analogy.[43]

The *Examiner*'s readiness to use the example of Haydon in the cause of reform must be seen in relation to the larger contradictions in its position. The paper placed a very high value on art and venerated artists as a social type – one of its fundamental complaints was that in contemporary British society money and rank counted more than 'mind', a position common in the discourse of bourgeois radicalism. It regularly voiced a patriotic enthusiasm for British art, and did not make such hostile assaults on the character of public exhibitions as the *Champion* and some other periodicals.[44] This sits somewhat uncomfortably with its denunciations of aristocratic taste and the corruption of patronage. It means that the blame for any larger deficiencies in contemporary artistic practice had to be attributed solely to the degeneracy of the aristocracy. Indeed, the *Examiner* explicitly denied that the artists were to blame for the failure of British painting to achieve a higher moral tone:

> It is said, and justly said, that they ought to endeavour to induce and lead an exalted public taste; they ought to try to infuse a public and a philosophical love of Art. This, we contend, they have in some measure been doing; perhaps as far as the sordid, because trading and mere money getting spirit, and enormously taxed condition, of the great mass of the people, would permit.[45]

It appears from this that Hunt placed no particular faith in middle-class patronage, and in fact he would have produced a more coherent and effective cultural critique had he been willing to do so, or to make a more severe assessment of contemporary art.

Hunt's insistence on the moral functions of painting and his attachment to High Art should be clear from what has been said so far: the idea that large historical paintings were indisputably the highest form of artistic practice was central to the *Examiner*'s critique of patronage, institutions, and the state, and underlay its support for West and Haydon. Because of his commitment to the academic hierarchy, Hunt favoured genre, as a painting of human figures and expression, above landscape; claiming that representation of the 'intellectual part of man' took 'more athletic powers of reflection and examination' than that of 'external and unconscious creation'.[46] Consistent with this position, he also estimated imaginative and ideal landscapes over views representing everyday scenes: the Epic/Imaginative over the 'Familiar' to use his terms. Like Hazlitt, Hunt maintained that the kind of mental vision which could discern and separate out the 'ideal' from the 'obvious' and 'ordinary' was rare:

> It is the poetry of Painting, and it is admitted that few indeed are born Poets.

Painting, like Music and Poetry, became more difficult but also more valuable as it moved further from the 'familiar' and approached the 'sublime'.[47]

It was partly the importance of 'expression' and the 'ideal' in Hunt's system which enabled him to make such a favourable assessment of Turner's work, although criteria of naturalism, formal harmony, and originality were also brought to bear. Initially his admiration for Turner was founded largely on verisimilitude. Thus he wrote of *Tabley the seat of Sir J. Leicester Bart. Windy Day* (University of Manchester, Tabley Collection), exhibited in 1809:

> A camera obscura reflecting the scene he represents, though it would exhibit more nicety in the details, would not be otherwise more lively or natural.

A similar criterion was applied in relation to *Frosty Morning* (Clore Gallery) in 1813, which was said to be 'among the nearest imitations of common nature'. By contrast, in 1812 *Hannibal* (Clore Gallery) lifted Turner into the 'highest rank of landscape painters' by reason of 'that main excellence of the Sister Arts, Invention'. Hunt's later reviews of Turner's 'imaginative' landscapes tended to mix a high level of praise with criticism of the drawing of the figures, unnatural colouring, and over-generalization: a type of criticism levelled at both *Dido and Aeneas* (National Gallery, London) in 1814 and *The Decline of the Carthaginian Empire* (Clore Gallery) in 1817. Like many critics, Hunt seems to have found it easier to accommodate Turner's innovation in the medium of water-colour than in his oil paintings.[48]

Hunt's concern with imagination and the ideal, also predisposed him to look favourably on Martin and Danby. Recognizing that their work did not really match the academic pattern of historical landscape painting, he used the term 'Poetic' to refer to landscapes of the type of Danby's *Delivery of Israel out of Egypt* (Harris Museum & Art Gallery, Preston), claiming that the latter was superior – a position which means that he had revised the academic hierarchy to comprehend the original aspects of modern art. His appraisal of both painters frequently emphasizes the power of their work over the spectator, and this is a corollary of his conception of the artist as a masculine heroic type.[49]

Given his enthusiasm for 'ideal' and 'poetic' landscape painting, Hunt showed a surprising ability to respond favourably to the new naturalism, which within his theory could not seize the imagination of the spectator in the same way. Thus he stated his admiration for a whole sequence of early works by John Linnell, although he disliked Linnell's choice of subject in some cases, and found his colouring harsh. *Kensington Gravel Pits* (*Plate 4*) was described in 1813 as:

> a landscape of first-rate merit. It is nature presented in its most agreeable and lively aspect as far as regards so novel and difficult a subject. In this commendation, we except the degree of harshness in the too strong contrast of the yellow ground with the bright blue sky

In the following year, Linnell's views were said to be 'natural' but 'without tastefulness of selection'. His objects were often 'the least pleasing that are to be seen', and his colouring was often harsh as a result of too strong contrasts. This is an interesting response to Linnell's originality, both to his representation of subjects so different from the conventional picturesque, drawn from the junctions of town and country on the outskirts of London, and to his attempt to use novel kinds of colour contrast to suggest the idea of bright sunlight. It is not surprising that Hunt found Mulready's early landscapes easier to accommodate, considering how much closer they were to the Dutch tradition, and for him as for many contemporary critics, it was the less innovative Callcott who represented a model of technique in the representation of everyday landscapes.[50]

Equally commonplace is Hunt's dislike of what he regarded as a 'slovenliness of brush' in landscape and other genres. Like Haydon and Hazlitt, Hunt was critical of Reynolds (the 'Sir R. WALPOLE of Painting'), who had corrupted British art by his example of a 'generalizing, careless, and unscientific style of execution'.[51] Consistent with this, while praising Cox's landscapes in 1814 for their richness of colour and 'affinity to the general effects of common Nature', he regretted what he saw as a disregard for 'the drawing of particulars'.[52] It is not surprising that Hunt was never entirely happy with Constable's technique, although he always recognized his talent and praised his work over many years. Hunt's basic assessment of Constable had been made by 1812: the 'natural' qualities in Constable's work were admirable but, like so many of his contemporaries he did not give enough attention to drawing and finish. Reviewing Constable's *A Water-Mill* (Private Collection, *Plate 83*) and other works at the Academy exhibition of 1812 he observed:

> Mr CONSTABLE has much originality and vigour of style, but bordering perhaps a little on crudeness of effect. I say perhaps, as it is doubtful whether if his general tone of colour was less cold, green, and grey, and his masses of light and shade less subdivided by a number of strong touches of both, he would not considerably diminish that originality and vigour so peculiar to himself.

Hunt made similar comments in 1815 and in 1817, but he seems to have responded to the growing scale of Constable's ambitions, because in a sequence of reviews of 1819–21 he praised his work more highly than before. However, while Hunt found paintings such as *Landscape – Noon* (*The Haywain*) came 'nearer to the actual look of rural nature than any modern landscape whatever', he was unable to find a 'sentiment' or 'soul' in his work.[53]

Considering his attachment to academic principles, Hunt made a surprisingly favourable assessment of water-colour painting, claiming that 'England' was unequalled in this type of art. None the less, he regarded the water-colour medium as inherently inferior to that of oil, and also described the Society of Painters in Water-Colours' exhibitions as 'little more than a landscape and edifical Exhibition of familiar scenes'. While praising their overall standard, he found them derivative and repetitious, some of the painters being 'too much in the habit of copying each other in what they find is pleasing and popular', and 'thus producing a rather monotonous character in the general display'. Elsewhere he complained of 'many artists' painting landscapes by 'regular receipts', which had little or nothing to do with 'nature'. Thus unlike critics strongly committed to water-colour painting, Hunt could recognize that its boasted 'truths' were also matters of convention.[54]

Along with many other critics, Hunt tended to regard brushwork of the type evident in Constable's work as a kind of mannerism, and like the majority of them he found it difficult to place a positive evaluation on style – although he was much clearer than most that it was the means of representation which produce pleasure. In 1813, he defined 'Mannerism' as:

> a sameness in the drawing, forms, and attitudes, the countenances, touches, colouring, and chiarascuro, by which one Artist may be readily distinguished from another

It was a quality found in the work of all artists, but was always a defect, because the objects of 'nature' are endlessly varied:

> In proportion as the Artist attains this variety, he will be less Mannered, though from the limitation of the human powers, he will be so inevitably.

Contradictorily, Haydon's *Judgment of Solomon* was praised in the following year as one of the very few pictures 'which are devoid of manner'. It is obvious that 'mannerism' is a kind of converse to the 'natural', and that 'style' can only be given a positive appraisal if in some sense it can be 'recognized' as true to nature.[55]

The concept of 'mannerism' plays a role in Hunt's criticism comparable in some respects to that it plays in Hazlitt's in which imitation of the works of other artists or even of oneself is a fault, and originality lies in the discovery of new views of 'nature'. On a number of occasions Hunt observed that 'good imitations' are better than 'indifferent originals', but he was not entirely consistent on this and he regularly stressed that 'imitation even of what is good is looked at with indifference by the right judge of art', unless it is unified with some 'self-derived' quality. The only 'just' and 'legitimate' objects of ambition in the liberal arts are a 'powerful attitude and eminent station of originality'. Thus in 1827, Hunt cited the work of Stark and Patrick Nasmyth as exemplifying the unfortunate side effects of the British Institution's 'Old Masters' exhibitions, which multiplied 'imitations', rather than fostering 'original talent'. Both were compared unfavourably with Constable. One of Hunt's underlying assumptions was that art is progressive, an idea which he maintained was illustrated by the examples of Greece and Italy:

> All art is progressive. What is discovered and done in the early stage of society is advanced upon in the next, and thus continues gradually improving, till it reaches the summit of capability.

This, of course, was not a view shared by Hazlitt, but it was being adopted by the Philosophic Radicals around the *Westminster Review*.[56]

In the political critique of the *Examiner*, there is no clear model of political progress, rather there is a concern to assert 'that spirit of equal justice which is the essence of the British constitution' (historically speaking), and which is threatened by corrupt elements in the political establishment. Rather than seeing contemporary political issues in terms of an antagonism between middle-class and aristocracy, the *Examiner* tended to see them as a struggle between 'the People' and an 'Oligarchy' sustained by the principle of 'Legitimacy'.[57] Equally, while a value can be attributed to some of the novel features of contemporary painting, the *Examiner* (like the *Champion*) remained fundamentally committed to a traditional notion of High Art. By contrast, the *London Magazine* of the mid 1820s clearly represented the 'middling classes' as the agent of political progress, and also directly challenged traditional norms of artistic excellence. A similar position was articulated in a less developed form in the *Literary Chronicle*. I surmise that this is because both were essentially magazines of the 1820s, which were able to draw on the increasingly coherent discourse of bourgeois progressivism articulated by the Philosophic Radicals. In short, they self-consciously took a class position on culture.[58]

The 'London Magazine'

The *London Magazine* has probably received more critical attention than any other magazine of the early nineteenth century. It was edited by John Scott from its first number in January 1820 up until his death in February 1821. In July 1821 John Taylor took over, and Thomas Hood became sub-editor leaving in 1824. At the end of that year, Taylor transferred the editorship to Henry Southern, and the magazine went into a new series which lasted until 1828. In September 1825, Taylor and Hessey sold the magazine to Southern, and from November art criticism was dropped from its range of contents. Charles Knight bought the *London* in April 1828, and he and Barry St Leger ran it until its demise in 1829. Art criticism was re-introduced in the third series of 1828–9. Although there is interesting material by Hazlitt, Scott, and T. G. Wainewright in the art notices of the first series, the most original and distinctive criticism of the *London*'s history was published in 1825, and 1828–9, and it is on this alone I shall concentrate.

Under Scott, the political tenor of the magazine was comparable to that of the *Champion* under his editorship, combining patriotism and reverence for British political institutions with indignation at contemporary corruption. John Taylor, the co-proprietor and editor 1821–4, was a more thorough-going liberal, and under him and subsequent editors the magazine never carried an apology for any monarch or defence of the aristocracy. It advocated parliamentary reform, legislation to ameliorate popular distress, and repeal of the Corn Laws, and it also began to give more coverage to political economy, with articles on Malthus and Ricardo in 1823–4. By 1824 the magazine had reached the same conclusions concerning the Whigs as the Utilitarians, and had written them off as a party. In late 1824 the Philosophic Radical Southern became editor, and after the sale of the magazine to him in September 1825 it became a different kind of publication.[59]

In Volumes 2 and 3 of the Second Series, covering May–December 1825, the magazine gave a surprising amount of space to the Fine Arts, including fourteen pages on the exhibition of the Society of British Artists, twelve on that of the Royal Academy exhibition, and no less than forty-eight, spread over three numbers on the retrospective exhibition of the British School at the British Institution. The notable feature of these reviews is that they contain the fullest attempt to elaborate a bourgeois aesthetic for painting that I have discovered in the periodical literature of this period. The social bases of this aesthetic are established by a savage critique of the pretensions of 'connoisseurs', who are the enemy of artists, and who tend to mislead the 'public'. Connoisseurs substitute a blind veneration for antiquity and traditional authorities for a real sensitivity to art and the public, when influenced by them, becomes incapable of judging modern art. The connoisseur as a social type is drawn from the aristocracy and the ranks of commercial wealth:

> In our own country, and elsewhere, it is most obvious, that whoever is born in the peerage, whoever is born to wealth, whoever has acquired it, becomes, as if instinctively, imbued with the knowledge of art – a connoisseur.

But taste is not to be bought with money and neither does it come by descent with a title – it is only attained by education. Although only painters can properly judge painting, they are often partial and imperfect judges, and technicalities apart:

> there is much more on which every man of literature, general taste, education, and habits of observation, is equally entitled to form an opinion[60]

This critic did not attack the general character of British art, and sought to explain the plethora of bad pictures in the Royal Academy exhibitions by referring to the character of a society in which the middle class possessed considerable wealth, but had deficient taste as a result of imperfect education – a position entirely consonant with that of the Philosophic Radicals. The production of bad art is explained by referring to the large demand for illustrated books and prints, and the numbers of poor artists encouraged by demand for drawing masters in female schools. However, there are some causes for optimism and the public will eventually escape the 'hereditary cant' of connoisseurship:

> the public will in time learn to judge for itself, because, when its shackles are removed, it will dare to think for itself, and it will seek for grounds of judgment where alone they are to be found. It is thinking for itself in politics and legislation, it is thinking for itself in morals and literature, and it will soon learn to think for itself in art.

In his own criticism, the critic claims to examine paintings according to 'the principles of common sense' – as we have seen it was precisely this principle patrician aesthetics claimed was inadequate.[61]

Predictably, the key criteria for this writer were 'nature' and 'originality', and the worst vice was 'manner'. Thus, he claims in his first review of the British School retrospective that the country has indeed a school of painting, because its art has a character of originality. No worthwhile art can be formed on an imitation of earlier artists. Indeed, taking a position close to that of Stendhal, who wrote a number of articles and reviews for the *London Magazine* in 1825–6, he stresses the need for artists to produce an art of and for their time:

> It is an important consideration to this great art, that it should keep pace with the progress of society, and yet it is one which seems scarcely to have attracted the attention which it claims. In the humblest departments, the face of nature itself, the whole physical world changes as civilization proceeds or modes alter. It is one part of the business of a painter to be the historian of the physical world before him, of the objects of art as they vary with the progress of man, of the more transient modes which caprice or fashion may cause and produce.

If the artist wants to be understood by his audience, if he wants to have the 'sympathy of his age', he must become its historian:

> Man himself changes. Not only do his pursuits vary in different periods of society, but his very feelings and thoughts change their cast and colour from age to age. It is true, unquestionably, as is commonly said, that human nature is always the same, and that human passions, being founded on our very constitution, must display themselves in the same manner in every country and every

> age. But if this be a truth, it is, like many more, too general for use, and like many more, one which misleads us by its wide generality. Human nature and human passions are mere words, under which are ranked a whole army of feelings, actions, and consequences, endlessly implicated, and endlessly modified. Whatever original foundation they may have in our constitution, it is by collision with the surrounding world, by the influence of external circumstances, that all these assume their characters, producing the endless moral appearances and effects by which they are recognized, and which constitute man and his history.

Man varies enormously 'in different countries and in different states of society', and whatever his original identity, he is not the same being in different ages and different places:

> the poet who would paint him knows that he must study him through these changes; knows that if he would paint him, his contemporary, he must study him, his contemporary. There also is the painter's duty.[62]

The painter must indeed indulge the tastes and fashions of his age, for without doing so he cannot attract the sympathy of his public. This open recognition and acceptance of necessary change in aesthetic standards makes a striking contrast with the universal norms which Alison and Knight sought to salvage, and depends on an extension of the franchise of taste far beyond the narrow limits of high society within which such theorists would contain it. Novelty is no longer a source of corruption, but a necessary accompaniment of progress and a sign of cultural health. By rejecting the universal in favour of the contemporary and particular, taste is theoretically democratized. Here is a sense of history comparable to that which runs through Stendhal's *Le Rouge et le Noir* and *La Chartreuse de Parme*, and which looks ahead to Baudelaire's *heroïsme de la vie moderne*.

One of the implications of this willingness to accept change and this demand for originality is an irreverent approach to the hierarchy of genres, and a belief that traditional models are irrelevant – indeed a hindrance. Thus the problem for the modern history painter is that:

> nearly every thing, in conception, style, colour, and much that we need not enumerate, has been so far anticipated by one or other of the great masters of the art, that it is not easy for a modern artist to be absolutely new, or to paint in a manner which shall be peculiarly his own.

Although Reynolds and Fuseli have shown that it is not impossible to treat traditional subjects in new ways, Hilton has taken on too much in trying to represent yet again *Christ Crowned with Thorns* – with such themes, British artists will never produce much more than imitations of Italian pictures. Elsewhere the critic suggests that religious themes are exhausted because they go against the feelings and fashions of the age, and recommends artists to turn to other varieties of historical subject. Linked with this critique of the shibboleths of High Art, is a rejection of the need for large scale. In Britain a large canvas has always been an excuse for 'careless execution', and the British School is compared unfavourably with that of France in relation to both drawing and painterly execution. The abuse of 'breadth' is, as usual, associated with the influence of Reynolds but this is a significant connection in the context considering Reynolds' identification with the landed oligarchy.[63]

The role of the concept of nature in the 1825 *London* reviews is comparable to that which it plays in Hazlitt's criticism. The artist is one who sees in nature what others can not see, and his representation conveys to the spectator the particular resonances it has for him. The painter, like the poet:

> searching the world around him, sees nature under all her forms and modes; extracts her most delicate varieties, her beauties, her subtleties; gives to them a colour derived from the constitution of his own mind, and records them by the powers of his art, that he may excite in the minds of others the impressions they have made on his own.

(Considering the emphasis on the 'powers' of art, and the characterization of nature as female, it seems appropriate to describe the artist as 'he' here.) Although it is to the art of the Italian Schools 'that we look most generally for the rules of art – for the models by which we judge our contemporaries', their example is only a guide. Connoisseurs mistake the effects of time on the work of artists such as Leonardo, Raphael, and Titian for the real effects they intended:

> If their works were not, like those of Claude in another department, the mere transcripts of the finest nature in her happiest moments, they were still the abstractions of fine nature viewed through the peculiarities of their own minds, or represented according to systems which they judged best adapted to produce the intended effects.

Thus since the value of works of art depends on this tincture of an original quality of the artist's mind, the artist must only study the works of other artists to find in what measure they have attempted to 'transfer their own feelings' about nature to the minds of the spectator, and 'should express his own feelings in his own language'. Rather than 'Michelangelo', the last word of Reynolds' *Discourses* should have been 'Nature'. It is this discovery of endless new qualities in nature, which explains the succession of schools:

> something marks a period of creation, of invention, the result of new minds seeing and thinking for themselves, and discovering new modes of recording their conceptions.

When a school has worn itself out as a result of 'successive imitations' and consequent deterioration, another arises to take its place, and this constant succession of novelties is 'always and necessarily entwined with the progress of society'. This combination of individualism and progressivism is entirely characteristic of the discourse of bourgeois radicalism in this period.[64]

The implications of this critical system when applied to an evaluation of contemporary painting were that it would be valued partly for its differences from earlier art, and partly for its qualities of expression and individuality. Just as for Hazlitt, adherence to nature did not imply a narrow naturalism. Thus, Wilkie's *Chelsea Pensioners reading the Waterloo Dispatch* (Wellington Museum, Apsley House) was praised as a 'great and laborious work', and although criticisms were made of aspects of its colouring, composition, lighting and drawing, yet had Wilkie in this one painting entirely surpassed the Dutch School. The critic found a quality of 'mind and soul' in the painting entirely lacking in those of Teniers and his contemporaries. In his review of the Royal Academy exhibition of this year, he was even more enthusiastic about Mulready's *Travelling Druggist* (location unknown) for the 'facsimilie fidelity' of its details, which worked together in 'one of the most brilliant pictures we have seen, and probably one of the most brilliant that ever was painted'.[65]

Surveying the retrospective at the British Institution, the *London* found landscape painting 'the most purely original portion' of the British School. Landscape painting showed particularly clearly that British artists had risen as long as they followed nature, and declined when they ceased to do so:

> All remember the progress of Havell, whom no Censure of ours can now reach, from excellence to absurdity. The history of Varley's career, is, like himself, still before our eyes. With the exception of Turner, and as yet of Fielding, and a few more, almost every one of our artists in landscape has risen till he became stationary, when his decline has been more rapid than this rise.

Such a position led the magazine to that contempt for Gilpin's picturesque which we noted in chapter 2. Landscape painters in particular have been misled by the concept of 'breadth', and have sacrificed the details of nature to produce this quality – which easily became an excuse for superficial dexterity:

> It is the great secret to be able to combine her beautiful parts, all her variety of grace in detail, with her graceful and splendid whole[66]

However, Turner apparently met these criteria – at least presuming that the author of the British Institution reviews and of the reviews of the Society of British Artists and Royal Academy exhibitions in May and June are one and the same. His *Harbour at Dieppe* (Frick Collection, New York), shown at the Academy in 1825, was praised in very high terms for its combination of topographical accuracy and romantic effect.[67] The *London*'s commitment to originality also probably explains its enthusiastic response to Danby's *Delivery of Israel out of Egypt*, and it is consistent with its criticism of the grove scenes of James Stark as pastiches of Hobbema. What is odd, however, is the magazine's violent hostility to Constable's work, which seems inconsistent, and possibly derived from some personal animosity.[68]

The *London Magazine*'s reviews of 1825 display an insistent historical awareness, combined with an attempt to set out ostensibly modern aesthetic criteria, and need to be seen in the context of a publication which explicitly presented itself as a product of the metropolis of the greatest commercial empire to date, and signified this in its name. They self-consciously articulated an aesthetic for a new kind of democratic culture. Although I have characterized their position as bourgeois, I do not mean by this that the criteria of 'nature', 'expression', and 'originality' were intrinsically bourgeois, but rather that they could be put to use within a sociology of taste which was clearly related to the critique of privilege and theories of education developed by bourgeois radicals of this period. Further, this aesthetic seems entirely congruous in a magazine which was increasingly dominated by the type of discourse associated with such radicals.

The *London*'s art notices in the Third Series of 1828–9 are not as copious as those of 1825, but they remained interesting and original. The 'Notes on Art' in the April number of 1828 begins with an expression of regret that English and French artists of the day seem so mutually prejudiced against each other, and stresses that English painters should concentrate on reforming their own errors, and in particular by:

> adding correct design to an eye for colour and light and shade, by filling up the details after having thrown in the masses, by aiming at truth of imitation as well as striking effect

Such criticism of the 'British School' is unoriginal, but the favour with which French art is regarded is comparatively rare. This anti-national position was reasserted in the review of the Academy's exhibition in June, when the critic stated bluntly that English art was basically inferior to that of France. The President of the Royal Academy is a mere portrait painter and no British history painter can compare with Géricault.[69]

In 'Notes on Art' in the April number, the critic had even committed the outrage (repeated in the Academy review) of asserting that Britain had no School of painting, and that one was unlikely to develop. He described the impediments to British achievements in the arts as (i) want of natural genius, (ii) historical circumstances, and (iii) patronage. In relation to the first, although the British do not lack an enthusiasm for works of genius as their literature demonstrates, they do not seem to find inspiration in the eye. Comparing the works of Opie, Romney, and Barry with those of Raphael and Titian, he finds them flat and dead. The latter produced works in which 'every part is instinct with life and feeling', whereas British artists simply don't have the same 'sympathy' with the objects of external nature and treat them as an obstacle, producing over-generalized images which do not suggest the textures of visible objects. Further, the character of the age is inimical to artistic achievements because of the pre-occupation with public events, which distract from the contemplation of objects of sense. This pre-occupation with great events induces young artists to attempt grandiose subjects before they are able. In fact 'works of art and fancy' flourish in the early stages of civilization:

> before philosophy and science have too much generalized or multiplied the ordinary topics of reflection.

Art tends to decline with the progress of knowledge, because it can not give a concrete representation of all that the latter suggests, and contemporary theories of art tend to confound images with the ideas of things. In the mid 1820s, Benthamite intellectuals were claiming that poetry was incompatible with 'the strict process of logical deduction', and since progress depends on the latter, the imaginative faculty was likely to find free play only in the earlier stages of society.[70] However, the *London Magazine*'s critic does not seem as hostile to the aesthetic principle as the critics of the *Westminster Review*, and his view of painting as a mode of apprehending the world in all its particularities resembles that of Hazlitt, who was equally critical of the over-generalizing tendency of British art.[71]

Equally reminiscent of Hazlitt are this critics' strictures on contemporary patronage, which is said to be deficient in quantity and forced. Its principle is that which motivates the English generally to want to see their names printed in lists of subscribers to charitable institutions:

> *Exclusion* seems to be the first thought and condition of British enjoyment ... and the patron of British art feeling no real enthusiasm or satisfaction in it, indemnifies himself for the sacrifice of time and money by giving himself an air over the person he professes to countenance, and from a mixture of jealousy and pride, making him feel his superiority in rank and fortune – the only superiority he has a thorough conviction of.

The review claimed that in Italy and Greece the patron of high art was not just religion and the state, it was the whole people. Patronage itself is ineffectual, because the artist is no more than a manifestation of the age:

> Genius is but a particle caught up and exalted by the general flame: no man is great or excellent but by sympathy with the spirit of the age or country in which he lives

This position, combining historicism with the democratic principle, was to be characteristic of radicals such as the MP Thomas Wyse, who turned their attention to the arts in the following decade.[72]

The key criterion which emerges from the April 'Notices of Art' is one of 'resemblance to nature', linked with expression of the distinctive character of the artist. This position is little different from that of the 1825 reviews, but it is applied in a rather different way, and the 1828 critic is less concerned with originality and novelty. His insistence that the pleasures of painting derived primarily from the imitation of sensuous appearances seems consistent with the favour with which he regarded the works of Roberts, Watts, and Stanfield, and his approval of the

Society of Painters in Water-Colours exhibitions: the 'most popular, because in its way most perfect' of all the British exhibitions. Constable, however, was guilty of 'manner', although the criticism of 1828–9 acknowledges his talent in a way that of 1825 does not. Thus, the *Beach at Brighton, the Chain Pier in the Distance* (Tate Gallery) was described in 1828 as:

> one of numberless productions by the same artist, under which it might be written, 'nature done in white lead, opal, or prussian blue ...' It is evident that Mr. Constable's landscapes are like nature, it is still more evident that they are paint.

This dislike of painterly surfaces also troubled the critic in his evaluation of Turner, and his rather narrow standard of truth caused him problems in the evaluation of 'imaginative' landscapes more generally. The review of the 1828 Academy describes Turner's *Dido Directing the Equipment of the Fleet* as 'literally like a great diaculum plaster spread over his canvas and tinged with you know not what shapes and meanings'. However, if he could not accommodate *Dido*, the critic temporarily suspended his usual standards in response to *Ulysses Deriding Polyphemus* (National Gallery, London) in the following year. While the effect was 'unnatural' it was so poetic that it convinced the spectator that whatever Mount Gibel might look like now, Turner had represented it as it looked in the time of the Greeks. While Constable's 'silvery aspect' was a 'manner'; Turner's 'gold' was a 'style'. Constable's 'manner' detracted from the 'truth'; whereas Turner's 'style' produced the 'poetry' of his. Such judgements suggest that different styles are appropriate to different types of subject, and may be regarded as a hangover from the academic system. A similar suspension of naturalistic criteria occurred when the critic was faced with Danby's *Attempt to Illustrate the Opening of the Sixth Seal* (National Gallery of Ireland) in 1828:

> we think his performance the triumph of this sort of apocalyptic painting, which is founded on faith, rather than reason; and which, instead of imitating, reverses all we know of nature. The antithesis, is, however, marked and intelligible. The sun is black, the moon red, the earth blue, the flesh green, &c. We know what we have to expect, there is sufficient unity and keeping in contradiction and absurdity, and not a mere aggregate of littleness and confusion. It is like Mr Shelley's poetry, fanatical and self-willed but better articulated and made out. We do not applaud the class; we cannot deny the merit of the execution.

It is consistent with the character of the *London* after 1825, a magazine which promoted popular education and Utilitarian reforms and opposed mysticism and superstition, that its art critic should find the subjects of apocalyptic landscape paintings obscurantist. He had made it clear that great art was not to be expected in an advanced stage of civilization, and he found a connection between Catholicism, absolute monarchy, and the highest achievements of painting: 'We prefer to all the glories of art, the light of freedom, and the sober gifts of its dry nurse, reason.'[73]

Whatever the limitations of the *London Magazine*'s judgements on individual works, its criticism from 1825 onwards has a coherence, originality, and polemical force which was almost unrivalled. This was partly because it drew confidently on what it understood as a progressive and coherent social doctrine and represented what it understood as the interests of a rising social class. In relation to my larger argument, it is striking that the magazine treated landscape painting as the most significant achievement of the 'British School', and that which matched best with its conceptions of taste and progress.

The 'Literary Chronicle'

The *Literary Chronicle* was a sixteen-page Saturday paper which ran from May 1819 to July 1828, and merged with the *Athenaeum* in August of that year. For the first six years of its existence its editor was Thomas Byerley, who was succeeded by John Watson Dalby, and who in turn gave way to F. D. Maurice in May 1828.[74] The magazine sold at the low price of 6d (raised to 1s in 1827), and it was intended that this should 'place it within the reach of all classes of society'. Unlike its conservative predecessor the *Literary Gazette*, it claimed to be above politics: to judge books and not authors, and not to care 'whether the writer is a Whig or a Tory, or what may be his moral or political creed, or his public or private character'.[75] Such a claim was of course naïve, but it means that the *Chronicle* was not a partisan of political reaction, and that it could, for example, give a sequence of relatively favourable reviews to Hazlitt's work, while distancing itself from his politics. The magazine did carry harsh reviews of the different numbers of *The Liberal*, but then that publication met with widespread hostility. In sum, no single political position characterizes the *Chronicle*, but the fact that it carried articles favourable to Hazlitt and that in 1820 pro-Catholic sentiments found a space within it indicates that it was not a Tory organ, and this is consistent with its aim to bring information to a wide audience.

Because it was a cheap weekly paper the *Chronicle* did not give the same space to exhibition reviews as the *London Magazine*, and it did not offer such extended statements of principle. As with the *London*, it is possible to identify a number of different 'voices' in the *Chronicle*'s art criticism, including 'C.E.', 'J.P.T.', 'R', 'T', William Henry Parry and C. A. Monck. The magazine's position on the calibre of British art, the state of patronage, and the character of art institutions, was varied over the years 1819–22.[76] From the point of view of my argument, the most interesting notices appeared in 1823. Like those of 1822, signed 'C. A. Monck', these were distinctly acerbic towards contemporary art institutions. Thus, in February the British Institution's show was said to contain 'the dregs of that of Somerset House last year' – such works generally were not worth seeing at all, and the Institution had become a refuge for pictures which should have been rejected by the Royal Academy. The notice on the Academy in May was equally harsh: it was said to be the worst for many years, and complaints about the overcrowding and favouritism of the hanging were renewed:

> We fear there is a system of exclusion and favouritism, and this perhaps, can only be annihilated by the formation of a new academy, which, if begun on liberal principles, and the art thrown fairly open to competition, would we doubt not, meet with ample patronage – we mean not individual but public patronage.

The reference to a 'new academy' presaged an announcement of the formation of the Society of British Artists in the next number, an institution of which the *Chronicle* was an ardent supporter. The announcement was accompanied by a further denunciation of the conditions at Somerset House, and contained the accusation which was to feature so largely in the evidence to the Parliamentary Select Committee on Arts and Manufactures in 1834–5, that exhibitors at the Academy received no share of the money taken in entrance charges.[77]

In relation to the assertions of widespread patronage which appeared in the magazine this year, it is notable that an obituary of J. J. Angerstein asserts that support for the arts has come from the ranks of commercial wealth:

> To the honour, probity, spirit, and enterprise of her merchants, is Great Britain indebted, in a great measure, for that rank which she holds in the scale of civilized nations, and for that prosperity and grandeur which enabled her at one time to brave the confederated force of Europe, and at last to close the contest with the applause of the world ... If the arts were indebted for their revival in Europe, to the merchants of Florence, with justice may it also be said, that to the English merchants are the arts indebted in this country.[78]

This statement seems to be an unfurling of the banners of the bourgeoisie, and it may be understood as part of the more general attempt of that class to justify its right to a political voice through a superior patriotism which we noted in chapter 3. It is striking that such claims for bourgeois patronage should appear in a magazine which also gave strong support to the Society of British Artists, an oppositional body founded to break the monopoly of the Academy, some of whose supporters described that institution as 'aristocratic' in principle, and called for 'free trade' in art.

The *Chronicle*'s view of the connections between the Society and bourgeois patronage are clearly set out in a report of August 1824. In this the Society was congratulated on the donations it had received and on the sale of nearly £4,000 worth of works from the exhibition. The sum had been raised:

> Not by what are usually denominated the higher and more polished orders of society; nor, on the other hand, by the nest of picture dealers, who appreciate

> talent only as they can make it subservient to their griping avarice – but by the middle and respectable classes of an opulent and well-educated British public – those who have, in spite of our much-traduced climate, taste and feeling enough to appreciate and reward native talent; and from whom it appears to be the characteristic of the country, that the success of every liberal institution should originally emanate.[79]

This view of patronage, and the *Chronicle*'s strong support for an institution dominated by landscape and genre painters, is consistent with the importance its reviews attributed to the water-colour medium and the amount of space it gave to notices of genre pictures in these years. Thus the review of the Society of Painters in Water-Colours exhibition in 1824 claimed that water-colour combined the force of oil painting with a vivid freshness of its own, and linked the medium to the taste and means of the social strata with which it identified:

> while the grander productions of the pencil constitute the embellishments of patrician salons, the more unassuming water-colour drawing may decorate the drawing-room of less opulent amateurs. Productions of this class are executed on a scale that adapts them for the parlour, the study, and the boudoir; or they may even be deposited within a portfolio.[80]

While this statement is not dismissive of High Art, it implies a sympathy for works geared to 'more unassuming' tastes.

The *Chronicle*'s enthusiasm for genre is indicated by the extremely favourable review it gave of Richter's *The Widow* and Rippingille's *Cross-examining the Witness*, both shown with the Society of British Artists in 1824. Like the *London Magazine* it appraised paintings according to criteria of 'naturalness' and originality, but showed some of the same difficulties in giving value to what were read as the signs of style. None the less, the main comment on Rippingille's picture reveals how the quality of naturalness attributed to representations was recognized as the result of particular techniques and conventions:

> There is an extraordinary degree of truth and naturalness, if we may use the term, in this picture. The artist seems not to have studied effect of any kind, but quietly to have copied the scene exactly as he saw it. There are no prominent figures, no artificial arrangement, no peculiar distribution of light, nothing striking in the colouring. Yet there is none of the crudity, harshness, and insipidity, which there must inevitably have been, had he not maturely considered his composition.[81]

Of course it is impossible to tell how much stress is intended to fall on the word 'seems' in the second sentence, and the third and fourth sentences are essentially inconsistent: the critic applying naive naturalistic criteria in the third, and then recalling that all paintings are inherently produced by artifice and depend upon conventions in the fourth. The same kind of hesitation occurs in two comments on Etty's work. Etty was frequently criticized for 'manner' in his use of colour, and the

Chronicle's critic objected to 'too much of affectation' in the colouring of his *Maternal Attention*, shown at the British Institution in 1824. However, while Etty's *Pandora*, shown at the Academy later in the year, provoked him to describe the artist as 'decidedly a mannerist in composition and execution', still 'his mannerism is fraught with much beauty, and his ideal colouring accords well with the poetry of his subjects'.[82]

That the pleasures produced by naturalistic landscape are not attributed to an unmediated truth of resemblance are clear from the following comment on *A Study from Nature* by John Wilson, exhibited in 1825:

> It consists of merely some dock-leaves, the stump of a tree, and some paling; but these are painted with a taste and feeling that leave nothing to be wished for; and, apparently uninteresting as such objects may be, yet, when thus executed, they are capable of awakening pleasing associations, and perhaps captivate more because they affect to promise so little.

The effect of the work is here attributed to a quality of 'taste and feeling' in the paintwork, and to associations which the work prompts in the mind of the spectator. Considering this kind of judgement, it is not surprising that the *Chronicle*'s critic in 1825 found Constable's work admirable – although he referred to it only in general terms. Also significant is a comment on Daguerre's Diorama of Holyrood Chapel, which was praised for its 'truth to effect', but found to suffer as a work of art thereby:

> Paradoxical as it may sound, the illusion is too complete to permit us to admire the paintings as paintings: we are rather affected by them as we should be by the real objects. This species of representation seems to be to painting in general what wax-works is to either painting or sculpture: the effect is too purely mechanical.[83]

Such a rejection of the 'too purely mechanical' is consistent with the idea expressed elsewhere that the power of art depends on it manifesting a quality of feeling in the mind of the artist.[84]

Although changes in the evaluation of some individual artists indicate that the art critic of the *Chronicle* changed in 1825, its position on institutions did not, and it continued to apply the same critical principles. The review of the Society of Painters in Water-Colours exhibition contained a general comment on the relations between art, nature, and the mind of the painter comparable to some of those in the *London Magazine* in 1825:

> One, among the highest delights that human perceptions are capable of exciting, is that which results from the various modes in which each painter contemplates the object of his imitation. Thus diversity depends upon what, perhaps, may be termed a creative power, and hence that originality or representation, which obtains for the author the distinctive appellative – his style.

When disciples emerge who aim at the style of another, then a school is in decline. The charm of the water-colour exhibition lay in its variety of styles.[85] This is one of the few instances of a positive use of the term 'style' I have discovered.

The *Chronicle* this year gave particularly extensive coverage to the Society's exhibition, and made very high claims for the achievements of the artists, asserting that 'in the principal attributes of painting', G. F. Robson and some other landscapists in water-colour, could 'vie' with 'all that the accumulated labours of the ancient masters have achieved, great and original as were their powers'. (This was precisely the kind of claim for modern art which was intolerable to Haydon and the High Art camp.) By contrast the usual litany of complaints was recited about the Royal Academy exhibition: it was overcrowded, much on show should not have been, and many works were hung too high to be seen properly. Consonant with the critic's positive appraisal of water-colour was a favourable view of the British mania for topography, which he linked with a more general characteristic of 'British taste'. There was no other country in which 'this delightful and interesting branch of study' was excelled, and 'to seek for the *vrai ressemblance* (sic)'; hence, portraiture, in all things, is preferred to the *beau idéal*.[86]

There are no statements in the *Literary Chronicle* which link what can be broadly described as the aesthetic of naturalism and originality with social progress as clearly as the *London Magazine* did. None the less, the articulation of that aesthetic in the *Chronicle* was framed by statements about patronage and institutions which indicated a critical stance towards the culture of the dominant élite. What has to be acknowledged, however, is that there was no necessary connection between the two. This conclusion is demanded by the evidence of the *Review of Publications of Art*, the *Magazine of the Fine Arts*, and the *Repository of Arts*, which I shall now briefly describe.[87] All of these publications made use of the naturalist aesthetic (with some variations), but none of them identified with progressive politics – although they did express some dissatisfaction with contemporary patronage. What they all have in common is that their proprietors/editors were directly involved with the business of topography and landscape art, and this distinguishes them from *The Artist* and the *Annals of the Fine Arts*, which were committed to the faction of history painters.

Art magazines

It is to be expected that the specialist art press would find no advantage in general denunciations of contemporary art, although some magazines criticized particular institutions or aspects of the exhibition scene from a variety of motives. *The Artist*, which was produced mainly by academicians, was a vehement champion of professional criticism and professional judgement against connoisseurs, and was probably established as a rival to *The Director* (January–July 1807), the house magazine of the British Institution.[88] It carried articles lamenting the deficiencies of patronage, which forced artists to waste their talents on 'trivial subjects, unworthy of their powers and below the dignity of art', and argued the need for art education of the wealthy, and government patronage to promote High Art.[89] The *Annals of the Fine Arts*, edited by Haydon's friend James Elmes, was a pro-Haydon organ, fiercely critical of the Academy as an institution which had sacrificed art and the national interest to the selfish interests of its members. However, although the *Annals* complained of the condition of patronage, its politics were if anything conservative.[90]

The Artist, which was not a reviewing magazine, gave no space to landscape painting; and the *Annals*, while it employed what can be regarded as naturalistic criteria in relation to both landscape and genre, inevitably treated them as lesser genres. The *Annals* was also sharply critical of the Water-Colour Society exhibitions, attacking both the pervasive high colouring of the drawings, and the monotony of the subjects.[91] Essentially, both magazines represented the interests of factions within the artistic community with no cause to question the traditional hierarchy – although the *Annals* did use a species of naturalism represented by Haydon and Wilkie to attack the Reynoldsian style of history painting.[92]

The *Review of Publications of Art* was edited by John Landseer, whose status as an engraver predisposed him to be critical towards the Academy, while his practice as an engraver of modern landscapes gave him an interest in the advancement of the genre. The *Review* contained complaints regarding the 'neglect of living merit' and the dearth of patronage for history painting, but in a dialogue which forms part of the review of the British Institution exhibition in 1808, the trend for artists to paint subjects representing contemporary life rather than epic subjects is treated sympathetically, and in a largely favourable review of the Society of Painters in Water-Colour's Exhibition, Landseer asserted:

> we are far from approving of that bigotted taste, or that fastidious mode of criticism which confines our approbation exclusively to a particular style of art.[93]

According to Landseer, the achievements of art transcend logic and judgement, and often depart from 'settled system or rule'. There seems to be an implicit criticism of academic principles here, and this is also suggested by some of Landseer's other positions.

Landseer claimed that modern everyday subjects were more likely to appeal to the contemporary public than historical subjects which frequently could only be understood by those with a sophisticated education, and were beyond the comprehension of many exhibition visitors. In his review of the British Institution exhibition of 1808, he strongly defended landscape subjects on the basis of the association of ideas, claiming with reference to the works of Wilson, Gainsborough, de Loutherbourg and Turner:

> ideas of the most interesting kind are associated with such subjects. The soul flies from the foul haunts of herded men, to scenes of native innocence, where hypocrisy appears not, and sincerity need not be restrained.

Landseer applied a similar logic to the modern-day genre subjects of Wilkie and others, and indeed the success of genre painting was closely connected with the success of naturalistic landscape painting. To judge from the dialogue which prefaces the British Institution review, Landseer did not deny the traditional ranking of genres, but he asserted that:

> If an artist addresses himself (by his works) to his contemporaries, he must deal in the kind of truth which those contemporaries understand, or he must teach them the language and the science of his superior art . . .

While he admired Haydon and accepted the merits of High Art, Landseer could equally discern qualities in the lesser genres which he evaluated in terms drawn from other discourses than that of the Academy.[94]

Landseer's most remarkable achievement as a critic was his eighteen-page review of Turner's Gallery, which is the most perceptive interpretation of the artist's work produced in the early nineteenth century. Although in this review he claims:

> Perhaps no landscape painter has ever before so successfully caught the living lustre of nature herself, under all her varying aspects and phenomena . . .

he also asserts that Turner's work, far more than that of his contemporaries, depends on the 'manifestation of mind', and less on 'dazzling and extrinsic qualities'. Whatever the brilliance of his colour or the striking effect of light and shade, these are always means to achieve some 'intellectual value', they are always subservient to 'some grand presiding mental purpose'. For Landseer, Turner is 'a master of the philosophy of his art'. Although the only aesthetician Landseer refers to in his review is Uvedale Price, in fact the aesthetic by which Turner is evaluated is not Price's 'picturesque', but the theory of association. Turner is particularly praised for his grasp of the 'unities of time and place', and his ability to bring together objects and effects which will co-operate to stimulate one great idea. Landseer develops this point most clearly in his account of *Pope's Villa at Twickenham* (Sudeley Castle, Gloucestershire, *Plate 74*), of which the overall effect is such that:

> we scarcely remember any picture that more powerfully imparts its prevailing tone of tranquillity to the mind of the beholder than this; or which more plainly shows that its author has developed the mysteries of the arcana of affinities between art and moral sentiment.[95]

It was appropriate that Turner's art was defended in relation to criteria of association and expression, but it was also symptomatic of the moment that it should be so. Naturalistic landscape had not yet acquired the distinct identity or numerical presence in exhibitions which would make it a 'cause', and the triumph of the landscape genre was only just beginning. By contrast, the *Magazine of Fine Arts* of 1821 appeared at a moment when naturalism was a well-established mode. It was published by the topographical entrepreneur John Britton, who is said to have written the exhibition reviews himself.[96] Although one of the earliest reviews in the *Magazine* asserted that the 'higher departments' of British art were improving, and argued that:

> English landscapes, and scenes of ordinary life, will never confer a very high character on a school . . .[97]

the tone of the review of the British Institution exhibition in the same number is more characteristic. This stresses that patronage in Britain comes from every class, 'from the monarch to the tradesman', and finds the variety of the exhibition evidence of 'much original thinking', despite the dearth of history paintings on show – a view which suggests an essentially positive and optimistic attitude to the prevailing social order. The *Magazine* was able to respond so favourably to contemporary art because it did not subscribe to the rigid academic definition of the hierarchy of merit which underlay the *Annals*:

> we cannot see any reason for the lamentations of certain periodical critics, who deplore the decline of the arts . . . When the canvas represents an interesting story or subject, it is of secondary importance whether it be tragedy or comedy, terrible or pathetic, calculated to excite imagination or mirth; it is always an appeal to the understanding. The degree of its power is that of its particular merit; but there is very little inequality between the classes of such works. The preference alternately given to them is arbitrary.[98]

West and Hogarth are both equally painters of history, and the distinctions between higher and lower classes of history are invidious and should be abandoned.

The *Magazine* thus sought to rebut the kind of criticism which junked whole areas of artistic production because the scale of work was small or its subject not sufficiently 'elevated'. It printed a regular column entitled 'Remarks on Contemporary Criticism' to counter some of the more 'irresponsible' attacks on contemporary art, by which it seems to allude to the criticism of the *Examiner* and the *Annals*, and it also contained a veiled critique of Haydon as 'a conceited imposter'.[99] By contrast with the *Annals'* repeated invective against the Water-Colour Society's exhibitions, the *Magazine* found that its 1821 display showed an 'extraordinary degree of excellence', and gave an eloquent defence of the virtues of the water-colour medium. Like a number of contemporary critics, Britton compared the overall effect of the exhibition on the visitor very favourably with that of the Royal Academy shows: 'neither Lord A., nor Bishop B., nor Lady C., distract his thoughts from the sublime and beautiful'. Instead 'he' feels that this is a place for 'investigation and reflection', since while 'local views' abound, they are generally well selected and treated with 'judgement':

> Few indeed, are the subjects, which the accomplished painters' command of colour, light and shade, and aerial effect, cannot render pleasing in a considerable degree; but those are the most excellent, in which the mechanical powers of the art are exerted with a particular sentiment and object, so as to produce a certain train of agreeable sensations. When the artist has attained this end, his work ranks high amongst the productions of art; and landscapes often possess this power, whilst pictures miscalled historical are frequently mere arrangements of colour, formed to impart a sensual pleasure to the eye.[100]

Given this appeal to picturesque and associationist principles to justify a critique of the academic hierarchy, it is somewhat surprising that the *Magazine* also printed the extended attack on association aesthetics I referred to in the previous chapter. Even such short-lived publications could speak with more than one voice.

While the *Magazine*'s general position on the value of the genres and water-colour is comparable to that of the *London Magazine* and *Literary Chronicle* at one level, within its pages it is unconnected to any larger attempt to define a progressive culture, and appears primarily as a stance taken in relation to the little politics of the art world. A similar aesthetic to that of the *Magazine of Fine Arts* had been articulated earlier in the *Repository of Arts*, where it was equally removed from social or political critique.

The '*Repository of Arts*'

Rudolf Ackermann's *Repository of Arts, Literature, Commerce, Manufactures, Fashions and Politics* ran from 1809 to 1828, and is the most important fashionable magazine of the early nineteenth century in relation to the arts. A lavish publication, at its height it sold only two thousand copies. Unlike most general magazines it did not carry notices of Theatrical Criticism, Bankruptcies, Accidents, &c., and neither did it carry much in the way of 'Commerce' and 'Politics' – indeed, by 1812 it was described as 'a Magazine which particularly recommends itself to the Fair Sex', which in terms of contemporary ideology justified its limited range. The *Repository* needs to be situated in relation to the more general pattern of Ackermann's activities as a publisher, print-seller, and art-dealer, and it took its name from his emporium in the Strand. Although Frederick Shoberl, one of the German emigrés employed by Ackermann, has been described as the editor, the character of the magazine is closely related to Ackermann's interests and concerns, particularly in the prominence it gave to water-colour and topographical art. The political stance of the early numbers of the *Repository* was conservative, and Ackermann was fiercely anti-French, acting as a kind of unofficial agent for the Saxon Court after 1818. Like other fashionable magazines it represented the prevailing social order as a satisfactory one.[101]

It is very probable that the articles on the arts in the *Repository* were written by a number of authors, including W. H. Pyne and the indefatigable William Carey in later years. At any rate, the art notices are not entirely consistent, although a distinctive dominant position clearly emerges which is highly favourable to topographical landscape. The *Repository*'s position on the general state of art in Britain can be related to Ackermann's involvement in the print market, to his commitment to the political establishment, and to his concern not to alienate a fashionable readership. After 1810, the magazine maintained an unfailingly positive view of the general talents of British artists, but often criticized the character of the exhibitions, and suggested the artists did not have the patronage they deserved. It regarded the Royal Academy as an institution with favour, and in 1813 claimed that it had talents of which any age would be proud in Turner, Callcott, Wilkie, Bird, and Ward. The *Repository* frequently regretted the predominance of portraits in the Academy's exhibitions, and referred to the 'Kaleidescope' effect of the display on the eye, but it also found that there were 'always' 'standard works' within them. The problems of the arts in Britain were attributed to the commercial character of the nation. The *Repository* lamented the absence of government patronage, and regularly praised the Directors of the British Institution – although in 1821 it noted that their concern to assist rising merit meant that they admitted work of inferior quality into their exhibitions. Offering an explanation of why Washington Allston's *The Dead Man Restored to Life by Touching the Bones of the Prophet Elisha* (Pennsylvania Academy of Fine Arts, Philadelphia) was not more admired, the *Repository* suggested that the exhibition public was essentially too light-hearted to appreciate such a work:

> The generality who form the gay scene presented by such a concourse of visitors, where few are disposed to be grave, must, in a great measure, look upon so solemn a subject as too great a check on their spirits to allow of their admiring it.

As we have seen, for those with a less sanguine view of the political order than the *Repository* the character of the exhibition scene was symptomatic of a much larger political and cultural malaise.[102]

In a review of the exhibition of the Society of Painters in Water-Colours in 1812, the *Repository*'s critic observed of a De Wint drawing, *A Corn Field*:

> That an intelligent mind does not depend upon the greatness of the subject to produce a fine work of art, may be boldly asserted from the picture before us. The shocks of wheat are grouped without apparent design; the figures are not placed in the field, but to pursue their occupation; the groups of clothes are not formally arranged; every thing is as it would appear were we suddenly to enter a harvest field amidst the blaze of noon. The colouring of the corn is brilliant and dazzling, the sky is heavenly serene, and the whole effect is replete with feeling of the chastest notions of art.

This statement indicates two things about the *Repository*'s critical stance. Firstly, as we would expect the high status it gave to landscape was linked to a refusal to be bound by a rigid hierarchy of genres:

> we object to no class of art, we are pleased with all, let but the images created be worthy of the artist's mind, and the representation be drawn from the best source of originality – nature.[103]

Secondly, the criterion of 'naturalism' did not simply relate to effects of light and atmosphere or the botanical truth of trees, it also related to the disposition of human activity and to composition, although this was rarely explicitly stated. It was the application of this criterion which partly licensed the *Repository* in championing the water-colour painters, who, it said, had 'raised a monument of honour to the British nation', and in 1812–13 it printed an important series of articles on the history of the medium.[104]

The *Repository* represented the changes in the character of water-colour painting in the eighteenth and early nineteenth centuries as a progress towards 'a strict and faithful imitation of nature', in which Girtin and Turner had played a key role.[105] On several occasions it expressed regret that there was so little topography in oil equivalent to that in water-colours. In 1815, it found that only some works by Mulready matched its ideas in this respect, perhaps referring to the landscapes Mulready had exhibited at the Academy in 1811. The magazine's commitment to naturalism is particularly clear from the very favourable review it gave to one of the most extraordinary examples of detailed representation of natural phenomena in a scene of everyday labour to be exhibited in the early nineteenth century: the young John Linnell's *Kensington Gravel Pits* (*Plate 4*), which was shown at the British Institution exhibition of 1813:

> This very pleasing representation of a gravel-pit, may be numbered amongst the finest pictures of the collection; the effect is bold, the colouring rich and clear, and the pencilling masterly. It is obvious, that the study for this natural composition must have been coloured upon the spot. Judging from this and various late specimens from the pencil of Mr Linnell, and other contemporary rising artists, we may hope, ere long, to see this department of art vie with the rural pictures of the best times, of the Flemish and Dutch Schools.[106]

Four points need to be noted in relation to this statement. Firstly, the commonplace idea, enshrined in academic theory, that the art of the Dutch and Flemish Schools represents the *ne plus ultra* of realism is still referred to, despite Linnell's departures from Dutch and Flemish precedents in some respects. Secondly, Linnell's work is seen as belonging to a more general tendency. Thirdly, the idea of verisimilitude is linked with a rather vague appraisal of technical qualities, which none the less indicates that the critic's understanding of the relationship between imitation and picture making is not altogether naive. Fourthly, the quality of the work is said to derive partly from the procedure of colouring on the spot. The *Repository* frequently made a linkage between naturalism, in both water-colour and oil painting, and the practice of painting outdoors, in relation to artists as diverse as Pugin, Girtin, and Glover. Although the magazine still referred to the Dutch and Flemish

Schools as a norm of accurate representation, it also printed Richter's radical attack on that principle in *Daylight: A Recent Discovery in the Art of Painting*. In this connection, it should be noted that the *Repository* commented of Panoramas in 1827 that while they were 'not thought very highly of by artists generally' because they depended on 'mechanical dexterity' and 'a sort of knack', yet 'many of the best and most studied rules of art' were necessary to their perfection.[107]

The idea of truthful imitation as a value inevitably led to problems with style. Clearly truthful imitation could take a variety of forms if the work of Glover, De Wint, and Linnell all represented it. As usual, the term used against those whose style could not be matched with the norm was 'manner', which was understood as a form of undue individualism or peculiarity:

> In the arts, the glowing enthusiasm of the mind must, for external representation, be regulated by the eye, and that organ must be true to nature. Men of all professions and studies may be originals, without being correct; or they may strike out a path for themselves, without violating the modesty of nature.

It seems to have been certain kinds of colour and vigorous brushwork which the *Repository*'s critic found unnatural, and it is perhaps significant that he found Constable's *Haywain* somewhat less satisfactory than the works of Callcott and Collins, who were regularly praised for their 'truthful' effects.[108]

For criticism in which the kind of criterion of naturalism outlined above was so central, the work of Turner and the imaginative landscapes of Martin and Danby might be expected to present some kind of problem. The *Repository* was generally favourable to Turner's work, describing his *Snowstorm. Hannibal and his Army* as an 'extraordinary work' and the artist himself as a 'Prospero of the graphic art'. In 1815 it found *Crossing the Brook* (Clore Gallery) the most 'elegant landscape' it had ever seen: 'every tree and shrub has a classic taste'. Significantly, it noted:

> We think his manner and execution are as purely original as the poetic forms which create his compositions.

Other reviews in the *Repository* also imply that there is a kind of imaginative art, which must be judged according to criteria of originality and the strength of its effect, as well as by naturalistic criteria. But if the artist depended too much on his imagination and departed too far from the works of nature 'in their ordinary shape', an unavoidable sameness resulted – as in the case of Martin. The difficulties which the *Repository*'s approach produced for the evaluation of landscape which was not topographical or naturalistic, were most clearly acknowledged in a review of Danby's *An Enchanted Island* (private collection) in 1825:

> There is a good deal of credit due to Mr Danby for his conception and execution of this subject: being a work of imagination, he could indulge, and he has indulged, his own fancy in the region of enchantment. We are not wizards enough to follow him thither for a closer examination of his work, not knowing the canons of criticism which rule the wand of the seer . . .[109]

This kind of problem with imaginative landscape was thus not invariably accompanied with the aversion to obscurantism which the *London Magazine*'s critic articulated in 1829, which indicates that the two positions were only consistent, and not connected by any binding cultural logic.

The criticism of these magazines suggests that material interests and the market success of some new types of landscape painting and topography, caused some early nineteenth-century critics to develop a kind of position which vindicated naturalism in some of its aspects. However, the larger ideological framework of such statements varied. There was nothing inherent in this kind of art which made it accord with a doctrine of political progress beyond the fact that it was new, original, and in some respects popular. The fact that it could be seen as specifically English and specifically modern was presumably the cause of its attraction to the critics of the *London Magazine* in the late 1820s – but this was precisely an instance of a non-class symbolic formation being appropriated in the interests of class politics.

Limits of cultural critique

Art criticism of *c.* 1805–30 may be considered *en bloc* as a kind of sub-field within the larger discourse of periodicals and newspapers, a sub-field in which a range of types of statement were put together in various combinations: statements drawn from the available discourses of academic theory, philosophical criticism, and increasingly art criticism itself (as the weight of precedent within this discourse accumulated), and applied in relation to particular works and particular views of the artistic scene and the social order. However, the definition of a morphology of statement types does not in itself explain their usage. One of the key issues in relation to early nineteenth-century criticism is indeed to explain the novelty of some of the statements which it produced: statements which were without precedent and the very converse of what seemed obvious and self-evident in eighteenth-century British art writing, such as that the hierarchy of genres was outmoded and irrelevant, that the ideal in art was nonsense, that a genre painter was a history painter, that water-colour was equal to oil painting and so on. I therefore consider this criticism as a *practice* of writing through which authors attempted to represent and make sense of a range of new circumstances on which they brought to bear a mass of hand-me-down conceptions which they fashioned anew.

In relation to the institutions of art, critics had to make sense of a very large expansion of the artistic profession and of artistic output, reflected in the growth of exhibition institutions and the scale of exhibitions, the proliferation of one-person shows accompanied by considerable publicity and self-advertisement in some cases, and the emergence of whole exhibitions devoted to what had hitherto been the minor medium of water-colour. In relation to the production of pictures, they had to contend with the growth in marketability and importance of genre painting, the increasing importance and changing practice of topographical and naturalistic landscape painting, and with marked innovations in the form, scale, and pretensions of 'imaginative' landscape painting. In sum, they had to make sense of large changes in the form, type, presentation, and consumption of works of art, which in many respects could only be evaluated negatively within the framework of eighteenth-century discourses on the arts. To an important extent, critics could only deal positively with these changes by inverting the academic hierarchies of value, or by modifying them, or by appeal to the theories of association or the picturesque.

These changes in the artistic field took place in a period of great social change and political unrest, and for contemporaries these different aspects of experience were not unrelated, as modern art historians generally represent them as having been. Political impartiality is a myth, and it was one which few periodicals or newspapers of the early nineteenth century even pretended to subscribe to. The clearest links between artistic and political discourse occur in papers far to the right or left of the political spectrum, such as the *Morning Post* or the *Examiner*, in which the alleged virtues or deficiencies of contemporary art and patronage were described as outer signs of the health or sickness of the social body. I do not claim that the cultural critique of the opposition press was a very profound one, but surely there are some contentions in the writings of Hunt, Hazlitt, and others which deserve serious consideration: that the taste of the dominant élite was generally shallow and unintellectual, that with a few exceptions it did not take the arts seriously, that exhibitions were market places in flattery and fashionable gatherings which reflected precisely the snobbery and adulation of rank and wealth with which the dominant groups in British society fuelled their self-esteem. Surely there were indeed connections between contemporary artistic practices and the corrupt and repressive oligarchy they served.

Jonathan Cook has suggested that the form which Hazlitt's work took resulted from the 'demands of writing for a literary market' which called for critical reviews and short essays, and that this set limits to the kinds of connection he could develop between his positions on politics and art:

> Thus, what we find in Hazlitt's work is a series of brilliant but dispersed criticisms of his culture rather than a sustained critique of it.[110]

This comment has a wider relevance, and it is true that the format and market of newspapers and periodical literature put restraints on what could be said, and tended to promote impassioned invective rather than 'sustained critique'. However, the problem seems to me more than just one of format. It was partly that the precedents for a book of sustained contemporary cultural criticism did not exist (although both Coleridge's *Biographia Literaria* and Hazlitt's *Spirit of the Age* could be seen as experiments in this direction) and the intellectual materials from which to build one could not be found within the English radical tradition. Scottish social theory, which could have provided some kinds of model in the writings of Ferguson, Hume, Kames, and Millar was probably too close to political economy and to Utilitarian philosophy, which romantics like Hazlitt saw as part of the problem, to be usable. Indeed, it has been suggested that romantic writers of liberal sympathies, such as Hazlitt, were affected by the wider aversion to 'generalization, system and even rational connected argument', which became a fashion from the late 1790s.[111]

Cook has also pointed to 'a problem of the relation between ethical and political idioms' in Hazlitt's writing, and this seems to me to point towards the other real issue – which is that the critique of corruption in radical discourse in the early nineteenth century was essentially couched in moral terms. Thompson has described the radicalism of 1815–20 as 'a generalized libertarian rhetoric', and most of radical discourse as 'concerned with the piecemeal exposure of the abuses of the "borough-mongering" or "fund-holding" system'.[112] This discourse simply did not provide the materials for 'sustained critique', partly because within it the dimension of class was present really only as a negative 'them'. It is for this reason that some of the articles in the *London Magazine* in the years 1823–5 seem to make rather more progress in articulating a convincing interpretation of contemporary culture, because they are written from the standpoint of 'us', the bourgeoisie. By identifying the novel qualities of modern painting in a positive way with a progressive bourgeois outlook, the criticism of the *London* was able to produce a more coherent and systematic representation of these developments, because it situated them within a clear historical perspective. By comparison with this, Hazlitt's observations tend to look fragmentary and splenetic, despite his philosophical insight and the quality of his writing.

Yet if art criticism in the early nineteenth century produced little sustained politico-cultural critique of contemporary art, art was perceived as a political matter. That is to say, early nineteenth-century critics wrote as whole individuals, aware that cultural artefacts do imply a range of values, and do endow these values on their possessors. They saw artistic institutions as part of a larger social fabric, and as directly implicated in struggles for power and influence among competing social groups. In this view of the politics of art, landscape painting plays a nebulous and shifting role. There was no genetic connection between landscape painting as a whole, or between any particular type of landscape painting and the values of any single social group. But because the political value of landscape painting was shifting and ambiguous this does not mean it did not have a political value – it had several. What is most striking is that despite the celebratory mythology of the rural which most landscape painters of British scenes apparently evoked, and which seems so obviously linked with the interests of landed society, even the bourgeois radicals closest to Utilitarianism do not appear to have produced any critique of this imagery of a rural order which was the foundation of the privileges against which they directed their main energies. They made no functional connection between this imagery and the hegemony of the 'aristocracy'.

(iii) The functions of naturalism

So far I have been attempting to situate landscape painting within the politics of painting at a high level of generality. I now want to consider what the study of criticism suggests about landscape painting as a mode of representing social life. The pictorial system of European painting was part of the doxa, in that it was inconceivable there could be any other mode for the truthful representation of visual experience than that of perspective and the related devices of Renaissance naturalism (in Gombrich's sense). Indeed there was remarkable unanimity as to what constituted the best means of attaining verisimilitude among the varieties of style on offer, despite some differences of opinion over issues of finish and colour. Thus critics measured sensory naturalism by the 'relationship between the system of representation employed in the picture and the standard system', as is neatly illustrated by the following observation on Turner's *'Now for the Painter', Passengers Going on Board* (Manchester City Art Gallery) of 1827:

> Mr Turner's pictures are everything they should be, except natural ... In the picture before us, for example, nothing can be more skilfully painted than the water. It is transparent, liquid, and in actual motion, so far as effect is concerned; but still it is not like the water of Vandervelde, or Backhuysen, or of nature; and the reason is, that the artist has essayed to make it more like 'real water' than that of either of the above.[113]

While most critics found it difficult to attribute a positive value to style, many implied that there could not be a picture without style – a perfect copy, and some indirectly acknowledged a value in style by describing the individuality of a painter's practice as the discovery of a new kind of truth in the representation of nature. Only thus could the range of styles which were admired all be described as truthful. The majority of critics showed some awareness that painting depended on the manipulation of codes of representation, and drew on the conceptualization of those codes within academic theory in terms of the categories of drawing, modelling, chiaroscuro, colouring, composition, and style. Thus if paintings were seen as a kind of natural sign, it was clearly understood that verisimilitude in the narrow sense was not the only or even the key measure of the value of a picture. It had to be combined with a truth of expression – that is with a truth to human nature and experience. Verisimilitude simply re-inforced and confirmed the ideology which was connoted via expression.

Of course there were differences as to what constituted 'truth of representation' in relation to the social world, as much as in relation to visual effects, and there was a continuum between the two. Thus while Gainsborough's 'fancy pictures' were much admired as images of the 'rustic character', with 'nothing of the clumsy or vulgar about them'; there were also criticisms such as Hazlitt's that his work represented 'an ideal of common life', and that it was 'mannered'.[114] With the appearance of paintings such as Collins' *The Disposal of a Favourite Lamb* (RA 1813), which effectively reworked Gainsborough's cottage door theme in a style which early nineteenth-century observers understood as 'natural', Gainsborough's work looked correspondingly 'artificial'.[115] However, while the standard mode for representing the working class changed, the mechanism of its effect remained the same: it was represented both as it was and as it ought to be at the same time. Thus in 1819 the *Observer* explicitly recognized the process of fabrication in Wilkie's painting:

> in the beauty of the pencilling, in the management of groupes, and in that most essential quality, the giving those very gestures and looks which, in actual life, best denote the thoughts and feelings he intends to express, he is unsurpassed

at the same time as it affirmed the representation was true:

> The longer we look at his works the more we like them, because they are such truthful images of our species, and because they reflect back upon us our own emotions and actions. They are not deceptions, but realities; not sophistications, but truths. They are nature.

Thus Wilkie's pictures are presented as an image of universal humanity. It is easy to see that this is *universal* humanity defined by a particular class interest, and this contradiction almost surfaced in the *Parthenon*'s observation in 1825 that the pictures of Collins, Constable and Wilkie:

> show us the features of Nature, and the scenes of domestic life in a magic glass, which seems to embellish, while it does but reflect their image.[116]

Wilkie was consistently said to have surpassed Dutch and Flemish genre painting through the moral truths represented in his work, but artists whose representations of the 'lower orders' did not meet these requirements were criticized – as the responses to Heaphy's exhibits of 1807–11 demonstrate. While Heaphy commanded high prices for his water-colours, and his talent was regularly acknowledged, critics in several magazines found his imagery 'degraded'. It was not that his representation of the poor was false, it was rather that he had chosen the wrong kind of truth. Thus *Le Beau Monde* complained in 1808 that 'he paints a detail of wickedness or a detail of virtue with the same interest or the same apathy', while three years later the *Repository of Arts* found his works 'deficient in that moral effect which alone can excuse the representation of vulgarity'.[117] Considering an image such as *Country Girl being Robbed by Two Boys* (*Plate 7*) one can understand this response. In this and other drawings, such as the *Family Doctress* (1809, Victoria & Albert Museum) and *Inattention* (1808, Yale Center for British Art), Heaphy suggests extreme passions, and unruly or vicious behaviour. In the drawing illustrated here, the boy on the right of the girl seems to be about to tear open her blouse, while the hand of the boy on the left violates her basket. The girl's strained pose and frightened look contrast with the suggestion of pleasure in the face of the left-hand boy. These features give to the drawing a kind of sexual menace which must have outraged the sensibilities of many early nineteenth-century spectators. Further, Heaphy shows vice and bad passions where they should not be: in the country – and to be precise, near Epsom, as the sign indicates. Such works are like a riposte to the saccharine narratives of Collins. Thus there was a kind of representation of the 'lower orders' which was true, but which was also unacceptable. The poor could and should be represented 'truthfully', but at the same time either de-vulgarized or represented in its vulgarity so as to demonstrate a self-evident moral truth – as in Wilkie's *Village Festival* (Tate Gallery) where the imagery of drunkards illustrated that drunkeness led to vice in various forms.

There was a kind of voyeuristic aspect – a kind of titillating exoticism – to viewing such imagery of the 'humble poor'; or so a comment in the self-styled Comte de Soligny's *Letters on England* (1823) suggests. This describes the subjects of Wilkie's pictures as restricted to:

> the higher classes of low life, where the habits and institutions of modern society have hitherto, in a great measure, failed to diffuse that artificial and conventional form of character, which, if it does not altogether preclude the *action* of the feelings, at least forbids the outward manifestation of them.

Had Wilkie used 'his peculiar and unrivalled power of depicting what *is*, to scenes in high, or even in middle life', his works would have been 'altogether feeble and worthless', for among these classes 'outward attributes' are:

> smoothed and polished down to a plain and colourless surface, which will not admit the passage of any thing from within, and from which everything without slides off like water-drops from the feathers of a bird.[118]

It thus seems that Wilkie's imagery of an animated 'peasantry' offered a vision of the free and natural expression of feelings, uncramped by norms of decorum, which could both appeal to middle-class fantasies, and at the same time strengthen that class's sense of its own identity.

The representation of the human figure was regarded as the most important aspect of expression in early nineteenth-century criticism, yet from reading it one would imagine that the figures in much naturalistic landscape painting were simply invisible, since such pictures were discussed almost exclusively in terms of a narrow verisimilitude. Thus none of the reviews I have discovered of Linnell's *Kensington Gravel Pits* mentions the prominent group of labourers within it, and the *Repository*'s comment on the verisimilitude of the figures in De Wint's *A Corn Field*, discussed earlier, is unusual. Constable's figures were almost invariably passed over without comment.[119]

The only paintings of the rural scene which elicited statements on the representation of the figures were those which can be seen as a hybrid between landscape and genre painting, and particularly those of Collins and Cristall, some of which will be analysed in detail in the next chapter. In paintings such as *The Reluctant Departure* (RA 1815, *Plate 8*), Collins combined a contemporary narrative (in this instance of mother making a reluctant farewell to her child) with an image of landscape in what was understood as a 'natural' style. Critics frequently commented on the 'appropriateness' of Collins' figures, and they were repeatedly said to match the kind of locality represented or the 'sentiment' of the scene. However, the essentially formulaic function of such figures as accompaniments to the image of British 'nature', is suggested by a review of 1822, which praised the artist for making his figures 'less prominent' and narratives 'less obtrusive' in recent pictures:

> We want a certain class of *figures* in his landscapes, that each may mutually enliven and illustrate the other; but we do not want the one to fix and engross our attention, to the neglect of the other.[120]

This may be understood partly as a comment on the proprieties of particular genres, as much as one on the proprieties of figure types. But the stress on 'figures', as opposed to character, at least suggests that the labourer in the landscape must not have an obtrusively individual presence.

The clearest discussions of the representation of rural figures occur in relation to the work of Cristall. In one type of Cristall water-colour, rural figures (usually women) in contemporary dress which signified the 'typical dress' of parts of either England, Scotland, or Wales are represented in the foreground against scenery which represented 'characteristic' landscapes of those regions.[121] In 1821, a review of an outline engraving after one of his pictures commented:

> His interesting studies of the peasantry are well known. This class of persons, in districts remote from cities, manufacturing towns, and seaports, retains a primeval health, strength and agility and produce numerous instances of beauty.

In movement they had a 'natural grace', while their 'rural costume' was 'destitute of the affectation of fashion or ornament', and came close to the beauties of drapery. Cristall had drawn his 'peasants':

> as we may suppose Michael Angelo would have drawn them, and [they] are valuable examples of the grand style in art.

Here we encounter a familiar elision: Cristall's figures are true to a healthy but vaguely remote peasantry – but they are also represented as Michelangelo would have drawn them. Writing in 1824, W. H. Pyne found Cristall's peasantry 'truly English', but also of a remote stock:

> They are selected from sequestered villages, yet uncontaminated by the vicinity of manufactories. The healthy offspring of retirement and content, a remnant of that race which once peopled a thousand villages and hamlets, that have now nothing left of their wanted simplicity but their ancient names.

Cristall's classicizing style was very different from the Dutch derived styles of Collins or Wilkie, but it was equally true – because he represented a different type of the labourer.[122]

One of the most revealing of the many discussions of Cristall's work, and one of the few in which the kind of commentary on his figures is extended to that of other painters occurs in the *Repository of Arts* in 1812. In this review a group of water colours by Cristall, Hills, and Uwins is said to represent the desirable form of the English 'yeomanry' or 'peasantry'. Thus Cristall's *Gleaners* were drawn from 'a race of healthy cottage children', such 'as we wish to meet in every village', while Uwins's *The Haymaker's Dinner* personified 'smiling peace' in its 'group of honest rustics':

> all the characters are stamped with nature; the former is an epitome of the independent English yeoman; his labourers are such as English peasantry should ever be – healthy, happy, and neat . . .

Underlying this emphasis on things as they ought to be, is an implication that things are changing, and that in many places they are not as they should be. Thus Francis Stevens' drawing of *Simpson's-Place Bromley* represented a manor house which reminded the *Repository* of an earlier period:

> when the squire lived in the midst of his tenantry, and administered to the wants of his humble neighbour, and his honoured lady made her way to church amidst the blessings of the poor.

Thus the work of Cristall, Uwins, and others was interpreted as representing either a remote and healthier rural order, or a healthier rural order which was passing or had passed away, of a time before *The Deserted Village*.[123] While such an attitude might seem to match best with the taste of the patrician gentleman we considered in chapters 4 and 5, it is important to remember that it was the class of capitalist agriculturalists which was bringing about the very changes to which the *Repository* referred; and there is abundant evidence that the nostalgic vision of an earlier unspoilt rural order appealed as much to the middle classes as to the gentry.

From an historical perspective, there is a case for regarding the naturalistic painting of the early nineteenth century as more 'realist' than the rural scenes of say Gainsborough or Westall, because such painting was interpreted as providing kinds of information about what was understood as the real nature of geography, botany, atmosphere, and agriculture in a way the latter was not. Spectators of Gainsborough's pictures in the late eighteenth and early nineteenth centuries understood works such as *The Cottage Door* (Huntington Collection) as generalized and ideal images of rural life. Therein lay their truth. By contrast, Constable's landscapes were understood to be specific representations of a part of Britain and of modern agricultural practices within it. However, at the same time as representing the landscapes of Suffolk or wherever, naturalistic landscapes without a topographical function also referred the spectator to a larger conception of 'nature' as a manifestation of the handiwork of an anglican deity, and to a conception of nature as the opposite of the town – to districts 'remote from cities, manufacturing towns, and seaports'. If naturalistic landscape paintings were understood as representations of specific places in the British countryside seen under specific conditions, it should be clear from the foregoing that they were also read as truthful representations of the social order as it was constructed in the nature poetry of Thomson, Crabbe, Bloomfield, et al. and in a wide range of class discourses. Yet whatever their general symbolism, their signification of an abundance of particular truths brings them far closer to a realist aesthetic.

One of the problems of the social history of art in its cruder forms is that it has a flattening effect, reducing diverse bodies of images to unmodulated manifestations of ideology and class interest. However, from the perspective of this study, ideologies are not large and tidy parcels of ideas to be neatly attributed to class groups. And the same applies to works of art. One of my basic premises is that paintings have no single reading, but always several, depending on what type of person is doing the reading, when, and for what purpose. Thus naturalistic landscapes were related to a complex range of ideas partly depending on 'context'. In early nineteenth-century criticism the works of Constable, De Wint, Linnell, et al. were referred to other types of pictorial practice; to theories of the picturesque and association; to criteria of verisimilitude in technique, colour, and composition; to an ill-defined notion of English rural nature; and to various perspectives on the condition of the national culture. They were not explicitly referred to the discourses of poetry, agricultural improvement, and political economy because it was not part of the ritual functions of criticism to refer them to those discourses. We can learn much of how pictures functioned as aesthetic signs from criticism, but to discover something of those complex chains of association which bound those functions to the larger experiences of the spectator we must turn to a different kind of evidence.

8 The imagery of seaside resorts and modern leisure

This chapter is concerned with the problems of representing the modern as constituted in the development of the seaside resort. It looks at the complex relationships between visual forms, aesthetic discourses, and social interests as they bore on the ambitions of landscape painters and on their commodity production. I shall begin by establishing the nature of some of the places which were represented (Brighton, Hastings, Margate, Great Yarmouth, etc.) and sketch the social forces which were at work in their growth and transformation. The aim of this is partly to suggest the forms that modernization took, and to explore the conflicting attitudes it prompted. It would be naive to expect that the physical character of the sites was the major factor determining the form taken by representations of them. Rather, what occurred was that established image types were adopted and sometimes modified to represent new realities, just as earlier forms of discourse are continually adapted to serve new functions.[1] In many cases, pictures were produced which were straightforward variations on seventeenth-century Dutch prototypes, and whose only connection with a specific site was their title. It is the exceptions to this pattern which are seen as having most aesthetic interest here.

The representation of the modern was not a problem as such. Indeed, the modern was widely represented in the lower levels of visual imagery such as tourist prints. But the higher the status of an image type was, the more it was understood to have a primary aesthetic function, and the more difficult representation of the modern became. Within academic theory, higher levels of imagery were seen as demanding the 'ideal' and therefore the mythical. An ambitious landscape painter could pursue originality by a 'truthful' representation which incorporated the modern, and hope that his work would be interpreted, within and without the artistic community, in relation to the new developments in theory and criticism which licensed such practice. However, it is indicative of the extent to which consumers were resistant to the combination of innovation in form and subject, that the most original beach scene of the period, that which came closest to rupturing the type of mythological connotations seen as appropriate to major oils, Constable's *The Beach at Brighton, the Chain Pier in the Distance* (*Plate 27*) was an apparently unsaleable work.

(i) Attitudes towards resort development

It is an historical commonplace that the development of seaside resorts is one of the most striking features of British urban development in the eighteenth and early nineteenth centuries. The 1851 census shows that between 1801 and 1851 the population of seaside towns had risen faster than that of any other type of town.[2] New watering places sprang up around the coasts, sometimes growing in places which had hitherto been little more than a few cottages, but which were seized on by ambitious developers of the type represented by Mr Parker in Jane Austen's *Sanditon*. This remarkable growth was influenced to some extent by developments in medical opinion, but it depended far more on an increasing demand for leisure facilities among gentry and bourgeois groups, and on an increasing awareness of leisure as a field for capital investment.[3] P. J. Corfield has described the resorts as 'in a sense showcases for the urban way of life', and they certainly became a prime symbol of its manners and frivolities.[4]

The major inland spas, which had been centres of fashionable amusement since the Restoration, were notoriously exclusive and originally catered for a small and homogeneous section of society. Already in the eighteenth century some of the bourgeoisie had begun to infiltrate into these places, and the distaste of older landed society at this intrusion is represented in Smollett's Squire Bramble in *Humphrey Clinker*, who complained of the 'men of low birth and no breeding', who having 'found themselves translated into a state of affluence unknown to former ages', appeared at Bath to mingle with the royalty and nobility. There were also a sizeable number of lesser spas which catered mainly for the class groups which could not afford to travel to Bath. The spas continued to prosper in the early nineteenth century when a number of new spa towns developed, but by 1840 Augustus Bozzi Granville, one of the leading authorities on water cures, could observe:

> No one can deny that mineral waters, have for the last thirty years, been growing out of fashion . . .[5]

The spas had lost out to the seaside, and changing leisure patterns were reflected in the extent to which royalty frequented the coast as opposed to the inland watering places: the Prince of Wales at Brighton from 1783 on, and George III at Weymouth from 1789. In the late eighteenth century Brighton had replaced Bath as the most fashionable town outside London.

Sea-bathing had been increasingly popular since the 1730s when Brighton, Margate, and Scarborough were already resorts. However, although it had been recommended as early as 1702 as a cure for certain complaints, sea-bathing did not gain widespread acceptance until after the publication of Dr Richard Russell's *Dissertation Concerning the Use of Sea-water in Diseases of the Glands* fifty years later. The remarkable change in habits to which this contributed caused one commentator to complain in 1769 of:

> an epidemical disorder that was formerly quite unknown and even now wants a name, which seizes whole families here in town at this season of the year . . . in a word, of whatever nature the complaint may be, it is imagined that nothing will remove it but spending the summer months in some dirty fishing town near the main shore.[6]

Although the developing seaside resorts modelled themselves on the inland spas and tried to provide the same kind of amenities in theatres, assembly rooms, circulating libraries and even mineral waters; their very growth reflected the fact that the old watering places could not provide sufficient facilities for the increasing number of the middle class with leisure. The seaside towns were thus largely unable to maintain the exclusiveness the great spas had once had, particularly after the creation of the railway system in the 1830s and 1840s. However, while the bourgeoisie arrived in droves, the resorts were largely inaccessible to the working class until working hours were reduced in the latter part of the century.

The presence of the professional and lower middle class at certain towns was noticed surprisingly early on. At Margate, which could be reached easily and cheaply from London by water, 'Many plain, unrefined characters, intermingled with the more polished crowd' in the late 1770s. In 1804, Farington heard that it was like Cheapside or Wapping, and in 1824 *The Times* noted that it had become unpopular with the fashionable world.[7] Blackpool, one of a group of northern resorts which developed to cater for the industrial centres of Lancashire, was by 1813 full of 'crowds of poor people from the manufacturing towns', although it is unlikely that these were yet working class.[8] Even Brighton, the most aristocratic of the resorts, was losing its exclusiveness by 1806, when Lady Jerningham compared it unfavourably with the spa town of Tunbridge Wells, 'that Elysium of quiet, pleasant, Sociable Intercourse'. Brighton, by contrast, she described as a 'great Staring, Bustling, Unsociable' place, where 'Judas might have survived his desperate intention'.[9] The last master of ceremonies was elected there in 1828, Queen Victoria did not like the place, and it had no royal visitors after 1845. In the letterpress to his *English Landscape Scenery*, Constable observed that Brighton had become:

> one of the largest, most splendid and gayest places in the kingdom; the resort of multitudes of every class of society.[10]

Of course, the 'multitudes' only appeared to be of 'every class of society' to one whose family connections and conservative outlook led him to identify closely with traditional landed society, but the remark is significant for what it tells us of a conservative view of the place in this period.

While there has been important research into the history of leisure in recent years, this has tended to focus on the changing character of working-class leisure, and on the efforts of the dominant social groups to mould it within their own ideological framework to counter any subversive or oppositional potential of leisure pursuits.[11] Far less attention has been given (understandably) to the friction between the bourgeoisie and landed society over the usage of the same leisure sites in the eighteenth and early nineteenth centuries. Yet tensions there undeniably were. When Farington's acquaintances compared Margate to Cheapside and Wapping they intended no compliment. The presence there of solicitors, lawyers, surgeons, doctors, undertakers, barbers, tailors, shopsellers, butchers, bakers, tea-dealers and representatives of other socially comparable occupations who William Robinson describes in *A Trip to Margate* (1805), meant inevitably that the place lost its *bon ton*, and that landed society, and the big bourgeoisie which moved in the same orbit, could not use visits there to demarcate their distinct status from groups lower down the social hierarchy. Thus, Richard Ayton in *A Voyage round Great Britain, Undertaken in the Summer of the Year 1813* (vol. VII, 1824) was quite explicit that Margate was a 'well-frequented' but not a 'fashionable' watering place, and that it attracted visitors from the 'intermediate rather than ... the opulent classes of society'. Ramsgate, by contrast, was a resort of the 'genteeler class'.[12]

For a paper as close to the world of fashion as the *Morning Post*, the development of the resorts was yet another cause for national self-congratulation. The *Post* regularly reported on the Watering Places as part of its general coverage of fashionable life, and in an article of 1825 it found that the rapid expansion of 'all the delightful little towns' along the South Coast provided yet another demonstration of that 'wonderful state of prosperity at which our country has arrived':

> At Hastings, rocks are hewn down, parades formed, noble rows of houses built, and all is bustle, improvements, and gaiety. But what can be said that shall give an adequate notion of the amazing increase of houses, inhabitants, public buildings, and places of amusement in Margate – bewitching, free and easy, funny, frolicsome Margate?

An idea of condescension is clearly intended here, and the writer then quotes from a satirical poem on the town, and pokes fun at visitors such as 'Mr Scrapecheese' from Tooley Street and 'Cockney's wives'.[13] From such a perspective, the only problem was how to ensure the exclusivity of some of the towns from the intrusion of such persons.

Evidence of direct conflict between social groups over use of the same urban space is provided by a fascinating report on Brighton, published in the *Morning Herald* in 1822. This begins by observing that Brighton was no longer 'the scene of rustic simplicity and fashionable frolic' it had once been, and that:

> For upwards of twenty years every thing had been growing up to the magnitude of a city; and the new improvements now going forward are calculated to make it a city in appearance as well as reality. The readers of this paper must recollect that the old Steyne was formerly a beautiful green lawn, open to pedestrians of all ranks, which was filled every fine afternoon with crowded parties, and upon which the fishermen exercised their right, from long usage, of drying their nets.

However, this intermingling of different social groups was to be brought to an end. Building work was going forward on the Steyne, which was to be laid out in walks and shrubberies. Iron palisades were to be erected round it and access would henceforth be restricted:

> Some people consider this as a grand improvement, while others view it as a modern refinement, introduced with a view of making an invidious distinction between the higher and the middling classes, and an encroachment on that freedom which had put all the visitors on a sort of equality with each other.

The fishermen too had complained about this violation of their customary rights, and became 'boisterously mutinous'. They were only bought off by the Lord of the Manor agreeing to waive the annual tribute he had been accustomed to receive from them. The *Herald*'s report illustrates graphically that the growing number of middle-class visitors at Brighton was not welcomed by those from the upper ranks of society who congregated there. Another indicator of this growing intrusion of vulgar persons and of the desire to avoid contact with them, was the building of an eight-foot-high wall, topped with iron palisades and boards, around the lawn of the royal palace where it bordered the Steyne – hitherto it had been only fenced off by a low wooden railing.[14]

The increasingly fashionable character of the more select resorts produced a mixed response from both conservative and liberal intellectuals. Fashion was directly connected with neglect of the responsibilities of rank and with dissipation in current ideologies, and Brighton in particular appeared a site of 'dissipation' and 'nonsense' to the (then Whig) *Morning Post* of 1785.[15] It did not improve subsequently. In a satirical poem of 1796, John Williams referred to it as:

> one of those numerous watering-places which beskirt this polluted island, and operate as apologies for idleness, sensuality, and nearly all the ramifications of social imposture . . .[16]

Williams refers repeatedly to the vice and social pretensions of the visitors. It was 'fashion' too, that Southey mocked in less severe terms in his account of Watering Places in *Letters from England*, observing that the 'tribes of wealth and fashion' are drawn to the seaside not by the 'beauty of the place' or by the bathing, but by their desire to mix in 'society', and be seen as part of the fashionable world; while a guide to Hastings of 1824 'principally' attributed to the same cause the fact that such places 'increase in extent and consequence, and become raised, from the huts and mean dwellings of fishermen, to be the abodes of wealth and splendour'.[17]

Useful to my purposes here, because of its clear contrast of old and new, is Charles Lamb's well-known essay 'The Old Margate Hoy', which was published in the *London Magazine* in 1823. This is an attack on the fashionable visitors seeking amusement, who do not really care for the sea, and who have spoiled the fishing villages. Lamb regrets the supersession of the Old Margate Hoy by the 'foppery and fresh-water niceness of the modern steam packet'.[18] He found the resorts themselves a detestable cross between town and country without the advantages of either. Of Hastings he writes:

> If it were what it was in its primitive shape, and what it ought to have remained, a fair honest fishing-town, and no more, it were something ...

But the visitors from the town who do not care for the sea, and who go there to say they have been, are his aversion. With them:

> All is false and hollow pretension. They come, because it is the fashion and to spoil the nature of the place.[19]

(It is interesting to note in connection with this that Ayton described the 'generally recognized' and 'endemic malady of a watering place' as 'ennui' – all the customary facilities of the resorts were designed to combat this malady.)[20] Lamb's critique is the view of a middle-class intellectual, for whom the development of the resorts represented a despoliation of a social order in which human beings lived in a proper and healthy relationship with nature, a despoliation which contradicted one of the fundamental strands of the literary culture of the period. It also appeared in the context of a periodical which frequently used cultural criticism as a way of lambasting the moral and intellectual shallowness of the dominant social groups.

The resort phenomenon was seen in its most advanced form at Brighton. The newness of the buildings there seemed both the quintessence of modernity and the anti-picturesque. This was vividly expressed by P. G. Patmore, who found its features to be 'not what can be called striking', but none the less 'very remarkable':

> There is no beauty or grandeur in the houses or public buildings. On the contrary, there is an air of smallness everywhere; but this is accompanied by a newness, a completeness, and a finish, which gives to the whole the effect of a picture. Any part that can be taken in by the eye at once, has the appearance of a newly painted scene on the stage. Most of the houses look as if they had been kept in a case, and were now just uncovered for some public occasion.[21]

In December 1820, a writer in the *London Magazine* observed 'a perfection in the ugliness of Brighton, which in some degree satisfies the imagination', so lacking was the coast in the picturesque, and the sea in shipping. Nature having nothing to offer, the beauty of Brighton was confined to its buildings, and the Chain Pier:

> It is true that its motion is apt to make one sea-sick, but it is an elegant little machine, a toy seemingly not sea-worthy; yet its very fragility of look and bending nature constitutes its strength.[22]

The currency of such comments indicates that Constable's revulsion from Brighton was hardly unique, and also shows how very daring was his ambition to render the most modern of seafronts with its 'elegant little machine' the subject of a major picturesque landscape.

In a famous letter to John Fisher of 1824, Constable described that promiscuous intermingling of social classes and improper display of womanhood that Williams had satirized in 1796, and emphasized his dislike of the place:

> Brighton is the receptacle of the fashion and offscouring of London. The magnificence of the sea, and its . . . everlasting voice, is drowned in the din & lost in the tumult of stage coaches – gigs – 'flys' &c. – and the beach is only Piccadilly . . . by the sea-side. Ladies dressed & *undressed* – gentlemen in morning gowns & slippers on, or without them altogether about *knee deep* in the breakers – footmen – children – nursery maids, dogs, boys, fishermen – *preventive service men* . . . rotten fish & those hideous amphibious animals the old bathing women, whose language both in oaths & voice resembles men – all are mixed up together in endless & indecent confusion. The genteeler part, the marine parade, is still more unnatural – with its trimmed and neat appearance & the dandy jetty or chain pier, with its long & elegant strides into the sea[23]

The contrasts of this letter were hardly Constable's invention – they derive from a far more widespread vein of feeling. Given the problems such a subject must present to the painter, and given that Constable found only the 'breakers' and the 'sky' fit materials for his brush (although he conceded the picturesqueness of the fishing boats too), a major question we must address is why he painted modern Brighton at all.

Finally if no voice of the working class has come down to us, we can at least have that of contemporary radicalism in Cobbett, who inevitably found in such fashionable places the obtrusive presence of 'Old Corruption' and its hangers-on. In a letter from Oxford of November 1821 he lumped Brighton, Margate, Ramsgate, and Worthing together with London, Cheltenham, and Bath, as places infected by the 'body-vermin' of 'tax-eaters'.[24] In 1822 he described Brighton as a very pleasant place for a 'wen'; and found its situation healthy, and its tradespeople 'very nice in all their concerns'. But after a brilliant verbal assault on Nash's trashy Pavilion, he continues:

> Brighton is naturally a place of resort for expectants, and a shifty ugly-looking swarm is of course assembled here.

In 1823 he referred to the presence of 'stock-jobbers' and their families, and in a most telling passage he defined the improvements on the fringes of London and along the Brighton road as emblems of the way 'the produce of labour is taken from the industrious, and given to the idler'.[25] We can thus assume that the 'splendours' which so dazzled the *Morning Post* as signs of contemporary opulence, had a very different meaning for Cobbett and those who thought like him.

Cobbett's writings also indicate another side to Brighton life, that is the presence there of a strong petty-bourgeoisie and artisanal radical element which helped to make it an important early centre of the Co-operative Movement.[26] In 1822, he spent the evening at Brighton in the company of reformers, 'plain tradesmen and mechanics'.[27] It is worth noting in this connection, that one of Constable's best-known outbursts against 'radicals' was prompted by an incident at Brighton, when one of his friends, Henry Phillips, tried to interfere in a working class meeting at the Carpenter's Arms:

> almost every mechanick, whether master or man, is a rebel and a blackguard – dissatisfied in proportion to his abilities, &c., &c., &c.[28]

For Constable, Brighton as an urban centre prompted the same kind of social anxieties as any other place where the working-class might be concentrated.

The real phenomena which produced these different and conflicting viewpoints were the physical development of the South Coast resorts and the intermixing of different social groups there. In such locations, the symbiotic relations between older and newer wealth were clearly apparent, as were the contrasts between the upper ranks and those petty-bourgeois and professional persons they regarded as their inferiors. The working class was of course there too – but not for the purpose of leisure. Some of them were engaged in their 'picturesque' and apparently worthy occupations in the fisheries, and they provided part of the spectacle for tourists. It was inevitably the case that the resorts were contested sites, where evidence of social change could hardly be avoided, as middle-class groups with new-found opportunities for leisure began to pursue amusements in the same place as their 'betters'. They were thus sites which produced different meanings depending on the interests and outlook of the spectator. This variety of viewpoints has some bearing on the forms taken by representations of the seaside resorts in the early nineteenth century, and on the ideas associated with them.

Together with an increasing number of the petty-bourgeoisie, artists visited the coasts for the conventional purposes: recuperation and pleasure. Thus George Morland, who spent about a year at Margate in 1785–6, went there initially to paint portraits for the season, but seems to have been attracted by the diversions of the place to stay longer. Joshua Cristall went to Hastings in 1807 to cure his 'nervous debility', Fuseli spent a month there in 1813 on the recommendation of his medical advisers to try and overcome fever and depression, Haydon made several trips to Brighton, Margate, and Hastings for reasons of health and recreation,[29] and Constable's presence in Brighton in the eighteen-twenties was the result of his wife's health.

The earliest seaside painting I know of is Francis Holman's *Shore Scene with Shipping* of 1778 (formerly on loan to the Tate Gallery), which already contains some of the customary markers of the theme: the bathing machine and the well-dressed figures mingled with fisher people selling fish. Benjamin West's *Bathing Place at Ramsgate* of *c.* 1787–8 (Yale Center of British Art) is unusual for an oil painting in the directness with which it focusses on the activity of bathing. Most paintings of the resorts concentrated on the landscape and the natives of the place rather than on fashionable visitors. West's picture is closer to the type of representations found in prints – and indeed the picture was engraved for a publication of 1789. The function of this work is unclear, since West did not sell it and hung it up in his London house, but considering its small size (33.5 × 44.5cm), it may well have been produced in the first place for his own amusement.[30] Another early visitor to the resorts was de Loutherbourg, who probably went to the South Coast in the summer of 1784, since he exhibited a picture *The Launching a Fishing Boat from the Shore at Brighthelmstone* at the Royal Academy in the following year. (This was the only specifically topographical view of the coast he showed, although he exhibited a number of generalized coastal views related in type to those of Vernet, Gainsborough, and Morland.) Other artists besides West produced works outside their normal line during stays at the seaside, such as the portrait painter William Beechey, who exhibited views of Margate and Southend at the British Institution in 1806 and 1808, and in 1804 showed *A Child Picking up Shells by the Seaside* at the Royal Academy. In 1806, his *A View near Margate* sold to a Mr Bernard (perhaps Thomas Bernard), but the status of such works can probably be judged from the comment in the *Review of Publications of Art* of 1808 that Beechey had sent his 'landscape playthings', 'his summer recreations on the sea-coast – sketchy, unelaborate productions'.[31] However, the fact that artists visited the resorts and painted there for amusement does not in itself explain why coastal landscapes became such an important pictorial type, or the particular pictorial form these representations took.

By 1824, Constable could write of the numerous pictures of fishing boats and fishing people then being exhibited:

> But these subjects are so hackneyed in the Exhibition, and are in fact so little capable of that beautiful sentiment that landscape is capable of or which rather belongs to landscape, that they have done a great deal of harm to the art – they form a class of art much easier than landscape & have in consequence almost supplanted it, and have drawn off many who would have encouraged the growth of a pastoral feel in their own minds – & paid others for pursuing it.[32]

I shall consider the grounds of Constable's animosity later; at this point I quote his remark simply to indicate how commonplace such subjects had become by the mid eighteen-twenties.

(ii) The imagery of prints

Of course, one of the reasons for artists to visit the resorts was a professional one – that is to meet the demand for images of these places from visitors, which led to a large output of prints. Such imagery fell into a variety of categories partly according to the various types of medium employed, and different modes of representation were seen as being appropriate to these different media. Copper-plate engravings, aquatints, etchings and lithographs tended to be used for fairly specific functions and these functions demanded somewhat different forms of imagery from those employed in oil painting. Many of the images which appeared in prints were based on water-colour drawings, but there were also types of water-colour drawing which did not serve straightforwardly topographical functions and were not made for reproduction in the first place. (There were also water-colour drawings made for engravings but also intended for exhibition.) The representation of the seaside resorts in prints and illustrated books is in itself a complex issue which I can not deal with comprehensively here, but some basic features of the common reproductive imagery need to be established to help define the distinguishing characteristics of the imagery of oil paintings and exhibition water-colours.

Aquatint was widely used for images of contemporary social life and for satires, one category of which was humorous commentaries on the fashion for the seaside such as Wigstead and Rowlandson's *An Excursion to Brighthelmstone, Made in the Year 1789* (1790) and Green's *Poetical Sketches of Scarborough: Illustrated by Twenty-one Engravings of Humorous Subjects* (1813).[33] In such illustrations, landscape was only ever a secondary or incidental feature, and the main emphasis was on what was implied to be the characteristic behaviour of the visitors. However, the aquatint, coloured or uncoloured, was also used for representations of both 'romantic' scenery and straightforwardly topographical views. Of the former category, de Loutherbourg's *Romantic and Picturesque Scenery of England and Wales* (1805) is an example, in which representations of Margate and Ramsgate are inserted among views of conventional picturesque sites in the Wye Valley, the Lakes, and Wales. But while the text about Margate emphasizes its character as a resort, the print, entitled *Storm off Margate*, is essentially a sea-piece composition with boats struggling in a stormy sea, which could be anywhere in terms of topography. Ramsgate, 'a bathing place of considerable importance' (and one still considered as 'select'), is represented through an apparently topographical view of the harbour entrance on a windy day, in which fashionably dressed men and women are shown prominently at the end of the harbour wall in the foreground. (The text explicitly emphasizes the importance of Ramsgate harbour as a haven for shipping in times of storm.) This particular image combines something of the humorous print of contemporary manners with elements of topography and the seascape. In fact, both these prints seem somewhat out of place in a publication devoted to 'picturesque scenery', but neither are they straightforward topography.[34]

Illustrated books which are straightforwardly topographical, and less oriented to the picturesque, included images which show the modern features of the resorts most directly. The best example of this category is the coloured aquatints after drawings by William Daniell in Richard Ayton's *A Voyage Round Great Britain undertaken in the Summer of 1813* (8 volumes, 1814–25). Daniell's illustrations match well with the unsentimental approach to modernization of Ayton's text. For example, in the volumes on Scotland (III, IV, and V) Ayton regularly praises the growth of commerce, agricultural improvement, and the modernizing of buildings, and draws attention to features of Daniell's images which refer to these things.[35] Thus, of the image of the herring fishery in *The Bay of Barriedale in Loch Houme* (1819), he writes:

> A votary of picturesque might have wished that these accessories had been of a more dignified kind ... unfortunately the genius of romance has not yet condescended to admit herring-busses and fishing-smacks into the compass of its machinery. A contemplative mind, however, would not pass by such objects with cold indifference or contemptuous disregard. Exclusive of the interests excited by the migration of the herrings, as a phenomena in natural history, there is abundant scope for reflection on the important influx of wealth which the migration annually brings to our shores.[36]

This tone is consistent with the emphasis on progressive associations throughout, and among views of the Southern Coast in Volume III (1824) there is an image of workshops at Sheerness, a view of the new developments at Brighton, and a plate explicitly intended to show Bognor in the process of development. In *Ramsgate*, a line of fashionably dressed people are pressed against a fence in the foreground looking over the sea view, while in *Pier at Margate* (*Plate 9*) a view from the cliffs shows modern houses and visitors, and a steam packet about to depart. *Hastings from near the White Rock* (*Plate 10*) again has fashionable people in the foreground, and clearly shows the modern houses of the town beyond.

In the hierarchy of print types in the early nineteenth century, copper-plate engraving came well above both aquatint and lithography. (Etching was seen as the print medium of original artistic expression *par excellence*.)[37] It was the technique seen as demanding the most dedication and skill, and copper-plate engravers such as John Landseer and the Cooke brothers were active in promoting the prestige and status of their craft. W. B. Cooke's *Picturesque Views on the Southern Coast of England* (1814–26), illustrated with engravings after water-colours by Turner, Havell, Edridge and other leading water-colourists, was widely regarded as a landmark in the history of landscape engraving, and immediately recognized as a production of outstanding quality. The virtual eulogy this publication received from the *New Monthly Magazine* confirms what we would expect from the appearance of the prints – that they should be seen as standing for a new naturalistic style in line engraving:

> Their lights, while sparkling, are worked with distinctness and affluence of touch, and they never sacrifice the true look of an object to a delusive clearness and dexterity of tooling. They are the reformists of art. They assert the genuine principles of its constitution. They give it us in its integrity, not its semblance. They give us truth. They give us Nature.[38]

This statement indicates that as the new style was understood as peculiarly English, so it could potentially have political connotations.

Within the *Southern Coast* and other works of the same type, landscape engravings were not intended to function simply as a topographical record: the title *Picturesque Views* was a clear sign that the engravings were intended to have a specific aesthetic character, above mere topography. Within the images themselves this difference was denoted by certain formal structures, the use of figures and atmospheric effects. The artists involved had to make views of real, visitable, and in some cases rapidly modernizing sites on the South Coast in such a way that they were topographically recognizable, but also had the character of 'picturesque' representation. Turner seems to have set the pattern for this in an inventive series of designs, of which a good example is *Brighthelmston, Sussex* (1825, *Plate 11*). In this there are plenty of signs of the development of the resort, and in the dead centre of the composition, bathed in light, is the Regent's Pavilion – a worthy symbol of the modish and dissipated character of what Wigstead called 'the English Baiae'. Also prominent in the composition is that triumph of modern technology the new Chain Pier, completed only two years before, on which people in fashionable dress promenade. Despite these unpicturesque materials, Turner redeemed the scene through the fishing boats in stormy waters off the pier's end, and through the dramatic atmospheric effect. This pattern was followed in a number of later topographical views of Brighton – although it is possible that Turner himself may have been influenced by R. Havell's aquatint *Brighton from the Sea* in E. W. Brayley's *Topographical Sketches of Brighthelmston* (1824). Another strategy, employed by Edridge in *The Beach at Brighton, Sussex* (*Plate 12*), was to concentrate entirely on the fishing industry at a resort, and to give no indication at all of the fashionable usages of the place – such beach scenes were licensed as picturesque subjects by a well-known type of seventeenth-century Dutch painting. A somewhat subtler approach was to represent some evidence of modernization, but to relegate it to the background and keep the foreground picturesque. This was what Turner did in his representations of Margate, Weymouth, and Lyme Regis, all of which are based around a composition in which a bay curves round the foreground into the distance. In the near plane, details such as figures of fishermen, women bathing, boats, baskets, and anchors suggest ideas of traditional occupations and communities, while in the distance the modern buildings of the town, sometimes with diminutive bathing machines on the beach in front of it, indicate changing usages (*Plate 13*). Because of the close connection between them, engravings of 'picturesque scenery' employed the same types of composition and effect as the more ambitious type of topographical water-colour, and as I shall show, some of the formats developed in this type of imagery were also adapted to oil paintings.

The relationship between the production of topographical imagery and the demand of visitors for visual souvenirs is seen at its most straightforward in the aquatints, lithographs, and cheap engravings, sold individually or in sets, and in the illustrated guides like Brayley's *Topographical Sketches* (twelve plates), which were available at the resorts or from London book and printsellers. In the 1820s, the most important medium for this type of image was probably the aquatint. This is certainly true of Brighton, which was represented in several series of crude aquatints, published for local libraries, printsellers, and booksellers in that decade, such as John Bruce's *Select Views of Brighton* (1824, second edition 1829) and C. & R. Sickelmore's publication of the same name (*c.*1827). These harshly coloured images made no concessions to the picturesque in their emphasis on Brighton's modern amenities and their insistent representations of fashionable visitors (*Plate 14*). Those things which a landscape painter could hardly hope to turn into an image of aesthetic significance (although they could just be fitted into the distance): the Regent's Pavilion, the houses of the Marine Parade, the Esplanade, the new developments of Kemptown and Brunswick Square were precisely the features to which such views gave prominence. A striking example of this celebration of modernity is provided by Westall's aquatint *Brighton from the Chain Pier* published by J. Dickenson of Bond Street, London, in 1833 (*Plate 15*).

To take another example relevant to later discussion, Hastings and its suburb Saint Leonard's, which had a reputation as lying in a particularly attractive scenic location, were represented in at least ten series of lithographs and aquatints between 1817 and about 1830.[39] Some of these were published and sold by, or in conjunction with, the proprietors of libraries in Hastings and Saint Leonard's; others were marketed by London firms such as Ackermann's. The topographical print at its most pedestrian and unpretentious is seen in G. Rowe's lithograph, *Hastings from the Sea* (Victoria & Albert Museum, *Plate 16*), which probably dates from about 1820, and was published by Rowe and a local printseller, G. Wooll of High Street, Hastings. Not only is modern development very clearly shown in this print, but there is no dramatic atmospheric effect or turbulent sea to distract from the bald features of the view. Rowe and Wooll also published a series of dreary lithographs, *Illustrations of Hastings and its Vicinity*, which concentrate to an important extent on local churches and new buildings in Saint Leonard's. The 1820s saw a spate of publications of coloured aquatints and lithographs of Hastings based on drawings by minor artists such as John Gendall, John Marten, Augustine Aglio, and Thomas Ross.[40] The last of these was a local drawing master, and his series is the most unequivocal and direct in its representation of modern amenities such as the Marine Parade and the Pleasure Gardens of St Leonards. H. Morton's twenty-five aquatint plates, *Views Illustrative of Hastings and its Vicinity* (1817), have more pretensions to artistic status, and are more various in subject and approach, including several views of decaying medieval buildings in the neighbourhood. Such prints indicate that the production of imagery of seaside resorts was only oriented around bald topographical representation at the lowest level. The visual souvenirs produced by artists with any ambitions as artists inevitably contained the signs of the aesthetic outlook – which at this time meant primarily the characteristics and effects which could be read as picturesque. Generally speaking, the more the image was conceived as a 'picturesque view', the more evidence of modernity had to be relegated to the background or simply omitted.

Topographical prints and drawings had a very low rank in the hierarchy of artistic production, and were seen as a different category of objects from most exhibition water-colours and oil paintings which had a comparatively high rank, providing that they were sufficiently distinguishable from 'mere topography'. Thus the kinds of ideological construction to which water-colours and oil paintings referred the spectator tended to be more complex, and to confer on the practice of those types of production far more prestige in the cultural field. Only some highly elaborate copper-plate engravings had anything like the same status, and even these achieved it primarily as a reflection of the drawings of the 'great artist'. In the Preface to his *History and Antiquities of the Town and Port of Hastings* (1824), William George Moss wrote of the tourist guides:

> The GUIDES to watering-places are, in general, trifling. They neither contain, nor indeed are expected to contain, any thing beyond subjects of mere fashionable or domestic information, such as rides, walks, libraries, public exhibitions, and amusements, with other minor details: which, though unquestionably pleasing as well as useful to the visitants, are still in themselves, as to subject, insignificant and uninteresting.[41]

Moss was careful to distinguish his own work as a 'History', and to point out that the 'study of history' had always been considered 'among enlightened nations' as a necessary part of the education of the 'scholar' and 'gentleman'. He described himself as 'Draughtsman' to the Duke of Cambridge, and his book is illustrated by good-quality copper-plate engravings after his own drawings: illustrations which mix the modern and the picturesque. Moss's distinction between the provinces of the 'Guide' and the 'History' might stand as an analogy with the distinction between the cheap tourist views and the more serious examples of picturesque topography, which were often accompanied by texts bristling with historical and social information, to which details in the prints could be related.

(iii) Early oil paintings and water-colours

The artists who stand out in the development of the resort theme in the early nineteenth century include Turner, Callcott, Cristall, and Collins. Turner's early coastal views were not associated with the resorts, and were part of a more general effort to produce a type of 'British' landscape, which would have something of the status of English nature poetry. Thus *Harlech Castle from Tygwyn Ferry* (Yale Centre for British Art), exhibited in 1799, represented a specific place in forms derived from Wilson and Claude, with a broad evening effect signifying a kind of contemplative mood. So that no one could miss the intended 'poetic' quality and the classical connotations of the design, Turner had some lines describing evening in classical terms from Milton's *Paradise Lost* printed along with the catalogue entry.[42]

The *Fishermen on a Lee Shore in Squally Weather* (Iveagh Bequest, Kenwood), exhibited in 1802, refers to no specific location through its title and should be seen as an attempt to emulate the type of stormy coast scenes produced by seventeenth-century Dutch artists such as William van de Velde and Jacob van Ruisdael. Equally, *Sun Rising through Vapour; Fishermen Cleaning and Selling Fish* (National Gallery, London), exhibited in 1807, has no evident topographical features, and can be seen again primarily in relation to Dutch prototypes, although the sunrise effect was inspired by Claude. However, some features of this picture, particularly the groups of fisher people engaged in labour, and the piece of jetty intruding from the right, were to be characteristic elements in the representation of resorts, and the picture would probably have been read in 1807 as an English view.

In the first decade of the century Turner produced at least three oils of specific resorts, which include *Old Margate Pier* (Private Collection), which was possibly exhibited at his own gallery in 1804, and *Margate* (Petworth House, *Plate 17*), exhibited there in 1808.[43] The former is a stormy seascape of straightforward Dutch provenance. The 1808 *Margate* is both a more original picture, and one to which we have an extended contemporary response. *Margate* is again essentially a seascape, although the figures in boats are rather more foregrounded and consequently more a focus of interest and sympathy than in most Dutch paintings of such scenes. Landseer's commentary on this picture in the *Review of Publications of Art* in 1808 indicates how difficult it was to reconcile ideas of the permanent qualities of human relations with nature, which landscape painting was supposed to produce, with the representation of a site like Margate, where fashion and development had overlaid the traditional occupations of the place, and changed its physical character, where nature could only be experienced in relation to modern 'conveniences'. It also clearly identifies the devices through which Turner had 'dignified' his subject:

> We had not imagined that any VIEW of MARGATE, under any circumstance, would have made a picture of so much importance as that which Mr Turner had painted of this subject: but, by introducing a rising sun and a rough sea; by keeping the town of Margate itself in a morning mist from which the pier is emerging; and by treating the cliffs as a bold promontory in shade, he has produced a grand picture

Landseer claimed that Turner had given 'a peculiar interest to his foreground' by the image of Margate wherries stopping a Hastings fishing boat on its way to the London market to buy fish – this characteristic incident was part of the painting's truth to locality. However, the modern features of the town were reduced to 'bolder forms' by the effect of morning mist, and the mill and brewery on the cliff reminded him of magnificent temples:

> The classic scholar who shall contemplate this picture, forgetting modern Margate, will probably be led to think of the temple of Minerva on the

> promontory of Sunium, which no Grecian mariner presumed to pass without an offering or a prayer.

As we saw in the previous chapter, Landseer's explanation of Turner's work was conceived within the framework of associationist aesthetics. Turner was praised both for achieving a unified emotional effect through a complex chain of associations, and also for producing an image of the modern which obscured many of the particularities of the contemporary. It was this feature of his work which distinguishes it from the more radical naturalism which emerged around 1810.[44] For Landseer, that modern Margate could only properly be represented in the distance in serious art is clear.

As we have seen, within the mode of the topographical but picturesque water-colour view, intended primarily for engraving but also seen in private exhibitions,[45] Turner found it far more appropriate to represent evidence of modernization, as the contrast between the Petworth *Margate* and the water-colour for the engraving in the *Southern Coast* (*Plate 13*) shows.[46] Within larger water-colours, designed specifically for a large public exhibition, modernization needed to be even more remote. In *Scarborough Town and Castle: Morning: Boys Catching Crabs* (Private Collection), which was probably exhibited at the Royal Academy in 1811,[47] the castle is clearly shown silhouetted on top of the distant cliff, but the modern town below it is a relatively insignificant feature of the design. Attention focusses primarily on the picturesque irregular forms of the decaying pier, the fishermen making their way down onto the beach, the boys catching crabs, and men unloading ships. These kinds of figures and actions, which are equivalent to the staffage of Dutch beach scenes, are given far more prominence in this exhibition work than they are in Turner's *Southern Coast* designs.

A painter whose development in the first and second decades of the century was closely linked with that of Turner was Callcott. Particularly important in relation to the coastal theme and the productive engagement with Dutch prototypes were his *A Sea-Coast, with Figures Bargaining for Fish* and *A Calm, with Figures Shrimping*, both works on an exhibition scale (122 × 183cm), exhibited at the Royal Academy in 1806.[48] The first of these has many characteristic features of beach scenes in general: the jetty entering the composition from one side with an expanse of ocean dotted with sailing craft on the other; men and women unloading fish from a boat; a distant gathering of figures, perhaps engaged in a fish auction; and the still-life element of dead fish, baskets, and rotting posts on the sand. Neither this work, nor *A Calm*, seem to have been anchored to specific locations. Callcott's contemporaries recognized the inspiration of Dutch artists such as Simon de Vlieger, whose *Beach Scene at Scheveningen* (1633, National Maritime Museum, Greenwich) and other works show fishmarkets. David Brown has appropriately linked *A Calm* with the coastal views of Jan van de Cappelle, while the posts emerging from the water on the right foreground emulate a device common in Jacob van Ruisdael's seascapes. However, in the context these pictures would have been seen as English views, and their derivation from Dutch pictorial types, together with the nature of their subject-matter and their coherent light effects, would have been read as guaranteeing a truthful representation of 'nature', and by extension of social life. Thus the *Morning Post* commented on *A Sea-Coast*:

> The picture ... is a very fine one; the group of figures is delightfully painted, and the general effect is truly that of Nature.[49]

In 1812, the *Repository of Arts* observed of Callcott's picture *Little Hampton Pier*, (*Plate 18*) exhibited at the Royal Academy in that year:

> The sand yet wet with the departed tide, is truly deceptive; and the group of fishermen is designed and painted with the most just attention to the character and habits of these rude inhabitants of the sea-coast.[50]

As I illustrated in the last chapter, the *Repository*'s reviews of this year are full of approving comments on pictures which represent agricultural labourers, and it particularly praised Callcott's picture *The Cottager's Relief* for its 'happy selection' in terms of subject: 'we do not remember a more pleasing picture of rural manners than this'.[51] There appears to have been a kind of ideological equivalence between the ideas produced by representations of agricultural workers by these artists, and those produced by their representations of fisher people. In both cases the pictures partly signified the myth of a 'rude' but 'healthy' and contended proletariat distant from urban areas, and served to illustrate an ideal of the social order.

(iv) Imagery of Hastings

A key figure in developing the painting of specific resort sites seems to have been Joshua Cristall, who made a number of studies of Hastings and Margate when he visited the South Coast for his health in 1807. At the Society of Painters in Water-Colours exhibition in 1808, Cristall showed eight drawings of the region, including the large water-colour *Fish-market on the Beach at Hastings* (Victoria and Albert Museum, 76.2 × 102.8cm, *Plate 19*). In May of that year, James Ward told Farington that Cristall's drawings had induced 'a Host of Artists' to consider going to Hastings. John Linnell went there in 1809, and in 1812 so did David Cox and William Havell. Other artists who were drawn to the place included Turner, Prout, and De Wint.[52]

Although Hastings had been a resort since 1770, its first guide only appeared in 1794, and in 1807 it was still in the very early stages of development, comparatively speaking. Knowles, writing in or before 1831, contrasted Hastings then with what it had been at the time of Fuseli's visit in 1813, and said it was hardly recognizable as the same place. Fuseli's own comments in one of his letters suggest he thought the place strikingly unsophisticated.[53] It is worth noting that the *Hastings Guide* of 1797 emphasized that the town had not yet succumbed to dissipation:

> One circumstance must, above all others, render Hastings dear to those who have a regard to morality; Vice has not yet erected her standard here, – the numerous tribe of professional gamblers, unhappy profligates, and fashionable swindlers, find employment and rapine elsewhere. Innocent recreational delight, card assemblies, billiards, riding, walking, reading, fishing, and other modes of pastime, banish care from the mind, whilst the salubrity of the atmosphere impels disease from the body.[54]

Ayton, in a volume published in 1824, could still comment on this absence of dissipation, but significantly the 1828 guide omitted any such claim, which must have been difficult to sustain after Hastings had become a garrison town.[55]

The 1797 guide states that a number of 'handsome modern built houses' had been put up, and that there were plans for more developments. At that time there were already several lodging houses, a bath house, assembly rooms, billiard rooms, and a library. The town had recently been paved, and a parade was projected, which was subsequently begun by the proprietor of the library and publisher of the guide, and completed by public subscription in 1812. The physical changes which impressed Knowles must have included Pelham Crescent, built in 1820–5, and the new town of Saint Leonard's, begun in 1828. In the 1797 guide, the population is estimated to be about three thousand, of which two to three hundred were fishermen or sailors, and the author comments on the great decline of the town's fisheries and trade over the previous thirty years. By 1828 the population was said to be over seven thousand, of whom between three and four hundred were fishermen and seamen, while an 1855 guide put the population at more than seventeen and a half thousand. This latter guide claimed that the fishing industry had involved ninety-seven boats in 1803, but was reduced to sixty-four by 1823, and also commented on the poverty of the fishing people.[56] However, in the 1828 guide the fisheries are still presented as a spectacle for the amusement of visitors, and it drew particular attention to the fishermen's skill in manoeuvring sloops and cutters of considerable weight up and down the Stade.[57] As the town grew, and became more oriented to its pleasure functions, the fishing industry increasingly assumed the character of a picturesque survival from an older social and economic order. For the guides, the 'increase of buildings' and the development of 'rows of handsome lodging houses' in what had been open fields prompted no unpleasant reflections – they were a necessary and welcome increase in amenities. This attitude is hardly surprising considering that the guides were mainly published for the proprietors of local lending libraries, for whom the image of modernization carried the promise of greater profits.[58]

Thus the Hastings Cristall visited in 1807 might claim to be less dissipated than Brighton and more exclusive than Margate, but the place was already becoming fashionable and there were unmistakable signs of development. One would never know this from Cristall's images, however, for he employed the same strategy as Edridge used slightly later in his views of Brighton beach for the *Southern Coast* and a now much-faded exhibition water-colour:[59] he represented Hastings as if no new 'handsome houses' were going up around it, and indeed, as if it was not a resort. The site of the Fish Market is marked on Moss's 1824 map (see map 1), and it was clearly adjacent to the buildings visible in Daniell's view (*Plate 10*). These were probably not new buildings, and were almost certainly there in 1807. Thus, to represent the beach looking west at this point, Cristall took a position from which the urban aspects of Hastings were reduced to a token presence.

In Cristall's bustling scene, there are no fashionable visitors,[60] and indeed if we were to take the picture as signifying the general character of the place, we would see it exclusively in terms of traditional occupations. For its contemporary audience it probably connoted ideas of a healthy, prosperous, and industrious local population, virtuously engaged in wresting a living from nature. The *Review of Publications of Art* found it:

> an excellent representation of the morning effect and general bustle of the Fish-Market at Hastings, and which is replete with those local incidents which show the accuracy of Mr Cristall's observation of Nature at this place.[61]

There is that familiar elision of 'Nature' and the social order here, and significantly Landseer found Cristall's images of fishing people, and his two rustic pictures:

> remind us of those rural mountain ballads in which Wordsworth reveals so much fine feeling and intimate converse with Nature.[62]

This response was partly produced, I suspect, by the formal qualities of Cristall's pictures. In *Fishmarket on the Beach at Hastings*, the clear perspective recession and balanced composition plainly refer to Claude's seaport pictures – a reference which inevitably produced ideas of the classical world to an informed spectator. The crisply drawn figures, firmly modelled in light and shade, and the statuesque poses, which look ahead to the more blatant Poussinesque references of Cristall's classical landscapes, reinforce the effect. The picture has a clear focus of interest in the academic grouping of men engaged in tipping out fish, and the round basket resting on the fisherman's shoulder (a virtual cornucopia) provides a formal and symbolic centre for the image. Other academic features of the design include the fisherman leaning against the pannier on the donkey at the right, and the woman and child in the left foreground, who might have come out of an Italian alterpiece. The theme of woman and child is repeated in the upper right, where a female figure with a child on her back stands among a mixed group around a fish basket. An element of romantic interest is provided by the sturdy male figure just right of centre, standing with his back to us, who looks towards the young woman with a basket, who appears to meet his gaze. By these means, Cristall 'dignified' and sentimentalized a scene of ordinary labour. As I showed in the last chapter, such 'dignification' of working-class types was characteristic of Cristall's work. Fittingly, the *Review of Publications of Art* found the 'principal sailor' in his *Coast of Sussex, with Seamen Pushing off a Boat to a Vessel in Distress* 'a figure of unsophisticated sympathy,

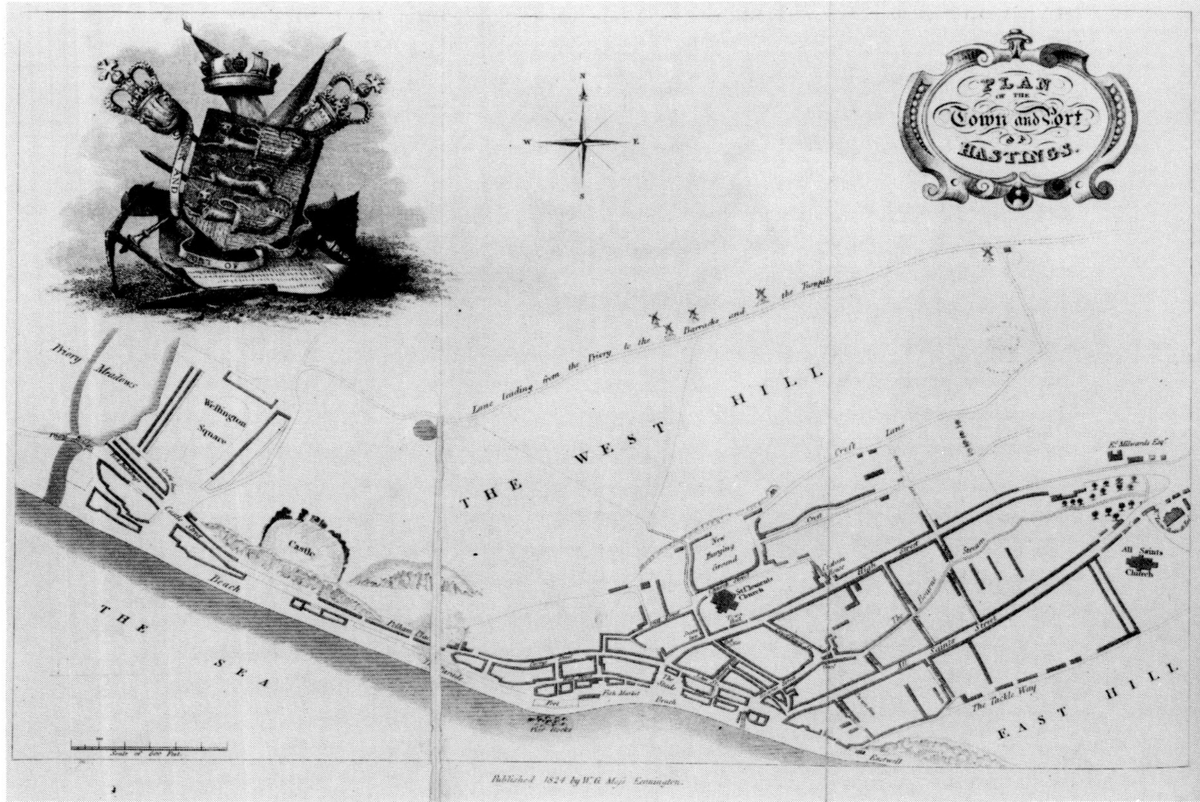

Map 1 *Plan of the Town and Port of Hastings*, from W. G. Moss, *History and Antiquities of . . . Hastings*, 1824

sustained by the conscious dignity of true greatness' – at this historical moment the ordinary sailor could be a hero for liberals like Landseer.

Such nationalist sentiments are also suggested by the *Fleet Sailing up Channel off Hastings* (National Gallery of Scotland, *Plate 20*), in which fisher people engage in industrious activity, appear to talk, or watch the spectacle through a telescope, while elegant young women, in poses derived from classical statuary, take care of children in a relaxed fashion, presumably secure in the knowledge that England's island 'home' is safe. However, the *Examiner* saw the ships rather as emblematic of commercial prosperity, and found that the drawing:

> suggests ideas of England's wealth, from the numerous fleets of merchandise that whiten the sea, and from the bold and busy swarm that people her coasts. A mass of these is well represented in various marine and mercantile employments on the beach.[63]

But in any case, ideas of national greatness and commercial prosperity were interrelated in poetry and other contemporary discourses. If Cristall's images evidently produced pleasing ideas for the liberal Hunt in the *Examiner*, they also produced them for the critic of the illiberal *New Monthly Magazine*, which described the drawing as 'truly English in its subject'.[64] This reminds us again that patriotism and the rural myth had positive functions in the ideology of radical and conservative alike.

Almost entirely through the titles of his works, Cristall anchored his confectionery of a modern marine peasantry to real sites on the South Coast: Hastings, Margate, and the Isle of Wight, thereby affirming their authenticity. But to make images which would (a) confirm current notions of the desirable character of the 'lower orders', and (b) be clearly distinguishable from mere topography, Cristall was obliged to exclude any prominent evidence of fashionable uses of these identifiable, visitable, places as resorts – to exclude signs of the kinds of experience most visitors would have of them. Whatever the changing material and social realities of Hastings, Cristall had no interest in using the available conventions to represent them. They were quite incongruent with the ideas of natural simplicity he evidently sought to evoke, and had he represented fashion and modernization, it is unlikely that his art would have had the critical success it initially achieved.

The success of Cristall's recipe with the critics and his fellow artists was perhaps the spur which prompted Turner to produce further variations on the fishmarket theme. The first of these, which was also titled *Hastings – Fishmarket on the Sands* (William Rockhill Nelson Gallery and Atkins Museum of Fine Arts, Kansas City), was exhibited at his own gallery in 1810, and bought by John Fuller, MP for Sussex 1801–12.[65] The picture refers unmistakably to seventeenth-century Dutch beach scenes such as the de Vlieger *Beach near Scheveningen* mentioned earlier and related works by Adriaen van de Velde and Jacob Esselins, and it gives no indication of the town of Hastings or its visitors. Only the title anchors it to Hastings, and only the declining fishing industry seems to characterize the place. In Turner's *Hastings*, the beach in the foreground slopes off to the left, where a boat, anchored just off shore, provides a balance to a group of fisher people right of centre. However, he used a more strongly centred composition, closer to Cristall's *Fishmarket* in *St Mawes at the Pilchard Season* (Clore Gallery), shown at his own gallery in 1812.[66] This work makes use of a centralized perspective recession, which like Cristall's water-colour owes something to Claude's seaport type. A group of buildings does appear in the background to the picture, but they suggest no ideas of modernization, and St Mawes appears simply the site of a peaceful profitable activity, which contrasts with the ideas of medieval strife suggested by the two decaying castles included. While these connotations seem consistent at a superficial level with the character of a remote Cornish fishing village, they seem less consistent with that of a fast-developing resort like Hastings.

However, the fishmarket theme was only one of several themes sanctified by precedent which could be reworked to make an 'English' painting, and thereby help to meet the perceived need for a national school. One of the most impressive coastal scenes of the first two decades, and a picture surprisingly little known, is J.J. Chalon's large *View of Hastings* (Victoria & Albert Museum, *Plate 21*), which was presumably the picture exhibited under that title at the Royal Academy in 1819, and again at the British Institution in the spring of 1820. The antecedents of this painting lie in a type of stormy, or at least windswept, coastal scene with fishermen struggling to bring in or put out boats, which had been developed from the shipwreck scenes of Claude-Joseph Vernet by artists working in late eighteenth-century England, and notably de Loutherbourg, Gainsborough, and Morland. Some artists had painted such scenes on quite a large scale, as for example in the unusual seascape by the portraitist John Hoppner in the Tate Gallery: *A Gale of Wind* (RA 1794? *Plate 22*). Eighteenth-century coastal scenes of this type generally contained few if any topographical features, and produced ideas of the sublime through stereotyped storm effects and the apparently hazardous situations of the seamen depicted. With their broken irregular outlines of waves, rocks, cliffs and decaying castles, and their rugged 'natural' figures, such scenes matched well with the aesthetic of the picturesque.

At first sight, Chalon's *View of Hastings* seems remote from such images, so different were the conventions of the naturalistic phase in British landscape painting from those of twenty or thirty years before. Not only are parts of the modern town of Hastings clearly represented, but there are several apparently well-observed fishing boats. The picture obviously justifies its title as a view of this specific place in a way which neither Cristall's or Turner's images of the fishmarket or beach do and seems to show the area near the Stade, looking east from the Pier Rocks, marked in Moss's map (see map 1). The distant headland and the buildings of the town have a kind of detail, irregularity, and variety which suggest direct recording of a particular site, whether or not they are accurate in terms of the conventional systems employed. In fact, the basic strategy is similar to that of topographical picturesque views such as Turner's *Southern Coast Margate* (*Plate 13*), although we seem much more immediately involved in Chalon's scene as a result of scale and the use of perspective. The foreground is made up of picturesque but convincing rocks, from which water drains off in a credible way – there is even a starfish. Slightly behind this are represented the 'natural' figures of local inhabitants pulling in a net, and beyond them a picturesque jumble of beached fishing boats and of boats at dramatic angles coming in through the surf. Out to sea, more boats are making their way in. Thus the activity of the fishermen provides the main action and figural interest with which a landscape painter was supposed to both enliven a picture and show the relationship between human beings and the natural order.

It is only behind and beyond these activities that Chalon fills in the signs which really sustain the claim made by the title that the work be read as an image of

Hastings. Yet although the physical evidence of the town's expansion are confined to the middle distance, it is clearly included, and indeed emphasized. Just below the centre of the picture, to the left, are two modern white houses, picked out in a beam of sunlight, while slightly further left, beyond the mass of darker and older houses along the beach, a lighter mass of modern houses with smoking chimneys is represented which also appear in Daniell's view (*Plate 10*). Further, while the picture foregrounds and therefore emphasizes the character of Hastings as a fishing town, fishermen are not the only kind of person whose presence is shown. Clearly visible in a space on the beach is a group of three figures in modern urban dress, two women and a man, watching the spectacle of the boats coming in, just as the guide books recommended.

Another key feature of this picture is the virtuoso light effect, which suggests most strikingly the dramatic contrasts of light and shadow produced by a stormy sky with breaks of sunshine, and which, with the figural activity, would have been central to Chalon's ambition to produce a major landscape painting as opposed to a mere topographical view. The strip of light paint denoting the distant sea to the right is also a particularly adept way of suggesting distance and creating surface variety, probably inspired by Turner's early seascapes. The surface of Chalon's painting is unusual in that although there is quite heavy impasto on parts of the sea and foreground, the drawing of details such as the rigging of the boats is extremely tight. This feature of the picture produced an unfavourable comment from the *Examiner* in 1819, which described the water as looking like 'a sea of cut brass and lead', and claimed it detracted from the praiseworthy light effect and the indications of rain and atmosphere. However, while the *New Monthly Magazine* also had some reservations, it found it a work of 'great science', and one of the finest 'local' views in the 1820 British Institution show.[67] Surprisingly, however, Chalon's *View of Hastings* received little notice in the press of 1819 or 1820, and no comment which linked it with the character of Hastings as a resort. Yet it came far nearer than the pictures of Cristall or Turner to suggesting something of the other aspects of Hastings, while continuing to perpetuate the mythical image of it as the preserve of a dauntless and hard-working fisherman. This kind of conjunction of old and new was to be central to the most impressive pictures of resorts of the 1820s.[68]

To conclude this discussion of images of Hastings, I want briefly to mention a few more water-colours, which confirm the pattern which is emerging. I have already mentioned David Cox's visit to Hastings in 1812, and it was presumably on studies made on this occasion that the aquatint etching of the *Fishmarket at Hastings* in his 1814 *Treatise on Landscape Painting* was based. This shows a view of the cliffs to the east of the town behind a foreground expanse of beach, on which boats and figures are the most prominent feature. There are no indications of modern development, and like Cristall, Cox bathed this scene of traditional industry in a morning glow of light. In 1816, Cox showed three drawings of Hastings at the exhibition of the Society of Painters in Water-Colours, one of which represented the fishmarket. He was back again in 1818, and in that year he exhibited a *Scene on the Beach, Hastings*, now in a private collection.[69] This shows a view from the beach over the sea with fishing boats coming in and a group of figures with horses and fishcarts in the foreground, using the same device as Turner's 1810 oil of looking seawards, away from any evidence of modernity. Another major water-colourist, Samuel Prout, sketched on the South Coast in 1812 and again in 1815. In his large exhibition drawing, *Hastings, Sussex* (Victoria & Albert Museum, *Plate 23*), which is dateable to about 1817, Prout represents a view from the east of the town, using the now familiar device of foregrounding the rubbish of the fishing industry – an abandoned capstan, broken baskets, and rusting chains; showing the local population through figures of women and girls in the dress of the fishing community; and indicating the presence of the town only through houses seen in the distance beyond a mass of land to the right of the composition. None of these images contains the modern boarding houses and tourist figures which are entirely commonplace in the guides and topographical prints, but which scarcely intrude in more ambitious forms of artistic practice.

In Constable's 1824 letter to Fisher, from which I quoted earlier, he seems particularly to associate coastal subjects with Callcott and Collins. In fact Callcott appears to have shown few beach scenes after his two 1806 exhibits, although he certainly maintained his reputation through river views and seascapes. Collins, on the other hand, exhibited a steady stream of views of the coasts of Devon, Norfolk, Kent, and later of places in France and Italy up until his death. These brought him a considerable degree of success and they deserve attention partly for that reason, but also because the use of imagery of fishing people and their children, together with the press response to them, suggests in the crudest form the myth of uncorrupted 'natural' communities of hard-working healthy folk, which I have argued was also a connotation of the work of Cristall, Turner, et al. For Constable, Collins' landscapes were 'far too pretty to be natural',[70] and it is to Constable's credit that he at least tried to represent more of the real experiences of the coast, and did not deal in this kind of confectionery. I shall argue that if his art has a special value, it partly lies in this, and in a kindred approach to the rural scene.

Despite Constable's aversion to Collins' work (and later to Collins himself), it is important to note that earlier they had been friends, and that Collins' approach to landscapes and rustic figures in the second decade of the century places him firmly within the naturalistic tendency.[71] His pictures were based on careful on-the-spot studies, and his journals of 1814–15 record a process of extended reflection on the connections between technique and effect, partly informed by dialogue with artists such as Constable, Havell, and Linnell.[72] (In fact, Constable regularly praised Collins' technique, even while he criticized his subjects.) At the time Collins produced a number of paintings which involved ambitious attempts to suggest novel atmospheric effects, including the *Bird-catchers – Morning* (RA 1814, Lord Lansdowne Collection), *Fishermen Coming Ashore before Sunrise* (RA 1817), and

Capstern at Work, Drawing up Fishing Boats (RA 1820).[73] In relation to the perceived value of 'finish' and the limitations of the sketch (as they were understood at this moment), it is worth recalling Collins' note to himself of 1817:

> A sketchy picture is easily done, because one is accustomed to overlook in it a hundred violations of truth, which are insisted upon in a finished picture. In making sketches, the very violation of the laws of nature is a proof of 'spirit' as it is called.[74]

It seems that the exhibition of his picture *Shrimp Boys – Cromer* at the Royal Academy in 1816 marked a turning point in Collins' career, although he was already an Associate member of that body. According to the biography by his son Wilkie Collins, the sale of the picture to Sir Thomas Heathcote helped him in a period of virtual penury, and its popularity stimulated him to produce more works of the same type. The picture was apparently based on studies Collins had made on a trip to Norfolk in 1815, when he had stayed with his friend the Norwich artist James Stark. According to Stark's later account, Collins was 'much delighted with the simple character of Cromer' and 'indefatigable in his pursuits' during the period of approximately two months they spent there. Stark had no recollection of Collins sketching from figures, although he remembered him studying the beach and cliffs. Collins himself had written from Cromer in September 1815:

> I have made some sketches of sea-shore scenery, etc.; but, although I have opened the door of every cottage in the place, I have not yet seen an interior good enough for Mrs Hand's picture.[75]

Interiors and landscapes were studied on location, but it seems likely that figures were often based on the articles of fishermen's clothing and the clay figure dressed as a fisherman which Collins kept in his studio. The 1816 picture, which I illustrate here through a print of 1820 (*Plate 24*), suggests the possible influence of John Crome's Yarmouth Jetty views (see *Plate 39*), although the genre element is much more important in Collins' landscape. Interestingly, the picture was hung next to Crome's *View near Norwich* at the Academy. The etching of 1816, which was worked over in mezzotint for the 1820 print, is comparable in technique to etchings Crome was making around this same time, and both the pictorial type and etching technique again derive from Dutch seventeenth-century art.

Collins frequently used groups of children in his work, and the ideological connotations of happy children in a 'natural' setting of rural scenery is fairly well-established from studies of the literature of the period. That Collins' paintings clearly referred to this mythology of childhood as a time of innocence and carefree joy is evident from the review of this picture in the *Examiner* in 1816:

> The pictures of the new Associate, Mr COLLINS, are more estimable than ever in their rich colour, sunny glow, delicate profusion of touch such as we see in vegetable nature, and in their disclosure of the moral and physical peculiarities

of the juvenile age. They always remind us of GAY's printed portraiture of infancy and youth:

> Theirs buxom health of rosy hue,
> With wit, invention ever new,
> And lively cheer of vigour born;
> The thoughtless day, the easy night,
> The spirits pure. The slumbers light
> That fly the approach of morn.[76]

The reiterated use of such childhood types over many years is illustrated by the *Prawn Fishers at Hastings* (1825, Royal Collection) and the Tate Gallery's *Prawn Catchers* of 1828 (*Plate 25*), which was perhaps number 371 in the 1829 Academy exhibition. This latter is a very similar conception to the 1816 picture. A group of three children are placed in the foreground next to a rock pool, from which one of them retrieves a prawn basket using a pole with a hook attached to it. In both pictures the smallest child appears to be a female onlooker. The children have the plump little faces, rosy cheeks, and tousled hair characteristic of the Collins 'type'. While it must be conceded that the effect of perspective and light and shade is convincing from a distance of six or seven feet, close-up the drawing of the picture seems slight and the brushwork does not have much variety or interest. The overall colouring of the pearly-blue sky with its pinkish-grey clouds, and the soft browns and greens of the shore, produce an overall prettiness of effect which matches the triteness of the children's figures. Such pictures do not have the originality and variety of some of Collins' work of the previous decade.

In *Prawn Catchers* and other Collins images of the same type, human beings are dwarfed by an over-arching natural order, which in contemporary aesthetic discourse signified the beneficent and omnipresent hand of the deity. The children shrimping are already preparing for the kind of industrious life their fathers pursue in the distant boats, while the little girls are already passive admirers of male achievements, destined for the domestic sphere. In such an environment, in contrast with that of the town, children will grow up to be healthy, industrious, and know their place in the social order. Collins' treatment of the theme of childhood in rural and coastal settings can be compared with that in contemporary pictures by Danby, Mulready, and others, and it seems likely that the theme had a strong ideological resonance in the early nineteenth century, partly as a result of its widespread usage in romantic poetry.[77]

In his biography of his father, Wilkie Collins wrote:

> Whatever intellectual rank Mr Collins's sea-pieces may be considered to hold, as original and popular works of Art, it is not to be doubted that from them his highest celebrity as a painter first arose . . .[78]

It was as a direct result of the success of the Cromer picture that Collins obtained a loan from Heathcote in 1816 to make a study visit to Hastings, where he lived in a fisherman's cottage for twenty-five shillings per week with food – a rent which was more than twice what some farm labourers received in weekly wages. Significantly, when in 1824 he was given a commission by George IV, the subject he chose was *Prawn Fishers*, and he returned to Hastings in that year to make fresh studies for the picture. However, whatever his direct contact with Hastings, Cromer, and other coastal places, Collins, like the other artists I have been discussing, generally represented the coast through images which suggested a particular mythical and harmonious interaction of the natural and social orders, and deliberately excluded any indicators of modernization.

As we saw in chapter 7, it was partly Collins' particular use of figures which brought him critical success. He himself regarded the subjects of the type of Dutch painting from which his own work was descended as generally 'gross, vulgar, and filthy', and the figures as 'such as degrade the human species below the level of the brute creation'.[79] The contemporary press gave his figures a similar response to that which it gave Cristall's. Thus the *Examiner* reporting on his *Morning, Fishermen on the Look Out* at the Royal Academy in 1819 observed:

> He always doubles the pleasure his scenes give us, by peopling them with men, women, and children, that expressly belong to them. They are never trifling accessories, as in most other, and even good landscapes, but important and essential additions.[80]

In 1827, the *Morning Post* commented on the foreground group in his *Buying Fish* at the Academy exhibition of that year that the 'expression of a moral sentiment is a happy addition to this class of picture', and that Collins was one of the few artists to attempt it.[81] However, to Constable, Collins' type of candy-box sentiment represented a failure to be 'natural', and his own major image of Brighton suggests ideas which explicitly contradicted the Collins type of mythology.

(v) Constable, Turner, and Brighton

Constable's own interest in coastal subjects is one of several neglected features of his output. My main concern here is inevitably with his major picture: *The Beach at Brighton, the Chain Pier in the Distance* (Tate Gallery, *Plate 27*), exhibited at the Royal Academy in 1827, and the British Institution in the following year. However, I want to look briefly at some of his earlier representations of the coast before giving a full analysis of that work.

As is well known, Constable's friend John Fisher obtained the vicarage at Osmington in Dorset in 1813, and went to live there in 1816. Constable and his wife visited them on several occasions, and in 1816 spent part of their honeymoon with the Fishers in the then secluded village. Fisher and Constable were both enthusiastic about some of the scenery around 'dear old Osmington', as Constable described it in a letter to his wife of 1823,[82] and Osmington and Weymouth bays provided the subjects for a number of oil studies and small pictures. One of these, entitled *Osmington Shore, near Weymouth*, was exhibited at the British Institution in 1819, and has traditionally been identified with a picture now in the Louvre, although this identification is not beyond doubt.[83] Whatever picture it was, it was not well received by the *New Monthly Magazine*, which compared it unfavourably with Constable's other exhibits, and described it as 'a sketch of barren sand without interest'.[84] The Louvre's *Weymouth Bay* (88.3 × 111.8cm) has a boat with nets on the beach in the immediate foreground, and two small figures, apparently fishermen, on the sands, while a shepherd with a flock of sheep enlivens the middle distance and adds a pastoral character to the scene. (The National Gallery's view of the same site also has a shepherd and flock, but does not have the foreground figure, and has a very different atmospheric effect.) Other views include the topographical panorama of *Osmington and Weymouth Bays* (Museum of Fine Arts, Boston, 55.9 × 76.9cm), and the Osmington Bay composition which exists in two variants in the Wadsworth Athenaeum and a private collection.[85] Although there are variations in the figures of these latter two pictures, they are in both cases figures of fishing people engaged in bringing boats to shore. None of these pictures contains any direct signs of the presence of the fashionable resort of Weymouth or its visitors. Only in a small oil sketch in the Victoria & Albert Museum (no. 330–1888), which has the same basic design as the National Gallery and Louvre pictures, are two diminutive figures of female strollers represented, one evidently holding a parasol. It is significant that in the more finished paintings, Constable preferred to use a shepherd and flock or fishermen, as he did in the mezzotint based on this composition in *English Landscape*. That Constable and Fisher may have felt some disdain for the general run of fashionable visitors is indicated by Fisher's comment in a letter of 1826, that the 'still genius' of the nearby wooded valley of Sutton and Preston was disturbed by 'fellows from Weymouth with padded chests & vacant faces', who went there and 'let off guns'.[86]

The other popular resort which Constable had represented in an exhibition painting prior to 1827 was Great Yarmouth in Norfolk. Constable exhibited a *Yarmouth Jetty* at the British Institution in 1823, and a *Yarmouth Pier* at the Academy in 1831, although this almost certainly represented the jetty too, since the 1823 composition was engraved with the 1831 title for *English Landscape*. Three versions of *Yarmouth Jetty* are known today, one signed and dated 1822 (Private Collection, *Plate 26*), which is thought to be the picture exhibited in the following year.[87] Unfortunately, the early history of these pictures is obscure, and it is not known when Constable visited Yarmouth, if he ever did so. It seems curious that not only is there no record of Constable ever having been there, but also that no drawing or oil sketch of Yarmouth has come to light, and it suggests the possibility that the composition was based on a sketch or print of the beach by another artist, however different this might be from his usual practice. The variations Constable made to the skies of his Weymouth Bay composition suggests his willingness to adapt sky studies for use in representations of places other than where they were made, and indeed there is clearly an important improvisational element in the skies of Constable's finished pictures, which do not have a direct relationship with his *plein air* studies.[88] In fact, the cloud forms in the Yarmouth pictures have a similar pattern to those of *Harwich Light-house* (known today in three versions). The sky in none of these resembles that slightly indicated in the pencil drawing in the Victoria & Albert Museum, on which the Harwich composition was based.[89]

Because of the importance of Yarmouth beach and jetty as subjects in Norwich painting, Constable's *Yarmouth Jetty* raises the question of Constable's relations with the Norwich artists. His only definite contact with a Norwich artist was with the feeble Crome imitator Joseph Paul in 1824, with whose work he was suitably unimpressed,[90] but considering the number of his friends and acquaintances who visited Norwich, the presence of Norwich paintings in the London exhibitions and the mounting prestige of the Norwich artists by the end of the second decade, he must have been familiar with some Norwich art by the time he produced the first version of this picture. Indeed, at the Academy exhibition of 1812 his *A Water-mill* (*9*) would have been more or less next to landscapes by Crome and Ladbrooke (*11* and *12*) and his *Landscape: A Recent Shower* (*133*) adjacent to Crome's *Landscape* (*132*). In 1815, his *Village in Suffolk (268)* was hung in the Anteroom next to Stark's *A Landscape* (*269*). Two years before Constable exhibited his *Yarmouth Jetty* at the British Institition, Crome's pupil George Vincent had exhibited *A Dutch Fair on Yarmouth Beach* (*Plate 42*) and a *Yarmouth Beach* at the same gallery. However, Vincent's *Dutch Fair* is partly a genre picture, and if his *Yarmouth Beach* was like his later representations of this subject (*Plate 41*), then it too contained a strong genre element. Constable was working much closer to the pattern of Ruisdael's beach scenes and concentrating more on effects of atmosphere, keeping human action and shipping as relatively small features. In this respect, Constable's composition is more like two slightly earlier works by Crome, now known as *Squall off Yarmouth* (*Plate 40*) and *Yarmouth Beach and Mill, looking North* (Lady Crathorne). The former may well be a picture exhibited in Norwich in 1818, while the latter is likely to date from around the same time.[91] Whether or not Constable saw either of these works is not known, but Crome seems to have exhibited no Yarmouth views in London to judge from the titles of works he showed there. However, either way, Constable's picture does not come off well in comparison. Crome's foregrounds are more effective, and more suggestive of direct observation, whereas Constable's boat, anchor, and Yarmouth cart are an utterly routine variation on the beach picturesque. Only the sky and the light effect really redeem Constable's picture, which is basically a Ruisdael theme updated by some miniscule figures in fashionable dress on the jetty. As I shall show, Crome's paintings are not only more interesting in formal terms, but also suggest far more of the modern character of Yarmouth. Constable's *Yarmouth Jetty* paintings are small pictures (all *c*.32 × 50cm), probably conceived to meet a market demand. Were we to judge Constable's contribution to the beach scene by his Weymouth and Yarmouth pictures, he would not seem the equivalent of Callcott, whose large compositions of 1806 are extremely impressive.

However, when Constable came to paint Brighton on the same scale as those works, he produced an image which was far more challenging and innovative than Callcott's Dutch pastiches. I am not concerned here with Constable's admirable but essentially private oil studies of Brighton, although it must be noted that some of them do clearly represent some of its fashionable and modern aspects. For example, in *Brighton Beach with Colliers* (Victoria & Albert Museum) the buildings of modern Brighton are seen on the left, while the black forms of the colliers are in themselves an indication of Brighton's urban expansion. In another sketch the beach is represented on a calm day, dotted with female figures carrying parasols, the mark of the visitor.[92] These studies have some resemblance to later French treatments of modern landscapes, but they simply could not be presented as finished works, and only had a kind of intimate and generative status. As I pointed out earlier, Constable had let visitors creep in to one of his Weymouth studies, but he had eradicated them from the finished pictures. At Brighton he took up the challenge of representing them.

In general, Constable's major compositions did not arise incidentally from his sketches, but were produced through a kind of concerted campaign, isolating a particular range of forms in the landscape which could be organized within a suitable perspectival arrangement, and then exploring different possibilities in drawings and closely related oil sketches. *The Beach at Brighton, the Chain Pier in the Distance* (127 × 183cm) seems to be based in the first instance on a pencil drawing with ink additions in the Victoria & Albert Museum.[93] This shows all of the details of houses, chain pier and bathing machines from the pump on the left of the composition to the end of the pier on the right, with the exception of some boats on the sea. The pump-house (which pumped water to the baths), treated as a 'picturesque' structure, featured in an engraving by W. B. Cooke after a drawing by Francia published in 1827, and entitled *The Pump-house Brighton*.[94] It also features quite clearly in a number of local views such as the *Marine Parade Brighton* in Sicklemore's *Select Views* (*Plate 14*), which confirms that the configuration of features in Constable's design related to well-established topographical patterns for representing Brighton beach. To return to the initial pencil drawing, even the faintly indicated figures on the beach near the bathing machines are like those in the finished picture, although the arrangement of boats on the shoreline on the left middle distance is slightly different. The composition of the picture has been altered through the removal of a section of the canvas on the left edge which included a large sail (much larger than the one that remains) and a standing figure to the left – the arrangement here was originally close to that of the bigger of the two oil sketches in the Philadelphia Museum of Art. As it appears from an engraving of 1829 (*Plate 28*), the composition with the additional fishing boat and sail was even more dominated by traditional occupations. By removing these items, Constable made more prominent the bulk of the Albion Hotel, which is seen behind the sail of the boat which enters the composition from the left. In the foreground, the detritus of the fishing industry is arrayed in picturesque profusion. The upturned boat, discarded anchors, ropes, hooks, bits of wood, drying nets, and an overturned basket in which a skate and some other ill-defined fish are just visible, all together give the near plane great visual diversity and interest.[95]

As in some views of coastal resorts by Turner for the *Southern Coast* which I referred to earlier, and as in Chalon's *View of Hastings*, the fishing industry is the largest feature in this composition. The man seated on a barrel to the left mending a net, with one of Constable's shepherd dogs nearby, is one of the closest working figures in Constable's art. Picked out by his white sleeves and red bonnet, he appears to look out of the picture as if accosting the leisured visitor who has turned him into a spectacle, and who threatens the character of his habitat. Two other, perhaps younger, figures, recline idly on the upturned boat, one of whom looks away towards inland, and who holds a bottle against his leg. Among the breakers, fishermen pull in a net, while a boy carries in the rope of the approaching boat to the right. Five foreground figures do not belong, or are not clearly marked as belonging, to the fishing community. A key figure is the young man in the centre of the composition, who wears white trousers and a short blue jacket, and who carries what appears to be a furled umbrella. His dress, and the fact that he is looking over the sea towards the boats and shipping suggests that he may be intended to represent a seaman. Two female figures turned away from the sea, one of whom carries a parasol, presumably represent visitors, as may the woman with a child near the breakers, although it is possible to read these latter as the wife and child of an incoming fisherman.

Thus Constable keeps old Brighton, the 'natural order', largely distinct from the new Brighton behind. Only the two women with their backs to the sea seem to mediate between the two. The distant bathing machines are not in use – the squally weather has reclaimed the beach for its traditional occupations. However, in contrast to say William Scott's *View of Brighton*, an oil of 1817 (Yale Center for British Art),[96] Constable's image does not allow the spectator to forget the modern. Although the line of houses is lightly brushed, their regular lines and colouring of pink, ochre, and white, together with the touches of green on the cliff in front of them, make them stand out in relation to the stronger blue-grey colours and soft shapes of the sky, and the darker brown irregular forms of the foreground beach. The Chain Pier, that triumph of modern technology, stands out by its straight dark lines and regular curves against the light sky and horizon. Although the houses along the Marine Parade, as seen from a distance, could be just about comprehended within the picturesque aesthetic in purely formal terms due to the variety of their shapes, this is not true of the Chain Pier. The Pier was both a utilitarian object, and 'a place of fashionable and luxurious promenade', which could stand as a symbolic antithesis of the picturesque, the natural, and the traditional.[97]

Comparing Constable's picture with the numerous cheap topographical views, picturesque views, and artists' etchings which represented the beach and pier, it becomes clear that it brings together distinctive features of different categories of representation. Thus, the topographical view, at its most unassuming, as in the collections of views published by Bruce and Sickelmore, or the small aquatints by R. Havell which illustrate Brayley's *Topographical Sketches of Brighthelmston* make little use of picturesque conventions. The images teem with fashionably dressed figures even when they represent the beach, as in Havell's *Chain Pier from the Sands at Low Water* (*Plate 29*). Further, images of the Marine Parade and houses near the Suspension Pier have a kind of regularity which clearly signified newness and modernity, and was precisely the contrary of the picturesque. The majority of such views of the Pier were like Constable's picture in that they showed it from the west, but unlike his picture, they showed it from the fashionable area above the beach where the Steyne met the cliff as in Sickelmore's aquatint of *c.* 1827 (*Plate 14*) (see also map 2). By taking a position on the beach, Constable adapted the viewpoint customary for artists making picturesque views, and Edridge, Francia, and Owen had all produced views from this level which had been engraved by the Cookes. The picturesque group of boats which Constable used in his left foreground (and which had greater importance in the original composition) was precisely the kind of object which E. W. Cooke used as the basis for numerous designs, the titles of which associated them with Brighton, Hastings, and other coastal resorts. In *Twelve Plates of Coast Sketches, Brighton*, a collection of etchings published by Longman in 1830, and apparently belonging to a series called the *Marine Character of the Coast of England*, two compositions have important elements of Constable's image. *Prawn Boats &c. Brighton Beach* (*Plate 30*) has a foreground mass of boats with houses including a bath house called 'Mahomed's' (the famous establishment of S. D. Mahomed) on the cliff to the left,[98] while the Chain Pier extends into the image behind the boats. In *Hog Boat on the Sands at Brighton* the boat is foregrounded to the right of centre, with children with prawn nets around it, and the Pier enters the image from the left. Such combinations of boats, rope houses, drying nets and sails, fishermen and children provided Cooke with the theme for almost limitless variations. But while the modern might occasionally intrude into the distance in such subjects, it would always, necessarily, remain distant and peripheral. This was also the kind of subject which Constable used as the basis for compositions in his pen and wash drawings of boats on Brighton beach, and in these too modernity was kept very much to the margins of the design.[99]

The fact that Cooke included the Chain Pier at all is an indication of the status which it had achieved as a symbol of Brighton by 1830. The mid 1820s had seen the publication of an enormous number of topographical prints of the Pier, and its importance is further shown by the fact that when W. B. Cooke's 1822 engraving *Brighton* (*Plate 31*), after a drawing by Edridge, was republished in 1827 the Pier was added to the distance. Yet although Edridge's view is a west–east view from the beach, and the composition is basically similar to that of Constable's picture, there is

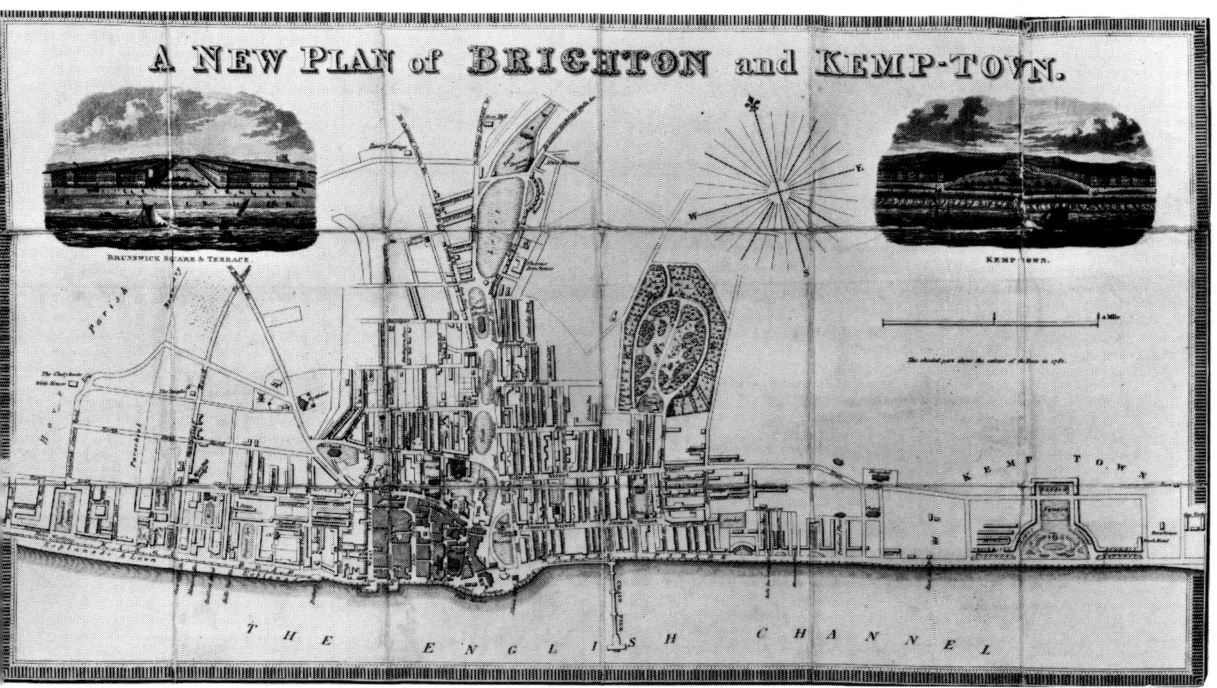

Map 2 *Plan of Brighton and Kemp-Town*, 1830

a fundamental difference in that the old houses on the left give no hint of the modern character of Brighton, which, but for the addition of the Pier, would seem a fishing town. This strategy of using the Pier to signify the topographical location, but keeping all evidence of modernization remote and reduced, is used even more strikingly in a steel engraving after a Copley Fielding *View of Brighton*, published in 1829.[100] Here the image seems essentially that of a scene of fishing boats being unloaded, and this activity dominates the foreground and the middle distance. Only in the far distance on the left are houses visible, and it is only by examining closely the area of distance right of centre that the shape of the Chain Pier can just be made out. Thus, if Constable kept his representation of Brighton in the middle distance, he did force it into a striking juxtaposition with the picturesque Brighton of the beach and fishing boats in a way less 'original' artists like Edridge and Cooke did not even attempt in etchings and water-colours. The only contemporry images which came close to throwing together picturesque and modern in this way are prints by minor topographical artists. The daring innovation of Constable's enterprise, was to unite topographical and picturesque modes in a dramatic large-scale painting.

In his letter to Fisher written from Brighton in late August 1824, Constable observed that: 'I am living here but I dislike the place . . . '. Having characterized the beach in the passage I quoted earlier, he continued:

> In short there is nothing here for a painter but the breakers – & sky[101]

It is clear that Constable chose not to show the 'indecent confusion' of fashionable people using the beach in his painting, partly by representing it as seen on an overcast and windy day, and partly by foregrounding the fishing boats, which he acknowledged to Fisher were 'picturesque', together with the seaside equivalent of the rotting stumps, dock leaves, and other plants which he used in the foregrounds of his rural scenes. With the exception of the two windswept strollers I mentioned earlier, fashionable people are denoted only by small marks of paint along the cliff top and on the Chain Pier itself. Leslie Parris and Conal Shields observed several years ago that in Constable's letter the 'natural and the artificial' are diametrically opposed, but claimed it could only be 'suspected' that this antithesis underlies the picture. To me it seems that it is more than just the natural and artificial, the sea and sky against the beach and town, which are contrasted here. It is also an older and more natural social order contrasted with the rapidly growing, and to Constable distasteful, new social order, which is signified by the physical evidences of modernization. Constable represented a site which for him was being both physically and morally spoiled, and I suspect he produced this answer to the coastal scenes of Callcott and Collins with a certain amount of irony.[102] His determination to confront the modern in his coastal scenes is further suggested by the small unfinished picture of *Hove Beach* (40.5 × 51cm, Musée Royaux des Beaux-Arts de Belgique), in which a group of fashionable strollers form the nearest and most prominent figures.[103]

As I demonstrated earlier, it was a commonplace of association aesthetics that the humble contemplation of nature led the mind to greater reverence for the deity, and refined morals. On the basis of such a position, Brighton and other fashionable resorts could only represent a despoliation of God's handiwork in the interests of frivolous and worldly pleasures. Evidence that such were its implications is provided by an article in the *Repository of Arts* in 1817, entitled 'On the Superiority of the Painter's Feelings'. This argued that while the beauties of nature imparted gladness even to those of 'the most common abilities', they did far more for painters and poets, who could see 'a thousand beauties in the most common scenery, which the vulgar traveller strides over uncautiously'. It continued:

> But Nature, simple unsophisticated Nature, thy charms are sought after even by the votaries of dissipation, but to no purpose: because they bring not with them those pure manners which are the only admissions to thy altar, their offerings are rejected; yet they would woo thee in the ruin, on the sparkling ocean, and on the evening promenade. For this are Bath, Brighton, and Cheltenham visited; while the charms of novelty pass for the fascinations of the true goddess. Soon the former leaves them, and they hasten to other scenes.[104]

That is to the ball-room, concert-room, or theatre. Constable would certainly have identified with such a view of the fashionable world and of the 'superiority' of the artist's feelings.

I am not trying to suggest that Constable's painting was produced as a form of social comment, although an element of this may have been involved. I take it as axiomatic that the intentions of an artist in producing an aesthetic object are (a) ultimately unknowable, and (b) ultimately irrelevant to its meaning and effects.[105] This does not of course preclude speculation as to the factors determining the artist's agency and motives, and it is curious that Constable should have made a major picture out of a type of subject which he regarded with such condescension. I have already quoted remarks which indicate this in his letter to Fisher of August 1824. In November he wrote to the same respondant:

> The sketchbook I am busy with a few days when I will send it – they are all boats – and coastal scenes – subjects of this kind seem to me more fit for execution than sentiment. I hold the genuine – pastoral – feel of landscape to be very rare & difficult of attainment – & by far the most lovely department of painting as well as of poetry.[106]

Yet in fact, two of Constable's most important pictures, that under discussion and *Whitehall Stairs, June 18th, 1817 (the Opening of Waterloo Bridge)* (Tate Gallery, 1832), were not pastoral scenes, but were explicitly contemporary urban landscapes, both of which contained prominent examples of modern technology – Rennie's Waterloo Bridge in the case of the latter.[107] I suspect that Constable's motivation was partly a desire to show that he was not restricted to one kind of landscape subject only, and that he could outshine his contemporaries in town and coastal subjects too. Fisher had advised him to 'diversify' his pictures as to time of day in 1824, and in 1827 told him that *The Beach at Brighton* represented a 'useful change of subject'. Fisher seems to have admired the painting greatly, and Constable himself reported that it had been praised at the 1827 Academy exhibition, and had attracted inquiries as to its price. However, the work remained in Constable's studio up until his death, and perhaps potential buyers were put off by what Fisher described as its 'ferocious beauties', and which he asked him to 'mellow' in a letter of December 1828.[108] Yet although the painting proved unsaleable, it seems likely that Constable was attempting to cash in on the vogue for such subjects at the same time as he sought to produce a more profound statement. While he disliked the generality of beach scenes, he evidently regarded his Brighton picture as an important work, and it attracted enough attention for the engraving after it by Frederic Smith to be published by Colnaghi in 1829 (*Plate 28*).

The contemporary press responses to the painting do not particularly help to sustain my interpretation. The *Morning Chronicle* admired the originality of this 'powerful picture':

> It is a masterly performance, original as all his works are, and destined to convince the generations to come, that there are 'Giants in our days'.

The *Morning Post*, however, disapproved of all Constable's Academy exhibits in 1827, and complained that the colouring of the picture was 'singularly defective;

one would say that there are streaks of ink dashed across it'. The *Examiner* held precisely the contrary view of the picture's colouring:

> with its blue and green sky and water on one side, changing nearly to a warm brown beach on the other; with its freshness of colour mellowed, [*it has*] the natural look of our English atmosphere, half-sullen and half-smiling.

It found Constable to be 'among the best of our painters of Familiar Landscape', and less of a 'mannerist' than most others. However, if these responses do not help to confirm that the differences between the foreground and middle distance of the picture were read as I have suggested, this may be because it was so obvious it hardly needed to be pointed out. The only review I have discovered which related Constable's image to the character of Brighton as a resort, is that in the *Repository of Arts*. This again is highly favourable, describing the picture as a 'capital local landscape with a connecting sea-view of particular interest'. It found the colouring of the houses on the front a little cold but suggested:

> The artist was, however, determined to have a cool promenade at Brighton; and how glad would the summer visitors of that town be, if they could imitate his example.[109]

This comment does at least serve as a reminder that it would not have been particularly appropriate for an early nineteenth-century artist to represent a resort as if seen on a hot sunny day, since visitors did not go to sunbathe, but to breathe an invigorating atmosphere and bathe in cold water. Taken together, the reviews indicate that Constable's 'originality' was widely recognized and appreciated by the critics. However, the fact remains that this impressive and ambitious picture did not sell, whereas Collins found a ready market for his anodyne wares. As Constable's career more generally illustrates, 'serious' landscape art did not have the same kind of appeal with the picture-buying public as less ambitious varieties.

Despite some variations in composition and format, Constable's approach to the representation of modern Brighton resembled that which was employed by Turner and others in picturesque views of some of the major resorts of the period. The novelty of Constable's picture was that it utilized this approach in a major exhibition landscape. Whereas Chalon had used a stormy atmospheric effect and contrasts of light and shade to give a dramatic force to a scene of fishing boats coming in; Constable, by his particular pictorial construction and contrasts of chiaroscuro and colour, dramatized the relationship between old and new. Unlike the pictures of Callcott and Collins, Constable's work represented explicit evidence of modernization, and forced a contrast between it and traditional occupations. That he felt obliged to represent the new, even if only from a distance, adds an element of dramatic tension to this picture which is absent from theirs. It is perhaps significant that the contrast was re-inforced in Smith's engraving after the picture. In this, the sailing boat close to the west side of the Pier's end in the painting is omitted, but what appears to represent a ball of smoke hangs over the side of the structure at this point. I suspect that this denotes the presence of a steamer moored on the east side of the pier, just as one is represented in the lithograph after R. H. Nibb's view *The Chain Pier, Brighton (from the Sea)*, published in Brighton in 1846.[110] That such is the case is further suggested by a small dark shape silhouetted against the lighter distance just beyond the Pier's end, which again does not appear in the painting. This shape can hardly represent a sailing ship or boat, but it does look like the shape of a steamer with smoke trail. Thus the print seems to refer to the fact that the primary function of the Pier was to provide a birth for the Brighton–Dieppe Ferry, although it was also used by an increasing number of other steam boats. The reason for these changes is suggested by the print having been published jointly by Colnaghi and 'Mr Folker' of Brighton, which indicates that it was aimed primarily at visitors to the resort, sympathetic to evidences of modernity.

To praise a work of art for its 'truth' seems a rather quaint and outmoded notion nowadays, and one deeply suspect – for the current vogue among our theoretical vanguard for denying the possibility of credible solutions to traditional epistemological problems makes such judgements simply redundant and naive, or evidence of an incipient authoritarianism. Personally, I am unconvinced by these assertions of an epistemological impasse, which seem to match so ill with the tones of certainty and authority assumed by some of those who make them. However, that truth is elusive and developmental, and not to be grasped by identity thinking I acknowledge. And if such is the case, then art may deserve a status as a mode of cognition which it is not widely given. If the aesthetic is to refer to something more than what Adorno dubbed 'culinary hedonism', then it can only be because it involves kinds of judgement which consist of more than a form of rarified sensual discrimination, and which rather engage our cognition as a whole, historically formed social beings. In the early stages of bourgeois society in which Constable worked, the antecedents of the Modernist project can be traced in the first calls for an art of originality and individuality, appropriate to its time, which would show something new. This notion may be clearer in Stendhal's statements or those of the *London Magazine*'s art critic of 1825 than it is in Constable's pronouncements, but it was realized in his practice none the less. Neither Constable nor any other early nineteenth-century painter produced art that denied and negated tradition as Modernism does, and no art of the period has quite that quality of dissonance which Adorno defined as Modernism's 'trademark' – although some works by Delacroix, Géricault, and Goya seem to approach it.[111] However, Constable's work does bespeak that urge to engage with the present, mixed up with an unease at the threat of relentless change, which has been commonly associated with Poe and Baudelaire. That is why Constable is at his very best when he deals with the urban. The fact that he would not have thought so is beside the point. Constable's work was intended by the artist to be didactic and propositional in some respects. The truths he proposed to tell were truisms of natural theology and the social doctrine associated with it by contemporary Toryism, although it is unlikely that he would have thought the value of a picture's effects could be reduced to their equivalence to such ideas. But truths can also be discovered in his work of which he was not perhaps fully conscious. They are truths related to the problems of thinking modernization through these ideologies, and working through their implications for pictorial forms. Constable worked at these contradictions more than any other contemporary landscape painter. Indeed, it can be argued that because of his particular formation as a class subject he worked at them obsessively. This granted him a kind of insight, but it was one which cost him dearly – or so the unresolved struggles and incoherence of some of his later pictures suggest. For whereas *The Beach at Brighton, the Chain Pier in the Distance* is a triumph, *Whitehall Stairs, June 18th, 1817*, despite the brilliance of its design, is a disaster. One may interpret the failure of this latter picture to produce the effect of transparent denotation of the former, as being the result of an obsessive worrying of surface textures in an effort to render the modern more picturesque, more aesthetic. In the earlier picture, Constable had perhaps accepted the disjunction between the two as unavoidable, if unappealing.

From this perspective there is a sense in which Constable's *The Beach at Brighton* can be judged a more profound and significant image than the beach scenes of Callcott or Collins. Reactionary that he was, Constable felt obliged to represent 'nature', whether in the form of the agricultural landscape of Suffolk or the South Coast, in ways which were true to his experience as he understood it. In the aesthetic discourses of his period, the terms 'natural' and 'true' were seen as having a direct equivalence, although within such discourses 'truth' was seen as a resemblance apprehended intuitively, and not susceptible to the kinds of demonstration utilized in the natural sciences. As I argued in chapter 2, it is a mistake to interpret Constable's conception of science in a positivistic sense or to regard him as a simple naturalist. Yet although Constable's 'nature' was a complex ideological construct, in which a primary concern with the humanly formed landscape of rural England as evidence of the hand of a provident creator was fused with assumptions about a 'natural' hierarchy in social relations, he none the less felt impelled to produce an art which abounded in signifiers which denoted a direct first-hand observation of the landscape and the interaction of humans with it and within it. Constable's 'pastorals' of Suffolk, although he referred them to kinds of poetry which expressed rank condescension to the lower classes, sought to acknowledge that the labouring population laboured in certain specific modern ways, while at the same time affirming that this was their inevitable lot. Equally, when it came to the coast, the working class had to be shown going about its proper business.

If to argue the 'truth value' of pictorial signs is indeed inherently problematic, from the moral and political standpoint of this study it seems valid to treat as a positive quality in them features which indicate a deep and complex engagement with historical and social circumstances. What can be said in relation to Constable's *The Beach at Brighton* is that (a) it represents fishermen engaged in various aspects of their occupation, (b) it combines this with a representation of a specific location in a way which was and remains readily understood as such, and (c) that location and a particular element within it, the Chain Pier, had connotations of modernization and of the social changes which accompanied it for a contemporary audience. Constable's picture is thus anchored to a real place, and suggests a basic formulation of contemporary social developments – it dramatizes the interplay of social forces through its formal structure. The pictures of Callcott, Collins, and some others to whom I have referred, indicate these developments only by occlusion. Their works connote a mythology of the coast and its inhabitants as it would have been nicer to think them, and were understood as so doing. Whereas other painters of the period largely confined themselves to re-hashing Dutch beach scenes with modifications to the genre figures and boat types, Constable looked to the example of contemporary topographical art and injected a new content within a Dutch format, at the same time modifying the formal pattern by working on a bigger scale and introducing broader brushwork and far richer arrangements of light and shade. It is the combination of these qualities which make his *Beach at Brighton* one of the most aesthetically significant landscape paintings of the early nineteenth century.

The only other representation of the South Coast resorts which can compare in formal achievement and modernity with Constable's *Beach at Brighton* is Turner's *Brighton from the Sea* (*Plate 32*) of *c.* 1828–9, which was one of four paintings commissioned from the artist by Lord Egremont for the Grinling Gibbons saloon at Petworth. It has been suggested that the Tate Gallery's sketch, which is slightly larger than the Petworth version (69 × 135cm compared with 63 × 132.1cm) was originally intended to fulfil the commission, but that Egremont demanded more finished brushwork, more figures and detail. However, while there seems indubitable evidence that the Tate's two Petworth views (TG559 and TG2701) were both *in situ* in the house in 1828 and then subsequently replaced, there is no such evidence that the Tate version of *Brighton from the Sea* was ever there, although it is not an unreasonable supposition that it was. The existence of the full-scale 'sketches' for the Petworth pictures has puzzled Turner scholars because they seem inconsistent with the general pattern of his practice. I do not presume to offer an explanation of this specialist problem, but it does seem to me improbable that the Tate *Brighton from the Sea* would have been regarded as a finished picture by Turner, let alone by Egremont. Attractive as it is, it simply does not have the depth and richness of Turner's finished pictures of this period, and the details which Turner added in the Petworth version: the foreground flotsam, and the greater marking out of the Chain Pier and the Brighton sea front greatly enhance the painting's capacity to produce meanings and the force of its effect.[112]

John Gage has shown that Egremont had financial interests in both the Chain Pier and the Chichester Canal (the subject of one of the other paintings), and taken together the four views might have seemed a straightforward celebration of Egremont's estate and his recent contributions to economic progress. The Chain

Pier was widely seen as a triumph of technological innovation and ingenuity, and a Brighton guide of *c.* 1824 vaunted its length of 1,250 feet and its durability – it had withstood the violent storm of 23 November 1824:

> The whole is handsomely painted, and is the finest specimen of architecture, of the kind, in the world.[113]

However, Turner's rich and impressive painting can not be reduced simply to a testimonial to Egremont's entrepreneurial vision, even if knowledge of his interests gives the picture a particular resonance to those who saw and see the picture in its Petworth context. As in the 1825 view from the *Southern Coast* (*Plate 11*), fishing boats are the closest objects to the viewer in terms of the picture's perspective, and the sails of the fishing boats on the right are initially the most prominent feature of the composition because of their scale. The prominent standing figure in the nearest boat on the left, who in the sketch appears to look towards the arriving steam packet, in the finished version appears to look out of the painting towards us as does his seated companion. The fishing boats, which function as signs of Brighton's traditional character, are contrasted with the intrusive modernity of the 'dandy jetty', as Constable called it, which forms a lattice-work against the declining sun. (This contrast is even clearer in the engraving after the picture.) It should be recalled that such a light and slender structure, which could yet withstand the force of the ocean, was still a visual novelty in this period. Another clear sign of the modern is the steam packet behind the fishing boats, bringing visitors to the pier, visitors who can be made out under the awning over its stern. Thus different social categories are shown in their different activities, work and leisure are juxtaposed. More visitors are visible in the form of promenaders represented on the Pier, and as small blobs of paint along the beach and cliff top in front of the modern houses on the right. Like Constable, Turner put picturesque details in the foreground – not just the irregular shapes and variegated contrasts of the fishing boats, but also the rubbish: the broken baskets and vegetables floating in the water on the right. The detail of this rubbish not only adds variety and interest to that part of the picture, but it helps to establish the perspective recession more effectively than in the Tate's sketch, and also reinforces the idea of the presence of a large town.

By comparison with the hard dark lines of Constable's representation of the Chain Pier, Turner's image suggests a more graceful structure. The picture has a wonderfully clear, blond light effect, and the dark shadows on the foreground water, which are deeper on the left, make the pinks and yellows of the buildings of modern Brighton look particularly ethereal. The radiant atmosphere works with the long horizontal shape of the composition and the gentle swell of the water, indicated by the slight lines of surf which appear to spread out from the sunset, to suggest more positive ideas of a benevolent physical and social environment than the colder colours, busy figures and windswept sea and clouds in Constable's picture. In Turner's Brighton old and new, work and leisure, seem to mingle together in a harmonious continuum, rather than being starkly contrasted as in Constable's gloomy vision.

Brighton from the Sea is an essentially Claudean picture, which combines Dutch-type details of fishing boats with a conception ultimately derived from Claude's seaports in its balanced receding masses arranged around a central avenue of light – although the design could also be related to the sunset estuary scenes of Cuyp, and the calms of Simon de Vlieger and Jan van de Capelle. Thus the symbols of modernity have been treated so as to make them into an aesthetic object appropriate for a major oil painting. The fact that this image seems calculated to suggest an optimistic and progressive view of the British social order, may remind us that even Tory noblemen like Egremont were also capitalists. The bourgeois radicals who criticized the principles of 'legitimacy' and 'aristocracy' in the name of progress had no copyright on that concept. Conservative interests, then as now, represented themselves as progressive – as any reading of the *Morning Post* will show. It was the nature of progress which was at issue.

It would be trite and theoretically indefensible to see Constable's *Brighton Beach* as simply the counterpoint to his reactionary and anxious view of the social order, and Turner's *Brighton from the Sea* as the counterpoint to a more progressive political perspective. Constructions of intentions and artists' attitudes are not the issue here. But having said this, it is the case that Constable's work lends itself to being read as a sign that old Brighthelmstone is giving way inexorably to new Brighton, and the evidence of the old, shunted away into the shadows on the left, does not produce positive connotations in the way that Turner's fishermen in their radiant ambience clearly tend to. Light and atmosphere soften all into harmony in Turner's image; in Constable's they make contrasts which are as much social as visual. I must acknowledge that there is no evidence in the press responses that Constable's contemporaries saw in his painting anything more than an original exercise in English landscape painting: a 'correct and pleasing' view with an interesting effect;[114] and I have discovered no contemporary responses to Turner's painting. However, if the press statements represented the whole sum of the critics' responses to the picture, then they not only failed to observe the social implications of the image as I have identified them, they equally missed the profound chain of associations which Constable could have consciously articulated in relation to the work. As I stressed in the last chapter, art criticism was a discourse largely confined within a limited pattern of types of statement – and extensive reflections on pictorial meaning were not usually part of the grist to its mill. Consequently, it is both necessary and legitimate to make use of the rare references to the construction of meaning developed in relation to a few works, to produce an account of that which was left unsaid in relation to the majority.

Bearing in mind the *Review of Publications of Art*'s response to Turner's *Margate*, it may be the case that Constable's innovative treatment of Brighton simply aestheticized a socially problematic object in the same way for many of his contemporaries. For such viewers, the differences in the social implications of his and Turner's pictures would be insignificant – all that would be significant would be the differences between formal references and the evocations of mood. However, the evidence I have advanced in relation to responses to the works of Collins and Cristall, seems to be sufficient to sustain the view that beach scenes had connotations which extend beyond the province of 'art'. The figures of Constable (or of Turner) were doubtless too small to provoke comment in their own right, but they were presumably accepted as 'natural' for such scenes – rather than producing the 'natural' but such 'as we wish to meet' effect of Cristall's types. It is at least reasonable to surmise that reflecting viewers of the conservative intellectual variety, or equally political radicals, might have admired the aesthetic character of Constable's performance, but also found in the work confirmation of their critical appraisal of the social and physical development of the resort towns. We may also note that the reactionary paper closest to the fashionable world, the *Morning Post*, did not give a favourable report of this picture.

Although the style of presentation and the method of my argument are somewhat different, it should be clear that it is of the same type as that advanced by T. J. Clark in relation to works by Courbet, Manet, and others.[115] That is to say, I am claiming that certain pictures represented contemporary social realities through formal devices which, by their differences from dominant pictorial norms, subverted some current mythological structures. This is to argue that they could give a kind of cognitive purchase on the social order. However, it should be clear that I am not making such strong claims for the effects of some of Constable's paintings as Clark makes for those of the heroes in his narratives. This is partly because the conditions of artistic practice and public reception in early nineteenth-century Britain did not allow paintings to function in quite the way they could (arguably) in France in the 1850s and 1860s. Given that Constable's pictures did not provoke controversy or divide opinion, it is only possible to argue that they had the potential for the kind of reading I've offered. I shall return to these issues in chapter 10.

(vi) Norwich artists and Great Yarmouth

I have argued elsewhere that the 'Norwich School' is a mystificatory concept, and it is unnecessary to set out these arguments again here.[116] Suffice it to say that while the term was in currency outside Norwich by 1819, it distinguished a centre of artistic training rather than a distinctive style. This is hardly surprising, since there are no common formal elements in paintings produced in Norwich in the early nineteenth century which could serve to distinguish them from those produced elsewhere. Further, the leading figures of the second generation of the 'School' so-called, Crome's pupils James Stark and George Vincent, were clearly ambitious to get out of the provincial artist/drawing master category, and establish themselves as professionals in the only centre which really counted – Stark had moved to London by 1816, when he entered the Academy Schools, and Vincent was there by 1818.[117] Although John Crome had exhibited in London occasionally in the years 1816–21, Stark and Vincent did so frequently in that period and continued to maintain their presence in the 1820s. By 1820 they had also sold works to major patrons such as Sir George Beaumont, Sir John Leicester, and the Marquis of Stafford.[118] Thus although the *Literary Chronicle* could describe them in 1818 as 'the two Norfolk heroes' (a jokey reference to Nelson) they were seen as major young artists whose only significant connection with Norwich lay in their having trained there.[119]

It is symptomatic of the responsiveness of Norwich-based artists to the general trends of the period, that they produced some ambitious pictures of resorts, but one thing which does distinguish their productions of this type is their concentration on the Norfolk resorts of Yarmouth and Cromer. I shall not discuss the Cromer pictures here, since relatively few survive and they do not offer any significant variations from the types already discussed. However, I shall argue that Yarmouth was a very different type of town from any of the Southern Coast resorts,[120] and that it necessarily produced a different range of associations. The distinctive features of the place seem to be the cause of distinctive elements in the types of picture developed by Crome and more especially by George Vincent.

The distinguishing aspect of Yarmouth's development is that it was not in any way a decayed and picturesque fishing village like Brighton or Hastings to begin with. It was a flourishing port, it had a large fishing industry, and employment was also to be found in the shipyards and breweries. In 1818 a silk mill was built on the denes, which relied on child labour. Thus Yarmouth's prosperity depended primarily on industry, and it did not experience the same dramatic expansion as most resorts. Its population, which was said to be about sixteen thousand in 1795, was barely over twenty-four thousand in 1849, whereas Brighton's population increased from just over seven thousand to sixty-five thousand between 1801 and 1851. The essentially commercial character of the place was already a subject for comment in the eighteenth century, and the strategy of local guide-books was to present its commercial features as an attraction. Thus according to a substantial guide of 1826:

> To such as delight in the bustle of mercantile pursuits, its noble quays, its wharfs, and its rivers, offer a rich field for improvement and speculation.[121]

Yarmouth first developed as a resort probably as a result of the sea-bathing craze inaugurated by Russell's treatise, for there seems no evidence of bathing there before the bath house was built in 1759. This cost nearly £2,000, and was enough of an event to be recorded in Blomefield's county history. Brighton's first guide had been published in 1761; Yarmouth's appeared in 1777, and was an amusing semi-satirical production by one James Rymer. At this time Yarmouth's amusements were evidently still in a fairly primitive state, and Rymer complained sardonically that this was not due to the:

> want of liberal sentiment, and absence of that spirit of genteelity and politeness which characterizes the inhabitants of other public places

but rather to:

> inattention by reason of the chief inhabitants being greatly engaged in the several departments of corn, flower, malt, mackerel and herring business: by all which money is to be made; but none by instituting fiddling, dancing, and dramatic entertainments.[122]

In fact this last assumption was a mistaken one, as developments in Yarmouth and elsewhere were clearly to show. In the following year, a Mr Fulcher of Ipswich built a theatre at a cost of £1,600, at which actors from Norwich performed. In 1788, public rooms were added to the bath house, where billiards, balls and public breakfasts all took place, and where concerts were performed in the early nineteenth century. The town obtained a Parliamentary Act for improving paving and lighting in 1809; a new wide east–west street, Regent Street, was built in 1813 at a cost of £30,000; and one hundred and fifty gas street lamps were lit for the first time in December 1824. By 1829, a public library, subscription rooms, a coffee room, a billiards room and concert room were all to be found on Yarmouth's quay. A contemporary guide book commented sententiously that:

> The improvements that have been made in recent years, and are still making are extensive, and excite astonishment in the mind of every stranger.[123]

Thus, early nineteenth-century Yarmouth was not only a flourishing commercial town, but also the leading resort of the East Anglian coast. It had a variety of amusements, and plenty of accommodation, and its guides claimed that there was much of antiquarian, picturesque, and natural interest in the neighbourhood. Visitors were assured that order was 'strictly preserved by a very active and efficient police', and one guide-book even boasted that there was 'NOT A BEGGAR TO BE SEEN, so admirably is the police conducted'[124] – the spectacle of prosperity and industry was not to be spoiled by visible evidence of surplus in the labour market, with its Malthusian associations.

The commercial workaday character of Yarmouth meant that it became a fundamentally bourgeois resort, which was visited primarily by people from nearby towns and especially Norwich, from which river transport was cheap and regular. G. S. Carey commented in his survey of watering places of 1801 that 'Yarmouth is not so fashionably attended as Southampton, Brightelmstone, or even Margate or Ramsgate'. It was much cheaper than these places, and consequently:

> many of the summer visitors ... are neighbours composed mostly of that description, who go more for an hour of relaxation, to look about them and to gratify their stomachs ... than swill themselves with the briny waters of the ocean.[125]

The upper ranks of Norfolk Society (if they did not go to the South Coast) went to the small and exclusive fishing village of Cromer, which had begun to be visited as a watering place about 1785. This had a population of a mere six hundred and seventy-six in 1801, and one of only one thousand three-hundred odd in 1851 – although it already had three inns catering to visitors by 1829. A topographical work of 1819 compared the two places thus:

> The company is select and respectable and if retirement be sought for, Cromer will afford this in perfection. The Norwich people mostly frequent Yarmouth, which is a gay, lively place – the Margate of Norfolk.[126]

It is probable that the accounts of the social complexion and attractions of the resorts given in general guides and topographies are far more reliable than those published locally, and Richard Beatniffe considerably exaggerated the gentility of Yarmouth in his *Norfolk Tour* of 1795.[127] A more important implication of this evidence is that not only was it impossible for Yarmouth to become a contested site for gentry and the middle classes (its character was already determined), but its beach provided a spectacle of thriving industry quite unlike that of Hastings or Brighton.

At this point it is worth noting the links between Norwich artists and Yarmouth's wealthier inhabitants. The overwhelming majority of the local patrons of Norwich artists came from different sectors of the Norfolk bourgeoisie – commercial, industrial and professional. Crome, Cotman, and several others worked as drawing masters in Yarmouth, and found important patrons there. J. H. Druery's account of Yarmouth, published in 1826, listed the residences of substantial citizens on the quay, and described their picture collections: this reveals that Dawson Turner, J. D. Palmer, Samuel Paget and the Reverend John Homfray all owned pictures by one or other of the Cromes, and the iron-founder William Yetts was later to own the Tate Gallery's *Mousehold Heath* if he did not already do so.[128] However, the titles given to works in these collections do not suggest that the Yarmouth bourgeoisie particularly wanted representations of Yarmouth – the only view of the place they seem to have had among them was a J. B. Crome *View on the River at Yarmouth*, which was in the collection of Samuel Paget. Of the six clearly identified views of Yarmouth lent to John Crome's memorial exhibition, all were lent by residents of Norwich. Thus it seems unlikely that there was much stimulus from Yarmouth patrons for the production of pictures of the place.

Before analysing some of the pictures which have survived, I want to say something about the different elements which went into the image of Yarmouth beach. The beach was backed by the view of the sea, dotted with ships and boats, and this was an important attraction of any resort.[129] While the North Sea resorts could not compete with those of the South Coast in terms of climate or proximity to London, they were more attractive in this respect. In the letterpress to *English Landscape* Constable noted that the view at Brighton was deficient for want of shipping; by contrast, Yarmouth was fortunate in that Yarmouth Roads offered the only secure anchorage between the Thames and the Humber, and in 1854 it was estimated that fifty thousand vessels passed through them every year.[130] This 'nautical panorama', as one guide-book called it, certainly impressed Parson Woodforde, who wrote in his diary in 1776:

> Nothing can beat what we saw today – immense sea Room, Ships and Boats passing and repassing – the Wind being rather high, the Waves like Mountains coming into the Shore.[131]

Yarmouth guides specifically recommended the jetty as 'one of the most fashionable promenades about Yarmouth', which offered a 'highly interesting view', and it is clear that it was the nub of social activity on the beach. There had been a jetty at Yarmouth since the sixteenth century, although it had needed repeated rebuilding and repairs due to the effects of the sea and storms. At the beginning of the nineteenth century, the jetty was 110 paces long and 24 feet wide at its head where there was a crane. By 1804, the crane had become so dilapidated that it had to be removed, and in 1805 the whole structure was largely destroyed by storm and tide. The new jetty, begun in 1808 and finished in 1809 at a cost of £5,000, was 453 feet long and 20 feet wide. It also differed from the earlier one in having side rails but no crane.[132] The best idea of the leisure functions of the jetty is suggested by Druery's text to Joseph Lambert's engraving of it, which comments:

> The extensive prospect the Jetty commands of the British ocean, the momentarily varied scene of commercial barks at anchor and under sail, the noble specimens of modern architecture on the Denes, with a fine view of the town, render this Jetty a spot of universal interest to the inhabitants of Yarmouth, and of particular gratification of its numerous visitors.

In relation to this claim, it needs to be noted that the jetty was very close to the bath house, where public breakfasts and balls were held in the summer months in a 'fine room' adjoining the original building, and where a billiards table was also available.[133] (See map 3.)

It should be evident from what I have said so far, that at Yarmouth the conflict between old and new usages which characterized Brighton or Hastings did not occur. The overall class composition of the visitors was different, and their activities mingled with those of the working inhabitants in contrast with the pattern of the South Coast resorts. As elsewhere, the work of the fishing community was part of the spectacle, particularly around the jetty which combined utilitarian and leisure functions. Thus Beatniffe described the fishing industry as another pleasing feature of the view:

> To those who take delight in seeing others pleased, without themselves being particularly interested in what is going forward, it must give much pleasure to behold the cheerful activity of the fishermen on the beach, when landing and carrying off the herrings.

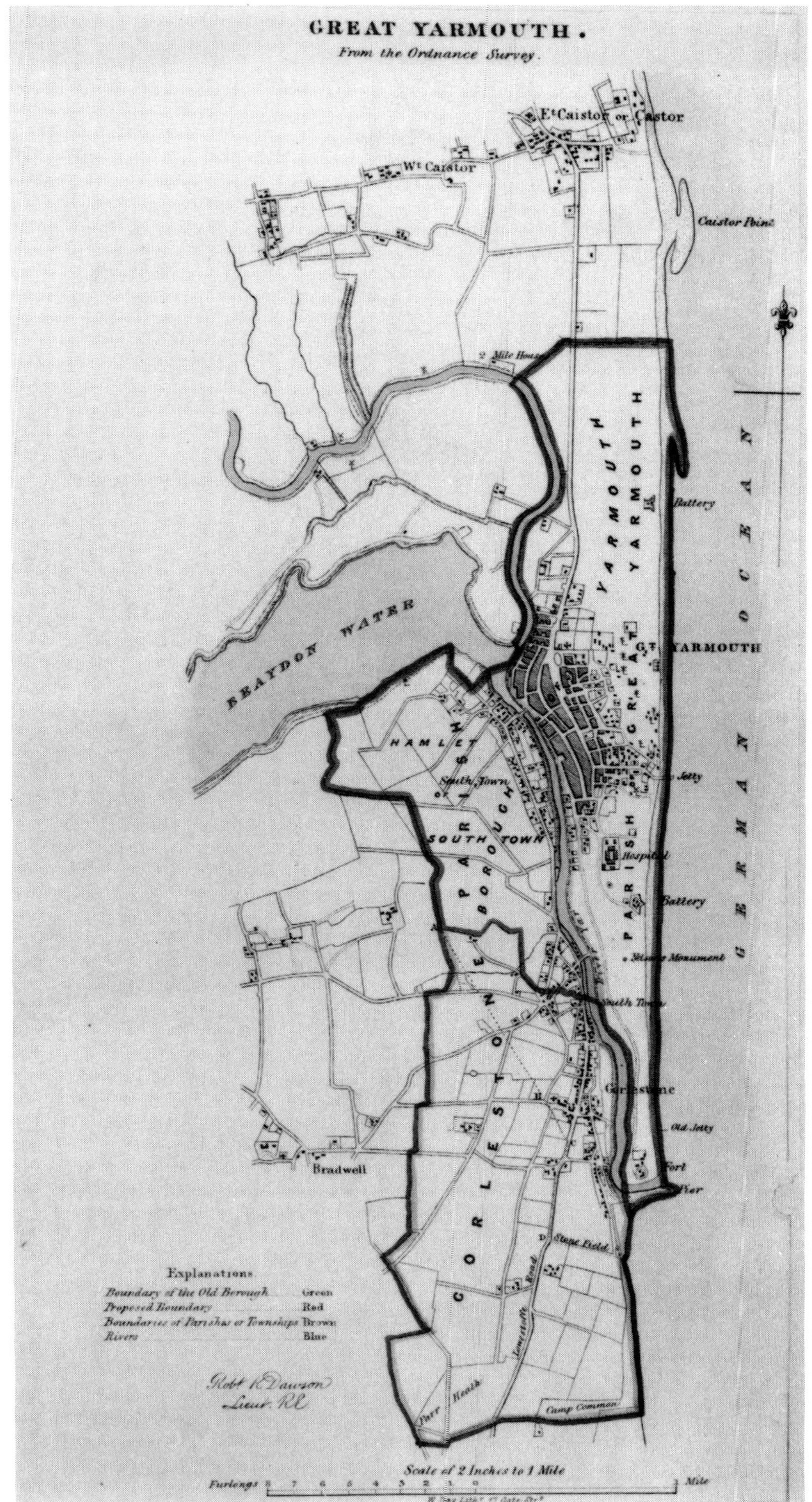

Map 3 R. K. Dawson, *Great Yarmouth from the Ordnance Survey*, early nineteenth century

It is of course only when viewed as a spectacle by those who do not work, that such activity falls into the category of 'cheerful'.[134]

Even more pertinent to the representations of fishing people by Norwich artists is the account of fishing at Cromer given by Edmund Bartell in his guide: *Cromer, Considered as a Watering Place; with Observations on the Picturesque Scenery in its Neighbourhood* (1800, second edition 1806). Bartell was a local physician and amateur artist, who published an essay on picturesque cottages in 1804. He was a member of the Norwich Society of Artists in 1808–10, and an honorary member and sometime donor until the Society's demise in 1833. *Cromer, Considered as a Watering Place* is as much an essay on picturesque landscape as it is a guide (each chapter describes an excursion), and it contains several references to art theorists including Gilpin, Shenstone, and de Piles.[135] For Bartell the constantly changing views of ships on Cromer beach gives interest to the scene, and the loading and unloading of coals is a picturesque activity. More generally:

> The fishery, independent of the pleasure we receive from the consideration of the support it brings to a numerous, hardy, and, in many instances, an industrious set of people, is not without its effect in a picturesque point of view. The different preparations for a voyage, the groups of figures employed in various ways, some carrying a boat down to the water's edge, some laden with nets, oars, masts, and sails, while others, in a greater state of forwardness, are actually pulling through the breakers, form a scene of the most busy, interesting and pleasing kind.[136]

Writing of the value of the sea as a motiv for artists, Bartell discusses the composition of a 'calm', but concludes that such scenes can only make 'a formal object', and:

> If you wish to make it picturesque, you must compose your foreground of some projecting rock or pier head, a boat or two lying on the shore, and a few appropriate figures; remove the ship in the foreground to the second distance, with others in the last distance to mark the horizon; and with these materials, if well managed, a very pleasing picture may be formed.[137]

This reads so like a recipe for one of Crome's Yarmouth jetty views, that it is not unreasonable to speculate that Bartell may have functioned as an aesthetician for the Norwich Society of Artists.

Like the Southern Coast resorts, Yarmouth was represented in a sequence of topographical prints and publications, although inevitably these were not as numerous as those related to Brighton and Hastings. A sign of its increasing importance as a leisure centre is the series of pleasingly crude aquatints based on paintings by J. Butcher, and published by J. Barnes of Yarmouth in 1790, to judge by the date on one of them. There are three of these in the Todd topographical collection in Norwich Museum, all representing key social sites of the town: the Market Place, the Quay, and the Jetty. The *North West View of the Jetty at Yarmouth* (*Plate 33*) conforms precisely to the pattern of tourist prints identified earlier in its emphasis on fashionable life, and hint of satire. Shipping, bathing machines, fashionable figures on the jetty, and visitors travelling in a Yarmouth cart (a special narrow cart developed to negotiate Yarmouth's notoriously narrow lanes), are all included. Workmen loading barrels, women selling fish, fishermen smoking, an embracing couple, and two women in conversation with a group of fishermen are juxtaposed with naval officers and more obviously well-to-do figures, all together suggest something of the mingling of social classes characteristic of the place. The type of stark imagery of the modern, so characteristic of guide-books, is well represented by the plates in *The Picture of Yarmouth* (1819) by John Preston, Yarmouth's Comptroller of customs. These are aquatints, partly executed by the Yarmouth printer C. Sloman, and based on Preston's own drawings. The main body of the text is devoted to Yarmouth's 'Public Establishments' and is celebratory in tone:

> No place perhaps in the united kingdom has altogether undergone more general improvement in a few years than Yarmouth, and, as a watering-place, it stands at this time unrivalled.[138]

In its political character it represented the cause 'of ORDER, of PROPERTY and of PEACE'. This progressivist and celebratory tone is matched by clear sharp images of the Town Hall, Custom House, Barracks, Gaol, &c. Fittingly, the jetty, as drawn by Preston, is a far from picturesque structure (*Plate 34*).

The more up-market topography of Yarmouth is represented by Joseph Lambert's series of *Graphic Illustrations of Great Yarmouth and its Environs* (1822). This consisted of twenty-four copper-plate line engravings, published and printed in Yarmouth, which were also available from shops in Norwich, Ipswich and Lowestoft. Although Lambert's drawings are unimpressive, and he was a pedestrian engraver, this was a publication with more artistic pretensions: large India paper copies were available at four shillings per number (of four numbers), while the standard size were three shillings per number.[139] Just as the Chain Pier functioned as a symbol for Brighton, so William Wilkins' Nelson Column functioned as one for Yarmouth – and it is clearly shown in the distance in Lambert's jetty view, poking above the horizontal of the platform on the right (*Plate 35*). There are far fewer indications of fashionable life in this than in Preston's images, and it has more pretensions to being a picturesque view in line with the more expensive and time-consuming medium in which it was executed. Finally, moving up to the top of the aesthetic scale in terms of prints (artist's etchings excluded), a steel engraving by Finden after E. W. Cooke's *Yarmouth Norfolk* (*Plate 36*), is precisely comparable with the Copley Fielding *View of Brighton* which I discussed earlier. The main activity of Yarmouth is represented through a fish market in the foreground, although its status as a port is also indicated. The Nelson Column, which is prominent in the background, was not a problematic object for representation in the way that the Chain Pier was. Although it inevitably detracted from the natural simplicity of the scene, it did represent a dignified and 'sublime' architectural object, and it was in harmony with the chain of associations produced by imagery of the hardy and industrious island race properly at work on the beach.

In relation to this body of images, and in contrast with the oils and water-colours of Brighton and Hastings I discussed earlier, it is striking how from the beginning Norwich artists were ready to integrate evidence of modernity into their imagery of the beach. Yet they made no contribution to the output of tourist views of Yarmouth. Cotman and Robert Ladbrooke both produced series of prints of the architecture of Norfolk, and Robert Dixon and James Stark published collections of picturesque views of the county.[140] Crome, Cotman, John Thirtle, Ladbrooke and others also produced a considerable number of oil and water-colour views and prints of Norwich. This probably indicates firstly that they regarded such ephemeral productions as beneath them, and secondly that, apart from the beach, Yarmouth itself, except for some isolated medieval structures, was too lacking in the picturesque to attract them.

It was probably the convenience of Yarmouth as a sketching site on the coast, together with their participation in middle-class leisure habits, which drew Norwich artists there. The more fashionable southern resorts were too far off to make a visit practicable when similar materials could be gathered so close at hand, and the only non-amateur representations of them shown at the Norwich Society exhibitions by local artists were Vincent's *Brighton Beach* in 1817 and David Hodgson's *View at Brighton* in 1820.[141] It seems reasonable to assume that the interest of the Norwich artists in beach scenes was sparked off by the success of Turner's *Sun Rising through Vapour* at the 1807 Academy and of Callcott's two coast scenes the year before. Crome's friend Robert Ladbrooke exhibited a *View of Yarmouth Jetty* and a sketch of the beach with the Norwich Society in 1806, and showed a *Mackerel Market on the Beach at Yarmouth* in 1810. Crome exhibited his first Yarmouth beach and jetty with the Norwich Society in 1807 together with a drawing of the subject, and exhibited six views of the beach thereafter. His son John Berney Crome began exhibiting views of it in 1809. Of later Norwich artists, George Vincent and the Stannard brothers, Joseph and Alfred, were those who produced the largest body of Yarmouth images.

The painting Ladbrooke exhibited in 1806 might be identified with the *Yarmouth Beach* now in Yarmouth Museum, but for the fact that this seems to represent the jetty constructed in 1808–9 to judge from its length and regularity (*Plate 37*). While this is a crudely executed variant on a well-known Dutch School pattern, it is an important prototype in so far as it juxtaposes the sphere of work, represented through the foreground fishmarket, with the sphere of leisure in the middle distance, represented through the bathing machines and the promenading figures on the starkly unnatural lines of the jetty. The *Mackerel Market* of 1810 can be more confidently identified with another picture in Yarmouth Museum, which has a composition representing more of the sea view, and the spectacle of fishing.[142] Both works must have contributed to establish the connection between fishmarket scenes and representations of Yarmouth beach, which Vincent was to develop in a sequence of later pictures.

The views of Yarmouth jetty which Crome exhibited in 1807 and 1809 must have represented the old jetty, and it is surely this structure which appears in the British Museum drawing (*Plate 38*). There are at least four oils of the jetty attributed to Crome which would have to be interpreted as early works (datable to *c.* 1805–8) because of their essentially picturesque colour range and rather formalized compositions. All these pictures are in poor condition, and are marginal to the category of naturalism. The best preserved, and most original of Crome's Yarmouth jetty paintings, and the only one I shall discuss here, is that illustrated in *Plate 39* (Norwich Castle Museum), which probably dates from around 1810–12. The jetty in all these paintings seems to be that which was swept away in 1805, for it has no hand-rails – however, it may be that Crome did represent the jetty built in 1808–9 in the later pictures, but omitted the rails in the interests of compositional unity.[143]

The Norwich painting clearly belongs to the naturalistic phase, and suggests a familiarity with both Callcott's *A Sea Coast*, and with Turner's seascapes, such as *Guardship at the Nore, Sheerness, &c.* (Clore Gallery, London). It also needs to be compared with Cotman's early oils such as *Sea View (Fishing Boats)* of around 1810 (Norwich Castle Museum). The fresh bright colours, the brilliant suggestions of light on the water and boats, and the innovative sketchy technique of representing water around the jetty and in the surf – all these qualities make it an exercise in the aesthetic of originality discussed in chapter 6, and link it with the experiments of Constable, Havell, Linnell, Turner, and others. Indeed, it is strikingly sketchy for such a small work (44.8 × 58.3cm), and Crome's pictures were occasionally criticized for their lack of finish in the Norwich newspapers.[144] It was partly this sketchy quality which gave the work the character of breadth, which Crome particularly stressed in a letter to James Stark of 1816 that contains the only significant aesthetic statement by him to have survived. In this Crome recommended that the sky should form part of 'one grand plan of light and shade' in the composition, and thus:

> Trifles in Nature must be overlooked that we may have our feelings raised by seeing the whole picture at a glance, not knowing how or why we are so charmed.[145]

Crome had thus well assimilated the view of the significance of breadth which had been articulated by Reynolds, Barry, and other academic theorists. That his practice manifested this quality for his contemporaries is clear from a number of comments in both the local and national press, which praised him for his 'peculiar talent of giving interest to local scenery by striking effects of sky and atmosphere'.[146] This comment was made in relation to a work exhibited in Norwich in 1818 with the title *Yarmouth Beach, from the Pier*, which I have tentatively identified with the picture illustrated in *Plate 40*. The bright daylight effects in this and *Yarmouth Jetty*, together with the bustling figures of the latter, again indicate the reconceptualization of the characteristics of breadth which accompanied the development of the naturalistic style.

Crome's *Yarmouth Jetty* is sufficiently close in its compositional conception to Callcott's *A Sea-Coast* to suggest that Crome was consciously responding to Callcott's example. But the differences between the two works are also extremely significant. Crome's picture represents a specific spot with clear signs of contemporaneity. Callcott's bit of beach is somewhere in England, but like his figures, it simply anglicizes a Dutch prototype. The figures in Callcott's foreground are either turned away from the spectator or seem absorbed in their haggling. Crome's nearest figures are significantly closer to the bottom edge of the canvas, and three of the figures in his boat look out of the picture in a way which implies an involvement with the spatial area on our side of the picture's frame. On the jetty itself, bourgeois and working figures clearly mix, for there are two female figures in full-length light coloured dresses, the nearest of whom seems to carry a parasol like the two figures in the British Museum's drawing (*Plate 38*). Every figure in Callcott's work seems oblivious to the sea, while Crome shows the presence of spectators enjoying the same spectacle as that represented in the painting. Silhouetted against the sky, the busy group on Crome's jetty makes contemporary social life the centre of the picture, in contrast to the formal arrangement of ships in the centre of Callcott's image. Crome's picture is about a third of the size of Callcott's, and this together with its sketchy surface, enhances the effect it produces of a piece of direct observation, whereas the latter appears a set-piece effort to dignify the lower levels of the landscape hierarchy. In sum, then, the formal properties of Crome's picture facilitate a reading of it as a direct representation of a modern seaside resort – although it should be noted that Crome chose not to represent the amenities near the jetty, and particularly not the bath house.

It has been a consistent emphasis of this chapter that artistic practices are determined more by inherited visual formulae and aesthetic discourses than they are by the individual experience of the artists, whether this is conceived as a social trajectory or as an isolated consciousness recording visual phenomena. However, the considerations on ideology in chapter 2 should also indicate that I believe discourses are being consistently measured against experience, and this can cause change and modification, both to an individual's sense of identity, and ultimately to discourses themselves. I do not see individuals as passive objects produced through ideologies, but as active agents.[147] On this basis it is at least worth considering how far Crome's particular class position and politics, together with his relations with his patrons, and the character of Yarmouth as a resort may help to explain the distinctive character of this view of the jetty. Crome was the son of a Norwich journeyman weaver who also kept an ale-house, and he thus came from the class group which was the first to develop a militant working-class politics, in a city notorious for its radicalism. His first employer, Dr Edward Rigby, was a substantial Norwich bourgeois who became mayor of the city in 1805. Rigby was an active Whig, who had visited France in 1789, and was a contributor to that remarkable radical publication *The Cabinet* (1795). In addition, he was a member of the Norwich Society of Artists from 1810–17, and a patron of the body from 1818 until his death in 1821. Other early patrons of Crome on the Whig side of Norwich politics included the Gurney family and the surgeon Philip Martineau.[148] Crome himself was a freemason, a member of a baptist church, and recorded himself as a liberal voter.[149] Dawson Turner's representation of Crome as a model of industry and virtue, who knew how to adapt to his proper role in the social order hardly stands up. R. N. Bacon, editor of the *Norwich Mercury*, described him as 'a wine bibber and improvident', and Turner's own wife referred to him as a 'great rascal' in a letter of 1815.[150] However, Turner was certainly one of the most important of Crome's patrons, and it should be noted that he too was a liberal in his political opinions.[151] Turner himself wrote of Crome's market:

> To attempt any enumeration of Crome's patrons were an endless task: it were in reality little less than to give a list of all those who knew him.[152]

He specifically singled out as the most notable the Jerninghams and the Gurneys, but as the Cliffords have noted, while Lady Jerningham lent three pictures to Crome's posthumous exhibition of 1821, the majority of Crome's patrons were considerably lower in the social scale.[153] Crome therefore moved primarily in a milieu of Norwich bourgeois and petty bourgeois, although he occasionally came into contact with landed society through his practice as a drawing master. He was primarily dependent on teaching for his living, and his paintings were generally small and cheap, and intended for the houses of local patrons rather than for big London exhibitions at which he showed a total of merely eighteen works. Those who lent pictures of Yarmouth to the posthumous exhibition included Francis Stone (architect and surveyor), Reverend E. Valpy (headmaster of Norwich Grammar School), Mrs de Rouillon (Norwich school teacher), Philip Barnes (builder), and Charles Turner (wine merchant).[154] It is very likely that all of these persons had a direct familiarity with the pleasures that Crome's picture referred to.

Thus my argument is as follows: Crome's *Yarmouth Jetty* represents the spectacle of contemporary leisure at the seaside resort in an intimate and direct way, which makes it seem closer to some French art of the 1860s and 1870s, than to most contemporary British representations of the coast. This willingness to insert the signs of leisure within compositions derived from Dutch models, but handled in an innovative style, is also demonstrated by the row of bathing machines in the middle distance in Crome's *Yarmouth Beach and Mill, Looking North* (Lady Crathorne). The factors which determined the production of such works included particularly the innovations in the theory of painting discussed in chapter 6, and the kind of direct sketching activities they promoted. (In this respect, it is worth noting that of all Crome's pictures, that in which the brushwork and colouring are most suggestive of *plein air* painting, the *Boulevard des Italiens* (Norwich Castle Museum), was said in the nineteenth century to have been begun on the spot. It is also Crome's most emphatically modern subject.)[155] However, Crome's interest in such a subject as Yarmouth jetty may be partly explained by his particular class position, his attitudes, and the attitudes of those whom he served. I am not suggesting that the picture be seen as either a simple manifestation of authorial consciousness or as a simple manifestation of the consciousness of its audience. Rather, Crome's class position and relations with his audience enabled him to produce a work, the formal properties of which permit it to be read as describing a kind of immediate engagement with contemporary social life, which has no real parallels in its unpretentious acceptance of the leisure usages of a particularly bourgeois resort. Other types of image which Crome produced of the same site indicate how vital was the naturalistic aesthetic to the image of the social constructed in this painting – such a work could not be validated by the kind of picturesque aesthetic which I surmise underlay Crome's paintings of the 1805–8 period.

The hypothesis that the scale and character of Crome's *Yarmouth Jetty* are directly related to its production for a local clientèle with a particularly intimate relationship with the site it represented is, I believe, supported by the character of George Vincent's views of it. Norwich Castle Museum has two oil paintings of fish auctions on Yarmouth beach by Vincent, one dated 1827 (*Plate 41*, 102.5 × 128.3cm) and the other 1828 (64 × 92.4cm).[156] The first of these includes the new jetty of 1808–9, the Nelson Column and three bathing machines. However, the main focus of attention in the image is the picturesque collection of objects in the foreground and the composition of boats, which may be compared with that in Crome's earlier *Yarmouth Jetty* in Norwich Museum (not illustrated here).[157] The busy scene of the fishmarket is relegated to the middle distance and the jetty is further off again. Figure activity in the foreground is confined to a simple genre incident of two men sharing a bottle, and the perspective recession of the picture from right to left does not offer a significant hierarchy of interest in the way that Constable's *Beach at Brighton* does. The modern is relegated to the distance, but it is hard to read any significance in to this beyond the fact that it is less picturesque than boats and fish auctions. The selling of fish occupies a more prominent place in the 1828 picture, in which the figure of the auctioneer is again centralized. With their detailed representations of boats and more complex perspectives, these pictures lack the immediacy of Crome's picture (*Plate 39*), and are essentially updated Dutch-type beach scenes with the genre element which tended to attract notice in London exhibitions. There is no record of Vincent exhibiting a view of Yarmouth after 1823, but he was living in London in straitened circumstances in 1827–8, and may have produced them for picture dealers.[158] It is possible that the 1827 picture is a repetition of the *Yarmouth Beach* Vincent exhibited in 1821 at the British Institution and Norwich Society – with a frame it would probably have been about the dimensions given in the British Institution catalogue.

These pictures are both less significant than the two major works Vincent exhibited in 1821 and 1823: A *Dutch Fair on Yarmouth Beach, held Annually in September* (Yarmouth Museum, 111.5 × 143.2cm, *Plate 42*), and A *View of Yarmouth Quay* (Norwich Castle Museum, 77.2 × 103cm, *Plate 43*). The first of these, which was shown at the British Institution in 1821, seems to have done much to confirm Vincent's reputation as a rising star in the landscape field, and was widely seen as one of his best pictures to date.

The Dutch Fair was held on the Sunday before 21 September when Dutch boats visited the port prior to the start of the fishing season. In his notes to Manship's *History of Great Yarmouth* (1854), C. J. Palmer printed an extensive account of the event from 1785, and said that it 'continued to be seen till the close of the eighteenth century', but that since the interruption of trade in the wars 'few of the Dutch Schuyts have entered the harbour'.[159] Palmer also described the booths, 'to which numbers of country people resorted, to purchase dried flounders and skate, pipes, ginger-bread, and domina-clumps', as going the 'whole length of the quay', whereas Vincent shows the fair taking place next to Wilkins' Nelson Column, set up in 1817–19 on a spot remote from the town. A report of the Column in the *Annals of the Fine Arts* in 1819 commented on the area around it:

> The features of the surrounding scenery are neither heroic, classical, nor picturesque, but of that tone – not to say vulgarly quotidian cast, that is but little calculated to awaken any very pleasurable associations in unison with the edifice itself.[160]

It is possible that by introducing the Dutch Fair, Vincent was able to give a picturesque interest to a picture of the Column, although he also relied on dramatic cloud patterns, and a rich interplay of light and shadow. In the picture the base of the Column is picked out by a shaft of sunlight, while the gilded figure of Britannia on top is silhouetted against a light patch of cloud. This emphatic presence would certainly have helped to anchor the picture topographically for a London audience, even if the placing of the Fair around the Column was a form of poetic licence. However, if this was the case the Norwich papers were strangely silent on the matter and indeed gave the picture surprisingly little attention. One informed contemporary observed in a letter that it presented 'every interesting feature of the place which it is possible to introduce in a general view'.[161]

In other respects, Vincent's painting seems to represent the view from south of the monument accurately (see map 3): on the far left are the distant buildings of Yarmouth itself, the large structure emerging from the right side of the monument's base is presumably the hospital, and the jetty is visible through the masts of the schuyts just right of centre. The picture thus brings together the picturesque and traditional with the modern – the modern being represented in this instance through the emblem of national greatness and maritime strength, the distant town, and the bathing machines picked out near the jetty. The conjunction of the victory monument and the commerce on the beach may well have been intended to imply that the Pax Britannica was a concomitant of peaceful trade. Further we cannot miss the presence of the modern visitor in the picture: the group in middle-class dress with a poodle near the most prominent of the schuyts are in bright clothes, and stand at the apex of a light filled foreground triangle, marked off by areas of shadow and darker colours. Beyond, in one of the brightest areas of middle distance, more middle-class figures swarm over the base of the monument. Thus townspeople and picturesque 'fisherfolk' mingle together in harmonious social interplay in an atmosphere of popular festival. This spectacle of busy figures needs to be seen in relation to the use of staffage in works such as Turner's *Dort or Dordrecht: The Dort Packet-boat from Rotterdam Becalmed* (Yale Center for British Art, exh. RA 1818) and *England: Richmond Hill, on the Prince Regent's Birthday* (Clore Gallery, exh. RA 1819).

The contemporary commentator I referred to earlier saw the picture at an early stage, and observed:

> It cannot fail to make an excellent Picture should he be successful in the figures for there must be something more than those which are introduced as the mere *austaffiring* of a Landscape

In the event, its success may be measured by the fact it received at least seven substantial comments in reviews, as well as a number of passing references.[162] A long notice in the *Sun* newspaper commented on the rich accumulation of detail:

> It would be impossible to enter into a minute description of the numerous particulars of which his picture is composed, and we shall, therefore in general terms say, that it will afford amusement to any one who will look into the different characters assembled on the beach – that bustle, gaiety, pervade the scene, that the Schuyts and Boats are correctly represented.

Like a number of other reviews, the *Sun* praised Vincent for moving away from the 'careless style' of his earlier works, but also found room for improvement. Robert Hunt, in the *Examiner*, particularly dwelt on what he described as the 'Venetian-like' use of colour:

> The dresses of a concourse of persons afforded him ample scope to present this concord of sweet colours, and frigid indeed must be that fancy that does not reflect it strongly and with delight. This pomp of colour is rendered doubly rich by the contrasted blue sky, while it is harmonized to it by the same blue in the figures and yellow in the clouds. The practice is Titianesque and triumphantly successful.

However, Hunt seems to have missed the larger significance which could be read into the scene, for he expressed the hope that Vincent would in future 'turn his attention to something more heartfelt than mere colour'. Although the *Monthly Magazine* found the Nelson Column 'a fine feature in the picture', and praised the 'truth and identity of character' of the effect, the only review which referred to the connotations of the subject, was that in the *Literary Chronicle* which found that the painting presented:

> a lively and amusing scene, which happily combines with it a national feeling, by the introduction of an object which never fails to recall pleasurable and proud recollections: we allude to the Nelson Pillar (sic), introduced in this picture.

The success of *A Dutch Fair on Yarmouth Beach* demonstrates how well Vincent had gauged his use of colour, scale, and figures to the requirements of the London exhibition audience. Crome's little pictures never made such a splash, and it is probable that the increased attention his two works at the British Institution of 1821 received was partly a spin-off from the success of Stark and Vincent. Of these, the *Sun* commented:

> this artist's style is calculated to produce very powerful effects on a larger scale than we have yet seen him attempt.[163]

The limitations of the exhibition reviews as a source are indicated by the fact that I have not been able to find a single notice of Vincent's *View of Yarmouth Quay*, shown at the Academy in 1823. This may be partly because reviews of the Academy exhibitions gave more attention to history pictures, portraits, and genre than did those of the British Institution's, presumably because there were more pictures of these types within them. Landscapes were more prominent at the British Institution, and in that context Vincent was a bigger fish than at the Academy. Since he was neither an academician nor an associate, and had not even been a student there, it is quite likely that his work was badly hung. In reviews of the Academy show of 1823 it was Turner's *Bay of Baiae* together with works by Collins and Constable which attracted most attention among the landscapes. In any case, *A View of Yarmouth Quay* is smaller and was less well-calculated to attract attention than *A Dutch Fair* had been.

Apart from the beach and jetty, the quay was Yarmouth's main promenade – although the market place and denes were also recommended to visitors. Rymer had commented on the 'agreeable and various' prospect from the quay, which he described as the 'chief seat of commercial business', and in his usual satirical tone he observed that:

> The gay world also mingle here with the crowd, in order to take an airing; to exercise the limbs; to display external charms; to attract, persuade, and captivate by various ways and motions.

Beatniffe described it as 'almost the only agreeable walk' in Yarmouth itself, and three years after Vincent's painting was exhibited, Druery's guide claimed that it was the 'principal object of attraction to visitors'. Preston commented in 1819 that its charm as a promenade had been much enhanced by the 'removal of the sand-pits, sheds, mastmakers', works, posts, &c. which formerly encumbered it – which suggests that the development of Yarmouth as a resort necessitated some cleaning up of its utilitarian features. Virtually every guide claimed that the quay was the second finest in Europe, inferior only to that of Seville, and Preston asserted it was 'deservedly the admiration of all strangers'. The quay was not only the commercial heart of the town, but also the centre of fashionable amusement, for the assembly rooms, library, and other facilities were mainly situated there. It was newly paved, and had some of the new mansions of the most important Yarmouth families.[164] At this point, however, it is necessary to distinguish between the representations of the guide-books and less interested views. In 1814, the *Repository of Arts* published an article on Yarmouth Quay, which specifically complained of the tendencies of Tours and Guides to 'mislead our opinion'. While agreeing that the site was 'susceptible to embellishment' the author found that Yarmouth Quay had 'not the least pretensions to beauty'. The houses were 'mere narrow strips' which formed a 'patchwork' with no 'picturesque variety', and 'it must indeed be confessed that architectural taste is at the very lowest ebb at Yarmouth'. The review of Wilkins' Nelson Column, to which I referred earlier, also commented scathingly on the pride of the inhabitants in the quay, and on the absence of 'elegant buildings'.[165]

In taking the quay as a subject, Vincent was following a precedent set by Crome and J. B. Crome, who had exhibited views of it with the Norwich Society in 1809 and 1812, 1813, 1816, and 1817 respectively. As far as I know, none of these have survived. Vincent's picture also needs to be seen in relation to the bustling urban scene of Crome's *Boulevard des Italiens*, which had been exhibited in Norwich in 1815. Scenes of ports were an important theme in landscape painting of the period, and the success of Callcott's *Entrance to the Pool of London* (Trustees of the Bowood Settlement, RA 1816) and *Rotterdam* (Private Collection, RA 1819) inspired imitation. However, the format of these is based on a type of Cuyp river scene, whereas Vincent's picture owes more to the townscapes of van der Heyden and quay scenes such as Ruisdael's *Quay at Rotterdam* (Frick Collection, New York). Vincent himself had achieved some favourable critical responses for his *View of Greenwich from Blackwall*, exhibited at the British Institution in 1820, and sold to James Wadmore; and his *London, from the Surrey Side of Waterloo-Bridge* exhibited with the Society of Painters in Oil and Water-Colours in the same year, and sold to Sir John Leicester for £62.[166] Mixing together townscape and port scene, Vincent's *Yarmouth Quay* is an extremely capable work, combining complex patterns of recession, an effective arrangement of cloud masses to balance the composition, a rich variety of light and dark, and figures picked out in bright colours to enliven the effect. (However, it should be noted that the colour range of the picture is less light and the handling of the tree foliage is less loose and suggestive than that of Crome's *Boulevard des Italiens*.) To judge from this picture, Vincent seems to have agreed with the view that there was little of the picturesque in the architecture of Yarmouth Quay, which only appears as a few glimpses of buildings seen through the trees. The main interest of the picture lies in the foreground groups of labour and the busy scene on the left, and thus it focusses on the traditional functions of the quay. The middle class are in the picture, but only as a receding line of promenading figures picked out in lighter colour among the trees, and barely visible in a black and white reproduction. There is also a surprising feature in the picture in that there are two beggars (contrary to the claims of the guide-book!): one seated on a barrel end, holding a cup, under the tree second from the right edge, and another seated on the pavement next to a standing male figure half hidden by the tree, who, to judge by his cocked hat, may represent some kind of constable. I can think of no obvious explanation for this inclusion, since while such figures had formed an element of staffage in the eighteenth century, they were not part of naturalistic landscape, and it is hard to read them except as a touch of ironic humour – of a piece with the sleeping dog in the centre of the foreground of this scene of industry. Whatever the significance of this anomaly, Vincent had chosen to represent precisely that part of the quay recommended by the guides as a promenade to its predominantly middle-class visitors. It is hard to imagine the persons of fashion who determined the character of Brighton and other upmarket resorts finding this spectacle of commercial activity quite so worthy of attention.

This same concentration on the utilitarian, day-to-day features of the town is seen in Vincent's remarkable *View of Yarmouth* (Private Collection, 111.8 × 174.2cm, *Plate 44*, which shows the town as seen from Gorlestone, near the river's mouth.[167] This is a large work, and it is surprising that there is no record of it having been exhibited. To judge from its technique and scale it dates from the early to mid 1820s, when Vincent produced his most ambitious and carefully executed paintings. Beyond the conventional picturesque of the foreground bank with its donkey and weeds, lies a patch of waste along the river's edge, on which are dotted various workshops. Men are shown working on boats on the right, and there is what appears to be carefully observed detail in the masts and rigging of moored vessels. It seems probable that the smoking chimney among the masts belongs to a steamer, although it might be part of a workshop. On the cliff on the left stand some prosaic and unpicturesque houses, behind which rises a modern water-tower. Various ships are picked out on the patch of light sea in the right distance, while in the centre the dark shapes of Yarmouth's churches and mills, and the Nelson Column are made out against the sky. This is a picture which precisely contradicts the standard aesthetic of the beach scene purveyed by Collins, Cristall, Prout, and others. The contrast between the conventional picturesque of the bank and the unglamorous vista beyond is striking, and again almost ironic. Even the least pretentious kind of topographical print would hardly tackle a subject so lacking in features of associative significance. Only the magnificent cloud effects and dancing patterns of light and dark redeem the image in terms of landscape aesthetics of the period.

Taken together, Vincent's *Dutch Fair on Yarmouth Beath, Yarmouth Quay*, and *View of Yarmouth* represent an attempt to render the modern picturesque, while yet remaining authentic to the character of a bustling modern port, which bore only lightly the marks of its development as a resort. In this respect these pictures stand comparison with Chalon's *View of Hastings* and Constable's *Beach at Brighton*, although only the *View of Yarmouth* suggests some of the tensions of the latter.

(vii) Conclusions

It will be evident from what I have said, and from the illustrations which accompany this chapter, that a wide variety of patterns were employed to represent seaside resorts. Many views of resorts were small unpretentious beach scenes, derived from well-known Dutch prototypes. However, even within the format of small-scale works there were attempts to give 'importance' to the subject by breadth, or by this quality plus sentimental or classical figure types. In works such as Turner's *St Mawes* and *Brighton from the Sea* Claudean references served a similar function. Large-scale works closer to the topographical tradition, such as Vincent's *Dutch Fair on Yarmouth Beach* or Constable's *Beach at Brighton* had to rely primarily on 'breadth' and use of colour to dignify the subject. All these strategies related primarily to the ambitions of painters within the artistic field; although success in this field also promised a social pay-off. Given the continuing conservatism of academic discourse, the most obvious route to a more 'dignified' style of representation was to do like Collins and Cristall: develop sentimentalized or ennobilized figures and play down references to place. The aesthetic of originality and naturalism which lay behind some works by Chalon, Constable, Crome, Turner, and Vincent relied on a different kind of discursive construction. It depended on a concept of truth to particulars with selection, it engaged with the real features of places and thus fed off topographical imagery, and possibly the natural sciences. It was because of this engagement with the particulars of places, that social position had a more direct effect on representation. Given the balance of class forces in this period, and the contradictory and shifting places occupied by artists in the social structure; and given the complex permutations of discourse around the processes of modernization and commercialization which the resorts were understood to represent, it was inevitable that approaches to representation were diverse. The diversity of pictorial types was also partly the product of the complex interaction of aesthetic with socio-political discourses. Within landscape painting, the responses to modernization were represented either by deliberate occlusion of the modern as in Collins and Cristall, or by rendering the modern picturesque and implicitly celebrating it as in the works by Vincent and Turner singled out earlier. Perhaps such images partly signified the repression of anxieties about the modernization of the coastal towns, so evident in some texts of the period. However, the only image which seems to give form to such feelings is Constable's *Beach at Brighton, the Chain Pier in the Distance*.

9 The contradictions of progress: imagery of rivers

(i) The symbolism of rivers

River scenery provided one of the major themes in the vastly increased output of landscapes of British scenes in the early nineteenth century. Turner's series of Thames views and Constable's views of the Stour are well known, but these need to be seen as part of a larger phenomenon, and the widespread attraction of this type of subject matter demands a more historical or sociological type of explanation than well-rehearsed references to personal circumstances, such as Turner's place of residence being near the Thames between 1804–5 and 1826, or Constable's upbringing on the banks of the Stour ('They made me a painter' etc.)[1] If rivers were an important focus for representation it was because, like seaside resorts, they had an ideological resonance which made them significant as a landscape subject. I want to suggest that two types of text have a particular explanatory value in relation to this: firstly, the symbolism of rivers, and particularly of the Thames, in English nature poetry, within which they were a major motiv; and secondly, the topographical genre of the history of rivers, which offered a form of narrative text on the significance of individual rivers, and elaborated a complex chain of associations around them. I shall examine the ideology which such texts offered in general terms, and define the visual modes of river topography as the basis for an analysis of some of the major river paintings of the period.

Before doing this, however, I want to consider briefly the play of social interests around rivers. If the social and physical characteristics of the developing seaside resorts made them a problematic subject for representation, this was not true of rivers – they did not represent the conjunctions of the modern and traditional, of work and leisure, of nature and fashion, of simple virtue and luxury with the same stark contrasts. Tradition might be symbolized by pastoral activities along the banks, and the modern by the presence of barges or figures in genteel dress at leisure, but there was little juxtaposition of the hard forms of contemporary urban development with nature in its pastoral state except at some industrial locations which were little represented. The vital role of rivers and canals in the development of the British economy and Britain's power as a nation state was well understood and widely celebrated. Thus the drawing master and topographer John Hassell observed in his *Tour of the Grand Junction* (1819) that:

> Inland navigation, to a manufacturing country, is the very heart's blood and soul of commerce, nor can we easily estimate the utility and importance of this mode of conveyance, in obviating the expense and tediousness of land carriage, or the more protracted delays invariably attendant on opposite winds and tides.[2]

Investment tended to derive from local sources, and noblemen such as the Duke of Bridgewater and the Earl of Egremont shared interests with more familiar types of capitalist in the 'patriotic' and profitable development of the canal and river system. While the development of rivers and canals had been taking place since the second half of the sixteenth century, its pace had hotted up in the years after 1750 to meet the needs of industrial growth and the expanding urban population. By this time, river improvements could no longer meet the economic requirements of some regions, and the main investment was in canals, leading to the so-called Canal Mania in the 1800–20 period.[3] Further, the development of navigation was intrinsically connected with the improved agriculture, as well as with the carriage of coal to manufacturing districts. The availability of coal in rural areas brought to an end the practice of burning valuable dung in open field regions, and barges carried fertilizer and livestock. They also carried timber for fencing which directly facilitated the process of enclosure. The barges in Constable's Stour landscapes thus have an important connection with the improved agriculture of the scenery: they are a sign of progress.[4]

Rivers stood as symbols of the nation's power, wealth and political health in a way that seaside resorts did not, and this was primarily because of their importance in eighteenth-century British poetry. Native literary achievements had been advanced as an appropriate 'ornament' to the progress of the nation's culture long before British painting. The poetry of Thomson, particularly *Liberty* (1735) and *The Seasons* (1726–46), had an enormous popularity in the late eighteenth and early nineteenth centuries, and this offered a construction of the national which depended heavily on landscape imagery.[5] Thomson consistently uses the geography of regions as metaphors of the societies which inhabit them. Thus, in *Liberty*, when the poem defines the extent of the Roman Empire, it is partly in terms of a sequence of rivers – the Tigris, Euphrates, Rhine, Danube, Volga, and Nile (Part III, lines 226–56). The vocabulary of the passage signifies the power of these rivers, and their power reflects on that of Rome, which has 'quell'd' tyrants and freed nations in the regions through which they flow. When the poem describes the 'barbarous' peoples which broke up the Empire, it likens them to their habitat:

> Hard like their soil, and like their climate fierce.

They come from:

A sullen land of lakes, and fens immense,
Of rocks, resounding torrents, gloomy heaths,
And cruel deserts black with sounding pine;
Where nature frowns
(Part III, lines 516–19)

Considering the use of this kind of crude equation between the character of peoples and the regions they inhabit, it was inevitable that English scenery would be described as having particularly fortunate qualities. This is well exemplified in the opening passage of Book V, 'The Prospect', where after acknowledging the assets of France, Tuscany, Arabia, and Peru in a cursory way, Thomson launches into a hymn of praise Britain, in the course of which there is an inevitable reference to rivers:

Where swarm the finny race ? Thee, chief, O Thames !
On whose each tide, glad with returning sails,
Flows in the mingled harvest of mankind ?
(Part V, lines 57–9)

That the Thames should stand as the 'chief' of British rivers was entirely logical, and its status as such was well established in poetry by the time Thomson produced *Liberty*.[6]

The Thames had been celebrated by a whole succession of poets since Denham in the seventeenth century. Perhaps most importantly, Pope had used the valley of the Thames as a setting in his *Pastorals*, specifically referring to 'Windsor's blissful Plains', while in *Windsor Forest* (published 1713), the Thames is already associated with a Pax Britannica:

Hail Sacred Peace ! hail long-expected Days
That Thames's Glory to the Stars shall raise ![7]

The rivers of other nations are compared unfavourably with the Thames, and the poem as a whole celebrates British power and influence and what Pope conceives of as British liberty. Pope was particularly associated with the Thames through his residence at Twickenham, and his house there was extensively represented in topographical prints. However, more important for artists was Thomson, who had lived at Richmond, and was buried in the church there.[8] In well-known lines in 'Summer' in *The Seasons*, Thomson invites the reader to view Nature from 'Thy hill, delightful Shene', that is from Richmond Hill. He then describes some of the delights of 'the matchless Vale of Thames', with particular reference to the estates of nobility and their 'worthy' and 'polish'd' proprietors. This 'Vale of bliss !' displays the 'wonders of toil', and the 'goodly prospect' of the countryside, and its towns and 'gilded Streams' leads him to the effusion:

Happy Britannia ! where the Queen of Arts,
Inspiring vigour, Liberty abroad
Walks, unconfined, even to they farthest cots,
And scatters plenty with unsparing hand.
(lines 142–5)

The continuing currency of such river symbolism is demonstrated by the appearance in 1810 of a major celebration of the national river in the form of Thomas Love Peacock's poem *The Genius of the Thames*. This follows the precedent of Pope and Thomson in listing the rivers of other nations, but then saying that they do not compare with those of Britain because:

tyrants foul, and trembling slaves,
Pollute their shores, and curse their waves

By contrast, on the banks of the Thames:

peace with freedom, hand in hand,
Walks forth along the sparkling strand;
And cheerful toil and glowing health,
Proclaim a patriot nation's wealth.[9]

Peacock explicitly celebrates the peace of the Thames valley in contrast with the 'wasted banks' of the Danube, and his poem suggests that the vast proliferation of nationalistic discourse during the Anglo-French Wars enhanced the resonance of river images as emblems of national and imperial identity. This may help to explain why Turner produced a major sequence of oil paintings representing the scenery of the Thames valley over the years 1805–12. At least, the artist's continuing concern with poetry and his frequent use of poetic quotations to suggest the particular frame of reference he intended works to evoke, support this conclusion.[10]

(ii) Histories, topographies, and prints

Topographical descriptions of rivers frequently referred to any poetry relating to them, and there was clearly an interplay between these two discourses, the general message of which was broadly similar. In his *General Account of all the Rivers of Note in Great Britain* of 1801, the gentleman traveller and tour writer Henry Skrine observed that:

> the banks of rivers and the heights which command them almost exclusively monopolise the beauty, and compose the characteristic features of every country; the nature of the stream and its surrounding objects deciding the qualities of romantic scenery, rich plains and pastures, abundant manufactures, and consequent population.

Not only were the mansions of the nobility, castles, abbeys, and cities found among them, but their scenery was particularly appealing to the eye:

> The spire of the rustic village no where looks so pleasing, nor have woods ever so strong an effect, as on the banks of rivers; the progress also of navigation, and the increase of a large stream to an estuary, present great variety of Scenery, and the ports which generally grace its exit to the sea, with their attendant shipping form interesting subjects.[11]

By the time this statement was published, the history of rivers was not a new concept. The 1790s had seen a number of publications based around this idea by the author and etcher Samuel Ireland, including volumes of *Picturesque Views* of the Thames (1792), Medway (1793), Avon (1795), and Wye (1797). A further publication based on Ireland's views of the Severn, with a text by Thomas Harrall, appeared in 1822–4. Ireland wrote his own texts for all except the Severn views, and these combined commentary on the qualities of the scenery with rather shallow historical notices. The illustrations tend to fall into a pattern of bridges, ancient monuments, and country houses, and take the form of crude coloured aquatints, with the exception of the Severn series which are lithographs. In the Preface to his Avon views, Ireland disavowed the theory of the picturesque, which he described as mere 'elegant essays', and he claimed to give only the 'delineation of truth' in his drawings. None the less, Ireland used the term 'picturesque' in his titles, and also in his text when he wished to recommend scenery as being exceptionally pleasing.[12]

The concept of a series of publications on English rivers seems also to have underlain Boydell's *History of the River Thames* (1794–6), two sumptuous volumes of tinted aquatints etched by J. C. Stadler after drawings by Farington, with a text by William Combe. The title page of this, with its dedication to George III, describes it as *An History of the Principal Rivers of Great Britain*, which suggests that other volumes were originally intended.[13] The sequence of views incorporates a number of purely picturesque objects from the upper reaches, such as *Ewen Mill* and *Langley Ware* (*Plate 45*), but thereafter the views are predominantly panoramic vistas derived from the Dutch topographical tradition of Siberchts and others, with occasional Claudean features. In a number of instances, Farington represented well-known views as seen from the parks of major houses, such as the woods and river at Cliveden viewed from one of the walks, with two gentlemen in the foreground (*Plate 46*), or the Walton bridges viewed from the grounds of the Duke of York's estate at Oatlands (*Plate 47*). This visual emphasis on the estates of the gentry and on the commanding prospect, is matched by Combe's text, which abounds with descriptions of estates and details of the families associated with them. The lower stretches of the river in the city of London are represented largely within the format of Canaletto type compositions. Although many of the river scenes contain representations of barges, there are few images of labour, partly because Farington concentrates on commanding views, in which figures are generally reduced and distanced. In his Preface, Combe makes the commonplace observation that while the scenery of the Thames valley had the beautiful in profusion, it was lacking in the sublime. By keeping well away from the banks for most of his views, Farington also avoided what was generally understood to constitute the picturesque.

In contrast to these substantial histories, there also appeared in the 1790s a set of picturesque views, unaccompanied by any text, which took a specific river as its theme. Over the years 1797–1802, Francis Jukes published a series of sixteen folio size aquatints after drawings by Edward Dayes, which are known as *Jukes's Views on the River Wye*. The series includes views of towns, monuments, bridges, and the river in the landscape, and has strong effects of light, shade, and atmosphere. Although Dayes included a number of classic picturesque objects such as Llanthony Abbey, Tintern Abbey, and Chepstow Castle, it is striking that he was also prepared to bring together the modern and the picturesque as in the stark utilitarian lines of the bridges in his *View of Monmouth* and *View of Chepstow Bridge*. In one of the most overtly picturesque of the plates, the *View of the Doward Rocks* (*Plate 48*), the dramatic cliffs and mass of mottled foliage, are fronted by a scene of three youths pulling a barge, and the plate is dedicated to the 'Proprietors and Owners of the River Wye Navigation'.[14]

These two types of publication, the histories and the picturesque views, continued to be produced in the early nineteenth century, but the range of types of print widened, and the functions and significance of these types varied. The most strikingly original and ambitious publication of this period is John George Wood's *The Principal Rivers of Wales Illustrated* (1813), a series of one hundred and fifty-five soft ground etchings, tinted in two tones of yellow and grey wash, accompanied by two hundred and eighty-four pages of text by the artist. The views can be roughly categorized into the following types: sources of rivers – usually solitary and desolate scenes, picturesque views of the course of rivers, usually taken from near or on the banks (*Plate 49*), bridges, mountains, antiquities, townscape vistas, and industrial scenes (*Plate 50*). The range of the series is impressive, and it moves between views which have no significant topographical features and depend on picturesque effect to give them their value, and direct and detailed delineations of iron works, copper works, and aquaducts. In the townscapes, Wood juxtaposed modern amenities with the gothic, and even included factory chimneys in his view of Chester. Despite a short-lived fashion for soft-ground experiments among landscape painters in the first two decades, the status of soft-ground was not high. It was seen primarily as an easy form of etching for amateurs, and was little used for topographical work.[15] Thus Wood's use of the medium is comparatively unusual, and his plates hover between topography and picturesque drawings.

I have already argued in chapter 8 that different print media tended to be used for different functions, and the print imagery of rivers confirms this. Line engraving tended to be used for picturesque topography, and aquatint and lithography (sometimes coloured) for views more concerned with the modern and with fashionable life. Thus one of the most uniformly picturesque sequences of river views is *The Thames: or Graphic Illustrations of Seats, Villas, Public Buildings, and Picturesque Scenery, on the Banks of that Noble River* (1811), engraved by W. B. Cooke after drawings by Samuel Owen, and published by the former. A second version of this, *Views on the Thames*, was published in 1822 with the same text and some additional plates. In the 1811 series the plates are primarily etched and there is relatively little use of the burin, so that they have a character close to artists' etchings. The introduction describes the aim of the publication as: 'to display a succession of picturesque scenery on the banks of the Thames', and although like Combe's *History of the River Thames* it gives considerable attention to the families and events associated with the 'seats' and 'Villas' along the river, they feature only in a small way in the engravings. In country house views, the house itself is frequently a small and inconspicuous feature, as in that of Oatlands (*Plate 51*), where a barge fills the foreground and the house is distanced. The series as a whole concentrates on locks (*Plate 52*), weirs, bridges, old houses, and country churches. Towns tend to be seen over water meadows from a distance, as in *Oxford from Ifley*, and there is a constant presence of barges, bargees, and fishermen. In contrast to Farington's approach, Owen's viewpoint is taken from down on the river banks, among the picturesque details of the scenery, and this is matched by the rich textures of Cooke's plates. When it comes to representing the lower reaches of the river, Owen provides some convincingly modern images of the capital, but many of them view it from among a mass of boats reminiscent of the composition of a Dutch sea-piece or river scene (*Plate 53*).

By contrast, the *Picturesque Tour of the River Thames*, a volume of coloured aquatints after drawings by Westall and Owen, which Ackermann published in 1828, has very little of the picturesque in it. While acknowledging debts to Combe's history, the text to this boasted that the illustrations:

> will furnish striking evidence of the extraordinary improvements made during the last thirty years in the getting-up, as it is called, of this kind of graphic embellishments.[16]

In fact, the effect of the plates is flashy and slick, and the technique is repetitive and finicky. The lack of any striking picturesque features is consistent with the emphasis of the views on the modern and fashionable, and the pervasive presence of bourgeois figures picked out in bright colours (*Plate 54*). The series features such modern amenities as the Suspension Bridge at Hammersmith, Southwark Bridge, and Waterloo Bridge; and in three of the plates showing the lower reaches of the river there are representations of steam boats. It is thus comparable in approach with some of the contemporary aquatint views of Brighton.

The status of aquatint in the early nineteenth century varied according to its character and function. Landseer represented it as an essentially 'mechanical process', and resented its status as a form of engraving.[17] Even T. H. Fielding, a practitioner in the medium, acknowledged the superiority of line engraving and lamented its degradation to the 'mere production of coloured prints'. Yet in a manual of 1841, he stressed the delicacy of aquatint, and claimed that it was 'the only style of engraving which can faithfully render the touches of the artist's brush'.[18] The aesthetic potential of aquatint in this respect, is illustrated by F. C. Lewis's series of thirty-five plates of *Picturesque Scenery on the River Dart, Devon* (1821). These were intended to be 'as nearly as possible Facsimiles of the Drawings', and thus 'to form A Set of Studies for the Learners of Landscape Drawing' – an aim which sits uncomfortably with their proclaimed topographical function. Although a note in the advertisement suggested that the work might 'contribute to illustrate the History of Devon by the Revd Danl. Lysons', it consisted primarily of sepia-toned views of river valleys and bridges, with little topographical interest. The technique suggests the effects of sketches rather than of finished drawings, and the publication is a hybrid of the artist's drawing book and the set of picturesque views.[19] Lewis followed up *Scenery on the River Dart* with a series of tinted etchings of the Tamar and the Tavy (1823), which are not germane to my purpose here except in so far as they illustrate the continuing hold of the river theme as an organizing principle, and its continuing marketability.[20]

From the point of view of the relationship between the imagery of rivers in prints and in paintings, the most important publication of this period is a series which is broadly similar in conception to *Jukes's Views on the River Wye*, that is Robert and Daniell Havell's twelve folio size coloured aquatints, *A Series of Picturesque Views of the River Thames, from the Drawings of Wm. Havell*, dedicated to the Commissioners of the Thames Navigation, and published initially in 1811–12, with a second edition in 1818. Stylistically these clearly reflect the transition from the drawing style of Dayes to the naturalistic water-colour mode of the early nineteenth century, and they are notable for their light colours and blond atmospheric effects. By 1810–11 when he made the drawings on which the plates were based, Havell had been producing views of the Thames valley since 1805 or possibly earlier.[21] In comparison with Dayes' views of the Wye, Havell's Thames scenes are notable for their persistent representation of labour, a characteristic which seems only consistent with their dedicatees. Thus, in *Wallingford Castle, taken in 1810 while the Bridge was Repairing* (*Plate* 55) the foreground scene of barges and workmen rebuilding a damaged pier receives most attention, while the castle of the title is an insignificant detail poking up behind some trees in the distance. Barges are also a prominent feature in *An Island on the Thames near Park Place, Oxfordshire* (*Plate* 56) and *Cliefden Spring and Woods, near Maidenhead* (*Plate* 57), in neither of which are the nearby country houses at all visible, so that the overall effect is one of the river as a commercial waterway. A barge is again prominent in the nearer part of the landscape of *Windsor Castle* (*Plate* 58), and the castle itself is shown in an unflattering way rising above houses with smoking chimneys. The Thames valley is thus represented as a busy workaday world, although there are pastoral touches, as in the

View of the Thames at Streatley, a panoramic view with a field of sheep and a recumbent shepherd, or still more overtly in the Gaspardesque composition of *Caversham Bridge near Reading*, where a shepherd and flock occupy a scrubby patch of foreground. Havell provided no images of antiquities or country houses, and his bright sunlit scenes of the river's prosaic activities are strikingly *unpicturesque*. It is this which makes them such a significant contribution to the currency of images in the 1810–20 period.

(iii) Turner's Thames Series

At the time Constable began his long preoccupation with views of the Stour valley around 1810, Turner was widely regarded as the most talented and innovative landscape painter around. One of my theses here is that the series of views of the Thames he had exhibited over the years 1805–12 are likely to have represented a major example, both thematically and formally, for those who saw their project as to produce a distinctively British type of landscape painting. The precise range of pictures which Turner exhibited in these years is impossible to ascertain, since most of the Thames pictures were shown at his own gallery at 64, Harley Street (opened in 1804), and the catalogues of this are only extant from 1809 and 1810, although some further information can be gleaned from exhibition reviews.[22] On this basis, the series may be described as follows.

It has been suggested by A. J. Finberg, and more recently by Martin Butlin and Evelyn Joll, that the two paintings of *Walton Bridges* (Loyd Collection, and National Gallery of Victoria, Melbourne), *The Thames near Windsor* (Petworth House), *Clieveden on Thames* (Clore Gallery), *The Mouth of the Thames* (destroyed), and *Sheerness and the Isle of Sheppey, with the Junction of the Thames and Medway from the Nore* (National Gallery, Washington DC) were probably exhibited over the years 1806–7. However, although we know he did show Thames views before 1808 there can be no real certainty about which ones they were. Landseer's detailed account of the Gallery in the *Review of Publications of Art* in that year makes it possible to identify the works then on show as the *Union of the Thames and Isis* (Clore Gallery), *The Thames at Eton* (Petworth House), *Pope's Villa at Twickenham* (Sudeley Castle), *Richmond Hill and Bridge* (Clore Gallery), *Purfleet and the Essex Shore* (Private Collection), *The Confluence of the Thames and the Medway* (Petworth House), and *Sheerness as seen from the Nore* (Loyd Collection).

Among the eighteen works listed in the catalogue for Turner's exhibition of 1809, the following are relevant: *Thomson's Aeolian Harp* (City Art Gallery, Manchester), *Near the Thames' Lock, Windsor* (Petworth House), *Ploughing up Turnips near Slough* (Clore Gallery), *Harvest Dinner, Kingston Bank* (Clore Gallery), *London* (Clore Gallery), *Shoeburyness Fishermen Hailing a Whitstable Hoy* (National Gallery of Canada, Ottawa), and *Guardship at the Great Nore, Sheerness, &c.* (Private

Collection), together with two works shown in 1808. New works exhibited in the following year included *Grand Junction Canal at Southall Mill* (Private Collection), *Dorchester Mead, Oxfordshire* (Clore Gallery), and the *View of the High-street, Oxford* (Loyd Collection) – although this latter did not represent the river, views of Oxford were a standard feature of Thames topographies. Three works which had been shown the year before were again on view.

There is no evidence as to whether Turner exhibited any new works at his gallery in 1811, and of the six known to have been on show at Harley Street in 1812, none related to the Thames.[23] Finberg's suggestion that *Windsor Castle from the Thames* (Petworth House) and the *Thames at Weybridge* (Petworth House) were among new works shown in 1813 is purely conjectural, and Butlin and Joll have redated these pictures to *c.* 1805 and *c.* 1807–10 respectively, which raises the possibility that they were exhibited in the years 1805–7. After the exhibition of *Frosty Morning* at the Academy in 1813, Turner abandoned the production of rustic landscapes conceived within Dutch School formats. However, the summation of his involvement with the Thames valley can be regarded as *England: Richmond Hill, on the Prince Regent's Birthday* (Clore Gallery), the massive canvas exhibited at the Academy in 1819.

Despite some uncertainties, it is clear that Turner exhibited at least seventeen paintings of the Thames valley in 1808–10, and made it the subject of eight more finished oils from around that time. This is entirely consistent with his view as recorded in a publication of 1809: 'that a landscape painter may find sufficient scope for his pencil by studying the scenery on the banks of the Thames'.[24] That Turner's main output of Thames pictures was in the years 1806–10, accords both with his campaigns of sketching on the Thames, as recorded in Sketchbooks XC, XCIII, XCIV, XCV, XCVI, and XCVII in Finberg's catalogue (dated 1804–7), and with the main sequence of Thames oil studies, which date from 1806–7 in Butlin and Joll's estimation, although John Gage has dated some as late as 1811.[25] Of course, it needs to be noted that the Thames views were only one element in the display at his gallery, but that they were recognizable as a major aspect of his output, unified by their particular theme, is clear from Landseer's comment that:

> The greater number of the pictures at present exhibited are views on the Thames, whose course Mr Turner has now studiously followed, with the eye and hand at once of a painter and a poet, almost from its source to where it mingles its waters with those of the German Ocean. 'f.n.' Including the pictures of Thames scenery which Mr Turner has formerly exhibited.[26]

As I have shown, in the eighteenth-century poetry Turner so admired rivers stood as emblems of the character of regions, and the Thames stood pre-eminently as a symbol of the pastoral prosperity and commercial wealth of Britain. In the topographies, rivers served as threads, along which all that was regarded as most attractive, interesting, and characteristic of a region was strung. In what follows, I shall argue that both kinds of discourse have a direct relevance to some of the pictures in Turner's series, and to the conception of the whole.

The earliest of Turner's Thames paintings is likely to have been the Petworth *Windsor Castle from the Thames* of *c.* 1805 (*Plate 59*). The classical structure of this work is matched by the serene atmospheric effect, the glow of the sun on the trees and water, and the statuesque group of men and women with sheep in the foreground. The bridge and sheep on the islet in the middle distance are further references to the Italianate landscape tradition, but Turner also includes barges to the right and left, which indicate the bustling commercial activity of the river, and refer the viewer to types of Dutch river scene. These barges, together with the rotting stumps and eel pots in the left foreground anticipate characteristic features of Constable's river views.

In 'Summer', Thomson refers to the 'glorious view', 'calmly magnificent', where:

> Majestic Windsor lifts his princely brow,

and the area around Windsor was endlessly celebrated in the topographies. A text of 1792 described the castle as standing on a hill, 'the base of which is washed by the most beautiful river in this or any other country'. As seen from the surrounding neighbourhood:

> Its solemn and majestic appearance impresses the mind of the beholder with awe and veneration; and its situation seems to have been pointed out by nature for the seat of monarchs.[27]

The topographies wove a complex web of associations around Windsor, and they also proclaimed its great beauty. Turner's picture appears to represent the corner of the north terrace at mid afternoon, as seen from Eton playing fields, across the river and the Little Park (see map 4). This would explain the presence of what appears to be the islet on the left of the composition. The picture is like a visual counterpart to Combe's description:

> The river, having passed Eton, winds around Windsor little park, with the castle rising on its brow, in every appearance of picturesque beauty and grandeur. Sometimes a range of battlements is seen above the trees; or a single tower appears through a casual opening in the branches . . . The park being surrounded by a wall, nothing is seen of it from the water but the trees that shade it; these, however, form very rich masses of foliage, and not only break the castle into various distinct parts, but sometimes form a verdant base to the whole of it.[28]

According to the text of W. B. Cooke's *The Thames*, the park of this 'charming domain' was animated by 'sheep, cattle, and a herd of royal deer'. The story of how George III had found the Great Park at Windsor in 1791 'a rough jewel', and shaped it into a model estate with the Flemish and Norfolk farms, was well-rehearsed, and the role of sheep in improving the soil of the Great Park was established folklore.[29]

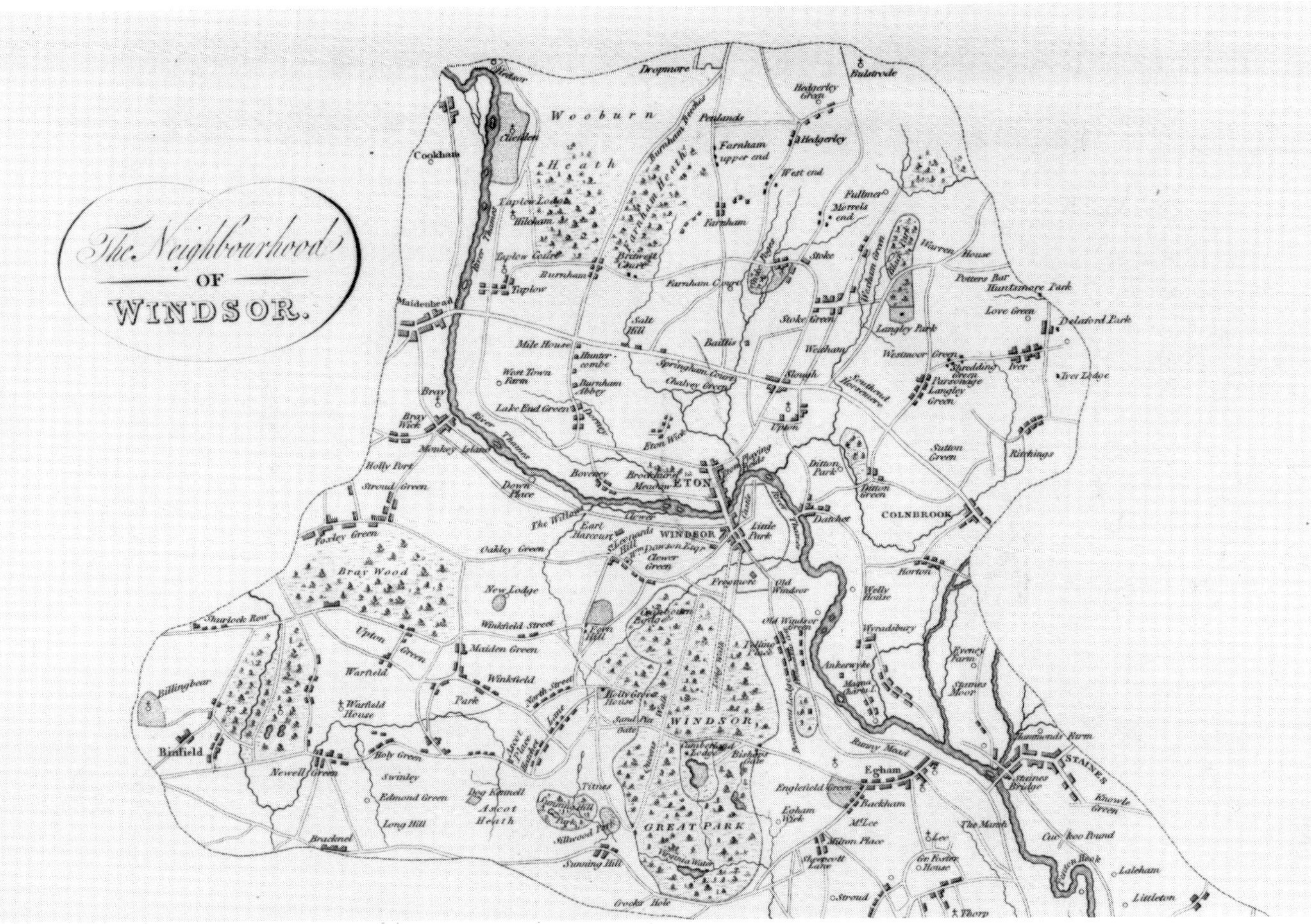

Map 4 *The Neighbourhood of Windsor*, from J. Hakewill, *The History of Windsor and its Neighbourhood*, 1813

It must be acknowledged that the relevance of George III's reputation in husbandry to the sheep of Turner's picture can not be confirmed. However, that they function as a pastoral symbol is certain, and they thus contribute to a mythical image of the Thames as a vale of peace and plenty, secured by a uniquely benevolent constitution, and a uniquely virtuous monarchy.

The next paintings in the series in terms of date, the two *Walton Bridges* (*Plates 60 and 61*) contain many of the same elements, but are less obviously related to the classical landscape tradition. It is possible to see the expansive wooded vista in which the scene is set, and the sunny effects, as referring to Claude's work, but the river scenes of Cuyp seem more immediately relevant. It is likely that Turner would have exhibited two such major works as these, and indeed I believe that they form a pair. (They are almost identical sizes, being 92.5 × 123.5cm, and 92 × 122.5cm respectively.) The land around Walton was flat and marshy, which was why a double bridge had been constructed in 1780, consisting of four main arches with stone facings, together with a flood bridge of fifteen brick arches connecting the bridge with Oatlands on the Surrey bank. The Loyd picture thus represents the bridges looking down river from the Middlesex side and facing roughly east. However, this is somewhat incongruous, since it seems to denote an evening view: in addition to the sky effect, there are the traditional signs of peace and tranquillity in the drinking cows and the barge horses being watered on the right. The barges themselves are moored up, and it appears that the sail of the nearmost one is being pulled in. The Melbourne picture shows the bridges from the opposite direction in the late morning, to judge from the fall of the shadows. Here all is bustle and energy, with a foreground scene of sheep-washing watched by a farmer on horseback and a shepherd with his dog.

The scenery around Walton was again noted for its beauty, and particularly for the view from Oatlands, an estate which had been bought by the Duke of York, who had enclosed the open fields and 'wastes' of Walton and Weybridge (amounting to almost one thousand acres) by two acts of 1800. Using a characteristically elevated viewpoint, Farington shows the bridges from Oatlands Park, as seen across a stretch of artificial water created by the previous resident, the Duke of Newcastle (*Plate 47*). The houses of Walton are visible beyond the trees, and there are houses at either end of the bridge.[30] No buildings whatsoever are represented in Turner's pictures, which by showing the scenery as if from a few feet above the waterline make it appear entirely given over to agricultural activities. The parkland of Oatlands is suggested only by the luxuriant masses of trees on the right of the Loyd picture and the left of the Melbourne one. While Farington's view is oriented to the gentleman tourist, concerned primarily with a succession of estates, Turner immerses the viewer in a world of georgic and commercial activities, and brings to our attention a mass of picturesque detail in the form of wooden bridges, plants, and stumps, in a way which again look forward to Constable's Stour scenes. It is as if

Turner had taken us to the bridge in the middle distance of one of Claude's Arcadian landscapes, and shows us that Arcadia is in fact Britain.

In terms of poetic resonance, it is easy to understand why Turner chose to represent a sheep-washing in the Melbourne picture, since Thomson gave a long description of sheep-washing and sheep-shearing in 'Summer', and claimed that on this 'simple scene' the 'solid grandeur' of Britain rested. The theme was subsequently developed in John Dyer's poem *The Fleece* (1757), in which livestock generally become emblems of the beauty, fecundity, and general superiority of the nation. As John Barrell has shown, although Dyer explicitly acknowledged the divisions in the contemporary social order, the poem sets out to show the harmony of interests among the different occupations and ranks within it.[31] An incessant nationalistic rhetoric emphasizes how well-off are both sheep and shepherds in Britain in comparison with their less fortunate counterparts in other nations. However, while sheep-washing was thus a poetically appropriate accompaniment to an image of the national river, it does not sit particularly well in the region depicted, since while there were large numbers of sheep on Hounslow Heath and Sunbury Common, which are very close to Walton, they were 'poor half-starved, ragged coated and wretched looking' creatures in the eyes of the progressive agriculturalist.[32]

The conjunction of pastoral and commercial elements which Turner concocted in the three works I have discussed also characterizes the *Dorchester Mead, Oxfordshire* (*Plate 62*) of 1810. Like the *Windsor Castle from the Thames*, this shows timber barges (a reference to Britain's 'oak walls' ?) and cattle cooling themselves, against a background which includes Culham Bridge and the spire of Abingdon church. The peaceful bucolic atmosphere is enhanced by the effect of mist and the low declining sun. This image corresponds with Combe's description of a view 'crowded with objects', where the river entered the town:

> Houses and gardens, with the various buildings, suited to the trades that require such a situation, alternately and on either side, cover the banks, which are united by a bridge of three arches, an ancient structure, that heightens the picturesque appearance of the scene.[33]

The view of this area was popular with artists, and the representations of it by Owen and Havell (*Plate 63*), which are almost contemporaneous, contain many of the same features. However, the differences are also striking. To enhance the poetic effect of the scene, Turner produces a rich breadth of light and shadow, organized around a central Claudean glow. By comparison with the topographical prints, he provides very little evidence of the urban features of the area, and his viewpoint is lower – once again the viewer is immersed directly among foreground groups, with the same kind of proximity as the herdsmen and cows of Cuyp's river bank scenes. Havell's image seems assertively modern and unpoetic by comparison.

Of the same size and importance (102 × 130cm) is *Ploughing up Turnips, near Slough* (*Plate 64*) of 1809, another misty morning scene of busy activity. *Ploughing up Turnips* includes a distant view of Windsor, with a silhouette quite similar to that used in the much nearer view in *Windsor Castle from the Thames*. Again Turner seems to have chosen a view recommended in the topographical literature, since in his *Topographical Survey of the Great Road from London to Bath and Bristol* (1792) Archibald Robertson had observed that near Slough:

> From the fields below, . . . the Castle appears to advantage; having the town and college of Eton in the valley on the right, and the distance closed by the royal forests on the south; forming a pleasing and picturesque scene.[34]

In the painting, the towers of Eton and the royal forests are clearly visible behind the foreground scene of agriculture. Michael Rosenthal has suggested that the view of Windsor was intended to suggest a cause and effect relationship between George III's patronage of progressive agriculture and the foreground activities, and that the golden colour was to evoke ideas of a Golden Age and to 'enhance the georgic completeness of it all'.[35] It is certainly true that the formal structure of the picture works so as to pull the eye from the foreground agricultural activity to the castle, and support for this interpretation is provided by the fact that the labourers are ploughing the round white Norfolk turnip, a crucial element in the new agriculture. However, the picture does not represent the royal farms, and as a representation of the improved agriculture it is inconsistent. In his report on Buckinghamshire for the Board of Agriculture of 1810, St John Priest refers specifically to a practice of farmers in the south of the country of leaving a border of grass around their fields, which 'afford(s) the means of carrying off part of a turnip crop without injury to the land', and also served as a resting place for sheep.[36] The foreground of Turner's picture can be read as a border of this type, here used by cows rather than sheep. However, the modernity of turnip husbandry seems contradicted by the two teams of horses in improbably close proximity in a small field, and Priest attacked the use of rows of four to five animals in the county as wasteful and unnecessary. Two horses were the norm in Suffolk and Norfolk, and in his *Landscape, Ploughing Scene in Suffolk* (Private Collection), exhibited in 1814, Constable showed a pair of horses abreast, and was praised for his accuracy in an Ipswich magazine review discovered by Rosenthal.[37] Turner further demonstrates his insensitivity to agricultural backwardness by showing the kind of 'foot-plough' generally used in Buckinghamshire, and specifically criticized by Priest. Constable, by contrast, shows the wheel plough used in Suffolk and Norfolk, and by progressive farmers such as George III elsewhere. Turner does seem to have based the scene on direct observation, in that there are several on-the-spot pencil studies of male and female labourers, cattle, teams of horses, and the plough, together with the landscape background, in his *Windsor, Eton Sketchbook*. However, the symbolism of the turnip, the topographical references and accumulation of details of husbandry, were probably more important to the painting's effect of contemporaneity than any local accuracy.[38]

It is unnecessary to my argument to consider all of Turner's series in the same degree of detail. It will be sufficient to note here that the same peaceful rustic atmosphere is evoked by the *Harvest Dinner, Kingston Bank*, with its calm expanse of water, in which Turner again utilizes a viewpoint on the bank among docks, reeds, and other plants, and brings us close to a group of 'contented peasantry' at rest. His pervasive concern with this mood is suggested by his uncharacteristic view of *Clieveden on Thames* (*Plate 65*). The stretch of river at Cliveden was much recommended for its beauty, and Robertson, Combe, Skrine, and Hakewill all singled it out for special attention, describing it in terms of the prospect from the gentleman's park.[39] The views looking down from the woods by Farington (*Plate 48*) and Hakewill are precisely equivalent to such descriptions. However, while the text to Cooke's *The Thames* gives a comparable description, Owen's view, as befits picturesque topography, is down at river level, while Havell places barges prominently on a placid expanse of river, with the woods rising in an undulating mass behind (*Plate 57*). Turner's view is even more placid and picturesque, with the river a lazy stream in which a few cattle are watering, and where the only barge is moored near an inn.[40]

It will be clear that while some of the works I have discussed contained distinctive and easily recognizable topographical signs, others such as *Harvest Dinner, Kingston Bank* and *Clieveden* depended on their titles to anchor them as Thames valley views, and establish their poetic/historical frame of reference. This is also true of another peaceful pastoral scene, the *Union of the Thames and the Isis* (*Plate 66*). Superficially this is just another rustic landscape, a picturesque scene of watering cows, riverside plants, and a wooden bridge. But the title refers it to a well-known myth, discussed in every topography I have read, which derived from a Latin poem, 'The Marriage of the Tame and the Isis', in William Camden's *Britannia* (1594). This claimed that the Thames above its junction with the little river Tame was really the Isis, and implied that 'Thames' was a corruption of Thamesis. (Turner's interest in this myth is confirmed by the fact that when the *Thames at Weybridge* composition was engraved for the *Liber Studorium*, it was given the title 'Isis', and by his reference to the 'Isis' as a sister of the Thames in a fragment of verse.)[41] Combe describes the spot in a passage which may have inspired Turner's image:

> The Tame, when it has passed beneath Dorchester Bridge, takes its course, half concealed by reeds and sedges, through the meadows, and soon mingles with the Thames, not as an equal, but a tributary stream. Indeed, so little does its appearance justify the alliance, which it has been said by fabling poetry, to form with the principal river, that were it not for a wooden bridge thrown across its mouth, as a communication between the meadows which are divided by it, the voyager might pass unnoticed the petty influx of water it receives from the Tame.[42]

By giving a pastoral and picturesque character to the scene, Turner seems precisely to emphasize the inconsequentiality of the tributary. Owen took the same strategy in his view in Cooke's *The Thames* (*Plate 67*).

The *Union of the Thames and the Isis* was an exercise in the mode of giving aesthetic significance to ordinary landscapes through breadth and atmospheric effect, which I have argued was a crucial element in the naturalistic strategy.[43] So too is a work even more germane to Constable's Stour views, the *Grand Junction Canal at Southall Mill* (*Plate 68*). Of course, this does not represent the Thames *per se*, but the Grand Junction joins with the River Brent at Hanwell, close to Turner's scene, and only a short distance from the Thames. No one with any knowledge of art in the early nineteenth century could have failed to compare the picture with *The Mill* (National Gallery, Washington), a celebrated picture then attributed to Rembrandt, which had been exhibited in London in 1799 and again in 1806. However, it is significant that Turner departs from Rembrandt's example in placing his mill against a light and expansive Claudean sunset, rather than silhouetted against a bright mass in a penumbra of darkness. This sky gives a serene, peaceful, and optimistic atmosphere to the work, which matches with the browsing horse and the bargee consuming his supper on the right, producing a unified chain of associations. Considering how much the theme of the picture and some of the details offer comparisons with Constable's work, it should be recalled that it was in 1810 that the latter made his first campaign of sketches at Flatford Mill, and that his first finished view of the site, *A Water-Mill* (Private Collection), which is primarily an image of a lock, was painted in 1811–12 and exhibited at the Royal Academy in 1812.[44]

All the works I have discussed so far have a marked agricultural or commercial element in them. I now want to consider four pictures in which no such features appear: *The Thames near Windsor* (*Plate 69*), *The Thames at Eton* (*Plate 70*), *Near the Thames' Lock, Windsor* (*Plate 71*), and *Richmond Hill and Bridge* (*Plate 72*). These were all probably produced in the years 1807–9, and the first three were sold to Lord Egremont, along with *Windsor Castle from the Thames* and *The Thames at Weybridge*. All four pictures are morning or evening views of the river, and *The Thames near Windsor* and *Richmond Hill and Bridge* are overtly Claudean compositions. It is self-evident from their titles that three of them represented the area around Windsor, which was incessantly associated with chivalry, aristocracy, and royalty in contemporary texts, and Richmond too had comparable connotations. The work which is probably the earliest of the four, *The Thames near Windsor*, has a foreground scene of fishermen pulling in nets, with a group of women, perhaps gathering mushrooms. To judge from the distant silhouette of the castle, this is probably a west–east view, looking downstream, although the bridge seems to be a poetic invention of Turner's since there were none on this stretch of the river.[45] A mass of elegant trees on the right, together with the receding mass on the left, frame the castle outlined against the glowing dawn. A pale sickle moon just left of centre is reflected in the water in the foreground, and the main warm colour in the lighting is a pinky tinge among the trees on the right, the rest of the sky being blues and grays. Even in the painting's present poor condition, it is possible to make out some buildings on the left bank and the small figure of a herdsman and cattle can just be seen amongst the trees. In this, as in other paintings of the group, Turner adopts a low viewpoint, and minimizes evidence of the urban development around Windsor.

Two of the paintings under consideration directly refer to Eton, 'the first school in the British empire', according to Combe, and a site which combined 'a happy union of monastic gloom and rural beauty' for Hakewill.[46] *The Thames at Eton* is less overtly Claudean than *The Thames near Windsor*, although it also has a composition in which masses of Italianate trees frame a slightly off-centre object with symbolic significance. It is smaller and more loosely painted, but again has a limited and subdued colour range with browns, grays, and dull greens predominating. Turner represents the twin towers of Eton's chapel's east end at twilight looking roughly north, with a pair of fishermen in a boat in the foreground, and a swan with cygnets near the right bank. Once again it appears that he has taken some liberties with the topography, since one would expect to see something of the buildings of Cloister Court and Brewhouse Yard, which are to the east of the chapel, from this angle. The area was pre-eminently associated with Thomas Gray, who had lived nearby at Stoke Poges where the graveyard of the *Elegy Written in a Country Churchyard* is situated. In his 1808 review, Landseer referred to the 'stately dignity' of the picture, and quoted from the *Ode. On a Distant Prospect of Eton College*. Indeed, it is hard to believe that Turner's picture was not deliberately designed to recall the poem, so apt does it seem as an equivalent to lines such as:

> Ye distant spires, ye antique towers,
> That crown the wat'ry glade, . . .

Its shadowy evening effect was precisely the kind of atmosphere seen as appropriate to meditations on mortality, such as those which make up both of Gray's most celebrated works.[47]

Equally Etonian is *Near the Thames' Lock, Windsor*, which shows the river in the deep shadow of late afternoon sunshine, with a group of boys swimming and playing in the water. Again, the colour range of this is very limited with a pervasive use of gray in the sky and castle, tinged with tones of yellow in the centre. The shadows of trees and water are very dark, and it is possible to see the black hole of the sluice gate on the left as faintly ominous. The background to this consists of parts of the castle, and Eton is not visible, although the view is taken from the playing fields. In case anyone should miss the connection with Gray, Turner included the first six lines from the third verse of the *Ode* in the catalogue entry for the picture and the frolicking figures again seem well adapted to suggest the mood of Gray's lines.[48] There is a striking contrast between Turner's image of the area around the lock, and the topographical representations. Both Farington and Owen took viewpoints near Eton Bridge, which enabled them to show the wooden structure and the mass of picturesque houses around it – Turner again deliberately focussed on the trees, river, and castle.

In his representations of Windsor, Turner thus directly avoided any imagery of the town: from all we might know from his pictures, Windsor was simply a castle among woods, in a paradisiacal region, peopled by an industrious population of 'peasants', fishermen, and passing bargees. This omission of the modern, and the use of visual trappings designed to evoke a bucolic atmosphere, is even more incongruous in the *Richmond Hill and Bridge*, a misty morning scene, with women washing clothes and sheep among the foreground trees. The picture was singled out for special praise by Landseer, who likened it to the 'morning pastorals of Theocritus', and noted that:

> By obscuring the detail of Richmond itself in the mistiness of morning; by introducing some sheep and the simple incident of women bathing a child near the foreground [...] Mr. Turner has given a pastoral character to a scene of polished and princely retirement.[49]

Yet in reality Richmond was notable primarily for its fashionable character, and even Landseer questioned the propriety of mixing pastoral elements with a theme of 'architectural elegance'.

As I have already indicated, Richmond was a site with a complex weave of associations around it. It had been the site of a royal palace and still had a royal park; it featured in a much-quoted passage in Thomson's *Seasons* and was also the burial spot of the poet, and no artist could forget that Reynolds had lived there and painted a well-known landscape of the view from the hill. In his *History of the Thames*, Combe gives two 'views' of Richmond, the first of which describes the prospect looking up river:

> Beneath the hill the Thames winds its silver stream through meads and gardens, where nature luxuriates, and which taste adorns; while the villas, seats, and villages that enrich its banks, with their blended beauty, heighten the enchanting scene.[50]

This is the prospect which features in *The Seasons*, from which Combe gives a lengthy quote, and it corresponds to one type of pictorial image of Richmond, to which I shall return. Turner's *Richmond Hill and Bridge* corresponds with another type, for which Combe again gives a verbal equivalent:

> In this part of the river the retrospective view possesses every charm of elegant landscape. The stream is divided by an island planted with poplars; the bridge appears with superior advantage beyond it, backed by Richmond hill, which rises in the intermingled possession of gaiety and grandeur; while the hanging wood of Petersham occupies the distance; the whole forming a picture of uncommon richness and beauty.[51]

Combe's account of the 'succession of villas' below the bridge, and of a scene which mingles 'gaiety and grandeur' is matched by Farington's view, which is taken from a position close to Turner's, and clearly shows modern Richmond, and includes fashionably dressed strollers in the foreground. Thus with the exception of the toll bridge, built by Payne in 1774–7, Turner has entirely hidden the modern features of the landscape behind his atmospheric effect.

It is interesting to note how sympathetic contemporaries could perceive the value of this device, by comparing the response to Turner's image with that to another major representation of the same site by a contemporary artist. In 1815, T. C. Hofland exhibited a *View of Richmond Hill from the Twickenham Meadows*, at the British Institution, which may be connected with the picture bought by John Todd of Moulsey Park and exhibited at Hofland's solo exhibition in 1821.[52] The publication of a large engraving after this picture in 1825 (*Plate 73*) prompted the critic of the *London Magazine* to compare it with Turner's 1808 exhibit, using an unacknowledged quotation from Landseer's review. He objected to what he described as the 'tamely-embellished boarding-school air' of Hofland's painting, and advised artists to avoid representing 'unpicturesque and unpoetical circumstances', by which he clearly meant the foreground scene of genteel leisure. Turner, by contrast, had divested the scene of its 'dressed and holiday aspect' and restored it to its 'primitive and pastoral character'.[53] When Turner did represent the modern buildings of Richmond in the large canvas of *Thomson's Aeolian Harp*, exhibited in 1809, he showed them scattered through the distance in a verdant Claudean river valley, which to Robert Hunt, writing in the *Examiner*, seemed so well matched to Thomson's description of the 'Inchanting Vale', with its succession of 'retreats', 'bowers', and walks. The foreground is dominated by elegant trees and classical fragments, accompanied with various figures: the nymphs dancing and adorning the harp, and the piping shepherd boy with his flock. This picture therefore equally de-modernized Richmond, but used yet more overtly classicizing devices.[54]

The blending of nostalgia, poetry, and nationalist associations in the Thames series is also illustrated by *Pope's Villa at Twickenham* (*Plate 74*), which partly evoked a person whom Combe called 'our great British bard', and whose house and garden he described as a 'classical spot'. Combe observed that the villa and grounds were still much as Pope had left them except for additions to the villa, which in Farington's print look neat and trim, nestling among willows that according to legend Pope had planted.[55] However, in 1807 Baroness Howe had ordered its demolition, and Turner represented it in a state of dilapidation. To enhance the moral message which might be read from this process of decay, Turner resorted to the traditional poetic and visual trope of contrasting the ruins of former splendour with timeless pastoral life. In the left foreground of his image, three rustics discuss some fragments of the structure, observed by a shepherd and his lover, while on the right of the composition are more sheep and two men with eel pots in a boat. (Landseer compared the figures with the 'hoary-headed swain' in Gray's *Elegy*.)

Amongst the picturesque weeds and clutter which occupy the nearest part of the picture plane is a dead tree, which is surely of symbolic significance. The painting is essentially Claudean in conception, and centres around a light-filled middle ground in which the crucial motiv is picked out by the declining sun. Landseer gave it an enthusiastic and lengthy commentary, in which he praised the way Turner had suggested different associated ideas which worked together to produce a unified effect of the mutability of human works:

> The tranquil state of the human intellect, like that of a river, is the time when it is most susceptible of reflection. At such a time the mind, willingly enthralled by a certain feeling of melancholy pleasure, is instinctively led to compare the permanency of Nature herself with the fluctuations of fashion and the vicissitudes of taste; and in the scene before us, the Thames flows on as it has ever flowed with silent majesty, while the mutable and multifarious works which human hands have erected on its banks have mournfully succeeded each other; and not even the taste, and the genius, and the reputation of Pope, could retard the operations of Time, the irksomeness of satiety, and the consequent desire of change.[56]

Rather than the conventional Christian concern with transience, the emphasis in this passage on the restlessness of human desires and the inevitability of change and decay seems informed by notions of the cyclical rise and fall of cultures which were so central to the social theory of the period. While the dominant vision of Britain in the Thames series is an optimistic one, like Thomson, and doubtless influenced by him, Turner could not entirely integrate this positive vision with the negative associations of some aspects of commercial society within the dominant culture.[57]

This is confirmed by the small evidence of urban life in the series. When Landseer claimed that Turner had followed the Thames from its source to the ocean, he did not observe that there was a major hiatus in his coverage of the river: Turner produced only one image of London (*Plate 75*), which does not seem to have been exhibited until the year after his review. Within the histories of the Thames the pictorial pleasures of London were well established. Combe provided an extensive account of the city as seen from the river, and described some of the sights and views with considerable enthusiasm, claiming, for example, that the 'magnificent prospect' from Westminster Bridge combined:

> such a happy intermixture of water and buildings, of permanent grandeur and varying scenery, as is not to be found in the view of any other river in the world.[58]

Farington devoted thirteen of his seventy-five views to London, mainly using compositions which transparently refer the viewer to Canaletto's townscapes. It is doubtful if he or his contemporaries read such views as picturesque, but that the city could be conceived in picturesque form in the following decade is shown by Owen's images of it for Cooke's *The Thames*. Yet while these etchings are conceived within the picturesque aesthetic, Owen incorporated far more nakedly modern and utilitarian elements than Farington, as in *West-India Docks*, with its regular line of stark warehouses, and the *Mast House in the Dock at Blackwall, formerly Perry's*. Owen's views are taken from down near the level of the river, and this means he gives far more idea of the towering tangled skyline of the city, and of its work life (*Plate 53*). In later years, Turner was to produce major views of ports, such as *Harbour of Dieppe (Changement de Domicile)* and *Cologne, the Arrival of a Packet Boat, Evening* (both Frick Collection, New York), but these belong to the 1820s vogue for continental townscapes. He may have felt that it was not possible to dignify a modern city sufficiently to make it an appropriate subject for a major oil, and he was never to make the commercial heart of London the subject of one.

I suspect that a basic reason for this was the ambivalent or negative status of cities, and especially of London, in English nature poetry. In the passage in 'Summer', after that describing the prospect from Richmond, the poem continues its 'Panegyric' on Britain:

> Full are they cities with the sons of Art;
> And Trade and Joy, in every busy street,
> Mingling are heard; e'en Drudgery himself,
> As at the car he sweats, or dusty hews
> The palace stone, looks gay, Thy crowded Ports,
> Where rising masts an endless prospect yield,
> With labour burn, and echo to the shouts
> Of hurried sailor, as he hearty waves
> His last adieu, and loosening every sheet,
> Resigns the spreading vessel to the wind.
>
> (lines 1457–66)

The poem here seems to be trying to convince the reader that while labour appears dusty and sweaty, it is in fact joyous. But 'Drudgery' only looks 'gay', and the 'crowded Ports' burn with work. The sailor is forced to make his 'last adieu', and the culminating image of the passage is a sad one of resignation. In the section in 'Autumn' which describes the development of civil society, the city is the site of commerce and luxury, of toil and of the arts of refinement:

> Then commerce brought into the public walk
> The busy Merchant; the big warehouse built;
> Raised the strong crane; choaked up the loaded street
> With foreign plenty; and thy stream, O Thames,
> Large, gentle, deep, majestic, king of floods!
> Chose for his grand resort . . .
>
> (lines 118–23)
>
> Then too the pillar'd Dome, magnific, heaved
> Its ample roof; and Luxury within
> Pour'd out her glittering stores . . .
>
> (lines 134–6)

If these are essentially positive images, Thomson's stress on labour and luxury is unmistakable, and in his description of the city in 'Winter', it appears as a centre of fashion, vice, and potential political corruption.[59] As within English nature poetry more generally, in *The Seasons* it is rural England, and more particularly the gentleman's estate, from which the moral and political virtue of the nation emanate, and it is rural England which is central to the extended analogy between geography ('nature') and political culture. That Turner had registered these negative elements in the poetic image of London is evident from two of his own verse fragments:

> This extended town far Stretching East and West
> The high raised Smoke no prototype of Rest
> Thy dim seen spires rais'd to Religion fair
> Seen first at moments th(r)o that World of Care
> Whose Vice and Virtue so commixing blends
> Tho one returns while one destruction sends
> Oer children's children whateer low & great
> Debase or noble here together meet
> To a concentrated focus hope together draws.

and:

> Where burthen'd Thames reflects the crowded sail,
> Commercial care and busy toils prevail,
> Whose murky veil, aspiring to the skies,
> Obscures thy beauty, and thy form denies,
> Save where they spires pierce the doubtful air,
> As gleams of hope amidst a world of care.

It was the second of these passages which Turner printed with the entry for *London* in the catalogue to his 1809 exhibition. The emphasis of both is on London as a world of toil, worry, and ambition, where persons of all classes mingle in uncertain struggles. As such, London was perhaps best seen from a distant hill, covered by a pall of smoke which was an equivalent to the uncertainty of those who were drawn there, and a physical manifestation of their exertions.[60]

The position from which Turner took his view again offered a well-known prospect, the subject of a water-colour by J. R. Cozens (*Plate 76*), and the painting represents and emphasizes some of its most significant landmarks: Greenwich Hospital, the Queen's House, and the dome of Saint Paul's.[61] Although Combe disliked the Queen's House he was effusive on the merits of the Hospital, claiming that its 'magnificence far transcends the palaces of our kings', and that in it 'the maimed and veteran sailor' found 'an harbour which national gratitude has prepared for him'.[62] Thus contemporary texts created a network of associations around the most prominent object in Turner's image, which connected it with the triumphs of the British navy, the stalwart character of its sailors, and royal munificence. It is possible to read this painting as a narrative, in which the hospital functions to symbolize the role of the navy in protecting the shipping and river beyond, on which depends the commercial wealth of London, symbolized by the dominating dome of Saint Paul's. Turner enhanced the spacious effect of his picture by the group of browsing deer in the foreground, which help to suggest scale, and the dramatic effect of light on the 'Silver Thames' curving away in perspective. Thus a foreground of parkland calm contrasts with the world of toil and business beyond, which, as in Turner's verse, is covered by a layer of smoke made up of impastoed off-white paint, denser in effect than the more thinly painted grey areas which denote buildings, and through which peak the spires of churches:

> As gleams of hope amidst a world of care.

In the foreground park, tiny figures of couples run and play among the trees. The smoking ragged forms of London are a rude intrusion into what is essentially a Claudean landscape perspective, lit by broken light effects, significantly different from Claude's serene Italianate skies, but reminiscent of those with which Konincks and Ruisdael backed their panoramic views of commercial Holland. None of the other well-known paintings of this view made it the basis for such a gloomy and dramatic image.[63]

It seems worth noting that Turner never did succeed in producing a major finished picture of the London river. While he made some sketches and studies of it at the time he was working on the Thames series, these did not lead on to finished works.[64] It was left to other painters to produce large-scale canvases of London's commercial heart: Callcott's placid Cuypian image of *The Entrance to the Pool of London* (Trustees of the Bowood Settlement, RA 1816), Vincent's *View of Greenwich from Blackwall* (BI 1820) and *London from the Surrey side of Waterloo Bridge* (Society of Painters in Oil and Water-Colours, 1820) and Hofland's *View of London from Somerset House* (BI 1822).[65] My explanation of the absence of views of this type from Turner's Thames series is that in 1806–10 modern cityscapes still fell outside Turner's aesthetic for major oils, and the connotations of London in English poetry were inconsistent with the benevolent myth of the Thames valley the bulk of the series was designed to suggest.

The list of Turner's Thames paintings exhibited, or believed exhibited, over the years 1807–9, indicates that seven of them represented the river below Greenwich, of which six focussed on the stretch of water known as the Nore between Shoeburyness in Essex and Sheerness in Kent, while one showed the Essex town of Purfleet as seen from the river. It is notable that Turner did not fix on any of the other places in the repertoire of the topographies such as Woolwich, Gravesend, or Tilbury Fort. He may have been attracted to Purfleet because Combe singled out its chalk quarries as serving 'to enliven for a moment the flat, inanimate shore' (a comment echoed in the text to Cooke's *The Thames*)[66] and even if he was not responding to Combe's recommendation, it is very likely that he would seek a scene with an established reputation for a pleasing effect. In *Purfleet and the Essex Shore*, the cliffs function simply as a strip of light in the distance on the right of the composition, and the main focus of interest is the foreground fishing activity, behind which are a loaded barge and an anchored ship, which probably represents one of the East India ships which stopped at Erith on the Kent shore to unload and lighten their cargo before proceeding up river. Like Turner's other pictures of the lower Thames this is more a sea-piece in the Dutch tradition than a topographical view, and it does not have the same symbolic resonance as the sea-pieces of the Nore.

In the early nineteenth century, the town of Sheerness at the mouth of the Medway had a fort, which was one of the key bastions in English coastal defences, and an important dockyard. According to Combe:

> Sheerness offers nothing picturesque in itself; but the rivers which it commands, and the various vessels in motion, or moored before it, compose a scene that may interest the painter as well as the politician.

At the Nore itself a hulk was moored with a light on it to guide shipping, and Cooke's *The Thames* described the scene here as follows:

> around it the guard-ships are stationary, while the scene is ever varying from the numerous vessels, which British commerce is increasingly receiving into its bosom; or dismissing, laden with its treasures, to every part of the world.

The junction of the Thames and Medway did feature in British poetry in the description of their 'bridal' in Spenser's *Faerie Queene*, but it was not used as a subject by any of the major eighteenth-century poets as far as I know.[67] Peacock directly referred to the area of the Nore in *The Genius of the Thames*,[68] and while this can not have influenced Turner's pre-1810 pictures, it indicates how his imagery related to a general pattern of poetic and topographical discourse around the river and its meanings.

In the four pictures in which it features, Sheerness is 'little more than mere threads of distance' to use Landseer's words, a strip of buildings picked out by light, being most prominent in *The Confluence of the Thames and Medway, Sheerness as seen from the Nore* (*Plate 77*) and *Guardship at the Great Nore, Sheerness &c.*. The less significant Shoeburyness appears similarly in the painting of that title. None the less, Landseer stressed how important this detail was in identifying the places represented, giving names to the pictures, and connecting them as a series.[69] All except *The Mouth of the Thames* feature warships at anchor, although in *Sheerness and the Isle of Sheppey* and *Shoeburyness Fishermen Hailing a Whitstable Hoy* the warships are mere distant masses. Appropriately for works conceived within the tradition of Dutch sea-pieces, the foreground in all are occupied by fishing boats. It is possible to read a direct cause and effect relationship between the presence of Sheerness and the peaceful activities of the sturdy fishermen going on under the protection of its batteries. The relationship is dramatized more by the massive forms of the warships in *The*

Confluence of the Thames and Medway and the *Guardship of the Great Nore*, and still more so in *Sheerness as seen from the Nore*, where the anchored ship is a dark mass against a red declining sun. In the *Confluence of the Thames and Medway*, the hulks frame the brightly lit strip of Sheerness, and their stability is emphasized by the barges and other boats moving round them. The British flag, just right of the centre, has not been placed there just for its colour.

It can not be argued that these works represent the peaceful path of British commerce, but in most instances they do refer to the guardian role of the navy and the coastal defences. While some are more visually eloquent in this respect than others, the words 'Nore' and 'Sheerness' in their titles would have profound associations for Turner's audience, in whichever of its social fractions we conceive it. Presumably most of that audience would have responded to the pictures simply as patriotic images, but it should be remembered that Sheerness could prompt alternative associations. In a topography of 1840 entitled *The Thames and its Tributaries*, Charles Mackay, a poet and journalist from a naval family, observed:

> The mutiny of the Nore will always render the confluence of the Thames and Medway a memorable spot in the annals of England.[70]

Richard Parker and the other leaders of the 1797 mutiny were hung from the yard arm opposite Sheerness. Doubtless Turner did not intend to call these particular associations to mind, and there is nothing in the images to prompt them beyond the location represented. Doubtless few, if any, liberals or radicals saw the pictures in Turner's gallery anyway. However, Mackay's comment at least reminds us that while different class groups shared much of a common mythology of Britishness in the early nineteenth century, they valorized aspects of it differently.

I suggested earlier that *England: Richmond Hill on the Prince Regent's Birthday* (*Plate 78*) could be regarded as the summation of Turner's involvement with the Thames valley. This huge painting (180 × 335cm) was exhibited at the Academy in 1819, with a catalogue entry which included the first eight lines of Thomson's passage on the prospect from Richmond in 'Summer' beginning: 'Which way, AMANDA, shall we bend our course?' The view had been the subject of numerous paintings and prints, and the idea of accompanying it with a reference to Thomson was not original – in 1815 and 1816 Hofland exhibited a large picture (now destroyed) entitled *View from Richmond Hill, Evening*, with lines beginning:

> Heav'ns, what a goodly prospect stretches round, etc.

which come slightly later. *England* has been the subject of a useful analysis by Charles Stuckey, who has argued that it can be seen as part of a deliberate ploy for royal patronage, based on a view redolent with royal and national associations. Stuckey has pointed to figures signifying the aftermath of a military band concert, and suggested that these, together with the figures of the widow and the boy with a wooden horse ('a Wellington of the future'), mean that the painting is an image of the 'welcome peace' after the Anglo-French Wars. More recently, Jean Golt has shown that whatever the fantasy elements in the image, it is likely to represent a real fête at Cardigan House in Richmond, which was organized in honour of the Regent's birthday by Lady Cardigan in August 1817.[71]

The painting was produced a decade after the last of the major paintings of the Thames series, after a phase in which Turner had exhibited some of his most effective classical subject pictures, and it is significantly different from the works I have discussed. It is far larger and more grandiloquent, as doubtless seemed proper for a picture which purported to represent 'England', and it is also more overtly Claudean than any except *Thomson's Aeolian Harp*. By comparison with the compositions of Farington, Owen or Hofland,[72] *England* dramatizes and emphasizes the panoramic effect, framing the river, a great inverted apostrophe running through an endless parkland, far more thickly wooded than Farington's or Owen's images suggest. (By the early 1820s, one commentator could complain of the intrusion of steam boats into this scene, which violated 'all one's most cherished notions of keeping and consistency'.)[73] The foreground scene of leisure is matched by a vista in which the '*Power of Cultivation*' and the 'wonders of his toil', of which Thomson made so much, are nowhere in evidence. Further, in the earlier pictures Turner had inserted figures which stand for the dutiful and loyal working folk of England going about their proper business. In this work he shows a different nation: those who live off their labour. The bulk of the figures are female, and Turner may have had in mind the passage in 'Summer' where the poem describes the beauty, elegance, and moral grace of the 'DAUGHTERS' of 'BRITANNIA' (lines 1580–94). There was also a well-established pattern of peopling topographical views of Richmond Hill with fashionably dressed figures.

The figures in the Thames pictures of 1806–10 mainly refer to a round of rural activities, which were understood to be natural and timeless. It is ironic that in the most grandiosely classical of his Thames views, Turner represented precisely the fashionable and the modern, so incongruous with the traditional theory of High Art. Jerrold Ziff has shown that some of the poses derive from studies Turner had made after Watteau's *L'Île enchantée*, and the picture has indeed the fairy land atmosphere of a *fête galante*: an endless afternoon of pleasure of the English ruling class, in which appears a glittering assemblage of ladies and gentlemen, straight out of the court reports of the *Morning Post*. However, it should be noted that some of the figures are difficult to give an identity to, particularly now that the foreground has deteriorated so much, and at the least there is a confusing mixture of social types and activities among the figures. (For instance, do the dark figure apparently slumped against a tree on the far left and the gesticulating figure holding his head next to him represent drunks?) None the less the overall character of the painting is clear. It is a work specifically designed for the social space and pictorial competition of the exhibition room. It offered a fantasmagoria of fashionable figures in a landscape setting in which topography has been saturated with poetic signifiers which translate it into the realm of myth: an image designed to give a corrupt court a flattering image of itself, and speak of a largely imaginary loyalty to its unglamorous and widely unpopular figurehead – a 'corpulent' and debauched 'Adonis' of fifty-seven, who symbolized the corruption of the political establishment more than any other individual.[74] It seems legitimate to read the earlier Thames paintings as proferring a patriotic message in a time of war, and despite their mythical dimension, some of them suggest down-to-earth realities of rural life. The idealized landscape of *England: Richmond Hill on the Prince Regent's Birthday* seems an appropriate symbol of the shift from the cross-class nationalism and loyalism of the war period to the shrill ideology of throne and altar articulated by conservatives in the social turmoil of the ensuing peace.

Reviews of the picture partly support my argument here. The *Repository of Arts* praised aspects of the landscape and did not mention the figures, while the *Examiner* admired the picture highly, but found a contradiction between the ideal image of England and the realities of the person it celebrated. For Hunt, the landscape was one of those 'select scenes' which gave 'full satisfaction to the mind':

> a pictorial display of the magnificence of England, as shown in its richly-fertilised land, its cultivated and high-spirited people of every degree . . .

The barb followed:

> It is a scene . . . in which it would be suitable to make holiday in honour of some truly great circumstance, of the birthday, not of a common-place Prince, who presides over measures which engulph a people in remediless expense and misery, but of a WASHINGTON or ALFRED, who executed measures which released their respective countries from base administrations, from vile aristocratic influence, from grinding taxation and misery.

The most telling observation on the figures appeared in the moderately liberal *Morning Herald*, which could not discover a 'single handsome person' among them:

> In truth it would appear that the various parties had all dined very heartily, and had not spared the juice of the vine-fruit, so disordered do they look in their dress, so odd in their attitudes. Nor do we well know from what classes of society they have been selected. Soldiers, officers, drummers, Royal servants, ladies intended to be gay and gentlemen designed to be gallant, fiddlers and ambulators, little boys and old grandmothers, all by the way with very rubicund countenances, are huddled together as if they had been shaken out of a dice-box. Whoever examines this painting closely, must regret, as we do, that such a lovely scene is profaned by the presence of such a motley congregation.[75]

This seems to me to point towards one of the problems of Turner's painting: although there were ways of representing the upper strata of English society as individuals in portraits or modern history paintings, there was no established formula for representing the world of fashion *en masse* outside the realm of caricature. Turner's choice of the *fête galante* prototype had an undeniable logic to it, and it was not without eighteenth-century precedents, such as Gainsborough's *The Mall* (Frick Collection, New York). But considering the current political climate, and the dominance of naturalistic norms for representing British landscape, such a blatantly theatrical device was bound to look a little odd. The final irony is that so committed an admirer of Thomson could have produced the picture at all, since however celebratory the image of England in *The Seasons* may be, the poem does not approve the world of fashion. That world was fundamentally at odds with the rural base of political and moral virtue the poem articulates. The reference to Thomson is as unsuitable as the inclusion of fashionable figures in a classical landscape. Turner's *England* is yet another instance of discursive constructions being adapted to incongruous new functions, and becoming farcical in the process. The painting was not bought by the Crown, and it may be some measure of its ludicrous and unconvincing aspect that it did not find a buyer. But then its size militated against its marketability, and it had no clear function outside the exhibition room or the grand gallery.

In this section I have argued that Turner's Thames pictures of 1806–10 lent themselves to being read as a series: that there was an implicit narrative in them, which derived in part from the poetic image of the river, and in part from the topographical histories of it. However, this narrative has major gaps, which partly arise from the constraints of the current system of pictorial forms, and the relative value the theory of painting accorded them. While Turner represented a whole sequence of scenes which the topographies endowed with complex associations (or the associations of which they reiterated and systematized), he avoided topographical modes of description, which had a low aesthetic value. Thus no country seats are included in the series, unless we count Windsor Castle, and this is not represented in the country house portrait mode, but always as a distant and partial silhouette. Turner picked out certain nodal points: the junction of the Thames and Isis, Windsor, Eton, Walton Bridges, Richmond, London from Greenwich, and the Nore, all of which had enormous poetic resonance with the exception of Walton Bridges. His series thus offered a somewhat different narrative from the topographies, or from any single poetic source – indeed the history of English poetry was part of its narrative. It was also a series which was not uniform or consistent in its modes: it moved from the apparently documentary detail of *Ploughing up Turnips near Slough* to the more overtly classicized references of *Richmond Hill and Bridge* and *Pope's Villa at Twickenham*. None the less, I wish to stress how very important it was in the development of a painting of English scenes which could yet stand as a serious and dignified art. The pictures were, of course, not without precedent in this respect, particularly in the work of Wilson. But in their use of Dutch modes and their accompanying concern with labour, in their selective use of topographical detail combined with great breadth of effect and innovative lighting, and in their range of poetic reference, they offered a new model. However, from the point of view of a radical naturalistic aesthetic, they could also be seen as having certain limitations, and some of the subsequent paintings which dealt with similar themes may stand as a critique of them.

(iv) Constable's Stour paintings

> He has none of the poetry of Nature like Mr TURNER, but he has more of her portraiture.[76]

The *Examiner*'s characterization of Constable and Turner now seems a truism, but it was not a truism in 1819, and neither is it a self-evident truth. It is necessary to relate the observation to the categories of the period, and Constable's practice to other practices, to understand why Hunt made such a judgement.

I have already pointed out that Constable began to produce his paintings of the Stour valley around 1810, when Turner's Thames series was probably available in its fullest development, and that some of the works he could have seen contain features which anticipate elements in his own river views. However, I am not concerned with the possibility of 'influence' here so much as with the currency of signs. What I wish to draw attention to is the way in which Constable's exhibited works implicitly related to a large body of images of similar subjects, both paintings and prints, which functioned in relation to a whole range of texts that endowed them with complex associations. My aim is to suggest how his pictures might have been read in relation to these larger patterns of imagery, and to see what light this sheds on their possible ideological functions.

Constable's *Dedham Vale, Morning* (Collection of Sir Richard Proby, Bart.), exhibited at the Academy in 1811, was his first major picture on the theme of the Stour valley, and Rosenthal has provided a useful analysis of its relationship with eighteenth-century landscape poetry and Turner's Claudean imagery of the Thames valley. However, the first exhibited picture which combined the motivs of river, lock, and barge was *A Water-Mill* (RA 1812, *Plate 83*), presuming that this is the picture formerly on loan to the Corcoran Gallery of Art in Washington.[77] This was followed by *Landscape – Boys Fishing* (Fairhaven Collection, Anglesey Abbey), shown at the Academy in 1813, and again with the title *Landscape: a Lock on the Stour* at the British Institution in 1814.[78] In both these pictures, the lock was treated primarily as a picturesque foreground object. *Boat-Building* (Victoria & Albert Museum), shown at the Academy in 1815, like other works from around this time such as *Landscape, Ploughing Scene in Suffolk* and the Boston *View of Dedham* (*Plate 3*), has its main figures at work. However, the labours of the river population only become a central element in the picture significantly titled *Scene on a Navigable River* (RA 1817, Tate Gallery, *Plate 82*), now usually referred to as *Flatford Mill*. In *A Mill* (Private Collection, now known as *Dedham Lock and Mill*), exhibited at the British Institution in 1819, the lock is treated primarily as part of a picturesque ensemble of trees and utilitarian objects, arranged around the church tower, while figure activity is small and does not immediately attract the eye. References to work are increased in the (probably) later versions in the Victoria & Albert Museum (*Plate 79*) and Currier Art Gallery by the inclusion of the prow and sail of a barge in the left foreground, and the grazing horse still attached to its tow-rope on the right.[79] Of the so-called 'large canal scenes', the sequence of six large canvases on Stour themes which Constable exhibited over the years 1819–25, *Landscape: Noon* or *The Haywain* (RA 1821, National Gallery) can not be considered as a canal scene at all, it is rather an updated Gainsborough pastoral. (Considering the distinction between navigable rivers and canals, the use of the latter term is inappropriate in relation to the Stour.) While barges and river work feature in the remaining five pictures, they are kept to the side of the image in *The White Horse* (RA 1819 as *Scene on the River Stour*, Frick Collection, New York), and in *Stratford Mill* (RA 1820, as *Landscape*, National Gallery, London), the main figure interest is the children angling in the foreground, and the barge moored on the right bank is a secondary object. Rosenthal and others have seen a change in Constable's treatment of the Stour after this work – an issue I shall return to later. Certainly the river's traffic only become the primary focus of attention in *View on the Stour, near Dedham* (RA 1822, Huntington Collection, San Marino, *Plate 87*), again a significantly titled picture. Although work is also the main figure interest in *A Boat Passing a Lock* (RA 1824, Collection of Baron Thyssen, *Plate 88*) and *The Leaping Horse* (RA 1825 as *Landscape*, Royal Academy, London, *Plate 89*), it is noteworthy that the titles of neither tied them to the Stour region. Constable may have felt that his theme was already recognizable from his previous exhibits, or he may have felt that a generalized title was more appropriate to works in which the topographical content was slight. It should be clear, at least, that while Constable had made the Stour a repeated theme in his exhibition offerings, and while he repeatedly illustrated its commercial use, the pictorial emphasis on its use varied, with implications for its semiotic value.

Constable would obviously not have conceived his Stour pictures as an account of the Stour navigation, and neither would he have conceived them as illustrations of scenes particularly dear to him. Such were not the functions of serious landscape art. They were conceived as public works by an artist whose grounding in academic theory and association aethetics would have made him reject particular individual associations as irrelevant to the lasting value of landscape painting, or any other type of art. That Constable's father owned Flatford Mill and worked Dedham Mill, that the barge in *Boat-Building* is being built on his father's land, and even that his father was a commissioner of the River Stour Navigation are facts which must have been unknown to the vast majority of Constable's audience, and are hence quite irrelevant to the picture's contemporary meaning, whatever has been made of them in subsequent biographical and critical narratives. Since I am investigating the public functions of Constable's paintings, it is the general associations of inland navigation, as represented by the Stour, which concern me.

The Stour was made navigable from Sudbury in Suffolk to Manningtree in Essex as a result of Acts of 1705 and 1781, which appointed commissioners with powers to set out towpaths along it.[80] Cromwell's *Excursions in the County of Suffolk* (1818) noted that 'a comparatively brisk trade in the commodities consumed by the neighbouring counties' was carried on the river, but that it had suffered from the post-war depression. Skrine described the stretch of river between Nayland and Harwich as 'passing through a pleasant part of the two counties it traverses' but was more enthusiastic about the Orwell, which meets the Stour at Harwich. It was the Orwell estuary which particularly impressed travellers such as Young and Cobbett, and which Cromwell found 'one of the finest salt-rivers in the kingdom'. That river, and not the Stour, was also the subject of a sonnet in *The Suffolk Garland*, a collection of poems and stories published in Ipswich in 1818. It seems that there was no really enthusiastic account of Suffolk scenery which included 'the charming valley of Dedham' until Suckling's *History and Antiquities of the County of Suffolk* of 1841, and this may well have been influenced by the national reputation of Constable's work.[81]

There was thus no magazine of poetic descriptions of the Stour valley, and no topographical histories of the river. There were no monuments or places along its banks which were connected with important historical events, with royalty, or the national poetry. However, by the time Constable began to make the Stour his principal subject, a massive body of river images in the form of both paintings and prints was in currency, which was so much connected with the discourses of poetry and topography, that almost any image of a commercial river would inevitably call to mind some of the ideas which made up the current construction of the 'British paradise'.[82] Almost any river could function as one of the 'family' of British rivers. At this point the passage I quoted from Skrine at the start of this chapter should be recalled: that the 'spire of the rustic church' and woods had their most pleasing effects from the banks of rivers, and that the 'progress of navigation' contributed to the variety of the scenery. The tower of Dedham Church, which features in the distance of *Dedham Mill* and the last three of the major Stour pictures, was not primarily a topographical feature for Constable's audience (few could have recognized it), and neither was it merely a way of emphasizing perspective effect – it stood symbolically as the focus of moral and social order in the traditional rural world.

The accumulation of imagery of rivers inevitably meant that the connections between them and the discourse of the picturesque were extended and strengthened. Despite his aversion to picturesque theory, Ireland identified a number of sites as 'truly picturesque', which tended to form the basis for images derived from Hobbema water-mill scenes. Describing the Medway near Brantridge in Kent, he observed that 'the various meanderings and recesses of the river' afforded 'perpetual scenes of that simplicity in nature, which produces the elegant in landscape'.[83] Topographies also identified the picturesque in river improvements. Thus Combe found the round tower used to store coals, which features in Farington's *Junction of the Thames Canal near Lechlade* (*Plate 80*), 'a very pleasing embellishment to the scene'. Still more significant are the plate of *Clarke's or Buck's Weir* and Combe's description of it. With its rotting stumps and irregular cottages nestling among trees, this image already has many of the ingredients of a Constable river scene, and Combe's description reads like a recipe for one. According to Combe, the sluice gate:

> affords variety to the view, breaks the line of the river, produces some kind of waterfall, and gives activity and eddy to the current. But these weirs are generally connected with various accessory and diversifying circumstances; the mill, the fisherman's hut, or the cottage of the person who collects the toll, sometimes imbowered in trees, but always connected with them, heighten and vary the character of the scene.

A comment on the stream 'fretting among the mossy timbers, or rushing over the aquatic plants that cling to the frame-work' brings to mind many of Constable's foreground details.[84] The text to Cooke's *Views on the Thames* is less revealing on the picturesque of river navigation, merely remarking that weirs gave 'a very pleasing variety' to the Thames's upper reaches. However, the sequence of plates commences with an Owen composition showing the Thames and Severn Canal and a pump-house at the source of the Thames, and it includes several images of locks and weirs, which bring together elements similar to those in Constable's paintings (*Plate 52*). All in all, Constable's enthusiasm for 'Mill dams', 'Willows, Old rotten Banks, slimy posts, brickwork' was far from unique.[85]

The picturesque of commercial waterways is articulated particularly clearly in John Hassell's *Tour of the Grand Junction* of 1819, which claimed that the canal offered 'a variety far exceeding that afforded by many rivers, as combining all the beauties of landscape'. Hassell's text predictably emphasizes the commercial usefulness of the waterway and describes the factories along its banks, but it also provides the conventional type of 'historical and topographical' information, and, more unusually, contains many descriptions of views considered as pictures. Thus Hassell writes of the area near King's Langley:

> At a short distance beyond this, we see the navigation making a deviation in the valley, exhibiting a succession of bridges and locks, passage boats, with horses and their drivers in different situations, having noble backgrounds and a profusion of wood, forming altogether, abundant incidents for the pencil of the artist.

While at Cowley Lock, near Uxbridge:

> The boats in motion at the opening and shutting of the locks, and the various avocations of the attendants, constitute very appropriate incidents, and form excellent embellishments for landscape.

Elsewhere, harvest fields are described as pictures in which labourers enact a narrative of healthy and cheerful labour. Hassell recommended particular attention to changing effects of light and atmosphere, and asserted that they should be:

> instantaneously copied, and ought to become the particular care of the artist; for whatever is coloured on the spot and from nature invariably forms the best picture.

He also re-iterates the commonplace that:

> the effects of light and shadow are the peculiar care of the artist, and often render a very humble composition of the highest interest.

Thus Hassell's conception of subject and his ideas on the practice of the landscape painter seem remarkably similar to those of Constable. I am not suggesting that Hassell's crude aquatints had any influence on Constable, who had been experimenting with the picturesque of river views almost a decade before they appeared. I cite the work rather to indicate how well established the interest in commercial waterways as a pictorial motiv had become by the time Constable produced his major Stour paintings.[86]

The publication of the Havells' *Picturesque Views of the River Thames* in 1811 only slightly post-dates the beginning of Constable's concentration on the Stour. Plates such as *An Island on the Thames near Park Place* (*Plate 56*) and *Cliefden Spring and Woods* (*Plate 57*) seem to match exactly with the emphasis of the topographies on the beauty (as opposed to grandeur and sublimity) of the valley through which the Thames 'swells into a majestic river, full of commercial craft, and glides in a broad silver mirror through the plain'.[87] By using compositions which suggest the river seen from a boat, and filling the foreground with an expanse of water, Havell produced an effect of a broad calm stream. The clear diagonals receding into the composition, the barges being towed up towards the horizon, and the lucid reflections enhance the effect of stillness and peace. Constable was always to make more animated and picturesque effects, partly through the more variegated surfaces possible in the oil medium. Neither would he give quite such prominence to labour as Havell did in *The Weir, from Marlow Bridge* (*Plate 81*) and *Wallingford Castle* (*Plate 55*); or include anything quite as modern and suburban looking as the neat white villas in the first of these. All of Constable's Stour scenes are remote from the signs of town life evident in some of Havell's images. Further, whereas the topography of the latter was specific and widely known, Constable's was of essentially local interest, and was to become increasingly insignificant and generalized. But the naturalistic conception of turning an agglomeration of everyday features of a real working landscape into a picturesque composition with bright daylight effects is very comparable to Constable's approach in *Flatford Mill* (*Plate 82*) and *Dedham Lock & Mill* (*Plate 79*). The differences in approach between them derive partly from the general differences between the practices of landscape in water-colour and oil.

Water-colour lent itself more easily to landscapes with a marked topographical element, whereas modern day-light scenes in oil needed to make more overt references to earlier pictorial forms if they were to achieve the status of significant art.

In the early nineteenth century Constable's pictures were inevitably categorized as deriving from the type of landscape painting developed by the Dutch School. Those which represented mills and locks would be seen as a development of subjects particularly associated with Hobbema. Constable said nothing on Hobbema in his Lectures and the sole judgement he made in his letters is not particularly favourable:

> Hobbima (sic) if he misses colour is very disagreeable as he has neither shapes nor composition.[88]

However, *A Water-Mill* of 1812 (*Plate 83*) could hardly escape comparison with Hobbema's mill scenes, such as that at Dulwich College (*Plate 84*). Although the Dulwich Picture Gallery was not opened to Academy students until 1815, the Bourgeois Collection was accessible earlier, and Constable must have known this type of Hobbema composition with the curving foreground, expanse of water, and mill buildings in the middle distance. His own composition is more balanced, calling to mind the perspective structure of Claude's seaports, but the similarities with Hobbema are unlikely to have been fortuitous. Similar comparisons may be made with *Landscape, Boys Fishing* and *Dedham Lock and Mill.* In *Flatford Mill* the curving lines of the path, stream, bank, and trees are reminiscent of a recurrent compositional device in Hobbema's work, and may be compared to that of the *Road on a Dyke* in the National Gallery of Ireland (*Plate 85*), which was shown at the British Institution in 1815.

I am not suggesting that Constable's paintings are pastiches of Hobbema's, but that they can be read, and would have been read, as Hobbema done again from nature.[89] They share this relationship with Dutch painting with the works of other participants in the naturalistic phase. In 1811–13 Mulready produced a sequence of bright sunlight scenes which up-dated Dutch models, including the two well-known views of Kensington Gravel Pits in the Victoria and Albert Museum (*Plate 91*).[90] More directly pertinent is John Linnell's *View on the River Kennet* (*Plate 86*), exhibited with the Society of Painters in Oil and Water-Colours in 1816, the year before Constable's *Flatford Mill* was painted. Along the towpath on the left of this composition, a team of men pull a barge which occupies the centre of the river. This work actively contrasts with the leisurely figures on the bridge and the boy fishing in the foreground – there is even a touch of humour here with the dog investigating the unconscious angler's lunch basket. The tight precise touch of the picture may be related to Linnell's familiarity with early Flemish paintings in the Aders Collection, but the composition derives from the river scenes of van Goyen and van Ruysdael.[91]

In the 1820s, Constable's relations with Linnell had some ups and downs, and he never seems to have been friendly with the Lewis–Linnell–Mulready–Varley circle, perhaps not surprisingly considering that their religious and social outlook seems to have been somewhat at odds with his own high Tory anglicanism. Considering Constable's distaste for the 'cockney's' view of nature, and the choice of subject of what Marcia Pointon has described as the 'Kensington School',[92] it is unlikely that he would have wholly sympathized with their type of imagery. On the other hand, it is striking that Constable's most topographically precise works, and those in which the theme of labour first plays an important role, date from the years 1814–17, thus coinciding with the main naturalistic works of Lewis and Linnell. While it gives less prominence to labour than Linnell's *Kensington Gravel Pits* (*Plate 4*) or Lewis's *Harvest Scene, Afternoon* (*Plate 5*), Constable's *Flatford Mill* gives it more than the *View on the River Kennet. Flatford Mill* has two barges close to the front of the picture plane, and a third in the distance, and labour is dramatized by the strenuous activity of the man poling the barge over to the towpath where the horse and boys are waiting. The spectator's eye is drawn to the horse by its white nose and the red band of the bridle, and is then directed back by the boy's posture and the rope – the direction of the horse's stance also points the eye towards the barge. Thus Constable reverses the order of the work–leisure contrast in Linnell's picture by foregrounding work and placing his young anglers in the middle distance. By comparison with the *River Kennet*, *Flatford Mill* emphatically signals the connections between the river and commerce: the line of the towpath forms the central avenue of recession, and it leads the eye to the distant mill buildings. However, figure activity is kept mainly to the periphery of the canvas so that most of the spectator's attention is initially absorbed by the receding mass of the river bank, with its accumulation of botanical detail, and by the contrasting forms of trees and clouds. The handling of paint is different from that of Linnell and Lewis in the way that Constable uses a great variety of fluid irregular strokes, which despite the picture's detail still look painterly – significantly the *Examiner* commented on the lack of finish in *Flatford Mill* and *Wivenhoe Park* (National Gallery of Art, Washington, DC) when they were shown at the Academy in 1817. This painterly quality can be read in one respect as an attempt to represent detail with breadth, the idea of which was so crucial to Haydon and Hazlitt at this time. Together with the complex cloud structure and the variety of light and shade, the surface helps to suggest the idea of movement, change, and vitality, and the animation of the landscape was basic to the conception of nature Constable derived from association aesthetics and natural theology.

Despite some differences, I want to suggest that the pictures I have been discussing represent an important shift from the type of river painting which made up Turner's Thames series, and this is related to their more radical naturalism. At the level of form, all these pictures have a degree of specificity in relation to ideas of natural phenomena and labour which is found in none of Turner's Thames pictures. Turner's handling is always broader and more suggestive, producing effects of mist, as in *Dorchester Mead* (*Plate 62*) and *Ploughing up Turnips* (*Plate 64*), and rendering distance insubstantial and vague. There is nothing which resembles the way enclosed fields are picked out on the distant hill to the right of Lewis's *Harvest Scene, Afternoon*, or the definition of incidental details of distant trees and mills in *Flatford Mill*. There is little in Turner's foreground details which compares with the definition of plant types in the foregrounds of *Flatford Mill* and the 1815 *View of Dedham*. Equally, the large number of male and female labourers in *Ploughing up Turnips*, some of them at ease and some in conversation, suggests a kind of sociable occasion, with nothing of the mechanical concentrated routine implied by Linnell's grouping in *Kensington Gravel Pits* or Constable's muck-spreaders in his *View of Dedham*. In *Dorchester Mead*, the woman with cows in the left foreground is a pastoral cliché, and the men moving timber from wagons to barge in the distance are rendered insubstantial by the looseness of the paint. While a combination of resting and working labourers is represented in both Lewis's *Harvest Scene* and De Wint's *Cornfield* (Victoria & Albert Museum), routine labour is clearly defined in the background to both, and women field hands glean in the latter. While De Wint's resting figures have something of the character of a picnic, in Lewis's image, the figures are standing thus suggesting a brief respite from work – they are also more detailed and emphatically modern than anything in Turner's range of rustic figures in the Thames pictures. In all of these works, no effects of mist or haze soften the definition of forms in sunshine.[93]

I am not trying to suggest that there is a straightforward disjunction between two mutually exclusive types of image here, but I am suggesting that there are significant differences within a continuum of possibilities. The harder lighting of those works by Constable, Linnell, and Lewis, and their more tightly particularized details remove them somewhat from the type of image which rendered English scenery poetic partly through generalized atmospheric effects, such as those with which Turner was particularly associated.[94] That Turner was less interested in the practice of painting in oil outdoors than these artists helps to explain these differences at the level of production techniques. That his thinking was more restrained within the theories of academic theory at this time is suggested by both his practice and by the text of his *Backgrounds* lecture. It is also significant, in this connection, that the Thames series were shown at his own gallery rather than at the Academy, where most of his major contributions in the first two decades of the century were historical landscapes.

As Landseer's 1808 review shows, the broad atmospheric effects and suppression of detail in Turner's Thames pictures were widely understood as endowing ordinary landscapes with a quality of poetry. The pictures of Constable, Lewis, and Linnell lacked this 'breadth' as it was commonly defined, although, as I suggested earlier, they may represent an attempt to redefine that quality. Further, Turner's series was linked with a common currency of poetic imagery and thus referred to a well-known literary construction of the British landscape as well as to familiar pictorial prototypes. While the landscapes of Constable, Linnell, and Lewis could be referred to poetic imagery, there was no single obvious strand in the national literary tradition to which to anchor them. Their references were thus less clearly poetic, both formally and thematically. This gave them a more reportorial quality, a more mundane and quotidian range of associations, and thereby condemned them to a lower status. But it also put a particular onus on the artist to make the means of representation tell. Cut off from any easily accessible framework of poetic meaning, technique achieved a new kind of semantic importance. Thus Constable's *Flatford Mill* is such a densely worked picture. Poetry came to depend partly on suggesting a kind of truth to feelings of vitality produced by immediate visual experience. But this quality was probably beyond the sensibilities of the exhibition audience, for this type of picture does not seem to have sold well.

The landscape which attracted most attention at the 1817 Academy exhibition was Turner's *The Decline of the Carthaginian Empire* (Clore Gallery), and Constable's *Flatford Mill* was little noticed in the exhibition reviews either then, or when it was shown at the British Institution in 1818.[95] In the latter year, the most reviewed landscapes at the Academy were Turner's *Dort* and Callcott's *The Mouth of the Tyne* (whereabouts unknown). To compete for attention with the works of Turner, Callcott, Martin, Vincent, and others, Constable needed to produce something larger and more eye-catching. To escape from the category of local views, his pictures needed to be more generalized and have fewer signs of specific locales. To achieve the suggestions of mood, which would raise their status in relation to both academic theory and association aesthetics, they needed more dramatic atmospheric effects and more striking arrangements of light and shadow. They also needed more prominent figures to give them 'interest' – a narrative content. The increased scale and dramatic qualities of the six large Stour scenes should be seen more as a response to this situation than as a logical continuation of Constable's formal development.

In order to give 'importance' to his landscapes, Constable needed to give figures a larger role. The figures were kept to the periphery of the composition in *The White Horse*, but the horse's colour and the lighter effect of the left of the canvas help to draw attention to it. Children fishing occupy the centre of the foreground plane in *Stratford Mill*, and the prominently placed wagon and team in *The Haywain* are emphasized partly by the lead horse's head being on a line running through the horizontal centre of the composition. In the three later pictures of the series, figure activity is not only centralized, it is also emphatic, and there is less in the way of picturesque buildings to distract from it. Labour is given a dramatic quality: the straining figure trying to move the barge in *A View on the Stour* (*Plate 87*) has this in a way the similar figure in *Flatford Mill* does not, both because he is more central and two other figures are straining near him, and because all the figure activity is adjacent to the trees which are by far the largest objects against the sky. *A Boat Passing a Lock* (*Plate 88*) has as its centre a figure picked out in red, his face hidden, his whole body thrown into muscular activity in a pose derived from those used in the academy life class. The writhing forms of the tree on the right echo the line of his body, which is also echoed in the wood of the lock, and in another straining figure on the right. The drama of this little scene of barge life is emphasized by the turbulent sky. A similar conjunction of exertion and atmosphere is constructed in *The Leaping Horse* (*Plate 89*), where the main tree again echoes the line of the principal figure.

The increasing importance of figure activity has been noted by Michael Rosenthal, who has argued that while figures are more prominent, their narrative significance has diminished. Indeed, he claims that the 'imagery' of *The Lock* picture makes no 'connections outside itself', and that its subject 'can be understood only in the limited context of Constable's own work'. Whereas in earlier pictures 'a horse being ferried on a barge' referred to an 'ideology of trade and work, which, in turn, transmitted the notions of value it embodied to the terrain pictured', in *The Lock* 'the imagery has been purged of any content'.[96] While Rosenthal is surely correct in arguing that the last three paintings of the Stour series do not refer clearly to specific locations, and instead suggest ideas of 'nature' as a 'general phenomenon', in my view this does not justify his conclusion. Further this move to generalization was already evident in the three earlier paintings, all of which aggrandize insignificant bits of landscape, and have less topographical information than the pre-1819 works. In relation to the narrative issue, it is hard to imagine anything more aimless than the position of horse and wagon in *The Haywain*, which point downstream and not across to the distant harvest field, and neither are the narratives of *The White Horse* and *Stratford Mill* more clearly significant than those of the later pictures.[97] For Rosenthal these latter are 'abstracted and picturesque' works, which are 'removed from significant concern with literary, topographical, political, social or other elements', by their surface and glittering effects, which produce ideas only of an animated 'nature': the paint surface signifies nothing but *surface* and the denoted objects.[98] However, while the marks of facture necessarily have a significatory value, once the signs of river traffic they make up are recognized as such, it is hard to see how the commercial connotations of the image can be blocked. While facture could signify individuality even in his own period, Constable's work can not be read historically as a self-contained semiotic system. It is true that by abandoning topographical codes Constable produced the idea of a more generalized English scenery he evidently aimed for, but the pictures remain unmistakably commercial river landscapes with all that implied.

Rosenthal tends to explain Constable's changing aesthetic by inserting it in the narrative of an individual psycho-history, in which the artist becomes increasingly estranged from the Stour valley which had nurtured his work hitherto, so that his art became 'a retreat from the real world, not the result of a confrontation with it'.[99] While I find his account of the changes in Constable's outlook in the early 1820s admirable and broadly convincing, I want to place more emphasis on the way factors within the artistic field may explain the changes in his practice.

At the level of public significance, in the last three of the large Stour pictures the commercial aspects of the river, its barges and bargees, had come to dominate Constable's imagery in a far more prominent way: an energetic and anonymous working population absorbed in its proper business. The counterpoint to his vigorous male figures is the family group of the mother, baby, and child, standing next to the mast of the barge in *The Leaping Horse*. This idealization of the bargee, which is unique to Constable, is ironic, for the proletariat of the rivers and canals was notoriously unruly and given to pilfering. In 1781, Golding Constable, the artist's father, and another of the Commissioners with whom he conducted a survey of the river, complained to the Board of Commissioners of the 'rudeness and ill-behaviour' of the bargemen, and the Board responded by ordering that such behaviour be 'punished with the utmost severity'.[100] In the latter part of the nineteenth century, the condition of the canal 'outcasts', their poverty, ignorance, immorality, irreligion, and drunkenness, was to lead to a campaign for their regulation which produced two Acts of Parliament, in 1877 and 1884.[101] (The domestic functions of Constable's barges are indicated by their smoking chimneys.) Conditions on the canals and rivers deteriorated as a result of competition from the railways, and it would be unwise to assume that they were as bad in the early 1820s as they were fifty years later. However, the increasingly dynamic character of labour in *A View on the Stour*, *The Leaping Horse*, and *The Lock*, and the frenzied character it is given in the latter two pictures, suggests the acute tensions implicit in an attempt to represent modernization within the category of pastoral landscape, as this might be conceived within the naturalistic mode.[102]

Such tensions seem to have passed unnoticed by the critics, for the changes in Constable's work coincided with his increasing critical acclaim. His concentration on a limited range of subject matter was the subject of comment in the *Champion* as early as 1819, which praised *A Mill* (probably *Dedham Lock and Mill*) as a 'very pleasing example' of what he could do with the 'scanty materials' of 'Water-Mills, Water-Locks, Navigable Canals, and a Flat Cultivated Country'.[103] The *Repository of Arts* noted in relation to *The Haywain* in 1822 that:

> The Scenery which Mr Constable selects is mostly common, and his landscapes generally resemble each other; a moist hue too often occurs in their tone.

In its review of the Academy of the same year the magazine observed that his pictures were usually 'transcripts of some favourite spot, which mostly happens to be familiar with the public' and which had 'great truth and simplicity'.[104] It may have been repeated comments on the sameness of Constable's subjects which induced him to develop new ones in the 1820s. Although occasional reviews found his pictures too close to Dutch models, the vast majority emphasized their local truth and essential 'Englishness'. Thus, in 1819, the *Literary Chronicle* found that *The White Horse* had a 'grasp of every thing beautiful in rural scenery', while it described *The Leaping Horse* in 1825 as 'a charming specimen of that fresh verdant scenery peculiar to this country'.[105] A notice on *The Lock* in the *London Magazine* in 1824 found the 'character' of Constable's 'style' 'peculiarly English', while the *Literary Gazette* commented on the way Constable, 'in a style peculiar to himself', regularly managed to achieve:

> the most perfect representations of the objects of his study, whether of foreground or of distance. The character of his details, like those of Wilson, appear, as if stuck out with a single touch; but this, we are well aware, comes only by great practice and much previous thought and calculation. In none of his former works have these essential qualities been more distinctly visible than in this picture. It is a fine type of the picturesque, with which its striking and powerful execution well accords.[106]

Thus the more overtly picturesque quality of Constable's work, and its broader paint work, did not detract from its appeal.

Unlike Turner's paintings, Constable's did not contain the obvious signifiers of poetic landscape, and Robert Hunt, who was probably the most consistent of Constable's admirers, made a logical assessment within the prevailing critical system in the passage with which I began this section. The changes in the artist's style made no difference to Hunt's assessment of his verisimilitude. *A View on the Stour* was singled out for special praise in contrast to the many 'counterfeits' of nature at the 1822 Academy, while in *The Lock* Constable had 'caught the portraiture of nature more powerfully, perhaps, than ever', and *The Leaping Horse* was almost certainly one of the pair of 'Nature's own landscapes', which Hunt praised in the 1825 Academy show.[107] Hunt gave no consideration of the meaning of Constable's landscapes beyond the observation that the *View on the Stour* offered the 'consoling recollection of the charms of nature'. Only W. H. Pyne in the *Somerset House Gazette* picked up the element of artfulness in Constable's work, 'the judicious mixture of truth and accomplished knowledge of the principles of art', that combination of:

> local truth and unsophisticated feeling displayed . . . in his scenes of inland rivers, where all is nature represented with that coolness and freshness of effect that operates upon every spectator, with the same commanding appeal to the approbation of his senses.[108]

What these various responses show is that Constable's regular exhibition of river scenes had, predictably, established him as a painter pre-occupied with such subjects: a Constable type had been defined. A number of comments also suggest that his atmospheric effects were not such as were the norm in images of the British 'paradise'. *Dedham Vale, Morning* (1811), *View of Dedham* (1814), and *Boat-Building* (1814) all have loosely Claudean structures and calm sunny skies, which can be read as a continuation of, and variation on, the kind of pastoral/georgic mode Turner had developed so successfully in the Walton Bridges pictures. Constable may have felt that such atmospheric effects were overdone, and something new was required to suggest the characteristic changeability of British weather. His stated concern with the sky as the chief 'Organ of Sentiment' in a letter of 1821,[109] probably signals his concern to move beyond the local scenes which had dominated his output of 1811–18, and to produce a more generalized and expressive landscape painting. In the big Stour pictures, Constable uses types of cloud formation derived from Dutch art (as much as observation), handled in a technique derived from Titian and Rubens.[110] These innovative effects were immediately accepted as representing an authentically English atmosphere, and indeed the last three pictures of the series, in which they are at their most extreme, were regarded as being as satisfactory, if not more so, than the earlier ones. However, whatever the originality of Constable's efforts to dramatize narratives of life on the waterways, there was a limited number of operations which could be represented, and none had any special significance. The fact that the Stour did not have a history (a written text), in the way the Thames or other rivers did, was ultimately disabling. I suspect that it was the limitations of its narrative possibilities which led Constable to recognize that the theme was exhausted.

(v) The imagery of the Norfolk rivers

Like Yarmouth, the rivers of Norfolk were a major source of subjects for Norwich painters. To judge from titles which are unambiguous in the Norwich Society catalogues, Crome exhibited views of the river at Norwich in 1806–8, 1810–12 (x2), 1812 (x3), 1813 (x2), 1814, 1816–19, and 1821. Many of these were described as views of or near the New Mills, or views in the region of St Martin's at Oak, in which they stand, and thus they represented the Wensum rather than the Yare. Confirmation of the river's importance for Crome is provided by its prominence in the output of his pupils. John Berney Crome showed river views with the Norwich Society in 1810–12, 1814, and 1818; Stark showed them in 1811 (x3), 1812, 1813 (x3), and 1821; and Vincent in 1814 (x3), 1815–18, 1822–3, and 1828. Stark and Vincent also exhibited some major river views in London. There has certainly been some confusion between pictures of this type by Crome and his pupils, and it is significant too that Crome's river pictures are among the works by him of which copies are known.[111]

(a) Crome's Wensum paintings

I suggested in the previous chapter that the distinctive character of Crome's Yarmouth views might be explained by the rather special conditions of patronage and exhibition in Norwich. The point of this section is similar in that it will be argued that Crome produced a distinctively intimate type of urban river scene, which like his pictures of the seaside resort focussed on leisure sites. But before considering Crome's images of the 'Norwich river', I want to introduce some information about Norwich as a city in the late eighteenth and early nineteenth centuries.[112]

Although Norwich's importance as an economic unit lay to a large extent in its function as the commercial and market centre of an agricultural region, its growth in the eighteenth century depended on its development as a centre of the worsted industry.[113] At the mid nineteenth century probably more than fifty per cent of its population were small craftsmen, traders, and skilled working class, and these groups are likely to have defined its social character throughout the century preceding. The development of the textiles industry in Norwich in the period from 1750 to 1850 followed a pattern which is standard when artisanal forms of production are transformed into more industrial and capital-intensive forms of organization. While there was relatively little use of power machinery and the city specialized in expensive quality goods, weaving firms grew in scale and involved increasingly large volumes of capital. By 1750, some manufacturers had already come to regard apprenticeship regulations as a nuisance which kept wage rates too high, and the century saw a gradual erosion of traditional restrictions and a decline in wages. While a few manufacturers grew very wealthy, the weavers were increasingly impoverished and there was growing antagonism between capital and labour. Like the artisans of other industrial cities, those of Norwich suffered from the relentless cycles of expansion and contraction, and because of their dependence on the export trade they were especially hard hit by the Anglo-French Wars. In the 1790s the city's population actually fell, and in the early nineteenth century the professional middle class began to supplant the manufacturers as leading figures in city government.[114]

The agricultural depression of the post-war period drove rural labourers into the city in search of work, and this trend was probably compounded by property-owners in neighbouring parishes pulling down their cottages to get rid of the poor and lower the poor rate. With such an abundant labour supply, manufacturers were increasingly unwilling to keep to the scale of agreed wages, and in 1813 the power of JPs to fix wages was brought to an end. From the early 1810s to the mid 1820s, the textiles industry enjoyed a boom, which came to a dramatic end in 1826 and was followed by a phase of violence, riots, and strikes against wage reductions. These intensifying class tensions, together with the polarization of political opinion among the propertied classes as a result of the French Revolution and Anglo-French Wars, served to make the political life of the city antagonistic and violent for much of this period.[115]

As I mentioned in the last chapter, Crome's life was involved with the Norwich manufacturer/merchant community in many ways. Dr Rigby, his first employer, was a leading figure both in city government and in Norwich's intellectual life – he was reported to be the driving force in the Norwich Philosophical Society of which Crome and J. B. Crome were members.[116] Crome's first major patron, Thomas Harvey, was a master weaver; and the most important of his early employers, the

Earlham branch of the Gurney family, derived their vast wealth originally from the textiles industry.[117] His pupil, James Stark, was the son of a major Norwich dyer and manufacturer, who made important contributions in a field of production in which Norwich had a considerable reputation, servicing other regions until after 1850.[118] Indeed, Crome's involvement with the apprenticeship system is itself symptomatic, since the system was the foundation of the city's government in the eighteenth century. Crome was apprenticed to the coach and sign painter Francis Whisler in 1783, and Stark and Vincent served three-year apprenticeships to him. Vincent was also sworn a freeman of Norwich in October 1817.

However, Crome's relations with respectable Norwich were ambiguous, and he was certainly not the model of bourgeois industry Dawson Turner made him out to be in his memoir. In a letter of 1858, the artist Henry Ladbrooke wrote of him that his 'habits were not those of a poor man – he kept a good, rather an extravagant house & lived like a fighting cock'.[119] He seems to have had a flourishing teaching practice, and his bank book of 1812–14 (Norwich Castle Museum) shows that his account was in credit to the sum of £415.94 at the start of 1814, so that the fact he was obliged to hold a sale of his books and prints in 1812 argues that he had large outgoings as well as a good income. Taken together, there is some evidence to suggest that the 'very awkward, uninformed, country lad', who Beechey recalled visiting his studio in the late 1780s, was never entirely assimilated to the polite culture of the Norwich bourgeoisie – perhaps partly because of his formation within an artisanal culture.[120]

The development of Norwich capitalism not only affected the wage levels and life expectancy of the working population, it was also imprinted on the urban environment. In 1660, Thomas Fuller had described Norwich as 'a City in an Orchard or an Orchard in a City', but although this phrase was frequently quoted in early nineteenth-century guides, by then the growth of its population had brought increasing spatial problems, and demanded considerable additions to its amenities. The needs of industry forced the municipal government to play an increasingly active role in maintaining and developing the physical fabric of the city. Between 1793 and 1795, eight of the twelve medieval gates were destroyed along with much of the wall. Several of the old bridges were rebuilt in the 1780s and 1790s, in 1800 a new bridge with a centre arch of iron was put up at St Michael Coslany, and the iron Carrow and timber Foundry bridges were begun in 1810. After 1780 there was increasing expenditure on street repairs, and overhanging gables were progressively removed. The market place had been paved in 1731, and in 1792 Gentleman's Walk, which runs along its lower edge, was paved in Scottish granite. Early nineteenth-century commentators remarked on the city's old-fashioned look, and the slow-down in the economy meant there was relatively little new building until the late 1810s. However, there was something of a building boom in the 1820s, and Stacy's guide-book of 1819 referred to the 'almost daily multiplication of buildings' outside the city's walls:

> built in humble imitation of those countless erections which astonish the stranger on his approach to the metropolis of England

at the same time as:

> each vacant space within the city, that circumstances permit, seems about to be appropriated to the use of the builder.

Thus despite the city's declining importance relative to other cities, it still underwent many of the same processes of modernization as its rivals.[121]

One of the central concerns of the city government was the river. The thirty-mile stretch of the Yare between Norwich and Great Yarmouth had been crucial to Norwich's industrial development, since it was from Yarmouth that its textile products were exported to the continent. An Act of 1669 set up the Yarmouth and Haven Pier Commission, which was empowered to levy duties on all cargoes entering Yarmouth to maintain the harbour and river. Further Acts followed, and that of 1723 authorized the Norwich Corporation to set up occasional commissions of sewers to inspect the river, and oblige those with land on the river front to maintain the banks. In the eighteenth century, the water system served the Norwich textiles industry well, but its growing reliance on cotton and wool spun in Lancashire and Yorkshire, put it at a disadvantage in relation to the manufacturers of those regions, which was particularly felt after 1815. Whereas the West Riding was increasingly advantaged by the development of the canal network in the north-west, Norwich faced growing problems in moving bulky freight to London. Breydon Water, which lies just west of Yarmouth, is very shallow, and could only accommodate boats with a draft of less than three feet. To reduce Norwich's dependence on Yarmouth and get round these problems, city interests proposed the Norwich and Lowestoft Navigation Bill of 1827, to make Norwich a port by linking Lowestoft to the river Waveney and the Waveney to the Yare, thereby avoiding Breydon Water. The route was opened in 1833, although returns on investment were poor, and its value was diminished by the opening of the Norwich and Yarmouth Railway in 1844.[122]

The river system was not only vital to the textiles industry, it also played an important role in Norfolk's progressive agriculture. R. N. Bacon, in his prize-winning *Report on the Agriculture of Norfolk* (1844) commented on the function of wherries (the local boat) in carrying marl and manure, particularly to the eastern districts of the county, and rushes and coarse hay from the marshes were also transported by them.[123] Within Norwich, the river was vital to the dyeing and brewing industries, and also, of course, for the water-supply. The New Mills of Crome's pictures were built by the corporation in the late sixteenth century and included a flour mill and water-raising complex. In the early nineteenth century, the power of the New Mills was harnessed to drive one of the city's new silk mills which was constructed by 1819, a five-floor building covering 220 square yards, which stood adjacent to them.[124] Crome's 'Norwich River' and 'New Mills' thus had major functions in the city's economy.

At one level, Crome's paintings and prints of the area around the New Mills can be slotted into a well-known category: the imagery of decaying cottages and urban buildings which was so popular with artists in the years around 1800. This imagery derived from a type of picture developed by seventeenth-century painters such as Ostade and de Hoogh, and was licensed by the currency of picturesque aesthetics. The closest parallel with Crome's river buildings is provided by Mulready's two views of the Kensington Gravel Pits area of *c.* 1812 (*Plate 91*). Indeed the similarities between Crome's and Mulready's developments are striking. Crome's early paintings of picturesque buildings such as *Carrow Abbey* (*c.* 1805, Norwich Castle Museum), and *The Blacksmith's Shop* (*c.* 1807–8, Philadelphia Museum of Art) have sombre, theatrical light effects, and relatively simple constructions. Like Mulready's cottage landscapes of *c.* 1806–8 (*Plate 90*), they suggest a nonspecific rural environment. By comparison, later works such as Norwich Museum's *View of St Martin's Gate* (*c.* 1810–12, *Plate 92*) and *Back of the New Mills* (*c.* 1816–17, *Plate 95*), like Mulready's Kensington pictures, have brighter colours, broad daylight light effects, and more complex arrangements of architectural forms, which clearly suggest an urban locale. In both cases, this transition can be read as one from a generalized picturesque to a more topographical and naturalistic mode.[125]

However, having established the general category in relation to which Crome's works would have been read, it is necessary to ask: what features do they have (if any) which distinguish them from other works in the same mode, and what inflections do such differences give to their meanings? My discussion here will focus on six paintings of somewhat different dates: the *View of St Martin's Gate* and *Back of the New Mills* mentioned above, the *New Mills: Men Wading* (*c.* 1812, Norwich Castle Museum, *Plate 94*), *The Wensum, Norwich* (*c.* 1813–14, *Plate 97*) and the so-called *Wensum at Thorpe, Boys Bathing* (*c.* 1817–18, *Plate 99*), both in the Yale Center for British Art, and *Norwich River: Afternoon* (*c.* 1819, collection of Max Michaelis, *Plate 100*). While it is impossible to identify these paintings with exhibited works with complete certainty, the *New Mills: Men Wading* may well have been *Creek Scene, near the New Mills, Norwich*, number 115 in the 1812 Norwich exhibition – this would tie in with the date of 1813 on the etching after the picture, and also with the etching's title of *Front of the New Mills*.[126] The Michaelis painting is likely to be *A Scene on the Norwich River – Afternoon*, which was number 48 in the 1819 exhibition.

Firstly, it needs to be noted that all of these pictures represent fragments of the urban scene in conjunction with the river. This in itself was far from original, and similar conjunctions can be found in topographical prints and water-colours such as Dayes' *View of Hereford* in *Jukes's Views on the River Wye* (*Plate 93*), or Girtin's numerous bridge compositions. *St Martin's Gate* has a remarkably complex pattern of shapes and forms, which denote spatial recession with little in the way of orthogonals.

Despite the markers of depth the picture tends to work almost like a sculptural relief composed of foreground, middle, and distant planes. There are problems with judging the picture's original effect from its present condition. As it is now, there is a marked contrast between the light colour of the sky and distant buildings, and the dark brown shadows of the foreground. Originally there was probably far more light colour in the lower part of the picture, which would have given it a less conventionally picturesque colour range. Yet there is still a marked change in use of colour between *St Martin's Gate* and the probably later *New Mills: Men Wading* and *Back of the New Mills*. In the last of these there is no dark brown colour at all, and there is very little in the second. Indeed to judge by technique, the two are closely related in date. The receding line of the bank is at a less acute angle with the picture plane in *New Mills: Men Wading* than in *St Martin's Gate*, and thus the picture has a less compressed recession. It is also lighter in colour, the effect of bright sunlight being suggested by details such as the thin streaks of yellow on the edges of the fence palings on the left. None the less, its overall effect is primarily one of bits of walls, fences, house-ends, gables and so on – a tangle of planes and different textures.

If Crome gives us a representation of the urban scene in these pictures, he suggests a quaint old town of humble picturesque buildings, in marked contrast to the impression of Norwich provided by say Cotman's *Norwich Market Place* (*Plate 96*). It was possible to represent Norwich in this way by concentrating on the parish of St Martin's at Oak at the north-west edge of the city (see map 5), as there can have been little river traffic there. Although the title of *View of St Martin's Gate* suggests that it represents part of the medieval fortifications, this is not the case. St Martin's Gate had been pulled down in 1793 and could not have been seen from the river anyway. The term was probably a name for the area, and presuming the title is correct, it is likely that it shows one of the streets which ran down from St Martin's at Oak Street to the river. *New Mills: Men Wading*, if it is the 1812 exhibit, probably shows the creek between the New Mills and Coslany Bridge, again visible in map 5. Crome's use of crumbling walls, jumbles of irregular old houses, and trees to represent the edge of the city, is seen also in the etching titled *Back of the New Mills, Norwich*, which probably shows the Wensum as it curves round towards Hellesdon, and may well be based on a lost painting.[127]

In his thirteenth *Discourse*, Reynolds advised the architect to 'take advantage *sometimes*' of the accidents of irregularity, which arose from piecemeal additions to houses, for 'as such buildings depart from regularity, they now and then acquire something of scenery by this accident'. He referred to the 'forms and turnings' of London streets, together with those of other old towns to illustrate the point. This passage was quoted by Edmund Bartell in his *Hints for Picturesque Improvements in Ornamented Cottages* (1804), and elsewhere in the text he emphasized the picturesque of tree-lined rivers and pools. Thus Bartell's writings can again be seen as offering an aesthetic theory for Norwich painting.[128]

In what I regard as the later pictures in the sequence, Crome's technique and

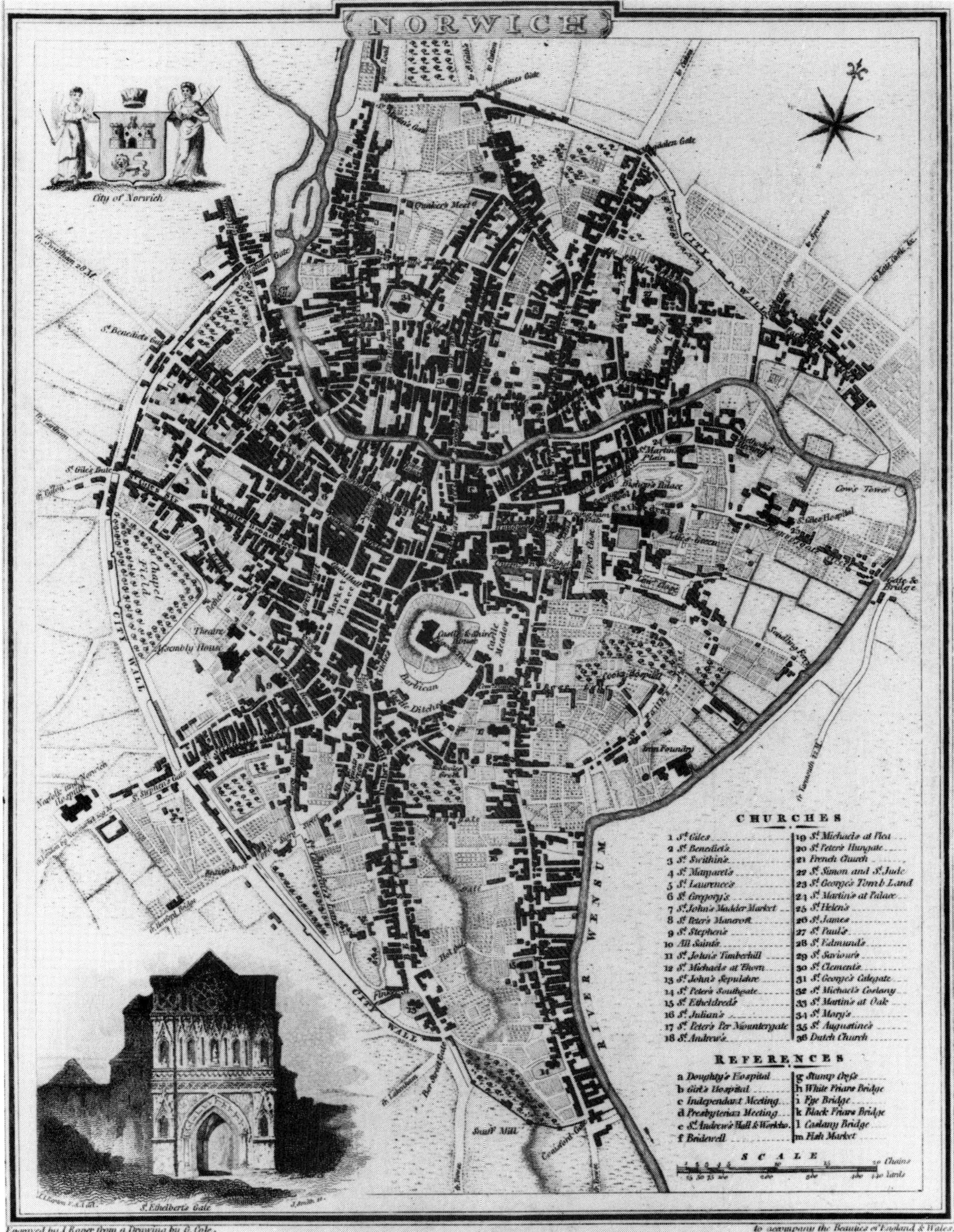

Map 5 J. Roper after G. Cole, *Norwich*, 1807, from Brayley & Britton's *Beauties of England and Wales*

approach changed somewhat. *The Wensum, Norwich* (*Plate 97*) is not only richer in colour than *St Martin's Gate*, it is a less formulaic exercise in picturesque architecture, and includes a large regular barn-like structure, with the tall roof of a factory or mill in the distance. The area represented may again be the creek which featured in the 1812 exhibit. This new willingness to include structures which did not of themselves meet picturesque requirements, and which were quite plainly utilitarian, is even clearer in the painting *Back of the New Mills* (*Plate 95*). Unlike the etching of this title, this shows the New Mills building and also loosely indicates the area of the city beyond it to the south. To see the mills in this way, Crome would have had to take a position on the east bank of the river somewhere just north of where it narrows down, or possibly he drew from a boat. To the left of the Mills is what appears to be a large factory, and another mill-like building juts into the composition behind the house on the left. (In this connection, it should be noted that Samuel Paget lent a picture to Crome's Memorial Exhibition in 1821 with the title *View of the back of New Mills near the Manufactory of C. Higgins Esq.*, dated to 1817.) To see how far Crome has moved from his approach of *c.* 1810–12, this house with its light pink and yellow colours and clear spatial presence, should be compared with the gable end of the main building in St Martin's Gate, which is defined almost exclusively through its picturesque outline. Equally, the overgrown walls and irregular fences of the latter picture, may be compared with the solid brickwork of the wall on the left of the former, the regularity of which is emphasized by the line of washing behind it – brick was not a material sanctioned in picturesque aesthetics. By filling the entire foreground with an expanse of water, the light effect of the picture is brightened, and the clearly defined reflections, together with the light-coloured sky, produce a placid sensation. The irregular line of forms curving round the composition from left to right accords with the usual movement of the eye, and also contributes to the tranquil atmosphere. In contrast with the cramped spatial construction of *St Martin's Gate*, depth in this picture is more strongly articulated by contrasts of light, dark, and colour in a series of receding planes: dark mill/light house/green mass and so on. *Back of the New Mills* is thus a modern urban view in a way the pictures of 1810–12 were not, and it may be compared with the effect of an anonymous topographical print of *c.* 1820 (*Plate 98*). However, Crome's concern with the picturesque and with breadth remains: although conventional picturesque colouring has been exchanged for a subtle range of pinks, greens, blues, and greys, there is still the same concern with variety and irregularity, but in a lighter key.

None of Crome's surviving oils of the Norwich river represent men clearly at work, except in the distance of *New Mills: Men Wading* where two men are cleaning the river from a boat. Instead, their male figures are boys playing and men relaxing or doing little. There are figures of women washing in both *St Martin's Gate* and *Back of the New Mills*, but this would probably have evoked the idea of domesticity rather than labour. In this respect, Crome seems to have shifted very slowly and incompletely from the aesthetic of the eighteenth-century picturesque to that of naturalistic landscape art. His river scenes may be compared with his rustic landscapes, in which figures are largely confined to the occasional herdsman and shepherd. The blatantly unimproved landscape of the Tate Gallery's *Mousehold Heath* (*c.* 1810–13) contrasts markedly with Cotman's attention to modern agricultural practices in water-colours such as the *Ploughed Field* (Leeds City Art Gallery) and the British Museum's *Mousehold Heath*. He seems to have found it easier to accommodate figures engaged in leisure activities than other types, and it is striking that the two paintings by him in which figures do play a prominent role are of continental subjects.[129]

The leisure element is most overt in the latest of the paintings. The picture erroneously titled *The Wensum at Thorpe* (*Plate 99*), was described by Dawson Turner, to whom Crome sold it, as a 'bright day-light scene at the back of the New Mills, on the Norwich river'.[130] It thus cannot represent Thorpe, which is below Norwich on the south-east of the city, and while it does represent the Wensum, it could not represent it at Thorpe since that river joins the Yare before reaching Thorpe. *Scene on the River at Norwich* (Turner's title) again shows an insignificant bit of waterfront, but its main subject is trees, and houses are confined to the distance. The combination of trees and the bathing boys, against an urban background, suggests a retreat from the city within the city. (It may be noted in this connection that there was a subscription bath-house on the Wensum near where it entered Norwich.)[131] This representation of carefree children in an urban environment is somewhat heterodox, since the usual setting for such figures was a 'healthy' rural scene, as in Constable's *Stratford Mill* or Crome's *Poringland Oak* (Tate Gallery). While children play in the foreground of Mulready's *The Mall, Kensington Gravel Pits* (Victoria & Albert Museum) the nakedness of Crome's boys makes them especially incongruous in an urban milieu, where the children of poor families worked from an early age.

The leisure of adults provides the main figure interest in *Norwich River: Afternoon* (*Plate 100*). In this the curve of the river round to the right is balanced by the leaning mass of trees, growing from the bank of what seems to be the entrance to the creek. The interplay of intricate shapes in the fences, foliage, and roof-lines fulfils the requirements of the picturesque, while the mills and houses beyond confirm the urban setting, and provide the backdrop to a pleasure boat excursion on a summer afternoon. The dress of the figures suggests they are from the lower end of the social hierarchy, and they thus fit in with the vernacular architecture of the location. The function of figures in picturesque landscape is again discussed by Bartell in his guide to Cromer, where writing of lanes he says:

> Figures in a road are another great source of amusement, and whether in motion or at rest, are equally pleasing; they create an interest in the mind by being strongly contrasted with inanimate objects. If at some distance, we are naturally

> led to inquire who they may be, or what their employment; and if a single figure happens to be reclining upon the bank, or leaning upon his staff, we probably form in our imagination the subject of his thoughts.[132]

If this kind of associationist semantics was extended to picturesque river views, Crome's figures do not just animate the scene, they also prompt reflections as to their occupations and state of mind. The placid effects of Crome's river scenes are thus of a piece with figure types which function to denote leisure, relaxation, and domestic life.

Crome's views of the Norwich river are not landscapes of 'nature' in the sense that Constable understood the term. To see this, *Back of the New Mills* should be compared with Constable's *A Water-Mill* of 1812 (*Plate 83*). While both pictures clearly develop from the Hobbema water-mill type, Crome emphatically urbanizes the form and smoothes out some of its picturesque qualities.[133] If Crome was not alone in selecting such semi-urban sites, he gave them a particular inflection, both by his consistent inclusion of the river, and by that of the New Mills and factory buildings. In themselves, Crome's boys bathing and his boats are nothing new: the distinctive feature of his use of figures is the way that working-class pleasures are represented in an urban picturesque setting. Given Crome's class origins, it is worth considering whether or not his decision to represent the city in this way may not have been determined by more than a narrow recognition that parts of it could be adapted to a current aesthetic. His background in artisan culture may have enabled him to feel a particular sympathy for such prosaic work-a-day surroundings, and to find a particular relish for leisure activities within them. However, Crome's outlook and the public meanings of his works are different things.

Unfortunately the Norwich newspapers provide very scanty exhibition reviews, and the only references to Crome's pictures of the Norwich river I have found are two brief comments in the *Norfolk Chronicle* in 1818 and 1819, which are purely technical and tell us nothing about the subject of the works.[134] Of the surviving oils, the only one whose provenance can be traced back to Crome's life-time is Dawson Turner's *Scene on the River at Norwich*. At least ten pictures of the 'Norwich river' were lent to Crome's memorial exhibition, the lenders I have identified being three members of the Paget family of Yarmouth; John Brightwen, a partner in the Gurney-Turner bank; the Reverend John Homfray, a Yarmouth clergyman; and the Reverend Edward Valpy, Headmaster of Norwich Grammar School. The class positions of these people are within the same range as those who bought Crome's Yarmouth beach pictures, and no significance can be deduced from this beyond the fact that his Norwich river pictures were clearly saleable to the local bourgeoisie.

In his text for Stark's *Rivers of Norfolk*, the Norwich worsted manufacturer, John Warden Robberds, observed in connection with the city's gothic remains:

> In the view of an ancient city, like Norwich, the most prominent places are filled by objects which naturally direct the mind to these considerations [i.e.

> *associations of gallantry and heroism*], and which are hence regarded with a warmth of feeling never excited by the tame regularity and cold elegance of modern terraces, crescents, and squares.[135]

While the buildings Crome represented had no such poetic associations, some of them were at least old and picturesque, and not tamely regular or coldly elegant. Robberds' text draws on a complex range of discourses, and displays a tension between a commitment to commerce, liberty, and progress, and a commitment to a model of the rural order as both picturesque and uncorrupted. To those sentimental bourgeois strung between these poles, Crome's work may have had a special appeal.

(b) John Thirtle's water-colours of the Norwich river

John Thirtle was a minor local artist whose main livelihood was probably his gilding and frame-making business. Like Crome, he was an individual with a wide range of employments, who came from a background in the Norwich trades, his father being a shoemaker. Although neither father nor son seems to have amassed much property, they were sufficiently respectable to be churchwardens and overseers of the poor.[136] Thirtle seems to have exhibited outside Norwich on one occasion only, and even in Norwich he did not make a big showing in the exhibitions, although his work was well-received in the local press. But if he was only a retiring provincial artist of negligible reputation, Thirtle produced a body of drawings of extremely high quality, which exemplify some of the most interesting dimensions of water-colour naturalism in the period.

It should be evident from the examples discussed in chapter 8 that the exhibition water-colour was not a pictorial form within which the modern could be rendered aesthetic, except in discreet snippets fitted into the distance. The smoking chimneys and hard regular forms of modern factories were represented contemporaneously in drawings such as De Wint's *Stockport* (*c.* 1816, Bodleian Library, Oxford) – but this was a small drawing made specifically for an engraving to illustrate a county history.[137] If one considers the various determining factors within the artistic field, this marginalization of the modern is not surprising. While exhibition water-colours necessarily had a relationship with the practice of topographical illustration, the exhibition drawing and drawing for engraving served different functions, even if the latter were sometimes exhibited and there was a continuum between the two. Exhibition water-colours, and particularly large ones, had to meet some of the requirements of landscape painting in oils if they were going to achieve the status of pictures and serious art. They had to meet the requirements of the picturesque (however reconstituted), and should preferably represent forms of social activity which were understood as 'natural', 'healthy', and traditional.

However, it seems that the very physical properties of the medium encouraged a kind of formal innovation. That working on a white surface in transparent colours, sometimes outdoors, suggested new possibilities in terms of colour effects and the relationship between drawing and painting was notably exemplified in Cotman's Greta drawings. There is nothing in the subjects of the Greta drawings which was not conformable to Uvedale Price's conception of the picturesque, as discovered in insignificant landscape motivs, but Cotman applied to such subjects a novel approach to colour and a fluid variegated brushwork, partly developed through outdoor sketches, which were licensed by the aesthetic of naturalism and originality, described in chapter 6.[138] To put the matter crudely, there is a kind of logic to some of the effects which experimental water-colour achieved in the early nineteenth century, which arose out of the way the discourses of contemporary aesthetics intersected with the possibilities of material and practice.

The complexity of Cotman's synthesis has made it easy to assimilate his work to the unique genius, ahead of his time, syndrome. However, it is important to note the variety of his output, and to recognize the way in which it was oriented to different tendencies in aesthetic discourse. Thus in Cotman's drawings of the first Norwich period, the aesthetics of the picturesque, of topography, of naturalism, and of classical landscape seem to play off against one another in a variety of combinations, ranging from the overt modernity of *Norwich Market Place* (which was intended as the basis for a print),[139] through the more picturesque *Trowse Hythe* (Norwich Castle Museum), to drawings such as the *Road to Capel Curig* (Victoria & Albert Museum), in which the aesthetic of classical landscape predominates. Although Cotman never managed to represent the face of Norwich's industry, a contrast of the Gothic and the modern can be read in the relationship between enclosed fields and the ruin in *Kett's Castle*, and the accretion of modern buildings around the east end of Norwich Cathedral in *St Luke's Chapel* (both drawings in Norwich Castle Museum).[140]

What I am arguing here is that there were tendencies in water-colour practice which were modern in their signification. I mean modern, but not, of course, Modernist. That is to say, the connection between the water-colour and the practice of topography meant it was somewhat easier to incorporate modern motivs within exhibition water-colours than it was within exhibition oil paintings, water-colour being understood as primarily an art of the 'view', despite the efforts of Cristall, Heaphy, Richter and others to extend its compass. (Modern motivs are understood here primarily as contemporary urban structures, but the term could be extended to the enclosed fields of the *Ploughed Field* and *Kett's Castle*.) It was also possible to make innovations in composition, colour, and technique somewhat more readily within the medium. I am not implying that modern urban motivs and formal innovation were not possible in oil painting, merely that in water-colour the scope for innovation was somewhat larger, and the medium itself encouraged it. The weight of tradition pressed down on and around water-colour practice, but not quite as heavily. It was in the area where modern topographical subject-matter, the aesthetic of naturalism, and the requirements of serious landscape art co-existed in a somewhat uneasy relationship with each other, that Thirtle's most interesting work can be seen to lie.

What is disconcerting about Thirtle's output, considered as an 'oeuvre', is the way it seems to involve such contrasting modes of working and visualizing. I am referring to the contrast between the vivid colouring of sketches such as *Thorpe, Norwich* (*Plate 101*), *A Norfolk Church* and *Sunset Landscape with Thorpe Hospital*, and the tame harmonies and bland surfaces of the finished drawings.[141] There is also a distinction between the modernity of the steam barge and modern villas in *A View of Thorpe, with Steam Barge working up – Evening* (exhibited in 1815, *Plate 102*) or the iron bridge in *Carrow Bridge* and the pastoral cliché of an *Evening River Scene*.[142] As can be seen from the examples of study and finished work illustrated here, the move from preparatory to final version usually involved extending the scope of the composition around the motiv, adding or making more emphatic framing devices, and extending the foreground and adding picturesque or genre details to it.[143] Such comparisons of sketch and finished work suggest the rough edges of impressions, somewhat untidily pressed into the mould of pictorial schema, had to be tidied up and smoothed off. Although it may seem indulging in a twentieth-century sensibility to see the transformation as one which leads to tameness, to argue that the transition from sketch to finished drawing involved fitting the conventions of observation within a framework of conventions more tightly governed by the rules of precedent does not seem unreasonable. It was not that the sketch did not involve conventions – how else could representation work? However, we may envisage the sketch allowing greater latitude to represent accidentals and to try out new variations.

Thirtle himself was emphatic about the advantages of finished drawings in his manuscript treatise on water-colour painting:

> once yr Eyes are opened to the beauties of a finished work & to the Everlasting delight of Folowg. nature in all her simplest minutiae – you will despise hasty sketches.[144]

This reminds us again that sketches simply did not have the same status in the early nineteenth century they have acquired since. Sketchiness, which in France in the latter part of the century came to signify qualities of individualism and originality, and modern sensibility, had not yet become associated with these values. At the level of reference, the modern was specified more clearly in finished works: the mess of commercial buildings and press of boats in *Rainbow Effect, on the River, King Street* (exhibited in 1817?, *Plate 103*), and the steam barge in *View of Thorpe*. However, it is arguable that some of the innovative, and hence modern technical elements in these drawings had been arrived at through experiments with the outdoor sketch.

Thirtle's finished water-colours incorporate the signs of the modern, in the form of trade, work, commercial buildings, and bridges around the edge of Norwich in a way Crome's oil paintings simply don't. *St Martin's Gate, New Mills: Men Wading*, and the *View on the Wensum* seem a precious and claustrophobic view of the edge of the city by comparison with *View of the River near Cow's Tower* (*Plate 105*), *Boat*

Builder's Yard (*Plate 106*), *Rainbow Effect on the River, King Street*, and other drawings. It is surely significant that Crome's approach is closest to Thirtle's in a water-colour of the commercial waterfront: *Houses and Wherries on the Wensum* (*c*. 1810–12, Manchester City Art Gallery, *Plate 104*).[145]

One of the staple tropes of topographical imagery in the early nineteenth century was the juxtaposition of the decay of medieval monuments with modern vernacular developments. Thirtle repeatedly organized his drawings of the edge of Norwich around this contrast. In the *Devil's Tower near King Street Gates – Evening* (not illustrated here), the silhouette of the medieval tower and its visual echo, the distant mass of Norwich castle, bracket the mess of the King Street waterfront. The composition of the finished drawing of *Rainbow Effect on the River, King Street* (*Plate 103*) was extended to include the medieval structure on the right, which is not present in the sketch. In *View of the River near Cow's Tower* (*Plate 105*) (which may be a drawing exhibited in 1810), the tower is juxtaposed with a modern villa, the unpicturesque line of poplars, the timber of the boatyard buildings, and a wherry with lowered mast, presumably prepared to negotiate Bishopsgate Bridge, downstream. The bulk of Cow Tower, with its ragged top, seems massive, useless, and forlorn in contrast to the sharp precise forms of the houses. The sprays of delicately touched foliage on the left, which belong to some trees outside the framework of the composition give it more of the quality of a sketch; and the apparently 'casual' compositional effect, is reinforced by the way in which Cow Tower is sliced in half. The image lacks any single clear focus of interest: the horizontal centre of the composition falls on the second poplar. *Boat-Builder's Yard near the Cow's Tower* (*Plate 106*), which was perhaps shown two years later, also has no clear hierarchy of interest. Indeed, there seems a balance between the activities of the labourers constructing the wherry in the left foreground, the boat coming ashore, the clutter of the yard, and the medieval relic on the opposite bank. The presence of Cow Tower is emphasized both by the framing effect of the clouds and light shafts, and also by the striking effect of the beam of sunlight streaming through the cruciform opening at the top. As one's eye moves along the mass of distant hill behind, it encounters another medieval structure in the shape of St Leonard's Priory, or Kett's Castle as it was known.

The most thematically daring of Thirtle's drawings is the *View of Thorpe, with Steam Barge working up* (*Plate 102*) of 1815. Thorpe was a fashionable suburb, and nestling in the long low line of hill rising from the valley are the new villas of the Norwich bourgeoisie. Between the sketch and the finished drawing, Thirtle has introduced a piece of land in the right foreground to provide a stronger framing effect than the reflection in the sketch. The reflection of the tree trunks, which gave an interest to the left foreground in the sketch, has been replaced by a narrative feature in the rowing boat, which makes a kind of contrast between human muscle overtaken by the product of mechanical ingenuity. The chimney of the boat is obscured by the sail, but the paddle wheel on the left is clearly visible, and the sails are small in proportion to the scale of the boat. The low view of this sleek expanse of water, together with the very wide angle formed by the orthogonals of the banks, helps to give a kind of pictorial force to the steam barge moving upstream and coming out of the composition almost head on. It is a design which, appropriate to its subject, makes little concession to the picturesque.

At one level, I do not want to suggest that there is anything unique about Thirtle's water-colours of the edge of Norwich – I instance them rather as examples of a particular kind of possibility in early nineteenth-century water-colour. Thus comparable juxtapositions of medieval bridges with the signs of modern trade can be found in the work of other artists of the period such as Girtin and De Wint. Varley represented a *Boat-Builder's Yard on the Thames* in a drawing of 1806 (Yale Centre for British Art), although it is not as large or ambitious as Thirtle's treatment of the theme. At Bristol too, artists were making some striking representations of the modern as it could be seen from the Avon within topographical water-colours such as Samuel Jackson's *View of Clifton from Rownham Meadows* (City of Bristol Art Gallery). Rivers also provided a motiv around which to locate contrasts of medieval and modern in some of Turner's well-known drawings for topographical publications of the 1820s and 1830s, including the *Newcastle-on-Tyne* (*c.* 1823, Tate Gallery) for W. B. and G. Cooke's *River Scenery of England* and *Dudley, Worcester* (*c.* 1832, Lever Art Gallery, Port Sunlight) for Heath's *England and Wales*. However, it must be noted that these latter are water-colours made for topographical publications, and not as independent exhibition drawings like those of Girtin and De Wint. This serves to explain why they are views of towns and cities, rather than studies of insignificant sites around their outskirts.[146]

Picturesque cottages, rustic scenes, coast views, medieval antiquities, the Lakes, North Wales, and after 1815, continental townscapes – such was the litany of titles in the Water-Colour exhibition catalogues in the early nineteenth century. That which fitted easily within the realm of the picturesque can be identified partly by its prominence in this litany. Conversely, the relative scarcity of imagery of London and other British cities indicates the difficulty of inserting such themes within this pictorial order. Forms could be found around the edges of London which might be treated picturesquely, as in Varley's *Cheyne Walk, Chelsea* (1811, Victoria & Albert Museum) or his *Millbank Penitentiary* (*c.* 1816, Museum of London), but they were occasional elements in an artist's output, not staples. It is because of the dominance of a particular definition of the picturesque that drawings such as those of Thirtle I have been discussing have a particular force. None of these drawings tests the boundaries of the picturesque in terms of colour, but they do so in terms of choice of motiv and composition. The selection of bits of the urban fringe, the commercial river, and the modern agricultural scene as the basis for finished works, is, as it was for the Impressionists, intrinsically related to the aesthetics of the sketch. However, sketchiness and the modern were not objectives for Thirtle, Cotman, and their contemporaries as they were for the latter. It was rather that the involvement with the sketch in the naturalistic phase allowed bits of the modern to creep in. So that if the figures of the modern bourgeoisie did not find representation in these works its houses and its transport conveniences did.

For a while in the years between about 1800 and 1830 it was possible for water-colour landscape painting, like landscape painting in oil, to do things which were unexpected. There was a kind of testing of the limits of what could be represented, as well as a testing of the schema of representation – a phenomenon which is seen in its most ambitious form in John Linnell's water-colour sketches of the edge of London.[147] The water-colour at this moment provided the conditions for a particularly episodic type of image construction, by comparison with which, large-scale exhibition pictures more clearly enunciated their references to established pictorial prototypes and landscape mythologies.

(c) The Valley of the Yare

There are marked differences between Crome's views of the river Wensum, and the views of the Yare produced by his pupils – differences which probably result from the different demands of provincial and metropolitan exhibitions and career ambitions. The sheer quantity of river paintings which Stark and Vincent contributed to the London exhibitions is noteworthy. At the British Institution, Stark exhibited a *Bishop's Bridge, Norwich* in 1818,[148] *Sailing Match at Wroxham, near Norwich* in the following year, *Banks of the Yare* in 1821, and *Moonlight on the Banks of the Yare* in 1824. Beginning in 1827, he showed a number of works connected with the engravings for the *Rivers of Norfolk*. His exhibits at the Royal Academy included *View on the King Street River, Norwich* in 1811, and a *View at Thorp, near Norwich* in 1821, which may have been the same as the picture shown at the Institution as *Banks of the Yare* earlier that year. He showed a *View on the Yare, at Thorp, near Norwich* at the Society of British Artists exhibition in 1824, and a *Reedham Mill, on the River Yare* with the same body in 1827, which was probably the basis for the engraving of the subject in *Rivers of Norfolk*. Vincent showed *On the River Yare, Afternoon* and *On the River Wensum* at the British Institution in 1819, and followed these with the *Vale of Thorpe, Norwich* in 1822 and *View on the River Yare* in 1826.[149] None of his Academy exhibits can be identified as river views with any certainty, but he exhibited a *View on the River Yare* with the Society of Painters in Oil and Water-Colours in 1818, and *A River Scene* with the Society of British Artists in 1829.

To judge from his surviving output, the river was a far more important theme for Vincent in the early part of his career than it was for Stark. In any case, Vincent was a more ambitious painter – or at least he continued to exhibit large works up until the mid 1820s, whereas Stark scaled down his ambitions after ill-health forced him to return to Norwich in 1819. For this reason, I shall consider only his works in detail here.

The most important of Vincent's surviving river landscapes are *On the River*

Yare, Afternoon (120.9 × 172.9cm, Private Collection, *Plate 107*),[150] *A View on the River Yare, near Norwich* (112.5 × 202cm, Southampton City Art Gallery, *Plate 108*), and *Trowse Meadows, near Norwich* (73 × 109.5cm, Norwich Castle Museum, *Plate 109*). The first of these is identifiable as the picture exhibited at the British Institution in 1819, and bought by the Countess de Gray for 120 gns – a patron who had already bought Stark's *Lambeth: Looking towards Westminster Bridge* (Yale Center for British Art) in the previous year, and was to buy J. B. Crome's *Rouen, looking from the base of Mount Catherine towards the Bridge of Boats* (Private Collection) in 1821.[151] It was a picture of sufficient importance for Vincent to have a mezzotint engraving made from it, in the vein of Turner's *Liber Studorium* prints.[152] The Southampton picture presents more problems of identification. The British Institution catalogues give the measurements of exhibits in their framed state, and it is too large to be any of these. Yet its scale suggests that it was a major exhibition picture, and it may have been the *View of Whitlingham, near Norwich* at the 1822 Academy, or the *River Scene* shown with the Society of British Artists in 1829. Stylistically, I would prefer the date of 1822, and it is less likely that Vincent would have produced a large canvas in the latter year, when he had not long been released from the Fleet Prison. However, one would have expected such a large picture to have attracted attention in the press, but I have found no references to it whatsoever.[153] *Trowse Meadows, near Norwich* can be identified fairly confidently with the *Norfolk Scenery* shown at the Norwich Society exhibition in 1828.[154] Although not on the same scale as the earlier London exhibition pictures, it shares some common features with them, and is one of the most successful of his later works.

In addition to the views '*at Thorpe*' or '*on the River Yare*' and so on, which Vincent exhibited in Norwich in 1818, 1822, 1823, and 1828, he also showed a number of smaller river subjects at the British Institution, together with sundry *Landscape*(s) and *Landscape*(s) *with Cattle*, which may or may not have been river views. A substantial number of smaller river scenes attributed to Vincent are in public collections or have passed through the sale rooms.[155]

It should be apparent from the illustrations of Vincent river views included here that not only are his major pictures considerably larger than any we know of Crome's, but they are full of bustling activity: they emphatically represent the river as a site of labour (if not very arduous labour), rather than as a site of leisure. Although Crome had represented the lower reaches of the river in a number of pictures from the first decade of the century, these were mainly generalized moonlight scenes, which redid Dutch prototypes in a broad painterly technique. Crome's only surviving day-light scene, the Leeds Art Gallery *Wherries on the Yare*, is fairly small, and lacks the kind of figure element which is so important in the large Yare pictures of Vincent.[156] It suggests a flat marshy scene with no clear signs of fertility. By contrast, like Turner's Thames series, Vincent's Yare landscapes represent the river as a flourishing commercial channel irrigating a fertile agricultural region.

The Yare is most clearly signalled as a commercial river in the 1819 picture (*Plate 107*), in which boats dominate the centre of the composition. It is difficult to work out why the nearmost boat is unloading at this point, but the episode provides a central figure interest, and the partly lowered sails make a contrast with the fuller ones of the timber wherry beyond. The destination of this carrying activity is indicated by the bulky shape of Norwich Castle and the spire of the cathedral in the distance on the right. These details give the image a kind of narrative reference which Constable's Stour scenes lack. The cows along the bank are appropriate to water meadows, and they, together with the stacked hay on the left, signify the region's agriculture. (In fact the cattle of the Yare valley provided leather for the city's tanning industry.) The windmill on the left edge of the canvas adds another characteristic feature of the Norfolk landscape. The painting was generally well-received by the press in 1819, being mentioned in at least seven reviews, and it clearly stood out as the most accomplished of Vincent's exhibits. The *New Monthly Magazine*'s observation is characteristic of the general tenor of the response:

> In composition, diversity of subject, truth and vigour of local colouring, admirable diffusion of day-light and richness of effect, [it] stands in the highest class in the rooms.[157]

The retitling of the picture in the *Morning Herald*'s review as *Canal Scene with a distant View of Norwich* is significant as indicating the type of reading the prominent boats induced.

In Southampton's *View on the River Yare* (*Plate 108*), the emphases of the 1819 picture are reversed: the pastoral provides the main focus, while the activities of the river are a secondary theme. On the left of the picture, the contrasting group of trees, twisted pollards, ragged picket fence, foreground weeds, and disproportionately small pair of asses is like a compendium of picturesque elements out of Crome's etchings; while the winding road and patches of luminous distance seen through the trees refer to the glade scenes of Hobbema, from which a number of Crome's compositions are derived. However, Vincent's signifiers of the pastoral are rather overdone: the combination of sheep, cattle, and haywaggon all together suggests a symbolic formula rather than a moment observed. On the river, the timber wherry, hay wherry, and two more distant sails suggest a line of (agricultural) trade through a productive landscape. Cattle browse on the far bank and smoke from a cottage drifts up in the distance. The church spire which pokes up rather uncomfortably above the hillside probably refers to Norwich cathedral, and below it a modest country house nestles among the trees. The picture produces pastoral associations partly because the figures are relatively inactive. Those on the hay wherry appear to be at rest, and the waggoner has seated himself on a log to talk to a fisherman, picked out by his red vest. The foremost cow and calf are stopping to drink from the streamlet which runs through the foreground, and the figure carrying a scythe among the trees on the upper left is presumably returning from work. The unusually long format of the canvas works with the long horizontal line of the cloud bank and the even surface of the water to produce a placid and peaceful effect. As in Constable's large canvases, the vitality of this picture derives partly from its wide colour range and complex interplay of light and shadow, and also from its loose painterly textures, particularly marked in the nearest of the moored wherries, in the hay barge, and in the upper sky on the right. (The canvas has been relined at least once, and much of the impasto has now been flattened, but in its original state it must have had an even more lively and vigorous effect.) But whereas Constable omitted the conventional signs of the pastoral from his major Stour scenes of 1822–5, thereby enhancing the effect of a moment observed, Vincent's imagery is securely normal in its agglomeration of stock devices.

The ideas of plenitude and harmony these pictures produce are equally suggested by *Trowse Meadows*, which as a narrative of harvest is more effective than Constable's *The Haywain*. Vincent's heavily loaded waggon is being pulled across the stream in a purposeful way towards the spectator, while the busy activity of harvesting continues behind. The imagery of rural harmony is pushed to the level of overkill by the inclusion of the milkmaid and cow in the foreground, and the family (?) group of the woman and child with a male figure on the right. The immediate foreground is littered with conventional picturesque objects: the broken tree stump, weeds, decaying fence, and eel pots. While the tree mass on the left is reminiscent of a Claudean repoussoir, the transformation of the Claudean scheme is significant: the absence of the balancing mass on the right, the low viewpoint and immediate engagement with rustic activities, are closer to Dutch prototypes. The painting thus combines a clear reference to the classical tradition with what was understood as the quotidian 'naturalness' of the Dutch School, and local English landscape is given connotations of the 'ideal'. A comparison between this compositional structure and that of De Wint's *A Cornfield* of 1815, or Lewis's *Harvest Scene* (*Plate* 5) of the following year, in which the absence of framing masses suggests a potentially wearying expansiveness, indicates how much more conventionally pastoral Vincent's conception was in relation to that of radical naturalism.

In sum then, I am suggesting that Vincent produced a group of large river landscapes with emphatic signs of commerce and agriculture, in marked contrast with Crome's small picturesque river scenes, because such works made more of an impact in London exhibition conditions. No contemporary critic, so far as I have discovered, made any comparison between Vincent's works and Turner's Thames series, or between them and Constable's Stour scenes, but this is not altogether surprising since such comparisons were not part of the general stock in trade of criticism.

Vincent's river pictures clearly offered some of the same kinds of messages as Constable's *Flatford Mill* and *Stratford Mill*, but it is striking that Constable's large pictures of the Stour Navigation suggest relatively episodic glimpses of the workings of the river, whereas Vincent combined signs of river traffic with more hackneyed motivs for signifying rural activities. Whereas Constable's field hands in his pictures of 1814–15 signify progressive agriculture by using modern ploughs or manuring, Vincent's haywaggons do not suggest the progressive aspects of Norfolk husbandry, and the contrived georgic/pastoral recipe of *Trowse Meadows*, which the artist apparently dignified as a representation of 'Norfolk Scenery', seems singularly inappropriate given the context of social disruption, which agricultural improvement and the post-war Depression was causing in rural Norfolk in the early nineteenth century. Since the bloodily suppressed uprisings around Ely and Downham Market in 1816, there had been a further outburst around Diss in 1822, which led to the imprisonment of at least two hundred men. Thomas Coke, Norfolk's leading agriculturalist, was an object of hostility for Anti-Corn Law demonstrators in Norwich in 1815–16, and Dr Rigby's essay on Holkham's agriculture, initially read at the Norwich Philosophical Society in December 1816, was intended to contradict charges made in the recent county elections that his practices as a landlord had deprived the poor of employment and made corn dear.[158]

It is perhaps because Vincent did not work from intensive studies of landscape details, as Constable, Linnell, and other naturalistic painters had in the preceding decade, that in his paintings the modern does not seem in tension with the pastoral. At any rate, his river Yare is not the scene of straining labour that Constable's Stour is, and offers a conventionally idealized imagery of Norfolk rural life. Doubtless this was partly because of the continuing appeal of poetic mythologies of the rural, and the prominence of pastoral and georgic imagery in contemporary exhibitions. However, Vincent's apparent acceptance of rural mythology may also have derived from his acquaintanceship with the conditions of urban artisans in Norwich, which as the son of a weaver and shawl 'manufacturer' he would have known well. Familiarity with the spectacle of urban squalor and intermittent extreme depravation may have led to the idea that the lot of the rural worker, however hard, was relatively healthy and appealing. Something of this attitude is suggested by a poem by Cotman's son Francis, 'To the Gentle Didlers of the Norwich River', which contrasts the happy condition of the labourers who cleaned the river with that of the Norwich weavers:

> Well may you pity Norwich weaver
> Who plies the loom in garret close;
> And, with his wife – he dare not leave her –
> Breathes once a week fresh air at Trowse.[159]

In conclusion to this section, it is enough to say that Norwich artists such as Vincent, Stark (*Plate 110*), and Stannard had produced an imagery of the Norfolk rivers, directly contemporary with Constable's major Stour scenes, which seems far less challenging and 'modern' by comparison.[160] Although they drew on no specific set of poetic discourse, they certainly owed something to the poetry of rivers more generally, and to various ideas about the Norfolk landscape which had a currency in topographical literature. The extent to which these paintings deliberately sought to draw on and give currency to a mythology of the Norfolk landscape as a region of lush agriculture and peaceful trade is indicated by James Stark's publication of thirty-six copper-plate engravings after a series of oil paintings he made in the late 1820s and early 1830s: *Scenery of the Rivers Yare and Waveney* (1834). This had a text by J. W. Robberds, and was dedicated to William IV. In contrast to some contemporary comments on the Norfolk landscape, Stark, not surprisingly, emphasized the beauty of local scenery in his 1827 prospectus for the work:

> The YARE, as it approaches NORWICH, possesses a character peculiarly its own; and, in its beautiful windings through the richly wooded and cultivated valleys of WHITLINGHAM, THORPE, and TROWSE, is not surpassed in the beauty and rural simplicity of its scenery, by any river in the kingdom.[161]

As the prospectus made clear, the publication was explicitly intended to record features of the Norfolk landscape which were likely to be changed as a result of the Norwich and Lowestoft Navigation Bill, and the text is partly an extended commentary on the mutability of the landscape – on the incompatibility of progress with the 'picturesque' and 'rustic'. Robberds describes the function of the artist as follows:

> Amidst the fluctuations of human affairs and the decay of all earthly forms, it is the province of the artist to snatch from utter oblivion those fleeting traits, on which depend some of the pleasures of the passing minute; and it is while he thus prolongs the vivid remembrance of our earlier enjoyments, that he helps to quicken in our bosoms the flow of generous feelings, and ministers to the kindliest impulses of our nature.[162]

As the reference to 'earlier enjoyments' in this passage suggests, Robberds tended to connect the enjoyment of rural scenery with childhood, as if it was likely to form part of the recollection of an audience who in adult life were destined to be town-dwellers.[163] Stark's plates themselves alternate between images which suggest this simple rustic condition through pictorial types derived from Hobbema, Ruysdael and other Dutch models (*Plates 111 and 112*), and a starker imagery of the port of Yarmouth and edges of Norwich (*Plates 113 and 114*). Produced only a few years later than Vincent's major paintings of the Yare valley, Stark's *Rivers of Norfolk* suggests again that there was a wilfully nostalgic and mythologizing element in the conception of those pictures.

(vi) Constructing social harmony: regattas and water frolics

One of the themes of this chapter has been that as in the nature poetry of Thomson, imagery of a harmonious and beautiful British (but actually English) 'nature' in early nineteenth-century landscape painting, functioned as the setting for representation of an ideal social order, the two being mutually expressive of each other. In the main, this social order was illustrated through a rural working population, and few signs of the superstructure of landed society which their labour supported were included. Turner's representation of a contemporary festival in *England: Richmond Hill on the Prince Regent's Birthday* is unusual in setting a scene of modern fashionable life in a major landscape, and there are no real parallels to it. Constable used a 'real' public ceremonial in a river setting for a large exhibition picture with potent connotations of patriotism and progress, which made the royal family the hub of social order, in *Whitehall Stairs, June 18th, 1817 (The Opening of Waterloo Bridge)*.[164] However, Constable found no such subjects in Suffolk, and significantly he represented the better-off social groups in an urban setting.

As in relation to themes of rivers more generally, the Norwich artists found locally a type of social occasion which paralleled subjects with more obvious national connotations represented by London-based artists. The 'water frolics' and regattas (the terms seem interchangeable), which were such a feature of the summer leisure activities of the Norfolk gentry and bourgeoisie offered a spectacle of the juxtaposition of different social classes, which could easily be turned into a symbol of a mythical social unity. In the period under consideration the main water frolics were held at Yarmouth, Thorpe, and Wroxham, although there are records of others at Beccles, Buckenham, Horning, Oulton, and Surlingham. They provided themes for three major exhibition pictures: Stark's *A Sailing Match at Wroxham near Norwich* (Private Collection, *Plate 115*),[165] exhibited at the British Institution in 1819; J. B. Crome's *Yarmouth Water Frolic – Evening – Boats assembling previous to the Rowing Match* (106 × 172.7cm Iveagh Bequest, Kenwood, *Plate 116*) exhibited with the Norwich Society in 1821; and Joseph Stannard's *Thorpe Water Frolic – Afternoon* (108 × 172.7cm Norwich Castle Museum, *Plate 117*), exhibited with the Society in 1825. These pictures are all large, ambitious works, but it is perhaps indicative of the fact that their meaning was somewhat localized that only the first was exhibited in London. I should acknowledge at this point that the social significance of these occasions has already been discussed by Trevor Fawcett in an article on Stannard's picture, and much of what I have to say elaborates his argument in rather broader terms.[166]

It is interesting that the earliest of these pictures was by James Stark, since it provides further evidence that Stark was a more ambitious and innovative painter during his London period than he was after his return to Norwich in 1819. Unfortunately, it is impossible to identify the picture with complete certainty, but the only Stark painting of a sailing match I know of is the so-called *View of St Bennet's Abbey on the River Bure*, illustrated here. At 34 × 54ins (88 × 138.5cm) this seems rather small for the 1819 exhibit, which was 53 × 74ins framed. Further, there are problems with relating the title to the motiv, since Saint Bennet's Abbey is approximately four miles from Wroxham Broad, and therefore could not be seen in proximity to it, as the image suggests. On the other hand, the river near the abbey would have been too narrow for a regatta. It is thus probable that Stark introduced the abbey to enhance the associations of the scene, and contrast modern leisure with an object symbolic of the national past to give the painting more effect for a London audience which would be unaware of the topographical discrepancy. In relation to this it is significant that a local gentleman who admired the picture in Stark's studio, also commented that it was 'no portrait of the Country'.[167]

A composite image of the Wroxham Frolic can be built up from succeeding reports in the Norwich papers. Its chief organizer seems to have been the vicar, the Revd John Humfrey, who gave a silver cup worth eight guineas in 1819, and also provided the refreshments. The *Norfolk Chronicle*'s report of 1817 does not provide much information about the occasion, but commented that heavy and continued rain took off much of the interest which the event derived in fine weather from the 'picturesque scenery' round about. That in the *Norfolk Chronicle* of 1818 recorded that the weather was 'remarkably fine' and that an excellent Norwich band entertained the visitors. In 1819 it gave a list of the 'fashionable' and 'genteel' parties present, which included Sir Thomas Preston and a bevy of local clergy. In 1820, the Earl of Albemarle, the Coke family, and Sir Robert Harvey were there among what was described as an 'unusual display of fashionable company'. Spectators lined the shore in 1819, and a 'numerous fleet of boats', 'decorated with flags, ribbons, &c. and having bands of music and many fashionable and genteel parties on board' assembled on the water. The following year:

> Numbers of wherries, laden with country folks in their holiday clothes, added much to the cheerfulness of the scene and the interest of the whole spectacle.

At Wroxham sailing matches seem to have gone on over two days and there are no reports of rowing matches – perhaps because it was sailors, artisans and petty bourgeois who made up the rowing crews from Yarmouth and Norwich, and there was no comparable social group in sufficient numbers near Wroxham. Even from these rather skimpy reports, it is clear that as at other festivals, the major events were sailing matches put on for the gentry and local bourgeois, but drawing crowds of the labouring population as spectators. Inevitably, the press reports only covered the entertainments of the former: the dinners in the Revd Humfrey's fishing house and the band entertainments. But the 1820 comment on the 'country folk' in 'holiday clothes' adding to the 'cheerfulness' of the scene is representative of a type of image such festivals which came to the fore in reporting of the larger occasions at Yarmouth and Thorpe.[168]

Stark's picture has a number of features which match the newspaper record, such as the group of musicians in the boat in the foreground, the mass of people packed into the large moored sailing boat beyond, and the refreshment tents in the right distance. Overall, it has a bright light effect, and spatial recession is indicated partly by making the sails on the left lighter than those on the right. The abbey and draining mill are framed by the masses of sailing boats on either side, and are thus an important element in the composition. They are also integrated with the event by the figures of spectators on the walkway round it. St Bennet's abbey was a major local landmark, and in the year after Stark exhibited his picture, William Taylor commented on the potency of its associations in a letter:

> Before the ruinous gate of St Benedict's Abbey spectres of the past rise in the mind – the rudeness of our courageous heathen ancestors, whom these monks came over to convert, to instruct, and civilise, – the pompous ceremonies of the Catholic church, which were guided in show solemnity under this archway . . .

and so on. 'Thus' Taylor continues in an exposition of association theory:

> we are pleased and delighted in the presence of the ruin, not by any inherent power of arousing the feelings, which broken and deciduous objects possess, but because certain interesting ideas are necessarily associated with peculiar remains of antiquity.[169]

By including an image of the abbey, Stark perhaps intended to refer to a wider conception of Norfolk as a region rich in medieval remains, a reference which many in the London exhibition audience could have been equipped to pick up on. At the least, it refers unmistakably to the historical associations of the British landscape in which this modern event takes place – a piquant contrast.[170]

Responses to Stark's 1819 painting from the London critics seem to have been somewhat mixed. The *Examiner* praised the contributions of Stark and Vincent to the British Institution in general terms as deserving 'little else but eulogy', but singled out Vincent's *On the River Yare, Afternoon* for special attention and said nothing specific on Stark's painting. The *New Monthly Magazine* was more enthusiastic claiming that:

> in happy reflection, variety of object, picturesque composition, light, shadow, colouring and executing, [it] ranks in the first class of landscape in the Gallery.

However, the *Repository of Arts* claimed that Stark was 'not so successful this year as he was in the last', while conceding that his pictures were 'always natural and pleasing'. Finally, Thelwall in the *Champion* made clear his dislike of Stark's subject. After praising his *Grove Scene* as an 'exquisite gem, possessing all the vigour and truth of Rydsdale' (sic), he was cooler on the *Sailing Match at Wroxham*:

> The subject is not good; but there are parts beautifully painted, and the whole displays a fine eye for colour.

While not wishing to make too much of a single response, it is interesting that Thelwall evidently preferred a kind of Stark composition which was going to be the staple of his output in the 1820s, when he seems to have concentrated on unambitious, but perhaps easy and readily saleable works. Of course, *Sailing Match at*

Wroxham, presuming I have identified it correctly, is clearly indebted to Dutch prototypes in the river scenes of Cuyp, and the *Literary Gazette* discerned in it 'a Flemish aspect'.[171] But with its modern-dressed figures and tents, it was a lot more emphatically contemporary in its connotations than Stark's grove scenes.

J. B. Crome's *Yarmouth Water Frolic – Evening* refers far more overtly to Cuyp's river scenes (*Plate 118*), a formula he repeated in *Rouen, looking from the base of Mount St Catherine*, exhibited in London in the same year. However, this does not mean that Crome was any less conscious of contemporary trends, since it was hardly possible for him to exhibit such a work without it suggesting comparisons with Callcott's *Pool of London* (RA 1816, Private Collection) and Turner's *Dort or Dordrecht* (RA 1818, Yale Centre for British Art). Francis Hawcroft has argued that the oil sketch for *Yarmouth Water Frolic* (Private Collection) is by John Crome senior, and that the Kenwood picture was begun by him and completed by his son.[172] While the foreground details of rowing boat, buoy, and wood in the finished painting detract from the design of the sketch, it remains a major work, rich in detail and effect. The even horizontal ripples drawn on the water, barely disturbing the reflections, the limp sails and drooping flags of the boats, the repeated triangles of the composition and the warm colours contribute to suggest ideas of a balmy summer evening. The composition is organized around the mast which is marginally right of centre, the boom of it leading the eye to the white ensign hanging from its stern, partly obscuring the richly gilded panel around the coat of arms. This centralized composition contrasts with asymmetrical arrangement of Callcott's and Turner's pictures, and seems to match with the 'Classical' aesthetic which J. B. Crome recommended in his Lecture on Painting and Poetry.[173] The boats themselves are crowded with figures, and figures line the banks to left and right. The most surprising feature of the picture is the steam boat moored to the right, which must be the earliest representation of a steam boat in a major oil by a British artist, and gives the work an emphatically modern character.[174] Steam boats were becoming a frequent sight on the Norfolk rivers in this decade, but when a 120-ton steam barge was taken to King's Lynn for the opening of the Eau Brink Cut in 1821, a correspondent of the *Norfolk Chronicle* commented that the boat drew 'a very great concourse of spectators to witness her arrival'.[175] J. B. Crome's steam boat (which does not appear in his father's sketch) is only a small river boat, but such machines were still modern mechanical marvels, which hardly fitted into the category of the picturesque, as the comment on the steam boats at Richmond, quoted earlier, illustrates.

Yarmouth Water Frolic was a more significant public event than that at Wroxham, with a more profound symbolism. This may partly explain why Stark and Crome chose such different types of effect – the liveliness of the former's picture contrasting with the relative solemnity of the latter's. In his biographical introduction to the *Collected Works* of Frank Sayers, William Taylor described the occasion as follows:

> Annually in July the Mayors of Norwich and Yarmouth meet in their state-barges on the river Yare, at Hardley-Cross, which separates their respective jurisdictions, and in the afternoon fall down into Breydon. This is a broad expanse of water, which receives three tributary streams, the Waveney, the Yare, and the Bure. All the many pleasure-boats kept on these rivers assemble; the commercial craft is in requisition to stow spectators, to waft music, to vend refreshments: such of the shipping, as ascends above the Yarmouth drawbridge, is moored within ken; there are sailing matches, rowing matches, and spontaneous evolutions of vessels of all sorts, a dance of ships, their streamers flying and their canvas spread. It is a fair afloat, where the voice of revelry resounds from every gliding tent. And when the tide begins to fall, and to condense this various fleet into the narrower waters, and the bridge and quays and balconies and windows of Yarmouth are thronged with innumerable spectators – and boys have climbed the masts and rigging of the moored ships, adding to the crowd on shore a rocking crowd above – and the gathering boats mingle their separate concerts in one chorus of jollity – and guns fire – and loyalty and liberty shout with rival glee – and the setting sun inflames the whole lake – the scene becomes surpassingly impressive, exhilarating and magnificent.[176]

The ideas that the event transformed the river, which was normally a site of labour, into a site of pleasure, and that the festival was a social concert are clearly drawn out. The spectators and participants of all classes mingle in this 'chorus of jollity', and the image of the sun setting on this 'broad expanse of water' suggests that nature is in harmony with the social atmosphere. Taylor's liberal politics is perhaps indicated by the phrase 'loyalty and liberty shout with rival glee'. More generally his account suggests the way a myth of the event had been developed – a myth to which Crome's picture, with its refulgent light, perhaps contributed. Like Taylor's account, which it precedes, it dignified the occasion as art.

According to correspondence printed in the *Norfolk Chronicle* in 1824, the custom of the Water Frolic had been given up in 1748 due to its expense, but then renewed, and given up again in 1793 as a result of an accident, not being revived until 1816.[177] This would suggest that it acquired a new importance as a festival in the context of the post-war victory celebrations. Presuming that Crome's picture was inspired by the Frolic of 1820, the following description of the event of that year is significant:

> In the evening, the company assembled on the adjacent shores and banks to witness the return of the boats from their aquatic excursion, was beyond calculation: nothing could be more pleasing or interesting: every spot commanding a view of the river being crowded with elegantly dressed females.

Such images of the Water Frolic were repeated year after year, frequently using the same phrases, and representing the evening 'scene' as a particularly pleasing one.[178] The patriotic significance of the occasion, denoted so clearly by the white ensign in Crome's painting, was demonstrated in 1821 by the band playing *God Save the King* as the mayor stepped aboard his barge in the morning, 'which had a very pleasing effect'.[179] The inclusion of the steam boat would have been more appropriate in 1823 or 1824, when the *Nelson Steam Packet* pulled the Yarmouth Corporation barge. Intriguingly, Stark made a steam boat the central motiv in a lost painting of *Yarmouth Regatta*, which provided the basis for an engraving in the *Rivers of Norfolk* (*Plate 119*).

How police was maintained at this large and diverse gathering is unclear. The only hints of more earthy delights come in the report of the 1824 Frolic, which commented that:

> The sports were prolonged until the shades of night began to veil the interest of the scene: the assembled multitude shortly quitted their stations on the banks and quietly returning to their homes surrendered the enjoyment of more protracted pleasures to a few choice spirits of the deep, who, regardless of the waning night continued to revel in uncontrolled felicity.

The class dimensions of the occasion were unwritten, but they are indicated by the omission of any account of popular pleasures, and by the discrepancy between reporting of the sailing matches and that of the rowing matches. The names of competing sail boats and their captains were at least partially recorded, while listings of the rowing competitors were generally impersonal and less detailed. In 1818, three 'salvage' boats from Gorleston raced for money prizes (as opposed to silver cups), and six 'gunning' boats raced for a gold-laced hat. The rowing match started so late in the evening in 1819 as 'to disappoint many thousands that had assembled on the occasion'. In 1820, the match was raced for a silver cup, and was won by an individual dignified simply as 'Boults'. In 1824, when the race was won by the *Cytherea* of Norwich, the *Chronicle*'s report did not even mention that the boat belonged to the Norwich artist Joseph Stannard.[180] As might be expected, there was a clear demarcation between the sport of 'gentlemen', and a sport which demanded a kind of lusty physicality which did not accord well with norms of middle-class masculinity.

The notices of J. B. Crome's picture in the Norwich press in 1821 were typically silent on the significance of subject matter, and limited to technical commentary. The *Norwich Mercury* singled out Vincent and Stark as 'foremost in the ranks of talent' after Crome's decease, but acknowledged J. B. Crome as also 'an able supporter of his father's school'. Of *Yarmouth Water Frolic* is only said the picture was 'remarkable for its brilliancy of effect'.[181] Reviews in the *Norfolk Chronicle* around this time were fuller and more reflective, and that of 1821 claimed the picture was a 'great credit' to its author, but found fault with aspects of its colour and handling, complaining of 'a hardness in the pencilling' which made it look unfinished, and a 'flaring mixture of red, green, and yellow in the centre vessel', disagreeable to the eye.[182] The absence of comment on the picture's subject should probably be taken as indicating that its suitability was self-evident. The blatant reference of the composition to Cuyp's prototype probably neutralized any disturbingly modern aspects of the theme, even if the style was still too up-to-the-minute for the *Chronicle*'s critic.[183]

In formal terms, Stannard's *Thorpe Water Frolic* is yet more challenging. There had been earlier water festivals in Norwich, and there were numerous informal sailing and rowing matches round about in the summer months: that which distinguished Thorpe Water Frolic was its scale and newness. The instigator of the Frolic was Lieutenant Colonel John Harvey, a Norwich cloth merchant and manufacturer, who had bought Thorpe Lodge in 1787 and landscaped the grounds around it. Harvey organized the first Frolic as a festive occasion in 1821, but in the following year he opened it up as a spectacle and entertainment to the labouring population, and by 1824 it seems to have been a public holiday for a large part of the city's workforce. Harvey was a major actor in the Norwich corporation and the police of Norfolk, and in this period of intense labour unrest liked to pose as 'the weaver's friend'. The Thorpe Frolic was, in all probability, deliberately orchestrated as a concert of social harmony, as 'some kind of social safety valve' to use Trevor Fawcett's phrase, but he has also emphasized the actual segregation of classes on the occasion: fashionable society being safely coralled in Harvey's grounds on the north bank of the river, the plebeian population being let loose in the meadows on the south bank. Harvey himself is clearly identifiable within Stannard's picture as the white-haired figure standing on the water-line just under the trees, framed between the stern of his boat *The Sylph*, and the gondola he had brought back as a souvenir from a trip to Venice. Fawcett has drawn attention to the following comment in the *Norwich Mercury*'s review of Stannard's picture in 1825:

> We believe there are very few artists now alive who could have produced a design where truth and fiction are so nicely blended . . .[184]

and emphasized the difference between the work and 'a literal transcript' or a 'documentary photograph'. But there could be no such thing as a 'literal transcript', except within an accepted set of conventions, and documentary photographs are as heavily coded as other forms of imagery. I want to look rather more closely at the developing imagery of Thorpe Water Frolic in the Norwich papers, and at the particular structures of Stannard's painting.[185]

In relation to the first of these areas, it is striking that the newspapers had already defined the Frolic as a spectacle in pictorial terms before Stannard gave material form to the image. In 1823, the account in the *Norfolk Chronicle* included the following passage:

> The appointed scene of action was a part of the Yare; where the meanderings of the stream form a delightfully picturesque feature in the varied beauties of a truly rich and interesting landscape. On the one side of the River's banks stands the charming village of Thorpe, on the other side the eye reposes on a verdant range of luxuriant meadows, to which the fine woods on the high grounds of Crown Point and Whitlingham form a noble background. Upon a spot next

> Thorpe Old Hall, beneath the protecting shades of some lofty and wide-spreading walnut-trees, Colonel Harvey, the patron and promoter of the *fête*, had caused a large marquee to be erected; in which his friends and visitors on this occasion, including many of the principal families of the city and county assembled to witness and enjoy the diversions.

The vocabulary of the picturesque travel guide is unmistakable in this passage. The 'eye' explores the scene, moving around the middle ground and then the background, returning to the '*fête*' shaded under the trees, which establishes the *bon ton* of the occasion. The sailing matches had taken place in the morning, after which the 'ladies and gentlemen' had a 'sumptuous dinner' in the marquee. In the late afternoon the rowing matches were held, by which time the numbers present were very large:

> the water's edge presented a most gratifying spectacle; upon the Thorpe side of the river the private gardens were filled with company, and Baxter's and Hinsby's, and other places of public resort were crowded with visitors; on the far side, the meadows from Thorpe as far down as Whitlingham were literally lined with spectators . . .

The different classes formed a display for each other from their opposite banks. If the 'ladies and gentlemen' were gratified by the sight of the 'multitude' enjoying themselves on the south bank (presumably in a decorous fashion), the multitude were to be edified by being permitted to watch the evening's dancing on the lawn of Harvey's house through the gates. The *Chronicle*'s report concluded by praising Harvey's public-spiritedness in providing 'so much innocent and healthful enjoyment', which could be so 'cheaply and easily . . . participated in by the industrious many'.[186]

The account of the 1824 Frolic in the *Chronicle* had an even more strikingly pictorial quality, and the paper called on Norwich artists to depict the event. The 'local advantages' of the view from Thorpe Lodge on this occasion, were said to demand 'a vivid representation by the pencil', in preference to one by 'the pen':

> The scene was altogether a subject for painters to study. And we should be glad to learn that it has been selected by our Artists as an appropriate task for next year's 'Exhibition'. – A foreground here offers itself, replete with handsome architectural objects, and enriched to the water's edge with the embellishments of horticulture. A sweeping bend of the stream displays these ornamented features with effect, as viewed from the promenade which was thronged with the young and the gay, the genteel and the graceful. The scene was moreover enlivened by numerous well-dressed groups of both sexes, stationed on the decks of pleasure-barges moored close to the shore; whilst a miscellaneous flotilla, of contrasted forms and dimensions, from the Steam Packet to the Venetian Gondola, from the Norwich keel of burthen, to the light sailing vessel and 'trim built wheryy' manned with motley crews, were traversing the

truculent bosom of old Yare. – A verdant expanse of meadows, backed by the rising grounds and well wooded heights of Crown Point and Whitlingham, completes the distant landscape: a combination, which, however it may be surpassed by others that might be named, certainly does not yield to any in luxuriance and varied loveliness.

There was again an emphasis on the social value of the occasion:

It has been remarked that of all modes of administering to the rational amusement of the people, a Regatta best serves to recreate the greatest number of persons. And the result of proceedings on Monday last, was such as entirely to bear out the observation.

The effect of social harmony was itself evoked in pictorial terms:

The general effect was at once both animated and orderly; bringing the personal distinctions of rank into harmonious approximation with the strong characteristic trait of popular manners: so happily blended without being confounded with each other, were the different divisions of the social fabric – in such good keeping were preserved the lights and shades and demi-tints, not only of the natural but the moral picture.

The *Chronicle*'s construction of this 'moral picture' clearly implies that there is a harmony between parts of the 'social fabric' which are unequal and necessarily different, so that they may be 'blended' but not 'confounded'; juxtaposed with propriety, but not mixed up. Significantly, the *Chronicle*'s desire to see popular manners at a safe distance came out most clearly in relation to gender. The final amusement of the day was to have been a rowing match between two 'women' for a muslin gown, although the competitors refused to row until it was dark. The newspaper signals a proper distaste for women behaving so contrary to norms of middle-class femininity, describing the competitors as 'two nymphs, not of the form fair, but from the marshes', who were 'better qualified to *wash* a gown than to row for one'.[187]

While the account of the 1824 Frolic in the *Norwich Mercury* was less overtly pictorial, it does draw attention to the increased scale of the occasion, and reveals that booths were put up on the south bank for the 'public at large'. It also connected the landscape setting with the holiday atmosphere and harmony of different ranks. At the same time as providing a party for Harvey's friends, the event lured:

the citizen from his toil to a day of healthful exercise – to bask in the bright sun-beams – to breathe the fresh air on verdant meadows, or to float in vacant ease along that element which raises so many high associations in the mind of an Englishman – to glad the eye with the prospect of a rich ornamented county, or with a busy changeful, and a gay scene – to hear alternate strains of soft animating music – to witness the eager contest of nautical skill and personal vigour – to join a multitude, all actors in the same pageant – in short, to feel all

> the enlivening elevation with which a succession of objects so pleasing can hardly fail to inspire a mind released from its ordinary cares . . .[188]

But, of course, the occasion is special, and such pleasures could only be occasional holiday pleasures, and the reality for the 'citizen' is one of 'toil' – and properly so for a paper close to Norwich manufacturing interests. By its very radiance, the event seems to atone for, or displace, the miseries – those 'ordinary cares' – of the Norwich weavers. The reports of the *Norwich Mercury* and *Norfolk Chronicle* alike are constructed from the social viewpoint of the respectable middle-class male. Both assume an *impersonal* spectator who is not part of either fashionable society or the 'multitude', both construct the event as a benevolent, paternalistic, and proper gesture by a social superior. Any aspects of the occasion which might have undermined such an interpretation went unreported.

It is, at least, most suggestive that in the very year when Stannard himself and his brother Alfred were among the crew of the winning boat, and the Frolic was bigger than ever before, the *Chronicle* should have called for an artist to record the occasion. In the circumstances, it seems likely that Stannard found the text around which to structure his image in the newspaper reports. The *Mercury*'s report gives quite substantial coverage to the artist's role in the spectacle, not only mentioning him as an oarsman in the *New Telegraph*, but also singling out for quite lengthy description his skiff *Cytherea* and the costumes of her crew. All-in-all, he must have seemed particularly well-qualified to answer the *Chronicle*'s call.

I now want to examine the way in which the painting *Thorpe Water Frolic* represents the event. Like the papers, Stannard made the hub of the occasion the figure of Harvey. The picture draws attention to him by the light colour of his head and stock, picked out against the relative shadow around him, and by less direct means: the boom of his boat, *The Sylph*, which dominates the centre of the composition, points towards him; and the heads of many spectators are turned in his direction. Particularly important among the latter are the group in the central rowing boat and the figure in the red coat shading his eyes, standing in the white boat with green stern on the right edge of the painting. The connection with Harvey is further emphasized by the presence of his house, Thorpe Hall – part of this is visible among the trees, and the building entering the composition from the left is the chapel belonging to it. In 1824, the *Mercury* recorded that a quay was formed below Thorpe Old Hall where the competing boats assembled, and there 'at the centre of the sports, was also the centre of the interest'. According to the *Chronicle*'s report of 1823, at about eight o'clock the crews of the winning boats assembled 'opposite the marquee' and Harvey presented them with silver cups. To the left of Harvey's figure in the painting men are depicted waving their hats, and it is thus likely it represents the moment when the Frolic's patron made his concluding speech. This interpretation matches the painting's late afternoon light effect.

Other features of Stannard's picture which invite comparison with the press reports are the crowding of vessels and figures within the design, which suggests the largeness of the gathering, the distinction of social types on the left and right, the musicians picked out in the stern of the rowboat behind that in the centre, and the modern houses of the 'populous and affluent village of Thorpe'. The spectacle of fashionably dressed women is also indicated. The figure at the centre of the composition in the stern of the rowboat is female, and behind her a prominent standing figure wears a large feathered hat. More women can be seen seated in *The Sylph*, and the *Norwich Mercury* reported in 1824 that Harvey and his son had taken a party of 'ladies' on a boat, while gentlemen formed masses of 'gloomy monotony' talking over 'men's' affairs. In the shadow in the left foreground are two women in a boat of provisions, who are probably of a lower social station since one has a bare arm. Significantly, perhaps, women are not given as much prominence on the plebeian side of the composition.

In formal terms, Stannard's *Thorpe Water Frolic* follows the example of J. B. Crome's *Yarmouth Water Frolic* in placing a mass of boats and sails in the centre rather than putting the largest boat to one side of the composition as Callcott and Turner did. Like all of these pictures, it implies a low viewpoint, as if the event was seen from a boat. The blue ensign drooping from the central rowing boat takes the place of the white flag in Crome's picture, in evoking those 'many high associations in the mind of an Englishman' which the *Norwich Mercury* had referred to. On the right of this mass of sails is an avenue of water framed by a receding perspective of smaller sails along the south bank. On the left there is a dark area, today far darker than it would have been in 1825 as a result of paint deterioration. In the picture's original state, the sail on the far left vessel would have helped to bring that side of the canvas more forward, and the area would have been less obscure in spatial recession. None the less, the left side must have always been darker, and this contributes to the general sweep of the picture through a perspective from left to right. The light effect is particularly vivid partly because of the light colour of the centremost sails, the pinks of the distant houses, the soft greens in the distance and the pervasive blues of the sky and water. The bright local colours of dresses and flags also help to give the image its festival quality. Stannard's handling of the areas representing water is much more varied and suggestive than that of J. B. Crome, and the style of the painting can be understood as that of the most advanced naturalism of the day. It is an impressive picture for one intended for a local audience.[189]

Neither of the local papers says that the work was painted for Harvey, but W. F. Dickes claimed it was in his 1905 study of the 'Norwich School', and Harvey is known to have owned pictures by the artist.[190] This is appropriate, considering that when Harvey gave the inaugural discourse at the First Artists' Conversazione in Norwich in 1830, he:

> lamented the penury of patronage under which painting and sculpture had so laboriously struggled, while he trusted that indifference had now passed away, and that 'the present morn of art would be succeeded in this country by its meridian splendour'.[191]

Interestingly, in listing the advantages necessary to constitute the 'great artist', Harvey referred to the 'association of ideas'.

Not surprisingly, the reviews of the picture in the Norwich press were extremely favourable. The *Chronicle* suggested that it would contribute to the 'celebrity' of the whole 'Norwich School', and went on to praise its composition, handling, and colour. The composition was 'intensely interesting, masterly, and elegant', while in colour it had 'all the force and harmony to be desired':

> As a whole, it is strongly stamped with truth and nature. The painter has most deeply felt his subject, and the pleasure throughout derived by him in the execution of the work is largely imparted to the spectator in viewing it.

The last sentence suggests again that there was felt to be a connection between Stannard's role in the Frolic and the character of his work, but it may also be the result of the critic's awareness of Romantic aesthetics demonstrated in some preliminary comments on manner and originality.[192] The *Mercury* found the picture:

> a work of great skill, whether the diversified disposition of such a multitude of objects of the same class, the lights and colouring, or the entire effect be considered.

It praised the trees as 'splendid instances of fine handling', but felt that the right side of the work was 'too blue', which may indicate that Stannard's use of colour was a little too progressive for the *Mercury*'s taste.

The ways in which the water frolics were constructed in the newspaper reports and in the paintings offer striking parallels. Thus the press had already defined the return of the boats in the evening at Yarmouth, which Crome chose to represent, as a particularly pleasing and social moment.[193] Equally, it emphasized the role of Harvey at Thorpe, and Stannard had selected a moment when the connection between that benefactor and the occasion would be most clearly symbolized. In Stark's picture, the only one in which racing is actually represented, sociability is suggested by the number of figures on the right of the composition, but the harmony of the occasion is not a strong meaning which can be read easily from the work. In Crome's *Yarmouth Water Frolic*, harmony is evoked by the effect of stillness, the placid evening sky, and the hieratic design within which the signs of the multitude are fitted. Stannard's *Thorpe Water Frolic* articulates this harmony most fully by putting a large number of detailed figures close to the picture plane. It clearly particularizes different social groups in the plurality of figure types, uniting them in the scene, while keeping them spatially distinct. It is also emphatically modern in form and reference. Crome's steam boat is an aside, easily missed, but it is impossible to ignore the modern villas and display of fashionable dress in Stannard's painting.

Throughout my analysis of *Thorpe Water Frolic* I have emphasized the congruities between the picture and the press reports, and the symbiotic relationship between the imagery of landscape and society in both. However, I do not want to collapse the two together, and the specificity of the picture must be given its due. The effect of *Thorpe Water Frolic* depends on the transformation of the Cuypian model: on the proliferation of incident and the crowding of the composition; on the introduction of contemporary circumstantial details; and on the vivid colour and complex light effect which mark it out as modern in style. If we consider that picture partly as the work of an individual social agent, a single eye-witness, then it must be assumed that there are features of it which derive from his own first-hand observations of boats, costumes, and setting. Presumably it was partly the recognition of these features within the framework of accepted pictorial conventions that helped convince the critics of the authenticity of the image. While the reference to the Cuyp prototype is just about recognizable, the mutation of the model transforms its meaning. It becomes insistently modern in a way that Callcott's *Pool of London*, Turner's *Dort of Dordrecht*, and Crome's *Yarmouth Water Frolic* are not.

Unlike these paintings, *Thorpe Water Frolic* purports to offer a conspectus of contemporary society. In this respect, the general import of the picture was essentially the same as that of the press reports. The contradictions which the press hinted at run through the middle of the image in the division between 'society' and the 'multitude' – this is one of the few landscapes of the period to juxtapose different classes. The point is, however, that these opposing actors in the social drama are represented at a holiday festival: they are represented through the exceptional, while the quotidian realities of urban toil have no place in art. Stannard's picture could seem to be 'truthful', at the same time as being reassuring. It offered a jolly image of leisure and fellowship: of Norwich society as it would be nice to think it on at least one day of the year, of 'human nature in its kindliest mood, released from care and anxiety, and . . . wholly devoted to present pleasure', as Robberds described the atmosphere of the Thorpe sailing matches. (Such an image would perhaps have been unthinkable thereafter, for in the following year the Norwich textiles industry entered a depression from which it never entirely recovered, and which led to immediate violence and a deepening immiseration of the workforce.) *Thorpe Water Frolic* is a brilliant contribution to a myth of social harmony and bourgeois benevolence. Its complete reworking of the Cuypian prototype to this end can be compared with Turner's reworking of Claude in *England: Richmond Hill on the Prince Regent's Birthday* – and Thorpe was known as the Richmond of Norfolk in the early nineteenth century. Like that picture it is somewhat garish, sugary (almost sickly), and over-wrought, and in both cases these qualities give an artificiality and preciousness, an almost fairy-tale tone, to the image of society they offer. But whereas Turner's painting articulates a patrician vision of society, Stannard's articulates one that is emphatically suburban and bourgeois.[194]

(vii) Conclusions

It should be clear from the foregoing that I am not arguing that the use of rivers as a referent conferred any kind of simple unity of meaning on landscapes of river scenes. Rather, I have tried to suggest that there was a widening range of visual forms available for the representation of rivers, and a complex ideology around them, which derived from several discourses. Thus there are marked differences between the significance of Turner's scenes of the Thames, Constable's of the Stour, Crome's of the Wensum, Vincent's of the Yare, and so on, and these are only partly the result of differences in the physical character and social functions of the regions concerned. Perhaps more they derive from that nebulous realm of myths around the nation and its local parts. Meanings varied too depending on the types of activity represented, ranging from those associated with the standard recipes of boats, men, and animals; through barges and locks; through edges of cities; through modern festivals, to warehouses and steam boats. None the less, the economic and social functions of waterways, and the sheer volume of discourses about them, overlapping and interlocking with one another, made rivers a crucial pictorial theme. Once again, it is paintings by Constable which stand out by their distance from the stock range of poetic references and their incongruous mixture of the modern and the picturesque, although some of Thirtle's water-colours are also notable in this respect. Constable's concern with the specificity of rural occupations and local landscape in works such as *Flatford Mill* and *A View on the Stour*, and his continuing use of narratives of labour in the 1820s, give a force to his Stour pictures which few of his contemporaries attained. John Linnell and G. R. Lewis attained it briefly in some paintings of around 1815, and it was in that short-lived experimental phase in the second decade that such effects were mainly produced. At this time, some artists seem to have thought, for a while, that they could dispense with overt references to the poetry of rural life, the clichés of pastoral imagery, and the received formulae for breadth. Quite why this kind of imagery could not be sustained, was, I argued in relation to Constable, partly the result of factors within the artistic field – the dominant conceptions of the artist's function and of artist's ambition, and the dominant conception of what constituted the poetic in art militated against such experiments. Quite a bit of weight should also be given to the demands of the exhibition context, since despite the popularity of experimental naturalistic painting with a section of the critics, large-scale, and frequently sensationalist, poetic landscapes seem to have made more of a splash with the public. Whether there may also have been determining factors outside the artistic field will be one of the subjects of my final chapter.

Conclusion: The passing of naturalism

The particular character of British art culture in the early nineteenth century, when compared with that of France, seems explainable largely through economic and institutional factors. The absence in Britain of any significant state direction in the Fine Arts or even of a national collection until 1824, the autonomy of the Academy as a professional body with merely nominal royal patronage, and the dominating power of the market over art production were aspects of the situation much remarked at the time. In these circumstances, public-spirited patricians and haut bourgeois felt obliged to take the state's functions on themselves by setting up the ostensibly national (but effectively oligarchic) British Institution, or by throwing their own *private* galleries open during the London season. Taken together, these circumstances meant that the ideology of High Art functioned as a set of imperatives even more remote from the realities of art practice than they were for French artists.

It seems reasonable to assume that it was these evident contradictions, together with the deep symbolism which had developed around landscape in the culture of the dominant social groups, which made it possible for landscape painting to become such a major field for artistic ambitions. In effect, we may interpret both the large scale adopted by artists such as Callcott, Constable, Hofland and Vincent; and the dramatic treatment of historical and poetic themes by Danby, Martin, and Turner; as equally representing a displacement of the ambitions of history painting as a public art into the lesser genre. While within the Academy's exhibitions figure paintings continued to dominate the Great Room – with landscapes playing a supporting role – the latter were prominent at the British Institution (set up to encourage 'Historical Pictures and Landscapes'), and dominant at the Society of British Artists' and the Water-Colour Societies' shows. However, the sheer volume of landscapes on display, and the critical status the genre acquired, did not mean that it could function as a vehicle for the public statement of central social values without problems. The absence of a national collection and of state patronage was as disabling for the ambitions of landscape painters as it was for those of history. Landscapes might perform an ephemeral public function in the exhibition room, but thereafter they were destined for the home, or the private picture gallery. The large scale of the properly public landscape made it expensive, and also less adaptable as a furnishing. Further, landscape could not displace history painting as the central didactic genre. Pastoral landscape became bizarre when it was given the pseudo-heroic narratives of a barge horse leaping an obstacle on a towpath, or a bargee straining to open a lock. In historical landscapes, the very format of the genre meant that the example of virtue inevitably became reduced to a detail. Even when the narrative informed the whole structure of the work, as in Turner's *Ulysses Deriding Polyphemus* (RA 1829, Tate Gallery) or *Regulus* (RA 1837, Tate Gallery),[1] human emotions could only be signified in a displaced form, which did not produce the same effects of empathy with individual agents. A continuing concern with the didactic functions of art, expressed in a range of discourses (including that of bourgeois progressivism), ensured that a moralizing painting of domestic life held a higher status than landscape with most critics, and that the dream of a national school of historical painting, which would articulate national values, continued to have a powerful appeal.

Given the pervasiveness of landscape mythologies, and their evident appeal to the middle classes, it can not be argued that landscape painting generally addressed the landed classes more than it did them. While it seems justifiable to assume that grand manner history painting, and portraiture in the more elaborate academic modes, tended to position the middle-class spectator as an inferior to the ideal addressee, landscape painting did not. Landscape had no clear role in relation to status differentiation, and it could be seen to stand for values antithetical to 'fashion', for values of naturalness and artistic integrity. Thus Hazlitt claimed of the Academy's exhibitions:

> The only pictures painted in any quantity as studies from nature, free from the glosses of sordid art and the tincture of vanity, are *portraits of places*; and it cannot be denied that there are many of these that have a true and powerful look of nature.[2]

Certainly there were critics who interpreted the rise of both landscape and genre painting as symptomatic of the influence of a particular social group. In 1816, the *Repository of Arts* suggested that:

> The love of what is antique, and the love of novelty, blind the taste of different classes in society, and cast a doubt over their opinions when judging works of art. One class will allow the modern no merit; the lovers of novelty, not rightly understanding perhaps the unvarying standard of nature, are equally fastidious in their judgment: thus between both, the artist suffers, and his art declines.[3]

It is not clear that the *Repository* is here establishing a distinction between classes of taste which also define broader class differences. In fact, most critics who disapproved of what T. G. Wainewright described as the 'barbarous horde of Vandals and Pictorial Radicals' and sought to promote the tradition of High Art, did so because of their commitment to some aspects of the academic system, to the principle of imagination, and the high calling of the artist – not because they associated High Art with patrician values.[4] Yet in the period we are concerned with, it was frequently alleged that the patrician class was disgraced by its failure to nurture a national school of historical painting, and the style and messages of history painting were undoubtedly seen as especially relevant to the nation's leaders, with whose education and culture they might seem ideally consonant – if not actually so. As the criticism of the *London Magazine* in 1825 so well illustrates, from a radical bourgeois perspective traditional history painting could seem anachronistic precisely because of its association with a social group which the march of progress was shunting aside. (When the education reformer Edward Edwards considered history painting, in a book prompted by the 1836 Parliamentary Report on the Fine Arts and Manufactures, he suggested that, like historical writing itself, it dealt too much with the 'dazzling exploits of the successful general and the shifty diplomatist', and too little with the 'peaceful triumphs of the patient inventor and the solitary student'.)[5] Landscape painting, by contrast, could seem both modern and egalitarian, however limited its class audience actually was.

I must emphasize that I am not suggesting that the growth of the bourgeois element in the art public called forth naturalistic landscape painting, or that it was self-consciously directed to that audience. In my view, the aesthetic of naturalism, with its emphasis on originality and the uniqueness of the artist's perceptions, is best understood in relation to the increasing autonomy of the intellectual field. While artists certainly did want to improve their social standing and material rewards, what they aspired to was not so much to 'live in ease and luxury', as to be given the opportunity for the 'production of excellence' – to secure recognition of a realm of qualitative values in a society dominated by commercial ones. Hence Shee's insistence that the principles of Smithian economics were irrelevant to art.[6] Hence Constable's commitment to large 'unprofitable canvas'(es), which he financed through the output of 'minor works'.[7] What artists wanted for their work was a serious audience, which would set a value on the evidence of 'mind' in it, and thus also accord a value to them as individuals. Those who Constable described disdainfully as 'Gentlemen and Ladies' showed no inclination to do this. As Fisher reminded him:

> wealthy people regard artists only as a superior sort of work people to be employed at their caprice: & have no notion of the mind & intellect & independent character of a man entering into his compositions.[8]

While Constable's paintings referred to a particular literary culture, it was not one which excluded those without a classical education. This was equally the case with the work of Callcott, Crome, De Wint, Linnell, Thirtle, Vincent, and the rest. It was a truism that taste for the higher beauties of nature required extensive knowledge to comprehend 'the signatures of Almighty Power' and 'Unfathomable

Design', and was therefore beyond the 'peasant'.[9] But it was equally a truism that the beauties of fertile landscape were understood by almost all. In theory, whereas the sublime and the wild picturesque were represented as exclusive tastes, that for a natural imitation of the useful was inclusive. Naturalistic landscape painting did not demand a profound knowledge of the art of the past, or of ancient history and literature. Its codes were as legible to the provincial bourgeois who bought pictures from the Norwich exhibitions as they were to Sir John Leicester and the Marquis of Lansdowne, who bought some of the larger exercises in the mode. Much has been made of Constable's political conservatism, although his paintings did not force a conservative reading and were popular with some radical critics. More weight should be given to the republicanism of Linnell, the links between Crome and Norwich radicalism, and to the democratic version of naturalism set out in Richter's *Daylight: A Recent Discovery in the Art of Painting*.

In the last three chapters I have argued that critical responses to landscape paintings suggest that there was no struggle over their meanings as social representations. For most critics of conservative and radical persuasions alike, the meaning of landscape painting as a category was something like Barry's account of the associations of Dutch rural scenes in his Second Lecture, where the life of the country is juxtaposed with that of the city in an altogether familiar way:

> the simple, laborious, honest hinds; the lowing herds, smooth lakes, and cool extended shades; the snug, warm cot, sufficient and independent; the distant hamlet, and the free, unconfined association between all the parts of nature, must ever afford a grateful prospect to the mind. No doubt much of our satisfaction results from contrasting this state of things with the dark, insidious, hypocritical disguises; the hateful enormities, vanities, affectations, and senseless pageantries, so frequently found in the courts of the great, and in large cities

And yet, almost inadvertently, the project of naturalism, premised on a valorizing of originality and a rejection or revision of the norms of the picturesque, led artists to deal with the modern. Much naturalistic landscape thus diverged sharply from the type of image Barry evoked. His vision sits uncomfortably in relation to Constable's 1815 *View of Dedham* or his *Flatford Mill*, and equally in relation to Linnell's *Kensington Gravel Pits* and *River Kennet at Newbury*. Certainly a new range of pictorial forms was developed which referred to established pastoral connotations, as in De Wint's *A Cornfield* or Lewis's *Harvest Scene, Afternoon*, but the very style of such works gave them a contemporaneity which was perhaps too emphatic. If it proved difficult to picture the most advanced husbandry in pastoral landscapes, or to make the modern central in the imagery of rivers and coasts, the signs of change did keep creeping in on the margins or in the distance. The evidence of this marginalization and evasion confirms that there were deep tensions between modernity and the project of landscape painting as traditionally conceived. These tensions were seldom dramatized within the images themselves, but their existence is testified by the failure of radical naturalism to find a market.[10] Such art may have been well-adapted to the comprehension of those without a university education, but it did not thereby necessarily meet what they perceived as the functions of pictures.

We are back again at the increasing autonomy of the artistic field, and the disjunction between the ambitions of artists and the needs and desires of their audience. Radical naturalism may stand in many respects as equivalent to the bourgeois ideal of order and knowledge, but this was increasingly dissociated from the realm of art by a public which looked to that realm more as a sphere in which the bourgeois *alter ego* of fantasy, passion, and violent primal forces would have free play. Or so the popularity of Byron, Scott, Martin, and Danby with the middle-class public suggests. The social infrastructure which would support a vanguard practice in later nineteenth-century France did not exist in Britain at this time, and the model of artistic personality crucial to such a practice was not available yet to painters, as it was becoming to writers.[11]

In the 1820s and 1830s, the discourses of radical democratic politics, Benthamite progressivism, and Romantic individualism mingled together producing sometimes surprising combinations. Thus the adventurer and poet R. H. Horne, who mixed in Benthamite circles around 1830, was at the same time an ardent admirer of Hazlitt – with Charles Wells he put up Hazlitt's tombstone. In Horne's writings, a Romantic conception of genius and artistic individualism is linked with a Benthamite concept of progress through the 'advancing March of Intellect' and education, which will together sweep away the 'cabalistic charters of slavery and intolerant selfishness'.[12] A similar mixture of ideas, welded into a less bizarre form, appears in the reviews of the *London Magazine* of 1825. For a critic who argued that 'new views, new conceptions, new modes' of painting were the source of its interest, and that which 'entwined' it with the progress of society, naturalism could be claimed as the art for a public which was daring to think for itself in 'politics' and 'legislation'. That is to say with the public of a model bourgeois democracy.[13] Yet by the time the *London* was praising Mulready for *not* producing pastiches of Ostade, and censuring Callcott for making Cuyps, and Stark for imitating Hobbema and Ruysdael, radical naturalism was over. The 1820s saw nothing to compare in daring with some of the works which Constable, Havell, Lewis, Linnell, and Mulready had painted in the previous decade. In the event, the middle-class audience which passed through the streets of the metropolis to the entertainment of the exhibition rooms, seems to have found triter formulae a more suitable furnishing than the individualistic experimental art of 1810–20 – or so the changes in the work of artists like Callcott, Collins, and Stark after 1820 suggest. The bulk of the middle classes proved as timid in taste as they were in politics.

A telling example of the emerging middle-class mythology of the national landscape is a long article, 'English Landscape', which appeared in the *New Monthly Magazine* in 1822. In the space of the postwar periodical press there was no room for the patrician and exclusive attitudes to landscape which informed eighteenth-century poetry and theories of the picturesque. None the less, this essay laments that the 'love of rural life' is 'losing ground among the better class of society', and praises 'English retirements in the country' for promoting habits of 'thought and reflection' to which are owed 'much of the steadiness and simplicity of the English Character'. These habits of thought are clearly only possible for the propertied and the leisured. But the landscape which inspires them is 'social and highly cultivated', for characteristic English scenery has none of the picturesque qualities which appeal to a superior taste. It is its intimate quality which makes English scenery so distinctive, and makes a profound imprint on national character:

> Close high-fenced fields surrounded by trees, houses buried in shrubberies and groves, beautiful cattle feeding among rich pasturages, and all in the smallest space, so that the eye can command them together, take a hold on the affections that an uninclosed country, large forests and immense buildings can never attain. We may admire the latter, but we cannot love them.

English scenery is thus beautiful and fertile, and suggests snugness, littleness and comfort – one might say it is positively feminized or domesticated. It is green and richly wooded, with 'masses of tufted trees rising amid an ocean of luxuriant vegetation'.[14]

Although the author finds the 'extensive and varied prospect of luxuriant scenery' antithetical to reflection, we may find his ideal of English scenery otherwise well represented in Vincent's huge painting, *A Distant View of Pevensey Bay, the Landing Place of King William the Conqueror* (Norwich Castle Museum, *Plate 120*), which was exhibited at the British Institution in 1824.[15] Considering the scale of this work, and the historical associations of the view, this can be read as a paradigm of the national landscape, comparable with Turner's *England: Richmond Hill on the Prince Regent's Birthday*, to which it may stand as a corrective. In contrast with the bloody associations of its title, the picture offers a *riant* view, which suggests that the Norman Conquest has laid the grounds for national prosperity. As well as being scattered with abundant trees, the scene is full of sheltering nooks and 'houses buried in shrubberies'. In the foreground, a faceless figure of 'Hodge' with shepherd's crook, is apparently conversing with his red-coated squire, whose gun and hound mark him out as the proprietor of the land. The squire might be read as a descendant of the Norman dukes, who has exchanged his forefather's martial weapons for the huntsman's gun; and the labourer could be read as a descendant of the Saxon peasantry, whom the Normans had subjugated and deprived of their traditional liberties according to one strand of radical ideology.[16] However, Robert Hunt did not notice this possibility, commenting only that the picture suggested 'a peaceful musing and retirement, the manna of good reflecting minds', and a relief from 'the sordidness, disappointments, and distractions of life'. W. H. Pyne in the *Somerset House Gazette* specifically set the picture in contrast to images of 'cloud capt mountains', 'frowning rocks', 'roaring torrents' and ruins, finding in it 'a healthy, and a happy region, animated by the substantial rural attributes of a golden age'. Yet it was not only beautiful, it was also apparently 'natural' and true:

> It is a pleasing and very faithful representation of a beautiful prospect, such indeed as a true English lord of a manor would pride himself upon pointing out to a foreigner, as a fair sample of the English pastoral.[17]

After the particularities and sharp-eyed observation of the small canvases of radical naturalism, *A Distant View of Pevensey Bay* takes us right back into the realm of the mythical and the generalized national landscape. This was probably almost inevitable with a work on this scale.

While neither the *New Monthly Magazine*'s essay or Vincent's picture can be construed as anti-industrial, both effectively offered an image of Englishness which stood in opposition to the urban and the modern. The currency of this image suggests that the British middle classes had already in the 1820s begun to adopt a vision of peaceful farmland as a synecdoche of national identity, even if this did not become dominant until the twentieth century. One of the key historical questions in relation to the culture of this period must be why the radical intelligentsia did not produce a critique of the dominant mythology of rural life to which so much landscape painting referred. The answer to this is likely to be found in the more general response of middle classes to what we have come to call tradition. The Benthamite radicals of the 1820s had no truck with tradition: their aim was to rebuild the social order on the principles of reason. Although their reason was capable of producing real insights into the mystificatory functions of culture, their underlying models of personality and institutions were reductive ones. They had failed to take on board the Burkean insight that the social order had already constructed the individuals with which any project of amelioration had to operate, and who could not just be made anew. Unlike those who invoked the 'principles of Saxon Liberty' against the descendants of the 'Norman oppressors', they had either not grasped that collective memories and myths can have a critical as well as a reactionary function, or spurned the possibility as unworthy of their higher aims.

The body of diverse discourses and beliefs which made up what we might understand as bourgeois ideology did not comprise a one-dimensional and crudely self-interested creed. Its legitimacy, then as now, depended on its claim to represent equally the interests of all. This inevitably meant it was composed of contradictory elements, which, in relation to landscape, may be epitomized through J. W. Robberds' letterpress to Stark's *Rivers of Norfolk*. That work is both a paean to the project to make Norwich a port, and thereby 'improve an important agricultural and manufacturing district', *and* a lament over the changes this will inevitably bring to the traditional order of rural Norfolk.[18] At one point, Robberds celebrates the decay of feudalism, which brought an end to 'tumultuary insurrections and civil strife', and released energies for 'useful industry', so that Britain could begin 'that career of commercial enterprise in which she has advanced to so proud and glorious an eminence'.[19] Elsewhere the passing of feudalism means:

> the birth of public opinion, and the first instance of that intelligent spirit of popular resistance to tyranny, which has so long distinguished this country[20]

Thus a democratic spirit is traditional and the national character is progressive. Yet the British are 'essentially' a 'Gothic people', and not only in their mode of building, for 'our institutions, our habits, our tastes, our character, our spirit, all are Gothic'.[21] Because Robberds has such a deeply historicized notion of the national culture, his attitude to modernization is ambiguous. Not only does he prefer gothic architecture to 'modern terraces, crescents, and squares' (as we saw earlier), but writing of the probable effect of increased trade on the small town of Beccles, he expressed the hope that it would never experience 'those rank and noxious impurities, by which the best fruits of commerce are too often corrupted and embittered'.[22] And in the text to the final plate of the book, Robberds lamented that what he called 'the spoilations of the spirit of improvement', symbolized in this instance by the enclosure of parts of Mousehold Heath on the outskirts of Norwich, had deprived the 'younger classes of a populous district' of a playground after their days in schools and factories.[23] Nowhere in his text does this Norwich worsted manufacturer make any tribute to the progressive agriculture of Norfolk. It seems that in his view of the world, the rural functions only as an idyllic realm to be contrasted with the harsher toil and struggles of urban life. This is at one level the conservative and interested critique of a bourgeois observer, whose fear of the 'ignorant and licentious rabble' is made abundantly clear in his commentary on Kett's Rebellion.[24] But it would be crudely functionalist to read the text only in this way. Despite Robberds' commitment to progress and property, his text also speaks a concern with the effects of commerce and urbanization on the human personality which was essentially critical – a concern which was partly grounded in that mythology of the rural to which the paintings of Stark and other contemporary landscape painters contributed.

History is one of the most important resources for alternative models of social organization, and much of the history of British social criticism in the early nineteenth century, both that of left and right, has to be written in terms of different uses of that resource.[25] As we have seen, at that time, landscape images like the cosy rustic scenes of Stark's *Rivers of Norfolk* (*Plates 111 and 112*) could be related to a range of critical perspectives on the social order. However, today the imagery of the English rural past is so commodified through media stereotypes, so drenched in kitsch, so infinitely distanced from any real phenomena, that it seems only the fuel for advertising campaigns and country cottage phantasies. Yet as Alex Potts has pointed out in an important essay, even in our own century the ideal of an ordered rural landscape has not functioned only as a vehicle for middle-class escapism – it has also stood as a symbol of aspirations towards an alternative *modern* culture.[26] The mythology of rural England may seem now to have a solely conservative function, but no ideology has a single meaning and effect.[27] While it may be difficult to appropriate it to a progressive politics, the effort must be made, for it is too powerful and pervasive to be ignored, and contained within it is the kernel of desire for a better life and a more healthy environment.

The presentation of British landscape painting within our dominant cultural institutions and the mass media is generally served up in a rancid sauce of nostalgia and nationalist sentiment. With notable exceptions, much academic writing underpins this cuisine. If the history of art is to make any contribution to dispelling the reactionary miasma around Romantic landscape painting, it will depend on analysis which investigates both the functions which landscape painting served within the turbulent social order of early nineteenth-century Britain; and how its practice involved an effort to produce forms of painting adequate to the cognition of the modern world – a world distinguished by 'constant revolutionizing of production, uninterrupted disturbance of all social conditions, everlasting uncertainty and agitation' – a world which traditional landscape painting, as Barry defined it, was unsuited to represent. If British landscape painters of that period deserve any credit, it is for their short-lived attempt to develop types of imagery which could comprehend some aspects of that world.

PLATES

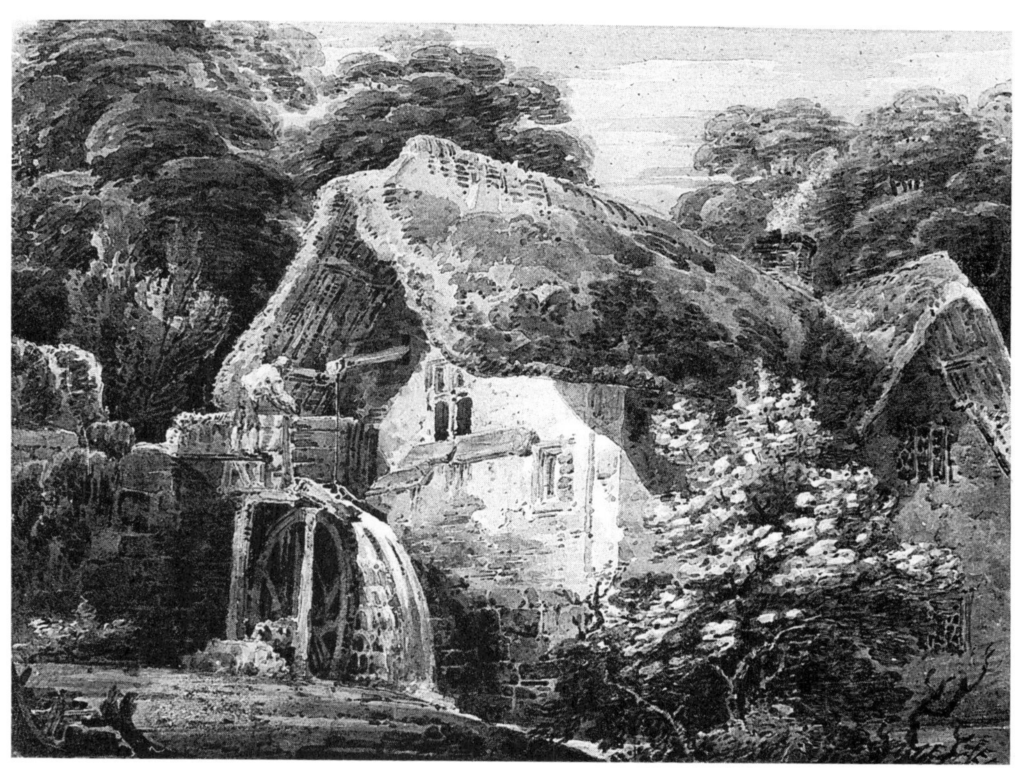

1 T. Girtin, *An Overshot Mill in Devon*, *c.* 1798, Leeds City Art Gallery

2 J. S. Cotman, *The Ploughed Field*, *c.* 1808–10, Leeds City Art Gallery

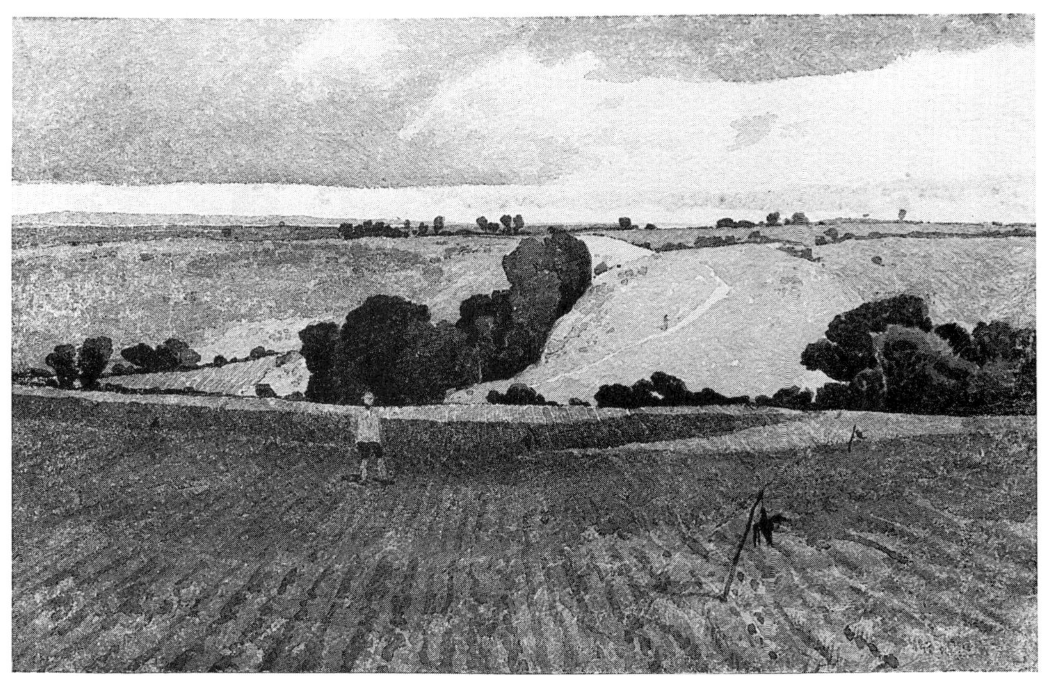

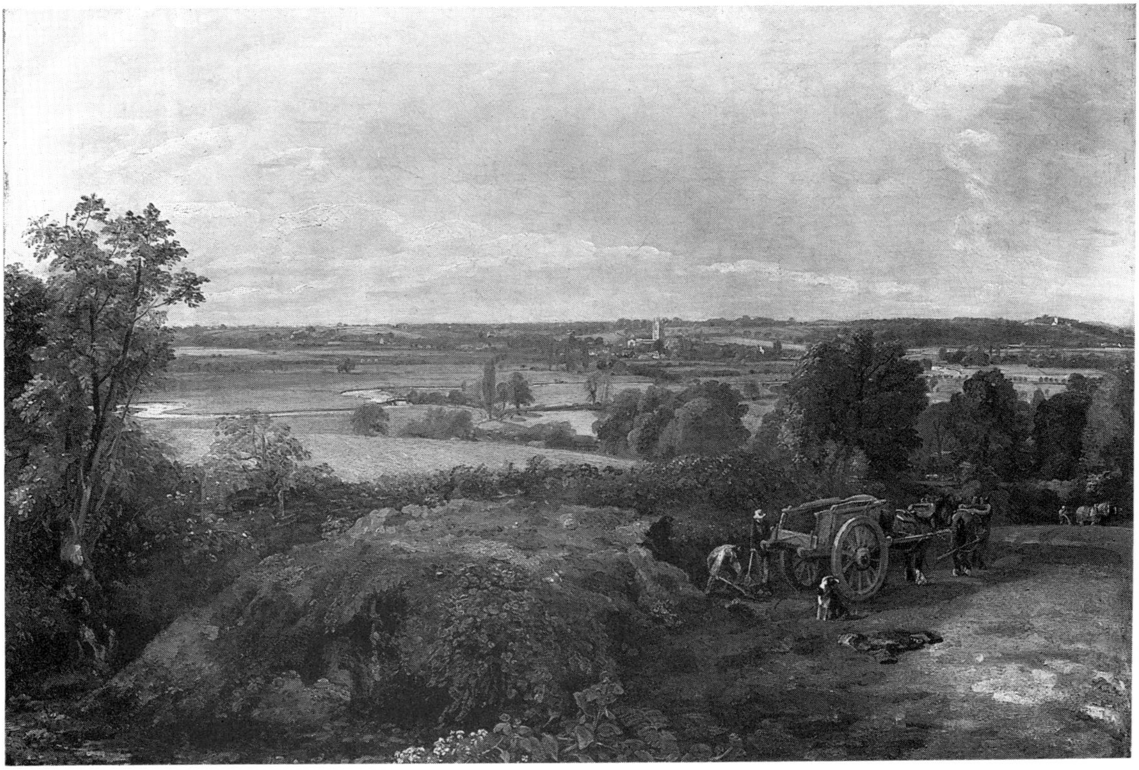

3 J. Constable, *View of Dedham*, 1814, Warren Collection, Courtesy of Museum of Fine Arts, Boston

4 J. Linnell, *Kensington Gravel Pits*, 1813, Tate Gallery

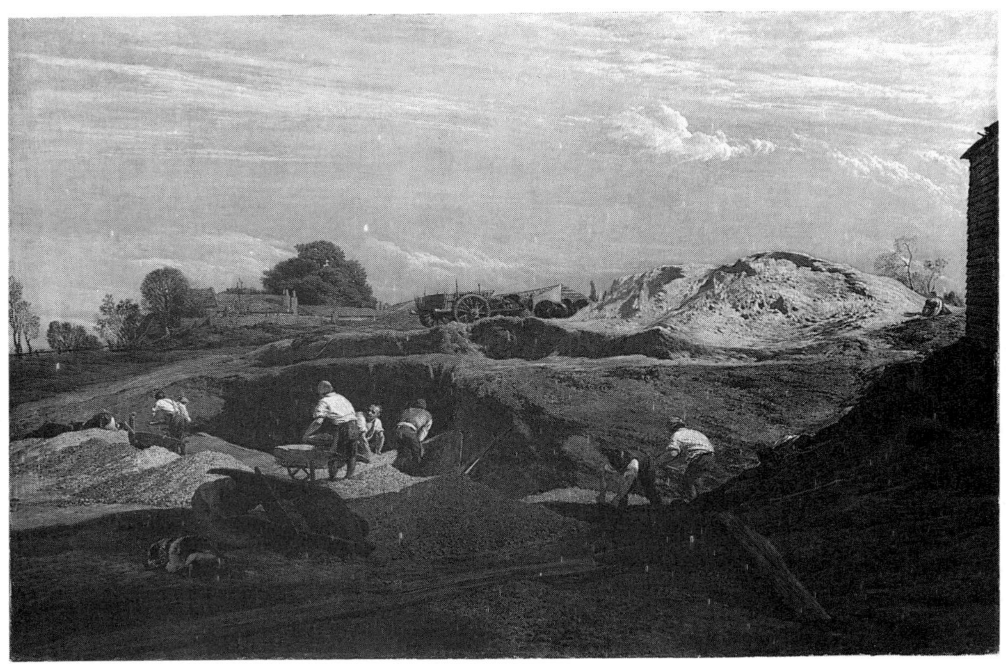

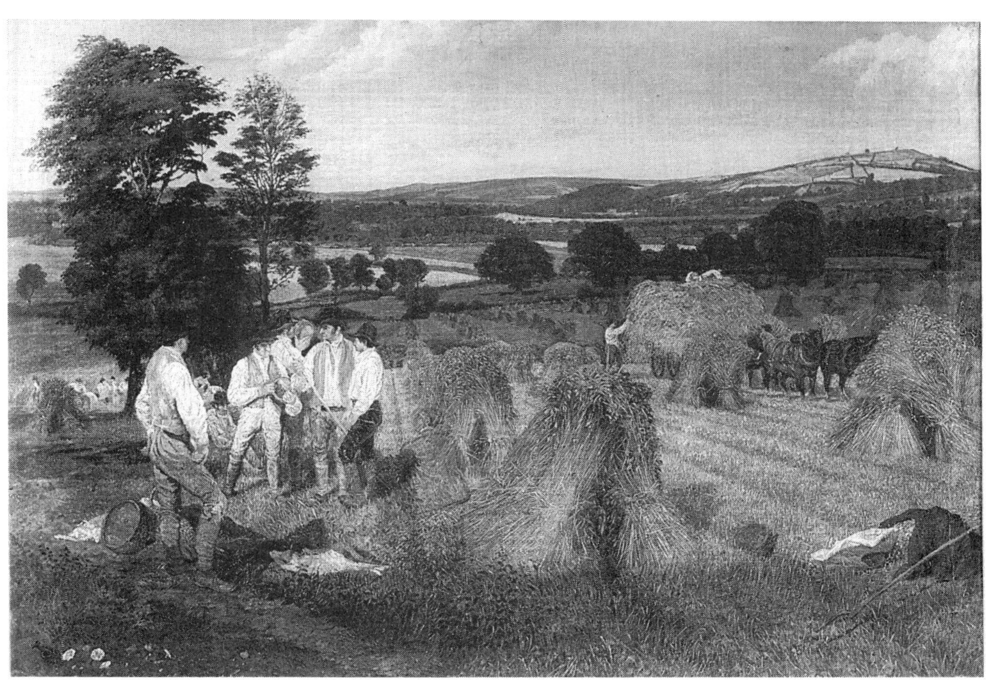

5 G. R. Lewis, *Hereford, Dynedor, and Malvern Hills, from the Haywood Lodge, Harvest Scene, Afternoon*, 1815, Tate Gallery

6 W. B. Cooke after J. M. W. Turner, *Battle Abbey, the Spot where Harold Fell*, copper-plate engraving, 1819

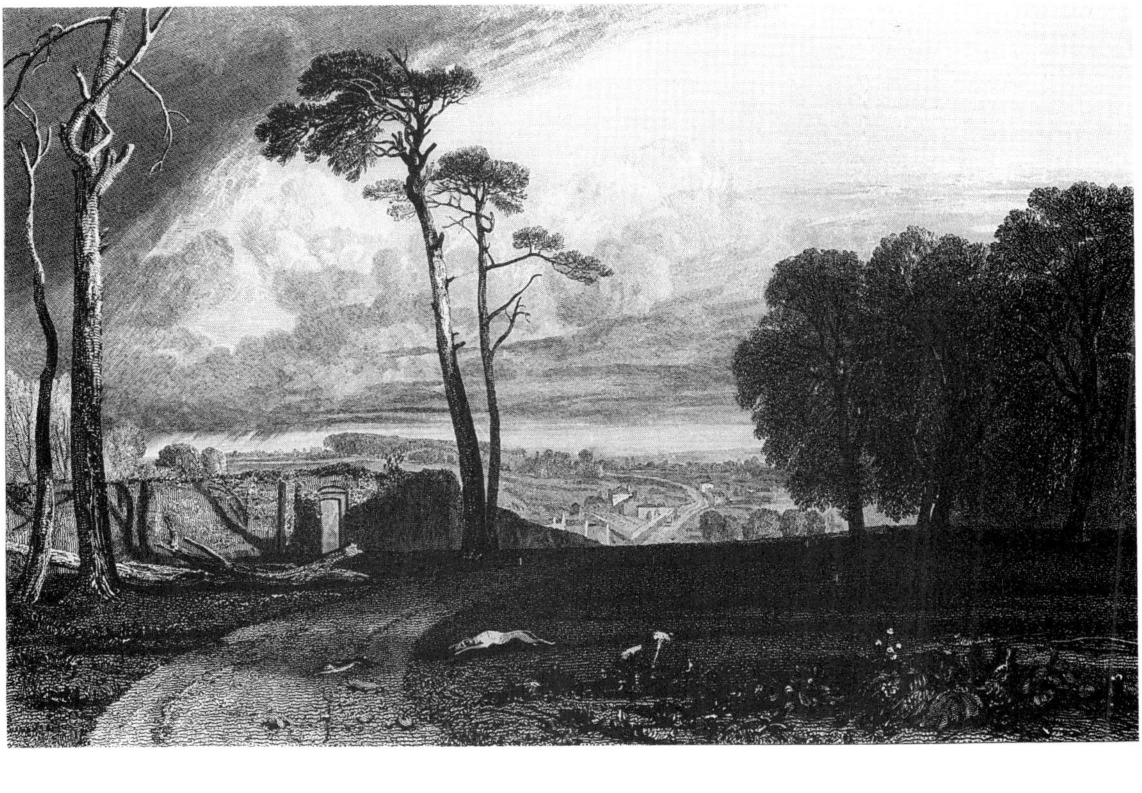

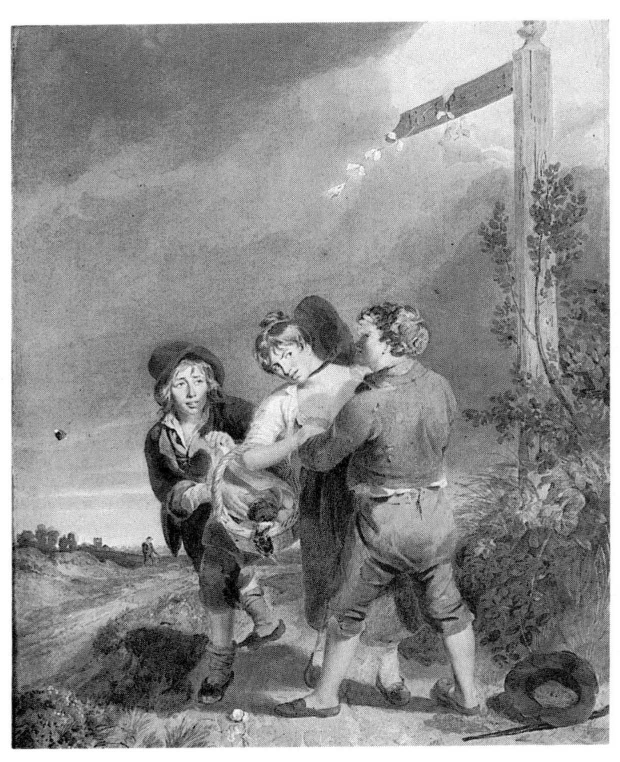

7 T. Heaphy, *A Country Girl being Robbed by Two Boys*, 1807, Private Collection, Scotland

8 W. Collins, *The Reluctant Departure*, 1814–15, Birmingham City Art Gallery

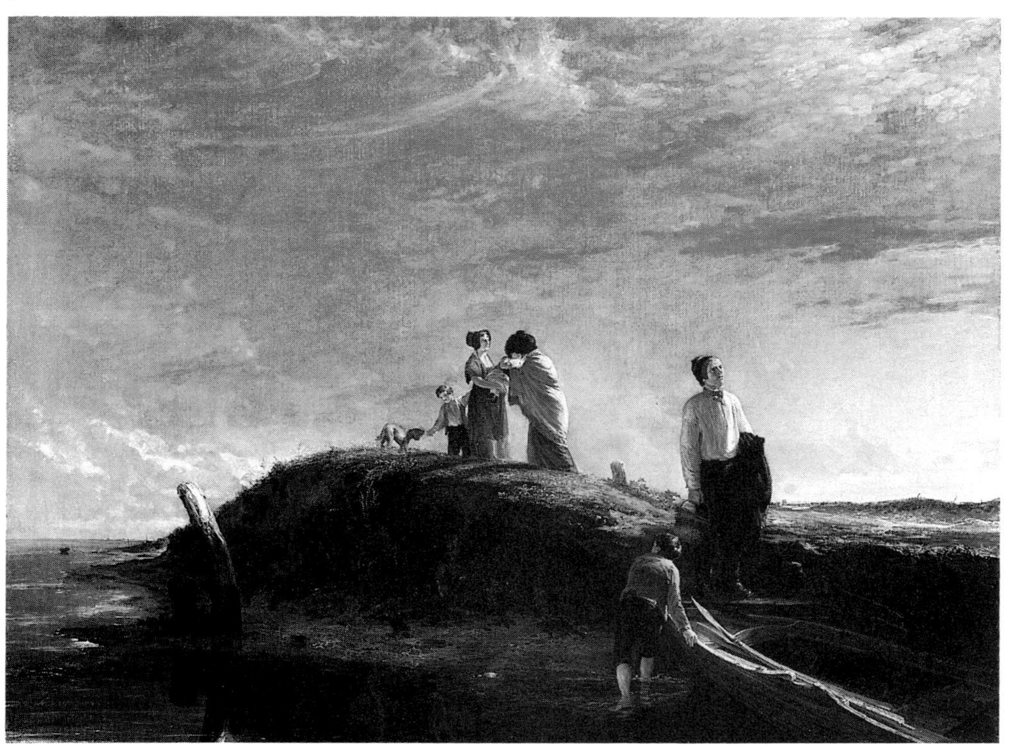

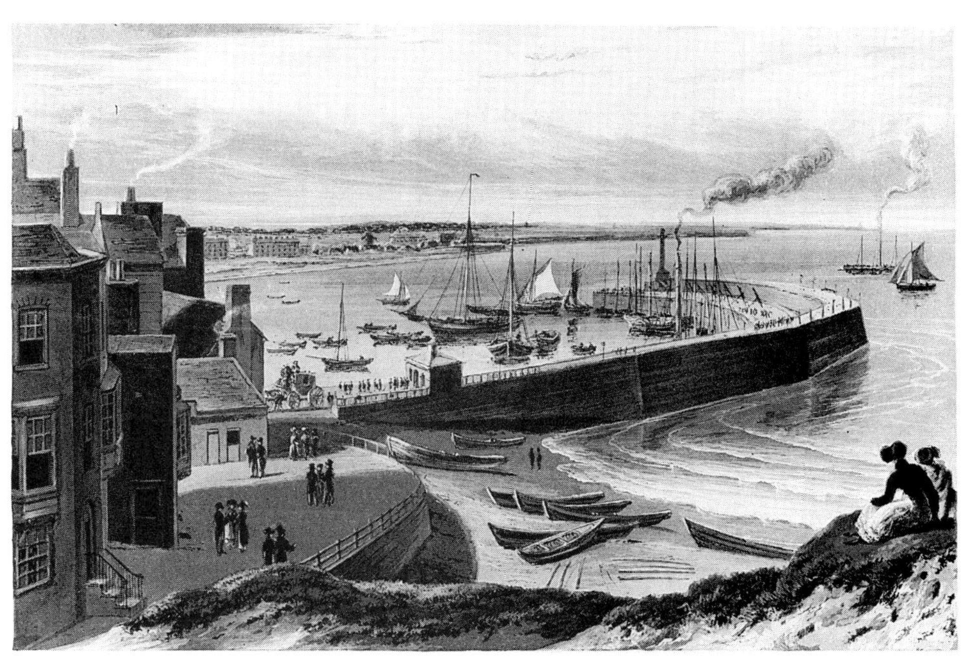

9 W. Daniell, *Pier at Margate*, aquatint, 1823

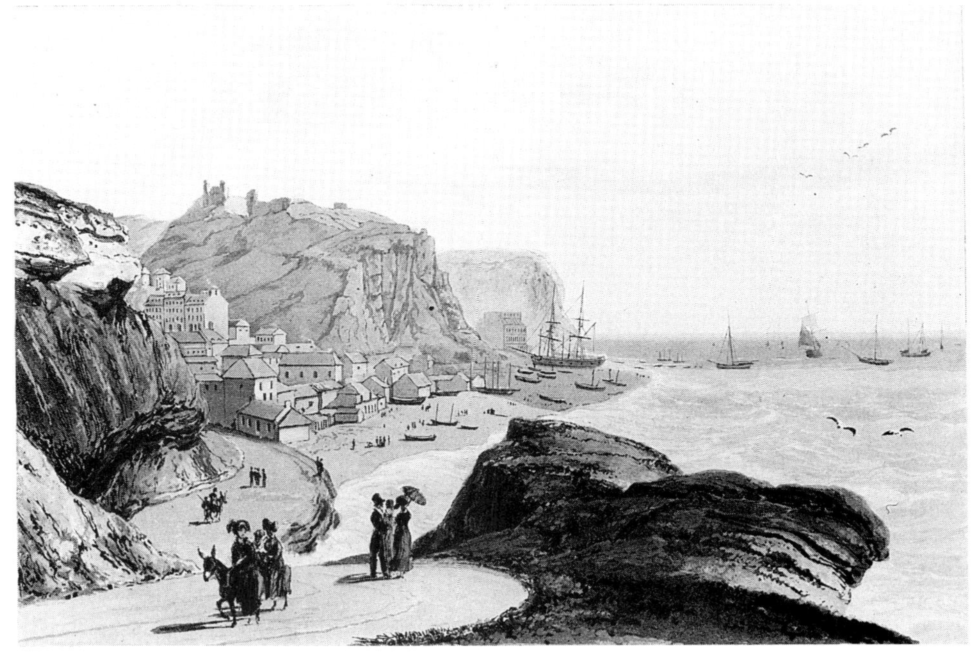

10 W. Daniell, *Hastings from near the White Rock*, aquatint, 1823

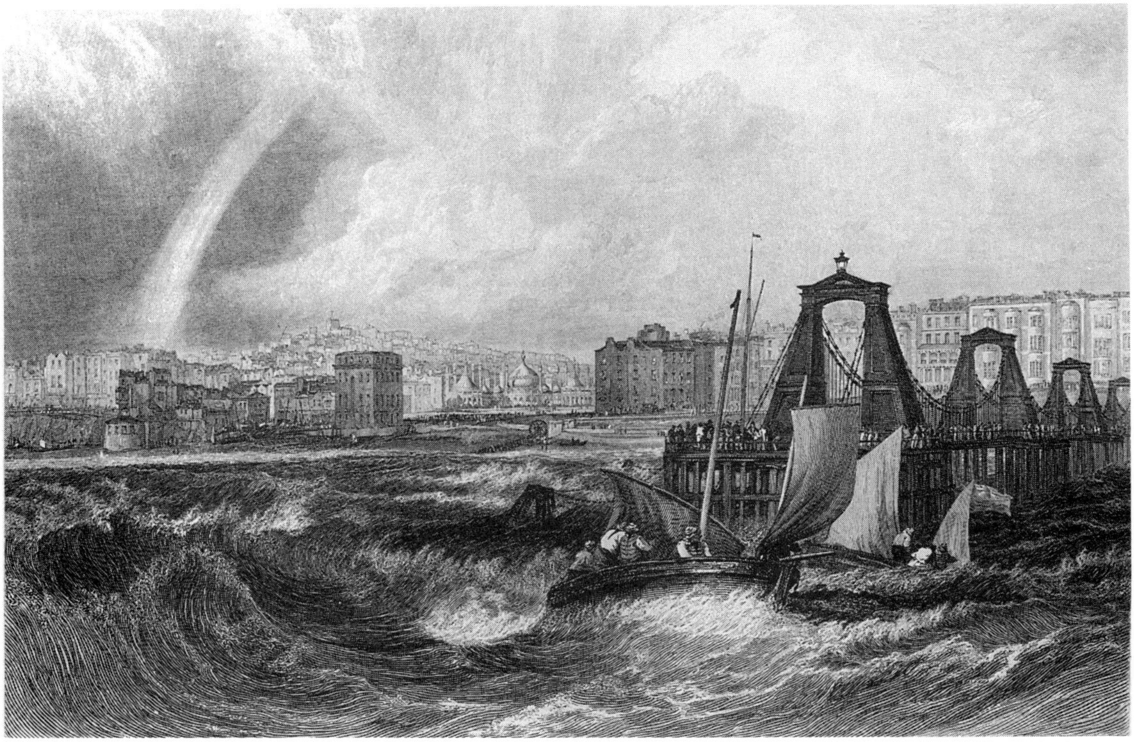

11 G. Cooke after J. M. W. Turner, *Brighthelmston, Sussex*, copper-plate engraving, 1825

12 G. Cooke after H. Edridge, *The Beach at Brighton, Sussex*, copper-plate engraving, 1814

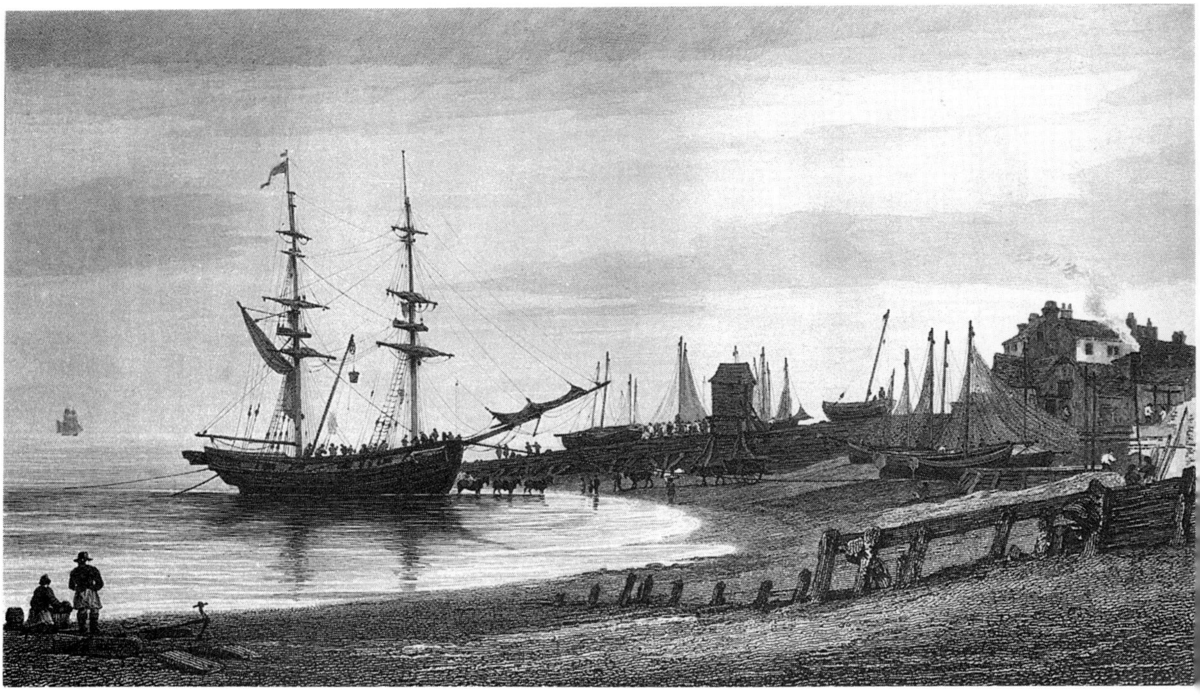

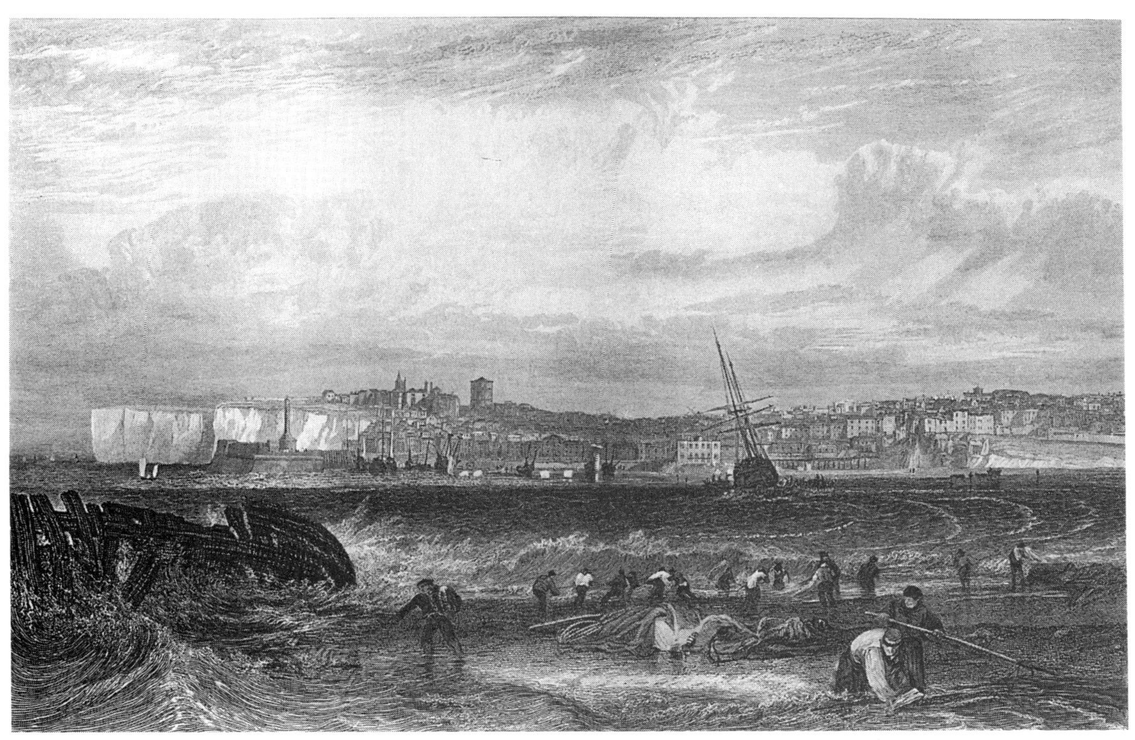

13 G. Cooke after J. M. W. Turner, *Margate, Kent*, copper-plate engraving, 1814

14 G. Hunt after E. Fox, *Marine Parade Brighton*, aquatint, *c.* 1827

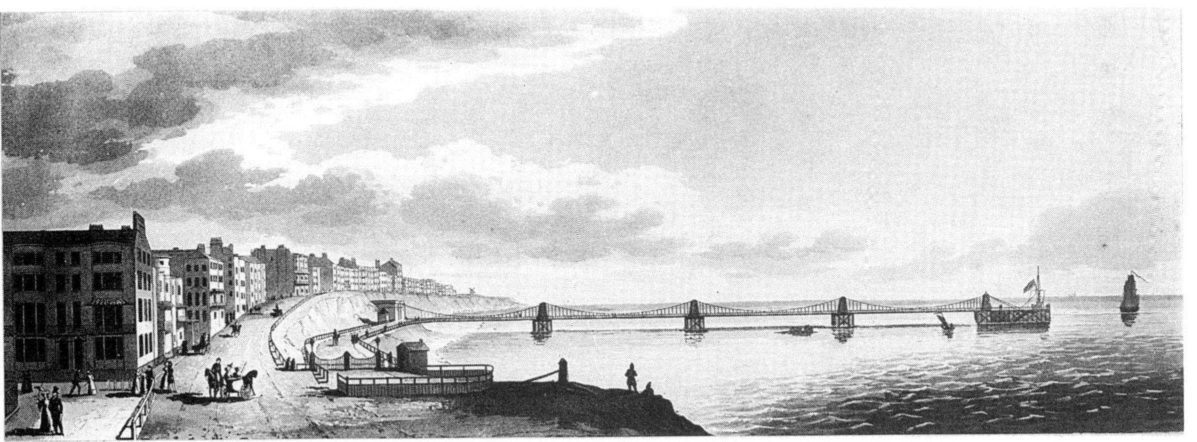

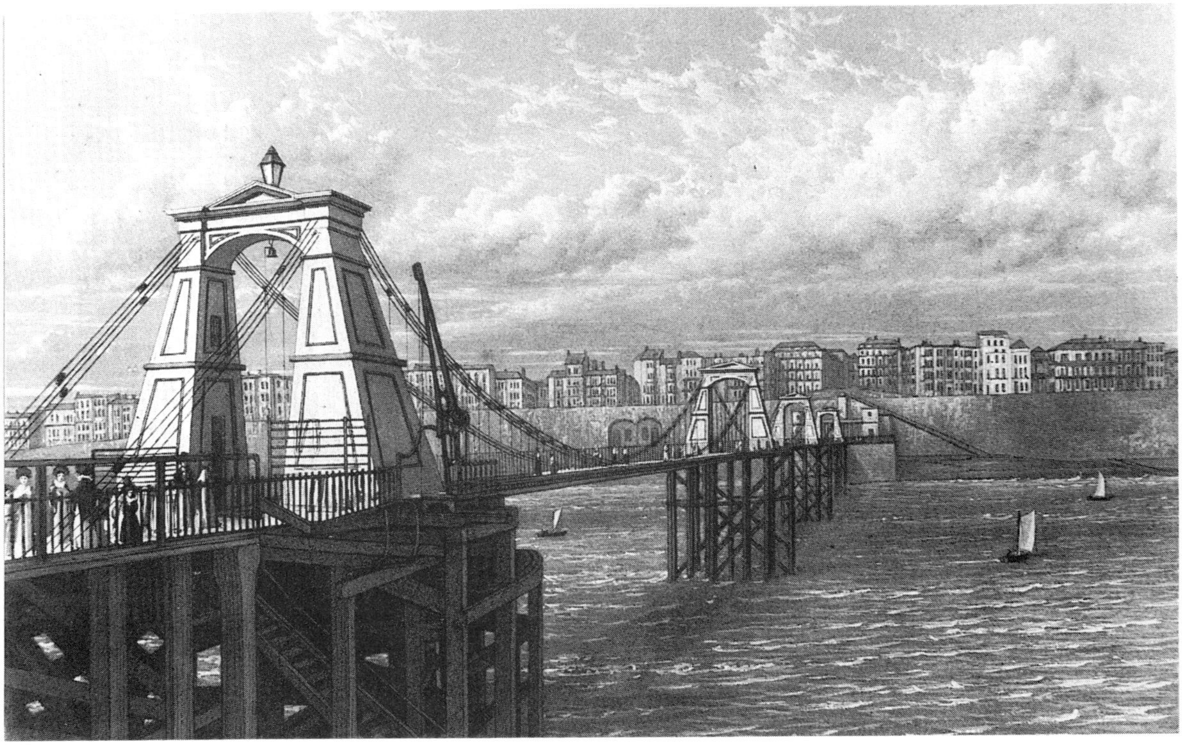

15 W. Westall, *Brighton from the Chain Pier*, aquatint, 1833, Brighton Art Gallery

16 G. Rowe, *Hastings from the Sea*, lithograph, *c.* 1820, Victoria & Albert Museum

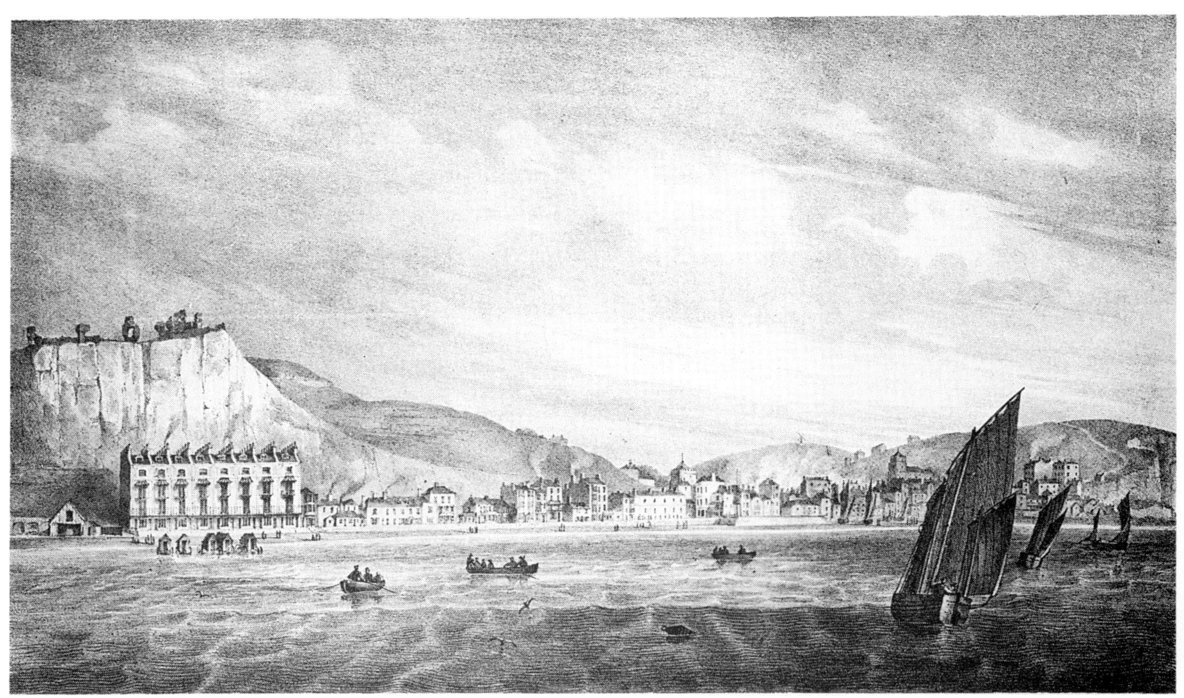

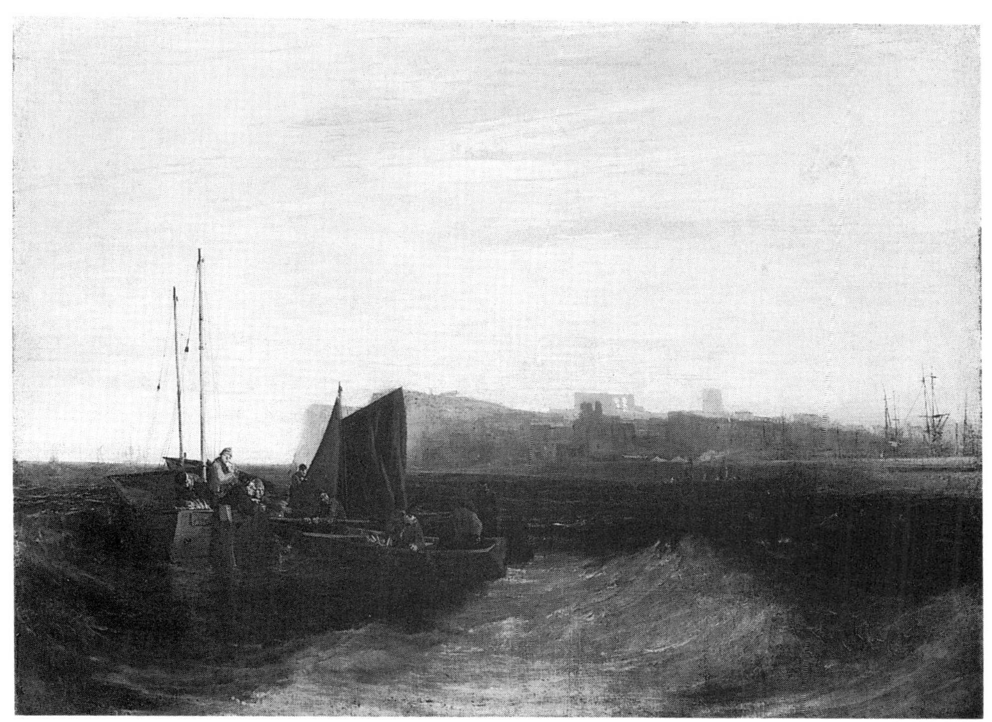

17 J. M. W. Turner, *Margate*, *c.* 1808, Petworth House

18 A. W. Callcott, *Little Hampton Pier*, *c.* 1812, Tate Gallery

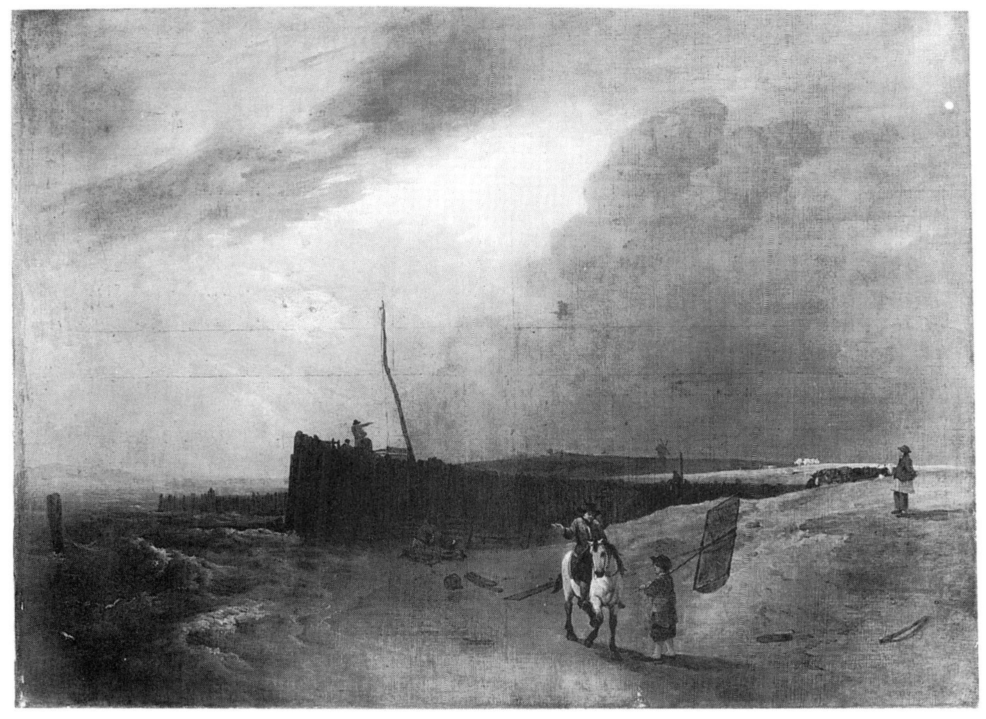

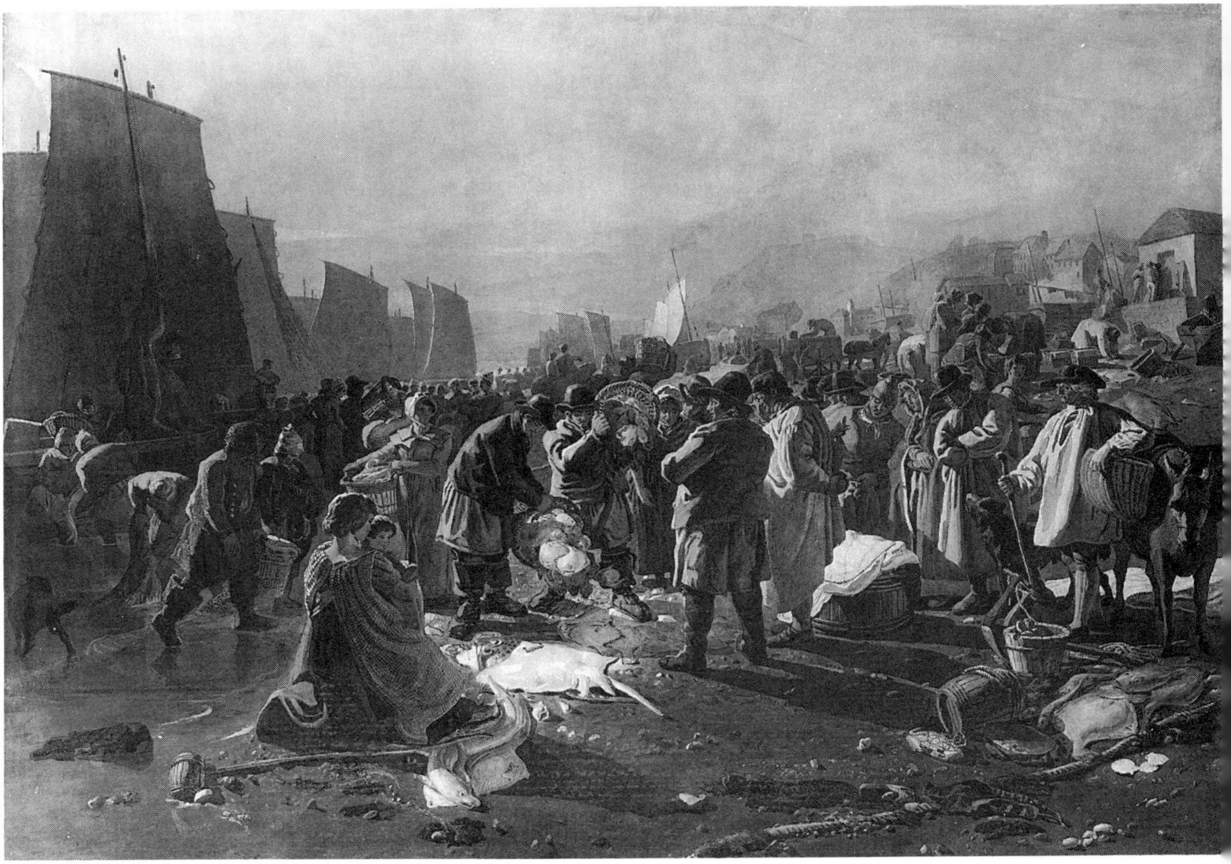

19 J. Cristall, *The Fish-market, Hastings*, 1808, Victoria & Albert Museum

20 J. Cristall, *Fleet Sailing up Channel off Hastings*, 1814, National Gallery of Scotland

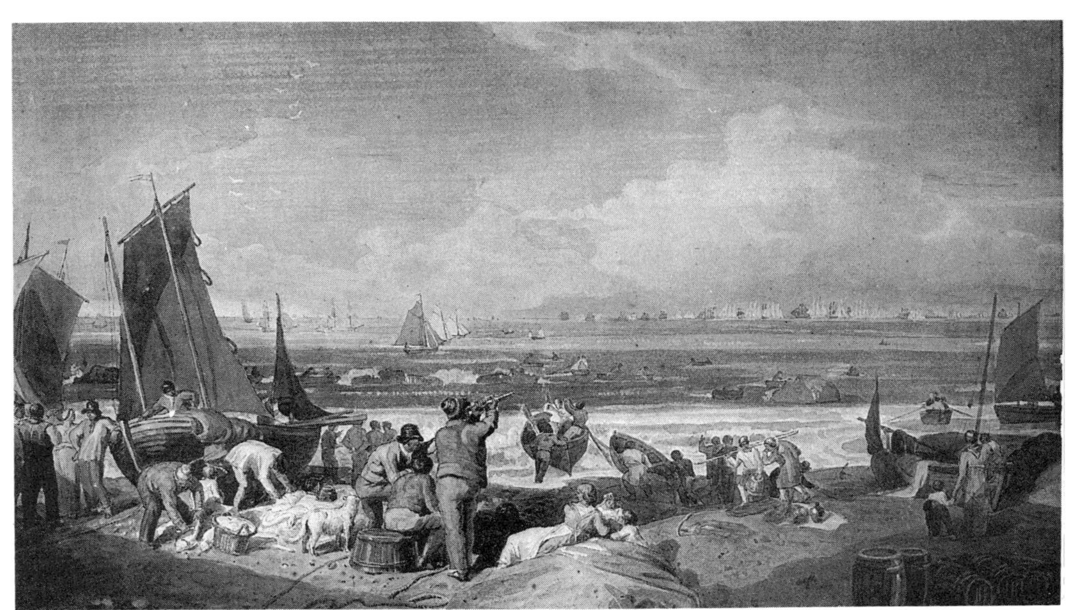

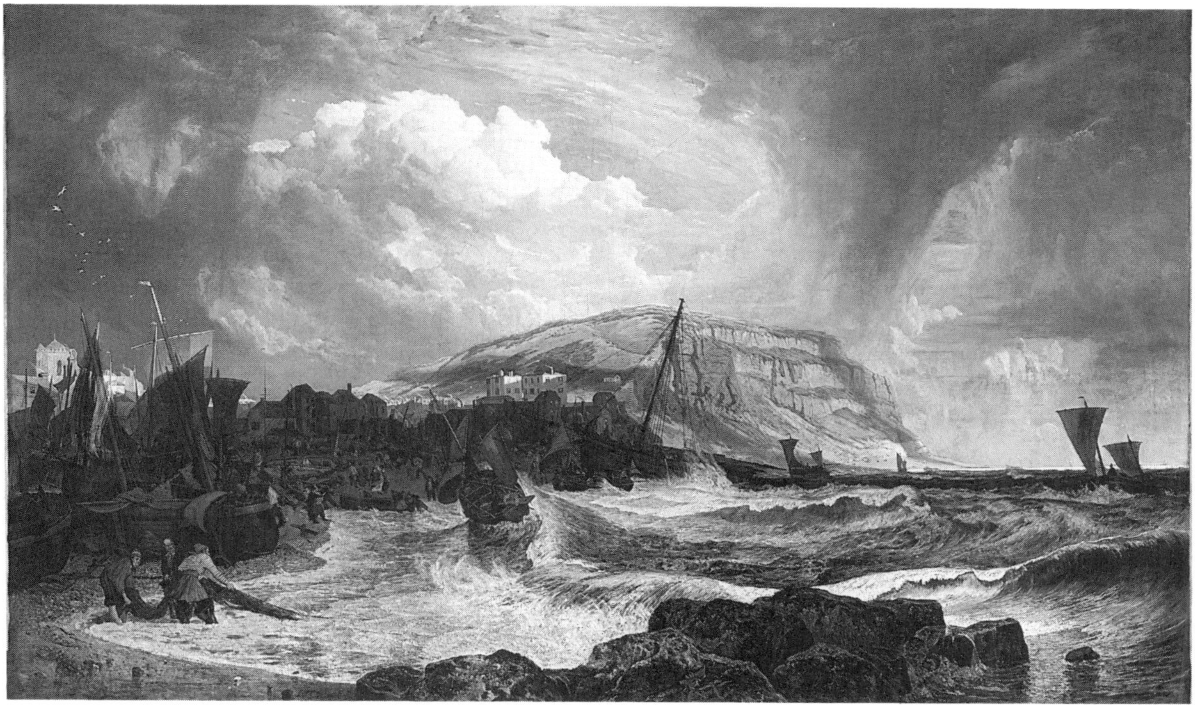

21 J. J. Chalon, *View of Hastings*, 1819, Victoria & Albert Museum

22 J. Hoppner, *A Gale of Wind*, RA 1794?, Tate Gallery

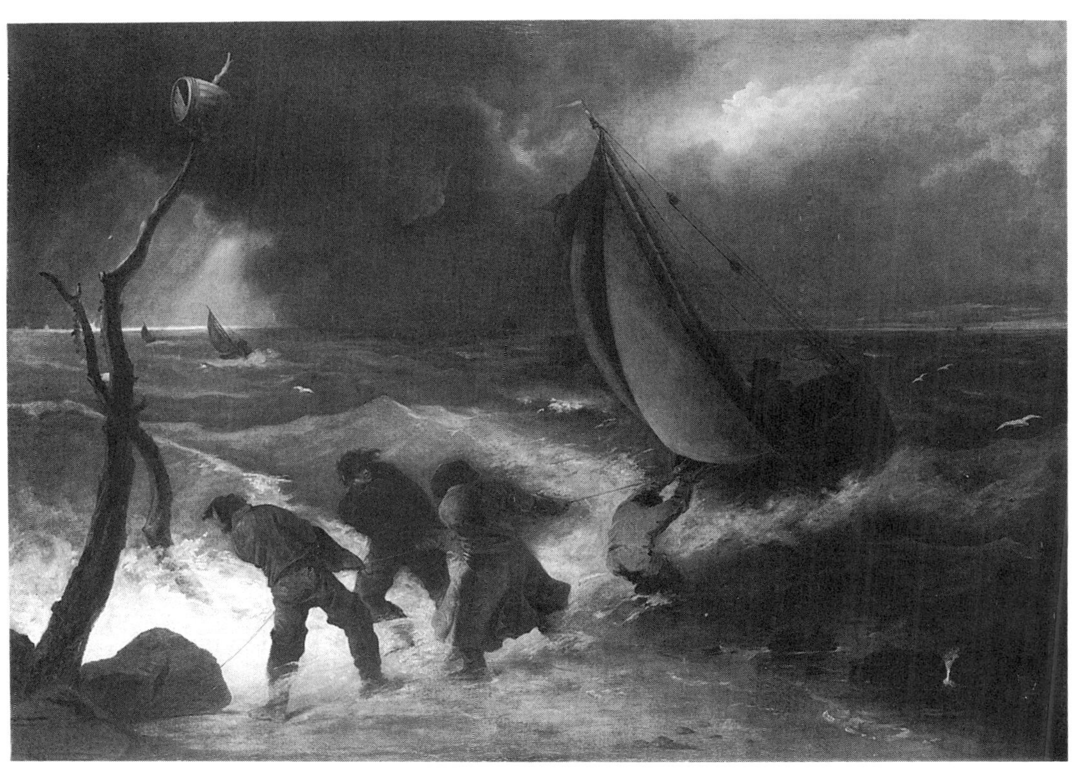

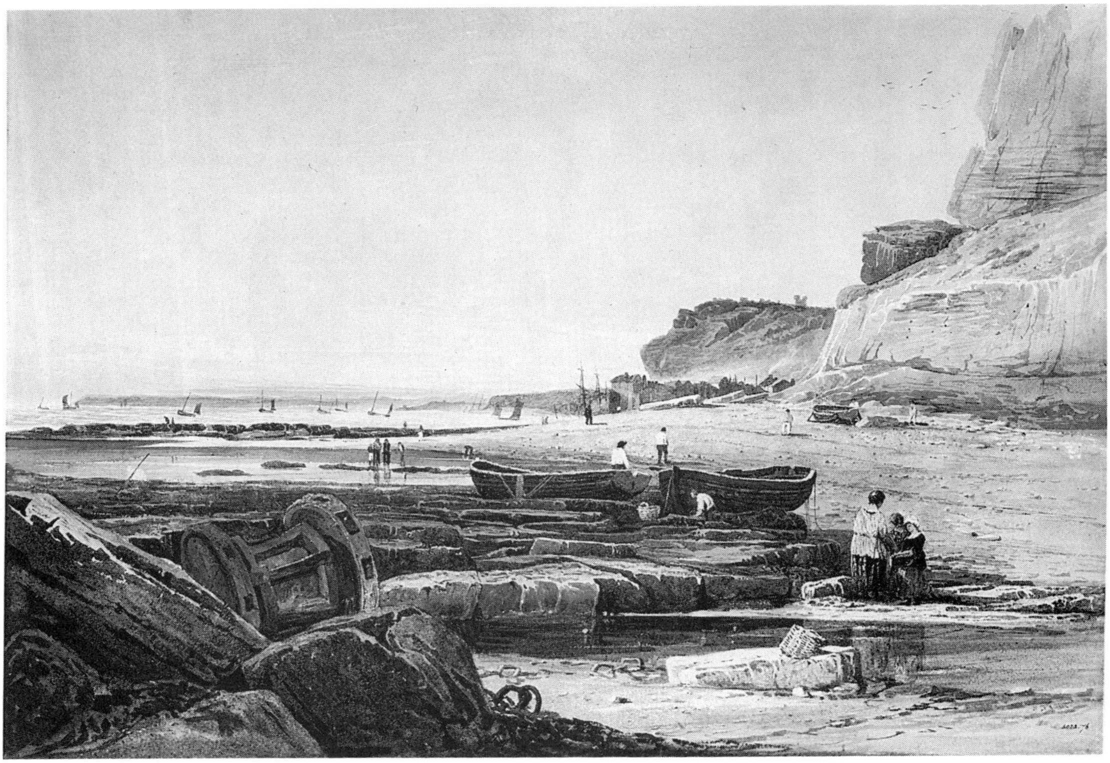

23 S. Prout, *The Beach, Hastings, Sussex*, 1817?, Victoria & Albert Museum

24 W. Collins, *Shrimp Boys at Cromer*, etching and mezzotint, 1820, British Museum

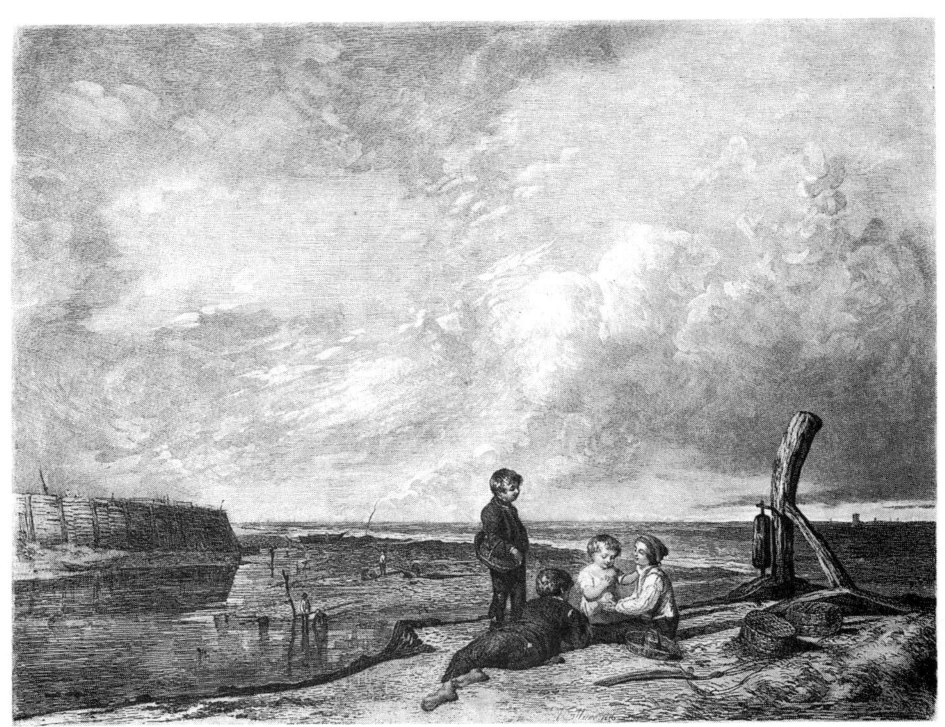

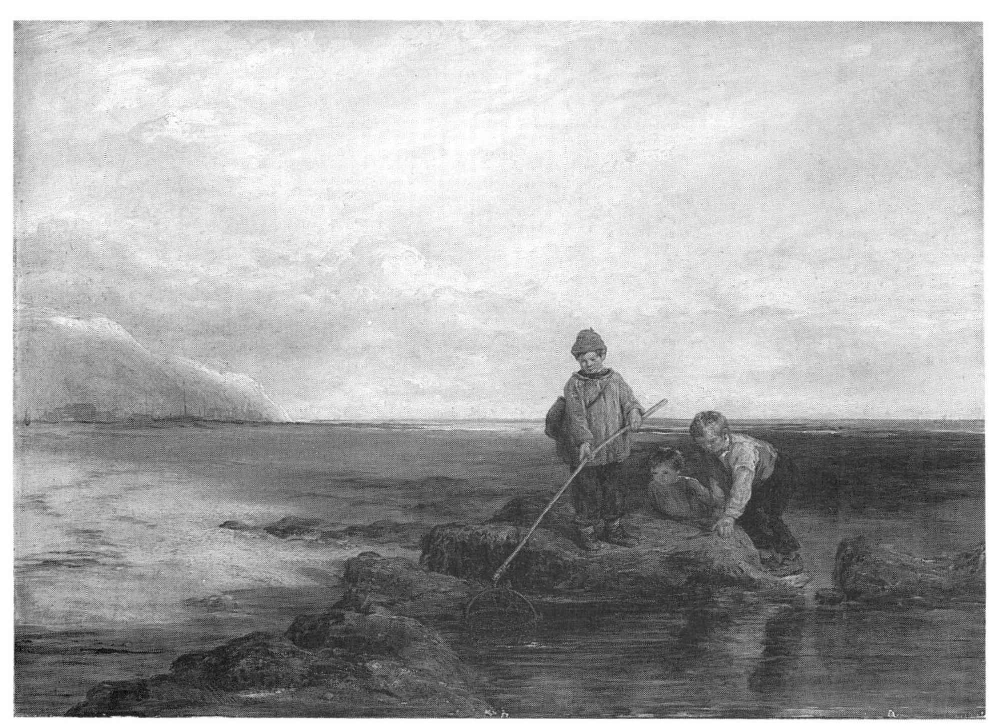

25 W. Collins, *The Prawn Catchers*, 1829?, Tate Gallery

26 J. Constable, *Yarmouth Jetty*, 1823, Private Collection

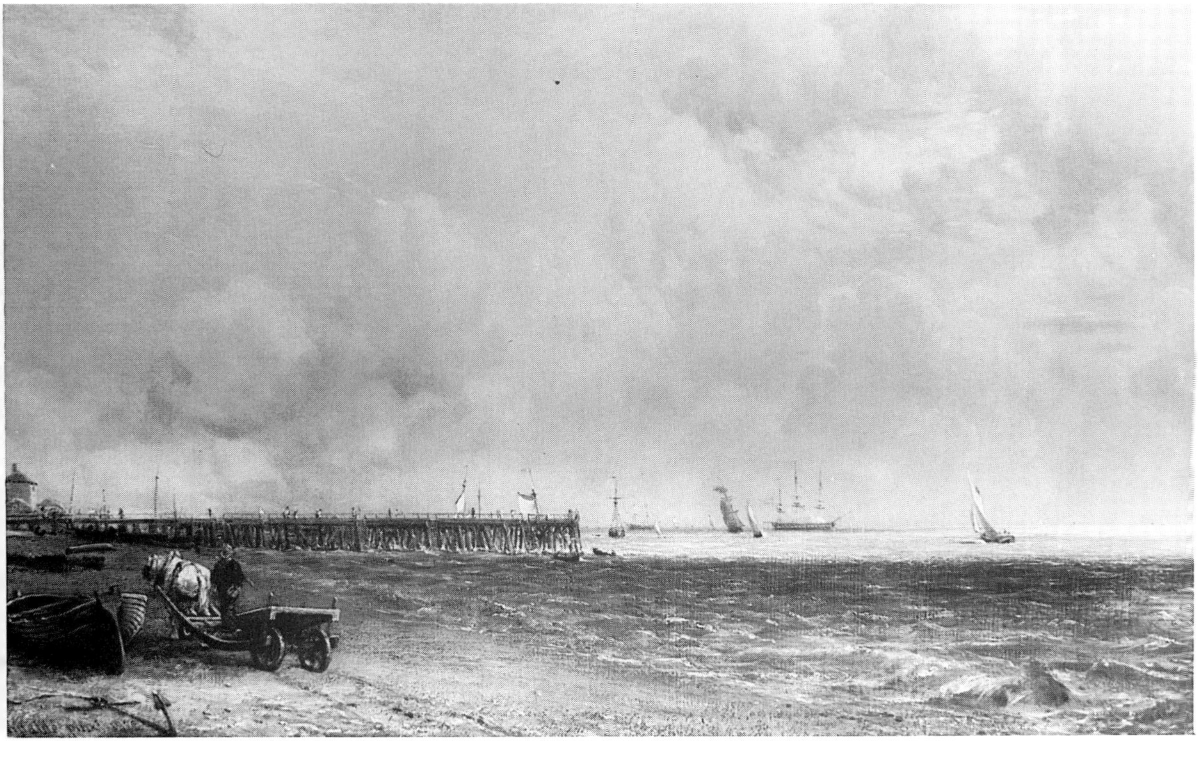

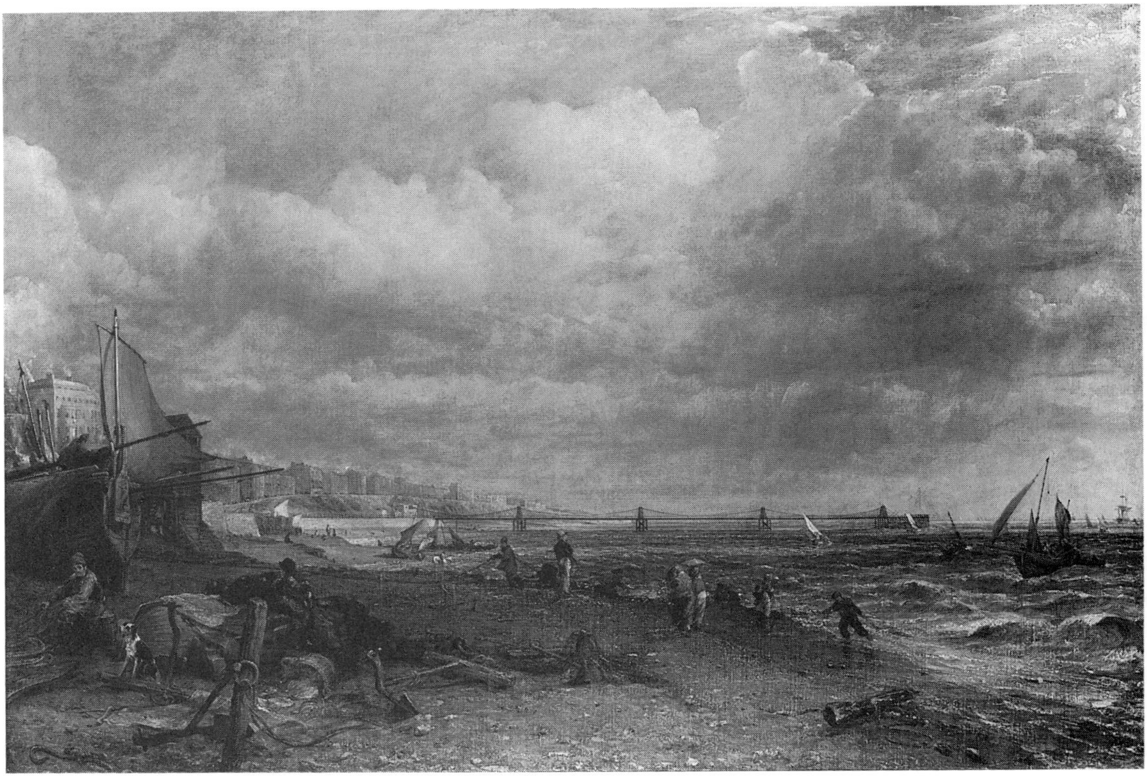

27 J. Constable, *The Beach at Brighton, the Chain Pier in the Distance*, 1826–7, Tate Gallery

28 F. Smith after J. Constable, *View of Brighton with Chain Pier*, copper-plate engraving, 1829, British Museum

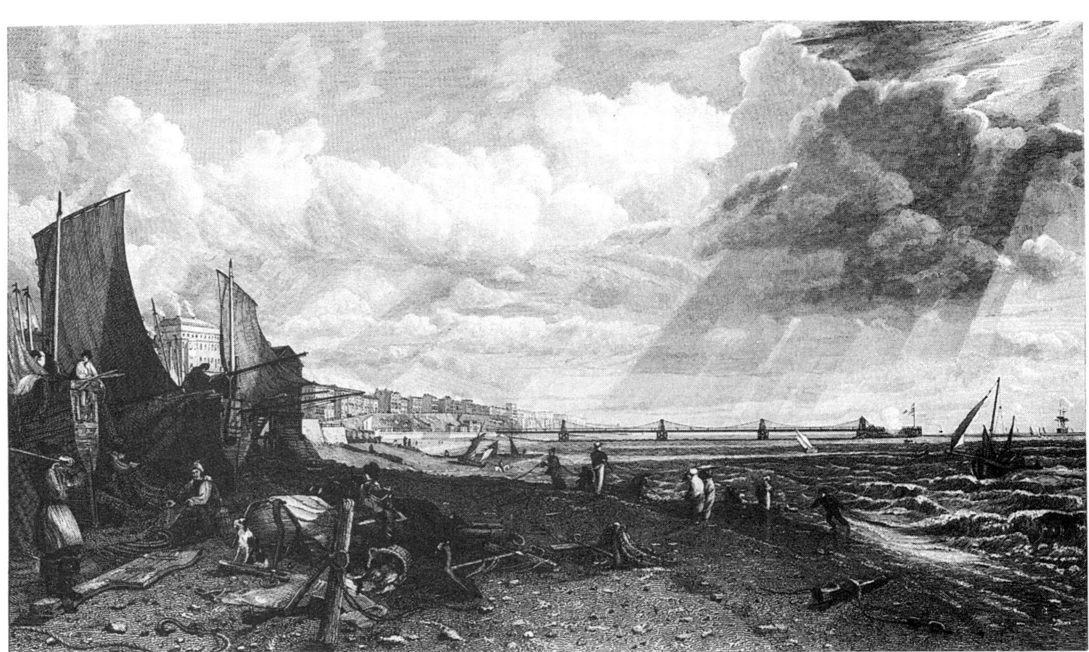

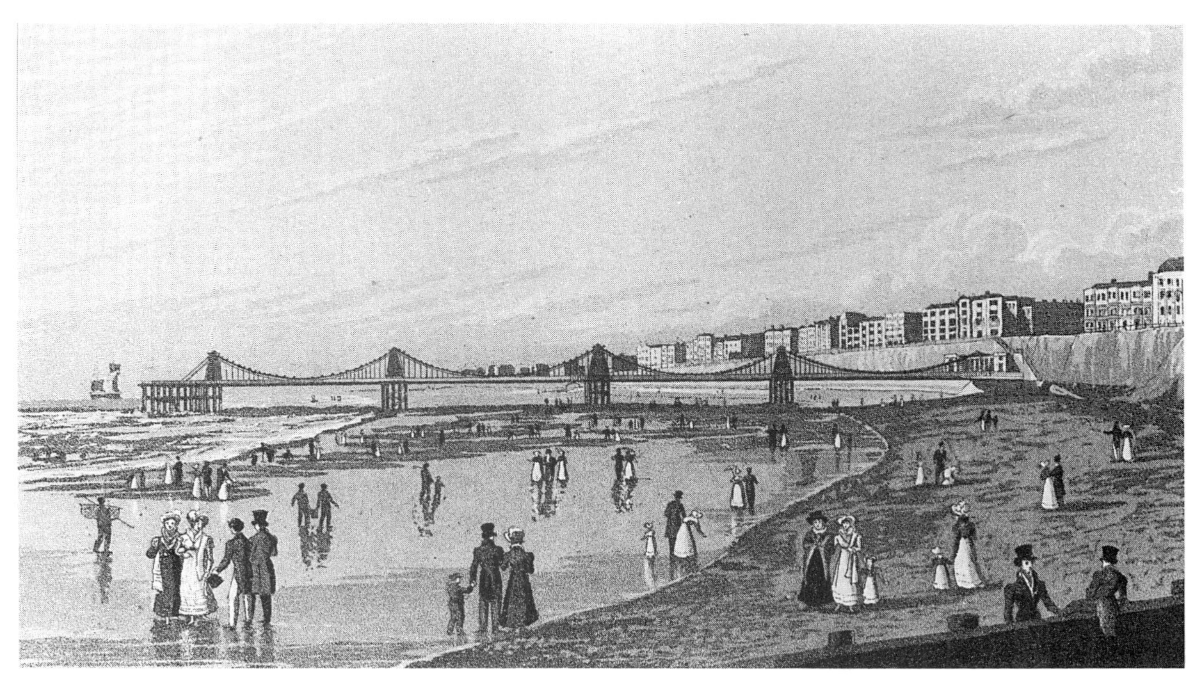

29 R. Havell, *Chain Pier from the Sands at Low Water*, aquatint, 1824

30 E. W. Cooke, *Prawn Boats &c. Brighton Beach*, etching, 1830

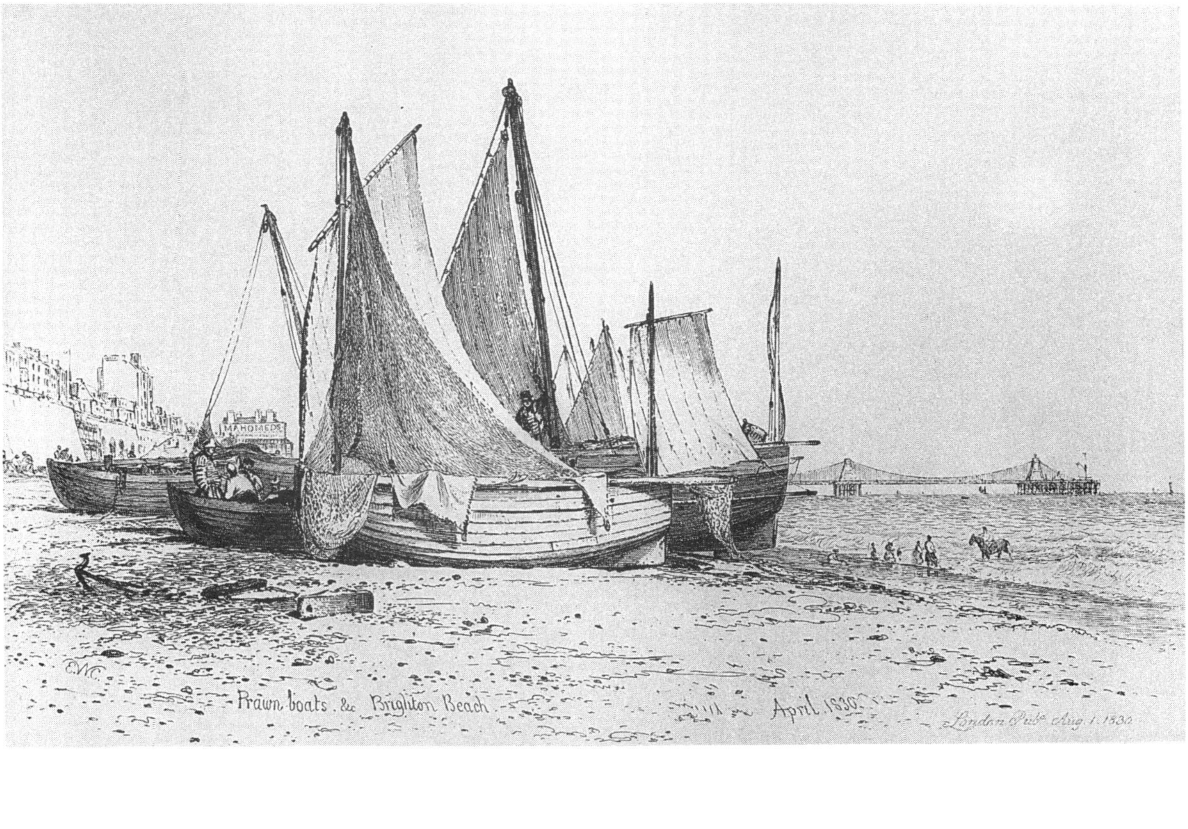

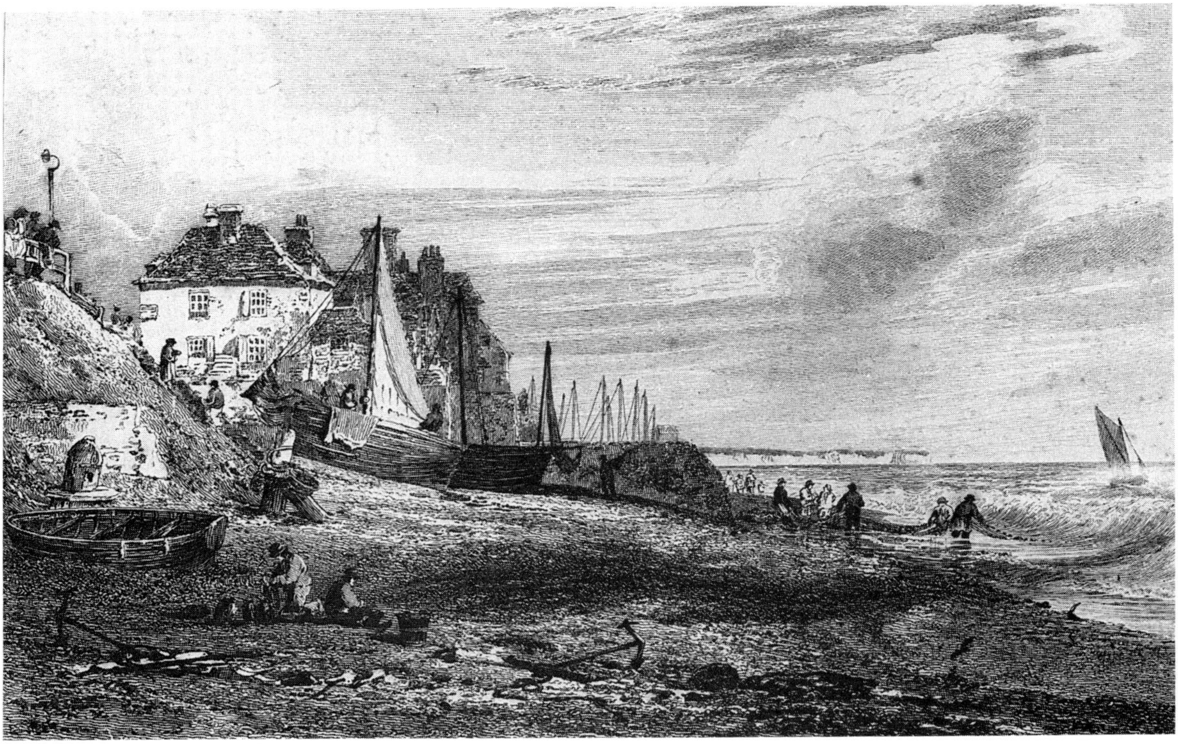

31 W. B. Cooke after H. Edridge, *Brighton*, copper-plate engraving, 1822

32 J. M. W. Turner, *Brighton from the Sea*, *c.* 1829, Petworth House

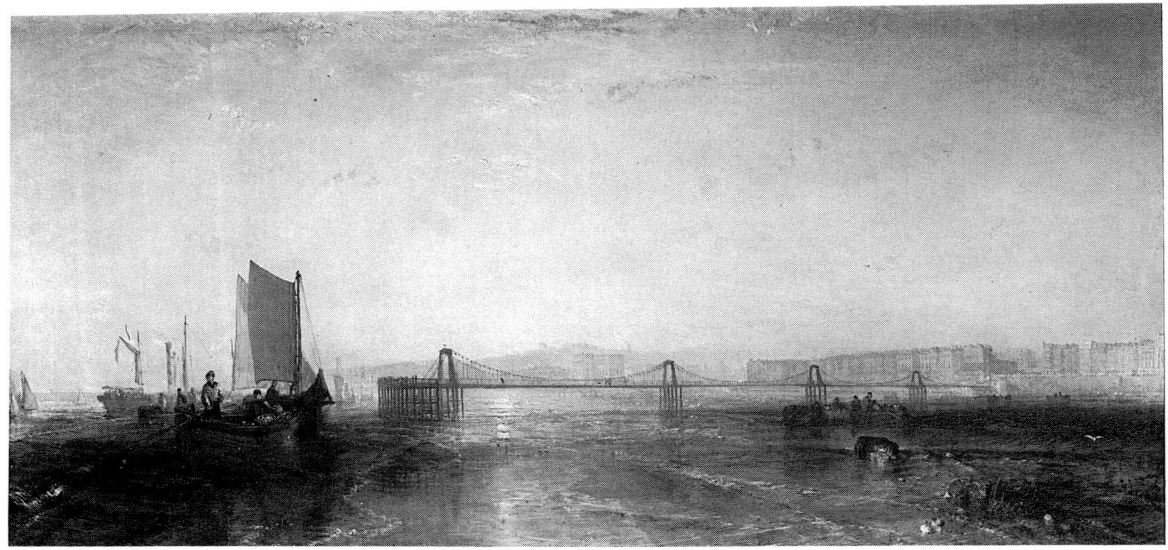

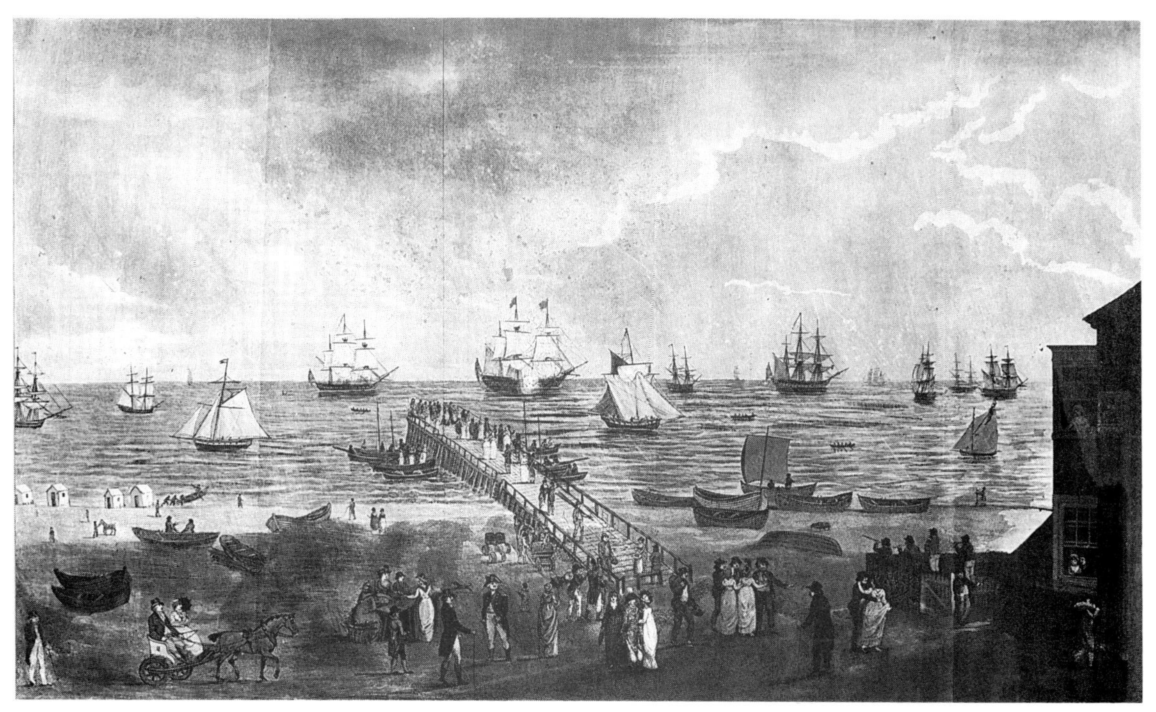

33 R. Pollard after J. Butcher, *A North West View of the Jetty at Yarmouth*, aquatint, *c.* 1790, Norwich Castle Museum

34 I. Clark after J. Preston, *Yarmouth Jetty and Roads*, aquatint, 1819, Norwich Castle Museum

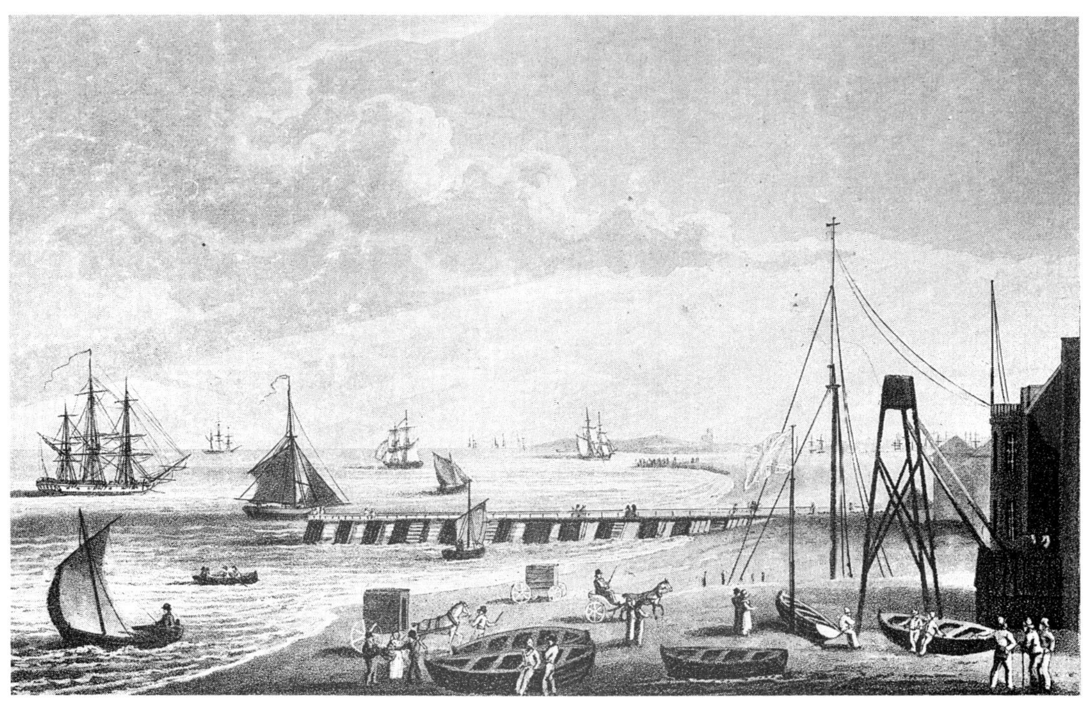

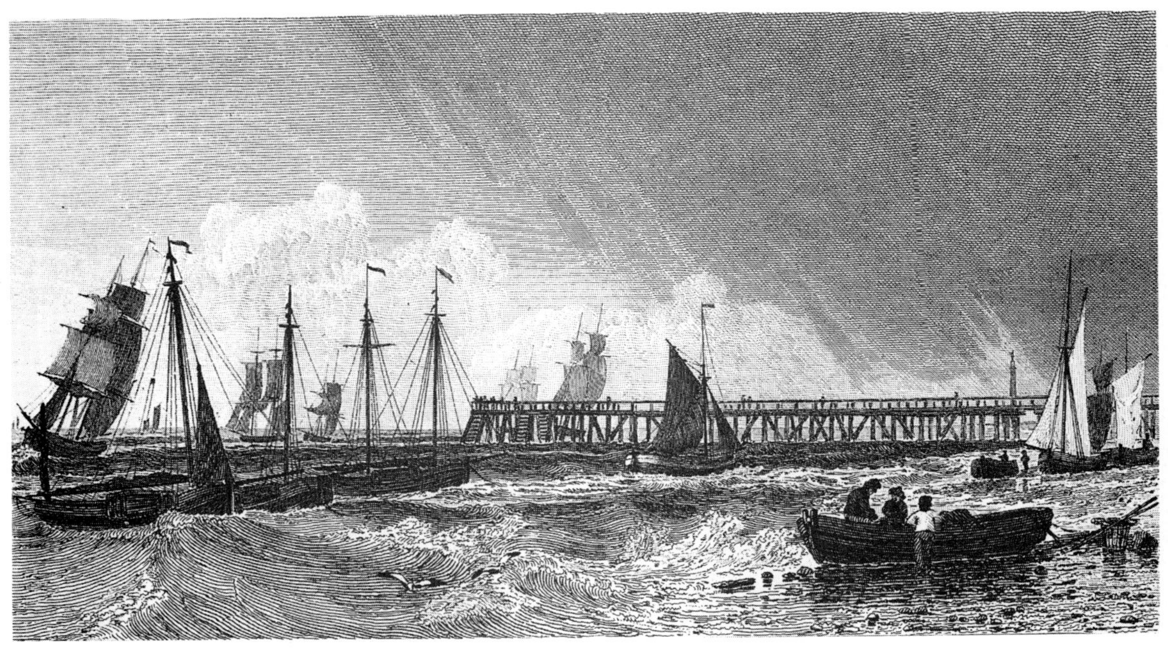

35 J. Lambert, *Yarmouth Jetty*, copper-plate engraving, 1822, Norwich Castle Museum

36 E. Finden after E. W. Cooke, *Yarmouth Norfolk*, steel engraving, *c.* 1830–5, Norwich Castle Museum

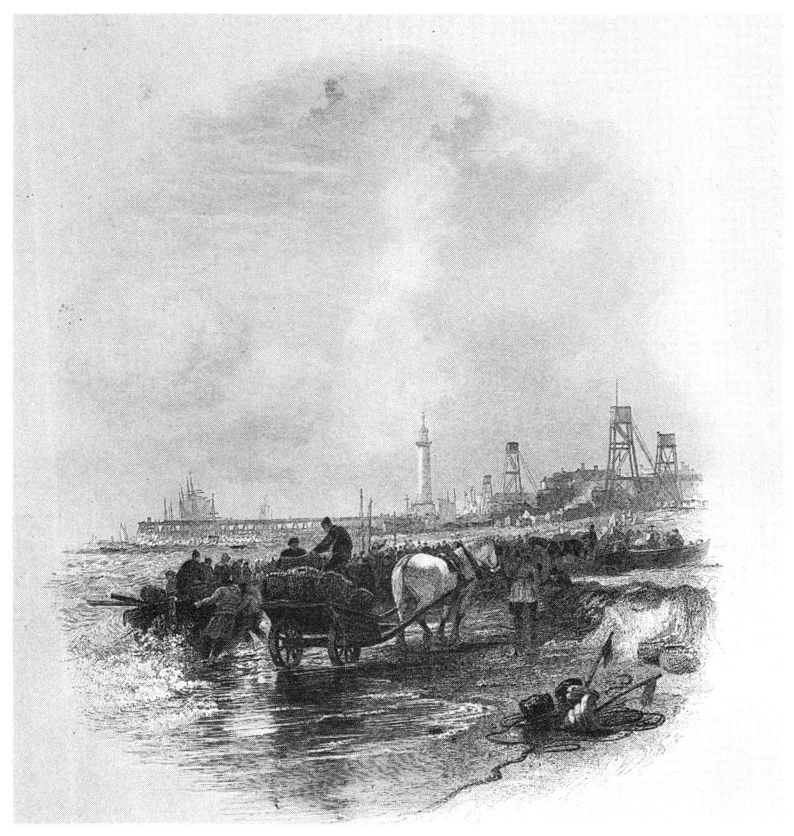

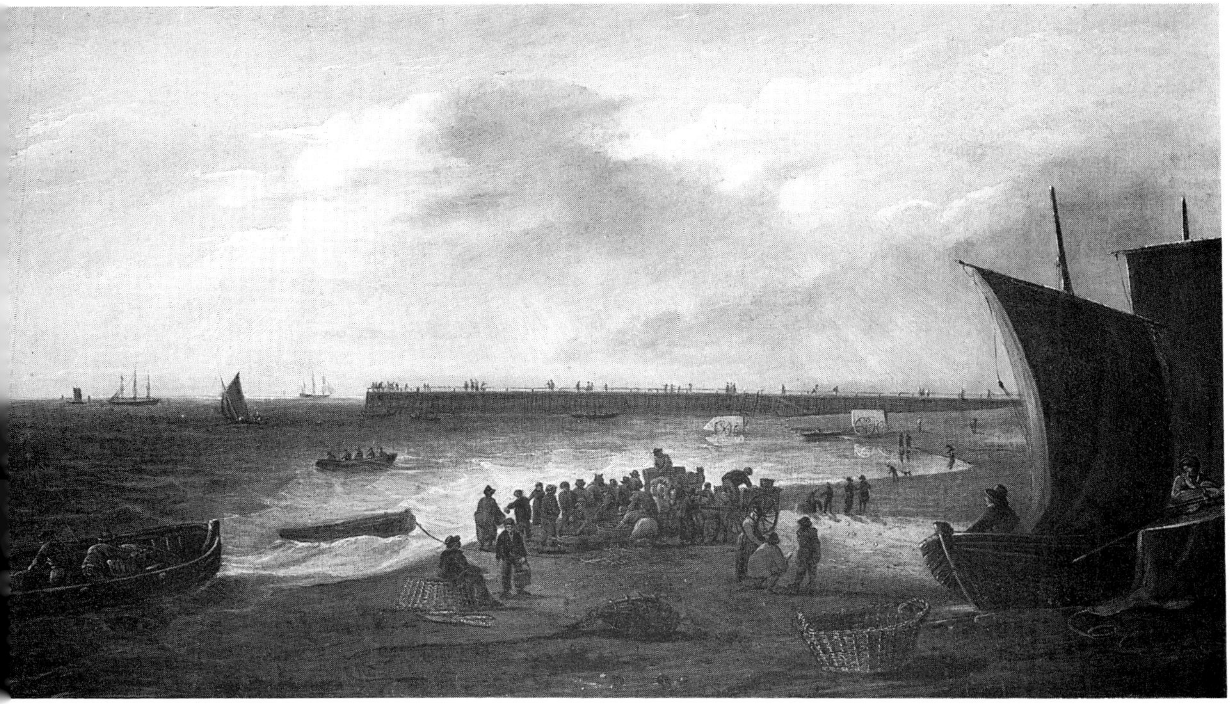

37 R. Ladbrooke, *Yarmouth Beach*, *c.* 1809, Great Yarmouth Museum

38 J. Crome, *Yarmouth Jetty*, *c.* 1806–7, British Museum

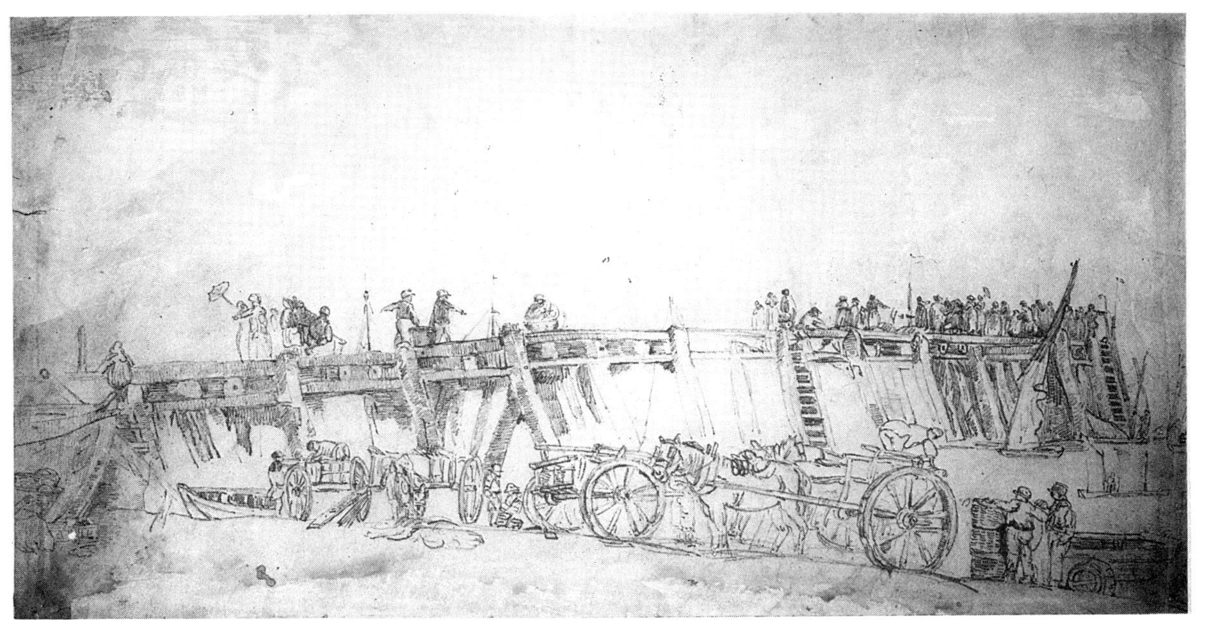

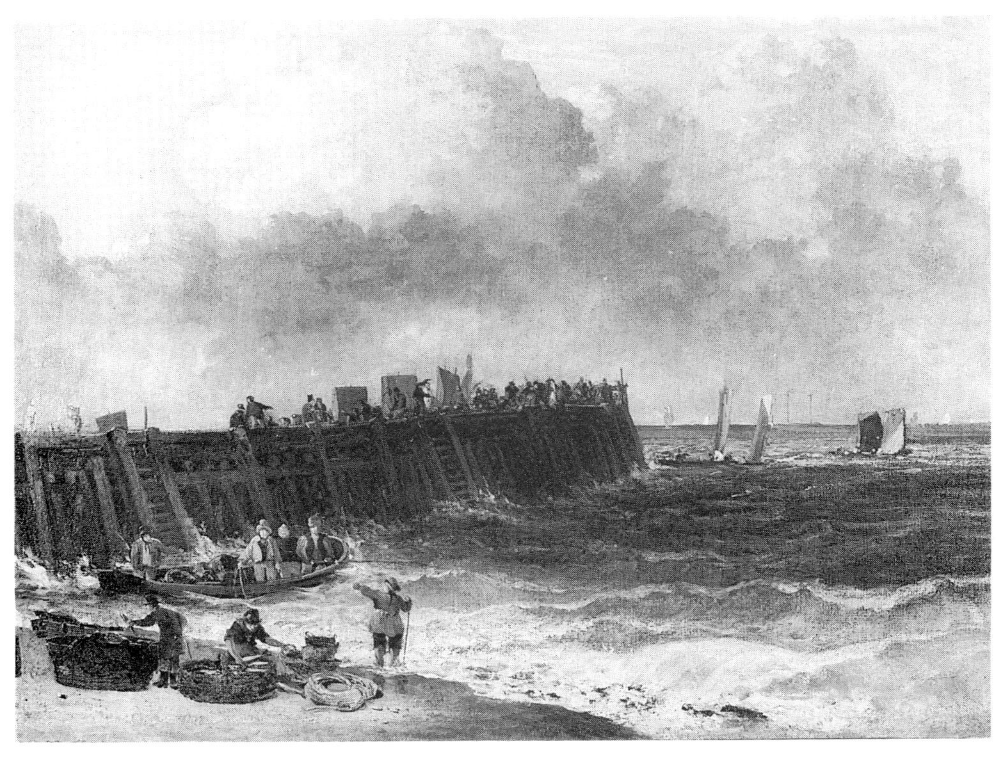

39 J. Crome, *Yarmouth Jetty*, *c.* 1812, Norwich Castle Museum

40 J. Crome, *Yarmouth Beach, from the Pier*, *c.* 1818?, Private Collection

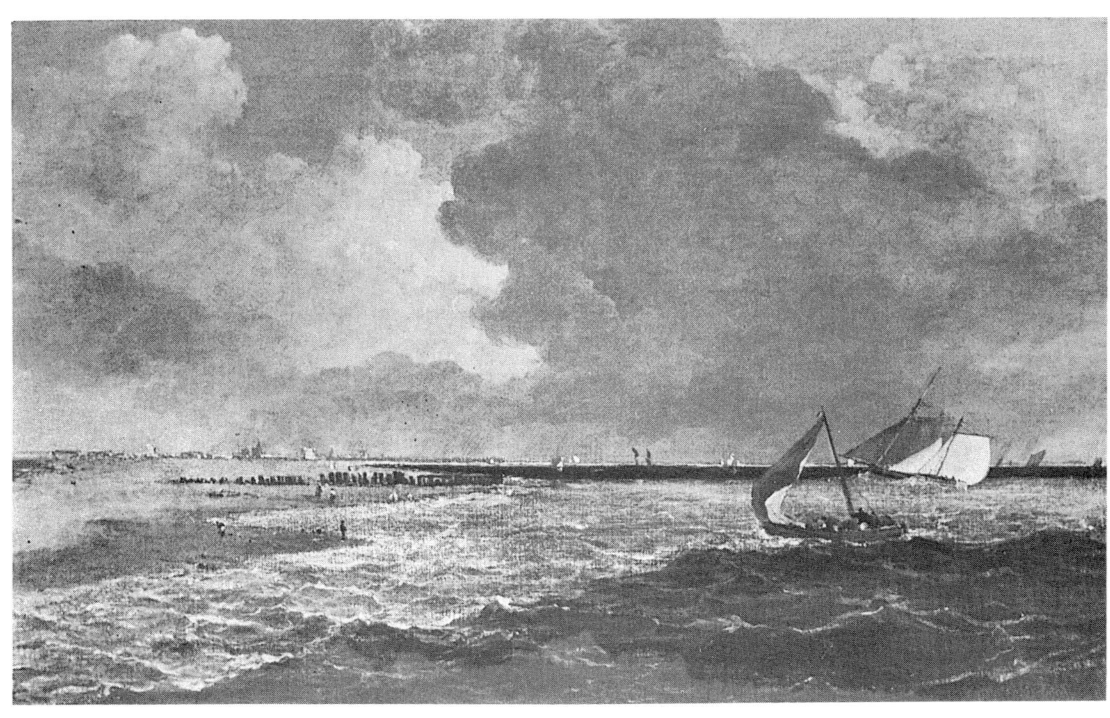

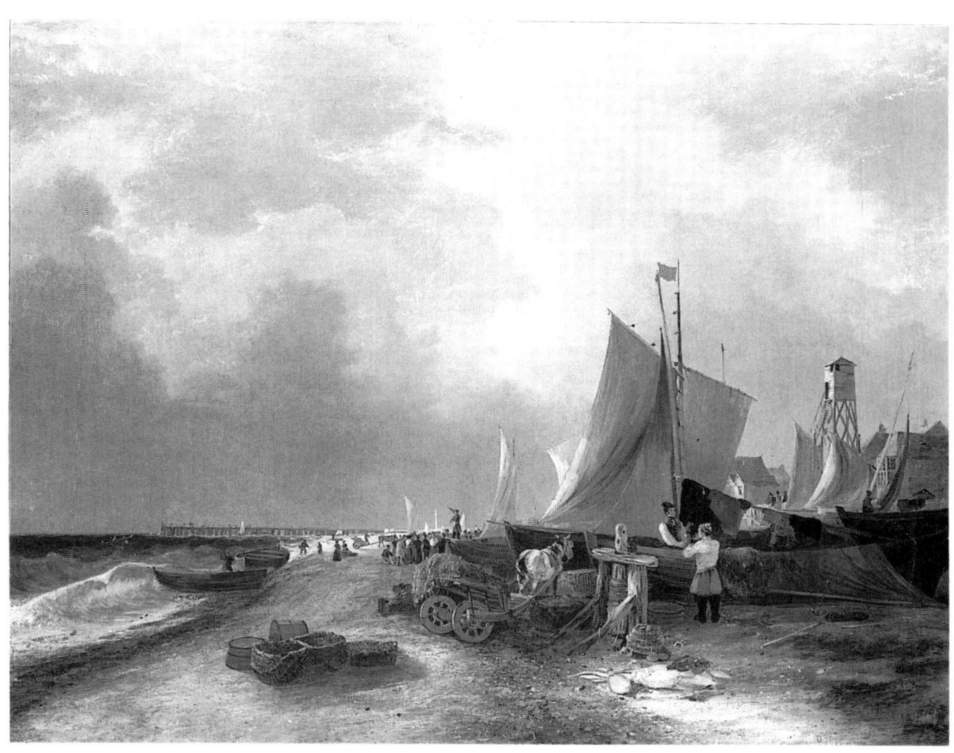

41 G. Vincent, *The Fish Auction, Yarmouth*, 1827, Norwich Castle Museum

42 G. Vincent, *Dutch Fair on Yarmouth Beach*, 1820–1, Great Yarmouth Museum

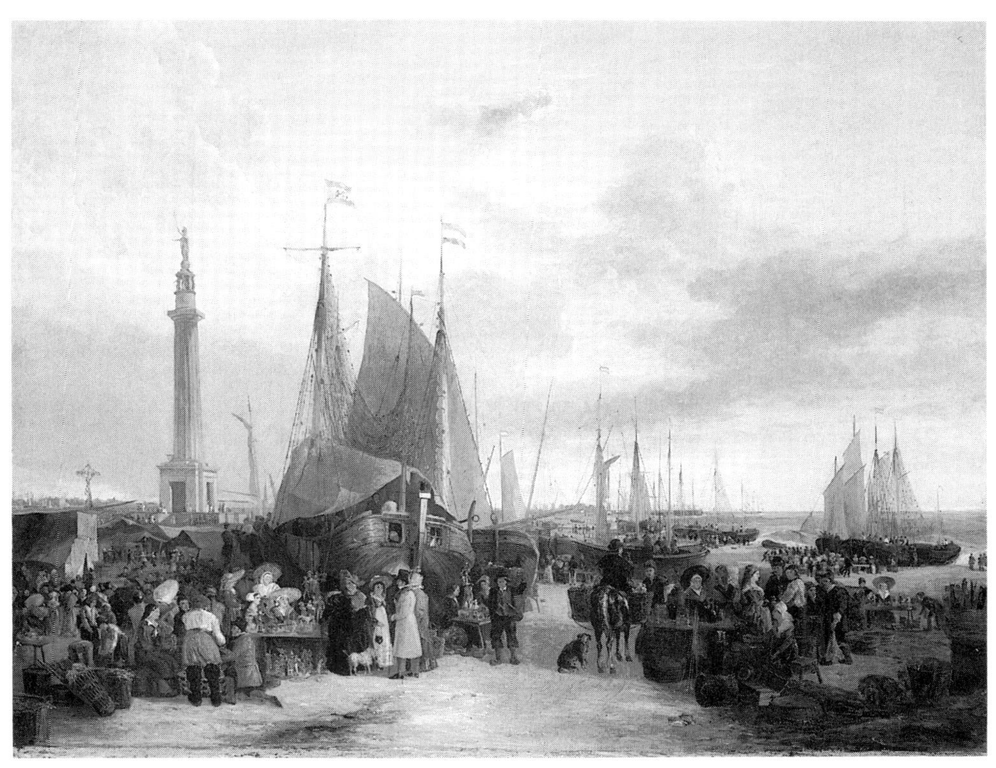

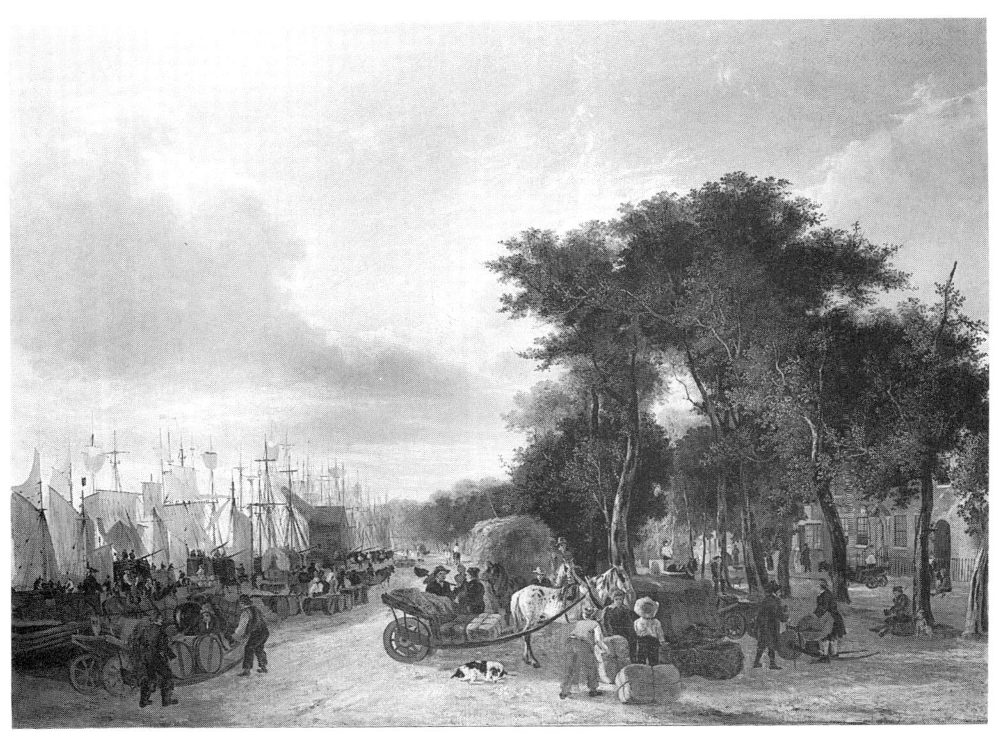

43 G. Vincent, *View of Yarmouth Quay*, 1823, Norwich Castle Museum

44 G. Vincent (?), *View of Yarmouth*, Private Collection

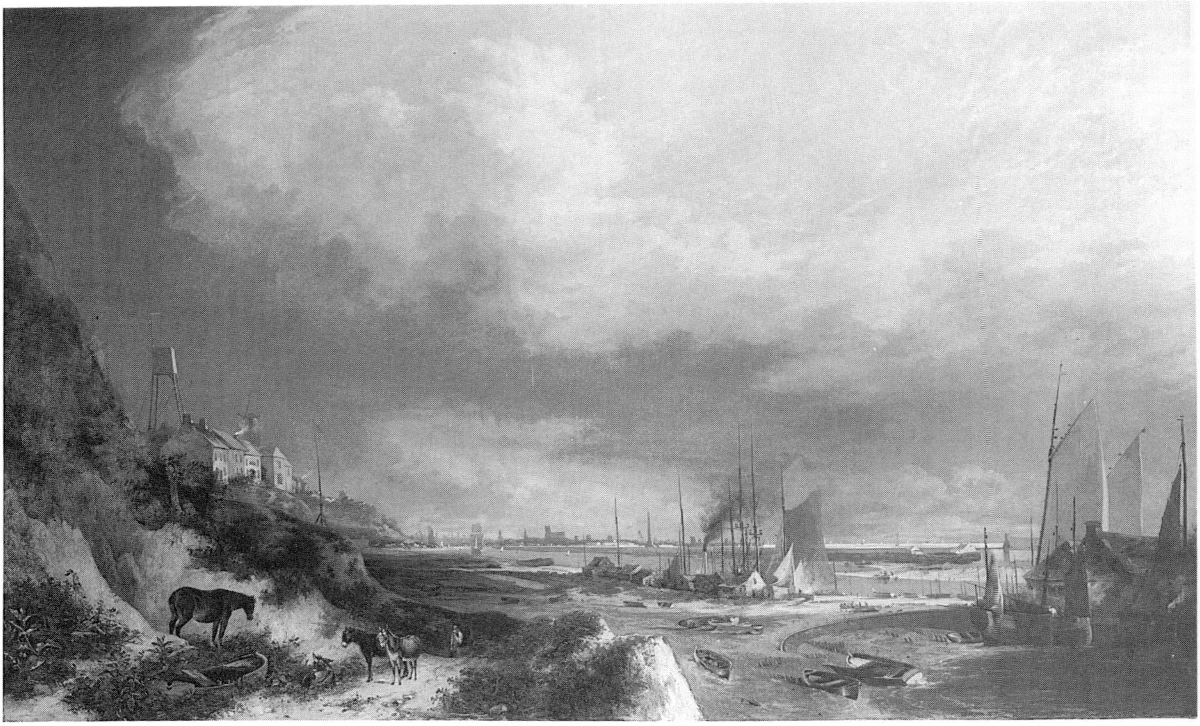

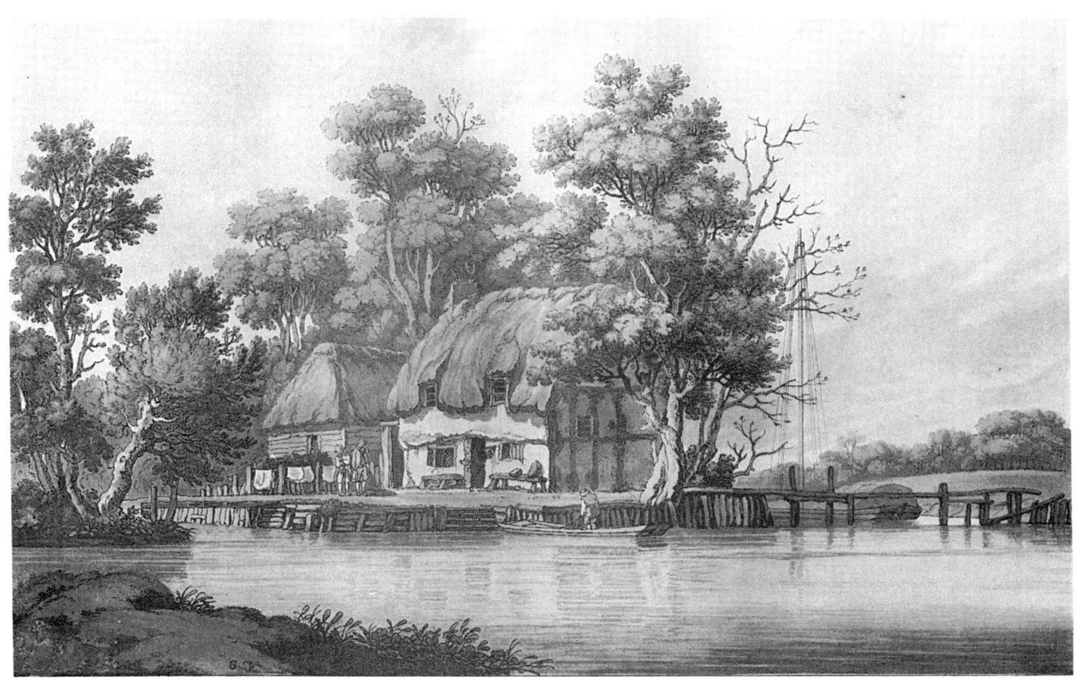

45 J. C. Stadler after J. Farington, *Langley Ware*, aquatint, 1793

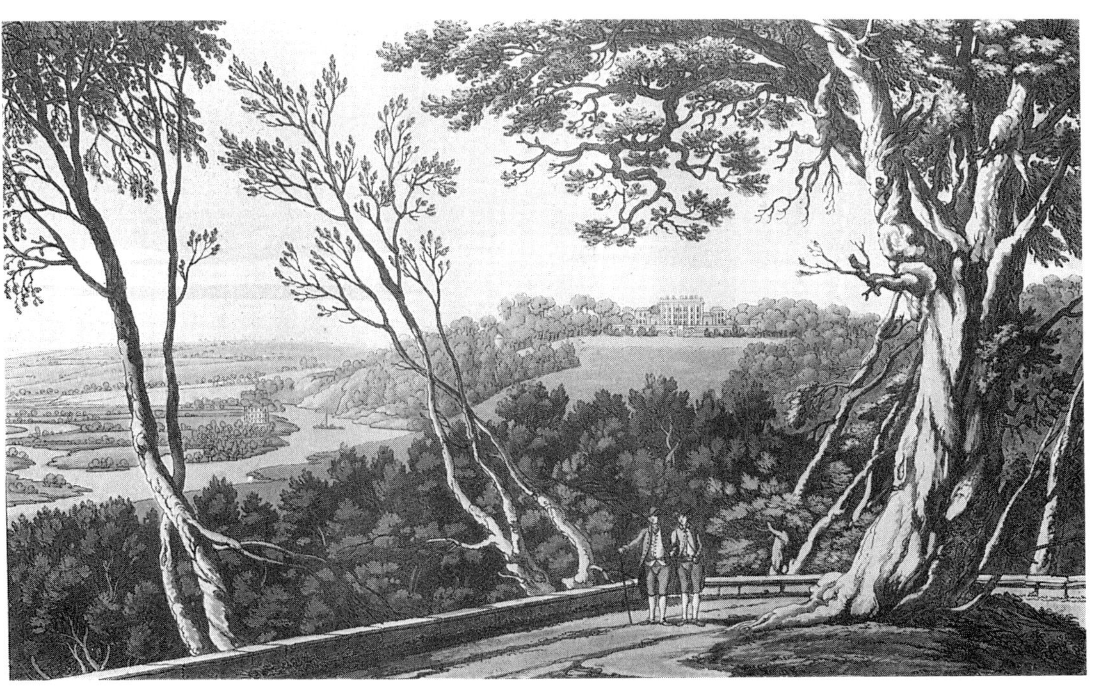

46 J. C. Stadler after J. Farington, *Cliefden*, aquatint, 1793

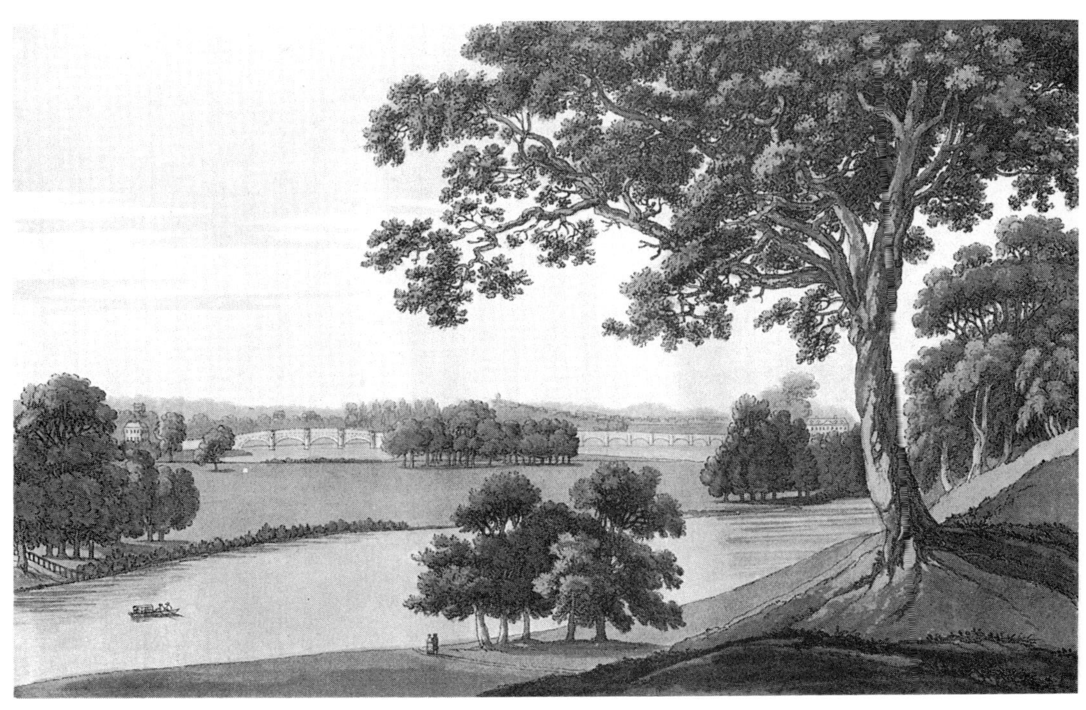

47 J. C. Stadler after J. Farington, *View of Walton Bridge from Oatlands*, aquatint, 1793

48 F. Jukes after E. Dayes, *View of the Doward Rocks*, aquatint, 1797–1802

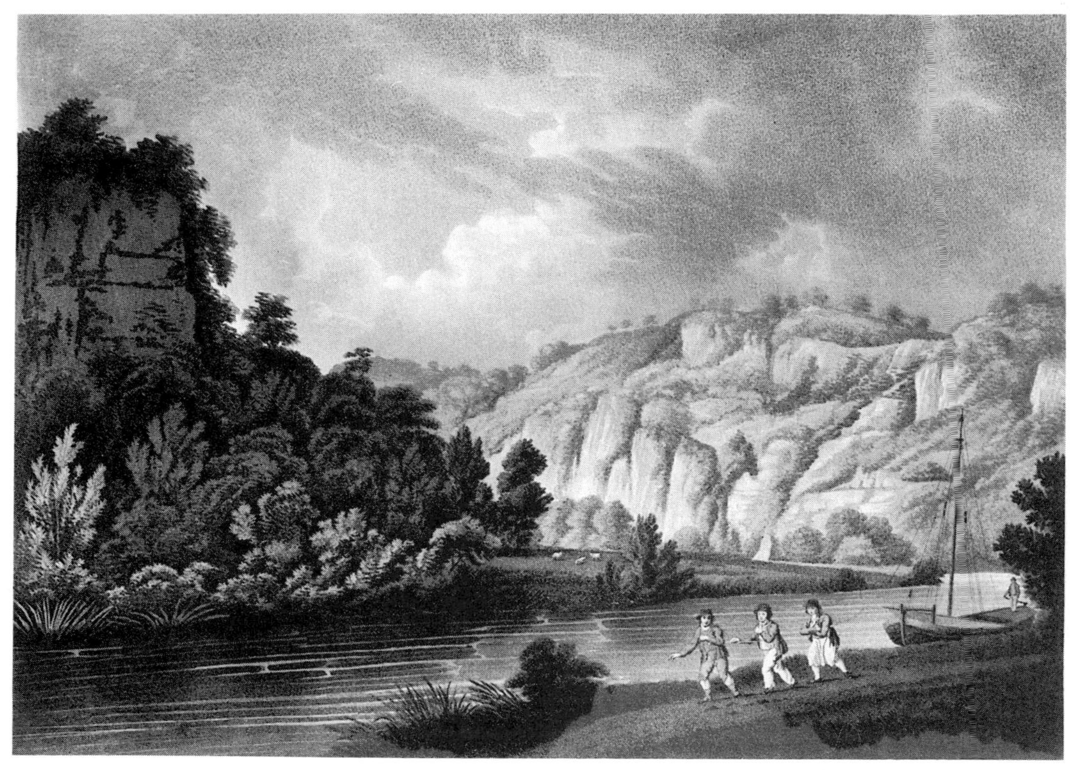

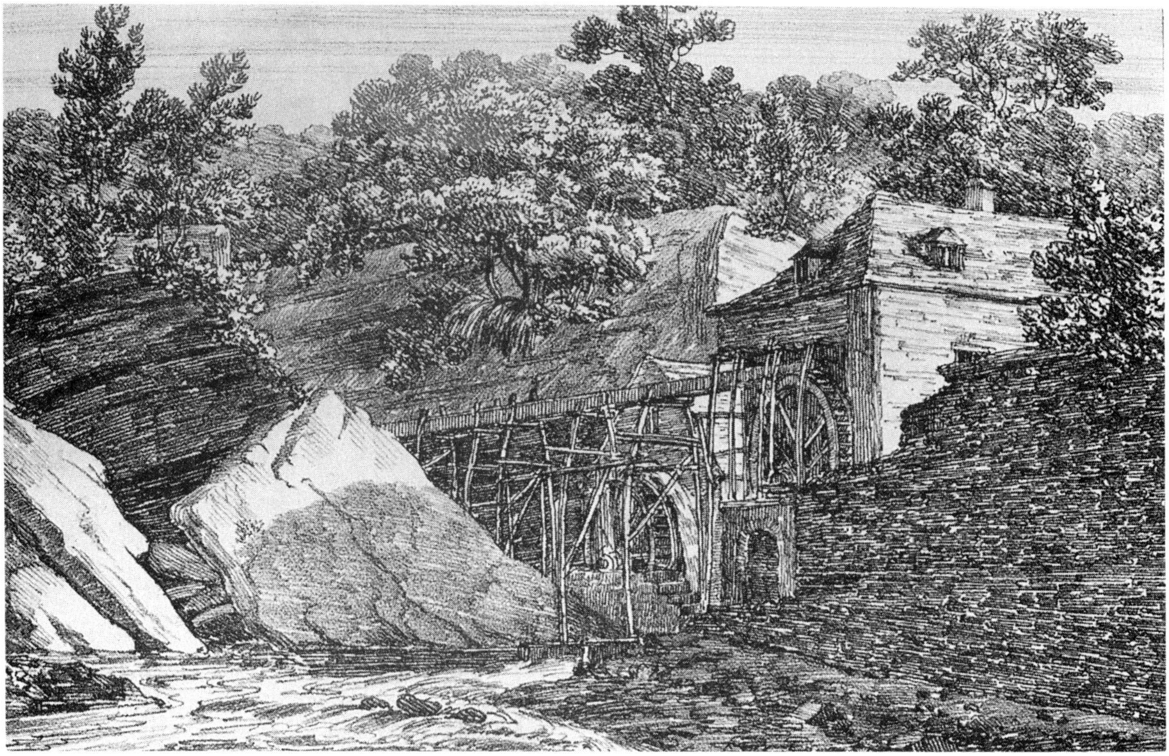

49 J. Wood, *Aber-Dulas Mill*, soft-ground etching, 1813

50 J. Wood, *Cyfarthfa Iron Works*, soft-ground etching, 1813

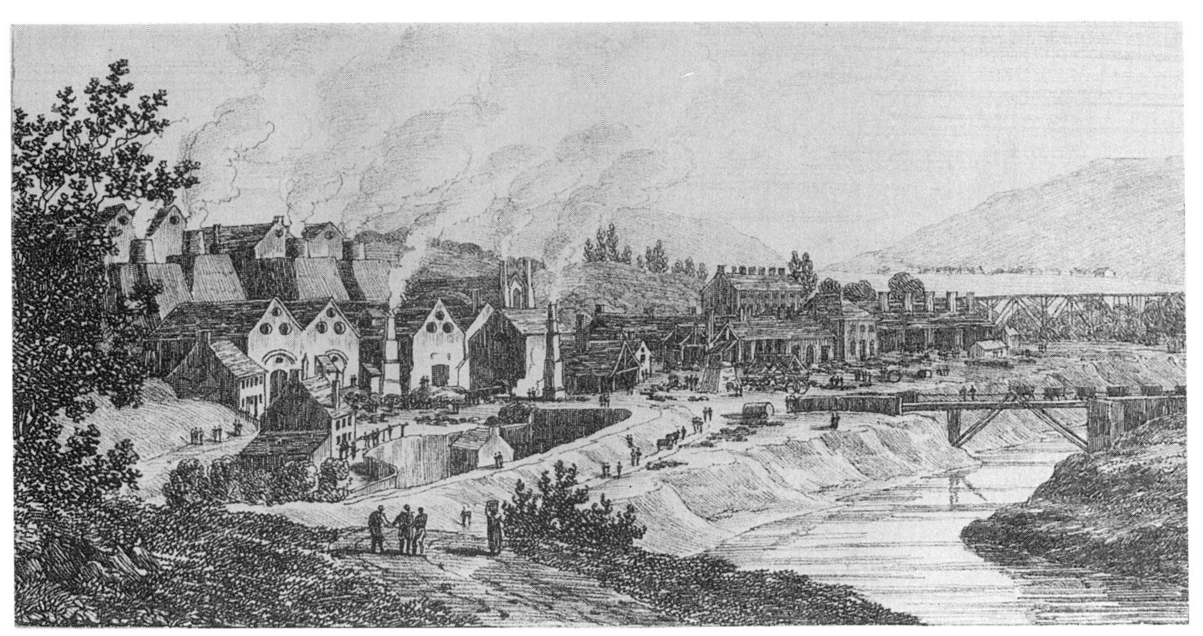

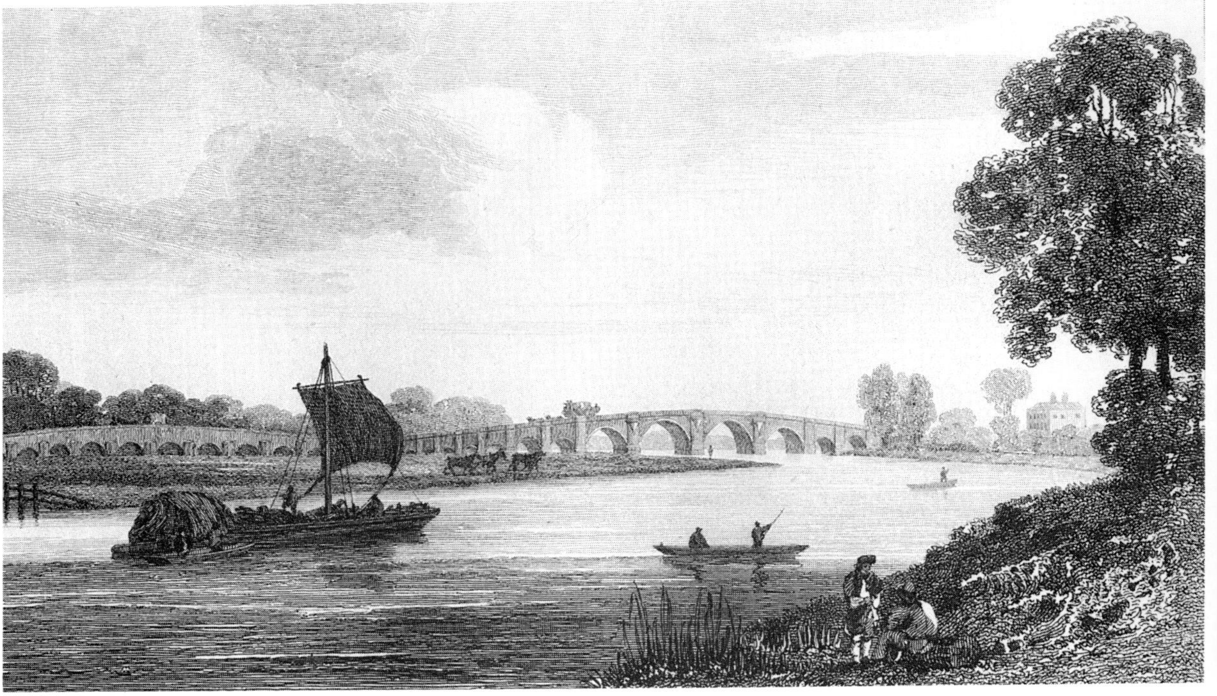

51 W. B. Cooke after S. Owen, *Walton Bridge*, etching, 1810

52 W. B. Cooke after S. Owen, *Shipmeadow Lock, A Paper Mill*, etching, 1811

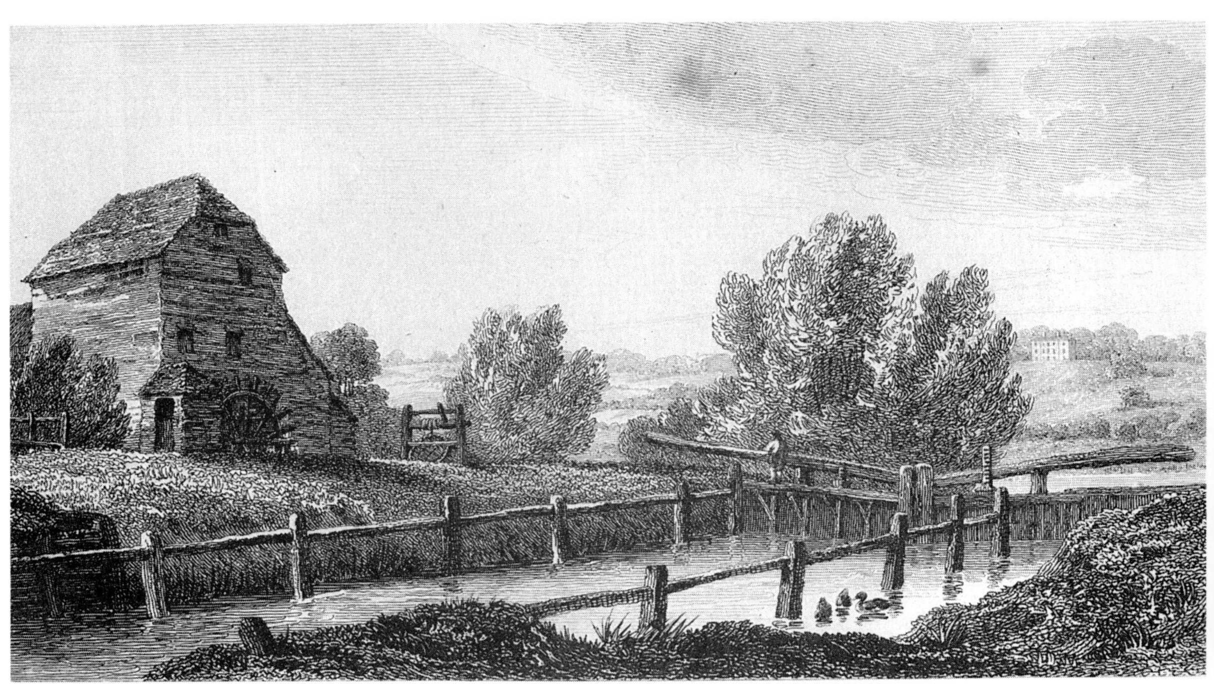

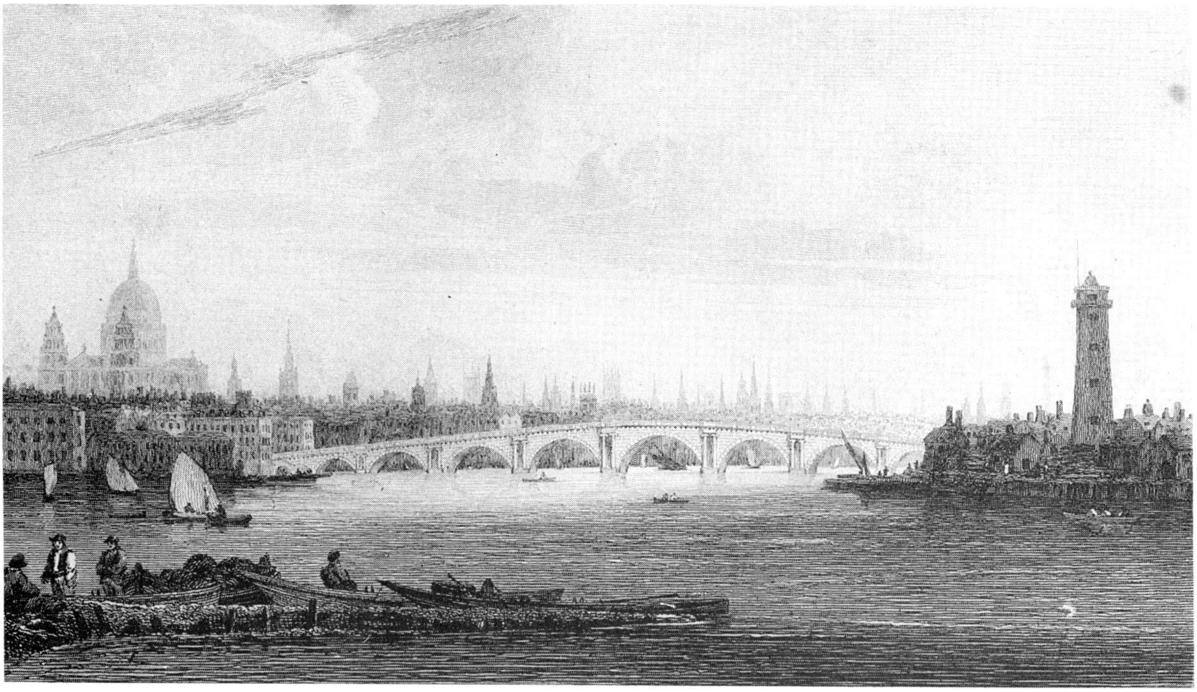

53 W. B. Cooke after S. Owen, *London & Blackfriars Bridge from Hungerford*, etching, 1811

54 R. G. Reeve after W. Westall, *Richmond*, coloured aquatint, 1828

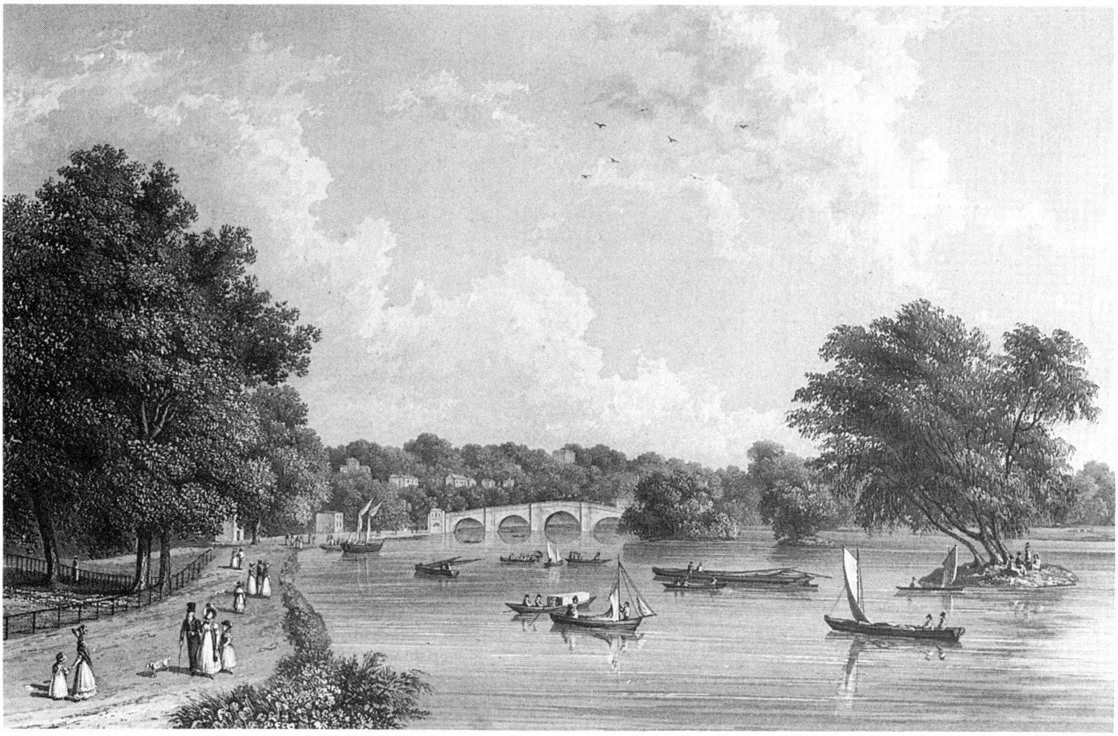

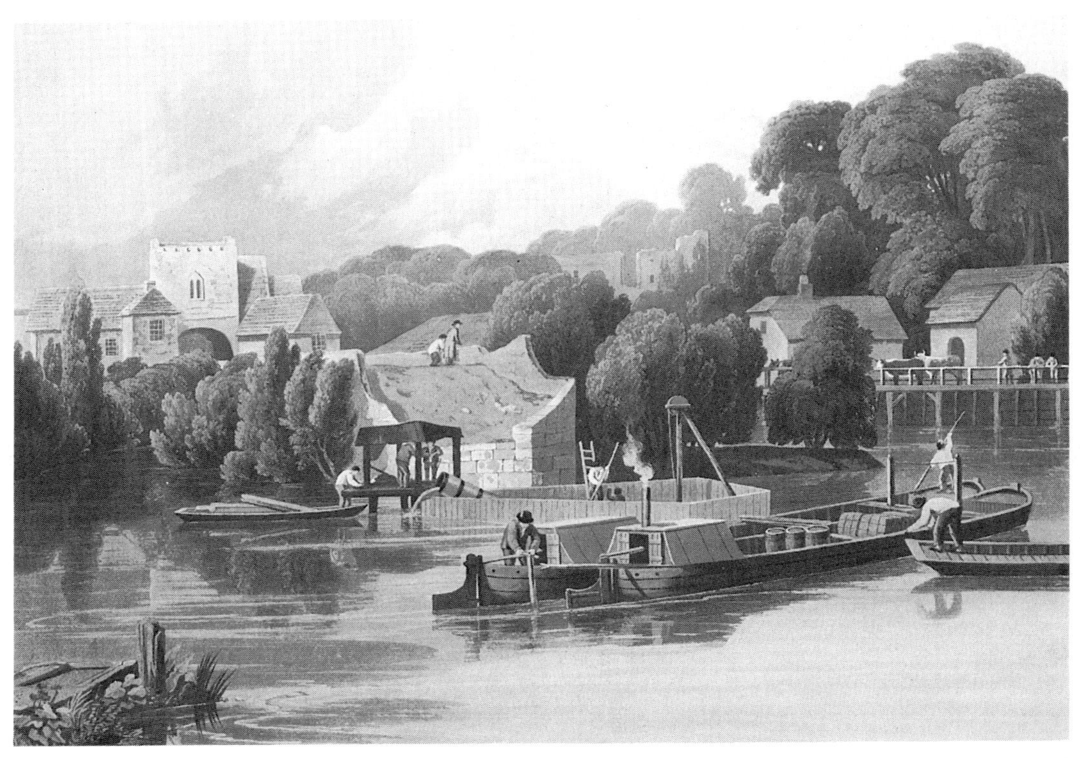

55 R. & D. Havell after W. Havell, *Wallingford Castle taken in 1810 while the Bridge was Repairing*, aquatint, 1811

56 R. & D. Havell after W. Havell, *An Island on the Thames near Park Place, Oxfordshire*, aquatint, 1811

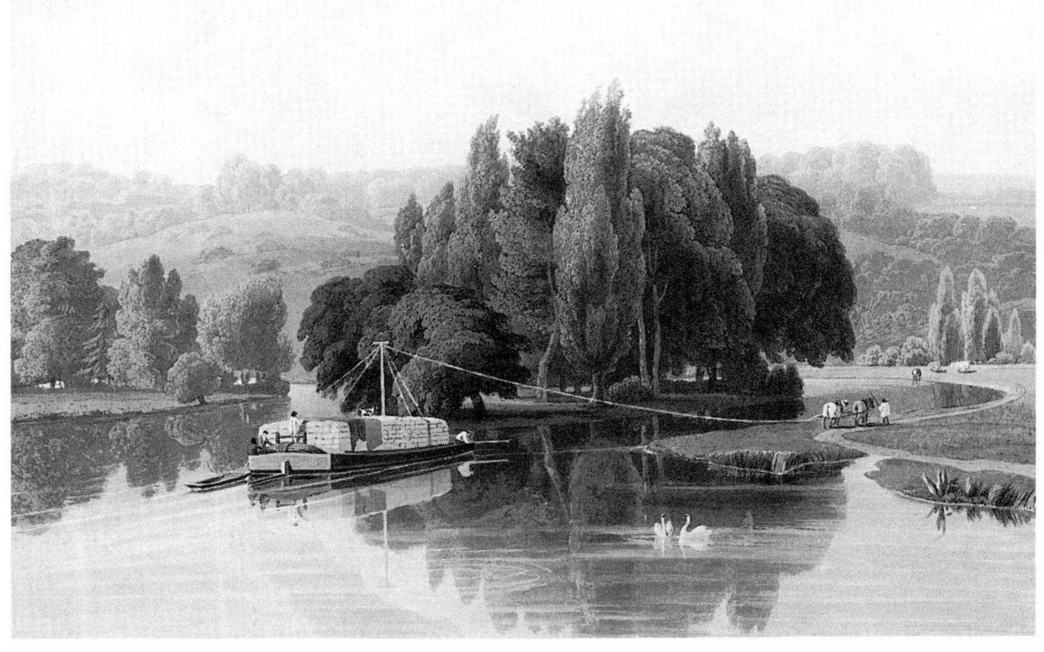

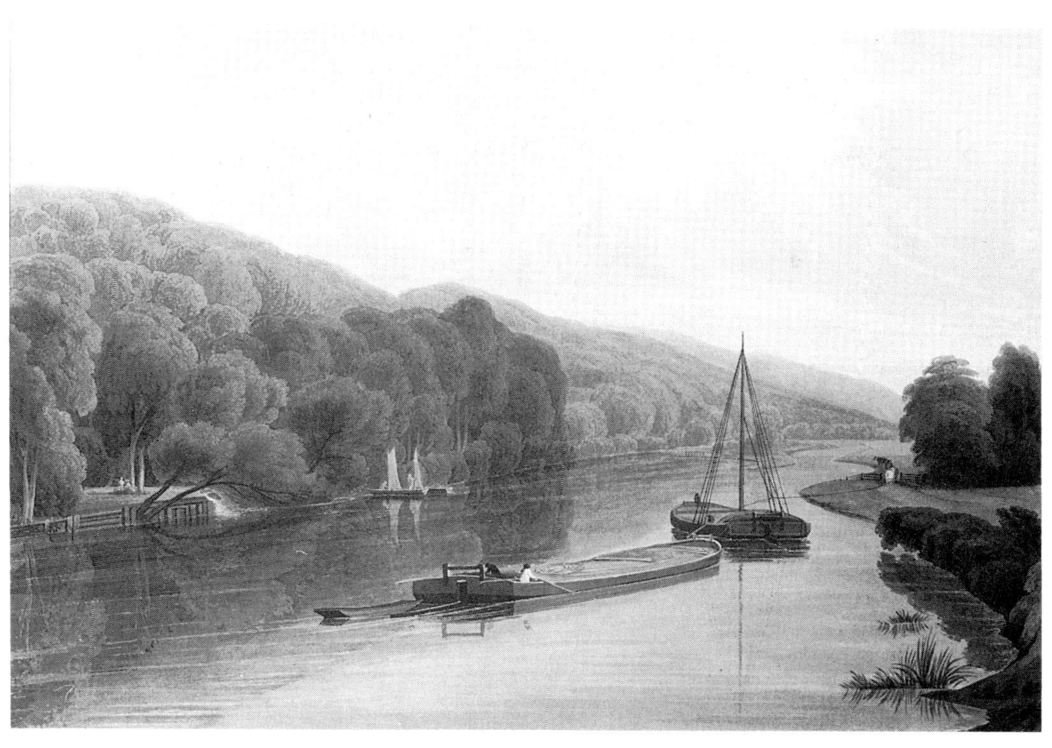

57 R. & D. Havell after W. Havell, *Cliefden Spring and Woods, near Maidenhead*, aquatint, 1811

58 R. & D. Havell after W. Havell, *Windsor Castle*, aquatint, 1811

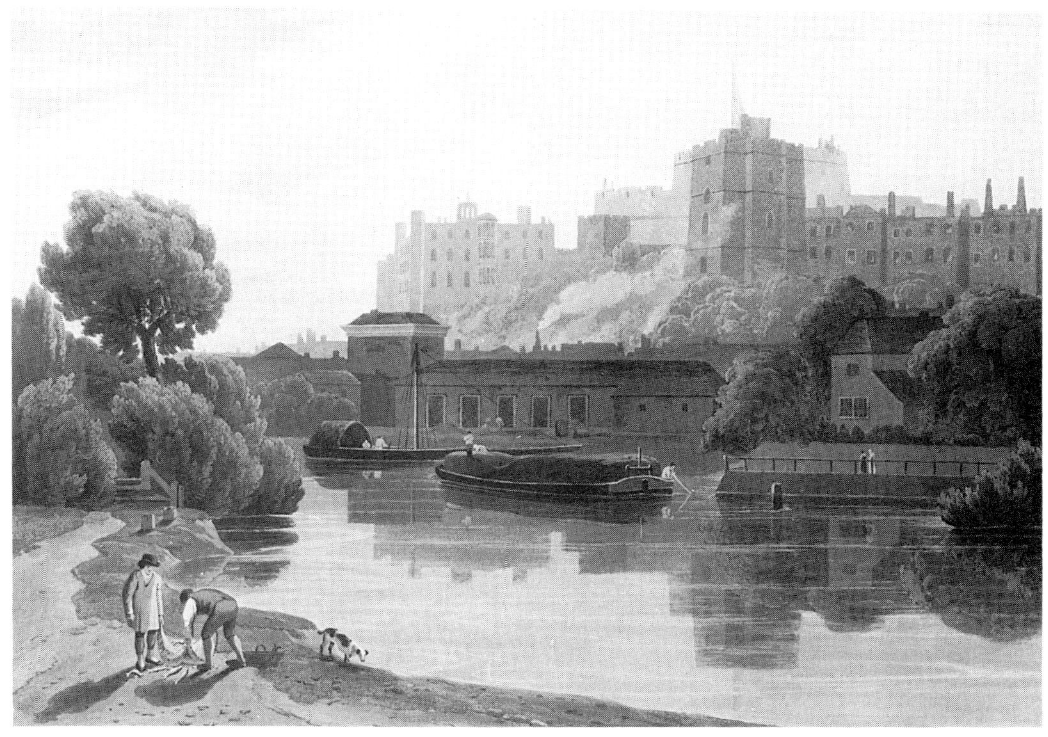

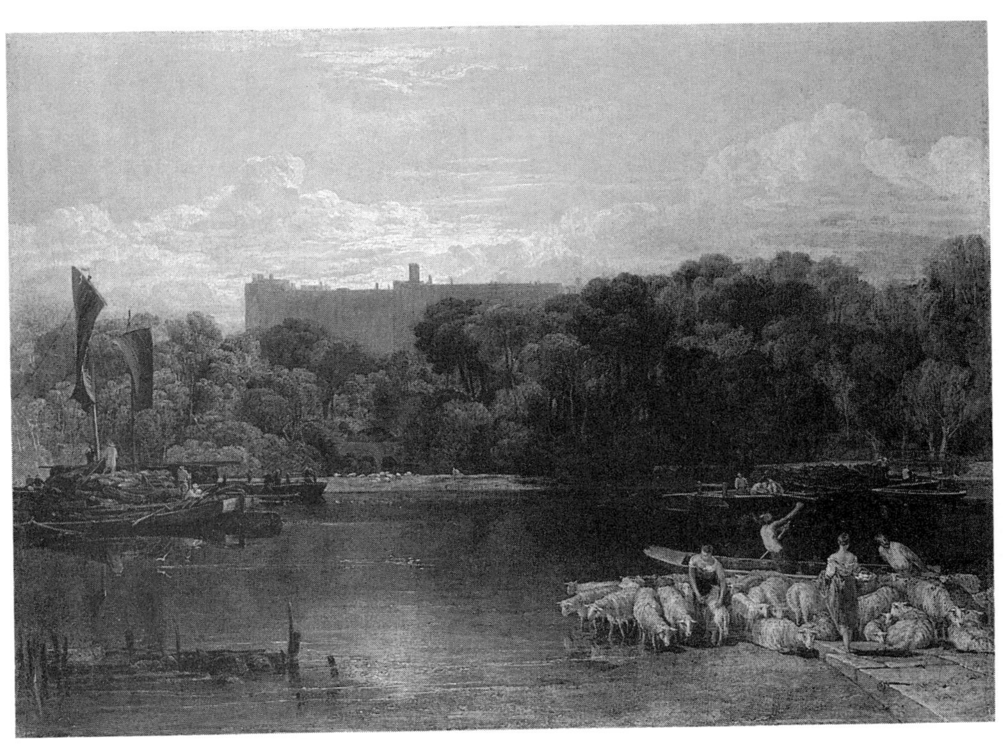

59 J. M. W. Turner, *Windsor Castle from the Thames*, *c.* 1805, Petworth House

60 J. M. W. Turner, *Walton Bridges*, *c.* 1806, Loyd Collection

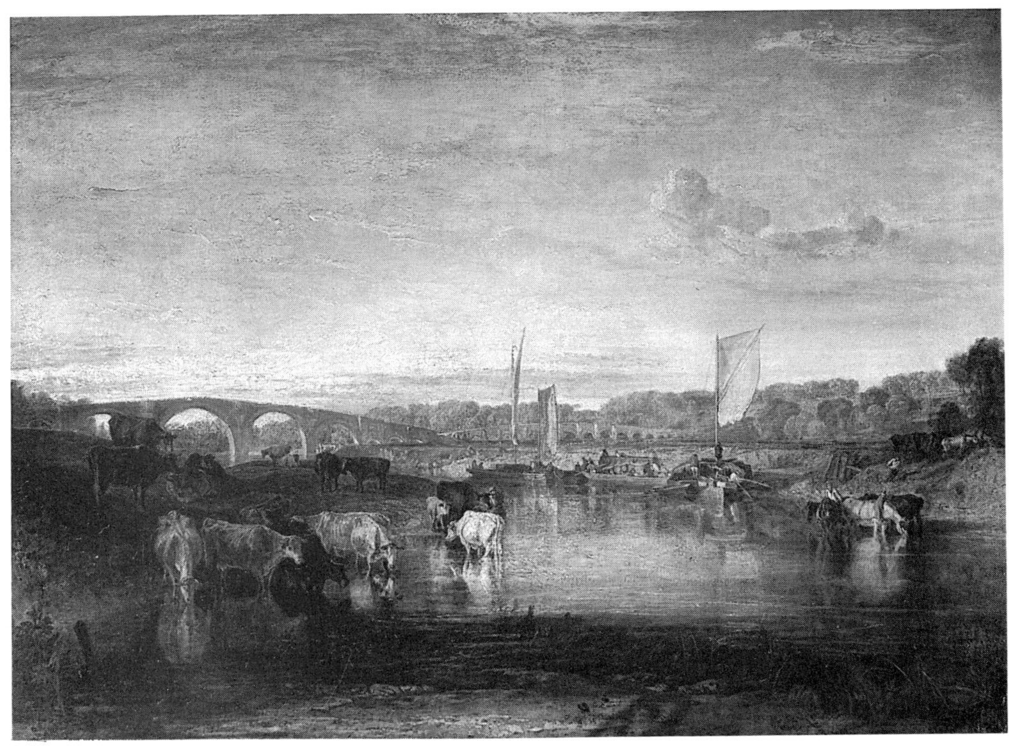

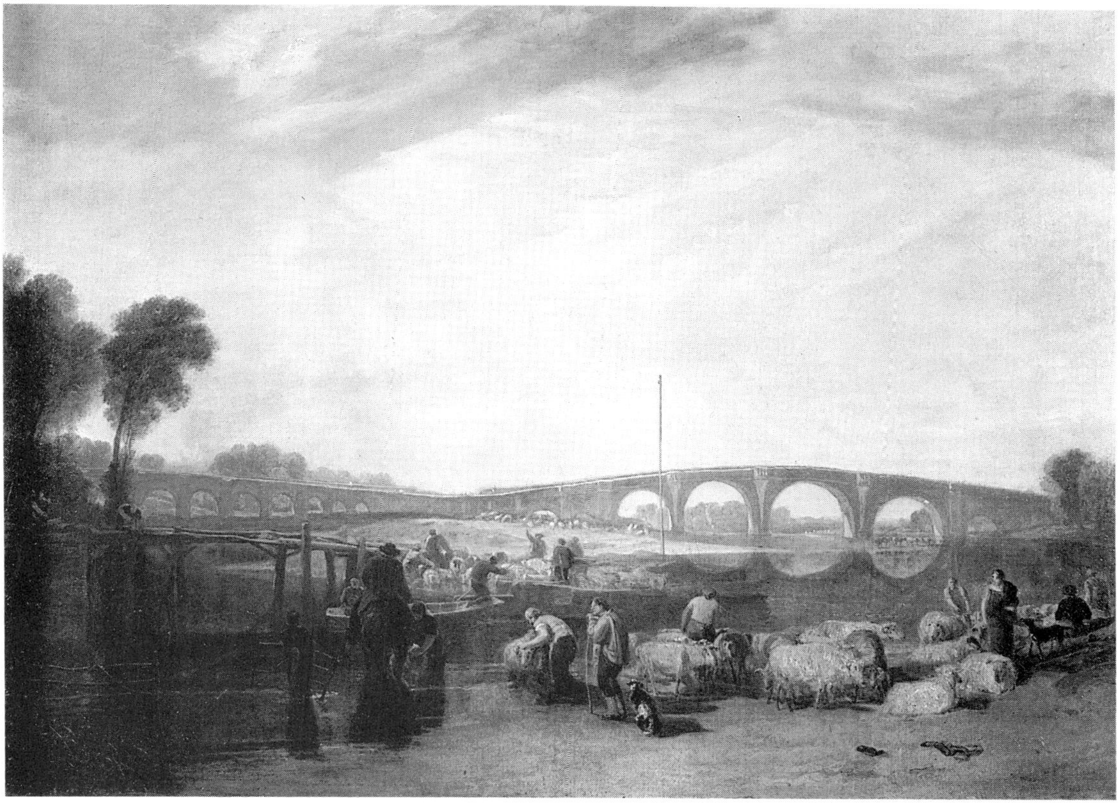

61 J. M. W. Turner, *Walton Bridges*, *c.* 1806, National Gallery, Victoria, Melbourne

62 J. M. W. Turner, *Dorchester Mead*, 1810, Clore Gallery for the Turner Collection, London

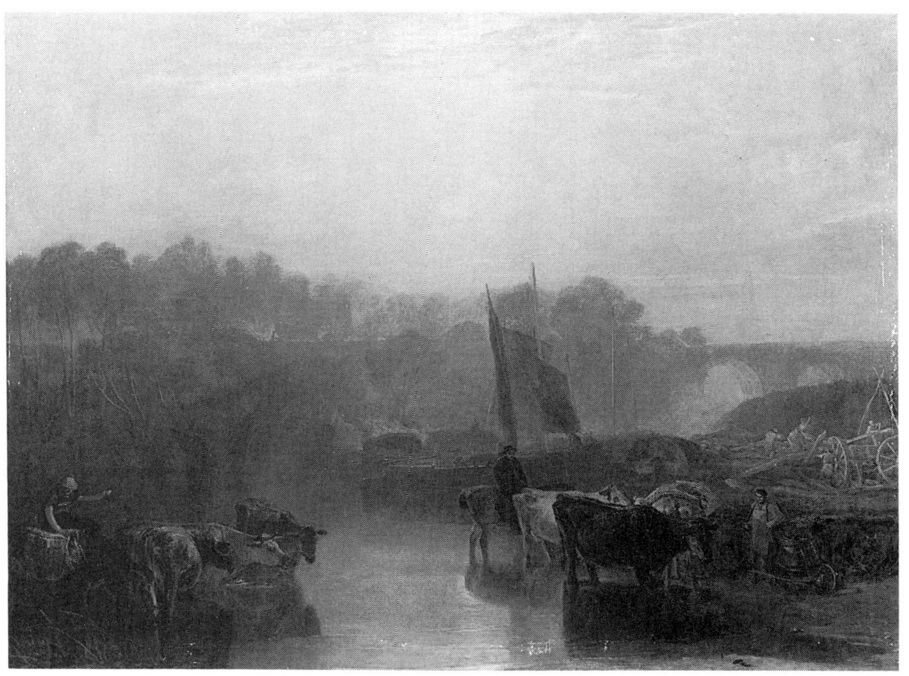

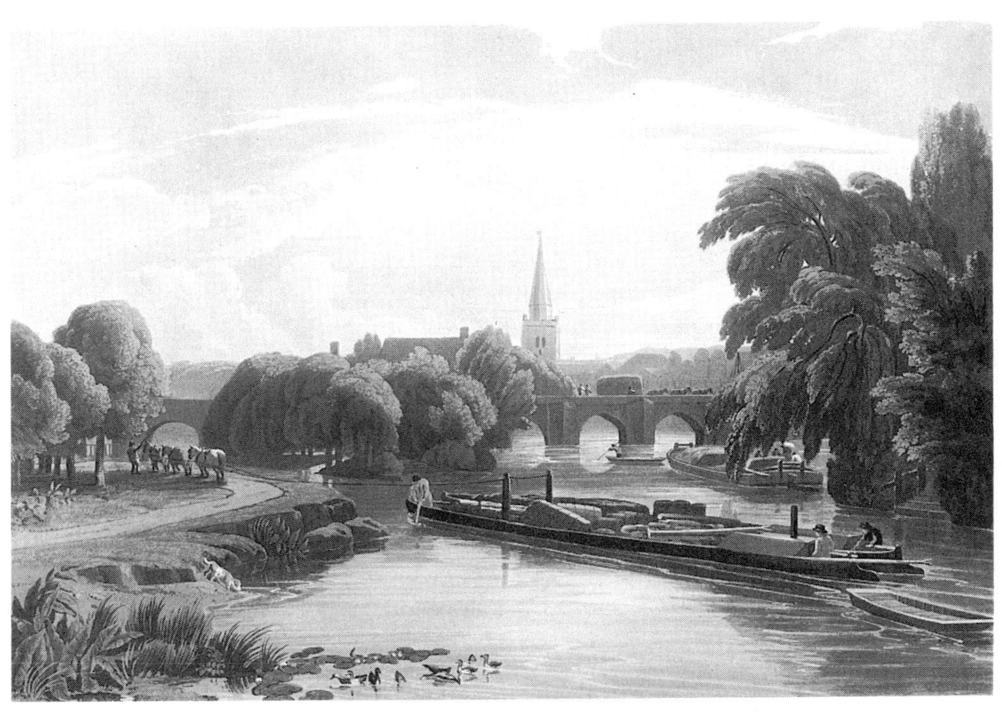

63 R. & D. Havell after W. Havell, *Abingdon Bridge and Church*, aquatint, 1811

64 J. M. W. Turner, *Ploughing up Turnips, near Slough*, 1809, Clore Gallery for the Turner Collection, London

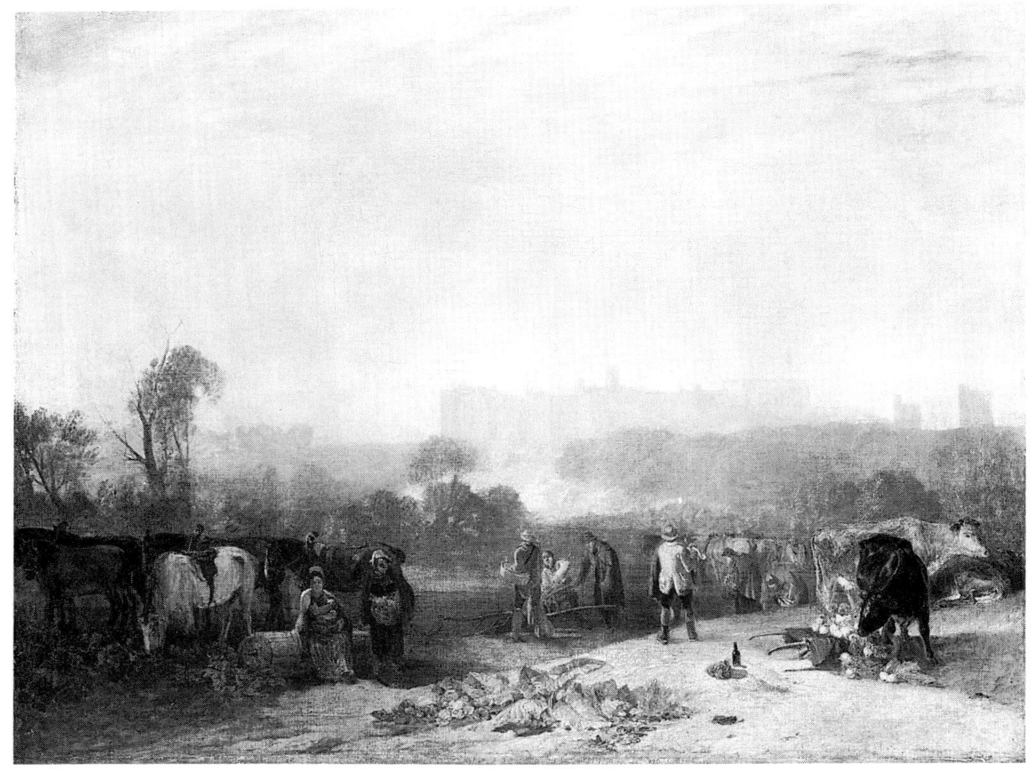

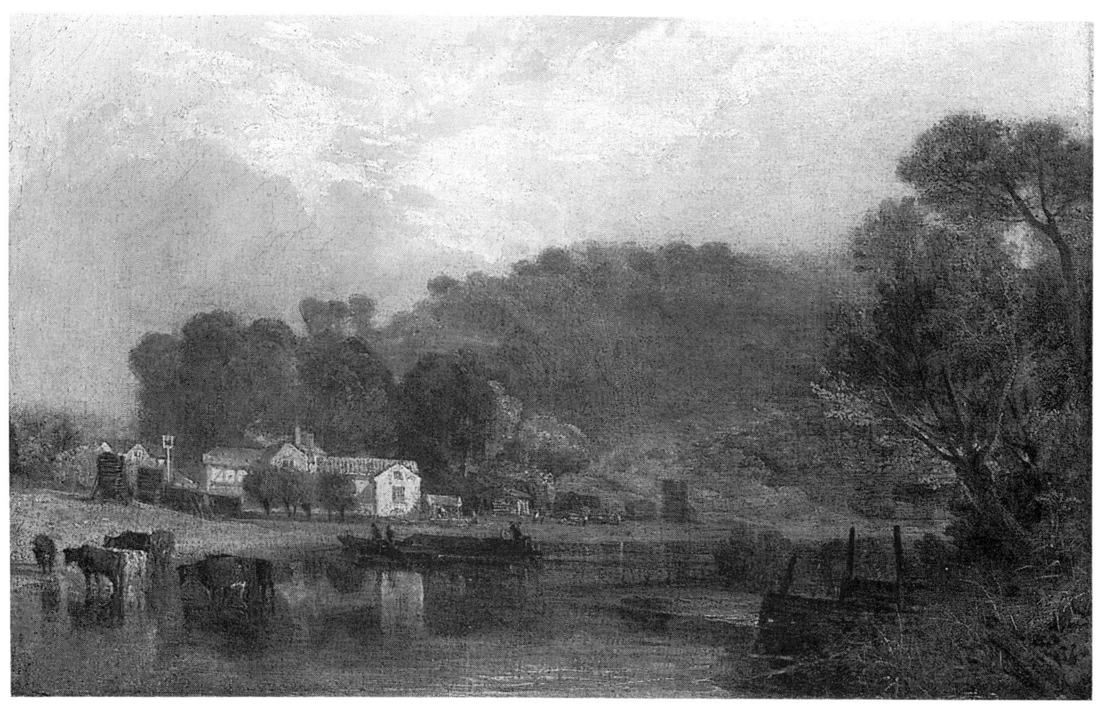

65 J. M. W. Turner, *Clieveden on Thames*, *c.* 1807, Clore Gallery for the Turner Collection, London

66 J. M. W. Turner, *Union of the Thames and the Isis*, 1808, Clore Gallery for the Turner Collection, London

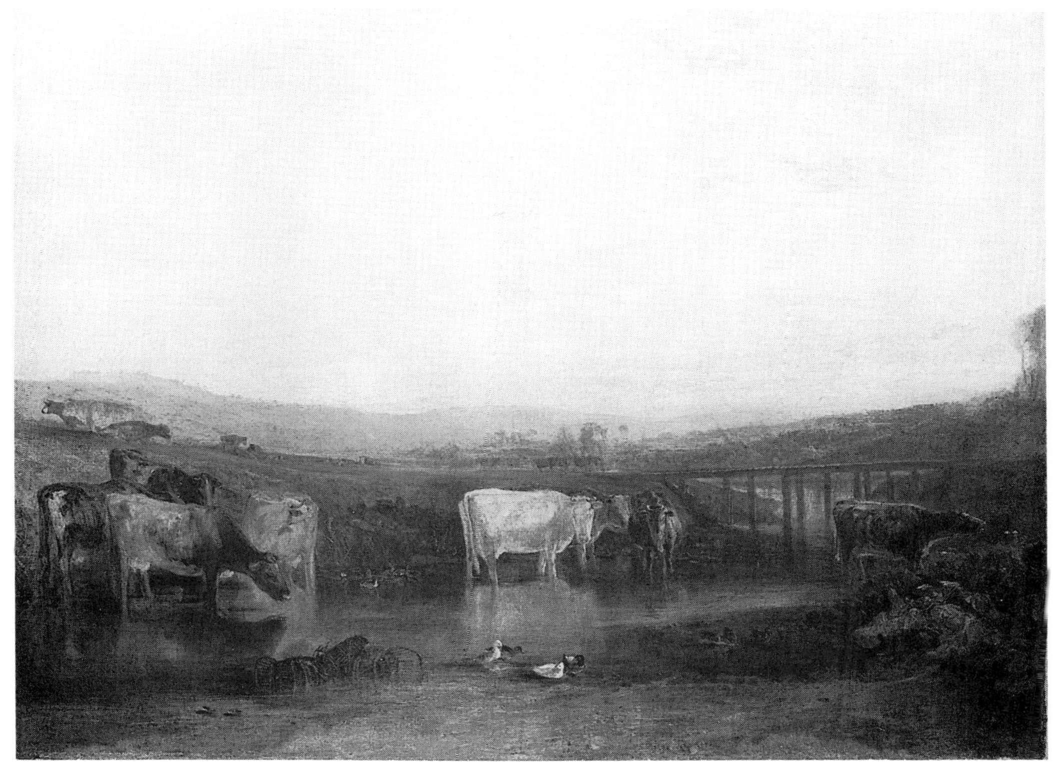

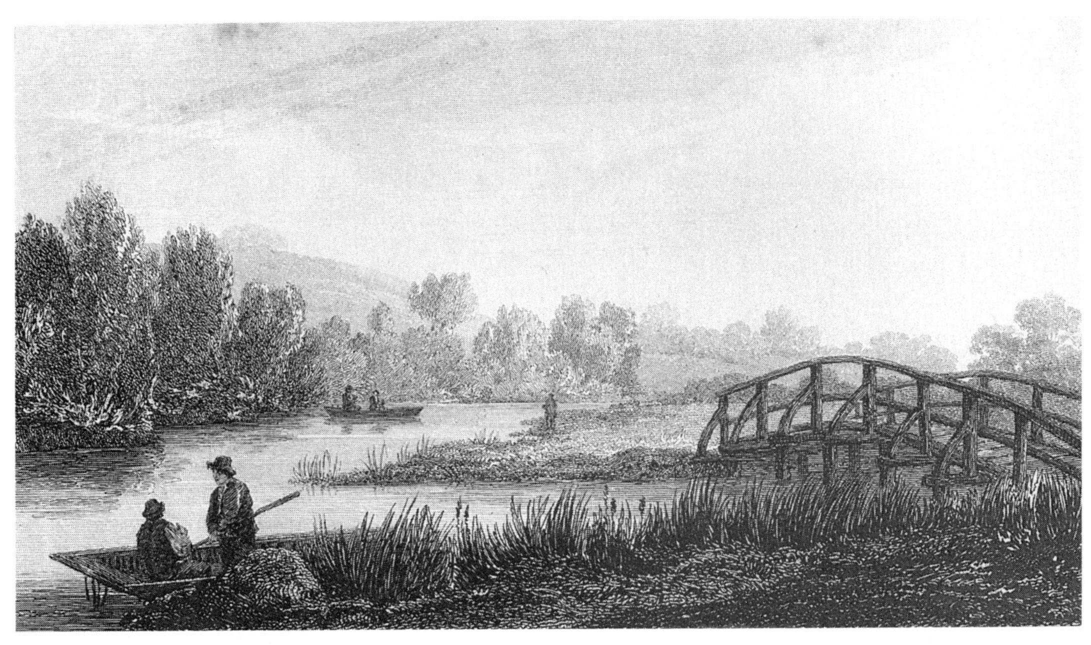

67 W. B. Cooke after S. Owen, *Junction of the Thames & Isis*, etching, 1811

68 J. M. W. Turner, *Grand Junction Canal at Southall Mill*, 1810, whereabouts unknown

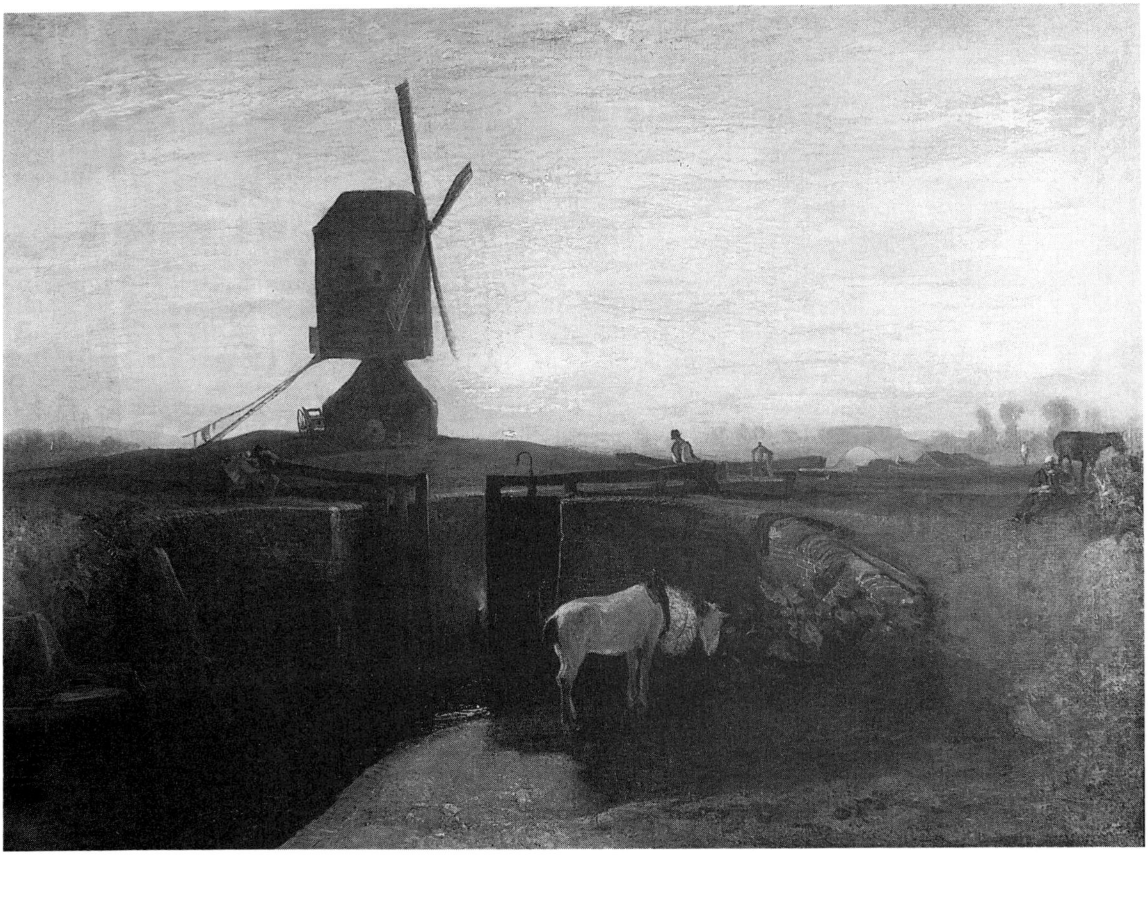

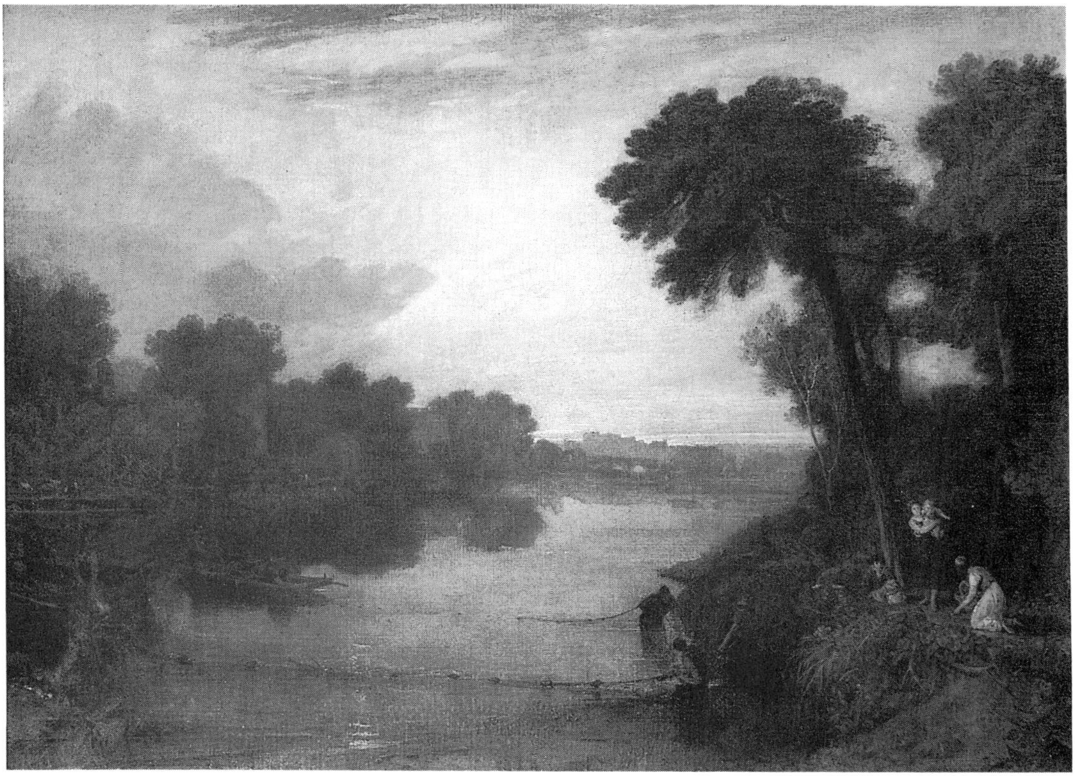

69 J. M. W. Turner, *The Thames near Windsor*, *c.* 1807, Petworth House

70 J. M. W. Turner, *The Thames at Eton*, 1808, Petworth House

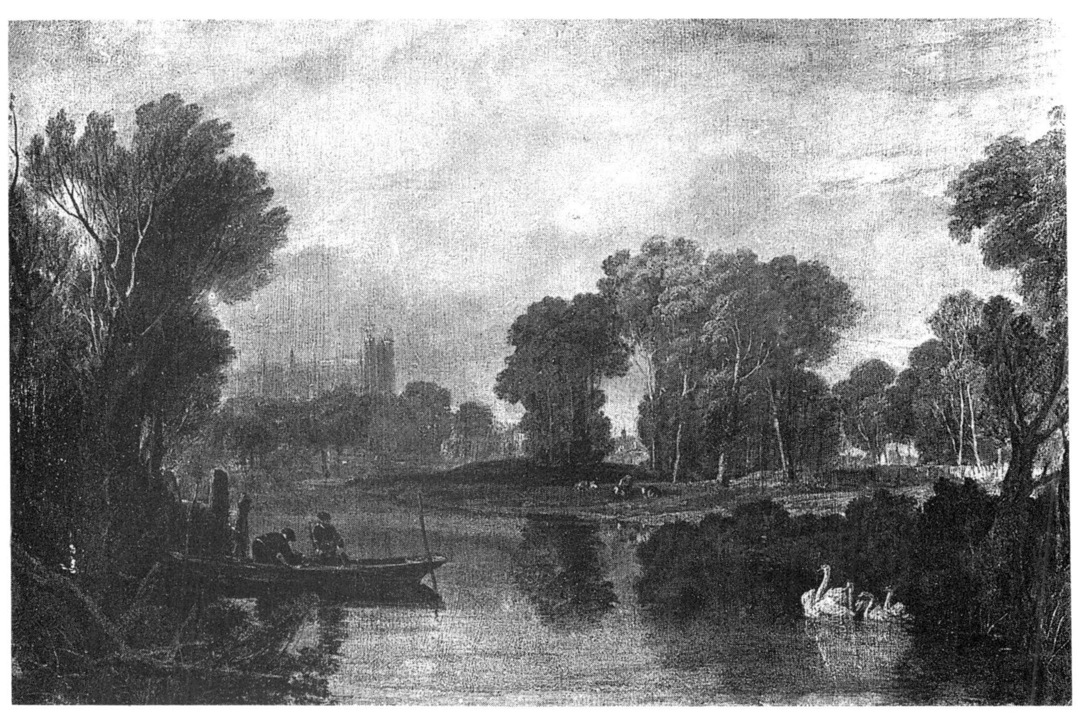

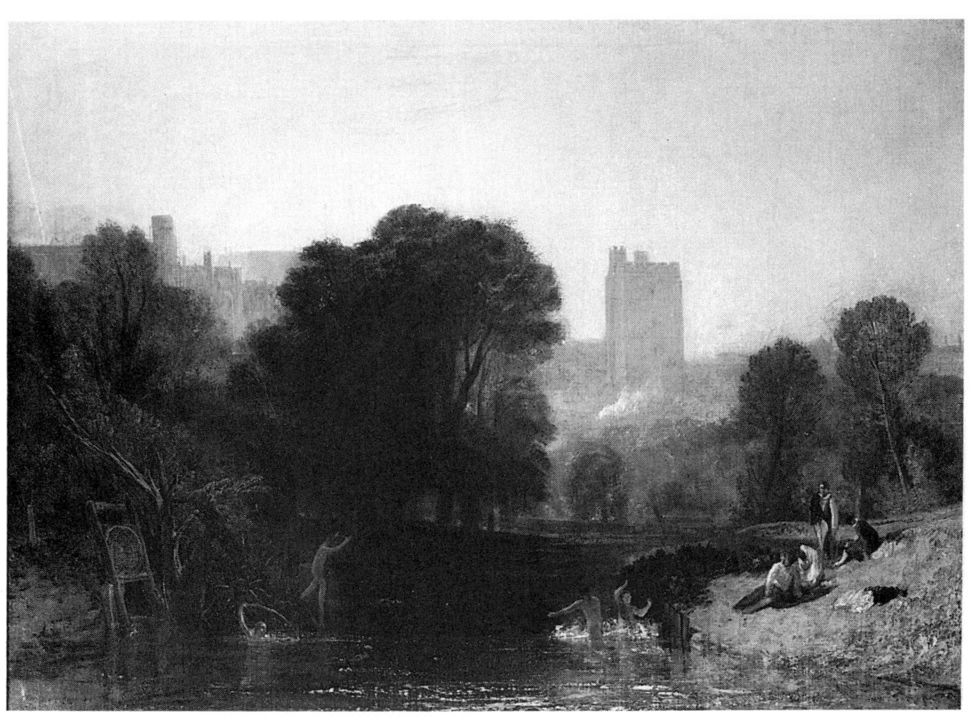

71 J. M. W. Turner, *Near the Thames' Lock, Windsor*, 1809, Petworth House

72 J. M. W. Turner, *Richmond Hill and Bridge*, 1808, Clore Gallery for the Turner Collection, London

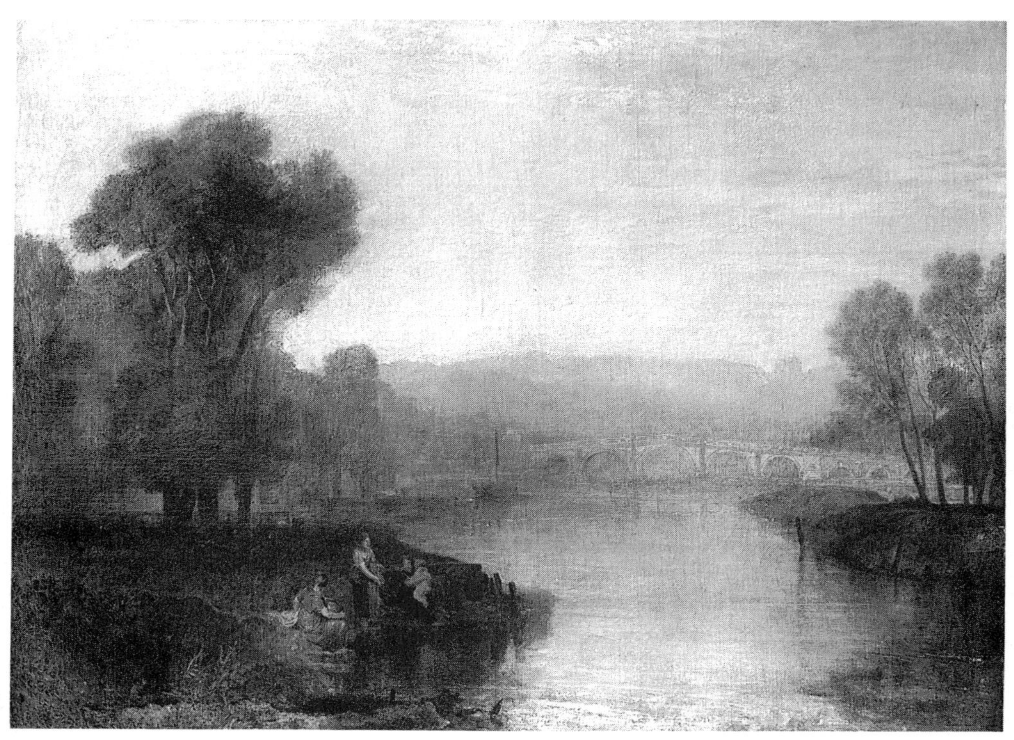

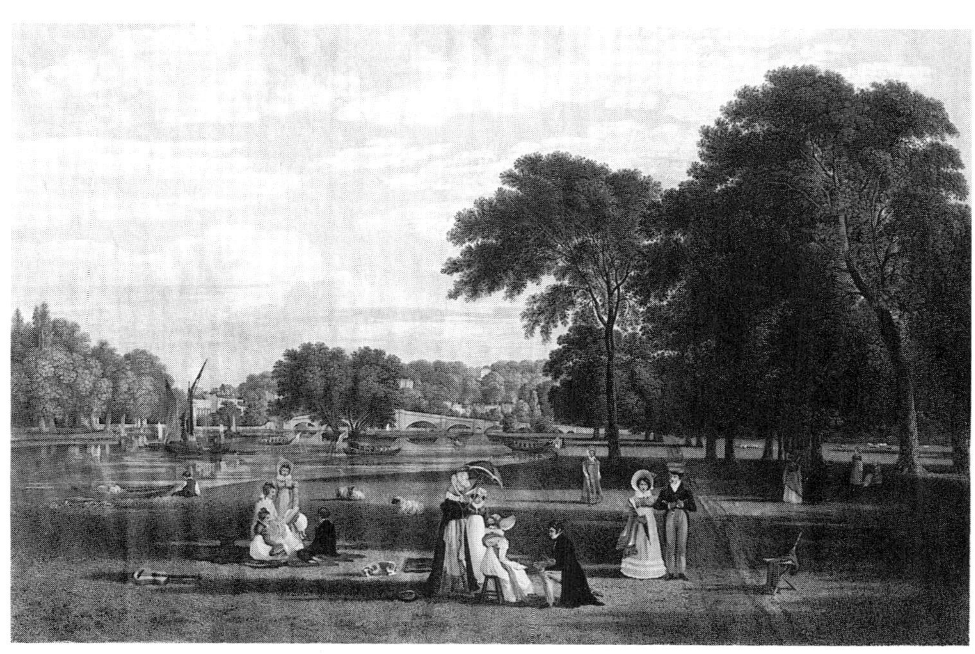

73 C. Heath after T. C. Hofland, *Richmond, From Twickenham Park*, copper-plate engraving, 1825

74 J. M. W. Turner, *View of Pope's Villa at Twickenham during its Dilapidation*, 1808, by kind permission of Lady Ashcombe, Sudeley Castle, Winchcombe, Gloucestershire

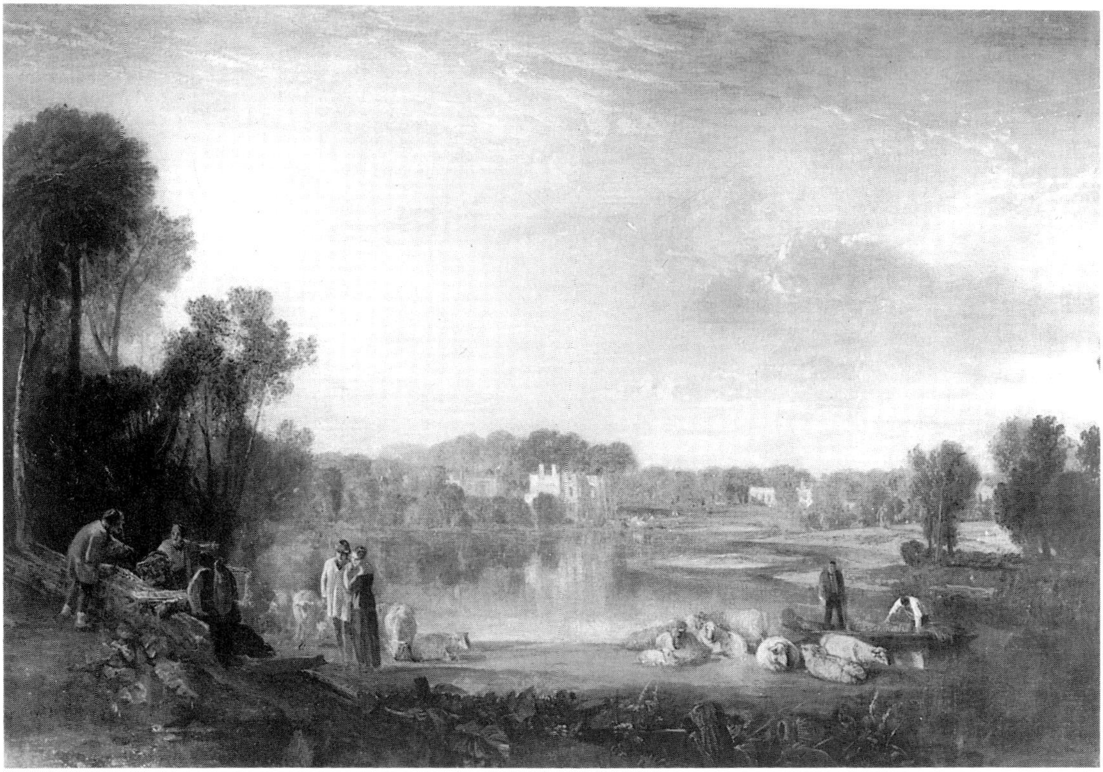

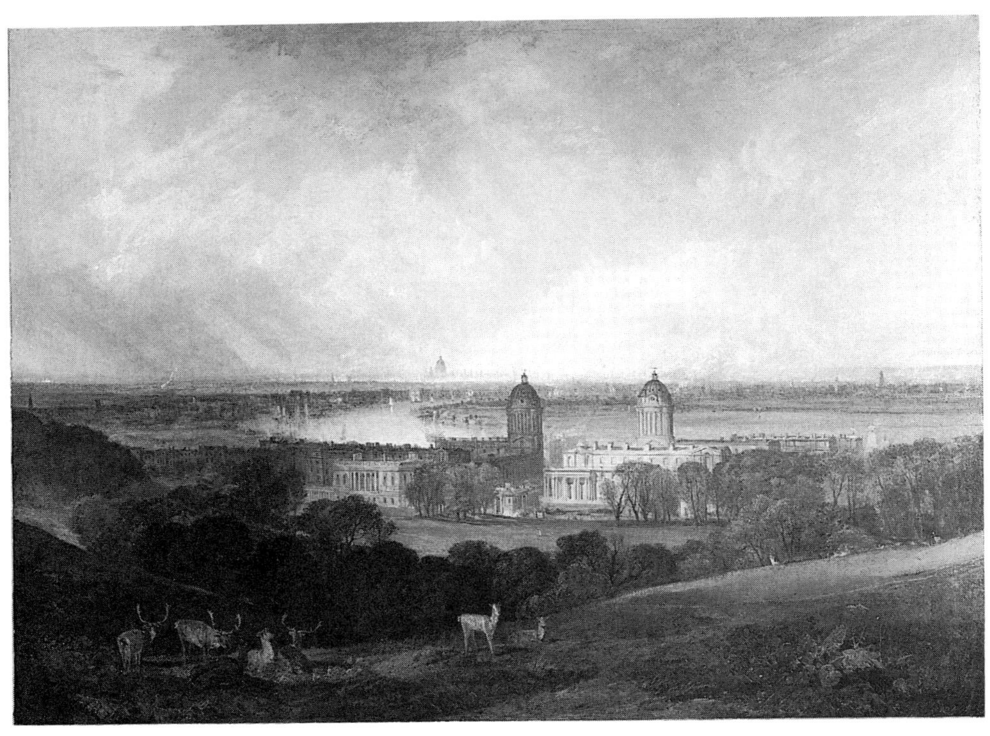

75 J. M. W. Turner, *London*, 1809, Clore Gallery for the Turner Collection, London

76 J. R. Cozens, *London from Greenwich Hill*, *c.* 1791, Yale Center for British Art

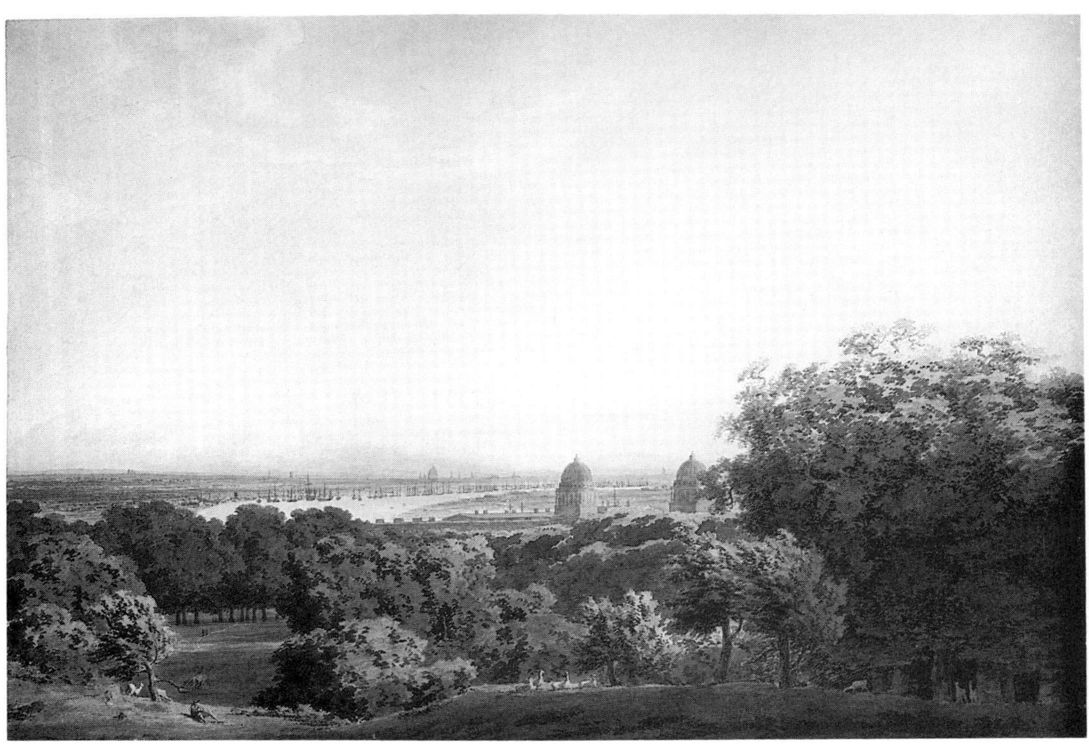

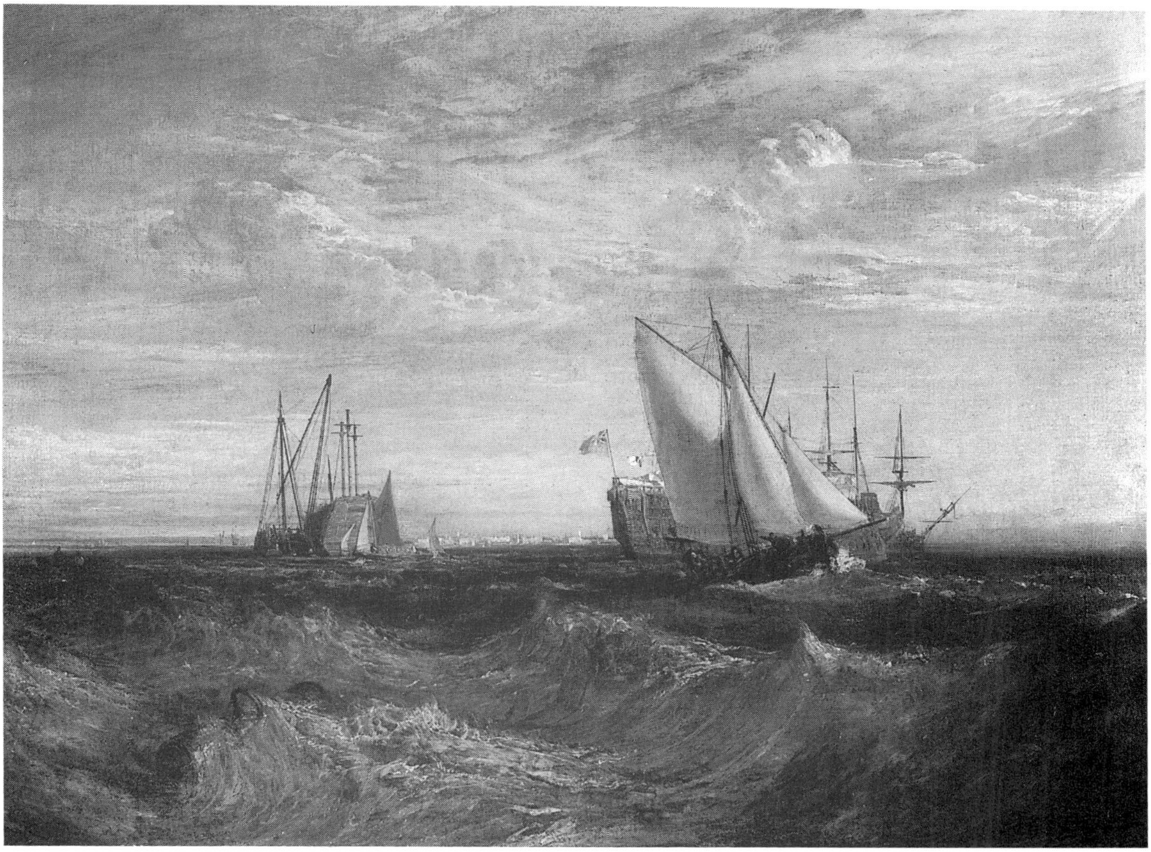

77 J. M. W. Turner, *The Confluence of the Thames and the Medway*, 1808, Petworth House

78 J. M. W. Turner, *England: Richmond Hill on the Prince Regent's Birthday*, 1819, Clore Gallery for the Turner Collection, London

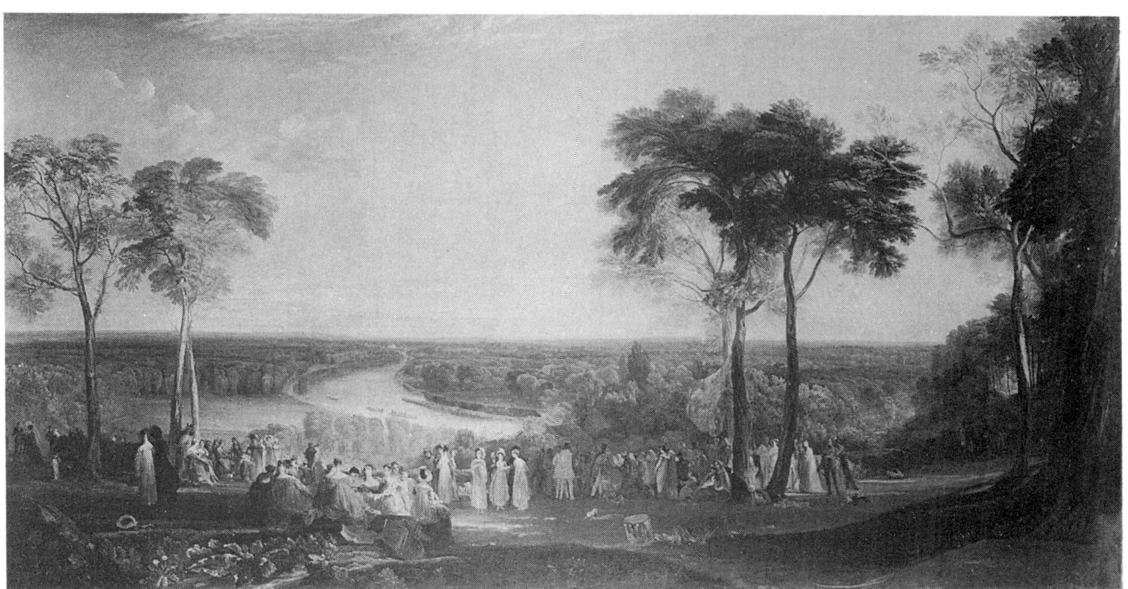

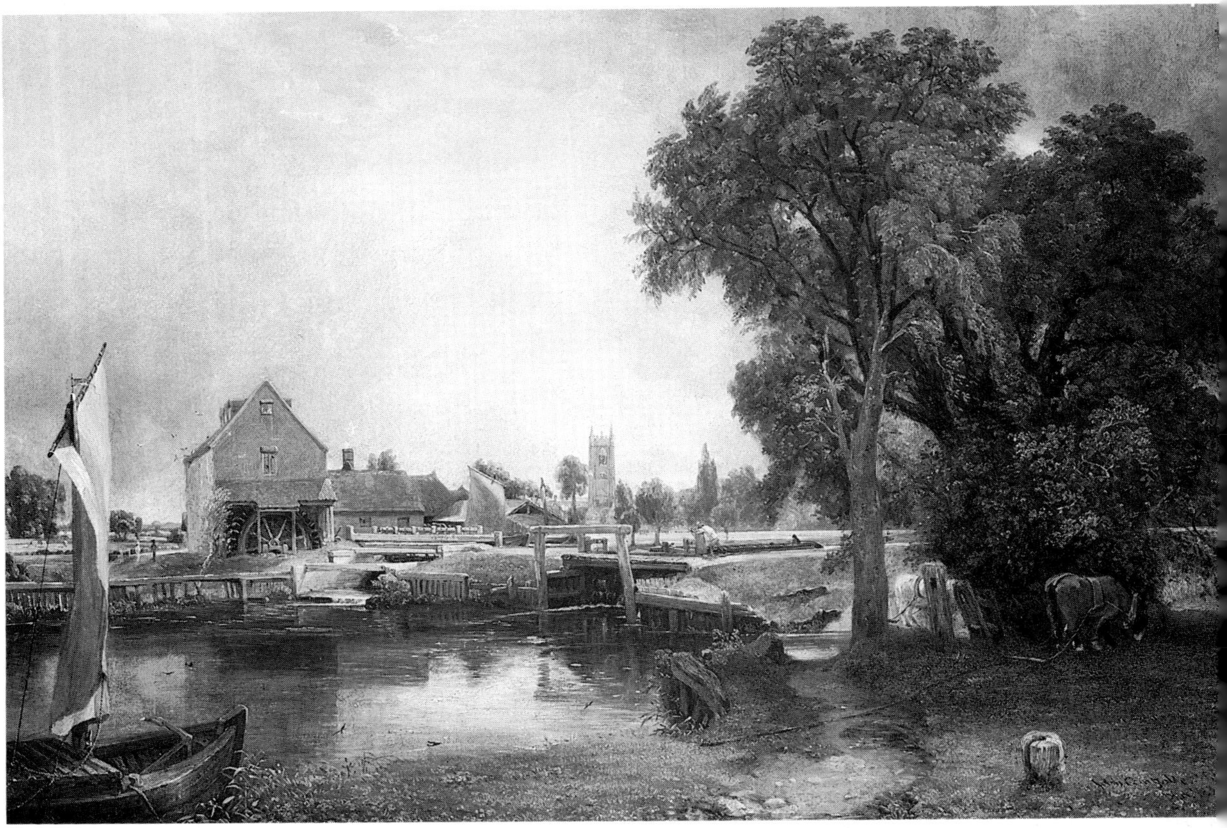

79 J. Constable, *Dedham Lock and Mill*, 1820, Victoria & Albert Museum

80 J. C. Stadler after J. Farington, *Junction of the Thames Canal near Lechdale*, aquatint, 1794

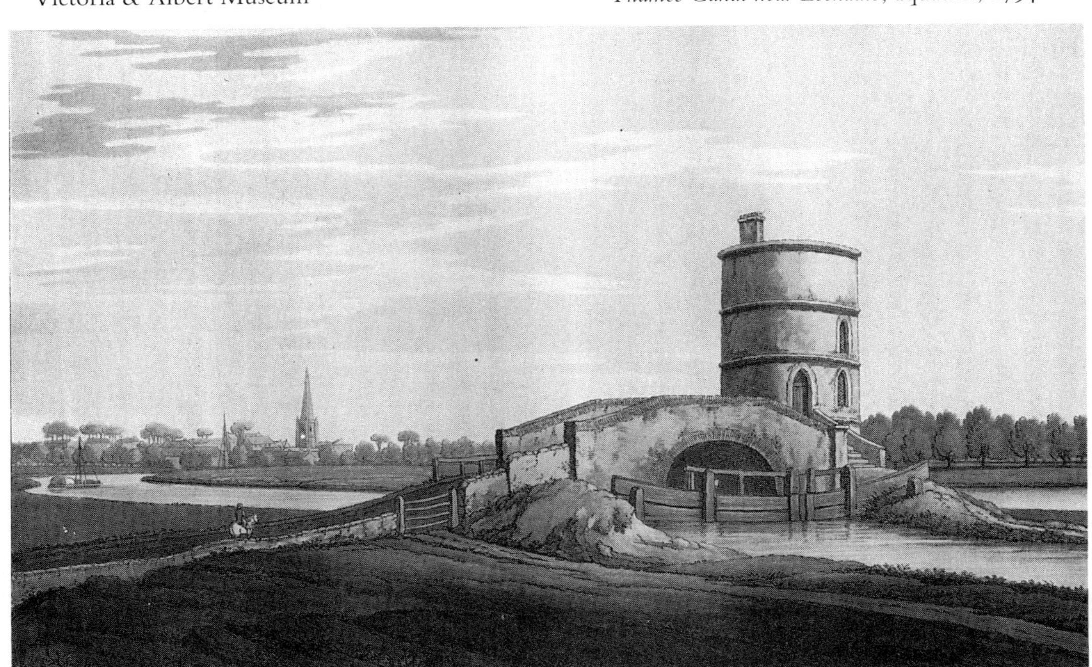

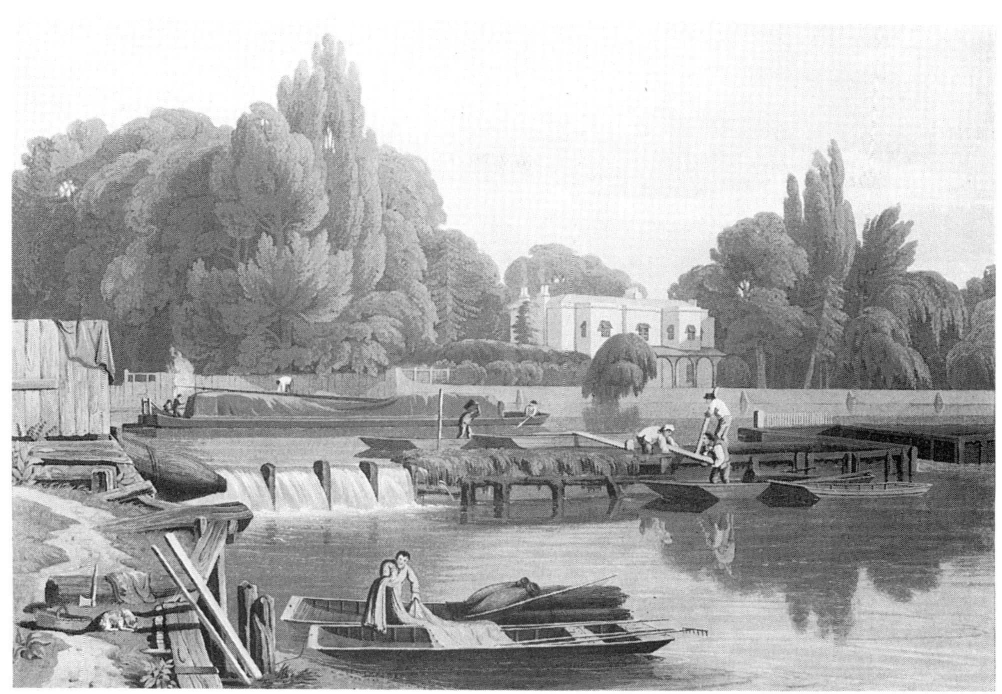

81 R. & D. Havell after W. Havell, *The Weir, from Marlow Bridge*, aquatint, 1811

82 J. Constable, *Scene on a Navigable River (Flatford Mill)*, 1817, Tate Gallery

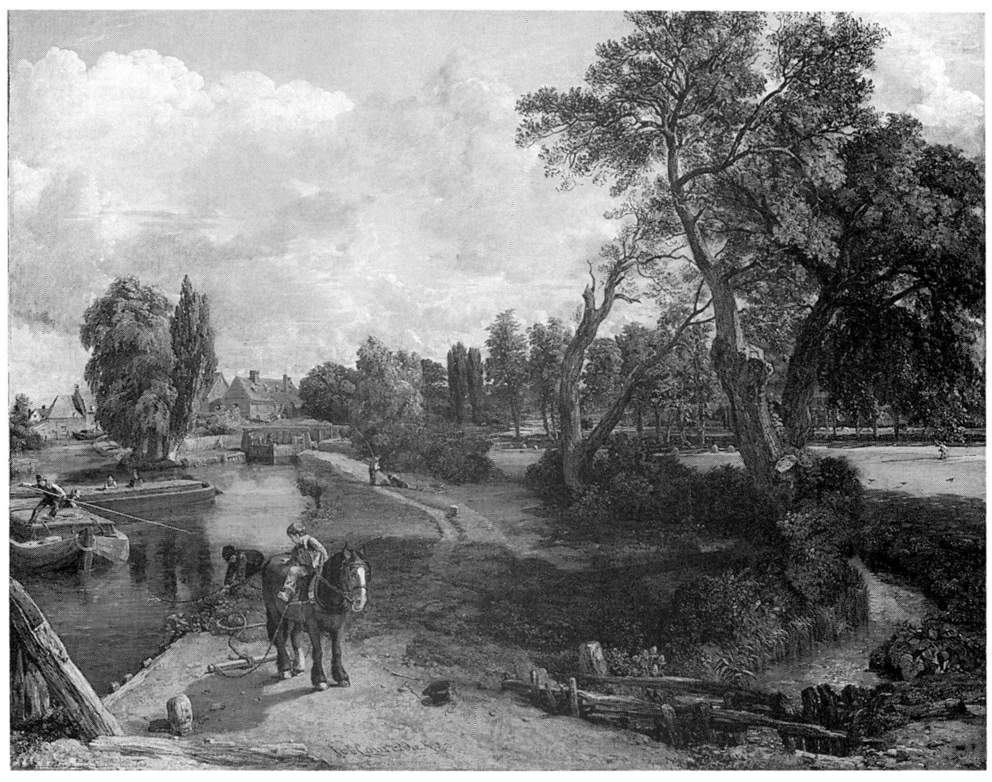

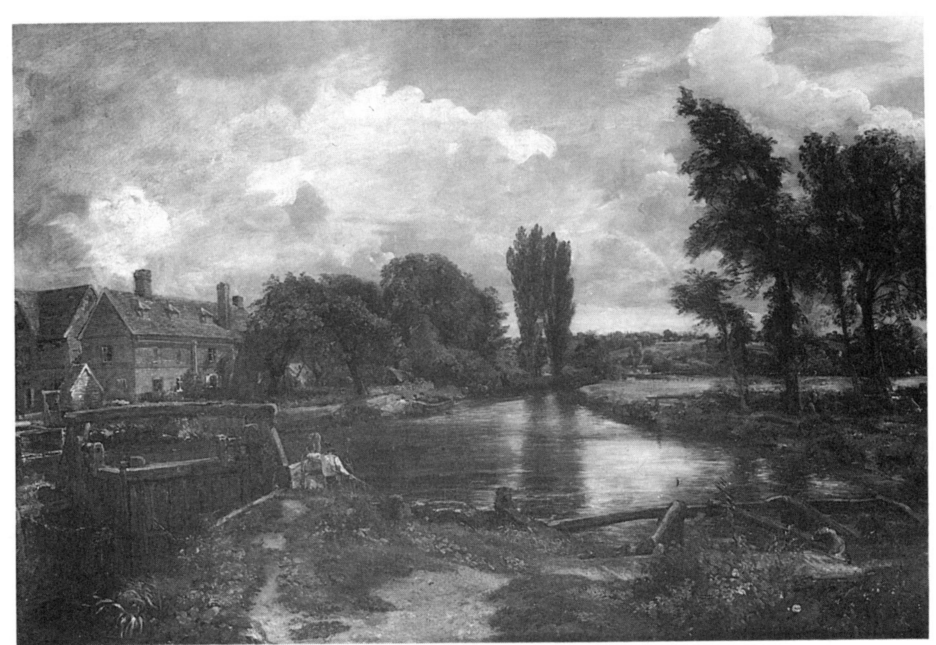

83 J. Constable, *A Water-Mill*, 1812, Private Collection

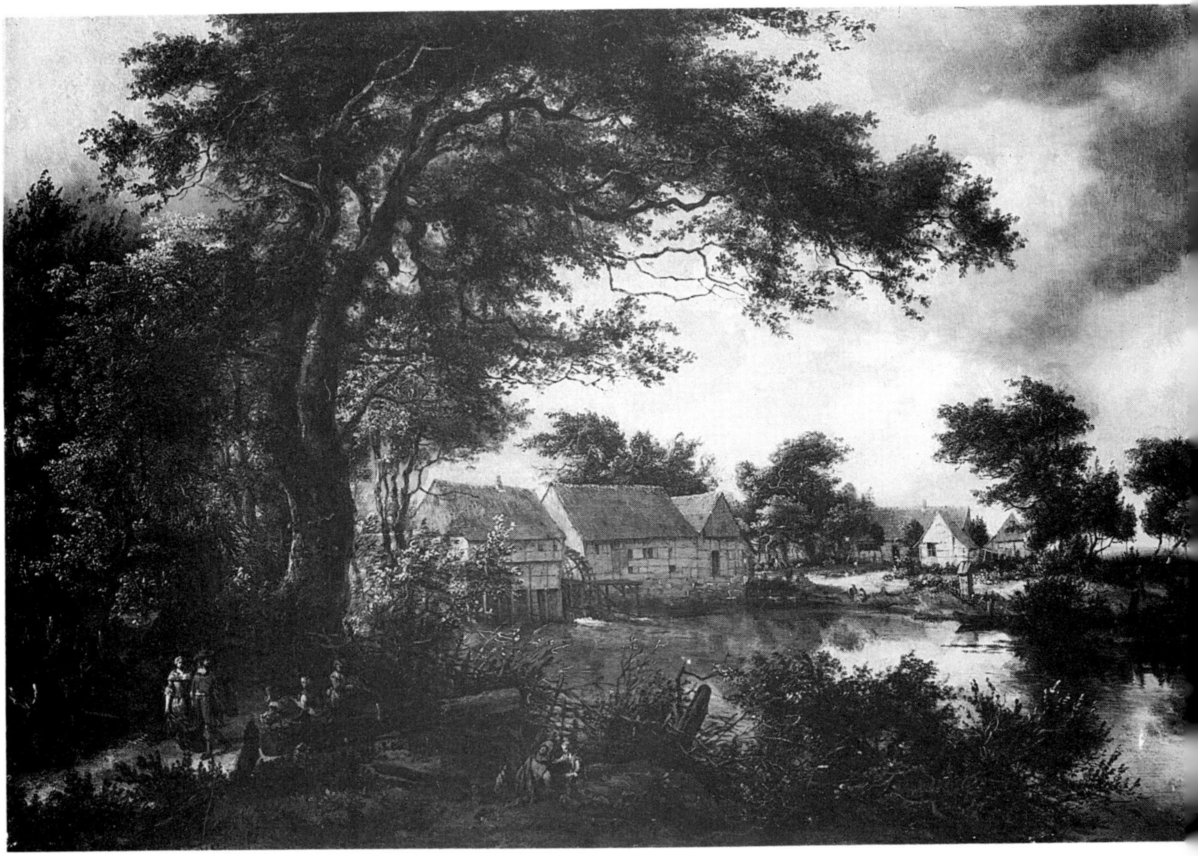

84 M. Hobbema, *Woody Landscape with Water-Mill*, Dulwich Picture Gallery

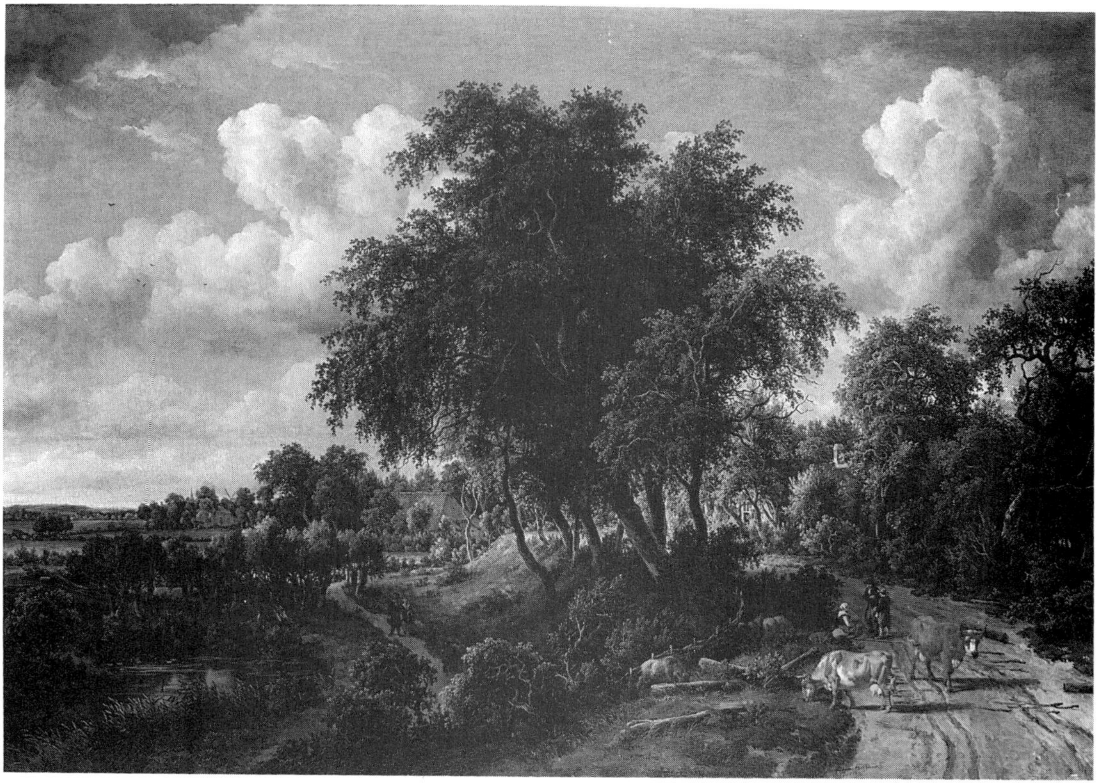

85 M. Hobbema, *Road on a Dyke*, 1663, National Gallery of Ireland, Dublin

86 J. Linnell, *The River Kennet, near Newbury*, 1815, Fitzwilliam Museum, Cambridge

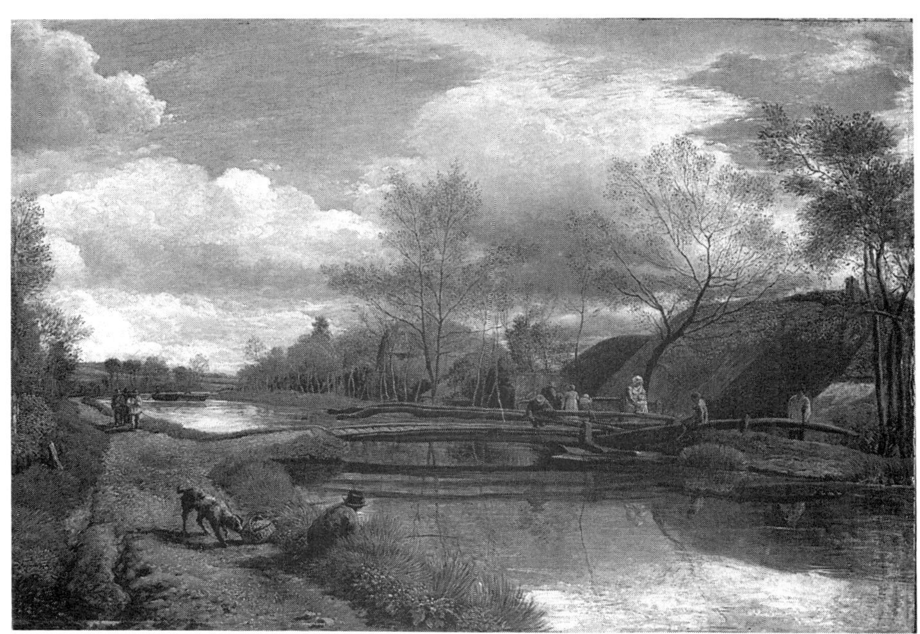

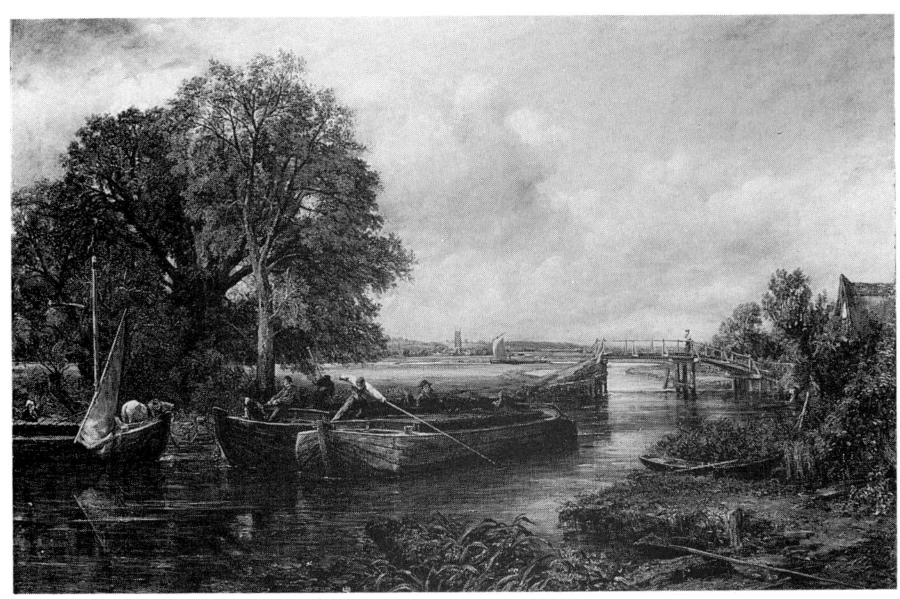

87 J. Constable, *A View on the Stour, near Dedham*, 1822, Huntington Art Gallery, San Marino, California

88 J. Constable, *A Boat Passing a Lock*, 1824, by kind permission of Lady Ashcombe, Sudeley Castle, Winchcombe, Gloucestershire

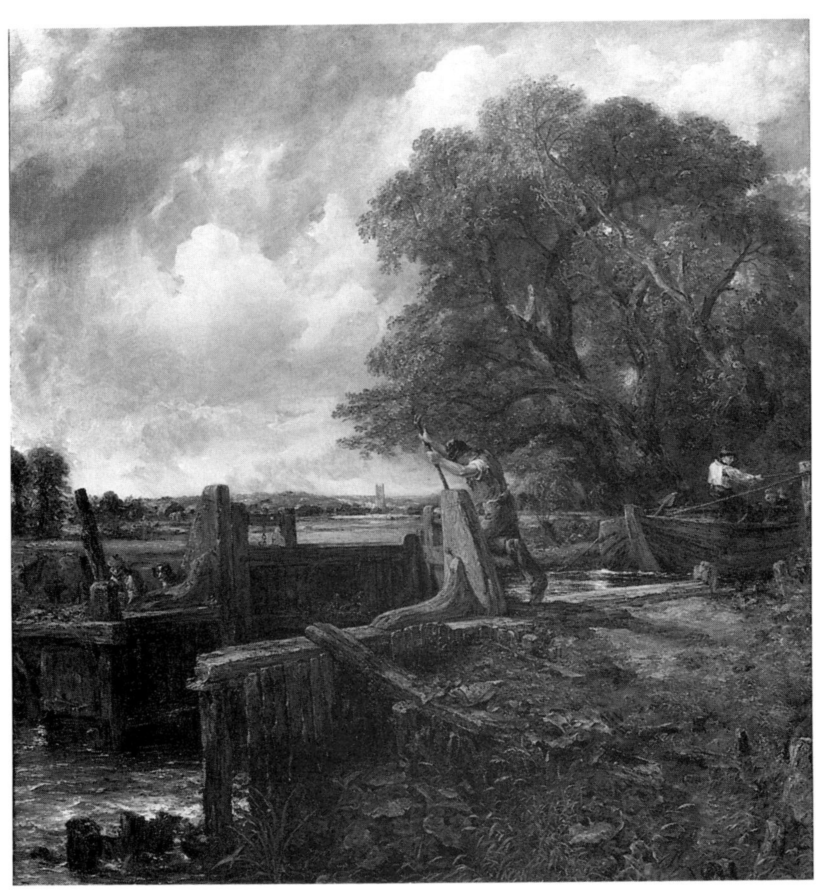

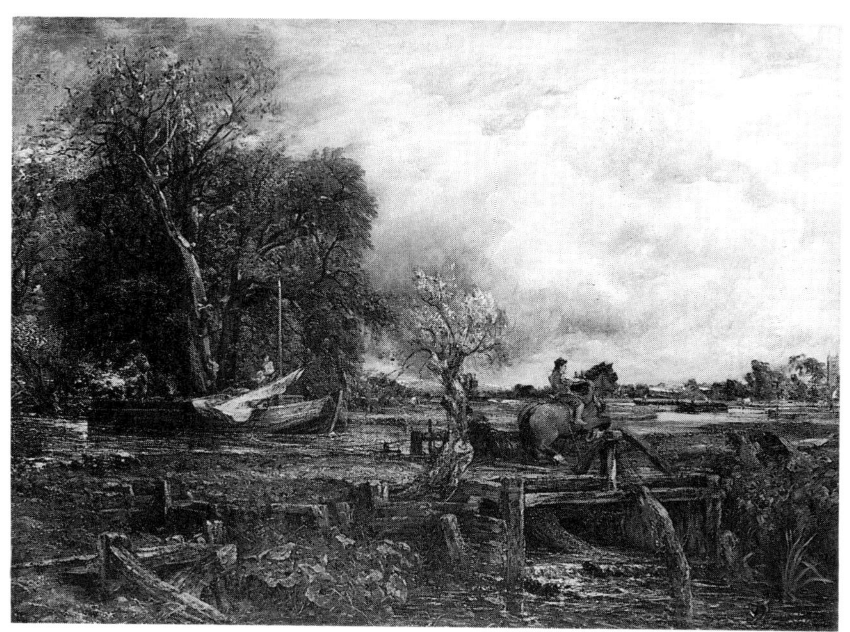

89 J. Constable, *Landscape* (*The Leaping Horse*), 1825, Royal Academy, London

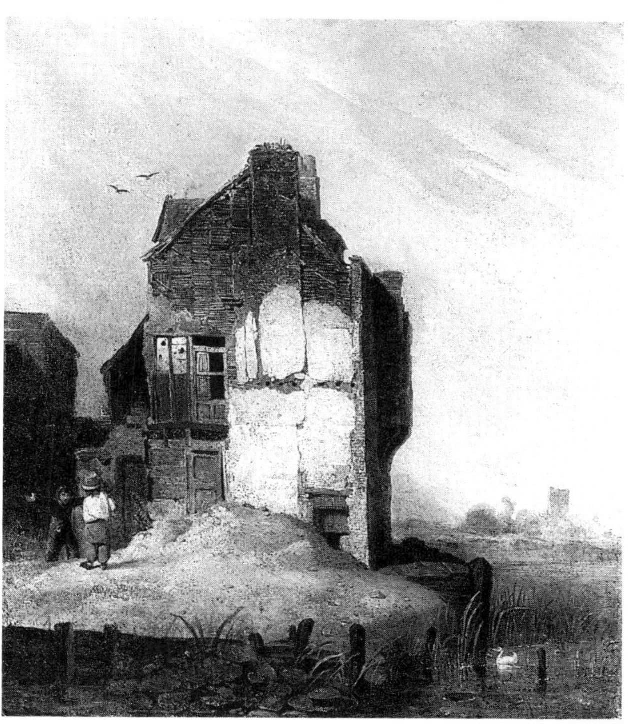

90 W. Mulready, *Cottage and Figures*, *c*. 1808, Tate Gallery

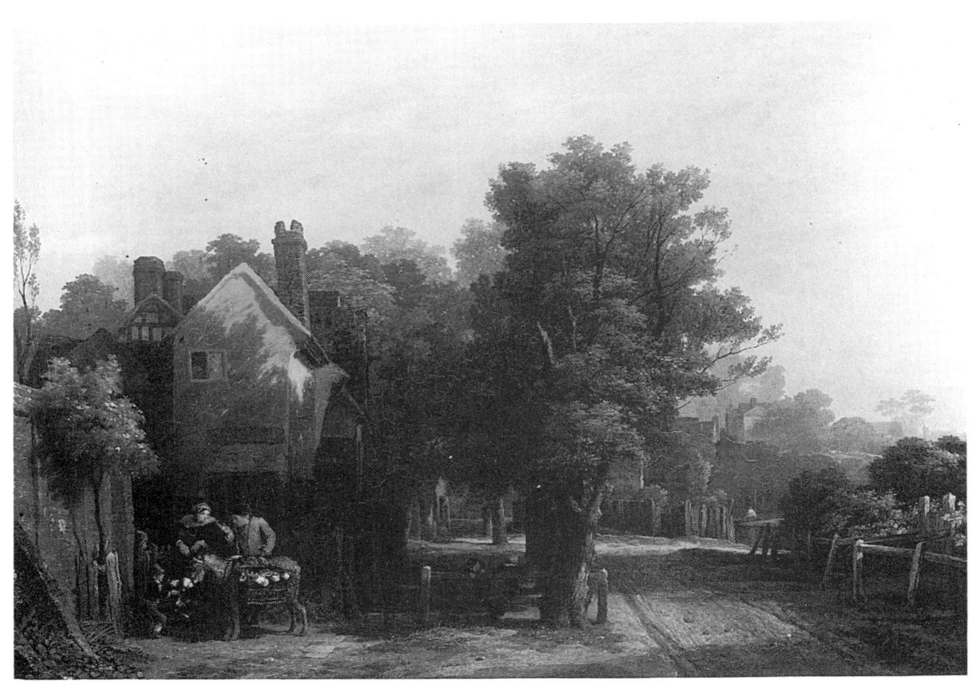

91 W. Mulready, *Near the Mall, Kensington Gravel Pits*, 1812–13, Victoria & Albert Museum

92 J. Crome, *View of St Martin's Gate, Norwich*, 1810–12, Norwich Castle Museum

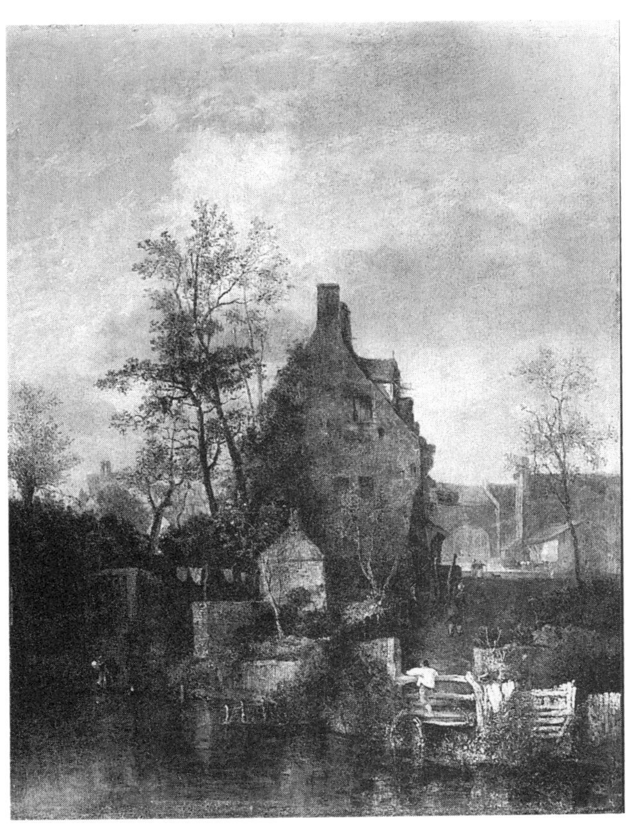

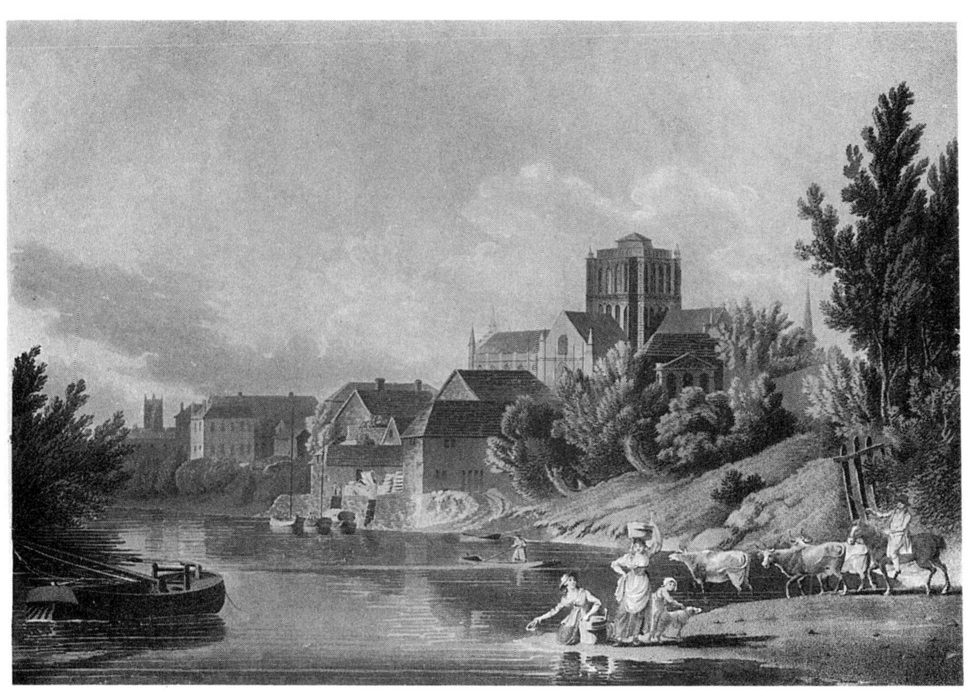

93 F. Jukes after E. Dayes, *View of Hereford*, aquatint, 1797–1802

94 J. Crome, *New Mills – Men Wading*, *c.* 1813? Norwich Castle Museum

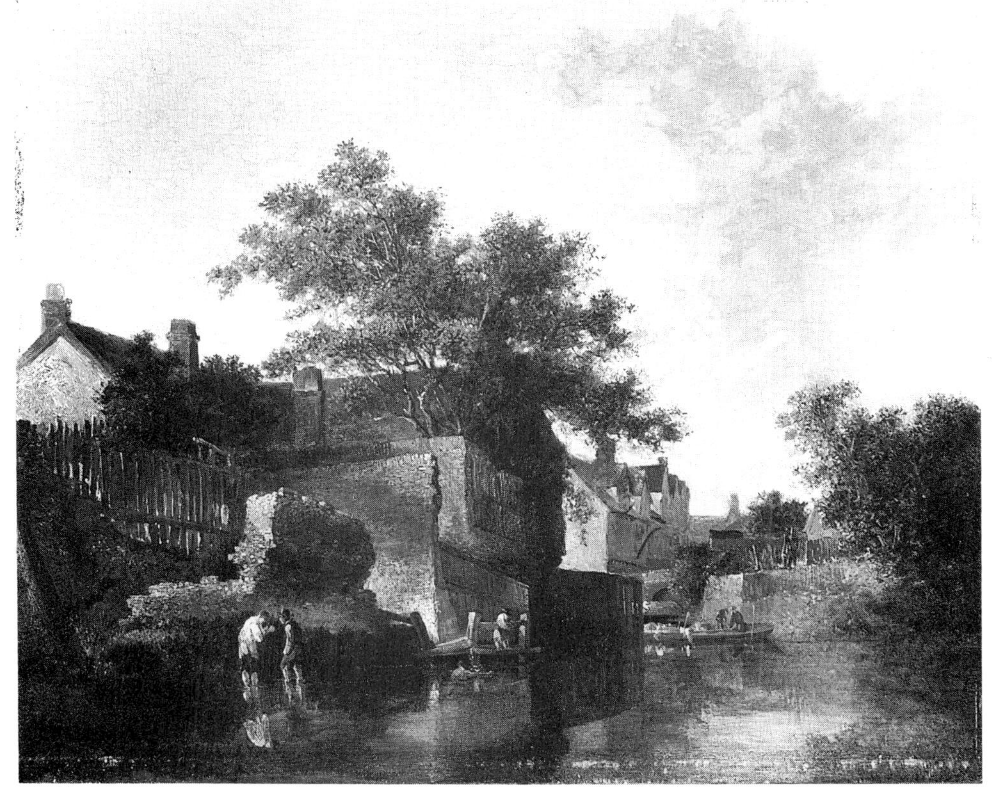

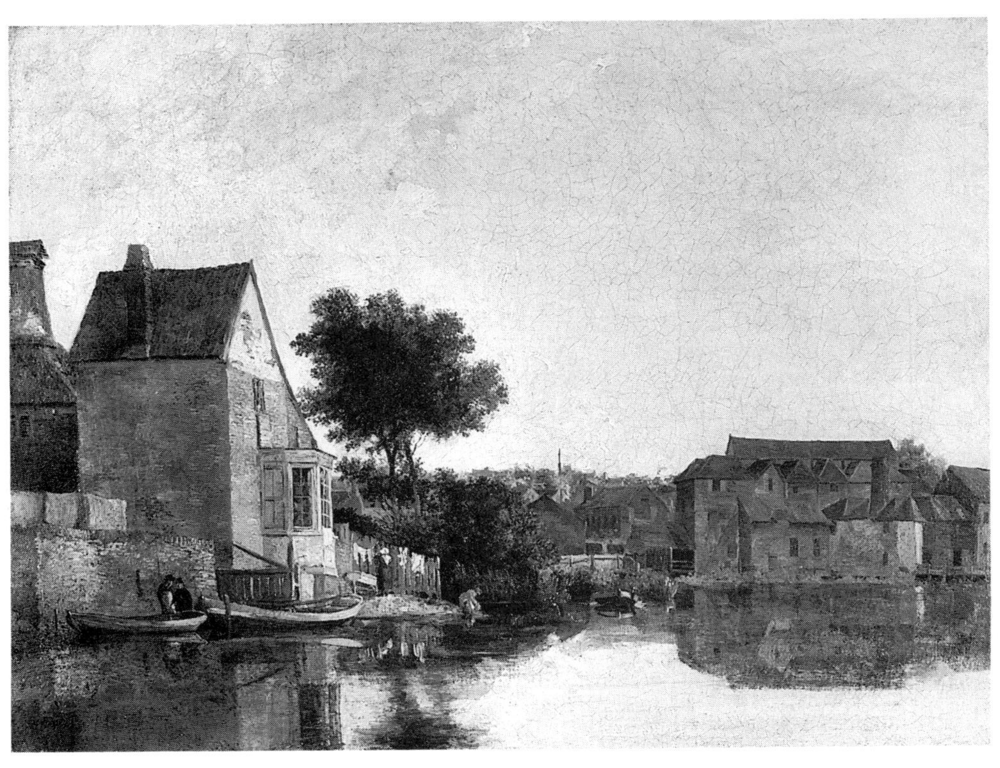

95 J. Crome, *Back of the New Mills, Norwich*, *c.* 1815, Norwich Castle Museum

96 J. S. Cotman, *Norwich Market Place*, 1809?, Tate Gallery

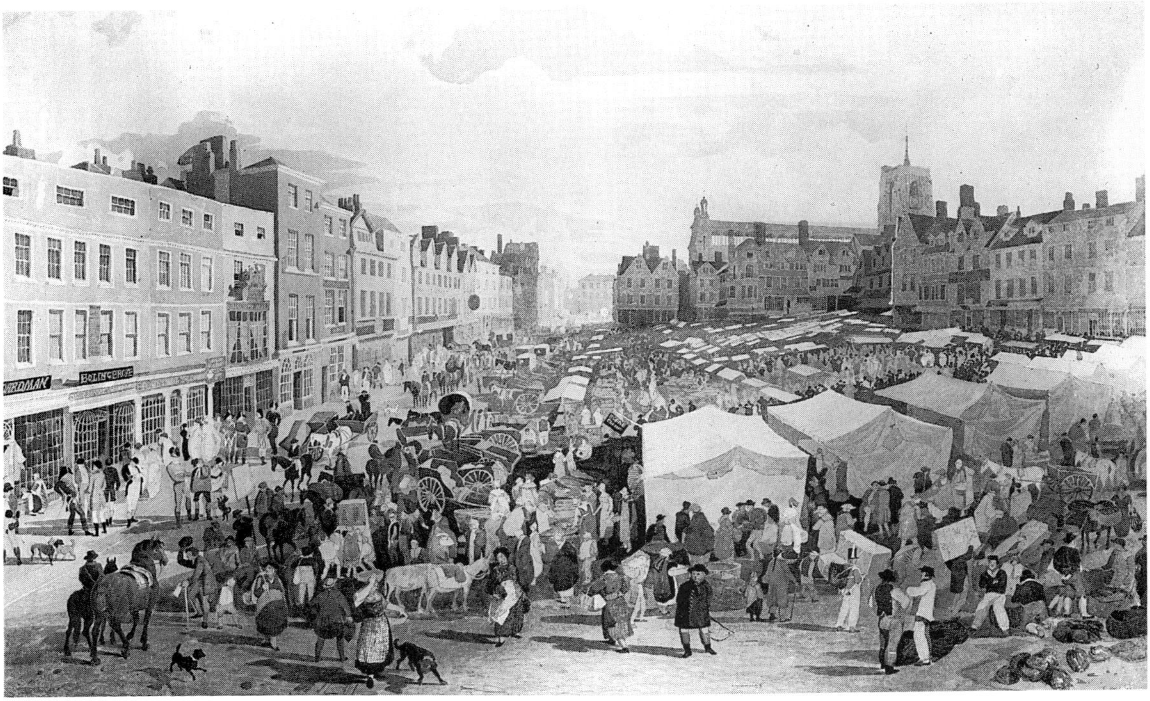

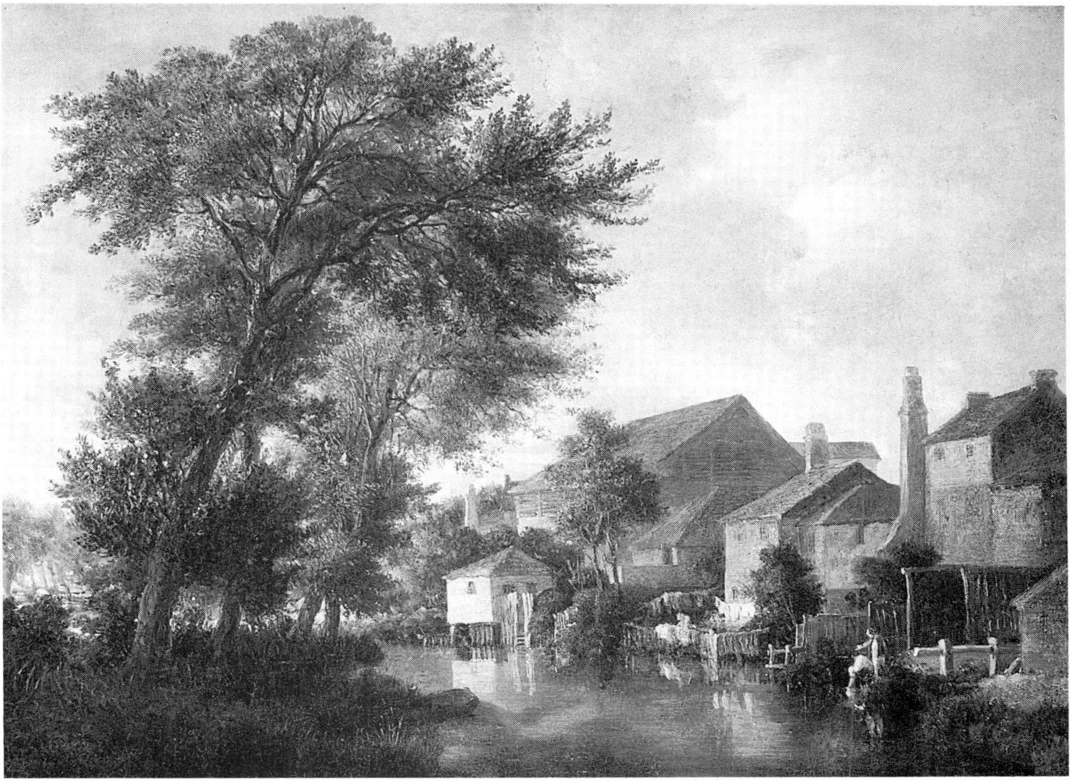

97 J. Crome, *The Wensum, Norwich*, *c.* 1815, Yale Center for British Art

98 Unknown artist, *View behind the New Mills, Norwich*, aquatint, *c.* 1815–20, Norwich Castle Museum

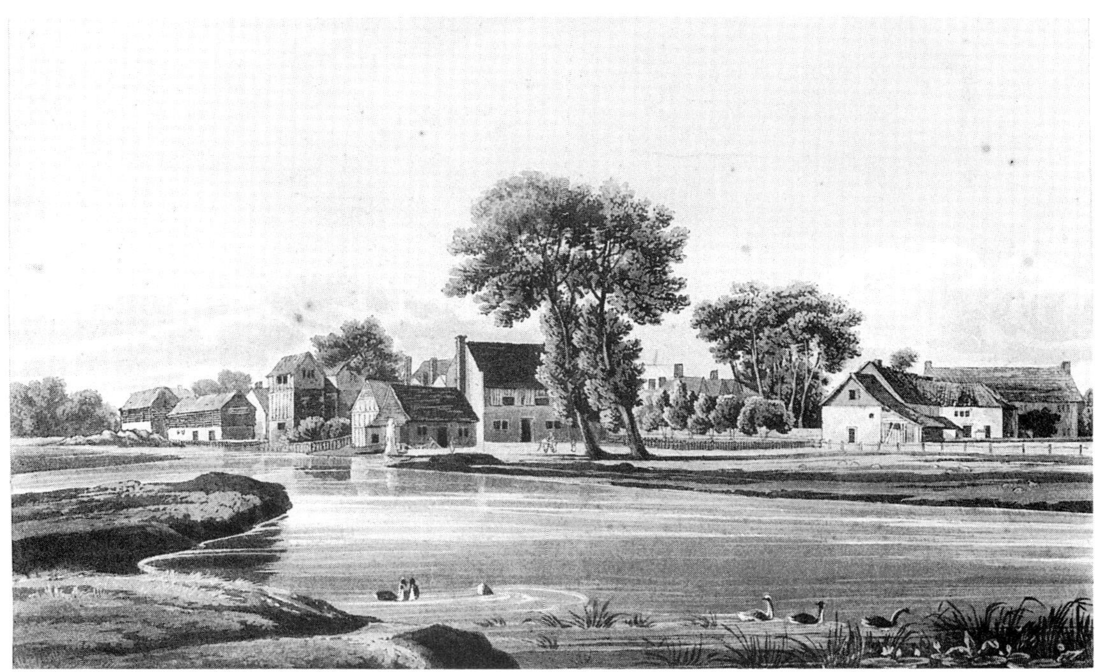

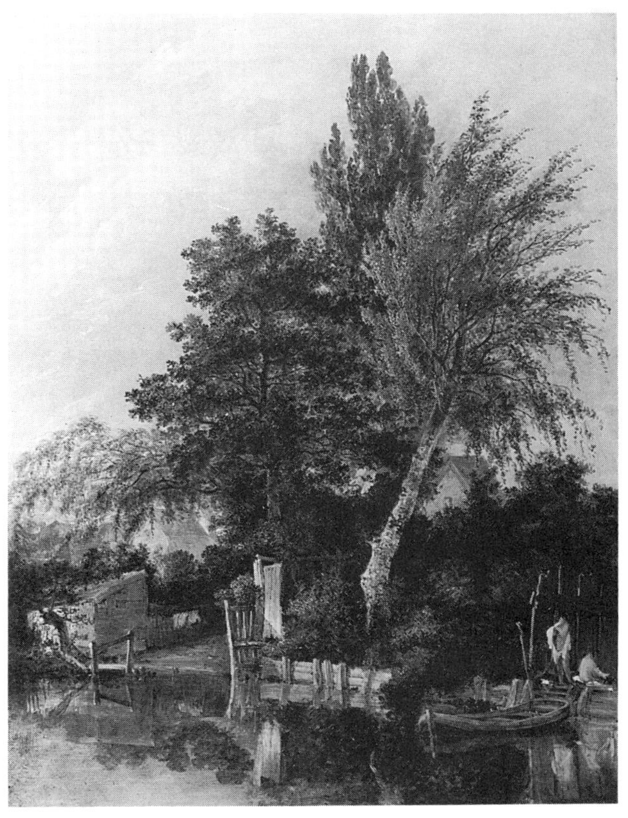

99 J. Crome, *Scene on the River at Norwich*, *c.* 1817, Yale Center for British Art

100 J. Crome, *Norwich River: Afternoon*, *c.* 1819, Private Collection

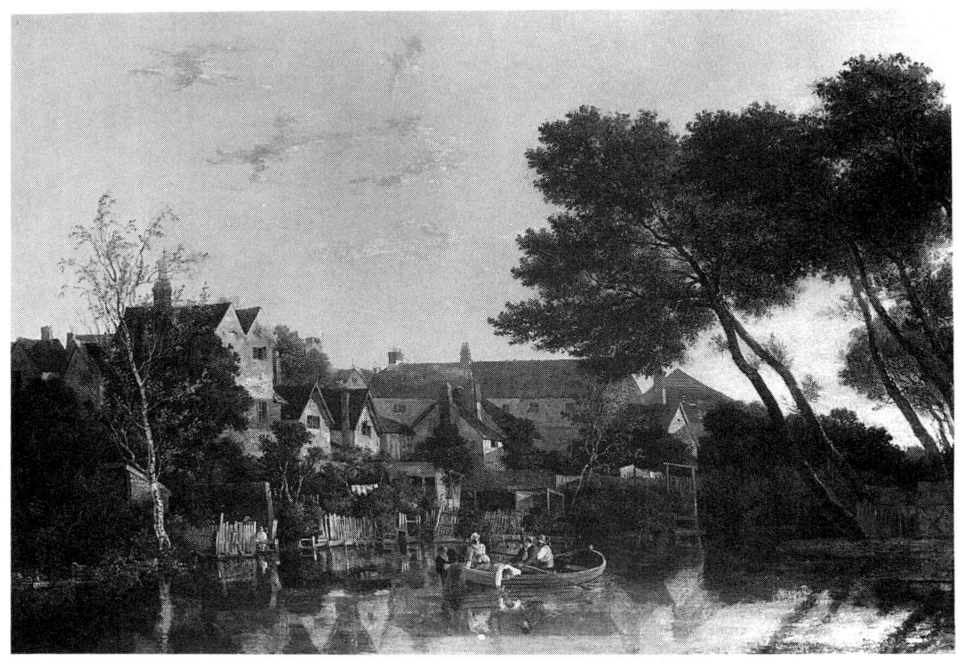

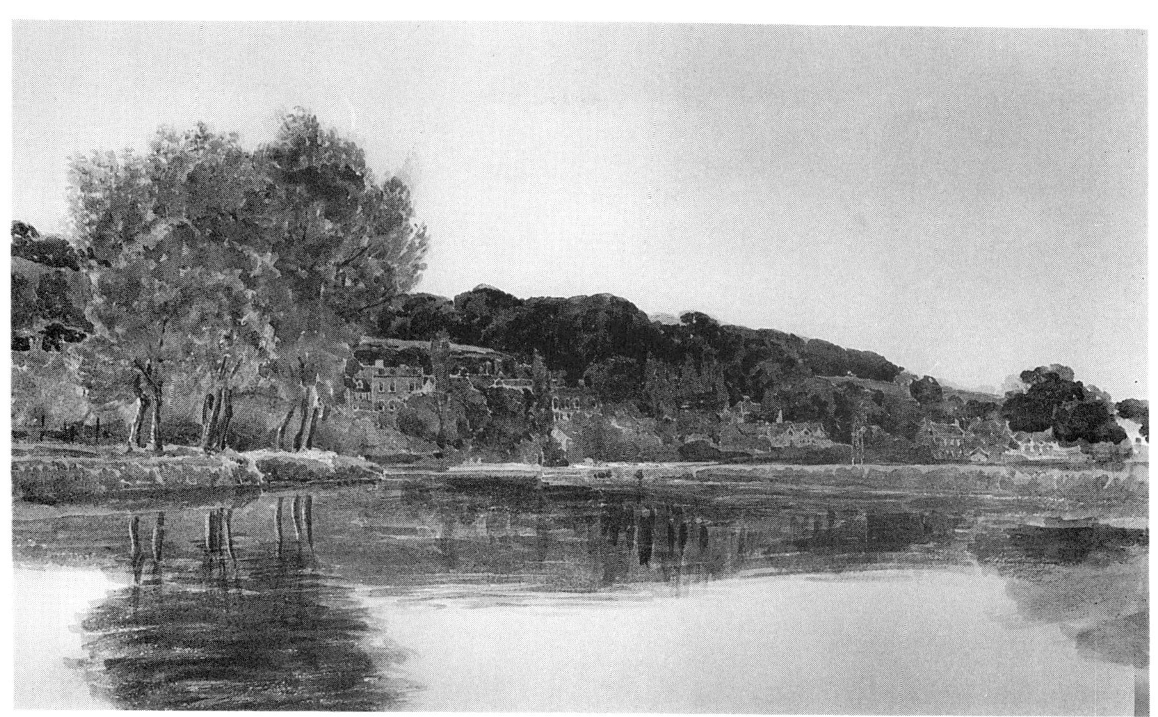

101 J. Thirtle, *Thorpe, Norwich*, *c.* 1815, Norwich Castle Museum

102 J. Thirtle, *A View of Thorpe, with Steam Barge working up – Evening*, 1815, Norwich Castle Museum

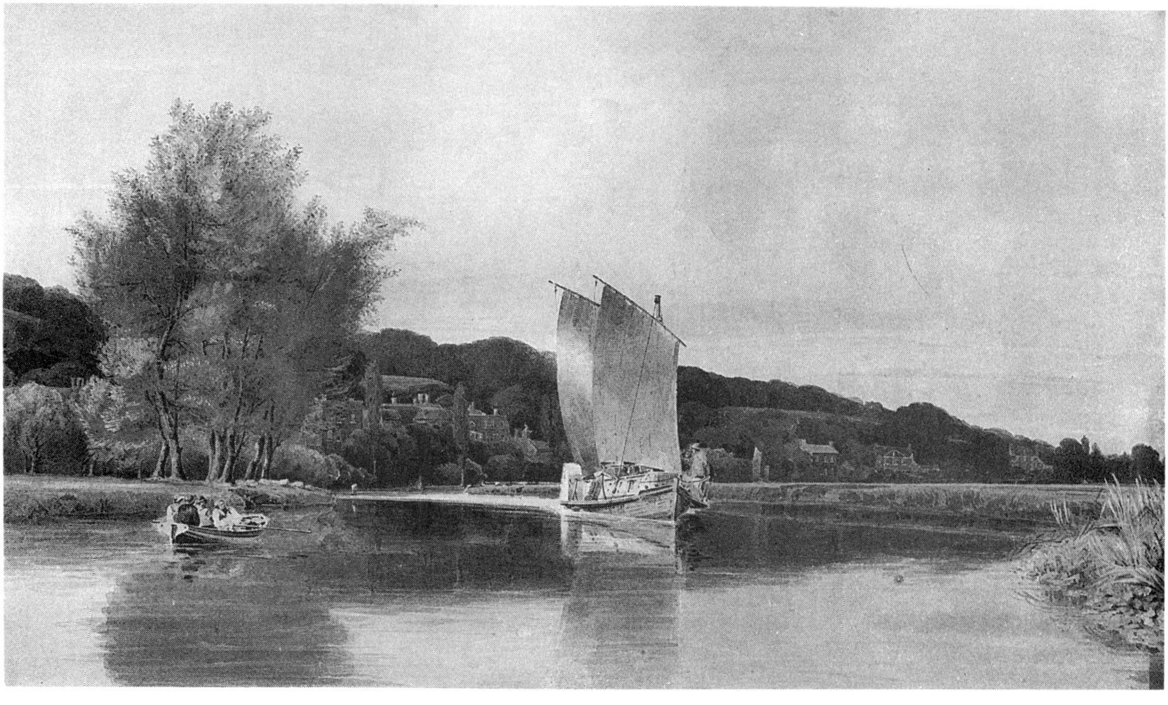

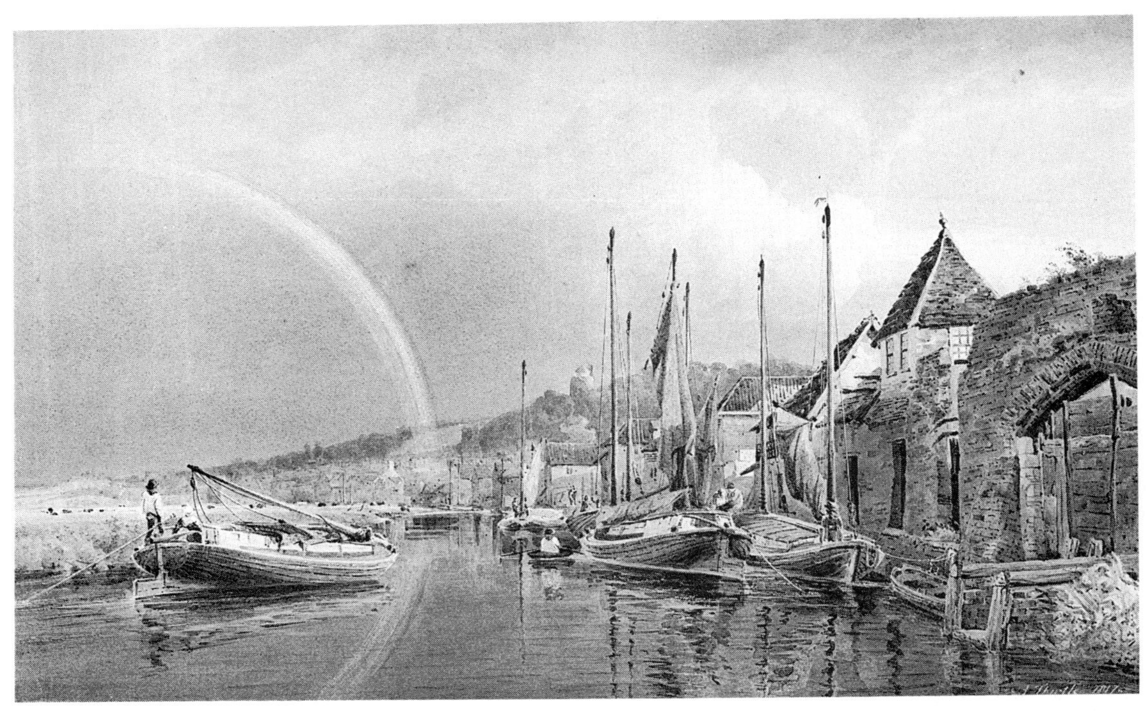

103 J. Thirtle, *Rainbow Effect on the River, King Street, Norwich*, 1817, Norwich Castle Museum

104 J. Crome?, *Houses and Wherries on the Wensum*, *c.* 1810, City Art Gallery, Manchester

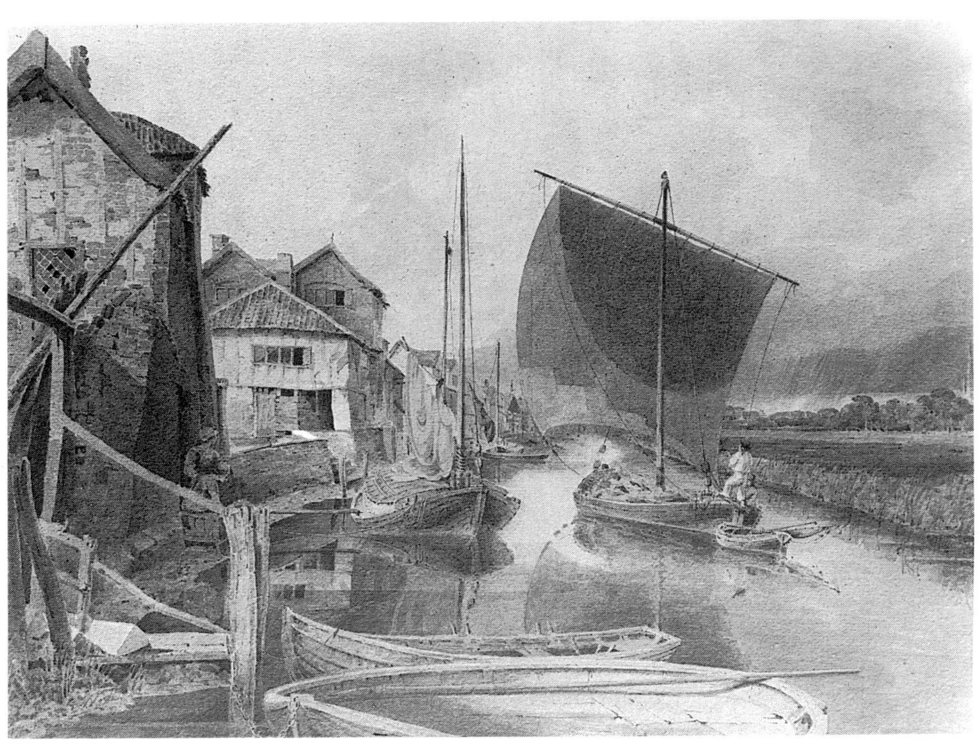

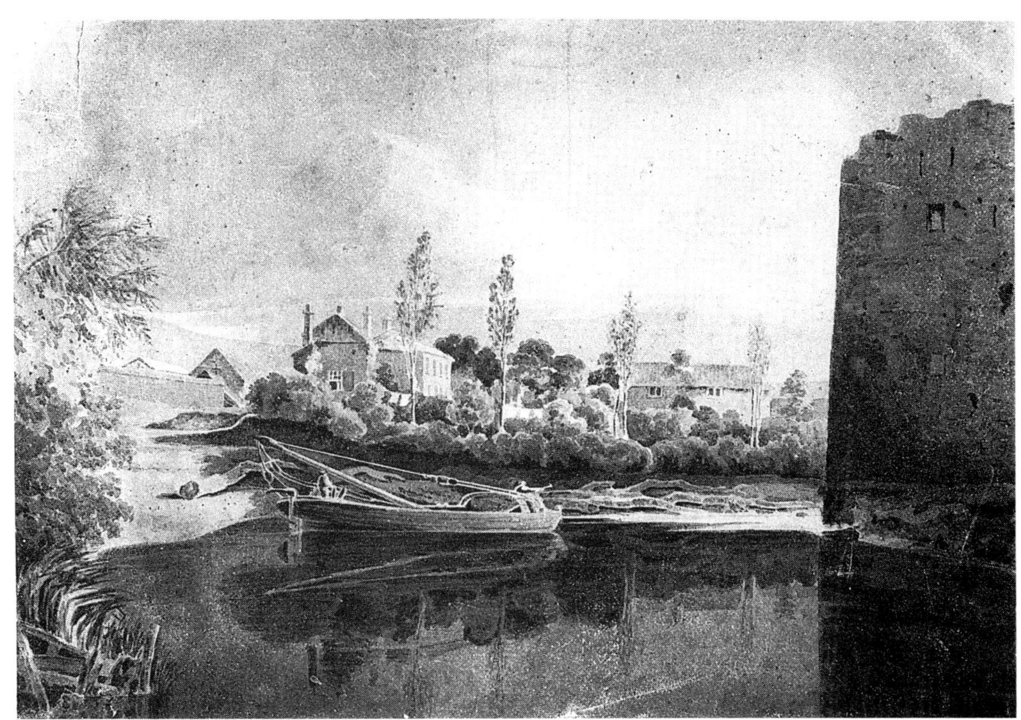

105 J. Thirtle, *View of the River near Cow's Tower*, 1810, Norwich Castle Museum

106 J. Thirtle, *Boat-Builder's Yard, near the Cow's Tower*, 1812, Norwich Castle Museum

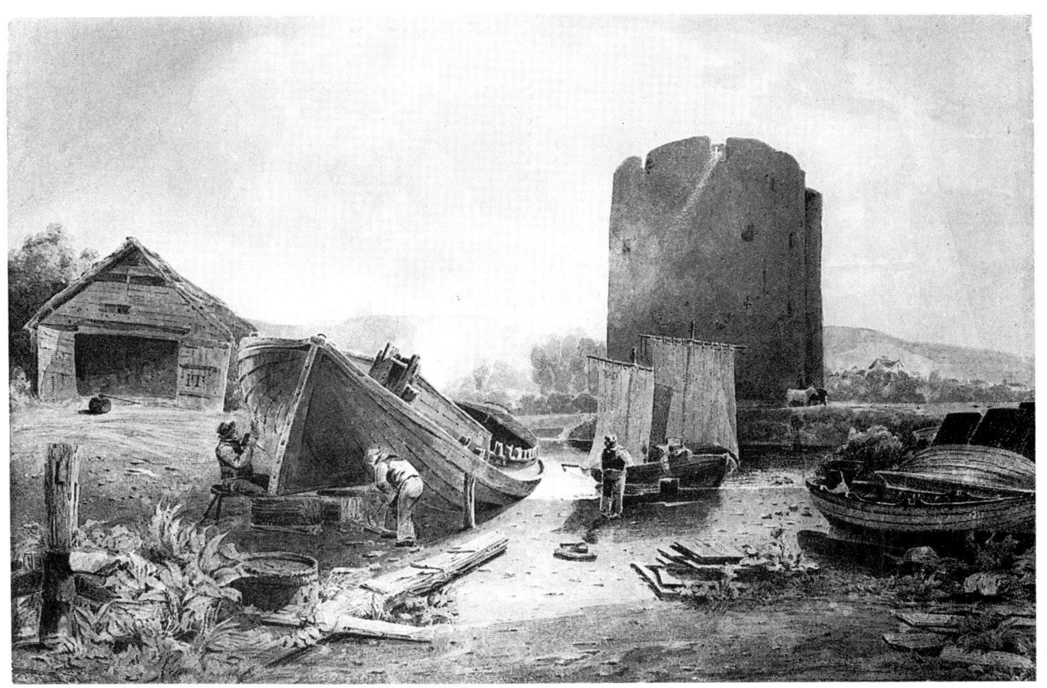

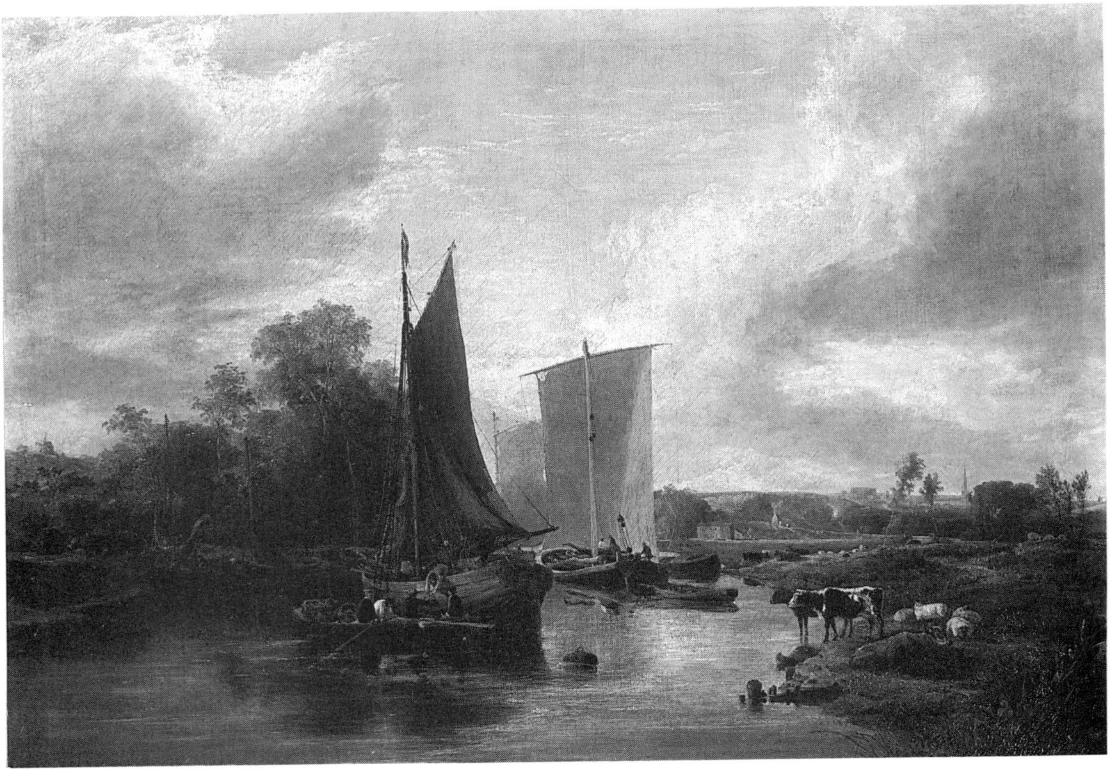

107 G. Vincent, *On the River Yare, Afternoon*, 1819, Christie's Sale, 16 November 1962 (81)

108 G. Vincent, *View on the River Yare near Norwich*, early 1820s, Southampton Art Gallery

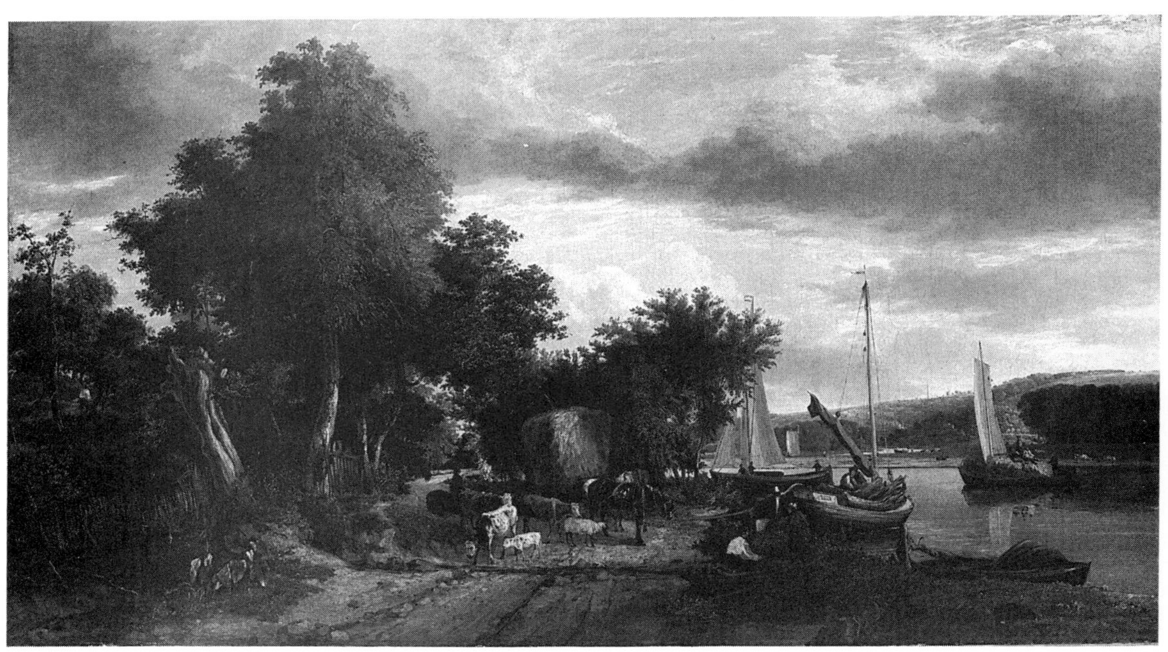

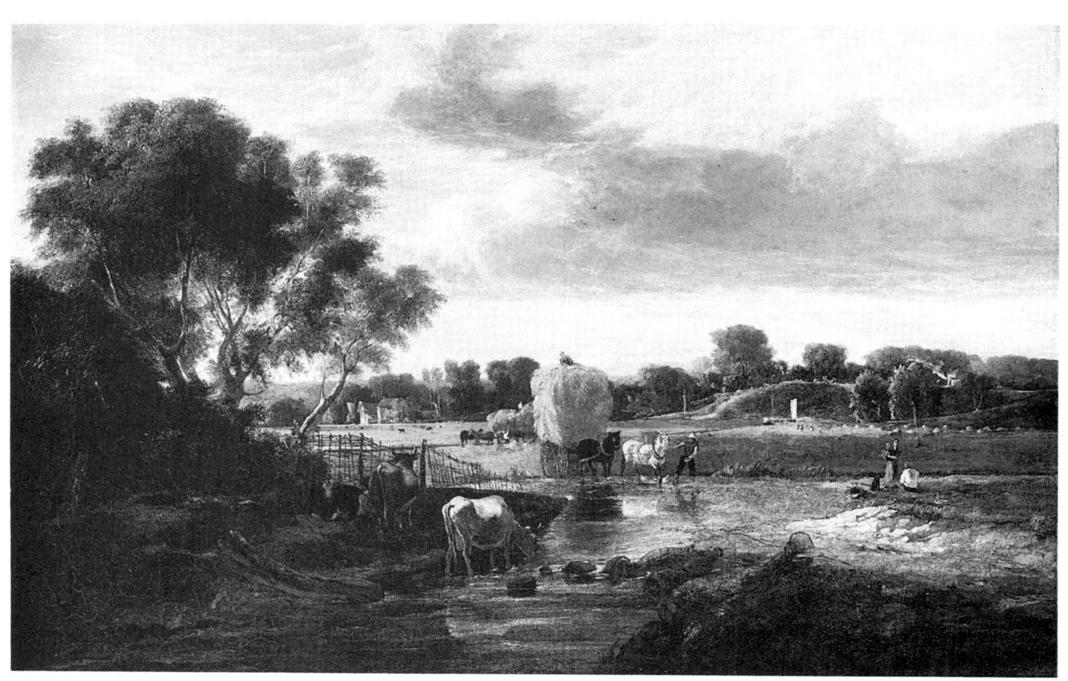

109 G. Vincent, *Trowse Meadows, near Norwich*, 1828?, Norwich Castle Museum

110 J. Stark, *Postwick Reach near Thorpe*, 1824?, photograph courtesy of Richard Green Gallery

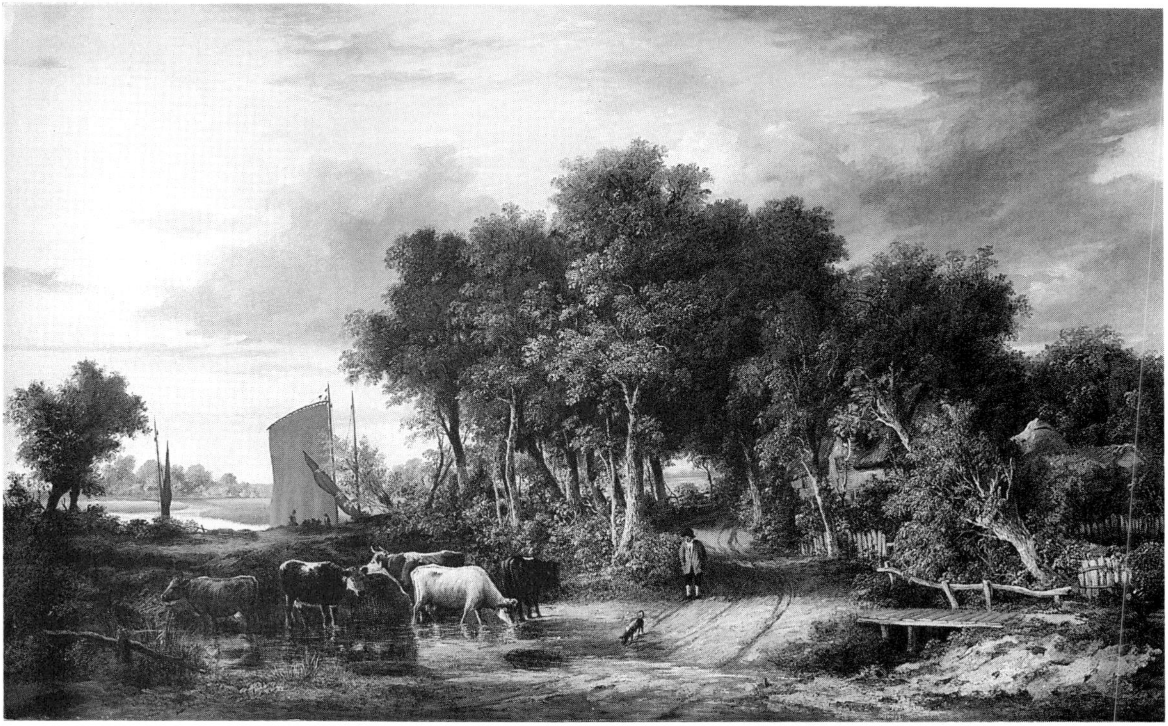

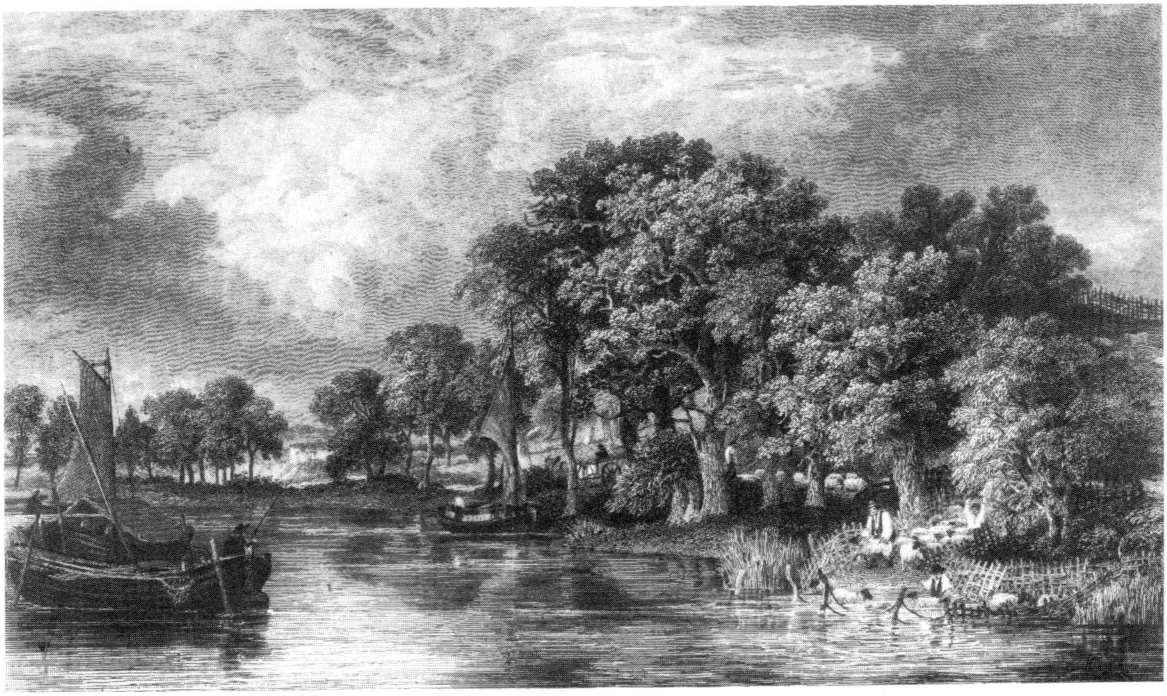

111 W. Forrest after J. Stark, *Postwick Grove*, copper-plate engraving

112 W. Forrest after J. Stark, *Shipmeadow Lock on the Waveney*, copper-plate engraving

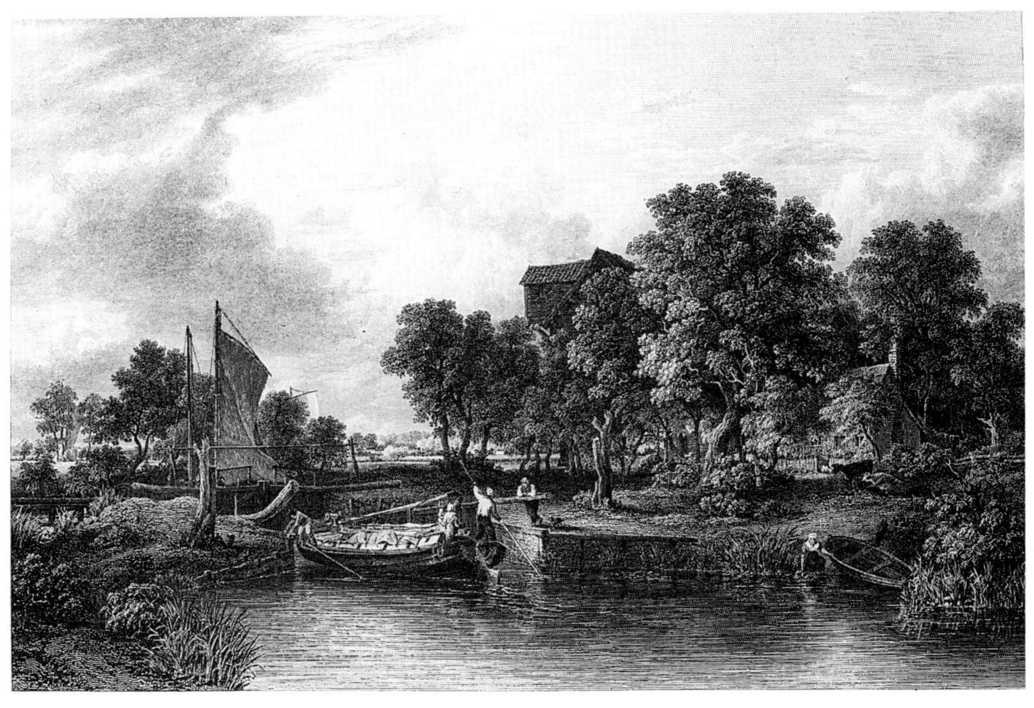

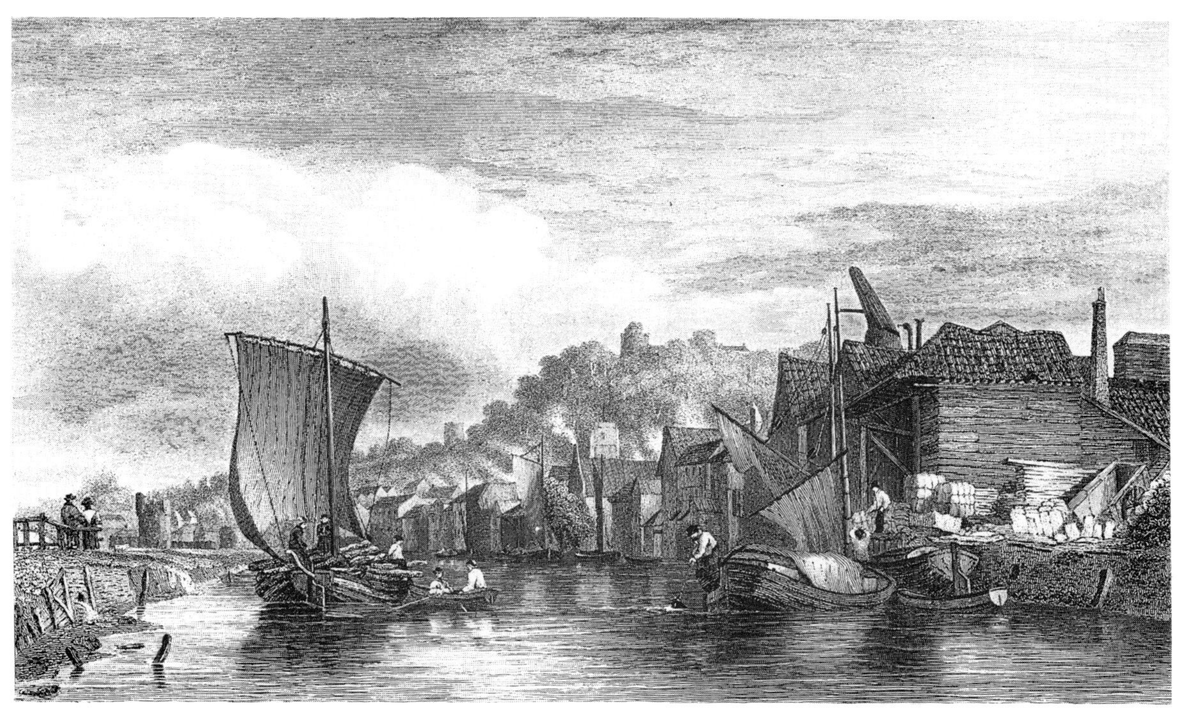

113 W. Brandard after J. Stark, *Harrison's Wharf, King Street, Norwich*, copper-plate engraving

114 G. Cooke after J. Stark, *Yarmouth Quay*, copper-plate engraving

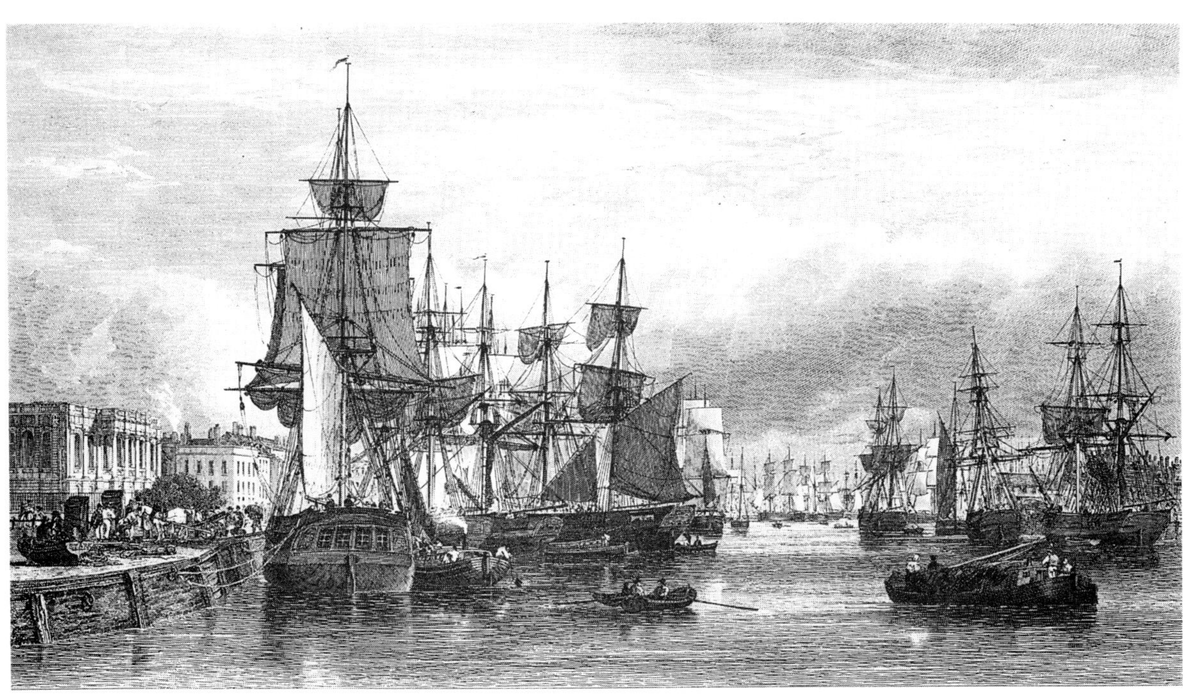

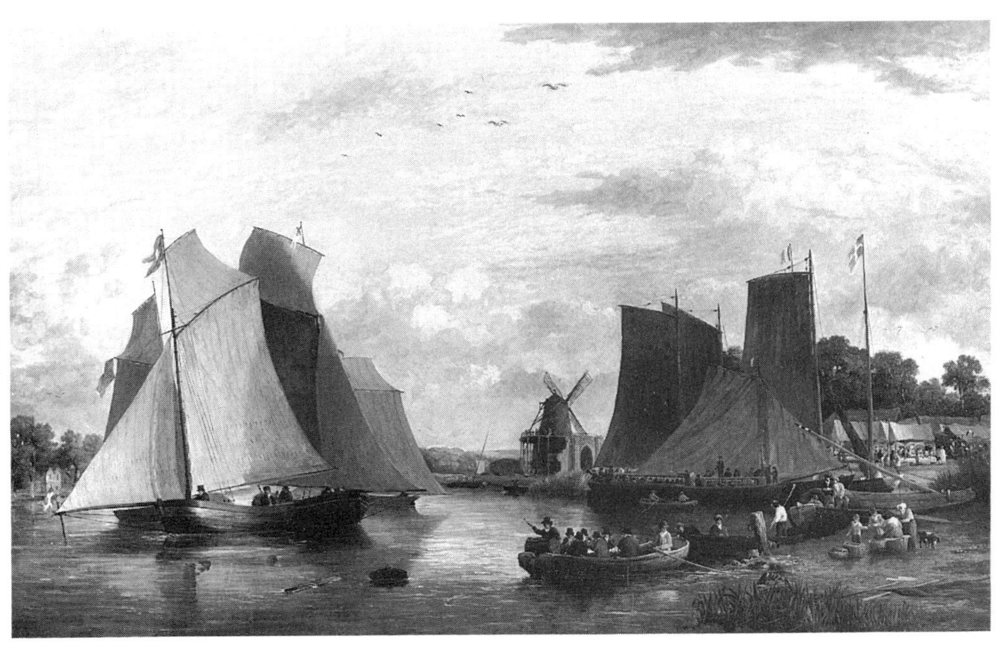

115 J. Stark, *Wroxham Regatta*, 1819? Christie's Sale, 26 November 1986 (61)

116 J. B. Crome, *Yarmouth Water Frolic*, 1820–1, Iveagh Bequest, Kenwood House, London

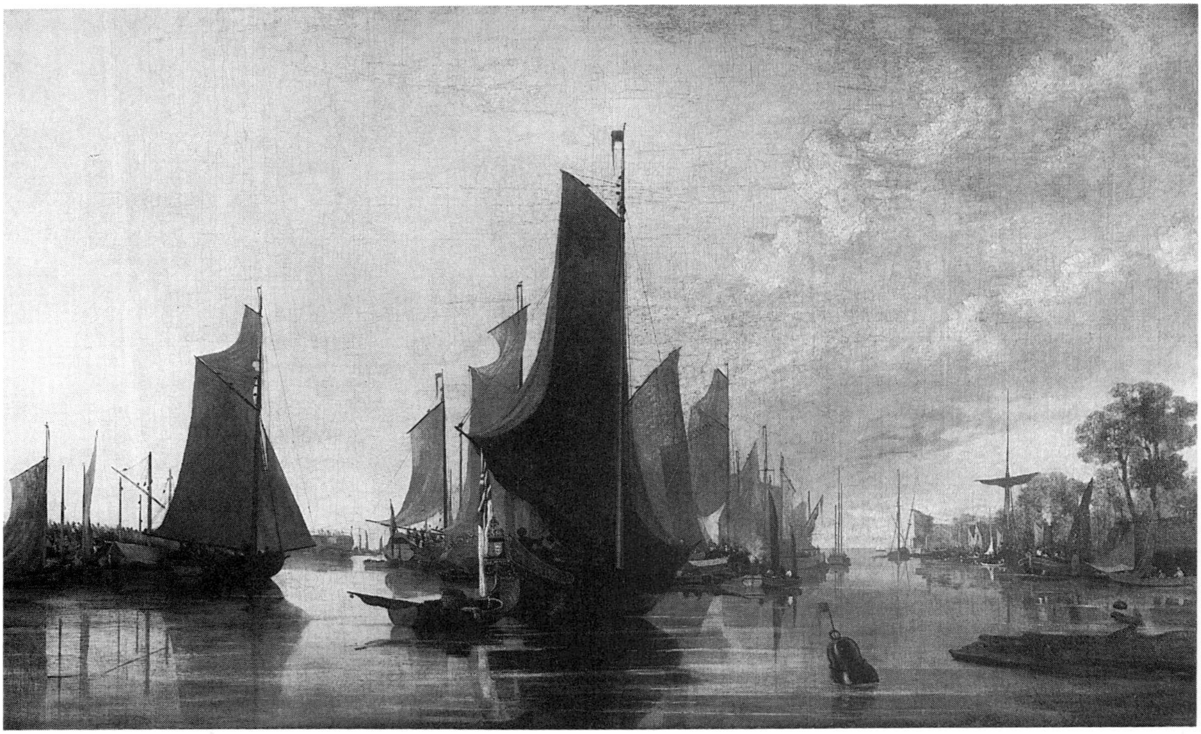

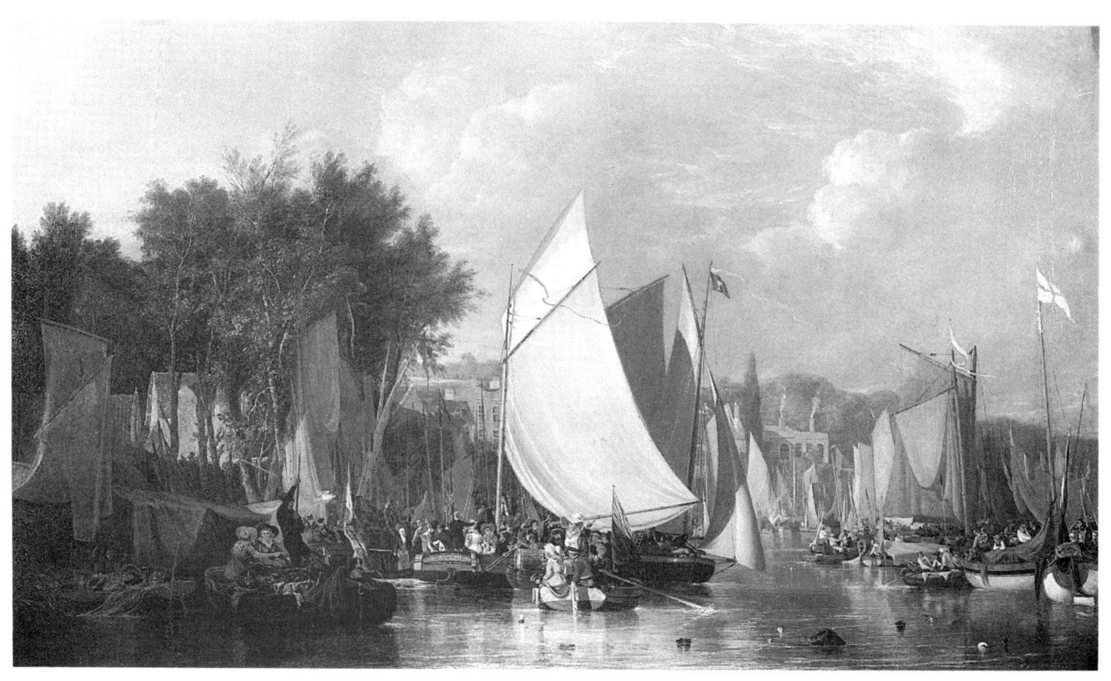

117 J. Stannard, *Thorpe Water Frolic – Afternoon*, 1825, Norwich Castle Museum

118 A. Cuyp, *View of Dordrecht*, *c.* 1655, Iveagh Bequest, Kenwood House, London

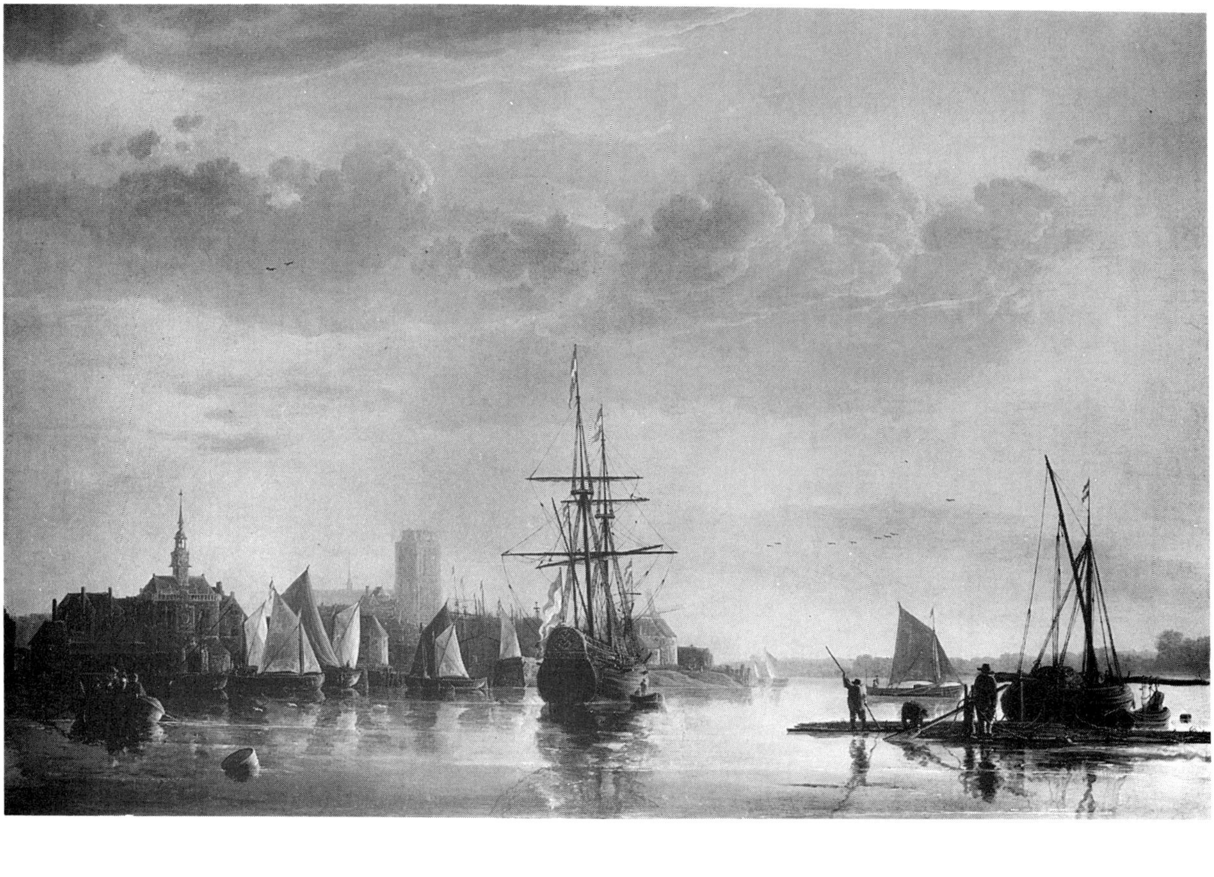

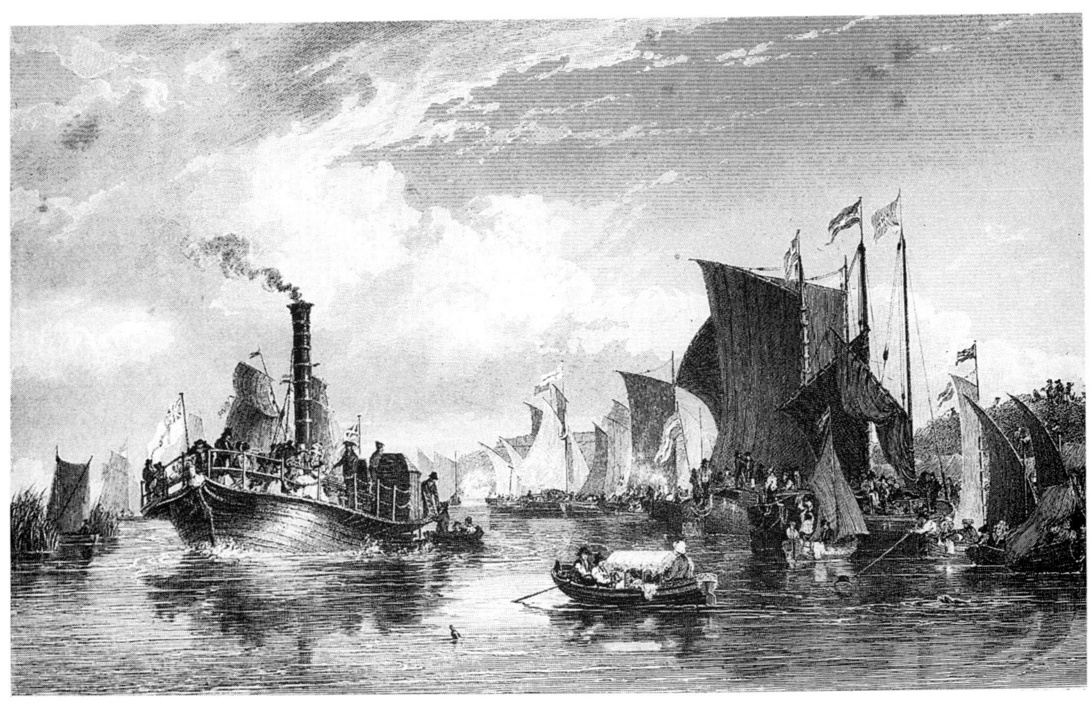

119 R. Brandard after J. Stark, *Yarmouth Regatta*, copper-plate engraving

120 G. Vincent, *Distant View of Pevensey Bay, the Landing Place of King William the Conqueror*, 1824, Norwich Castle Museum

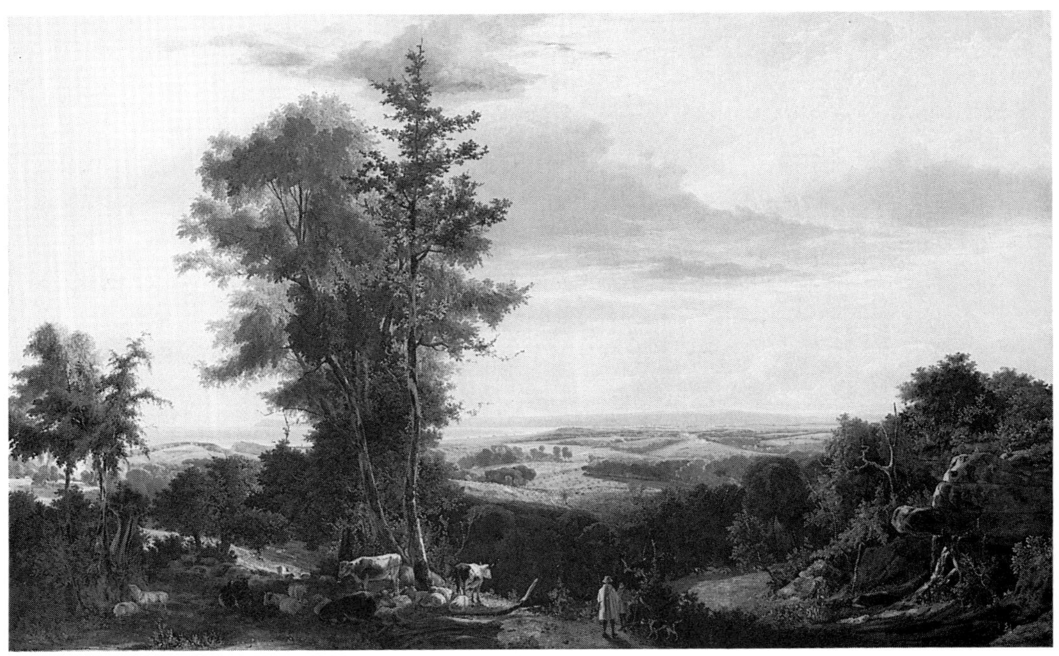

Photographic acknowledgements

Thomas Agnew & Sons Ltd, 26; Birmingham Museum & Art Gallery, 8; Royal Pavilion, Art Gallery and Museums, Brighton, 14, 15, 29, 30; Warren Collection, Courtesy Museum of Fine Arts Boston, 3; by permission of the British Library, 6, 9, 10, maps 2 & 4; Trustees of the British Museum, 24, 28, 38; Christie's, Manson & Woods Ltd, 83, 107, 115; Courtauld Institute of Art, 70, 71; by permission of the Governors of Dulwich Picture Gallery, 84; East Sussex County Library, map 1; English Heritage, The Iveagh Bequest, Kenwood, 116, 118; reproduced by permission of the Syndics of the Fitzwilliam Museum, Cambridge, 86; courtesy Richard Green Gallery, 110; Huntington Library & Art Collections, 87; courtesy of Oscar & Peter Johnson Ltd., Lowndes Lodge Gallery, 44; Manchester City Art Galleries, 104; Leeds City Art Galleries, 1, 2; Paul Mellon Centre for Studies in British Art, 32, 60, 68, 69, 77; National Gallery of Ireland, 85; National Gallery of Scotland, 20; reproduced by permission of the National Gallery of Victoria, Melbourne, 61; Norfolk Museums Service (Norwich Castle Museum) 33, 34, 35, 36, 37, 39, 41, 42, 43, 92, 94, 95, 98, 101, 102, 103, 105, 106, 109, 111, 112, 113, 114, 117, 119, 120, maps 3 & 5; Phaidon Press Ltd, 40, 100; Royal Academy of Arts, London, 89; Scottish National Portrait Gallery, 7; Southampton Art Gallery, 108; by kind permission of Lady Ashcombe, Sudeley Castle , Winchcombe, Gloucestershire, 74, 88; The Tate Gallery, London, 4, 5, 17, 18, 22, 25, 27, 59, 62, 64, 65, 66, 72, 75, 78, 82, 90, 96; by courtesy of the Board of Trustees of the Victoria & Albert Museum, 16, 19, 21, 23, 79, 91; Yale Center for British Art, Paul Mellon Collection, 76, 97, 99. Photographs by the author: 11, 12, 13, 31, 45, 46, 47, 48, 49, 50, 51, 52, 53, 54, 55, 56, 57, 58, 63, 67, 73, 80, 81, 93.

Notes

1 Art as seen

1 R. Southey, *Letters from England*, ed. J. Simmons, London 1951, pp. 153, 70. For a sketch of the growth and social geography of the city, see G. Rudé, *Hanoverian London 1714–1808*, London 1971, ch. 1.

2 'New Churches', *New Monthly Magazine*, series 2, vol. 6, September 1822, 447. Cf. 'Public Buildings', *New Monthly Magazine*, series 2, vol. 3, October 1821, 501–3. Even guide-books complained about 'the general style of public buildings' and the lack of 'monument of the arts' in the 'noblest situations'. See *The Picture of London, for 1810; Being a Correct Guide to all the Curiosities, Amusements, Exhibitions, Public Establishments, and Remarkable Objects, in and near London*, London 1810, p. 50.

3 Southey, *Letters*, pp. 49–50, 69, 78, 51. See also pp. 168–9 on the suburbs. Some of the same themes appear in Victoire Comte de Soligny (P. G. Patmore), *Letters on England*, 2 vols. London 1823, Letters LIV and LV, vol. II, pp. 128–71.

4 Southey, *Letters*, p. 83. Letter XLIX. Note also on the mania for consumer gadgets, pp. 94–5. On the growth of consumerism, see N. McKendrick, J. Brewer. J. H. Plumb, *The Birth of a Consumer Society: The Commercialisation of Eighteenth-Century England*, London 1983.

5 For an extended and brilliant analysis of the development of the public sphere framing art practice in the late seventeenth and eighteenth centuries in France, see T. Crow, *Painters and Public Life in Eighteenth-Century Paris*, New Haven and London 1985.

6 'Royal Academy', *Literary Gazette*, no. 278, 18 May 1822, 313.

7 Comments on exhibitions in contemporary diaries and letters are generally less extended and less informative.

8 For a contemporary perception of Somerset House as a public building, see Soligny, *Letters*, vol. I, p. 23: 'This is the *only* public building in London which can be said to have any pretensions to the character of grandeur and magnificence' (my emphasis).

9 'British Gallery', 7 April 1807.

10 'Exhibition of the Royal Academy, 1817', *New Monthly Magazine*, no. 41, 1 June 1817.

11 'Royal Academy', *Literary Gazette*, no. 278, 18 May 1822; no. 279, 25 May 1822. The critic was W. H. Pyne.

12 These estimates are based on receipts of £2,742 13s 0d, £4,591 7s 0d, and £3,501 16s 0d respectively. I am grateful to the Royal Academy, London, for allowing me access to the account books of 1769–1819 and 1819–49.

13 'The great exhibition has several times been crowded to the doors, and numbers could not obtain admission for want of room.' 'The Sixth Exhibition of the Works of British Artists', *Monthly Magazine*, no. 212, May 1811.

14 For example, the respective number of exhibits at the British Institution and the Academy in selected years were as follows: 1806: 257, 938; 1810: 318, 905; 1815: 235, 908; 1820: 323, 1072; 1825: 415, 1072; 1829: 541, 1223. Attendance estimates are based

on figures for exhibition receipts in the Institution's Minute Books, in the library of the Victoria & Albert Museum.

15 Estimates from Rudé, *Hanoverian London*, ch. 3.

16 'Royal Academy', *Literary Gazette*, no. 277, 11 May 1822; review of Payne Knight's *Analytical Inquiry into the Principles of Taste*, *Edinburgh Review*, vol. 7, June 1806, 302.

17 'Review and Register', *New Monthly Magazine*, 1 August 1816 (my emphasis). The 'battle pieces' referred to here were probably the sketches for paintings of the Battle of Waterloo, which had been shown at the spring exhibition that year.

18 Royal Academy, *The Daily Advertiser, Oracle and True Briton*, 7 May 1806.

19 'British Gallery', *Morning Post*, 23 May 1807.

20 'Fine Arts, Whether they are promoted by Academies and Public Institutions', *Champion*, 28 August, 11 September, 2 October 1814. Reprinted in *The Complete Works of William Hazlitt in Twenty-One Volumes*, ed. P. P. Howe, London and Toronto 1930–4, vol. XVIII, p. 46.

21 'The Exhibition at the Royal Academy', *Champion*, no. 175, 12 May 1816.

22 'Royal Academy', *Literary Gazette*, no. 381, 8 May 1824.

23 *Annals of the Fine Arts*, vol. III, 1818, Preface p. 5.

24 'Catalogue Raisonné of the British Institution', *Examiner*, no. 462, 3 November 1816. Reprinted in Hazlitt, *Complete Works*, vol. XVIII, p. 106.

25 Some publications which were essentially conservative in their overall position were equally critical of the exhibition experience. See, for instance: 'Exhibition at Somerset House', *New Monthly Magazine*, vol. 9, 1 June 1818; and 'British Institution', vol. 21, April 1827; 'Exhibition of the Royal Academy', *Repository of Arts*, series 2, vol. 1, 1 June 1816; and 'Exhibition at the Leicester Gallery', series 2, vol. 7, 1 April 1819.

26 'The British Institution', *London Magazine*, series 1, vol. 4, April 1821; 'On the Exhibition at Somerset House', series 1, vol. 3, June 1820.

27 'British Sculpture', *New Monthly Magazine*, vol. 3, 1 June 1821, p. 279. 'Among us the number who possess even a limited taste is very small compared with the bulk of our population, who have not a remote feeling of it.'

28 'The Exhibition at the Royal Academy', *London Magazine*, series 1, vol. 1, June 1820.

29 'Royal Academy, no. V', *Champion*, no. 441, 16 June 1821.

30 'Royal Academy', *Champion*, no. 227, 11 May 1817.

31 'The Exhibition of the Royal Academy', *London Magazine*, series 3, vol. 1, June 1828.

32 The argument of this chapter is partly modelled on that of C. Duncan & A. Wallach, 'The Museum of Modern Art as Late Capitalist Ritual: An Iconographic Analysis', *Marxist Perspectives*, vol. 1, no. 4, 1978; and 'The Universal Survey Museum', *Art History*, vol. 3, no. 4, December 1980.

2 Ideology and naturalism

1 That nineteenth-century landscape painting is an essentially urban phenomenon has received more attention from historians of French art. See University of East Anglia and Hazlitt, Gooden & Fox, *Théodore Rousseau 1812–1867* (exhibition catalogue by N. Green), London 1982, pp. 17–24; R. L. Herbert, 'Industry in the Changing Landscape from Daubigny to Monet', in J. M. Merriman, ed., *French Cities in the Nineteenth Century*, London 1982.

2 R. Williams, *Culture*, Glasgow 1981.

3 The general model of class is derived from E. O. Wright, *Classes*, London 1985. On gender and class, see L. Davidoff & C. Hall, *Family Fortunes: Men and Women of the English Middle Class 1780–1850*, London 1987, especially pp. 28–35.

4 Pierre Bourdieu has argued that class position is defined through a concatenation of variables, none of which are reducible to the effects of a single cause. However, he still makes volume and composition of capital the 'most determinant property'. See especially: P. Bourdieu, *Distinction: A Social Critique of the Judgement of Taste*, tr. R. Nice, London and New York 1984.

5 V. N. Vološinov, *Marxism and the Philosophy of Language* (1930), tr. L. Matejka & I. R. Titunik, New York and London 1973, p. 15.

6 The differences hinge largely on the difficulty of establishing standard units in complex pictorial imagery which are equivalent to speech phonemes. The meaning of visual units in pictures seems to be far more contextual, and has been described as depending on analogical relationships, as compared with the digital relationships of language. On this issue see N. Goodman, *Languages of Art*, Brighton 1981; M. Schapiro, 'On Some Problems in the Semiotics of Visual Art: Field and Vehicle in Image-Signs', *Semiotica*, vol. 1, no. 3, 1969; U. Eco, 'Critique of Iconism', in *A Theory of Semiotics*, London and Basingstoke 1977, pp. 191–217.

7 Vološinov, *Marxism*, p. 23.

8 J. Barrell, *The Political Theory of Painting from Reynolds to Hazlitt, 'The Body of the Public'*, New Haven and London 1986. I have set out my objections to Barrell's approach in my review: 'The Political Theory of Painting without the Politics', *Art History*, vol. 10, no. 3, September 1987.

9 On the relations between art, modernity, and the city in the nineteenth century see M. Berman, *All That Is Solid Melts Into Air: The Experience of Modernity*, London 1983. For an important critique of Berman, see P. Anderson, 'Modernity and Revolution', *New Left Review*, no. 144, March/April 1984.

10 I. Watt, *The Rise of the Novel*, Harmondsworth 1972, esp. ch. 2.

11 The sense of a sharp distinction between the landscape painting of the nineteenth century and that of the 'old masters' underlies, of course, Ruskin's *Modern Painters* – although 'modernity' is a negative category for Ruskin.

12 See J. Larrain, *The Concept of Ideology*, London 1979, for a general history of the concept. For its Marxist variants, see J. Larrain, *Marxism and Ideology*, London 1983.

13 G. Therborn, *The Ideology of Power and the Power of Ideology*, London 1980, esp. pp. 2, 77–81.

14 Therborn, *Ideology*, pp. 39, 2–3, 15–20. While I accept Therborn's critique of ideology as 'false consciousness', I feel he goes too far in his rejection of the notion of 'interests'. On this issue see A. Callinicos, *Marxism and Philosophy*, Oxford 1983, p. 166, n. 32; and Wright, *Classes*, pp. 248–9.

15 M. Foucault, *The Archaeology of Knowledge*, London 1974, p. 117.

16 Foucault made little use of the concept of ideology, which he seems to have equated with its vulgar Marxist version, see his *Power/Knowledge*, Brighton 1980, p. 118. On the general problems of Foucault's work, see P. Dews, *Logics of Disintegration: Post-Structuralist Thought and the Claims of Critical Theory*, London and New York 1987, chs. 5–7.

17 P. Bourdieu, *The Cultural Field and the Economic Field*, tr. R. Nice, CCCS Stencilled Paper No. 46, University of Birmingham 1977, pp. 3–4. On 'cultural capital', see 'Introduction' in Bourdieu, *Distinction*, although this offers no definition of the term as such.

18 For a critique of functionalist models of ideology, see N. Abercrombie, B. Hill, & S. Turner, *The Dominant Ideology Thesis*, London 1980.

19 P. Bourdieu, *Outline of a Theory of Practice*, Cambridge 1977, pp. 82–7; Bourdieu, *Distinction*, II, 3. In Bourdieu's social theory ideologies are 'illusions' consistent with interest, and he systematically downgrades their cognitive functions, stressing instead the efficacy of the institutional mechanisms through which they function. The power to state is more important than what is stated. This draws attention to the importance of institutions in conferring authority on ideological statements, but Bourdieu's approach is ultimately reductive, making all symbolic systems function one-dimensionally as classificatory schemes in the competition for social status, regardless of their content.

20 Notably Nelson Goodman. For a useful appraisal of Gombrich and Goodman, see W. J. T. Mitchell, *Iconology: Image, Text, Ideology*, Chicago and London 1986, chapters 2 and 3.

21 M. A. Shee, *Elements of Art*, London 1809, p. 273. Cf. Samuel Palmer's well-known remark to George Richmond in 1828: 'Though I am making studies for Mr Linnell, I will, God help me, never be a naturalist by profession.' R. Lister, ed., *The Letters of Samuel Palmer*, 2 vols., London 1974, vol. I, p. 36.

22 On the history of the term, see: R. Williams, *Keywords*, revised edition, London 1983, pp. 216–19. See also R. Wellek, 'The Concept of Realism in Literary Criticism', in *Concepts of Criticism*, New Haven 1963; and L. R. Furst & P. N. Skrine, *Naturalism*, London 1971, pp. 4–5.

23 Norwich Castle Museum, *A Decade of English Naturalism 1810–1820*, text by J. Gage, Norwich 1969, pp. 16, 24, 30.

24 Gombrich's *Art and Illusion*, in which the work of Constable is used several times to support the main hypothesis, was one of the two books recommended for 'Further Reading'. Gombrich uses the terms 'naturalistic' and 'realistic' almost interchangeably, but defines neither.

25 J. Gage, 'Constable and the Natural Sciences', read at a symposium on Constable held to coincide with the Tate Gallery's bicentenary exhibition (unpublished).

26 Williams, *Keywords*, pp. 276–80.

27 R. B. Beckett, ed., *John Constable's Discourses*, Ipswich 1970, p. 69.

28 R. R. Wark, ed., *Sir Joshua Reynolds, Discourses on Art*, New Haven and London 1975, Disc. VII, l.6–9; Disc. XI, l.108–12; Disc. XIII, l.91–104; R. N. Wornum, ed., *Lectures on Painting by the Royal Academicians. Barry, Opie, and Fuseli*, London 1848, pp. 295–6.

29 Beckett, *Discourses*, p. 57.

30 Beckett, *Discourses*, p. 83.

31 N. Goodman, 'The Status of Style', in *Ways of World Making*, Hassocks 1978, p. 27. See also his 'On Being in Style', in *On Mind and Other Matters*, Cambridge, Mass. & London 1984, pp. 130–4.

32 In 1827, a review of *Picturesque Views of the English Cities, from Drawings by G. F. Robson* described topography as: 'one of the most engaging of modern sciences, and peculiar . . . to this country; for not only do the British artists excel all others in this branch of the art, but the British people excel those of all other nations in their fondness for the same.' See *Literary Chronicle*, no. 430, 11 August 1827.

33 In this respect, my emphasis is different from that of Ann Bermingham, who sees an easy transition from the theory of Gilpin and the work of Gainsborough to the new aesthetic. See her *Landscape and Ideology: The English Rustic Tradition, 1740–1860*, Berkeley, Los Angeles, and London 1986.

34 W. Gilpin, *Observations on the River Wye*, London 1782, pp. 1–2.

35 W. Gilpin, *Three Essays; On Picturesque Beauty; On Picturesque Travel; and On Sketching Landscape* (1792) London 1794, p. i. For the history of the term 'picturesque' see Hipple 1957, pp. 185–8. On Gilpin generally see C. P. Barbier, *William Gilpin: His Drawings, Teaching, and Theory of the Picturesque*, Oxford 1963.

36 Gilpin, *Three Essays*, pp. 49–50.

37 The 'search after beauty should naturally lead the mind to the great origin of all beauty' – Gilpin, *Three Essays*, pp. 46–7. For Gilpin's natural theology, see his *Remarks on Forest Scenery*, 2 vols., London 1808: 'How does everything around us bring its lesson to our minds! Nature is the great book of God. In every page is instruction to those, who read.' (vol. I, p. 108).

38 Quoted in Barbier, *William Gilpin*, p. 103. For Gilpin's enthusiasm for Rosa, see ibid., p. 33; on his commitment to the sublime, p. 113. On the variety of nature, see Gilpin, *Forest Scenery*, vol. II, p. 248. On his objections to naturalism, see ibid., vol. I, p. 247, vol. II, pp. 232–6. See also Barbier, *William Gilpin*, pp. 133–5.

39 Gilpin, *Forest Scenery*, vol. II, p. 166; vol. I, p. 308. This stands in direct contrast to Hume's famous remark that the beauty of a field depends on its utility: 'nothing renders a field more agreeable than its fertility' – D. Hume, *A Treatise of Human Nature*, ed. L. A. Selby-Bigge & P. H. Nidditch, Oxford 1978, p. 364.

40 See, for example, Young's passage on Northamptonshire, quoted in E. Moir, *The*

Discovery of Britain: The English Tourists 1540–1840, London 1964, p. 116. At a number of points, Thomas West's famous *Guide to the Lakes* (1778) refers to 'sweet' enclosures and white farmhouses with slate roofs as contributing to the picturesque effects of the scenery.

41 Gilpin, *Three Essays*, p. ii; Gilpin, *Forest Scenery*, vol. II, p. 80; Barbier, *William Gilpin*, p. 103, p. 144 n. 3; pp. 112–13, 144.

42 Barbier, *William Gilpin*, p. 144. See also p. 24, n. 5. Cf. Gilpin's comments on Dutch seventeenth-century artists in his *Essay on Prints*, London 1802, pp. 58–9, 84, 104, 108–11, 147–9.

43 J. Barrell, *The Idea of Landscape and the Sense of Place 1730–1840*, Cambridge 1972 – especially ch. 2, 'The Landscape of Agricultural Improvement'.

44 Gilpin, *Forest Scenery*, vol. II, p. 123. U. Price, *Essays on the Picturesque, as Compared with the Sublime and the Beautiful: and, on the Use of Studying Pictures, for the Purpose of Improving Real Landscape*, 3 vols. London 1810, vol. III, p. 101. (Price had used the same title for essays in the collection published originally in 1794 and 1798.)

45 Price, *Essays*, vol. I, pp. 21–37.

46 Price, *Essays*, vol. I, pp. 293–4. Cf. vol. I, pp. 31–2, vol. II, p. 8 n.

47 William West had already noted the appeal of the Lakes to artists in his 1778 guide. See also J. H. Pott, *An Essay on Landscape Painting*, London 1782, pp. 62–3. For a range of artistic responses see Fitzwilliam Museum, Cambridge, *Beauty, Horror and Immensity: Picturesque Landscape in Britain 1750–1850*, Cambridge 1981; Victoria & Albert Museum, *The Discovery of the Lake District: A Northern Arcadia and its Uses*, London 1984.

48 For example, see Francis Stevens, *Views of Cottages and Farmhouses in England and Wales: Etched by Francis Stevens from the Designs of the Most Celebrated Artists*, published by R. Ackermann, London 1815.

49 J. T. Smith, *Remarks on Rural Scenery*, London 1797, pp. 6–7, 9, 12, 18, 19. For Gilpin's aversion to white and his general views on colour, see 'On the Art of Sketching Landscape', in Gilpin, *Three Essays*, especially pp. 83–4, 94, and lines 348–51.

50 Ann Bermingham has made the important point that Smith's archetype of the picturesque cottage conflicted with Constable's attachment to the values of agricultural improvement, which contributed to his move to naturalism (Bermingham, *Landscape and Ideology*, pp. 107–9). I agree with this, but wish to situate Constable's practice in relation to a larger aesthetic shift.

51 Review of Payne Knight's *Analytical Inquiry into the Principles of Taste*. *Edinburgh Review*, vol. 7, 1806, 314–15; 'The British Institution', *London Magazine*, series 2, vol. 3, November 1825, 356.

52 'On the Picturesque and the Ideal – A Fragment', in Hazlitt, *Complete Works*, vol. VIII, pp. 317–18.

53 Hazlitt, *Complete Works*, vol. IV, p. 74.

54 E. Robertson, ed., *Letters and Papers of Andrew Robertson 1777–1845*, London 1897, p. 84.

55 H. Richter, *Daylight: A Recent Discovery in the Art of Painting*, London 1817, pp. 5, 10; T. Phillips, *Lectures on the History and Principles of Painting*, London 1833, p. 371. *Daylight* was first published in part in the *Repository of Arts*, series 2, vol. II, November 1816 – Rudolph Ackermann being the publisher of both. It is possible that Richter's pamphlet was partly a response to the rejection of William Havells' *Wallnut Gathering at Petersham near Richmond* by the British Institution in 1815. In Havell's words, this was an attempt 'to represent my own beautiful country without referring to other painters, ancient or modern', and 'to paint the splendour of day-light and sunshine, the glory of Art and Nature'. See 'Mr Havell's Picture', *Examiner*, no. 384, 7 May 1815; and F. Owen, 'William Havell', *Connoisseur*, vol. 197, no. 792, February 1978, p. 101.

56 Richter, *Daylight*, p. 17.

57 Richter was the son of a German engraver who had settled in London, and the brother of the radical politician John Richter, who was imprisoned in the Tower in 1794.

58 'The facility with which this artist [i.e. Girtin] executed his coloured studies from nature, surprised all those who accompanied him on his travels, and who witnessed his practice.' – 'Observations on the Rise and Progress of Painting in Water Colours', *Repository of Arts*, vol. 9, February 1813, 93.

59 The Prague School theorist Jan Mukařovský suggested that works of art operate as both autonomous signs (within an aesthetic order) and informational signs, these two aspects functioning in a 'dialectical antinomy'. See his 'Art as Semiotic Fact', in L. Matejka & I. R. Titunik, eds., *Semiotics of Art*, Cambridge, Mass. 1984. Goodman and Schapiro have elaborated similar concepts.

60 On syntagm, see R. Barthes, *Elements of Semiology*, New York 1968, Part III; and *Image–Music–Text*, New York 1977, p. 51.

3 Artists in British society 1800–1830

1 The general conception of British historical development I use here is that set out in P. Corrigan & D. Sayer, *The Great Arch: English State Formation as Cultural Revolution*, Oxford 1985. This develops on marxist debates around the nature of class hegemony in Britain which began in the 1960s, and to which Perry Anderson, Tom Nairn, and E. P. Thompson were the main contributors (see bibliography). Like Corrigan and Sayer, I assume that despite the continuing importance of aristocratic influence in politics and culture, it is wrong to imagine that the British bourgeoisie failed to achieve the kind of hegemony achieved by that class elsewhere, or that Britain lacks a bourgeois revolution it should have had.

2 For an overblown view of the *ancien régime*, see J. C. D. Clark, *English Society 1688–1832*, Cambridge 1985, and the review by A. Ryan, 'Tory History', *London Review of Books*, 23 January 1986.

3 E. P. Thompson, 'The Peculiarities of the English', in *The Poverty of Theory*, London 1978, pp. 48–51. See also his 'Eighteenth-century English Society: Class Struggle without Class?', *Social History*, vol. 3, no. 2, May 1978. On Queen Caroline, see T. W. Laqueur, 'The Queen Caroline Affair: Politics as Art in the Reign of George IV', *Journal of Modern History*, no. 54, September 1982.

4 I make no strong distinction in this study between 'bourgeoisie' and 'middle class', and to some extent I have alternated between these terms for reasons of variety. However, I tend to use 'bourgeois' to signify the primary structural distinction between capital and labour, and 'middle class' to refer to the actual variety of class positions which are available to individuals who belong to neither the proletariat nor artisanal occupations. Whereas 'middle class' may sometimes incorporate what we would call the petty bourgeoisie, 'bourgeois' does not.

5 E. P. Thompson, *The Making of the English Working Class*, Harmondsworth, 1980, Part One; and also his 'Patrician Society, Plebeian Culture', *Journal of Social History*, vol. 7, 1973–4; and Thompson, *Social History*, 1978, pp. 162–5.

6 Davidoff & Hall, *Family Fortunes*, pp. 96–7.

7 L. Colley, 'Whose Nation? Class and National Consciousness in Britain 1750–1830', *Past and Present*, no. 113, November 1986.

8 Most notably in the campaign against the orders in Council and East India Company monopoly in 1812. See C. Emsley, *English Society and the French Wars 1793–1815*, London and Basingstoke 1979, pp. 159–61.

9 A. Briggs, 'Middle-Class Consciousness in English Politics, 1780–1846', *Past and Present*, no. 9, April 1956. By contrast with the manufacturing and professional bourgeoisie, the financial and commercial bourgeoisie seems to have been socially and culturally closer to landed society. See N. Rogers, 'Money, Land and Lineage: the Big Bourgeoisie of Hanoverian London', *Social History*, vol. 4, no. 3, October 1979.

10 J. E. Cookson, *The Friends of Peace: Anti-War Liberalism in England 1793–1815*, Cambridge 1982, ch. 1 – an invaluable study of the ideology of this period.

11 The role of Evangelical Christianity in the formation of middle-class identity must also

be noted, but this tended to lead to political quietism. See Davidoff & Hall, *Family Fortunes*, pt. 1, ch. 1.

12 Cookson, *Friends of Peace*, chs. 2–4.

13 Thompson, *Making*, chs. 14 & 16; J. J. Foster, *Industrial Revolution and Class Struggle: Early Industrial Capitalism in Three English Towns*, London 1974, especially pp. 34–43, 49–61. I. Prothero, *Artisans and Politics in Early Nineteenth-Century London: John Gast and his Times*, London 1981.

14 G. Nesbitt, *Benthamite Reviewing: The First Twelve Years of the Westminster Review 1824–1836*, New York 1934. W. Thomas, *The Philosophic Radicals: Nine Studies in Theory and Practice 1817–1841*, Oxford 1979. On Utilitarianism more generally see: E. Halévy, *The Growth of Philosophic Radicalism*, London 1972, esp. pt. 2, ch. 3; pt. 3, ch. 4.

15 See, for instance, the review of Lady Morgan's *The Book of the Boudoir*, *Westminster Review*, vol. 11, no. 22, art. 6, October 1829, which blames fashion for the corruption of 'new wealth', which instead of struggling against the 'aristocracy', becomes sycophantic to it. For a rather more light-handed critique of fashion as a social ontology, see 'On Fashions', *London Magazine*, series 2, vol. 1, no. 8, August 1825, especially 586–7. For a direct critique of the sexual morality of the aristocracy, see 'High-Life Morality', *Examiner*, no. 919, 11 September 1825 – despite 'many honorable exceptions', 'as a class, an equally frivolous, heartless, insolent, and sensual body does not exist under the sun' (576–7).

16 Review of Bentham's *Chrestomathia* and *Public Education*, *Westminster Review*, vol. 1, no. 1, January 1824, 68–9.

17 Review of *Men and Things in 1823* by J. A. Boone, *Westminster Review*, vol. 1, no. 1, January 1824, p. 5 – 'The one great thing on which we are intent, is getting money; and our politics, religion, literature, are only branches of that pursuit.'

18 See, for example: 'Desperation of the Corrupt', *Examiner*, no. 678, 24 December 1820; 'Proposed Royal Academy of Literature', *Examiner*, no. 709, 5 August 1821; 'Education of the People', *London Magazine*, series 3, vol. 1, no. 1, April 1828; 'A Comparative View of the State of Trade in the Years 1826, 7, & 8', *London Magazine*, series 3, vol. 2, no. 7, October 1828.

19 Review of C. Mills' *The History of Chivalry, or Knighthood and its Times*, *Westminster Review*, vol. 5, no. 9, art. 3, January 1826, 81. For a rather more conservative definition of gender characters, see the review of *The Loves of the Poets*, *Westminster Review*, vol. 11, no. 22, art. 10, October 1829.

20 Davidoff & Hall, *Family Fortunes*, pt. 1, ch. 2. The magazines of the liberal intelligentsia did not, however, take the kind of feminist position of elements in the Owenite movement – see B. Taylor, *Eve and the New Jerusalem, Socialism and Feminism in the Nineteenth Century*, London 1983.

21 Review of W. Godwin, *History of the Commonwealth of England*, *Westminster Review*, vol. 8, no. 16, art. 3, p. 330; 'Radical Reform', *Westminster Review*, vol. 12, no. 23, art. 12, January 1830.

22 On the influence of Cowper and More, see Davidoff & Hall, *Family Fortunes*, pp. 162–72.

23 See Watt, *Rise of the Novel*; E. D. Mackerness, *A Social History of English Music*, London 1966, chs. 2 and 3; J. H. Plumb, 'The Public, Literature and the Arts in the Eighteenth Century', in *The Emergence of Leisure*, ed. M. R. Marrus, New York, 1974.

24 I. Pears, *The Discovery of Painting: The Growth of Interest in the Arts in England, 1680–1768*, New Haven and London 1988.

25 McKendrick, Brewer & Plumb, *Birth of a Consumer Society*, pp. 49–56.

26 P. Bourdieu, 'Intellectual Field and Creative Project', in M. F. D. Young, ed., *Knowledge and Control*, London 1971.

27 R. Williams, *Culture and Society 1780–1950*, Harmondsworth 1961, ch. 2 'The Romantic Artist'; Williams, *Culture*, ch. 2 'Institutions'. See also M. Butler, *Romantics,*

Rebels, & Reactionaries: English Literature and its Background 1760–1830, Oxford 1981, chs. 5 and 8.

28 David Cox seems to have made extensive use of dealers – see N. N. Solly, *Memoir of the Life of David Cox* (1873) London 1973, pp. 24–5, 42, 46. But cf. De Wint's dislike of them – H. Smith, *Peter De Wint 1784–1849*, London 1982, p. 81.

29 A. Yarrington, 'Nelson the Citizen Hero: State and Public Patronage of Monumental Sculpture 1805–18', *Art History*, vol. 6, no. 3, September 1983.

30 On the decline of traditional patronage forms, see Pears, *Discovery of Painting*, ch. 5.

31 'Original Communications, On the Patronage of the Arts', *New Monthly Magazine*, vol. I, no. 2, March 1814, 121–2.

32 'The Rise and Progress of Water-Colour Painting in England, No. VII', *Somerset House Gazette*, no. 11, 20 December 1823, 161.

33 J. J. Prown, *J. S. Copley*, Cambridge, Mass. 1966, vol. II, pp. 289–90, 306; J. Pye, *The Patronage of British Art, An Historical Sketch*, London 1845, pp. 243–4; A. Cunningham, *The Life of Sir David Wilkie*, 3 vols., London 1843, II, pp. 40–1. For a general comment, see S. Uwins, *A Memoir of Thomas Uwins R.A.*, 2 vols., London 1858, vol. II, pp. 150–1.

34 For claims as to Boydell's importance, see Pye, *Patronage of British Art*, p. 249, n. 60. Reynolds is quoted in T. Balston, 'John Boydell, Publisher, "The Commercial Maecenas"', *Signature*, n.s. 8, 1949. In any case the scheme did not produce public art of the type the more ambitious artists wanted.

35 J. Landseer, *Lectures on the Art of Engraving delivered at the Royal Institution of Great Britain*, London 1807, pp. xxxvii, 309–10,n. Cf. his *Letter to the Royal Academy* (1807), quoted in Pye, *Patronage of British Art*, pp. 254–7. This attack was part of a larger critique of the privatized, individualistic culture of the dominant elite.

36 On the politics of engraving in the early nineteenth century, see J. Gage, 'An Early Exhibition and the Politics of British Printmaking, 1800–1812', *Print Quarterly*, vol. 6, no. 2, June 1989.

37 J. Farington, *The Diary of Joseph Farington*, ed. K. Garlick & A. Mackintyre; K. Cave, New Haven & London 1978–84, vol. IV, p. 1517.

38 A. J. Finberg, *The Life of J. M. W. Turner, R. A.*, Oxford 1961, p. 215; J. Gage, ed., *Collected Correspondence of J. M. W. Turner*, Oxford 1980, pp. 104–6; E. Shanes, 'New Light on the "England and Wales" Series', *Turner Studies*, vol. 4, no. 1, Summer 1984, 52–4.

39 T. E. Jones, *A Descriptive Account of the Literary Works of John Britton, F.S.A.*, London 1849, pp. 70–1.

40 The position of women as art patrons in this period is obscure. The British Institution had a small number of substantial female subscribers (i.e. of 100 guineas), and several women among both its Hereditary and Life Governors. In addition to the rather infrequent records of individual picture buyers such as the Countess de Gray and Mrs Hand, the role of women in organizing domestic interiors and their contacts with artists as drawing masters deserve consideration.

41 Cunningham, *Life of Wilkie*, p. 80; W. W. Collins, *Memoirs of the Life of William Collins, Esq., R.A.*, 2 vols., London 1848, vol. I, p. 205. For discussion of this phenomenon, see J. Gear, *Masters or Servants? A Study of Selected English Painters and Their Patrons of the Late Eighteenth and Early Nineteenth Centuries*, New York and London 1977, pp. 254–5.

42 T. Fawcett, *The Rise of English Provincial Art: Artists, Patrons, and Institutions outside London, 1800–1830*, Oxford 1974, ch. 3.

43 Uwins, *Memoir*, vol. II, p. 276. Cf. J. Linnell to S. Palmer 11 June 1839, in A. H. Palmer, *The Life and Letters of Samuel Palmer*, London 1892, p. 66.

44 R. B. Beckett, ed., *John Constable's Correspondence*, 6 vols., Ipswich 1962–8, vol. V, p. 35. Cf. W. Collins to S. Joseph, 28 January 1822, in Collins, *Memoirs*, vol. I, p. 187.

45 Uwins, *Memoir*, vol. II, pp. 264, 262, 235; vol. I, pp. 106, 124–5.

46 Cunningham, *Life of Wilkie*, vol. III, pp. 11–12, 143–5, 147–8, 180–1. Cf. Gear, *Masters or Servants?*, pp. 233–4, 283.
47 Farington, *Diary*, vol. IV, p. 1133.
48 T. Veblen, *The Theory of the Leisure Class* (1899), London 1970, p. 88.
49 M. A. Shee, *Rhymes on Art; or, the Remonstrance of a Painter*, London 1805, p. xxxv; M. A. Shee, *A Letter to the President and Directors of the British Institution*, London 1809, p. 57. In his *Discourse* of 1771, Reynolds had said that painting could be addressed either to the 'noblest faculties', or it could become a 'mere matter of ornament', 'of furnishing our apartments with elegance'. (*Discourse IV*, lines 4–8.)
50 H. Repton, *Sketches and Hints on Landscape Gardening* (1795), in *The Landscape Gardening and Landscape Architecture of the Late Humphry Repton, Esq.*, ed. J. C. Loudon, London 1840, p. 95.
51 M. Pointon, 'Portrait-painting as a Business Enterprise in London in the 1780s', *Art History*, vol. 7, no. 2, June 1984.
52 Uwins, *Memoir*, vol. I, p. 38.
53 See A. Hemingway, 'Academic Theory versus Association Aesthetics: the Ideological Forms of a Conflict of Interests in the early Nineteenth Century', *Ideas and Production*, Issue 5, 1986, 26–35.
54 Gear, *Masters or Servants?*, p. 128; Collins, *Memoirs*, vol. I, pp. 118–31.
55 House of Commons, *Report from the Select Committee on Arts and their Connection with Manufacturers*, 1836. Part II 'Minutes of Evidence and Appendix', p. 108, Q1284; cf. John Martin, p. 78; George Foggo, p. 120, Q1380. A call to end the injustice of the Academy's limited membership was made in the *New Monthly Magazine* in 1815 – see 'Exhibition . . . of the British Institution', vol. 3, no. 15, April 1815, 251.
56 C. M. Kauffmann, *John Varley 1778–1842*, London 1984, p. 33. On Wilkie's campaign to raise his prices in 1807–8, see Gear, *Masters or Servants?*, p. 267. In 1808, Hewlett sold a fruit piece for 400 guineas, and a flower piece for 800 guineas. See 'British Institution', *The Oracle*, 3 March 1808. Cf. the prices of 400 guineas, 180 guineas, and 130 guineas Heaphy achieved for water-colours in 1809–10 – W. T. Whitley, *Thomas Heaphy (1775–1835), First President of the Society of British Artists*, London 1933, pp. 17–18.
57 For sample prices of Turner and Callcott in this period, see D. Hall, 'The Tabley House Paper', *Walpole Society*, vol. 38, 1960–2, 113–14, 120. Crome's receipt is reproduced in N. L. Goldberg, *John Crome the Elder*, 2 vols., Oxford 1978, vol. I, p. 154; S. D. Kitson, *The Life of John Sell Cotman*, London 1937, p. 252.
58 For Collins' prices, see the list of his works in Collins, *Memoirs*, vol. II, pp. 341–52.
59 *Annals of the Fine Arts*, vol. IV, 1819, p. 121. Two years later Crome sold a small *Heath Scene near Norwich* from the British Institution to Sir J. E. Swinburne for thirty guineas – see 'British Gallery', *Literary Gazette*, no. 216, 10 March 1821. The highest price Crome is recorded as receiving is forty guineas from Samuel Paget for *Marlingford Grove* (Lady Lever Art Gallery, Port Sunlight). See C. J. Palmer, *The Perlustration of Great Yarmouth*, Yarmouth 1874, vol. II, p. 397.
60 Fawcett, *Provincial Art*, ch. 1, sections b, c.
61 Farington, *Diary*, vol. IV, p. 1568.
62 Cotman's views on the obloquy of the occupation are well-known, see Kitson, *Life of Cotman*, pp. 158, 272–3. Cf. Farington on the decision of his pupil Henry Salt to become a portrait painter: 'He wd. rather run any risk of difficulties than devote himself to the employ of a drawing master', Farington, *Diary*, vol. IV, p. 1129. In a letter of 1803, Francis Towne repudiated bitterly the stigma of being called 'a provincial drawing master', A. Bury, *Francis Towne, Lone Star of Water-Colour Painting*, London, 1962, p. 51.
63 R. Parker & G. Pollock, *Old Mistresses: Women, Art and Ideology*, London and Henley 1981, pp. 9, 33–5, 90–2, 99.
64 Although women could not study in the Academy life class, they did study in the school of painting provided by the British Institution's 'Old Master' shows.

65 *The Times*, 16 April 1806; 'Angelica Kaufman', *Examiner*, no. 3, 17 January 1808. Comment on *Judith Attended by her Maid* by 'Miss H. A. E. Jackson', 'Exhibition of the British Institution', *New Monthly Magazine*, vol. 1, no. 3, April 1814, 278.

66 'Miss Linwood's Exhibition', *Literary Chronicle*, no. 178, 12 October 1822. Cf. 'Miss Linwood's Pictures in Needlework', *Examiner*, no. 66, 2 April 1809: 'Some of her Pictures are exhibited with scenic effect which, though puerile to the truly tasteful, amuses the million.' For a description of her exhibition, see *The Picture of London, for 1810*, and later editions of that work.

67 'Miss Linwood's Exhibition', *Literary Chronicle*, no. 217, 12 July 1823. 'Mrs Ansley has a remarkable picture, *for a female artist*, and having parts of uncommon vigor, viz. 229, Satan borne back after having been wounded by the Arch-Angel Michael ...', *Literary Gazette*, no. 226, 19 May 1821 (my emphasis). For other references to this artist see: British Institution, *Champion*, no. 267, 15 February 1818; Royal Academy, *Repository of Arts*, series 2, vol. 11, June 1821. On the aptitude of women as water-colourists, see Society of Painters In Water-Colours, *Examiner*, no. 1161, 2 May 1830.

68 Review of Gouldsmith's publication of etchings, *Four Views of Claremont in Surrey, residence of Prince Leopold of Saxe Coburg*, in *Monthly Magazine*, vol. 40, no. 348, January 1820, 567.

69 The only evidence I have discovered which indicates that women artists tried to defend their talents, is a spirited plea against the exclusion of women from the Academy's Lectures on Painting, published in 1822, and signed 'Angelica Appelles': 'Surely, it is not from the superiority of man alone, that science has mounted her lofty throne, and derived all her strength and beauty. Examples of past and present days would throng to place a wreath on the brows of woman, and though we boast not the designating beard, or the brawny sinew, or the mind formed for councils deep, and deeds of high enterprise; yet we may claim the vivid intellect, the brilliant thought, and the refinement of taste; and if we are cast in a more delicate mould, still the fairy form may inclose a mind, in the cultivation of the Fine Arts, worthy to share the palm with the first of creation.' – 'Female Artists', *Morning Post*, 21 February 1822.

70 A partial exception is Bristol-based genre painter Rolinda Sharples. See Bristol City Art Gallery, *The Bristol School of Artists: Francis Danby and Painting in Bristol 1810–1840*, text by Francis Greenacre, Bristol 1973, pp. 211–17.

71 For a contemporary listing of major patrons of British art, see the 'Introductory Address' to J. Britton, *Fine Arts of the English School*, London 1812. Sir Thomas Bernard, Bart., the prime mover in the British Institution, was also very much a product of landed society. See J. Baker, *The Life of Sir Thomas Bernard, Baronet*, London 1819.

72 For Rogers' collection, see J. D. Passavant, *Tour of a German Artist in England*, 2 vols., London 1836, vol. 1, pp. 190–5; and for his taste, see J. R. Hale, *The Italian Journal of Samuel Rogers*, London 1956, especially pp. 188–234. S. Deuchar, *Paintings Politics & Porter: Samuel Whitbread II (1764–1815) and British Art*, London 1984. It has been plausibly suggested that Angerstein's attempt to sell of his collection to the nation at a knock-down price should be interpreted as an exercise in bourgeois 'patriotic activism', designed to assert parity with, if not superiority over, the landed classes. See Colley, *Past & Present* 1986, pp. 110–11.

73 For Davison, see *Annals of the Fine Arts*, vol. 1, no. 2, Art 16, 1816; 'Mr Davison's Pictures', *Literary Chronicle*, no. 216, 5 July 1823.

74 Fawcett, *Provincial Art*, ch. 2; Bristol City Art Gallery, *Bristol School of Artists*.

75 For a discussion of some early collections, see M. Clarke, *The Tempting Prospect: A Social History of English Watercolours*, London 1981, ch. 7.

76 The social position of artists is likely to mean that many of them were affected by the larger conservative shift in middle-class opinion from the mid 1790s, and that those who were not kept quiet about their radical sympathies. See D. Bindman, *The Shadow of the Guillotine: Britain and the French Revolution*, London 1989, pp. 66–74. On the conservative shift among writers, see Butler, *Romantics, Rebels and Reactionaries*, chs. 2–3.

77 Haydon maintained a careful distance from radical politics until the 1830s, and contemporary reports emphasized that his artistic reformism was unconnected with any political reformism. See 'Proposed Royal Academy of Literature', *Examiner*, no. 709, 5 August 1821, 482; and 'Fine Arts', *Monthly Magazine*, vol. 14, no. 83, December 1820, 605.

78 Sir John Leicester's Gallery, *Examiner*, no. 539, 26 April 1818.

4 Philosophical criticism's man of taste

1 P. O. Kristeller, 'The Modern System of the Arts', in *Renaissance Thought II, Papers on Humanism and the Arts*, New York 1965. The main surveys of this literature are: W. J. Hipple, *The Beautiful, the Sublime, & the Picturesque in Eighteenth-Century British Aesthetic Theory*, Carbondale, Ill. 1957; and J. Dobai, *Die Kunstliteratur des Klassizismus und der Romantik in England 1700–1840*, 3 vols., Bern 1974–7.

2 Addison's essays *On the Pleasures of the Imagination* (published in the *Spectator* in 1712), and Frances Hutcheson's *An Inquiry Concerning Beauty, Order, Harmony, Design* (1725) have both been claimed as the first modern aesthetic treatise.

3 The dominant model was, of course, that of Locke's *Essay Concerning Human Understanding* (1690). For the influence of this on eighteenth-century aesthetics, see: E. Tuveson, *The Imagination as a Means of Grace*, Berkeley and Los Angeles 1960, especially ch. I; J. Stolnitz, 'Locke and the Categories of Value in Eighteenth-Century British Aesthetic Theory', *Philosophy*, vol. 38, January 1963. On the emergence of epistemology as the central concern of philosophy in the seventeenth century, see R. Rorty, *Philosophy and the Mirror of Nature*, Princeton, NJ 1979, chs. 1 and 3.

4 According to a review of Alison's *Essays on Taste*, published in 1790: 'all our knowledge is derived by experience; and as it has been from the patient method of experiment and observation that the great discoveries in physical science have been made, it is reasonable to suppose that the same method of research will be equally successful in the philosophy of the human mind' – *Monthly Review*, n.s. vol. 3, December 1790, 361.

5 Compare the concept of the subject which John Barrell has suggested underpins the poetry of James Thomson. See J. Barrell, *English Literature 1730–80: An Equal Wide Survey*, London 1983, ch. 1.

6 I have developed this argument in more detail in my article 'The "Sociology" of Taste in the Scottish Enlightenment', *Oxford Art Journal*, vol. 12, no. 2, 1989.

7 R. L. Meek, *Social Science and the Ignoble Savage*, Cambridge 1976; I. Hont & M. Ignatieff, eds., *Wealth and Virtue: The Shaping of Political Economy in the Scottish Enlightenment*, Cambridge 1983.

8 See A. C. Chitnis, *The Scottish Enlightenment: A Social History*, London 1976; and the bibliography to this work.

9 N. Phillipson, 'Culture and Society in the 18th Century Province: The Case of Edinburgh and the Scottish Enlightenment', in L. Stone, ed., *The University in Society*, 2 vols., London 1975, vol. II, pp. 407–48.

10 N. Phillipson, 'Adam Smith as Civic Moralist', in Hont & Ignatieff, *Wealth and Virtue*. For a brief definition of 'civic humanism', see J. G. A. Pocock, *Politics, Language and Time: Essays on Political Thought and History*, London 1972, ch. 3 'Civic Humanism and its Role in Anglo-American Thought'.

11 For an instance of the naturalization of progress, see J. Millar, *The Origin of the Distinction of Ranks* (1771), reprinted in W. C. Lehmann, *John Millar of Glasgow 1735–1801: His Life and Thought and his Contributions to Sociological Analysis*, Cambridge 1960, pp. 176, 218. On the propensity of *all* human societies to pass through the same pattern of development, see p. 280.

12 A. Smith, *An Inquiry into the Nature and Causes of the Wealth of Nations*, ed. R. H. Campbell & A. S. Skinner; and W. B. Todd, 2 vols., Oxford 1976, vol. I, p. 99.

13 For Hume on the 'middling rank', see D. Forbes, *Hume's Philosophical Politics*,

Cambridge 1975, pp. 176–7; for Smith's characterization of the 'three great orders of society', see Smith *Wealth of Nations*, vol. I, pp. 265–7. For a qualified appraisal of the benefits of urban life and commerce, see: J. Millar, *An Historical View of the English Government*, 4 vols., London 1803, vol. IV, pp. 100, 124–5, 144–56, 246–51. For the critical view of urban commercial culture, see A. Ferguson, *An Essay on the History of Civil Society 1767*, ed. D. Forbes, Edinburgh 1966, pp. 39–40, 56, 145.

14 Ferguson is ultimately contemptuous of periods of refinement, in which the diversions of taste are really only a distraction 'to fill up the blanks of a listless life', and a way of avoiding 'any positive service to ... country, or to mankind.' (*Essay*, pp. 56–7, 256. Cf. pp. 231–2.)

15 Millar, *Historical View*, vol. IV, pp. 144–58, 230. For Millar's politics, see Lehmann, *John Millar*, ch. 7.

16 Millar, *Historical View*, vol. IV, p. 174. Cf. p. 311: 'The diversions and amusements of any people are usually conformable to the progress they have made in the common arts of life.'

17 See Hemingway, *Oxford Art Journal* 1989, for some discussion of these.

18 R. P. Knight, *An Analytical Inquiry into the Principles of Taste* (1805), London 1808, p. 235. Alison had earlier argued that there was potentially no limit to the objects of taste. See A. Alison, *Essays on the Nature and Principles of Taste* (1790, revised edn 1811), 2 vols., Edinburgh 1815, vol. II, p. 433.

19 H. Home (Lord Kames), *Elements of Criticism* (1762), 2 vols., Edinburgh 1785, vol. I p. 333.

20 Ibid., vol. I, p. v. Cf. pp. 11, 100.

21 Ibid., vol. I, p. vii.

22 H. Home, *Sketches of the History of Man* (1774), 4 vols., Edinburgh 1788, vol. I, pp. 214, 277.

23 On this, see for example Smith, *Wealth of Nations*, vol. I, p. 181.

24 Home, *Sketches*, vol. I, p. 282.

25 Ibid., pp. 210–11.

26 Home, *Sketches*, vol. II, pp. 330, 334, 135–53, 339.

27 It is notable that Smith alleged it was weak men who are drawn to the Fine Arts, exemplifying the point through the person of Shaftesbury. See A. Smith, *Lectures on Rhetoric and Belles Lettres*, ed. J. C. Bryce, Oxford 1983, p. 57.

28 M. Kallich, *The Association of Ideas and Critical Theory in Eighteenth-Century England*, The Hague and Paris 1970.

29 For example, see 'The Modern Athens', *London Magazine*, series 2, vol. 2, no. 8, August 1825, 505–7.

30 Alison, *Essays*, vol. I, p. xv.

31 Alison, *Essays*, vol. II, pp. 108–14.

32 Ibid., pp. 116–17; cf. Home, *Elements*, vol. I, p. 358.

33 Alison, *Essays*, vol. II, pp. 199–200.

34 Ibid., pp. 254–7, 433.

35 Ibid., pp. 274–6, 363, 393, 408.

36 Alison, *Essays*, vol. I, p. 63.

37 Ibid., p. 89. Cf. vol. II, p. 160.

38 Alison, *Essays*, vol. I, p. 10.

39 Royal Academy, *Repository of Arts*, series 2, vol. I, June 1816, 354, 352.

40 On Knight, see J. Messmann, *Richard Payne Knight: The Twilight of Virtuosity*, The Hague 1974; M. Clarke & N. Penny, eds., *The Arrogant Connoisseur: Richard Payne Knight 1751–1824*, Manchester 1982 – and the review by A. Potts, 'A Man of Taste's Picturesque', *Oxford Art Journal*, vol. 5, no. 1, 1982.

41 Knight, *Analytical Inquiry*, p. 1. Cf. on the vague and extensive 'usage of the term "beauty"', p. 9.

42 Ibid., p. 294.

43 A review of the *Analytical Inquiry* in the *Monthly Review*, vol. 40, June 1806, implied Knight had not acknowledged his debts to Hartley (149).

44 Knight, *Analytical Inquiry*, pp. 18, 95, 99.
45 Ibid., p. 146.
46 Ibid., pp. 293–4; and Knight's review of J. Northcote, *The Life of Sir Joshua Reynolds*, *Edinburgh Review*, vol. 23, September 1814, 263.
47 Knight, *Edinburgh Review* 1814, p. 276. For Knight's essentially pessimistic vision of the prospects of British society, which accords well with J. G. A. Pocock's 'civic humanist' paradigm, see his *Progress of Civil Society, A Didactic Poem in Six Books*, London 1796, especially pp. 134–53. On the insatiable character of human desires, see p. 79.
48 Knight, *Analytical Inquiry*, pp. 457–60, 18, 475–6. For Knight's 'Almighty universal soul' which 'Lives in each part and regulates the whole', see his *A Monody on the Death of the Right Honourable Charles James Fox*, London 1806–7, p. 12.
49 Knight, *Analytical Inquiry*, pp. 252, 263–5.
50 Ibid., pp. 234–5.
51 Ibid., pp. 240–1. For Knight on academies see also *Edinburgh Review* 1814, 279–80. In his review of Northcote's *Life of Reynolds*, Knight praises some contemporary British art and criticizes the government for wasting money on victory fêtes 'to attract the stupid gaze of a dissolute populace' when it would not support the British Institution (287–9). Yet in his review of Barry's *Works* (*Edinburgh Review*, vol. 17, August 1810), he asserts that British painters have not lacked patronage (309–10), and expresses doubts as to the effectivity of the British Institution (324), partly because he saw it as committed to a misguided concept of High Art.
52 Knight, *Analytical Inquiry*, p. 151.
53 Ibid., p. 308. Cf. Knight, *Edinburgh Review* 1814, 285–7.
54 Knight, *Analytical Inquiry*, p. 310.
55 Ibid., pp. 418–19.
56 Ibid., pp. 311–12.
57 R. P. Knight, *The Landscape, A Didactic Poem in Three Books*, (1794) London 1795, pp. 84–6.
58 See Hemingway, *Ideas and Production* 1986. On Knight's patronage of contemporary art see Clarke & Penny, *Arrogant Connoisseur*, ch. 7. In 1815, the academician Thomas Phillips referred to 'the presumption & self sufficiency with which his dogmas have been issued', and such a view was commonplace among artists. See T. Phillips to D. Turner, 25 June 1815, Dawson Turner Correspondence. Phillips' letters to Turner provide a clear record of academic resentment towards the British Institution.
59 A. Smith, *The Theory of Moral Sentiments*, ed. D. D. Raphael & A. L. Macfie, Oxford 1976, p. 190; Lehmann, *John Millar*, pp. 219–20.
60 Kames, *Sketches*, vol. II, p. 3; 'Of Essay Writing' in D. Hume, *Essays, Moral, Political and Literary*, Oxford 1963.
61 An indication of the suspect connotations of the term taste is provided by Mary Wollstonecraft's repeated insistence that taste without judgement is merely emotion. See M. Wollstonecraft, *A Vindication of the Rights of Woman*, ed. M. Brody, Harmondsworth 1975, pp. 160, 166, 183, 223, 277, 284–5.

5 Philosophical criticism and the science of landscape

1 See J. Stolnitz, '"Beauty", Some Stages in the History of An Idea', *Journal of the History of Ideas*, vol. 22, no. 2, 1961; S. H. Monk, *The Sublime: A Study of Critical Theories in XVIII–Century England*, Ann Arbor 1960.
2 J. Redwood, *Reason, Ridicule and Religion: The Age of Enlightenment in England 1660–1750*, London 1976, chs. 4–6.
3 M. H. Nicolson, *Mountain Gloom and Mountain Glory: The Development of the Aesthetics of the Infinite*, Ithaca 1959, especially chs. 2–6; Redwood, *Reason, Ridicule, and Religion*, ch. 5.
4 *The Spectator*, vol. 3, no. 412.
5 E. Burke, *A Philosophical Enquiry into the Origin of our Ideas of the Sublime and Beautiful* 1759, Menston 1970, pp. 127–9.

6 Nicolson, *Mountain Gloom and Mountain Glory*, ch. 8, 'A New Descriptive Poetry'.

7 J. Butler, *The Analogy of Religion, Natural and Revealed, to the Constitution and Course of Nature*, London 1736, p. 181.

8 W. Paley, *Natural Theology: or, Evidences of the Existence and Attributes of the Deity, Collected from the Appearance of Nature*, London 1803, especially pp. 524–6. (This work went through twenty editions, 1802–20.) On the social functions of the Anglican Church, see A. D. Gilbert, *Religion and Society in Industrial England: Church, Chapel, and Social Change, 1740–1914*, London and New York 1976, pp. 74–81.

9 A. Cooper, *Characteristics of Men, Opinions, Times* (1711, revised edition 1714), 3 vols., London 1714, vol. II, pp. 345, 372; Redwood, *Reason, Ridicule, and Religion*, p. 84.

10 Alison, *Essays*, vol. II, pp. 38, 196.

11 Ibid., p. 146; vol. I, p. 179. Reid makes the apprehension of beauty dependent on an 'internal taste', but suggests that 'grandeur' results from the effects of objects as signs. See his 'Of Taste', in *Essays on the Intellectual Powers of Man*, Edinburgh and London 1785, pp. 714–20, 730–3, 749. In his unpublished lectures, Reid makes knowledge of some signs innate, while others have to be learned. See P. Kivy, *Thomas Reid's Lectures on the Fine Arts*, The Hague 1973, pp. 3, 9, 29–34. Dobai has described Reid's theory as 'protosemiologische' (*Kunstliteratur*, Bd. II, p. 141).

12 Alison, *Essays*, vol. I, p. 37.

13 Ibid., p. 90.

14 Ibid., p. 121.

15 Ibid., pp. 125–6.

16 J. Constable to M. Bicknell, 28 August 1814: 'I am delighted with Alison's book on the nature and principles of Taste. I prefer it to Mr Burke's as I think it more just and its conclusions more sublime – indeed the conclusion of the last Essay "of the Final Cause and of the Constitution of our Nature" is by far the most beautifull thing, I ever read.' Beckett, *Constable Correspondence*, vol. II, p. 131.

17 Alison, *Essays*, vol. II, pp. 96–103.

18 Ibid., p. 444.

19 Although Payne Knight makes ideas of infinity and immensity productive of sublime emotions (Knight, *Analytical Inquiry*, p. 368), he gives far more attention to power, moral sympathy, and pathos as causes. This lack of concern with natural theology is consistent with his scepticism.

20 F. Jeffrey, review of Alison's *Essays on Taste, Edinburgh Review*, vol. 18, May 1811, 15. The same point is made in Hallam's review of Payne Knight's *Analytical Inquiry, Edinburgh Review*, vol. 7, January 1806, 324.

21 W. Wordsworth, *Wordsworth's Guide to the Lakes*, ed. E. de Selincourt, Oxford 1977, pp. 152, 162–4. See also Nicolson, *Mountain Gloom and Mountain Glory*, 'Epilogue'.

22 Nigel Everett has demonstrated the profound homology between the landscape aesthetics of William Gilpin and Uvedale Price and contemporary thinking on rural social problems, while Stephen Daniells has shown how developments in Humphry Repton's theory of landscape gardening were related to his increasing political conservatism and distaste for the social changes engendered by the Anglo-French Wars. See N. H. Everett, 'Country Justice: The Literature of Landscape Improvement and English Conservatism, with Particular Reference to the 1790s', unpublished Ph.D. thesis, University of Cambridge 1977; S. Daniels, 'The Political Landscape', in G. Carter, P. Goode, & K. Laurie, eds., *Humphry Repton, Landscape Gardener 1752–1818*, (catalogue to an exhibition at the University of East Anglia) Norwich 1982. See also Daniels' excellent essay 'The Political Iconography of Woodland in later Georgian England', in D. Cosgrove & S. Daniels, eds., *The Iconography of Landscape: Essays on the Symbolic Representation, Design and Use of Past Environments*, Cambridge 1988.

23 Price, *Essays*, vol. I, pp. viii, 93.

24 Everett, 'Country Justice', p. 111. For Price's social vision, see his *Thoughts on the Defense of Property, Addressed to the County of Hereford*, Hereford 1797; and Everett, Section 2, ch. 1 – 'Uvedale Price and the Politics of the Picturesque'.

25 Repton's 1794 letter is printed in Price, *Essays*, vol. III, pp. 3–22. For Price's response to the political analogy, see vol. III, p. 178. Cf. Price, *Thoughts*, pp. 17–18. For Repton on 'GENERAL UTILITY', see *Landscape Gardening*, p. 124; on agricultural landscape, see pp. 210–11.

26 Price, *Essays*, vol. II, p. 394. This theme was taken up in E. Bartell, *Hints for Picturesque Improvements in Ornamented Cottages and their Scenery: Including Some Observations on the Labourer and his Cottage, in Three Essays*, London 1804 – Essay III.

27 On Burke's rejection of associationism see M. Kallich, 'The Argument against the Association of Ideas in Eighteenth-Century Aesthetics', *Modern Language Quarterly*, vol. 15, March 1954.

28 Price, *Essays*, vol. I, pp. 50–1. Cf. pp. 22–3, vol. I, p. 218; vol. II, p. 247.

29 For Price's admiration for Reynolds and the *Discourses*, see Price, *Essays*, vol. I, p. 236; vol. III, pp. 208–9.

30 Price, *Essays*, vol. I, pp. xii–xiii, vol. II, p. 309, vol. I, pp. 41–2, vol. II, pp. 324–6, 335, vol. I, pp. 154–5, 129, 134.

31 Knight, *Analytical Inquiry*, p. 377. Cf. pp. 27, 59–60.

32 Ibid., p. 63.

33 Ibid., pp. 95, 152–4. Thus 'if the scale of imitation in that art should be hereafter extended, the boundaries of the picturesque will be extended in the same proportion'. (p. 154).

34 Knight, *The Landscape*, pp. 26–9, 42. Like Price, Knight seems to envisage a smooth transition from park to farmland here.

35 Knight, *The Landscape*, p. 46. Cf. *Edinburgh Review*, vol. 7, January 1806, 314–15: 'There is a good deal of narrowness and pedantry in the race of professional artists, which leads them to depreciate everything that will not easily bear delineation [. . .] With these chime in, of course, the children of poetry and romance, who admire nothing but rural simplicity; and sicken at all appearance of those terrible things art and opulence.'

36 Review of Payne Knight's *Analytical Inquiry, British Critic*, vol. 29, January 1807, 17.

37 *Edinburgh Review*, vol. 18, May 1811, 39.

38 I. Fleming-Williams, 'A Runnover Dungle and a Possible Date for "Spring"', *Burlington Magazine*, vol. 114, June 1972; M. Rosenthal, *Constable: The Painter and his Landscape*, New Haven and London 1983, pp. 82–7.

39 D. Stewart, *Philosophical Essays*, Edinburgh and London 1816, pp. 305–7.

40 Stewart, *Philosophical Essays*, pp. 330, 516–17. In what seems like a premonition of Vološinov, Stewart argued the primary role of language in establishing associations: '*Language* serves as a common channel or organ for uniting all the agreeable impressions of which the senses, the understanding, and the heart, are susceptible' (p. 359).

41 Halévy, *Philosophic Radicalism*, pp. 6–11.

42 Payne Knight did acknowledge that pleasurable associations were generated by 'marts thronged with the bustle of commerce, seaports crowded with shipping, plains enriched by culture and population', Knight, *Analytical Inquiry*, p. 196.

43 F. W. Stokoe, *German Influence in the English Romantic Period 1788–1818*, Cambridge 1926, ch. 3. Taylor published about 1,750 articles 1793–1824. The main source on Taylor is J. W. Robberds, *A Memoir of the Life and Writings of the Late William Taylor of Norwich*, 2 vols., London 1843.

44 W. Taylor, 'Outlines of a Discourse on a History and Theory of Prospect Painting', *Monthly Magazine*, vol. 37, 405–9; vol. 38, 211–15, 499–503, 1814, vol. 37, 407.

45 *Monthly Magazine*, vol. 37, 408.

46 This is consistent with views Taylor expressed in his correspondence. See Taylor to Thomas Dyson, in Robberds, *Memoir*, vol. II, p. 460; Taylor to Southey, 30 November 1802, vol. I, pp. 432–3; and Taylor to Southey, 1 March 1815, vol. II, p. 455.

47 *Monthly Magazine*, vol. 38, 500–3.

48 'The Colosseum', *London Magazine*, series 3, vol. 3, no. 11, February 1829, 105–8.

49 On the middle class and the suburbs, see Davidoff & Hall, *Family Fortunes*.

50 See J. Hoppner, review of Payne Knight's *Analytical Inquiry*, *The Artist*, vol. I, no. 11; 'On the Principles of Taste' (a critique of Alison's *Essays on Taste*), *Magazine of the Fine Arts*, vol. I, nos. 5–6, 1821; 'On Beauty', Lecture Fourteen in B. R. Haydon, *Lectures on Painting and Design*, 2 vols., London 1844, 1846. I have discussed these texts in Hemingway, *Ideas and Production*, 1986.

51 Turner seems to have engaged with association theory in the course of preparing his Lectures on Perspective, and he refers to the principle in a lecture of 1812. (See J. Gage, *Colour in Turner: Poetry and Truth*, London 1969, p. 200.) It is symptomatic of the fundamentally academic orientation of his thought at this time, that he rejected Payne Knight's argument that the association of ideas produced an emotional response, whereas nature in itself could not. See B. Venning, 'Turner's Annotated Books: Opie's "Lectures on Painting" and Shee's "Elements of Art"' (Parts I and III), *Turner Studies*, vol. 2, no. 1, 39–40, 45–6, n. 45; vol. 3, no. 1, 38–9.

52 In *English Landscape*, Constable refers to 'all its endearing associations' (Beckett, *Discourses*, p. 9), and the text to the plate of Old Sarum is explicitly an account of the associations of the scene.

53 J. Varley, *A Treatise on the Principles of Landscape Design*, London 1816–17. This passage should be compared with David Cox's argument in his *Treatise on Landscape Painting and Effect in Water Colours* (London 1814). Cox emphasizes that the artist should strive to keep his different works 'subservient' to the 'principal object' which initially attracted him to the view they represent, avoiding all 'objects which are not in character with the scene'. Cox makes no explicit reference to the association principle in his *Treatise*, and while his emphasis on the unified character of the scene is comparable with Varley's, he seems to envisage this being apprehended in a more intuitive way through the artist achieving 'a proper feeling' for the subject.

54 W. B. Cooke, *Views in Sussex, Drawn by J. M. W. Turner, R.A. and Engraved by W. B. Cooke* (text by R. R. Reinagle), London 1819. John Gage has discussed the significance of Reinagle's text from a slightly different perspective in Gage, *Colour in Turner*, p. 134.

6 Naturalism and the academic ideal

1 This was understood by Haydon's supporter James Elmes, editor of the *Annals of the Fine Arts*. In 1820 the magazine claimed that the innovations of Haydon and Wilkie had produced a reform in British art exemplified by the work of Callcott, Cooper, Collins, Mulready, Sharpe and Constable – see 'Royal Academy', vol. 5, 1820, 388–9. Although the claim is absurd, it demonstrates that naturalism in landscape painting was perceived as part of a wider tendency.

2 This veneration of Reynolds is well illustrated in Lawrence's *Address to the Students of the Royal Academy . . . 10th December 1823*, London 1824, p. 7.

3 See, for instance, Wark, *Reynolds*, *Disc. VII*, lines 209–12.

4 The phrase comes from R. H. Horne, *Exposition of the False Medium and Barriers Excluding Men of Genius from the Public*, London 1833, p. 26. This contains an extended critique of the Academy, pp. 73–84, 224–33. See also 'The Royal Academy Exposed', *New Monthly Magazine*, vol. 38, July-August 1833 (by George Foggo); and Houses of Commons, *Report from the Select Committee on Arts and Their Connection with Manufacturers*, Part II, 1836 – evidence of Foggo, Haydon, Hofland, Hurlstone, Martin, Rennie.

5 C. A. Du Fresnoy, *The Art of Painting*, tr. J. Dryden, London 1769, pp. lxi, xxxiv. On the sources of Reynolds' theory, see F. W. Hilles, *The Literary Career of Sir Joshua Reynolds*, Cambridge 1936 (1967 reprint), ch. 7; R. W. Lee, *'Ut pictura poesis': The Humanistic Theory of Painting*, New York 1970. On the Empiricist and Rationalist paradigms, see M. C. Beardsley, *Aesthetics from Classical Greece to the Present*, Alabama 1975, chs. 7, 8.

6 Wark, *Reynolds*, *Disc. VI*, lines 151–8.

7 Du Fresnoy, *Art*, p. 9; R. De Piles, *The Art of Painting* (tr. B. Buckeridge), London n.d., ch. 22, 'Of the Licenses'. Cf. Richardson: 'Rules may be established so clearly derived from reason as to be utterly indisputable.' – J. Richardson, *The Works of Mr Jonathan Richardson*, ed. J. Richardson, jun., London 1772, p. 303.

8 E. Young, *Conjectures on Original Composition*, London 1759 (1966 reprint), p. 28; J. Reynolds, *The Works of Sir Joshua Reynolds*, ed. E. Malone, London 1809, vol. II. In some of his other writings, Reynolds' emphasis on the limitations of rules is even stronger. For example, see his *Notes on the Art of Painting*, ibid., pp. 181–2.

9 For example, Richardson in his *Essay on Criticism*: 'Whatever authorities there may be for any proposition, the single values of these themselves consists in their being derived from reason . . . ' (Richardson, *Works*, pp. 173–4).

10 Wark, *Reynolds*, *Disc. VII*, lines 333–41.

11 For example, Wark, *Reynolds*, *Disc. XIII*, lines 209–15.

12 Wark, *Reynolds*, *Disc. II*, lines 122–3. A. O. Lovejoy, '"Nature" as Aesthetic Norm', ch. 5 in *Essays in the History of Ideas*, Baltimore 1948; M. Macklem, 'Reynolds and the Ambiguities of Neo-Classical Criticism', *Philological Quarterly*, vol. 31, October 1952.

13 John Barrell has argued that Reynolds' political outlook led him to advocate a norm of taste founded on abstract reason in the first six of his *Discourses*, but that thereafter changes in his political orientation made him increasingly represent taste as the product of custom, feeling, and imagination. I have argued against this interpretation elsewhere. See Barrell, *Political Theory*, ch. I; Hemingway, *Art History*, 1987, pp. 384–8.

14 Reynolds, *Works*, vol. II, p. 242.

15 Wark, *Reynolds*, *Disc. VII*, lines 181–5. For a discussion of Reynolds' use of associationism see Wark's Introduction pp. xxiv–xxxv.

16 J. Barry, *The Works of James Barry*, ed. J. Fryer, 2 vols., London 1809. For the norm of beauty, see vol. I, pp. 393–403. For a use of association, see vol. I, p. 405.

17 Wornum, *Lectures*, pp. 245–6, 276.

18 J. Knowles, *The Life and Writings of Henry Fuseli*, 3 vols., London 1831, vol. II, pp. 21–2, vol. III, p. 41–2, vol. II, pp. 134–5, 306. Fuseli found unacceptable Alison's proposition that matter is in itself incapable of producing emotion, but only functions as a sign for emotions with which it had become connected by convention and habit; and especially 'specious' his 'controverting the beauty of forms'. See his review of Alison's *Essays on Taste*, *Analytical Review*, series I, vol. 7, May 1790, 28.

19 T. Phillips, *Lectures on the History and Principles of Painting*, London 1833, pp. 265–6, 254, 300–1, 423. H. Howard, *A Course of Lectures on Painting Delivered at the Royal Academy of Fine Arts*, ed. F. Howard, London 1848, pp. 25, 69–71, 93, 64–5.

20 J. Galt, *The Life and Studies of Benjamin West*, 2 parts, London 1816, 1820, part II, p. 91. Cf. Opie on drawing, Wornum, *Lectures*, p. 249.

21 'we shall continue to think that positive beauty resides in form, independently of any mental qualities and passions, and capable of expressing them all'. 'On the Principles of Taste', *Magazine of the Fine Arts*, vol. I, 1821, 418.

22 Wark, *Reynolds*, *Disc. XV*, lines 362–8. For Reynolds, the sublime style is the product of genius beyond the realm of rules.

23 See his letter to Gilpin in Gilpin, *Three Essays*. Reynolds uses the term picturesque in a way consonant with the views he set out in the letter in *Discourse X* of 1780.

24 Howard, *Lectures*, pp. 141, 144–5.

25 Wark, *Reynolds*, *Disc. IX*, lines 80–6.

26 Wark, *Reynolds*, *Disc. III*, lines 292–5. On the refining mission of painting, see also Barry to C. J. Fox, 5 October 1800, Barry, *Works*, vol. I, p. 287; Fuseli in Knowles, *Life*, vol. II, pp. 331–2; J. Flaxman, *Lectures on Sculpture*, London and New York 1892, p. 192.

27 Wark, *Reynolds*, *Disc. III*, lines 284–5.

28 The source for the hierarchy of genres in Reynolds' writing is French theory. See A. Félibien, *Seven Conferences Held in the King of France's Cabinet of Paintings*, tr. T. Cooper, London 1740, pp. xxvii–xxviii.

29 For example, Fuseli in Knowles, *Life*, pp. 134–5, 305–6; Phillips, *Lectures*, pp. 254, 333.
30 Knowles, *Life*, vol. II, p. 217; Phillips, *Lectures*, p. 284.
31 J. Ziff, '"Backgrounds: Introduction of Architecture and Landscape": A Lecture by J. M. W. Turner', *Journal of the Warburg and Courtauld Institutes*, vol. 26, 1963, 133, 145–6.
32 Knowles, *Life*, vol. II, p. 341–2; Opie in Wornum, *Lectures*, pp. 326–7.
33 Du Fresnoy, *Art of Painting*, p. 40; Richardson, 'Of Composition' (although he does not use the term breadth), Richardson, *Works*, pp. 64ff.; W. Hogarth, *The Analysis of Beauty*, London 1753, p. 112; Reynolds in 'Notes on The Art of Painting', *Works*, vol. III, pp. 150–1.
34 Barry, *Works*, vol. I, p. 487.
35 See, for example, the contrast of British and French art in 'New York Academy Exhibition', *Annals of the Fine Arts*, vol. 3, 1818, 489–90; Howard, *Lectures*, p. 141.
36 'On Composition in Painting', *The Artist*, vol. II, 1809, pp. 155–6.
37 See J. Crome to J. Stark, 1816, in D. & T. Clifford, *John Crome*, London 1968, p. 90; Beckett, *Discourses*, pp. 9, 24.
38 Barry, *Works*, vol. I, pp. 243, 286–91; vol. II, pp. 571–4. On Barry's politics, see Barrell, *Political Theory*, ch. 2; Hemingway, *Art History*, 1987, pp. 388–9.
39 Wark, *Reynolds*, *Disc. V*, lines 419–23. On exhibitions and taste, see also Barry, *Works*, vol. II, pp. 254–5. On the exclusion of 'inferior people' from art exhibitions, see Pye, *Patronage of British Art*, pp. 96, 172–3.
40 Wark, *Reynolds*, *Disc. III*, lines 136–41.
41 Wark, *Reynolds*, *Disc. V*, lines 404–7.
42 On the vulgarity of the Dutch, see Barry, *Works*, vol. I, p. 376. Knowles, *Life*, vol. II, pp. 122, 192, 389; Phillips, *Lectures*, pp. 145–6.
43 Wark, *Reynolds*, *Disc. IV*, lines 1–8.
44 Wark, *Reynolds*, *Disc. I*, lines 10–12. Reynolds was almost certainly referring to the mercantile argument put forward in the 1755 Circular *Plan of an Academy* which argued it was a disgrace that the 'commonwealth' should import anything which it could properly produce itself. (Printed in Pye, *Patronage of Art*, pp. 75–6.)
45 See, for example, Shee, on the status of the artist in the Ancient World, in M. A. Shee, *Rhymes on Art: or, the Remonstrance of a Painter*, London 1805, pp. xxxv–xxxvi. Flaxman makes the point particularly clearly in his 'Memorial Address on Thomas Banks' (1805), quoting Rollin's *Introduction to the Arts and Sciences*, that in the 'assemblage of the learned', 'the plebeian finds himself on a level with the nobleman, the subject with the prince, nay, often his superior'. Flaxman, *Lectures*, pp. 277–8.
46 For Reynolds' politics, see Royal Academy, *Reynolds* (catalogue by N. Penny et al.), London 1986, pp. 34–5.
47 'The Ironical Discourse' in F. W. Hilles, *Portraits by Sir Joshua Reynolds*, London 1952, Appendix II, p. 128. This was inspired by Burke's *Reflections on the French Revolution* of the same year. Cf. Burke on the social composition of the Tiers Etat, in E. Burke, *Reflections on the French Revolution*, London and New York 1910 (Everyman edn), pp. 39–40; and their method of legislation, pp. 181–2.
48 On Burke and Reynolds, see Hilles, *Portraits*, pp. 123–46; and also R. W. Uphaus, 'The Ideology of Reynolds's Discourses on Art', *Eighteenth-Century Studies*, vol. 12, Fall 1978. For Burke on the inherited wisdom of political institutions, see Burke, *Reflections*, pp. 164–6.
49 Lee, '*Ut pictura poesis*', pp. 5–7.
50 Barry, *Works*, vol. II, p. 248.
51 M. A. Shee, *A Letter to the President and Directors of the British Institution*, London 1809, p. 7.
52 Shee, *Rhymes*, p. 26n. See Barry to C. J. Fox, 5 October 1800, on his aims to 'raise the reputation of the country even in despite of the patronage of it'. Barry, *Works*, vol. I, p. 287. On the martyrology of British art, see Shee, *Rhymes*, pp. 12–13; Haydon, *Lectures*, vol. I, pp. 41, 104.

53 For an example, see 'Royal Academy Exhibition', *Examiner*, no. 697, 13 May 1821.

54 In Haydon's case, his views were set out in articles in the *Champion*, *Examiner*, *London Magazine*, and *Annals of the Fine Arts* from 1812 onwards. Constable's position was developed only in his correspondence.

55 Beckett, *Discourses*, pp. 48, 57.

56 Haydon, *Lectures*, vol. I, p. 321; vol. II, p. 194. For further comments on Reynolds, see vol. I, pp. 169–70, 177–9, 193–4, 245, vol. II, p. 34. The idea that the great work of art is the equivalent of some quality in the mind of the genius, or some emotion *he* has experienced, is a commonplace of Romantic criticism. See, for example, Hazlitt 'On Gusto', *Complete Works*, vol. IV.

57 Haydon, *Lectures*, vol. I, pp. 178–9, 127. For Hazlitt, the Elgin Marbles had 'every appearance of absolute fac-similes or casts taken from nature'. *Complete Works*, vol. XVIII, p. 145.

58 Haydon, *Lectures*, vol. I, pp. 208, 257–8, 7.

59 Beckett, *Discourses*, p. 48. By contrast he recommended the example of Titian, who with 'equal breadth' made 'every touch a representation of reality'. Constable's view of Titian's achievement was strikingly close to Payne Knight's – see *Edinburgh Review*, 1814, 285.

60 Beckett, *Constable's Correspondence*, vol. V, p. 30.

61 Beckett, *Discourses*, p. 58. Cf. pp. 60–1. For an account of Constable's theory, see L. Hawes, *John Constable's Writings on Art*, Ph.D. thesis, Princeton University 1963, (Ann Arbor University Microfilms 1964). On manner, see ch. 1, section 3.

62 For example, Shee, *Elements*, p. 269n. See also the discussion of use of the term in art criticism in ch. 7.

63 Beckett, *Discourses*, p. 68.

64 Ibid., pp. 68, 83, 46, 58, 53. Constable regarded Claude's *Landscape with Goatherd and Goats* (National Gallery, London), as a 'study from nature', Beckett, *Constable's Correspondence*, vol. VI, p. 139. Cf. Hazlitt: 'Claude could only have painted his landscapes in the open air; and the Greek statues were little more than copies from living everyday forms.' *Complete Works*, vol. XVI, p. 196.

65 Louis Hawes has aptly likened Constable's approach of selecting from observations of everyday life to that of Wordsworth, and his critique of the academic ideal, manner, and grand subjects to Hazlitt's theory. See Hawes, *Constable's Writings*, pp. 106, 118–20; and more generally chs. 5 and 6.

66 Haydon, *Lectures*, vol. I, pp. 301, 310–11, 316.

67 Beckett, *Constable's Correspondence*, vol. III, pp. 18–19; vol. VI, p. 181.

68 Beckett, *Discourses*, p. 40.

69 The resentments felt by landscape painters over the hierarchical distinctions within the artistic profession seem to have been shared by genre painters like Wilkie and Mulready, and led to a reformulation of academic theory in the Lectures of Constable's friend and biographer, the genre painter Leslie (Professor 1847–52). In the *Handbook for Young Painters*, which he based on his lectures, Leslie repeatedly criticized the whole principle of 'Classification'. See C. R. Leslie, *Handbook for Young Painters* (1855), London 1887, pp. 50, 58, 255–6, 281–2. He claimed that Constable shared his view – see C. R. Leslie, *Memoirs of the Life of John Constable*, ed. B. Nicolson, London 1949, p. 303.

70 Cf. Barry, *Works*, vol. I, pp. 547–8, 553–7; Knowles, *Life*, vol. II, pp. 107–13, vol. III, pp. 35–6.

71 Haydon, *Lectures*, vol. II, pp. 91, 156.

72 Beckett, *Discourses*, pp. 46, 65, 63. In his lecture on Painting and Poetry, read before the Norwich Philosophical Society in 1818, John Berney Crome took a similar line, referring particularly to Ruisdael and Hobbema – although he also acknowledged the Reynoldsian principle of general form. (Manuscript in Norwich Castle Museum, pp. 4–5, 9–10.)

73 Constable's work of the 1820s presented problems for some critics precisely because his

broken surfaces and shimmering light effects seemed to lack unity or breadth. Thus the *Literary Gazette* observed of *The Haywain*: 'Notwithstanding the excellence of the composition, and some beautiful touches of nature, there is a want of effect in this landscape, arising principally from those scattered and glittering lights that pervade every part' (no. 228, 2 June 1821, 346).

74 Beckett, *Discourses*, pp. 62–3. Cf. pp. 53, 87. It should be noted that Uvedale Price had recommended the work of Ostade and Dou as exemplifying the unity of detail with breadth, Price, *Essays*, vol. I, p. 156.

75 For a definition, see M. H. Abrams, *The Mirror and the Lamp: Romantic Theory and the Critical Tradition*, Oxford 1971, p. 22.

76 Young, *Conjectures*, p. 10.

77 Hazlitt, *Complete Works*, vol. XX, p. 302.

78 Beckett, *Discourses*, p. 39, 67, 65, 10, 82–3. Writing of Wilson in a letter to Fisher of 1823, Constable says: 'He was one of the great appointments to shew to the world the hidden stores and beauties of Nature. One of the great men to shew to the world what exists in nature but which was not known till his time.' – Beckett, *Constable's Correspondence*, vol. VI, p. 117.

79 Beckett, *Discourses*, p. 9. See for example, Beckett, *Constable's Correspondence*, vol. V, p. 35; vol. VI, pp. 63, 103.

80 Beckett, *Discourses*, pp. 69–71.

81 *Rhymes on Art* went through two editions in 1805. For reviews, see *Morning Herald*, 23 February 1805, 28 March 1805; and the *London Review*, vol. 2, 1809, 372–406 (largely negative).

82 Shee, *Elements*, p. 363; Shee, *Rhymes*, pp. xii–xiii, 31n., xx–xxi.

83 Shee, *Rhymes*, pp. lvi, lvii. (Cf. p. 85, and Shee, *Elements*, pp. 226–8); *Rhymes*, pp. 50–3. (Cf. *Elements*, pp. 376, 385); *Rhymes*, pp. 55–62.

84 Shee, *Elements*, pp. 379–80. Cf. Shee, *Rhymes*, p. lix.

85 Shee, *Letter*, pp. 81–2n.; Shee, *Elements*, pp. xxxv–xxxvi; Shee, *Rhymes*, pp. 42–43n. 80; *Elements*, p. 347n.

86 Knowles, *Life*, vol. III, pp. 43–4, 53–4, 47–8; vol. II, pp. 216–18; vol. III, pp. 56–7.

87 Phillips, *Lectures*, p. 426. Cf. pp. 202, 222.

88 On 'public' and 'private' patronage, see Haydon, *Lectures*, vol. II, pp. 94–5; on the limitations of aristocratic patronage, see vol. II, p. 144; on the taste of the middle classes, see on Martin, vol. I, p. 319; on art and 'the people', see vol. II, p. 100.

89 Haydon, *Lectures*, vol. I, p. 323. Kensington Gravel Pits was a subject associated with Linnell and Mulready.

90 Richter, *Daylight*, pp. 54, 57.

91 Hilles, *Portraits*, p. 144.

92 For instance, Gilpin claimed of the sketch: 'And in those happy moments when the enthusiasm of his art is upon him, he [i.e. the "master"] often produces from the glow of his imagination, with a few bold strokes, such wonderful effusions of genius, as the more sober and correct productions of his pencil cannot equal.' – Gilpin, *Three Essays*, p. 62. Cf. Knight, *Analytical Inquiry*, pp. 103–4.

7 Art criticism and the politics of landscape

1 The literature on art criticism in Britain is very slight. See Dobai, *Kunstliteratur*, Bd. III, Pt I, 8 'Zeitschristen'; H. E. Roberts, 'Exhibition and review: the periodical press and the Victorian art exhibition system', in J. Shattock & M. Wolff, eds., *The Victorian Periodical Press: Samplings and Soundings*, Leicester and Toronto 1982. A significant recent contribution is J. C. Ivy, *Constable and the Critics 1802–1837*, Woodbridge and Rochester, NY 1991. Literary historians have done useful work in charting the periodical field, see: J. O. Hayden, *The Romantic Reviewers 1802–24*, London 1969; A. Sullivan, *British Literary Magazines: The Romantic Age 1789–1836*, Westport, Conn. 1983.

2 Information from: W. F. Ward, 'Periodical Literature', in J. V. Logan et al., eds., *Some British Romantics: A Collection of Essays*, Ohio State 1966; I. R. Christie, 'British Newspapers in the Later Georgian Age', in *Myth and Reality in Late-Eighteenth-Century British Politics and Other Papers*, London 1970; S. Koss, *The Rise and Fall of the Political Press in Britain*, vol. I, London 1981.

3 Thompson, *Making*, pp. 788–806; W. H. Wickwar, *The Struggle for the Freedom of the Press, 1819–1832*, London 1928.

4 J. Habermas, 'The Public Sphere: An Encyclopedia Article (1964)', *New German Critique*, vol. I, no. 3, Autumn 1974.

5 For hostility to critics, see for example Knight, *Progress*, p. 64; S. T. Coleridge, *Biographia Literaria*, ed. G. Watson, London & New York 1956 (Everyman edn), pp. 21, 28, 33–4; J. S. Mill, 'On the Present State of Literature' (1827–8), in E. Alexander, ed., *J. S. Mill, Literary Essays*, Indianapolis, New York and Kansas City 1967.

6 *Repository of Arts*, series 3, vol. XI, p. 84. Cf. 'On Criticism, Virtù, and the Rewards of Poets and Painters', *The Artist*, vol. I, 9 May 1807; *Somerset House Gazette*, no. VII, 22 November 1823, p. 29; and also the spoof letter from 'Horace Handy', in 'Original Communications', *Weekly Literary Register*, no. I, 6 July 1822 – which satirizes the lack of qualifications of contemporary art critics.

7 Hazlitt, *Complete Works*, vol. IV, pp. 76–7.

8 'Sketches of Society', *Literary Gazette*, no. 263, 2 February 1822.

9 'The Wishing Cap, No. IV. A Walk in the City', *Examiner*, no. 847, 25 April 1824.

10 'Life in London: A Sketch', *New Monthly Magazine*, vol. 13, no. 72, January 1820. Cf. 'London and the Country', series 2, vol. 5, 273–7.

11 One such philosophical onlooker was De Quincey, who in *Confessions of an English Opium Eater* describes his frequent walks through the city as 'a solitary and contemplative man', conscious of the miseries of the city, but somehow above them. See also: Leigh Hunt, 'Of the Sight of Shops', in *The Indicator, and the Companion; A Miscellany for the Fields and the Fireside*, 2 vols., London 1834, vol. I, p. 300.

12 Both the *Monthly Magazine*, and *New Monthly Magazine* carried sections on the Fine Arts, which were fullest during the sequence of public exhibitions from the end of January until July. They also carried reports on institutional business and Academy lectures, together with reviews of print publications. The art critic of the *Monthly Magazine* from 1806–12 was James Elmes, who returned to the magazine briefly from December 1820 until near the end of 1821. Between 1812 and 1820 the *Monthly* dropped its 'Monthly Retrospect of the Fine Arts', and art reports were much briefer, and ceased in some years. The *New Monthly Magazine*'s 'Review and Register of the Fine Arts' was both more regular and generally longer than the *Monthly*'s reports. Some of its criticism around 1820 was signed by William Carey, who launched a sequence of attacks on the *Annals of the Fine Arts* within its pages, but it is unclear how long he was with the magazine. The politics of the *New Monthly* became markedly more liberal after Thomas Campbell took over as editor in 1821, but even in its conservative phase, it never went in for the sycophancy and formulaic fashionable criticism of the *Morning Post*. The *New Monthly* carried extensive reports on landscape painting, and proved markedly sympathetic to some of the naturalistic painting of the period.

13 The *Literary Gazette* was a conservative periodical, and its political position was manifested more clearly in its art criticism than was that of the *New Monthly Magazine*. The *Gazette*'s critic was probably the water-colour painter W. H. Pyne (1769–1843), considering that the magazine published his 'Wine and Walnuts', and that the critical line is comparable to that of the *Somerset House Gazette*, which he edited. This means that the magazine gave extensive and favourable coverage of the water-colour exhibitions, and claimed the value of topography.

14 Begun in 1813 as *Drakard's Paper*, it became the *Champion* in the following year.

15 For analysis of the *Morning Chronicle*, and *Champion*, see my 'Discourses of Art and Social Interests: The Representation of Landscape in Britain *c.* 1800–1830', unpublished Ph.D. thesis, University of London 1989, pp. 220–8, 229–37.

16 I. Asquith, 'The Whig Party and the Press in the early Nineteenth Century', *Bulletin of the Institute of Historical Research*, vol. 49, 1976; Christie, *Myth and Reality*, ch. 16.

17 Most notably, it published Hazlitt's essay 'Why the Arts are not Progressive?' in two parts in January 1814. See Hazlitt, *Complete Works*, vol. 18, pp. 5–10.

18 The political characterization of papers is based largely on A. Aspinall, *Politics and the Press c. 1750–1850*, London 1949; and Koss, *Rise and Fall*. On the fashionable character of the *Post*, see Soligny, *Letters*, vol. II, p. 238.

19 'British Gallery', *Morning Post*, 31 March 1809; Royal Academy, 8 May 1821.

20 British Institution, *Morning Post*, 24 March 1806; 22 May 1816; 23 July 1806. Among numerous other examples, see reports on the Institution of 8 April 1807; 22 March 1810; 4 February 1815; 28 January 1822.

21 British Institution, *Morning Post*, 5, 17, and 22 March 1810; 28 January 1822; Royal Academy, 29 April 1815, 8 May 1821.

22 Society of British Artists, *Morning Post*, 28 March 1825. The antagonism of leading figures in the Society towards the Academy is clear from their evidence in the House of Commons *Report of the Select Committee on Arts and their Connection with Manufactures* – see that of F. Hurlstone (President), pt. II, pp. 63–7; and T. C. Hofland (Secretary), pp. 105–6.

23 British Institution, *Morning Post*, 22 May 1816.

24 *Sun*, 13 February 1807; 11 February 1808; *Oracle*, 15 February, 18 February, 15 April 1808; 20 February, 6 March, 5 April 1809.

25 'Sir Joshua Reynolds's Pictures', *Morning Post*, 20 May, 27 May 1813. Other notices on the exhibition appeared on 7, 10, 13, 18, 24, May; 8, 18, 21, 29 June; 12, 9, 24 July; 3, 5, 12, 13, 23, August 1813. British Institution, 8 February 1814; 26 April 1811. For further notices on West's picture see: 11, 20 March; 15, 17, 21, 22, 26, 27 April; 2, 7, 31 May 1811. 'West's Gallery', 22 May, 23 May 1829. For further notices on the Gallery, see 9, 20, 25, 26 May; 23 June 1829.

26 'Mr Haydon's Picture', *Morning Post*, 22, 30 March 1820.

27 Royal Academy, *Morning Post*, 29 April 1815; Sir Thomas Lawrence, 9 January 1830.

28 Royal Academy, *Morning Post*, 5 May 1821; 12 May 1807; 'The School of Hogarth', 7 May 1811; British Institution, 20 March 1809; 19 February 1816; 6 February 1830.

29 British Institution, *Morning Post*, 7 March 1815; 30 January 1813; 7 March 1816. On Callcott, see Royal Academy, 4 May 1822. On Hofland, see British Institution, 23 February 1816; 7 April 1817. On Constable, see Royal Academy, 13 April 1824; 20 June 1827; 4 May 1830. On Turner, see Royal Academy, 4, 6, 8 May 1809, 30 April 1810; 2 May 1811; 13 June 1812; 29 April 1815; 7 May 1823; 15 June 1827; 29 May 1829; 4 May 1830.

30 Royal Academy, *Morning Post*, 20 June 1827.

31 G. D. Stout, *The Political History of Leigh Hunt's Examiner*, Washington University Studies, n.s., Language and Literature, no. 19, Saint Louis, Mo. 1949, especially pp. 38–42.

32 Stout, *Political History*, chs. 5 and 6.

33 Ibid., pp. 37–8.

34 'State of the Arts in Great Britain', *Examiner*, no. 2, 10 January 1808; 'Prospective State of Historic Art in England', no. 161, 27 January 1811.

35 See Scott's articles: 'Reflections on the Patronage of Fine Art', *Champion*, no. 123, 14 May 1815; 'Public Tate: – Canova's Visit', no. 150, 19 November 1815; 'The Emancipation of the Works of Art from their Captivity in the Louvre', no. 146, 22 October 1815.

36 'David's Pictures now Exhibiting', *Examiner*, no. 338, 30 April 1815; Le Thière's Brutus, no. 443, 23 June 1816; 'M. JERRICAULT'S GREAT PICTURE', no. 665, 17 July 1820; 'British Gallery', no. 1045, 10 February 1828. He looked less favourably on David's *Couronnement* (Louvre) when that picture was exhibited in 1822, finding it valuable as a documentary record but its celebration of Napoleon's imperial trimmings morally degraded – 'Mr David's Picture of the Coronation of Napoleon', no. 779, 30 December 1822.

37 'State of the Arts in Great Britain', see note 56; 'Patronage of the Arts the Policy of Governments', *Examiner*, no. 91, 24 September 1809; British Institution, no. 197, 6 October 1811. On the flogging issue, see Stout 1949, pp. 14–16.
38 Report of the Prince of Wales' visit to Delahante's collection of 'Old Masters', *Examiner*, no. 174, 28 April 1811; 'State of British Art as evinced by our late exhibitions', no. 74, 27 July 1809; Prospective State of Historic Art in England – see note 34; 'Suggestions on the best Mode of encouraging History Painting in England', no. 134, 22 July 1820. See also: 'On the Benefit of the Arts from Government Encouragement', no. 40, 2 October 1808.
39 Royal Academy, *Examiner*, no. 73, 21 May 1809; 'Election of a Professor of Anatomy to the Royal Academy', no. 50, 11 December 1808; Royal Academy, no. 101, 3 December 1809; no. 104, 24 December 1809. On the Duke of York affair, see Stout, *Political History*, ch. 3.
40 British Institution, *Examiner*, no. 6, 7 February 1808; 'Rejection of Cooke's King William and Queen Mary receiving the Bill of Rights', no. 67, 9 April 1809; British Institution, no. 233, 14 June 1812; no. 234, 21 June 1812; 'Mr Havell's Picture', no. 384, 7 May 1815. On Havell and the *Examiner*, see Owen, *Connoisseur*, 1978, pp. 99–101.
41 British Institution, *Examiner*, no. 538, 8 February 1818; no. 590, 7 February 1819; 'Efficient Patronage of Art', no. 681, 21 January 1821; British Institution, no. 888, 6 February 1825.
42 Royal Academy, *Examiner* no. 597, 6 June 1819; no. 849, 10 May 1824; no. 901, 8 May 1825; 'A Brief Sketch of the State of the Arts', no. 934, 1 January 1826. Cf. Royal Academy, no. 1006, 13 May 1827. Society of British Artists, no. 820, 13 October 1823; no. 1001, 8 April 1827.
43 'Want of a Public Gallery of Paintings', *Examiner*, no. 728, 7 January 1822; 'A Brief Sketch of the State of the Arts' – see note 42. Haydon is also described as a 'reformer' in Royal Academy, no. 1033, 18 November 1827.
44 Under the editorship of both John Scott (January 1813 – July 1817) and the radical John Thelwall (January 1819 – December 1821), the *Champion* made scathing attacks on the Academy's exhibitions, treating them as a mirror of the corruption of fashionable taste. However, in Thelwall's criticism this critique of corruption was linked with the cause of reform in a way it was not in Scott's. See for instance: Royal Academy, *Champion*, no. 70, 7 May 1814; no. 436, 12 May 1821; no. 441, 16 June 1821.
45 Royal Academy, *Examiner*, no. 384, 7 May 1815.
46 Royal Academy, *Examiner*, no. 388, 4 June 1815.
47 Society of Painters in Water-Colours, *Examiner*, no. 747, 20 May 1822; no. 1008, 27 May 1827; Royal Academy, no. 1007, 20 May 1827. Cf. 'On the Picturesque and the Ideal – A Fragment', Hazlitt, *Complete Works*, vol. VIII, pp. 317–21.
48 Royal Academy, *Examiner*, no. 75, 4 June 1809; no. 283, 30 May 1813; no. 232, 7 June 1812; no. 335, 29 May 1814; no. 492, 1 June 1817; 'Exhibition of Drawings in Soho Square', no. 802, 9 June 1823.
49 For Hunt on Danby, see: Royal Academy, *Examiner*, no. 854, 14 June 1824; no. 902, 15 May 1825; British Institution, no. 889, 13 Feb. 1825. For characteristic responses to Martin, see British Institution, *Examiner*, no. 580, 7 February 1819; British Institution, no. 683, 4 February 1821.
50 British Institution, *Examiner*, no. 271, 7 March 1813; Society of Painters in Oil and Water-Colours, no. 332, 8 May 1814 – cf. the same, no. 383, 30 April 1815. On Mulready, see Royal Academy, no. 184, 7 July 1811. On Callcott, see British Institution, no. 170, 31 March 1811; no. 233, 5 April 1812.
51 British Institution, *Examiner*, no. 542, 8 March 1818.
52 Society of Painters in Oil and Water-Colours, *Examiner*, no. 332, 8 May 1814 – cf. the same, no. 663, 3 July 1820.
53 Royal Academy, *Examiner*, no. 232, 7 June 1812. Cf. comments on brushwork etc. in Royal Academy, no. 283, 30 May 1813; no. 387, 28 May 1815; no. 496, 29 June 1817.

54 Spring Gardens, *Examiner*, 22 May 1820; Exhibition of the Society of Painters in Water-Colours, no. 1004, 29 April 1827; Spring Gardens, no. 663, 3 July 1820.

55 Royal Academy, *Examiner*, no. 283, 23 May 1813; Haydon's *Judgment of Solomon*, no. 331, 1 May 1814.

56 British Institution, *Examiner*, no. 1004, 29 April 1827 – cf. on J. B. Lane's *Eutychus*, in British Institution, no. 324, 13 March 1814. On Stark and Nasmyth, see British Institution, no. 1002, 15 April 1827; Society of British Artists, no. 1003, 22 April 1827.

57 For representative statements, see: 'On the Inequality of our Taxation, and the Importance of Sustaining the Middling Class of the Community', *Examiner*, no. 18, 1 May 1808; 'State of Public Affairs', no. 729, 23 December 1821; 'Reform of Parliament – Representation of Edinburgh', no. 950, 16 April 1826.

58 For a brilliant Benthamite critique of the relations between class status and high culture, see the review of 'Tales of a Traveller, By Geoffrey Crayon Gent', *Westminster Review*, October 1824. This has been discussed in Nesbitt, *Benthamite Reviewing*, pp. 102–3.

59 For the history of the magazine see J. Bauer, *The London Magazine 1820–29*, *Anglistica*, vol. 1, Copenhagen 1953.

60 The British Institution, *London Magazine*, series 2, vol. 2, July 1825, 398; vol. 3, November 1825, 347.

61 *London Magazine*, series 2, vol. 3, September 1825, 49–50; vol. 2, July 1825, 397; vol. 3, November 1825, 353. For an earlier pro-middle-class critique of aristocratic patronage in the *London*, see the review of *Rhodes Peak Scenery*, series 1, vol. 8, December 1823, 616–17.

62 *London Magazine*, series 2, vol. 2, July 1825, 392–3. Cf. 'The Salon of 1824' in D. Wakefield, ed., *Stendhal on the Arts*, London 1973, pp. 93–4, 120.

63 *London Magazine*, series 2, vol. 2, July 1825, 389–90; 394 – cf. June 1825, 259 and vol. 3, November 1825, 345–7. On breadth and careless execution: vol. 3, November 1825, 349, 350–2.

64 *London Magazine*, series 2, vol. 2, July 1825, 391. On the Italian Schools, see vol. 3, November 1825, 342. On originality, nature, progress: vol. 2, July 1825, 395–6, 392.

65 *London Magazine*, series 2, vol. 3, September 1825, 60–2; Royal Academy, vol. 2, June 1825, p. 259.

66 *London Magazine*, series 2, vol. 2, July 1825, 400; vol. 3, November 1825, 355.

67 Royal Academy, *London Magazine*, series 2, vol. 2, June 1825, 260. On Turner, see also the extremely favourable comparison between Turner's *Richmond Hill and Bridge* (Clore Gallery) and Hofland's Richmond views, in 'Two Engravings', vol. 2, May 1825, 124–7. This draws on, and partly quotes, Landseer's review of Turner's Gallery in the *Review of Publications of Art*, of 1808.

68 Royal Academy, *London Magazine*, series 2, vol. 2, June 1825, 265–7. British Institution, vol. 3, September 1825, 54. Constable was described as having a 'peculiar affection for the dullest subjects' which he rendered alike by the repetitiveness of his 'disagreeable execution and colouring'. He was dismissed as a hopeless case: 'this is a hand that cannot mend: there is no mind to guide it'. (66)

69 Notes on Art, *London Magazine*, series 3, vol. 1, April 1828, 18 ff.; Royal Academy, vol. I, June 1828. On French art, see also the favourable review of Delacroix's *Marino Faliero*, in review of British Institution, April 1828; and 'French Pictures Exhibiting in Pall-Mall', vol. 2, September 1828.

70 Review of 'Fables for the Holy Alliance, Rhymes on the Road, etc. etc', *Westminster Review*, vol. 1, January 1824, p. 18.

71 On Hazlitt's view of the opposition between the aesthetic and scientific thought, and his critique of Benthamism, see R. Park, *Hazlitt and the Spirit of the Age: Abstraction and Critical Theory*, Oxford, 1971, Introduction, chapters 1–2.

72 Notes on Art, *London Magazine*, series 3, vol. I, April 1828. For Wyse, see his speech to a meeting of artists at the Freemasons' Tavern in 1842, printed in Pye, *Patronage of Art*,

pp. 176–85; and G. Foggo, *Report on the Proceedings at a Public Meeting, Held at the Freemasons' Hall, on the 29th of May 1837*, London 1837, pp. 20–4.

73 British Institution, *London Magazine*, series 3, vol. 1, April 1828; Royal Academy, vol. 1, June 1828; Royal Academy, vol. 3, June 1829.

74 Sullivan, *British Literary Magazines*, pp. 230 ff.

75 'Address to the Public', *Literary Chronicle*, no. 1, 1819; 'Address to the Public', no. 190, 1823.

76 On the limitations of patronage, see review of Sir John Leicester's Gallery, *Literary Chronicle*, no. 4, 12 June 1819. For a critique of aristocratic picture collections, see British Gallery, no. 3, 5 June 1819.

77 British Institution, *Literary Chronicle*, no. 196, 15 February 1823; Royal Academy, no. 209, 17 May 1823; 'Proposed New Institution for the Fine Arts, British Gallery', no. 210, 24 May 1823.

78 John Julius Angerstein Esq., *Literary Chronicle*, no. 195, 8 February 1823.

79 Society of British Artists, *Literary Chronicle*, no. 275, 21 August 1824. Cf. Society of British Artists, no. 246, 31 January 1824; Gallery of British Artists, no. 257, 17 April 1824.

80 Society of Painters in Water-Colours, *Literary Chronicle*, no. 259. 1 May 1824.

81 Gallery of British Artists, *Literary Chronicle*, no. 257, 17 April 1824. See also: no. 258, 24 April 1824, and the *Chronicle*'s defence of the subjects of these pictures against hostile criticism – 'The Exhibitions – Blackwoods', no. 264, 5 June 1824.

82 British Institution, *Literary Chronicle*, no. 252, 13 March 1824; Royal Academy, no. 261, 15 May 1824.

83 Society of British Artists, *Literary Chronicle*, no. 309, 16 April 1825; Royal Academy, no. 313, 14 May 1825; 'Late Exhibitions of the British Gallery', no. 327, 20 August 1825; 'The Diorama', no. 307, 2 April 1925.

84 This is clear in a sequence of favourable comments on Danby's works of 1824–5, the *Delivery of Israel out of Egypt*, *Sunset at Sea After a Storm* (Bristol Museum & Art Gallery), and *An Enchanted Island* (Private Collection). See: Royal Academy, *Literary Chronicle*, no. 313, 14 May 1825; Royal Academy, no. 261, 15 May 1824; and British Institution, no. 305, 19 March 1825.

85 Society of Painters in Water-Colours, *Literary Chronicle*, no. 416, 5 May 1827. The *Chronicle* also illustrates the popular dissemination of the association principle in relation to landscape – see 'On Taste in Works of Art', no. 400, 13 January 1827.

86 Society of Painters in Water-Colours – see previous note; Royal Academy, no. 417, 12 May 1827; 'Engravings – Topography', no. 422, 16 June 1827.

87 The same argument can be extended to the *Somerset House Gazette* (1823–4), edited by the water-colour painter W. H. Pyne.

88 *The Director*, 1 vol., London 1807, – 24 nos. from 24 January 1807 – 4 July 1807, edited by T. F. Dibdin. See T. F. Dibdin, *Reminiscences of a Literary Life*, London, 1836, vol. 1, pp. 249–52.

89 'On Originality in Painting: Imitators; and Collectors', *The Artist*, vol. 1, 21 March 1807, 7–8 (James Northcote). See, for example: 'On Instruction in Design, and the Requisite Qualifications for Judging of Public Works of Art', 2 May 1807 (Thomas Hope).

90 Or at least this is suggested by the extremely harsh review of the artist Henry Sass's *A Journey to Rome and Naples performed in 1817* (1818). Sass's politics were overtly liberal, and the *Annals* damned him as one of the 'little people of this great metropolis', satirizing his middle-class appearance, and suggesting he was of the type who read Cobbett's *Political Register*, the *Black Dwarf*, and *Independent Whig*, in the London coffee houses – *Annals of the Fine Arts*, vol. 3, 1818, Art. 14.

91 See for instance: Society of Painters in Water-Colours, *Annals*, vol. 4, 1819, 319. Cf. vol. 1, 1816, 87; vol. 5, 1820, 415.

92 On Haydon's 'more natural style of drawing and of form', see 'Memoirs of B. R.

Haydon', *Annals*, vol. 5, 1820, 373. A review of 1817 connected 'freshness and natural colouring' with painting from nature in relation to the works of Glover and Hofland, 'both of whom dare to paint nature as they see her' and not like Claude, Poussin or 'Ruysdael' (sic) – Royal Academy, *Annals*, vol. 2, 1817, 71. However, while it openly championed Wilkie, the magazine was not generally favourable to naturalism and complained elsewhere that 'Mulready and his followers' did not give sufficient attention to breadth – a complaint also levelled against Constable's *Stratford Mill* (National Gallery, London).

93 'Mr Turner's Gallery', *Review of Publications of Art* (1 vol. only), 1808, 152, 166.

94 Ibid., 80–2.

95 Ibid., 161, 157–8.

96 T. E. Jones, *A Descriptive Account of the Literary Works of John Britton*, London 1849, Part II, p. 181. For more on this magazine, see letters from W. C. Leeds to Dawson Turner, 30 July 1821, 30 August 1821, 30 December 1821 – in the Dawson Turner Correspondence, Trinity College Library, Cambridge.

97 Review of J. T. James, *The Italian Schools of Painting, with Observations on the Present State of the Art*, *Magazine of Fine Arts*, 20.

98 British Institution, *Magazine of Fine Arts*, 45–6. For a different view, see the notice on an engraving after Cristall's *Jupiter in the Isle of Crete*, pp. 452–8.

99 'Remarks on Cotemporary [*sic*] Criticism', *Magazine of Fine Arts*, 164.

100 Society of Painters in Water-Colours, *Magazine of Fine Arts*, 114–15.

101 J. Ford, *ACKERMANN 1783–1983 The Business of Art*, London 1983, especially pp. 77–83.

102 'On the Arts, and the Means of Improving them in this Country', *Repository of Arts*, series I, vol. 3, January 1810. On the need for state patronage, see: 'Observations on the Rise and Progress of Painting in Water-Colours', series 1, vol. 9, January 1813, 24–5. On Allston's *Dead Man Restored*, see Royal Academy, series 2, vol. 1, June 1816, 354.

103 Society of Painters in Water-Colours, *Repository*, series 1, vol. 7, May 1812, 301–10.

104 'Observations on the Rise and Progress of Painting in Water-Colours', *Repository*, series I, vol. 8, November, December 1812; vol. 9, January, February, March, April 1813. Cf. the series 'The Rise and Progress of Water-Colour Painting in England', in the *Somerset House Gazette*.

105 For example, see Society of Painters in Water-Colours, *Repository*, series 3, vol. 1, June 1823, p. 360.

106 British Institution, *Repository*, series 1, vol. 9, April 1813, 217 ff. Cf. the comments on Linnell in British Institution, vol. 5, March 1811, 155 ff.

107 For Pugin, see Society of Painters in Water-Colours – note 103; for Girtin, see 'Observations on the Rise and Progress of Painting in Water-Colours', *Repository*, series 1, vol. 9, 1813, 93; for Glover, see 'Mr Glover's Exhibition', series 3, vol. 1, May 1823, p. 301. 'Panorama of Geneva', series 3, vol. 9, no. 53, May 1827. Cf. the still more emphatic defence of panoramas in the *New Monthly Magazine*, December 1822, pp. 542–5.

108 Society of Painters in Water-Colours, *Repository*, series 3, vol. 9, June 1827, 359. On Constable, see British Institution, series 2, vol. 13, March 1822, 167; on Constable and Callcott, see Royal Academy, vol. 11, June 1821, 366–7; on Collins, see Royal Academy, series 3, vol. 5, June 1825, 353.

109 Royal Academy, *Repository*, series 1, vol. 7, June 1812, p. 340; vol. 13, June 1815, 338. Cf. on *Rome from the Vatican*, and *Bay of Baiae*, series 2, vol. 9, June 1820, 356 ff.; series 3, vol. 1, June 1823, 355. On Danby, see British Institution, series 3, vol. 5, March 1825, 176.

110 J. Cook, 'Hazlitt: Criticism and Ideology', in J. Aers, J. Cook, D. Punter, *Romanticism and Ideology*, London and Henley 1981, p. 154; Cf. Hazlitt's comment on publishers' preference for essays over books, in 'The Periodical Press', Hazlitt, *Complete Works*, vol. 16, p. 221.

111 On this, see Butler, *Romantics, Rebels, and Reactionaries*, pp. 169–73.
112 Aers, Cook, & Punter, *Romanticism and Ideology*, p. 148; Thompson, *Making*, pp. 660–1.
113 Goodman, *Languages of Art*, p. 38; Royal Academy, *New Monthly Magazine*, July 1827, 291.
114 Robert Hunt on Gainsborough's *Cottage Door* (Huntington Art Gallery, San Marino, Cal.), in 'Sir John Leicester's Gallery', *Examiner*, no. 586, 21 March 1819. On the same picture, see John Britton, in his *Fine Arts of the English School*: 'It has the true character of pastoral simplicity; but like the eclogues of the poets it heightens and exaggerates natural objects: the female figure is rather more Arcadian than English, and the colouring and effect are more imaginary than real. Nature never presented such a scene . . .' For Hazlitt on Gainsborough, see 'On Gainsborough's Pictures', and 'British Institution' (*Morning Chronicle*, 10 May 1814), in Hazlitt, *Complete Works*, vol. XVIII. Similar objections were levelled at the rustic pictures of Richard Westall – see, for example, *Review of Publications of Art*, p. 85.
115 Collins' *The Disposal of a Favourite Lamb* was in Sotheby's Sale, 29 November 1978 – photograph in Witt Library. For Hazlitt's enthusiastic response to this picture, see his review of the 1814 British Institution exhibition, Hazlitt, *Complete Works*, vol. XVIII, pp. 101–16.
116 Royal Academy, *Observer*, 7 June 1819; 'Historical Painting', *Parthenon*, no. 10, 13 August 1825, 151–3. For further examples see: Royal Academy, *Champion*, no. 175, 12 May 1816; Royal Academy, No. 3, *Literary Chronicle*, no. 163, 29 June 1822.
117 *Le Beau Monde*, quoted in Whitley, *Thomas Heaphy*, p. 16; 'Water-Colour Exhibitions', *Repository of Arts*, series 1, vol. 5, June 1811, 345. It is probably significant that these comments appeared in fashionable magazines aimed primarily at women, and other reviews remarked on the artist's popularity: *Repository*, series 1, vol. 3, 1810, 429; *New Monthly Magazine*, vol. I, no. 1, February 1814, 68. But it is also important to note that Heaphy sold no works from the Society of Painters in Water-Colours show of 1811, and concentrated on portraiture thereafter. *Country Girl being Robbed by Two Boys* is likely to be the *Robbing a Market Girl*, which the artist sold to Lord Kinnaird for 35gns from the exhibition of 1807 – see Whitley, ibid., p. 15.
118 Soligny, *Letters*, vol. 1, pp. 166–7.
119 Hunt referred to the 'pure pastoral' of Constable's *The Cornfield* (National Gallery, London), in relation to the shepherd boy and flock – see Royal Academy, *Examiner*, no. 961, 2 July 1826.
120 Royal Academy, *New Monthly Magazine*, series 2, vol. 6, May 1822, 256.
121 For representative examples, see 'Country Figures' in Victoria & Albert Museum, *Joshua Cristall 1768–1847*, text by B. Taylor, London 1975.
122 'Jupiter Nursed in the Isle of Crete', *Magazine of Fine Arts*, 457–8; Exhibition of Drawings, No. 9. Soho Square, *Somerset House Gazette*, no. 35, 5 June 1824, 130. A contemporary critique of this tendency to idealize rustic character was offered by Coleridge in his comments on Wordsworth's contributions to *Lyrical Ballads* – see Coleridge, *Biographia Literaria*, pp. 190–1.
123 Society of Painters in Water Colours, *Repository*, series 1, vol. 7, April 1812, pp. 301–10. Similar proprieties existed in relation to the imagery of urban figures. Thus a review of Cooke's *London and its Vicinity* praised the 'purely English' character of the social types represented, which raised the value of the work 'from a mere pictorial to a moral purpose' – *New Monthly Magazine*, series 2, vol. 21, 195.

8 The imagery of seaside resorts and modern leisure

1 This issue is dealt with particularly well in Larrain, *Marxism and Ideology*, pp. 197–200.
2 J. A. R. Pimlott, *The Englishman's Holiday: A Social History* (1947), Brighton 1976, p. 96. See also J. Walvin, *Beside the Seaside: A Social History of the Popular Seaside Holiday*, London 1978, pp. 39–40; P. J. Corfield, *The Impact of English Towns 1700–1800*, Oxford 1982, ch. 5.

3 Pimlott, *Englishman's Holiday*, ch. 3. See also J. Whyman, 'A Hanoverian Watering Place: Margate before the Railway', in A. Everitt, ed., *Perspectives in English Urban History*, London 1973, pp. 138–60.
4 Corfield, *Impact of English Towns*, p. 64.
5 Quoted in Pimlott, *Englishman's Holiday*, p. 101.
6 Quoted in Everitt, *Perspectives*, p. 147.
7 Everitt, *Perspectives*, p. 156. Cf. Peter Pindar's 'Ode to a Margate Hoy', printed in *A Picture of Margate, being a Complete Guide to all Persons Visiting Margate, Ramsgate and Broadstairs*, London 1809, pp. 117–20.
8 Walvin, *Beside the Seaside*, p. 31.
9 E. Castle, ed., *The Jerningham Letters 1780–1843*, London 1896, p. 285.
10 Beckett, *Discourses*, p. 20.
11 E.g. P. Bailey, *Leisure and Class in Victorian England*, London 1978.
12 R. Ayton, *A Voyage round Great Britain, Undertaken in the Summer of the Year 1813*, vol. VII, London 1824, pp. 6, 10.
13 'Sketches from the Coast II', *Morning Post*, 7 June 1825.
14 *Morning Herald*, 30 January 1822.
15 Pimlott, *Englishman's Holiday*, p. 60. For an incident of 'dissipation', see P. Quennell, ed., *Byron, A Self-Portrait*, New York 1967, pp. 637–8.
16 A. Pasquin (John Williams), *The New Brighton Guide; Involving a Complete, Authentic and Honorable Solution to the Recent Mysteries of Carlton House*, 4th edn, London 1796. This is a commentary on the Prince Regent, and not a guide at all. My thanks to Dian Kriz for this reference.
17 Southey, *Letters*, p. 164; W. G. Moss, *The History and Antiquities of the Town and Port of Hastings*, London 1824, p. 167.
18 One of these, the 'London Engineer', was represented in a coloured aquatint in the *Repository of Arts* for August 1819, acompanied by a text which praised its accommodation and facilities.
19 'The Old Margate Hoy', *London Magzine*, vol. 8, July 1823, 21, 24.
20 Ayton, *A Voyage*, vol. VII, p. 11. On the fashionable life of the resorts and the boredom, see also Soligny, *Letters*, vol. I, pp. 26–33.
21 Soligny, *Letters*, vol. I, p. 13.
22 'A Visit to Brighton', *London Magazine*, series 2, vol. 7, December 1826, p. 463.
23 Beckett, *Constable's Correspondence*, vol. VI, p. 171. For Haydon, who also saw in Brighton a scene of dissipation, the spectacle of wealth and display was a pleasurable diversion; see B. R. Haydon, *The Diary of Benjamin Robert Haydon*, ed. W. B. Pope, 5 vols., Cambridge, Mass. 1960–3, vol. II, p. 475.
24 W. Cobbett, *Rural Rides*, 2 vols., London 1912 (Everyman edn), vol. I, p. 74.
25 Cobbett, *Rural Rides*, vol. I, p. 160. Cf. pp. 33–4.
26 Prothero, *Artisans and Politics*, pp. 241–2.
27 Cobbett, *Rural Rides*, vol. I, p. 74.
28 Journal entry of 22 October 1825, in the form of a letter to Maria Constable, in Beckett, *Constable's Correspondence*, vol. II, p. 403.
29 G. Dawe, *The Life of George Morland*, intro. J. J. Foster, London n.d., pp. 18–31; Victoria & Albert Museum, *Joshua Cristall*, p. 44.
30 L. Hawes, *Presences of Nature, British Landscape 1780–1830*, New Haven 1982, cat. no. II, 3.
31 British Institution, *Review of Publications of Art*, 1808, 115.
32 Beckett, *Constable's Correspondence*, vol. VI, p. 171.
33 *An Excursion to Brighthelmstone, Made in the Year 1789, by Henry Wigstead and Thomas Rowlandson*, London 1790 – including eight aquatint plates, dedicated to the Prince of Wales. *Poetical Sketches of Scarborough: Illustrated by Twenty-one Engravings of Humorous Subjects*, London 1813 – published by Ackermann, drawings by Green, coloured aquatints etched by Rowlandson.
34 *Romantic and Picturesque Scenery of England and Wales, from drawings . . . by P. J. de*

Loutherbourg, Esq. R.A., London 1805. Plates engraved by W. Pickett and coloured by J. Clark, text in French and English.

35 See for example Ayton, *A Voyage*, vol. III, 1818, pp. 17, 58.

36 Ayton, *A Voyage*, vol. IV, 1820, p. 9.

37 Landseer, *Lectures*, pp. 120, 237–8.

38 'Recent Engravings, and the Present Superiority of our Engravers over those of the Continent', *New Monthly Magazine*, n.s., vol. 3, November 1821, 560.

39 J. R. Abbey, *Scenery of Great Britain and Ireland in Aquatint and Lithography 1770–1860 from the Library of J. R. Abbey*, London 1952, pp. 98–103.

40 John Gendall, *Six Views of Hastings*, aquatints, 1822; John Marten, *Hastings Delineated*, six lithographs, 1823; Augustine Aglio, *Six Views of Hastings*, lithographs, 1823; and Thomas Ross, *Views of Hastings and St Leonards*, nine lithographs, *c.*1830.

41 Moss, *History and Antiquities*, p. vii.

42 On the significance of such quotations, see J. Ziff, 'Turner's First Poetic Quotations: an Examination of Intentions', *Turner Studies*, vol. 2, no. 1, Summer 1982.

43 M. Butlin & E. Joll, *The Paintings of J. M. W. Turner*, New Haven & London 1977, nos. 51 and 78.

44 *Review of Publications of Art*, 1808, pp. 165–6. Cf. Landseer on J. C. Smith's *View of Ramsgate*, p. 294.

45 Notably in those of W. B. Cooke and Walter Fawkes. See Finberg, *Life of Turner*, for some account of these.

46 The water-colour is in the collection of Yale Center for British Art, and is reproduced in Hawes, *Presences*, Pl.20.

47 Tate Gallery, *Turner 1775–1851*, London 1975, no. 113. This drawing is 68.7 × 101.6cm. compared with the 15.6 × 23.6cm. of the Yale Center's *Margate*.

48 Tate Gallery, *Augustus Wall Callcott*, catalogue by D. B. Brown, London 1981, nos. 3 & 4.

49 Royal Academy, *Morning Post*, 9 May 1806.

50 Royal Academy, *Repository of Arts*, series 1, vol. VII, June 1812, p. 343.

51 *Repository of Arts*, June 1812, pp. 342–3.

52 Victoria & Albert Museum, *Joshua Cristall*, pp. 24–6, 44–52; Solly, *David Cox*, pp. 25–6.

53 Knowles, *Life*, vol. I, pp. 307–8.

54 Anon., *The Hastings Guide; or a Description of that Ancient Town and Port and its Environs*, 2nd edn, London 1797 (printed for James Barry, Circulating Library, Hastings), pp. 1–2.

55 Ayton, *A Voyage*, vol. VII, 1824, p. 44.

56 Anon. (M. M. Howard), *Hastings, Past and Present: with Notices of the most Remarkable Places in the Neighbourhood*, Hastings and London 1855, p. 72. The decline of the fisheries was noted as early as 1810 – see G. A. Cooke, *Topographical and Statistical Description of the County of Sussex*, London 1810, p. 156.

57 *The Hastings Guide*, 6th edn, 1828, p. 37.

58 Another *Hastings Guide*, in its 2nd edition in 1819, was published by P. M. Powell, the Library, Marine Parade.

59 *Brighton Beach*, Victoria & Albert Museum, 2939–1876.

60 By contrast, Heaphy showed 'a well dressed lady, apparently of the metropolis' bargaining with 'an honest fishmonger and his wife for a turbot' in a lost drawing of Hastings shown in the following year, and sold for 400 gns. This seems typical of Heaphy's infractions against good taste. The description of the picture is from a review in *Le Beau Monde*, quoted in Whitley, *Thomas Heaphy*, p. 16.

61 'The Bond-Street Exhibition of Pictures in Water-Colours', *Review of Publications of Art*, 1808, p. 183.

62 *Review of Publications of Art*, p. 184.

63 'Spring Gardens Exhibition', *Examiner*, no. 332, 8 May 1814.

64 'Review and Register of the Fine Arts', *New Monthly Magazine*, vol. I, no. 4, May 1814.

65 Butlin & Joll, *Paintings of Turner*, no. 105. Cf. Adrian van de Velde, *The Beach at Scheveningen*, 1658, Kassel Staatliche Kunst-sammlungen.
66 Butlin & Joll, *Paintings of Turner*, no. 123.
67 Royal Academy, *Examiner*, no. 600, 28 June 1819; 'Fine Arts', *New Monthly Magazine*, vol. II, no. 65, 1 June 1819; vol. 132, no. 75, April 1820. The second of the *New Monthly Magazine*'s reviews reveals that the picture was well hung at the Academy, but placed too high at the Institution. Chalon is a major artist, whose works receive far too little attention. The interesting use of modern figure types in the *View of Hastings* is paralleled in other pictures, such as *A Common: a Gamekeeper Questioning some Cow Boys on their being found with a Sporting Dog* (RA 1818, BI 1819, Phillips' Sale, 21 October 1974), and *Brocket Hall, near Hatfield* (Christie's Sale, 22 June 1979) – photographs of both are in the Yale Center for British Art Photograph Archive.
68 For Constable's friendship with J. J. Chalon, and admiration for his work, see Beckett, *Constable's Correspondence*, vol. IV, pp. 275–8; vol. III, pp. 52, 83, 87.
69 Solly, *David Cox*, pl. 6.
70 Beckett, *Constable's Correspondence*, vol. VI, p. 122.
71 For Collins and Constable, see Beckett, *Constable's Correspondence*, vol. IV, pp. 285–96.
72 Collins, *Memoirs*, vol. I, pp. 56–9, 70–1; cf. from 1817, pp. 113–14.
73 *Fishermen Coming Ashore before Sunrise*, Sotheby's Sale, 15 December 1981; *Capstern at Work, Drawing up Fishing Boats*, O. & P. Johnson's Sale, November 1962 – photographs of both are in the Witt Library.
74 Collins, *Memoirs*, vol. I, p. 115.
75 Collins, *Memoirs*, vol. I, p. 79.
76 Royal Academy, *Examiner*, no. 438, 19 May 1816.
77 L. Davidoff, J. L'Esperence, & H. Newby, 'Landscape with Figures: Home and Community in English Society', in J. Mitchell & A. Oakley, eds., *The Rights and Wrongs of Women*, Harmondsworth 1976; J. Cook, 'Romantic Literature and Childhood', in Aers, Cook & Punter, *Romanticism and Ideology*.
78 Collins, *Memoirs*, vol. I, p. 85.
79 Collins, *Memoirs*, vol. I, p. 112.
80 Royal Academy, *Examiner*, no. 600, 28 June 1819.
81 Royal Academy No. 9, *Morning Post*, 20 June 1827.
82 Beckett, *Constable's Correspondence*, vol. II, p. 284.
83 Tate Gallery, *Constable Paintings, Watercolours & Drawings*, London 1976, p. 100.
84 Quoted in Beckett, *Constable's Correspondence*, vol. VI, p. 40. The *Champion* also disapproved: 'British Gallery IV', in No. 329, 7 March 1819.
85 Tate Gallery, *Constable*, nos. 147 and 150.
86 Beckett, *Constable's Correspondence*, vol. VI, pp. 218–19.
87 Tate Gallery, *Constable*, nos. 213–15.
88 See the note on a Hampstead Cloud Study of 1822 in the National Gallery of Victoria, Melbourne: 'very appropriate for the Coast at Osmington' – Tate Gallery, *Constable*, p. 127.
89 Tate Gallery, *Constable*, nos. 178–9; G. Reynolds, *Victoria and Albert Museum, Catalogue of the Constable Collection*, London 1973, no. 142.
90 Beckett, *Constable's Correspondence*, vol. II, pp. 316, 341.
91 I have argued this elsewhere on the basis of an 1818 exhibition review, which refers to a picture called *Yarmouth Beach, from the Pier*. See A. F. Hemingway, 'Subject-Matter in the Paintings of John Crome', *Landscape Research*, vol. 9, no. 3, Winter 1984, 30–1.
92 Reynolds, *Constable Collection*, no. 266, no. 267.
93 Ibid., no. 289.
94 An impression of this is in Brighton Art Gallery. For a survey of representations, see J. & G. Ford, *Images of Brighton*, Richmond-upon-Thames 1981.
95 The possibilities of beach debris as a picturesque motiv were explored by a number of artists in this period. See for example, M. Rajnai & M. Allthorpe-Guyton, *John Sell*

Cotman 1782–1842. Early Drawings (1798–1812) in Norwich Castle Museum, Norwich 1979, nos. 75–9, 81–2.

96 Hawes, *Presences*, cat. no. II. 7.

97 'Capt. Brown's Suspension Pier at Brighton', *New Monthly Magazine*, no. 373, October 1822, p. 242. This described the pier as an 'indispensable convenience', which would also 'add a luxury to the town'. The plan of erecting piers on many parts of the coast was 'of the highest social importance' for 'commerce and communication'.

98 See Anon., *Shampooing: or Benefits Resulting from the Use of the Indian Medicated Vapour Bath, as Introduced in this Country, by S. D. Mahomed*, Brighton 1822, dedicated to George IV.

99 Reynolds, *Constable Collection*, nos. 274, 276, 279.

100 Ford, *Images of Brighton*, no. 78.

101 Beckett, *Constable's Correspondence*, vol. VI, p. 171.

102 Fisher observed of the picture in a letter to his wife: 'Turner, Callcott and Collins will not like it.' – Beckett, *Constable's Correspondence*, vol. VI, p. 230. C. Shields & L. Parris, *John Constable 1776–1837* (Tate Gallery Little Book Series), London 1969, p. 17.

103 G. Reynolds, *The Late Paintings and Drawings of John Constable*, 2 vols., New Haven & London 1984, no. 24. 72.

104 *Repository of Arts*, series 2, vol. 3, March 1817, 141–2.

105 For a famous commentary on this issue, see W. K. Wimsatt, Jr & M. Beardsley, 'The Intentional Fallacy', in J. Margolis, ed., *Philosophy Looks at the Arts: Contemporary Readings in Aesthetics*, New York 1962.

106 Beckett, *Constable's Correspondence*, vol. VI, p. 182.

107 For a discussion of the bridge as a symbol of modern capital and technology, see *Repository of Arts*, series 2, vol. 2, November 1816, 288. For the history of the picture, see Tate Gallery, *Constable*, pp. 166–8. As early as 1821, the *Monthly Magazine* (vol. 51, April 1821, 276) announced that Constable's 'The opening of Waterloo Bridge' would be shown at the Academy in that year – in fact it took him another decade to bring to completion.

108 Beckett, *Constable's Correspondence*, vol. IV, p. 165; vol. VI, pp. 231, 241.

109 'Fine Arts', *Morning Chronicle*, 12 April 1827; Royal Academy, *Morning Post*, 20 June 1827; Royal Academy, *Examiner*, no. 1013, 1 July 1827; Royal Academy, *Repository of Arts*, series 3, vol. 9, June 1827, 353. Interestingly, the *New Monthly Magazine* observed that Constable's style was inappropriate to his new subject; 'Mr Constable's style is rural, and adapted to rural objects almost exclusively' and he needed to change it, 'if he would meet with success in general subjects'. – Royal Academy, vol. 21, 1 Sept. 1827, 378. As we saw in chapter 7, the technique of the picture was also strongly criticized in the *London Magazine* in 1828.

110 Ford, *Images of Brighton*, no. 170.

111 T. W. Adorno, *Aesthetic Theory*, tr. C. Lenhardt, London and New York 1986, pp. 70, 160–2.

112 Tate Gallery, *Turner*, no. 328, pp. 105–6. National Trust, *The Picture Collection at Peterworth House*, n.d., pp. 18–19.

113 Anon., *Brighton and its Environs; A Brief but Comprehensive History and Guide*, 6th edn, Brighton 1825 (?), p. 48.

114 British Institution, *Repository of Arts*, series 3, vol. 11, March 1828, 179.

115 T. J. Clark, *Image of the People: Gustave Courbet and the 1848 Revolution*, London 1973; *The Painting of Modern Life: Paris in the Art of Manet and his Followers*, London 1985.

116 A. F. Hemingway, 'Cultural Philanthropy and the Invention of the Norwich School', *Oxford Art Journal*, vol. 11, no. 2, 1988.

117 In the 1817 Norwich Society catalogue, Vincent's address is still given as 'Norwich', while in that of 1818 it is London – '86 Newman St', next door to Joseph Clover and James Stark at 85.

118 A list of Stark's early patrons is found in J. Chambers, *A General History of the County*

of Norfolk, Intended to Convey all the Information of a Norfolk Tour, Norwich and London 1829, pp. 1119–20. This is a very useful source on the Norwich painters.

119 Society of Painters in Oil and Water-Colours, *Literary Chronicle*, no. 12, 15 June 1818.

120 Except, perhaps, Southampton, which does not figure prominently in landscape iconography of the period.

121 J. H. Druery, *Historical and Topographical Notices of Great Yarmouth*, London 1826, p. 99.

122 J. Rymer, *A Sketch of Great Yarmouth . . . with Some Reflections on Cold Bathing*, London 1777, pp. 21–2.

123 Quoted in G. Nobbs, *Bygone Yarmouth: An Illustrated History of a Seaside Resort*, Norwich 1971, p. 9.

124 Nobbs, *Bygone Yarmouth*, p. 9; Druery, *Notices of Great Yarmouth*, pp. 75–6.

125 G. S. Carey, *The Balnea; or, An Impartial Description of all the Popular Watering Places in England*, 3rd edn, London 1801, pp. 232–3. The anonymous *A Guide to all the Watering and Sea-Bathing Places*, London 1805, also emphasized its cheapness, p. 392.

126 T. K. Cromwell, *Excursions in the County of Norfolk*, 2 vols., London 1818, 1819, vol. I, p. 151. Cf. *A Guide to all the Watering and Sea-Bathing Places*, p. 192; and Chambers, *A General History*, pp. 151–4.

127 R. Beatniffe, *The Norfolk Tour: or Traveller's Pocket Companion*, 5th edn, Norwich 1795, p. 15.

128 Druery, *Notices of Great Yarmouth*, pp. 80–6, 79* – 86*. An interesting letter from J. S. Cotman to Yetts, dated 19 November 1829, is bound into a grangerized copy of C. J. Palmer's *The Perlustration of Great Yarmouth*, 3 vols., Great Yarmouth 1874, in Yarmouth Central Library – vol. III, opp. p. 280.

129 S. Lewis, *A Topographical Dictionary of England . . . with Historical and Statistical Descriptions*, 7th edn, London 1849, vol. IV, p. 712.

130 Beckett, *Discourses*, p. 21; H. Manship, *The History of Great Yarmouth*, ed. C. J. Palmer, Yarmouth 1854, p. 293.

131 J. Beresford, ed., *The Diary of a Country Parson: The Reverend James Woodforde*, 5 vols., Oxford 1924–31, vol. I, p. 188.

132 Beatniffe, *Norfolk Tour*, p. 19; Palmer, *Perlustration*, vol. III, p. 131; Chambers, *A General History*, p. 278; Druery, *Notices of Great Yarmouth*, p. 86.

133 J. Lambert, *Graphic Illustrations of Great Yarmouth and its Environs*, text by J. H. Druery, Great Yarmouth 1822, text to Pl. XI.

134 Beatniffe, *Norfolk Tour*, pp. 19, 11; Druery, *Notices of Great Yarmouth*, p. 86.

135 E. Bartell, *Cromer, Considered as a Watering Place; with Observations on the Picturesque Scenery in its Neighbourhood*, 2nd edn, London 1806, pp. 31, 44, 57, 80.

136 Bartell, *Cromer*, pp. 17–18. I have suggested elsewhere that Bartell may have had a direct influence on a group of drawings of such subjects which Robert Dixon produced in 1809–10. See A. F. Hemingway, *The Norwich School of Painters 1803–33*, Oxford 1979, pp. 29–33.

137 Bartell, *Cromer*, p. 29. Cf. Gilpin, *Forest Scenery*, vol. II, p. 247, on the picturesque of the coast; on van der Velde, see Gilpin, *Three Essays*, p. 27.

138 J. Preston, *The Picture of Yarmouth: Being a Comprehensive History and Description of all the Public Establishments within that Borough*, Yarmouth 1819, p. 248.

139 Information from original paper wrapper, bound into a copy in the Local Studies Library, Norwich.

140 J. S. Cotman, *Architectural Antiquities of Norfolk*, London, Norwich and Yarmouth 1818; R. Dixon, *Sketches Illustrative of ye Picturesque Scenery of Norfolk*, Norwich 1811; R. Ladbrooke, *Views of the Churches of Norfolk*, Norwich 1843; J. W. Robberds, *Scenery of the Rivers of Norfolk, from Pictures painted by James Stark*, Norwich and London 1834. John Crome announced his intention to publish his etchings in a prospectus of 1812, although in the event they were only published posthumously as *Etchings of Views in Norfolk by the Late John Crome*, 1838.

141 There is a photograph of a view of Brighton Beach attributed to Vincent in the Witt Library, which was with Agnew's in 1957.

142 Illustrated in Hemingway, *Norwich School*, pl. 8.
143 These paintings, all now known as '*Yarmouth Jetty*', are P23, P23a, P41, P42, P45, P46 in the Clifford's catalogue. For a discussion of their dating, see Hemingway, 'Discourses of Art', pp. 376–8. For the general problems of attribution and dating with Crome's work, see my review of N. L. Goldberg, *John Crome the Elder*, *Burlington Magazine*, vol. 121, no. 914, May 1979.
144 See A. F. Hemingway, 'Meaning in Cotman's Norfolk Subjects', *Art History*, vol. 7, no. 1, March 1984, 30–2.
145 Clifford's *John Crome*, p. 90. Cf. John Berney Crome: '*It is not the display of minutiae* but rather the knowledge of making one part subordinate to another that shews the skill of Art.' 'Breadth, which is so great an energy to the peculiar lovers of minutiae, is not only compatible with grandeur, but often the cause of it.' J. B. Crome, *Essay on Painting and Poetry* (MS, Norwich Castle Museum), pp. 8, 10–11. See also pp. 12–13.
146 *Norfolk Chronicle*, 8 August 1818. Cf. British Institution, *Sun*, 30 January 1821; and British Institution, *Champion*, no. 432, 14 April 1821.
147 On agency, see R. Bhaskar, *The Possibility of Naturalism*, Brighton 1979, ch. 3.
148 For Rigby, see C. B. Jewson, *The Jacobin City, A Portrait of Norwich in its Reaction to the French Revolution 1788–1802*, Glasgow and London 1975. For Gurney, see D. E. Swift, *Joseph John Gurney, Banker, Reformer, and Quaker*, Middleton, Conn. 1962, pp. 91–117. On *The Cabinet*, see Cookson, *Friends of Peace*, ch. 4. On Norwich intellectual life generally, see Robberds, *Memoir of Taylor*, vol. 1, pp. 44–46; T. Fawcett, 'The culture of later Georgian Norwich: a conflict of evidence', *UEA Bulletin*, vol. 4, no. 4, March 1972; and P. Mosley, 'Much ado about Norwich?', *UEA Bulletin*, vol. 5, no. 5, June 1973.
149 Lord Amherst & H. Le Strange, 'The Rise of Freemasonry in Norwich', *Norfolk and Norwich Notes and Queries*, series 1, 1898, 419–21; N. L. Goldberg, 'John Crome and the Norwich Cathedral: an Enigma', *Connoisseur Year Book*, London 1962.
150 D. Turner, 'Memoir of Crome', In J. Wodderspoon, *John Crome and his Works*, Norwich 1876, p. 7; R. & S. Redgrave, *A Century of British Painters*, London 1947, p. 351. Mary Turner to Dawson Turner, 14 October 1815 (m.s. letter, Private Collection.)
151 For Dawson Turner's picture collection, see his *Outlines in Lithography from a Small Collection of Pictures*, Great Yarmouth 1840; and the documents transcribed by Warren R. Dawson, B.M. Add.MS 56294, vol. 37(40), pp. 166r–168v; 171v–173r.
152 Wodderspoon, *John Crome*, p. 8.
153 The catalogue is printed as Appendix D, in Cliffords, *John Crome*. Except for Hudson Gurney's purchase of *Boulevard des Italiens* and *Fishmarket at Boulogne* (both Norwich Castle Museum), the Gurney family seem to have bought no major pictures. Although the Earlham branch employed him as a drawing master for the Gurney girls, it seems likely that their Quakerism inhibited them from buying his pictures.
154 On C. Turner as a patron, see Chambers, *A General History*, pp. 1116–17. The Cliffords identify *Yarmouth Jetty* (P42) with a picture of 1808 in de Rouillon's collection listed in the catalogue to Crome's posthumous exhibition (p. 199). This date seems too early, and the authors give no evidence to support their identification.
155 The picture seemed so different from Crome's other works, that doubts were expressed about its authenticity when it was exhibited in Norwich in 1860 (see 'The Exhibition', *Norwich Mercury*, 12 September 1860). In response a correspondent wrote to the paper: 'I remember seeing him [i.e. Crome] at work upon it, and I believe that the greater part was painted on the spot in the early part of the summer of 1814.' See 'The Exhibition', *Norwich Mercury*, 15 September 1860.
156 Another version of the 1827 picture was with Agnew's in 1949, and there is also a pencil drawing for the composition (photographs, Witt Library).
157 Cliffords, *John Crome*, P81b.
158 W. F. Dickes, *The Norwich School of Painting*, London and Norwich 1905, remains the basic source on Vincent. For Vincent's entanglement with picture dealers see *Arnold's*

Magazine, September 1833, 413 – I owe this reference to M. Pidgley, 'Cotman's Patrons and the Romantic Subject Picture', unpublished Ph.D. thesis, University of East Anglia 1975.

159 Manship, *History of Great Yarmouth*, pp. 311–12.

160 'An Amateur', 'A Critical Examination of the Architecture of the Nelson Column erected at Yarmouth 1817–19. W. Wilkins Esq. Architect', *Annals of the Fine Arts*, vol. 4, no. 15, 1819.

161 For a review, see *Norwich Mercury*, 29 July 1821. Vincent did go to Yarmouth to make studies for the picture. See his letter to Sir John Leicester, 6 October 1820, referred to in D. Hall, 'The Tabley House Papers', *The Walpole Society*, vol. 38, 1960–2, p. 94. The contemporary was the journalist and translator. W. C. Leeds, who saw a sketch for the picture, and the large canvas 'laid in' in Vincent's studio in late 1820. See W. C. Leeds to Dawson Turner, 30 October 1820, Dawson Turner Correspondence, Trinity College Library, Cambridge. In a letter to Turner of 24 October 1821, Leeds reported that Vincent proposed to make 'elaborate' etchings from his 'principal pictures', and observed: 'also, I presume that his view of Yarmouth Beach is to be engraved'. It seems unlikely that it was.

162 The longer notices appeared in reviews of the British Institution exhibition in: *Literary Chronicle*, no. 95, 10 March 1821; *Repository of Arts*, series 2, vol. 11, 1 March 1821; *Champion*, no. 432, 14 April 1821; *Examiner*, no. 687, 25 March 1821; *Guardian*, 11 February 1821; *Monthly Magazine*, vol. 51, March 1821, p. 174; *Sun*, 31 January 1821. Shorter notices appeared in the *Morning Herald*, 29 January 1821; *Literary Gazette*, no. 210, 27 January 1821, no. 211, 3 February 1821; *London Magazine*, vol. 3, April 1821; *Magazine of Fine Arts*, vol. 1, September 1821.

163 British Institution, *Sun*, 30 January 1821. According to the Institution's catalogue, the measurements of Crome's pictures with frames in this year were 29 × 28ins and 23 × 38ins. Although Crome's *Scene at Wittingham, near Norwich*, exhibited in 1820, was 60 × 54ins, this seems to have attracted no attention in the press (except for a passing reference in the *Examiner*, 31 January 1820), whereas works by J. B. Crome, Stark and Vincent in the same exhibition did.

164 Rymer, *Sketch of Great Yarmouth*, p. 9; Beatniffe, *Norfolk Tour*, p. 17; Druery, *Notices of Great Yarmouth*, p. 50. Cf. Chambers, *A General History*, p. 276, and F. Skill, *A Guide to Yarmouth*, Great Yarmouth 1835, p. 22; Preston, *Picture of Yarmouth*, p. 223.

165 'Yarmouth Quay', *Repository of Arts*, vol. 12, September 1814, pp. 131–2.

166 For the *View of Greenwich from Blackwall*, see *Annals of the Fine Arts*, vol. 5, 1820, pp. 153, 221; *Morning Herald*, 4 March 1820; *New Monthly Magazine*, vol. 13, April 1820, p. 466 (a very favourable comment). For *London, from the Surrey side of Waterloo Bridge* see reviews of the Society of Painters in Oil and Water-Colours exhibition in *The Times*, 27 April 1820; *Examiner*, 3 July 1820; *Literary Gazette*, no. 220, 7 April 1821, p. 219.

167 Exhibited in Oscar & Peter Johnson Ltd, *The Influence of Crome*, 1968, no. 54. I have been unable to see this picture. To judge from photographs the attribution is plausible, but it is worth noting that J. B. Crome exhibited a *View, looking from Gorleston towards Yarmouth*, with the Norwich Society of Artists in 1823 (no.65). Whether the picture is by Vincent or J. B. Crome makes no difference to my argument.

9 The contradictions of progress: imagery of rivers

1 Beckett, *Constable's Correspondence*, vol. VI, p. 78.

2 J. Hassell, *Tour of the Grand Junction*, London 1819, p. 1.

3 P. S. Bagwell, *The Transport Revolution from 1770*, London 1974, pp. 13–17.

4 Bagwell, *Transport Revolution*, p. 24; P. Horn, *The Rural World 1780–1850: Social Change in the English Countryside*, London 1980, pp. 18–19.

5 R. Williams, *The Country and the City*, St Albans 1973, pp. 87–91; Barrell, *English Literature 1730–80*, pp. 51–79.

6 All references to Thomson refer to *The Complete Poetical Works of James Thomson*, ed. J. L. Robertson, Oxford 1908. For Thomson on canals and improved rivers, see *Liberty*, Part v, lines 709–11.

7 A. Pope, *The Poems of Alexander Pope*, ed. E. Audra & A. Williams, London 1961, vol. I, p. 184.

8 On Turner and Thomson, see J. Lindsay, *J. M. W. Turner: A Critical Biography*, London 1966, esp. pp. 57–64. For references to Thomson in Turner's own verse, see J. Lindsay, ed., *The Sunset Ship: The Poems of J. M. W. Turner*, London 1966, nos. 6, 52, 53, 54.

9 T. L. Peacock, *The Genius of the Thames, Palmyra, and other Poems*, London 1812, pp. 23–4. When Coleridge attracted the attention of a government spy in 1797, while he was '*making studies*, as the artists call them' on the Quantocks, he was working on a never completed poem, *The Brook*, which was to trace the course of a stream from its source to the 'manufactories and the sea-port'. See Coleridge, *Biographia Literaria*, p. 108.

10 Ziff, *Turner Studies*, 1982. For the precedent of Wilson's Thames views, see D. Solkin, *Richard Wilson: The Landscape of Reaction*, catalogue to an exhibition at the Tate Gallery, London 1982, pp. 77–88, 204–7, 213–14.

11 H. Skrine, *A General Account of all the Rivers of Note in Great Britain*, London 1801, p. 3. Cf. W. Tombleson & W. G. Fearnside, *Tombleson's Thames*, London 1834, p. i.

12 S. Ireland, *Picturesque Views on the Upper, or Warwickshire Avon*, London 1795, pp. xiv–xv.

13 W. Combe, *Boydell's History of the River Thames*, 2 vols., London 1794–6. On the nature of the history of rivers, see Preface, p. ix.

14 E. Dayes & F. Jukes, *Views on the River Wye*, London 1797–1802.

15 J. G. Wood, *The Principal Rivers of Wales Illustrated*, 2 vols., London 1813. For the status of soft-ground etching, see Landseer, *Lectures*, p. 144; and also his review of *Seventy-eight Studies from Nature, Engraved by William Green, from Drawings made by himself*, in *London Review*, vol. 2, no. 3, August 1809, 356–7.

16 W. Westall & S. Owen, *Picturesque Tour of the River Thames: Illustrated by Twenty-four Coloured Views*, London 1828, p. iv.

17 Landseer, *Lectures*, pp. 132–6.

18 T. H. Fielding, *The Art of Engraving*, London 1841, p. 39. On Turner's decision not to use aquatint for the *Liber Studorium*, see G. Wilkinson, *Turner on Landscape*, London 1982, pp. 34–5.

19 F. C. Lewis, *Picturesque Scenery on the River Dart, Devon*, London 1821. Callcott, Collins, Cotman, Stark and Vincent were among the subscribers.

20 F. C. Lewis, *The Scenery of the Rivers Tamar and Tavy*, London 1823. A series of letters from F. C. Lewis to Dawson Turner concerning these publications is among the Dawson Turner Correspondence at Trinity College Library, Cambridge (21 March 1822; 23 May 1822; 10 July 1923; 25 July 1827; 17 September 1823.)

21 Reading Museum & Art Gallery, *William Havell 1782–1857*, text by F. Owen and E. Stanford, Reading 1981, nos. 34–76.

22 For the 1809 catalogue, see R. N. Wornum, *The Turner Gallery: A Series of Sixty Engravings*, London 1859, pp. xi–xiii; H. F. Finberg, 'Turner's Gallery in 1810', *Burlington Magazine*, vol. 93, December 1951.

23 Finberg, *Life of Turner*, p. 190.

24 Quoted in J. Gage, *J. M. W. Turner: 'A Wonderful Range of Mind'*, New Haven and London 1987, p. 127.

25 Butlin & Joll, *Paintings of Turner*, vol. 1, p. 120.

26 'Mr Turner's Gallery', *Review of Publications of Art*, 1808, p. 152.

27 A. Robertson, *A Topographical Survey of the Great Road from London to Bath and Bristol*, London 1792, pp. 65–6. Cf. J. Hakewill, *The History of Windsor and its Neighbourhood*, London 1813, pp. v–viii.

28 Combe, *Boydell's History*, vol. 1, pp. 293–4.

29 N. Kent, *Some Particulars of the King's Farm at Windsor*, Oxford 1798; W. Mavor, *General View of the Agriculture of Berkshire*, London 1808, pp. 334–42.
30 Combe recommends the bridge and park as seen from the river, *Boydell's History*, vol. I, p. 304. Skrine found the bridge too plain for a structure of its 'importance', and complained that its effect was lessened by the white house on the left of Farington's view. See Skrine, *General Account*, p. 367.
31 Barrell, *English Literature 1730–1780*, pp. 90–109.
32 J. Middleton, *General View of the Agriculture of Middlesex*, London 1807, p. 435.
33 Combe, *Boydell's History*, vol. I, p. 207; cf. Westall & Owen, *Picturesque Tour*, p. 63.
34 Robertson, *Topographical Survey*, p. 63.
35 M.Rosenthal, *British Landscape Painting*, Oxford 1982, p. 98.
36 St John Priest, *General View of the Agriculture of Buckinghamshire*, London 1810, p. 210. However, Priest insists that milch cows were not generally fed on turnips in Buckinghamshire, since it was believed to taint the milk (pp. 292–3).
37 M. Rosenthal, *Constable: The Painter and his Landscape*, New Haven and London 1983, p. 19.
38 John Barrell has suggested that the picture slips between the georgic and pastoral modes. See his *The Dark Side of the Landscape: The Rural Poor in English Painting 1730–1840*, Cambridge 1980, p. 153.
39 See especially Robertson, *Topographical Survey*, pp. 85–6; W. B. & G. Cooke, *Views on the Thames; Engraved by W. B. Cooke and George Cooke*, London 1822, text to 'Cliefden'.
40 It is possible that the inn refers to Pope's description in the *Epistle to Bathurst* of the end of the depraved George Villiers, second Duke of Buckingham, who had founded Cliveden. See Hemingway, 'Discourses of Art', p. 419.
41 Lindsay, *Sunset Ship*, p. 117.
42 Combe, *Boydell's History*, vol. I, p. 218.
43 See Landseer's laudatory review, in *Review of Publications of Art*, 1808, p. 153.
44 It has been pointed out that the lock in Turner's picture is opening the wrong way – Butlin & Joll, *Paintings of Turner*, vol. I, p. 73.
45 Windsor Bridge was a wooden bridge and could not have appeared in such a conjunction with the castle. The nearest bridge upstream at Maidenhead is improbably distant; and Datchet Bridge, downstream, was in ruins at this time. See Hakewill, *History of Windsor*, p. 328.
46 Combe, *Boydell's History*, vol. I, p. 291; Hakewill, *History of Windsor*, p. 201. Egremont who bought them had attended Westminster and not Eton, but Gray's poetry was part of the common culture of his class.
47 *Review of Publications of Art*, 1808, p. 154.
48 A letter from Lawrence to the Yarmouth collector, Thomas Penrice, shows the figures were read as Eton students. See Butlin & Joll, *Paintings of Turner*, vol. I, p. 66.
49 *Review of Publications of Art*, 1808, pp. 159–60.
50 Combe, *Boydell's History*, vol. II, p. 25.
51 Combe, *Boydell's History*, vol. II, p. 29. On fashionable Richmond, see Skrine, *General Account*, pp. 378–9.
52 This picture may well be the *View on the Thames with Richmond Bridge* (148.5 × 224.6cms.), which was lot 87 in Christie's Sale in December 1971 (photo in Witt Library). The cattle and sheep which occupy the foreground in this appear to have been painted over the fashionable figures which are there in the print.
53 'The Engravings', *London Magazine*, series 2, vol. II, May 1825, pp. 124–5. Criticism of the 'tameness' of Hofland's work was commonplace.
54 Butlin & Joll, *Paintings of Turner*, vol. I, pp. 64–5 summarizes scholarship on the picture. For favourable responses, see Royal Academy, *Examiner*, no. 75, 4 April 1809; 'The Arts', *Sun*, 6 June 1809.
55 Combe, *Boydell's History*, vol. II, p. 3.
56 *Review of Publications of Art*, 1808, p. 158. The description of the picture by John

Britton in his *Fine Arts of the English School* of 1812 is similar in its stress on the pensive associations it evoked, pp. 19–20. Britton sought Turner's advice in writing this text – see Turner to Britton, November 1811, in Gage, *Correspondence of Turner*, pp. 50–1.

57 The painting needs to be compared with *The Thames at Weybridge* (Petworth House) which dates from around the same time, and is comparable in theme. The signs of decay and transience in this picture make sense if the traditional title is correct, and it represents the grounds of Ham House near Weybridge. See Hemingway, 'Discourses of Art', pp. 427–8. Cf. Butlin & Joll, *Paintings of Turner*, vol. I, p. 126.

58 Combe, *Boydell's History*, vol. II, p. 158.

59 On Thomson's ambiguous response, see Williams, *Country and the City*, pp. 176–8.

60 Lindsay, *Sunset Ship*, p. 99. For an interpretation with a slightly different emphasis, see A. Potts, 'Picturing the Modern Metropolis: Images of London in the Nineteenth Century', *History Workshop Journal*, Issue 26, Autumn 1988, pp. 30–1.

61 For images of the same view by J. R. Cozens, J. Feary (1779), and G. Samuel (1816), see Hawes, *Presences*, nos. VI.14, VI.15, VI.16.

62 Combe, *Boydell's History*, vol. II, p. 245.

63 Cf. Soligny, *Letters*, vol. I, p. 40, who describes the view from about a league's distance: 'All that can be seen of the city itself is the immense dome of its cathedral; the rest, apparently for leagues on every side, is one dead immoveable mass of thick dun-yellow smoke, not hanging over, but rising out of it, and more and more dense as it approaches the earth . . . ' The views by Cozens and Samuel produce a serene effect, as does that by Hofland (Yale Center for British Art, B1976. 7. 122).

64 In sketchbooks XCIII and CV in Finberg's catalogue. A large oil painting from the early 1830s of *The Thames above Waterloo Bridge* (Butlin & Joll, *Paintings of Turner*, no. 523) was never brought to completion. This includes a twin-funnelled steam-boat.

65 For Turner's small number of water-colours of London from the 1820s, see E. Shanes, 'Turner's "Unknown" London Series', *Turner Studies*, vol. I, no. 2, 1981.

66 Combe, *Boydell's History*, vol. II, p. 263.

67 Ibid., p. 293; W. B. & G. Cooke, *The Thames*, text to 'South End'.

68 Peacock, *Genius*, pp. 88–9.

69 *Review of Publications of Art*, 1808, p. 162.

70 C. Mackay, *The Thames and its Tributaries*, 2 vols., London 1840, vol. II, p. 253, and more generally pp. 253–73. On the mutinies, see Thompson, *Making*, pp. 183–5.

71 C. F. Stuckey, 'Turner's Birthdays', *Turner Society News*, no. 21, April 1981; J. Golt, 'Beauty and Meaning on Richmond Hill: New Light on Turner's Masterpiece of 1819', *Turner Studies*, vol. 7, no. 2, Winter 1987.

72 For a discussion of Hofland's work and a reproduction of the engraving after it, see Golt, *Turner Studies*, 1987, pp. 15, 19–20.

73 Soligny, *Letters*, vol. II, p. 263.

74 On Turner's politics, see Gage, '*A Wonderful Range of Mind*', pp. 211–16; and on his pursuit of royal patronage, see pp. 176–80.

75 Royal Academy, *Repository of Arts*, series 2, vol. 7, June 1819; *Examiner*, no. 600, 28 June 1819; *Morning Herald*, 20 May 1819.

76 Royal Academy, *Examiner*, no. 600, 27 June 1819.

77 Rosenthal, *Constable*, pp. 52–9.

78 Tate Gallery, *Constable*, p. 84.

79 Ibid., nos. 166 and 180.

80 J. Priestley, *An Historical Account of the Navigable Rivers, Canals, and Railways, throughout Great Britain* (1831), Newton Abbott 1969, pp. 597–8. A. J. Waller, *The Suffolk Stour*, Ipswich 1957, p. 13.

81 T. K. Cromwell, *Excursions in the County of Suffolk*, 2 vols., London 1818, 1819, vol. I, p. 142; A. Suckling, *History and Antiquities of the County of Suffolk*, 2 vols., London 1841, vol. I, pp. iv–v.

82 Cf. S. Ireland, *Picturesque Views on the Upper, or Warwickshire Avon*, London 1795, p. 243, on the vale of Evesham.

83 S. Ireland, *Picturesque Views on the River Medway*, London 1793, p. 153.
84 Combe, *Boydell's History*, vol. I, pp. 56–7. Cf. Westall & Owen, *Picturesque Tour*, pp. 15–16.
85 Beckett, *Constable's Correspondence*, vol. VI, p. 77.
86 Hassell, *Tour*, pp. 29–30, 39, 48, 73, 87. On the picturesque, see pp. 88–9.
87 Skrine, *General Account*, p. 333.
88 Beckett, *Constable's Correspondence*, vol. III, p. 58. Cf. the more ambiguous comment p. 126.
89 In 1821, Constable's *Haywain* was read by the *Observer*'s reviewer as modelled on Ruisdael: 'It is however original enough to escape the servility with which imitators are generally branded ... ' – quoted in Beckett, *Constable's Correspondence*, vol. I, p. 201. Cf. the comment on *Stratford Mill*: 'The interest of this, as well as of all the works of this artist, arises from its truth and locality. But it is a truth and locality as given by a Ruysdael or a Hobbima [*sic*], not the everyday representation of pictorial scenery.' – 'Royal Academy', *Literary Gazette*, no. 172, 6 May 1820. See also: Royal Academy, *New Monthly Magazine*, series 2, vol. 3, July 1821, 334–5; Royal Academy, *London Magazine*, series I, vol. 7, June 1823, 701, 704.
90 M. Pointon, *William Mulready 1786–1863*, London 1986, nos. 11, 22.
91 It should be noted that Linnell retouched the picture in 1868 – Fitzwilliam Museum, Cambridge, *John Linnell: A Centennial Exhibition*, text by K. Crouan, Cambridge 1982, p. 14. For reviews, see Society of Painters in Oil and Water-Colours, *New Monthly Magazine*, no. 29, 1 June 1816; and *Repository of Arts*, series 2, vol. I, April 1816.
92 Pointon, *Mulready*, pp. 29–41. For Constable's later view of Mulready and Linnell (1832), see Beckett, *Constable's Correspondence*, vol. III, pp. 85, 92.
93 Versions of De Wint's picture are in the Victoria and Albert Museum, and Usher Art Gallery, Lincoln. Hugh Prince has described Lewis's picture as 'reassuringly old-fashioned' in its image of agricultural labour. While I accept his account of the iconography of the picture, his analysis does not give sufficient weight to style. The clear-eyed mode of representation which characterizes the picture must have looked startlingly unpicturesque and modern in 1816. See H. Prince, 'Art and agrarian change, 1710–1815', in Cosgrove & Daniels, *Iconography of Landscape*, pp. 112–14.
94 Something of the controversial nature of this type of painting may be indicated by the remark of Ramsay Richard Reinagle in a letter of this time; 'Claude was an admirable imitator of nature, but not a servile one. He was a Philosopher in his art – but your topographical mongers who fear adding or leaving out a stone or twig, are the very excrescences of art.' R. R. Reinagle to D. Turner, 18 November 1816, Dawson Turner Correspondence.
95 There were passing references to it in Royal Academy, *Examiner*, no. 496, 29 June 1817; British Institution, *Sun*, 2 Feb. 1818.
96 Rosenthal, *Constable*, p. 155. Cf. pp. 138–41.
97 For an explanation of what the wagon is doing, see A. Smart & A. Brooks, *Constable and his Country*, London 1976, p. 135.
98 Rosenthal, *Constable*, p. 166, and more generally pp. 166–70.
99 Ibid., p. 146.
100 Waller, *Suffolk Stour*, p. 12.
101 Bagwell, *Transport Revolution*, p. 34.
102 For suggestive interpretations of the imagery of labour in Constable's Stour scenes, see Barrell, *Dark Side*, ch. 3; and Bermingham, *Landscape and Ideology*, pp. 136–47. It will be evident that I prefer an account of their significance which is less centred around the experience of Constable as subject, and works more from the relationship between his pictures and a larger currency of signs.
103 British Institution, *Champion*, no. 329, 7 March 1819.
104 British Institution, *Repository of Arts*, series 2, vol. 13, March 1822, 167. Cf. Royal Academy, vol. 11, June 1821, 367; Royal Academy, *Repository of Arts*, series 2, vol. 13, June 1822, 354.

105 'Fine Arts', *Literary Chronicle*, no. 2, 29 May 1819; 'Exhibition at Somerset House', no. 313, 14 May 1825.

106 Royal Academy, *London Magazine*, series 1, vol. 9, June 1824, 668; Royal Academy, *Literary Gazette*, no. 387, 19 June 1824. The *Literary Gazette*, while generally favourable to Constable in the early 1820s, had problems with his finish and handling of detail. See the somewhat less favourable comment on *A View on the Stour* – Royal Academy, no. 281, 8 June 1822, 361.

107 Royal Academy, *Examiner*, no. 746, 13 May 1822; no. 849, 10 May 1824; no. 901, 8 May 1825. Cf. *Morning Post*, 13 April 1824; *Morning Chronicle*, 7 May 1822.

108 British Institution, *Somerset House Gazette*, no. 19, 14 February 1824.

109 Constable to John Fisher, 23 October 1821 – Beckett, *Constable's Correspondence*, vol. VI, pp. 76–8.

110 The *Literary Gazette* noted the Flemish aspect of *A View on the Stour*, in 'Royal Academy', no. 281, 8 June 1822, 361. See also R. E. G. Tyler, 'Rubens and "The Hay Wain"', *Connoisseur*, vol. 179, August 1975.

111 E.g.: *Scene on the Wensum* (Cliffords, *John Crome*: P66, P66a). In my view the Cliffords were right to doubt the authenticity of the Norwich Museum version (P66), whereas I regard the Yale version (P66a) as authentic. *View on the Yare* (P67) and *Old Houses at Norwich* (P85) have recently passed through the salerooms reattributed to James Stark: Sotheby's 17 March 1982, no. 53; Sotheby's 18 November 1981, no. 6.

112 Based primarily on: J. K. Edwards, 'The Economic Development of Norwich, 1750–1850, with Special Reference to the Worsted Industry', unpublished Ph.D. thesis, University of Leeds 1963; J. K. Edwards, 'The Decline of the Norwich Textiles Industry', *Yorkshire Bulletin of Economic and Social Research*, vol. 16, no. 1, May 1964; J. K. Edwards, 'Communications and the Economic Development of Norwich 1750–1850', *Journal of Transport History*, vol. 7, no. 2, November 1965; J. K. Edwards, 'Norwich in the Eighteenth Century: A Study in Social and Economic Organisation', 1972. Manuscript in Local Studies Library, Norwich; P. J. Corfield, 'The Social and Economic History of Norwich 1650–1850: a Study in Urban Growth', unpublished Ph.D. thesis, University of London 1976.

113 Edwards, *Yorkshire Bulletin of Economic and Social Research*, 1964, pp. 40–1.

114 Corfield, *Impact*, ch. 9.

115 Edwards, 'Economic Development of Norwich', appendix VII; Edwards, 'Norwich in the Eighteenth Century' – 'Relief of the Poor'; Jewson, *Jacobin City*; Bayne, *Comprehensive History*, pp. 392–4.

116 A report on the Norwich Philosophical Society in *New Monthly Magazine*, vol. 9, March 1818, emphasized the centrality of Rigby's role in it.

117 F. W. Hawcroft, 'Crome and his Patron; Thomas Harvey of Catton', *Connoisseur*, vol. 144, December 1959; Cliffords, *John Crome*, chs. 1–2.

118 C. Mackie, *Norfolk Annals*, 2 vols., Norwich 1901, vol. 1, p. 304; Edwards, 'Economic Development of Norwich', pp. 319, 482.

119 H. Ladbrooke to J. B. Ladbrooke (1858), in *Norwich Artists Deceased to 1898*, m.s. volume, British Museum Print Room. Crome's drinking habits are documented in some degree by surviving wine bills – see S. C. Kaines Smith, *John Crome*, London 1923, p. 35; Cliffords, *John Crome*, p. 81.

120 Quoted in Cliffords, *John Crome*, pp. 30–1.

121 'Public Works' and 'Local Government' in Edwards, 'Norwich in the Eighteenth Century'; Corfield, 'Social and Economic History of Norwich', pp. 448–63; J. Stacy, *A Topographical Study and Historical Account of the City and County of Norwich*, Norwich 1819, pp. 41–2.

122 Edwards, *Journal of Transport History*, 1965.

123 R. N. Bacon, *Report on the Agriculture of Norfolk*, London 1844, pp. 6–7. On the importance of manures, see p. 267.

124 Edwards, 'Norwich in the Eighteenth Century' – 'Water Supply'; Stacy, *Topographical Study*, p. 123.

125 For Mulready's development, see Pointon, *Mulready*, cat. nos. 1, 25, 30, 22, 23; and p. 32. A similar transition can be read in Callcott's work from *The Water Mill* (1805) to *A Rural Scene; the Entrance to a Village* (*c.* 1812). See Tate Gallery, *Callcott*, cat. nos. 2 & 14.

126 Cliffords, *John Crome*, E5.

127 Cliffords, *John Crome*, E4. A chalk and wash drawing of this composition, possibly based on a lost painting, is in Norwich Castle Museum (28.59.935).

128 Wark, *Reynolds, Disc. XIII*, lines 438–55; Bartell, *Hints for Picturesque Improvements*, pp. 125, 72–6.

129 I have discussed Cotman's images of Norfolk agriculture in my article *Art History* 1984.

130 Turner, *Outlines in Lithography*, text accompanying the lithograph from this picture.

131 Robberds, *Life of Taylor*, vol. II, p. 60.

132 Bartell, *Cromer*, p. 109. Bartell's description is like a recipe for Crome's *Marlingford Grove* (Lady Lever Art Gallery, Port Sunlight).

133 On Crome's enthusiasm for Hobbema, see Turner's comments in Wodderspoon, *John Crome*, pp. 7, 9.

134 *Norfolk Chronicle*, 8 August 1818; 14 August 1819.

135 Robberds, *Rivers of Norfolk*, text to *Bishop's Bridge*.

136 Biographical details from M. Allthorpe-Guyton, *John Thirtle 1777–1839, Drawings in Norwich Castle Museum*, Norwich 1977.

137 Smith, *Peter De Wint*, colour plate 4, p. 77.

138 I regard as outdoor sketches, drawings such as *Near Brandsby* (Ashmolean Museum), *In Rokeby Park* (Yale Center for British Art), and *Duncombe Park* (British Museum).

139 Kitson, *Life of Cotman*, p. 110.

140 I discuss these drawings in Hemingway, *Art History*, 1984.

141 Allthorpe-Guyton, *John Thirtle*, nos. 62 & 120. All the Thirtle drawings referred to are in Norwich Castle Museum.

142 Allthorpe-Guyton, *John Thirtle*, nos. 111 & 47.

143 Cf. in Allthorpe-Guyton, *John Thirtle*, the drawings *Devil's Tower, Norwich* (nos. 13 & 14); *St Benet's Abbey*, (nos. 24 & 23); and *Dilham Staithe* (nos. 116 & 115).

144 *Hints on Water-Colour Painting by John Thirtle Artist*, in Allthorpe-Guyton, *John Thirtle*, p. 34.

145 Cliffords, *John Crome*, D52. Doubts have been expressed as to the authenticity of this drawing, which has been seen as inferior to a large sketch version in the Whitworth Art Gallery, Manchester (D51). (e.g., see F. Hawcroft, review of Cliffords, *John Crome*, in *Burlington Magazine*, vol. 111, no. 801, December 1969.) The differences between the two could be interpreted as comparable to that between Thirtle's sketches and finished drawings, and D52 may well be by Crome.

146 Varley's *Boat Builder's Yard* is illustrated in Kauffmann, *John Varley*, fig. 20; Jackson's *Clifton from Rownham Meadows* is illustrated in Bristol, City Art Gallery, *Bristol School of Artists*, p. 154. For Turner, see, for example, S. Daniels, 'The Implications of Industry: Turner and Leeds', *Turner Studies*, vol. 6, no. 1, 1986.

147 For examples, see Martyn Gregory Gallery, *John Linnell: Truth to Nature (A Centennial Exhibition)*, text by K. Crouan, London 1982, catalogue nos. 14 & 15; Fitzwilliam Museum, *John Linnell*, catalogue nos. 17–21.

148 The picture received little attention in the reviews, but the *Examiner* referred to its 'beautiful simplicity of composition' and 'rich Cuypish colour', British Institution, no. 532, 8 March 1818.

149 The *Vale of Thorpe, Norwich*, was sold from the 1822 British Institution show to C. Harvey, Esq. MP (a Norwich patron) for £31. – *Literary Gazette*, no. 275, 27 April 1822, 264.

150 Lot 81, Christie's Sale, 16 November 1962.

151 Lot 21, Sotheby's Sale, 17 June 1981, 43 × 72ins. On these purchases see respectively, *Annals of the Fine Arts*, vol. 4, 1819, 121; vol. 3, 1818, 75; *Magazine of Fine Arts*, 151.

152 There is an impression of this in Norwich Castle Museum (66.939). In 1821, Vincent

was proposing to 'etch in an elaborate manner [. . .] a series of compositions from his principal pictures', a plan which again confirms the scale of his ambitions at this moment. See W. C. Leeds to D. Turner, 24 October 1821, Dawson Turner Correspondence.

153 The work may have been badly hung at the Academy, and Vincent did not exhibit there after 1823. Considering that Stark and Vincent had been much praised in the *Annals of the Fine Arts*, it is possible they had become associated with the faction of critics of the Academy in the artistic community. Vincent seems to have been close to the artists who formed the Society of British Artists, being among those who solicited support for that body in January 1824 (*Morning Post*, 13 January 1824). Although he was neither a member or a subscriber, this may well have been due to his financial difficulties. (On which, see his correspondence in Dickes 1905, pp. 499–505; and the letter from A. J. Stark to L. G. Bolingbroke, 1882, in the George Vincent Historical File, Norwich Castle Museum.) The Norwich-based artists, J. B. Crome, S. D. Colkett, and A. & J. Stannard all exhibited with the Society in the 1820s, and works by Vincent (then deceased) were lent to the Winter Exhibitions of 1832–4.

154 A. Moore, *The Norwich School of Artists*, Norwich 1985, p. 46.

155 For example, Norwich Museum's *On the River Yare* (also known as *Thorpe Staithe*), which probably dates from the later 1820s.

156 Cliffords, *John Crome*, p. 130. The Cliffords regarded the picture as inauthentic, but the attribution was reaffirmed by Hawcroft, *Burlington Magazine*, 1969.

157 'British Gallery', *New Monthly Magazine*, no. 62, 1 March 1819. Cf. *Annals of the Fine Arts*, vol. 4, 1819, 121; *Repository of Arts*, series 2, vol. 7, 169; *Champion*, no. 329, 7 March 1819; *Examiner*, no. 582, 21 February 1819; *Morning Herald*, 1 February 1819. The main negative response suggested that 'a little nature' was 'made to serve a great deal of art' in Vincent's work, and described him as a 'mannerist'. See *Literary Gazette*, 13 February 1819, in George Vincent Historical File, Norwich Castle Museum.

158 E. J. Hobsbawn & G. Rudé, *Captain Swing*, Harmondsworth 1973, pp. 60–1. The *Norfolk Chronicle* in the summer months of 1818 is full of reports of incendiarism. See also the letters from Dawson Turner to William Roscoe, 11 April 1822; 10 September 1822 (Liverpool Public Library, MSS 4913, 4918).

159 'Letters of the Cotman Family of Norwich' (British Museum, Add. MS 37029) pp. 103–4. The poem probably dates from *c.*1834.

160 Stark's so-called *Postwick Reach near Thorpe* (63 × 102.7cm, Richard Green Gallery) is possibly the *View on the Yare, at Thorpe* shown at the Society of British Artists exhibition in 1824, or the *Scene near Norwich* shown at the British Institution in that year. (For a description which supports the latter identification, see *Examiner*, no. 841, 15 March 1824). Stannard's *River at Thorpe* (Norwich Castle Museum) is his major exercise in this vein. This does not seem to be any of the pictures he exhibited with the British Institution or Society of British Artists, and is likely to be the *Scene on the Wensum – the Sun breaking out after a Storm*, shown with the Norwich Society in 1822.

161 For adverse opinions on the scenery of the county see, Chambers, *General History*, vol. 1, cii; N. Kent, *A General View of the Agriculture of the County of Norfolk*, London 1794, p. 6.

162 Robberds, *Rivers of Norfolk*, text to Pl.2, *Mouth of the Yare*.

163 Robberds, *Rivers of Norfolk*, text to Pl.24, *Shipmeadow Lock*. Robberds found the 'rudeness' and 'simplicity' of this lock 'in perfect keeping with the rustic scenery' around it. Such imagery is strikingly close to that of Constable, who subscribed for proofs of the *Rivers of Norfolk*.

164 On Waterloo Bridge as a modern political symbol, see *Repository of Arts*, series 2, vol. 2, November 1816, 288.

165 Number 61 in Christie's sale of 21 November 1986.

166 T. Fawcett, 'Thorpe Water Frolic', *Norfolk Archaeology*, vol. 36, Pt.IV, 1977.

167 Diary of Thomas Blofeld, quoted in Allthorpe-Guyton, *John Thirtle*, p. 18. Stark sold

his 1819 exhibit to J. J. Bullock for 60 gns, and it is possible that the picture with Christie's in 1986 is a slightly smaller repetition executed for another patron.

168 Reports of Wroxham Water Frolic, in *Norfolk Chronicle*, 9 August 1817; 12 September 1818; 17 July 1819; 29 July 1820.

169 Taylor to J. H. Payne, 24 October 1820, in Robberds, *Life of Taylor*, vol. II, pp. 510–11. On the associations of the ruin, see also Robberds, *Rivers of Norfolk*, text to Plate 6.

170 The abbey does not appear in the water-colour sketch of Wroxham Regatta in Norwich Castle Museum, attributed to Crome (Cliffords, *John Crome*, D100). This drawing is possibly by Stark, having affinities with some early drawings by him.

171 *Examiner*, no. 582, 21 February 1819; *New Monthly Magazine*, no. 62, 1 March 1819; *Repository of Arts*, series 2, vol. 7, March 1819; *Champion*, no. 318, 7 February 1819; *Literary Gazette*, 20 March 1819.

172 F. Hawcroft, 'John Crome and the "Yarmouth Water Frolic"', *Burlington Magazine*, vol. 150, July/August 1959.

173 'Poetical representations must be formed from the highest probable perfection that the work will admit of; external nature must in them be more elegant than in reality – every situation, every incident, every character, must be better accomplished in those qualities that raise our admiration & interest our passions.' – J. B. Crome, MS Lecture on Painting and Poetry, pp. 3–4.

174 J. B. Crome had already represented a boat of this type in the remarkable painting in Manchester City Art Gallery known as *The Steam Packet*, which probably dates from 1813–17. See T. Clifford, 'John Crome's *Steam Packet*', *Connoisseur*, vol. 185, March 1984. I don't accept Clifford's reattribution of the picture to Crome senior.

175 *Norfolk Chronicle*, 4 August 1821. Cf. the report of the Kingston Steam Packet, *Norfolk Chronicle*, 16 August 1821.

176 F. Sayers, *The Collective Works of Dr Frank Sayers*, ed. W. Taylor, Norwich 1823.

177 *Norfolk Chronicle*, 31 July 1824.

178 *Norfolk Chronicle*, 5 August 1820. Cf. report of 31 July 1819.

179 *Norfolk Chronicle*, 28 July 1821.

180 *Norfolk Chronicle*, 24 July 1824; 25 July 1818; 31 July 1819, 5 August 1820.

181 *Norwich Mercury*, 18 August 1821.

182 *Norfolk Chronicle*, 18 August 1821.

183 The painting has been tentatively identified with a *Wroxham Water Frolic* in J. B. Crome's 1834 Sale (Cliffords, *John Crome*, p. 239), but it seems odd that J. B. Crome should make a mistake with the title of his own painting. At the moment it is therefore uncertain whether or not the work was saleable.

184 *Norwich Mercury*, 6 August 1824.

185 Joseph Stannard (1797–1830) is an obscure figure, who never joined the Norwich Society of Artists, probably because of his pupilage to Robert Ladbrooke, and involvement in the short-lived Norfolk and Norwich Society of Artists, which held exhibitions in rivalry with the former's in 1816–18. The main account of Stannard is in Dickes, *Norwich School*, pp. 525–34. That he found it hard to make a living in Norfolk is indicated both by his obituary (*Norwich Mercury*, 11 December 1830), and by a letter from him to a 'Mr Cooke', dated 26 December 1823, in the Reeve Collection, British Museum Department of Prints & Drawings.

186 *Norfolk Chronicle*, 30 August 1823. This report estimated 10,000 persons were present.

187 *Norfolk Chronicle*, 28 August 1824. The *Mercury* estimated 20,000 were present this year, and Harvey's dinner had 400–500 guests. On Stannard's other rowing activities, see 'Rowing', *Norfolk Chronicle*, 19 June 1824.

188 *Norwich Mercury*, 28 August 1824.

189 For other works by Stannard in a comparable mode, see *Buckenham Ferry* (1826, Yale Center for British Art) and *Boats on the Yare, Bramerton, Norfolk* (1828, Fitzwilliam Museum, Cambridge) – Hemingway, *Norwich School*, Pls. 58 & 60.

190 On Stannard's patrons, see Chambers, *General History*, pp. 759, 847, 1118–19.

191 *Norwich Mercury*, 23 January 1830. The Conversaziones of 1830–2 were a last-ditch

attempt by the Norwich artists to stimulate local patronage. They are well-reported in the *Norwich Mercury*.

192 *Norfolk Chronicle*, 6 August 1825.

193 See especially, *Norfolk Chronicle*, 5 August 1820.

194 It seems particularly appropriate that J. J. Colman, the city's leading industrial magnate and philanthropist, should give this picture to the city for the opening of its new picture gallery in the Castle Museum in 1894. See Hemingway, *Oxford Art Journal*, 1988, 27–31.

Conclusion: The passing of naturalism

1 On this see Gage, *Colour in Turner*, ch. 8.

2 Hazlitt, *Complete Works*, vol. XVI, p. 205.

3 Royal Academy, *Repository of Arts*, series 2, vol. I, June 1816, p. 352.

4 'Janus's Jumble', *London Magazine*, series 1, vol. I, June 1820.

5 E. Edwards, *The Fine Arts in England; Their State and Prospects Considered Relatively to National Education*, London 1840, p. 238. For Edwards see *Dictionary of National Biography*.

6 Shee, *Rhymes on Art*, pp. li–lii, lvi.

7 J. Constable to J. Fisher, 17 April 1822, in Beckett, *Constable's Correspondence*, vol. VI, p. 90.

8 J. Fisher to J. Constable, 12 November 1822, in Beckett, *Constable's Correspondence*, vol. VI, p. 103.

9 Stewart, *Philosophical Essays*, pp. 284–5.

10 Constable's *Boat-building at Flatford Mill* was in his posthumous sale. *Golding Constable's Flower Garden*, *Golding Constable's Vegetable Garden* (both in Ipswich Museum) and *Hampstead Heath* (Tate Gallery, TG 1236), all of which have the marks of outdoor painting, remained in the Constable family until 1887. His 1815 *View of Dedham* and *Landscape: Ploughing Scene in Suffolk* may be best understood as works for a local clientele, like some of Crome's small pictures of Norwich and Yarmouth beach. On the relative lack of success of Lewis, Linnell and Mulready, see Tate Gallery, *Landscape in Britain 1750–1850*, text by L. Parris and C. Shields, London 1974, cat. nos. 240, 245, 248.

11 See Butler, *Romantics, Rebels, and Reactionaries*, especially ch. 3.

12 R. H. Horne, *Exposition of the False Medium and Barriers Excluding Men of Genius from the Public*, London 1833, p. 273. On Horne, see C. Pearl, *Always Morning: The Life of Richard Henry 'Orion' Horne*, Melbourne 1960.

13 British Institution, *London Magazine*, series 2, vol. II, July 1825, 392, 397.

14 'English Landscape', *New Monthly Magazine*, vol. 4, 1822, 535–6.

15 Illustrated in colour in Moore, *Norwich School*, p. 44.

16 C. Hill, 'The Norman Yoke', in J. Saville, ed., *Democracy and the Labour Movement: Essays in Honour of Dona Torr*, London 1954, especially pp. 42–54. For a contemporary example, see J. Thelwall, 'On the Saxon Origin of the English Constitution', *Champion*, no. 315, 17 January 1819.

17 British Institution, *Examiner*, no. 843, 29 March 1824; *Somerset House Gazette*, no. 20, 21 February 1824.

18 Robberds, *Rivers of Norfolk*, Dedication to William IV.

19 Ibid., text to Plate 15.

20 Ibid., text to Plate 13.

21 Ibid., text to Plate 19.

22 Ibid., text to Plate 28.

23 Ibid., text to Plate 36.

24 Ibid., text to Plate 35.

25 Williams, *Culture and Society*, chs. 1, 3, 4, 7.

26 A. Potts, '"Constable Country" between the Wars', in R. Samuel, ed., *Patriotism: The Making and Unmaking of British National Identity*, vol. III, London 1989.

27 The cult of the English landscape is defined as one of the chief cultural factors which has hampered Britain's 'progress' since the late nineteenth century in Martin Wiener's *English Culture and the Decline of the Industrial Spirit*, Cambridge 1981. But this seems to assume that a modern culture is only urban, and that 'progress' depends on a kind of free market productivism, which can tolerate no concern with qualitative values.

Select bibliography

Note: Some works referred to in passing in the notes are not listed here. The bibliography is divided between works published before 1900 and those published after 1900 (including Ph.D. theses). While this is intended to divide source materials from interpretative literature, modern editions of authors such as Coleridge and Reynolds fall into the second category.

Primary sources

John Berney Crome, 'Essay on Painting and Poetry', MS, Norwich Castle Museum.

Warren R. Dawson Manuscripts relating to Dawson Turner, BM Add. MSS 56290–4.

'James Stark 1794–1859', bound volume of letters and notes in the Bradfer Lawrence Collection, Norfolk & Norwich Record Office.

L. G. Bolingbroke, 'James Stark', MS volume in Norwich Castle Museum.

James Reeve, collection of materials relating to Norfolk & Norwich artists, 7 volumes in the British Museum Print Room, 2 volumes in the Colman & Rye Library, Norwich Central Library.

Dawson Turner Correspondence, Trinity College Library, University of Cambridge.

Literature published before 1900

Algarotti, F., *An Essay on Painting*, London 1764.

Alison, A., *Essays on the Nature and Principles of Taste* (1790; 2nd revised edn 1811), 2 vols., Edinburgh 1815.

Anon.,

Brighton and its Environs; A Brief but Comprehensive History and Guide, 6th edn printed & published by C. &. R. Sickelmore, Brighton 1825 (?).

A Guide to all the Watering and Sea-Bathing Places, London 1805.

The Hastings Guide; or a Description of that Ancient Town and Port and its Environs, 2nd edn, London 1797; and 6th edn, London 1828.

London: A Descriptive Poem, London 1811.

(M. M. Howard), *Hastings, Past and Present; with Notices of the most Remarkable Places in the Neighbourhood*, Hastings and London 1855.

The Picture of London, for 1810; being a Correct Guide to all the Curiosities, Amusements,

Exhibitions, Public Establishments, and Remarkable Objects, in and Near London, London 1810.

Picture of Margate, being a Complete Guide to all Persons Visiting Margate, Ramsgate, and Broadstairs, London 1809.

Ayton, R., *A Voyage Round Great Britain, Undertaken in the Summer of the Year 1813*, 8 vols., London 1814–25.

Bacon, R. N., *Report on the Agriculture of Norfolk*, London 1844.

Barry, J., *The Works of James Barry*, ed. J. Fryer, 2 vols., London 1809.

Bartell, E., *Hints for Picturesque Improvements in Ornamented Cottages and their Scenery*, London 1804.

Cromer, Considered as a Watering Place; with Observations on the Picturesque Scenery in its Neighbourhood, 2nd edn, London 1806.

Bayne, A. D., *A Comprehensive History of Norwich*, London and Norwich 1869.

Beatniffe, R., *The Norfolk Tour: or Traveller's Pocket Companion*, 5th edn, Norwich 1795.

Britton, J., *The Fine Arts of the English School*, London 1812.

Burke, E., *A Philosophical Enquiry into the Origin of Our Ideas of the Sublime and Beautiful*, (1757) 2nd edn 1759.

Burnet, J., *Practical Essays on Art* (1822, 1826, 1837), Bradford and London 1893.

Butler, J., *The Analogy of Religion, Natural and Revealed, to the Constitution and Course of Nature*, London 1736.

Carey, G. S., *The Balnea: or, An Impartial Description of all the Popular Watering Places in England*, 3rd edn, London 1801.

Chambers, J., *A General History of the County of Norfolk*, Norwich and London 1829.

Combe, W., *Boydell's History of the River Thames*, 2 vols., London 1794–6.

Cooke, W. B., *The Thames; or Graphic Illustrations of the Seats, Villas, Public Buildings, and Picturesque Scenery on the Banks of that Noble River*, London 1811.

Views in Sussex, Drawn by J. M. W. Turner, R.A. and Engraved by W. B. Cooke, text by R. R. Reinagle, London 1819.

Cooke, W. B. and G., *Picturesque Views on the Southern Coast of England; Engraved by W. B. Cooke, G. Cooke, etc.*, London 1814–26.

Collins, W. W., *Memoirs of the Life of William Collins, Esq., R.A.*, 2 vols., London 1848.

Cox, D., *A Treatise on Landscape Painting and Effect in Water Colours*, London 1814.

Cunningham, A., *The Life of Sir David Wilkie*, 3 vols., London 1843.

Druery, J. H., *Historical and Topographical Notices of Great Yarmouth*, London 1826.

Du Fresnoy, C., *The Art of Painting*, tr. J. Dryden, London 1769.

Edwards, E., *The Fine Arts in England; Their State and Prospects Considered Relatively to National Education*, London 1840.

Félibien, A., *Seven Conferences Held in the King of France's Cabinet of Paintings*, tr. T. Cooper, London 1740.

Foggo, G., 'The Royal Academy Exposed', *New Monthly Magazine*, vol. xxxviii, July–August 1833.

Galt, J., *The Life and Studies of Benjamin West*, 2 parts, London 1816, 1820.

Gilpin, W., *Three Essays: On Picturesque Beauty; On Picturesque Travel; and On Sketching Landscape* (1792) London 1794.

Remarks on Forest Scenery, 2 vols., London 1808.

Hakewill, J., *The History of Windsor and its Neighbourhood*, London 1813.
Hallam, H., Review of Payne Knight's *Analytical Inquiry, Edinburgh Review*, vol. VII, January 1806.
Hartley, D., *Observations on Man* (1749), 2 parts, London 1791, 1801.
Hassell, J., *A Tour of the Grand Junction*, London 1819.
Haydon, B. R., *Lectures on Painting and Design*, 2 vols., London 1844, 1846.
Home, H. (Lord Kames), *Elements of Criticism* (1762), 2 vols., Edinburgh 1785.
Sketches of the History of Man (1774), 4 vols., Edinburgh 1788.
Horne, R. H., *Exposition of the False Medium and Barriers Excluding Men of Genius from the Public*, London 1833.
House of Commons, *Report from the Select Committee on Arts and their Connection with the Manufactures*, Parts I & II, London 1835, 1836.
Howard, H., *A Course of Lectures on Painting Delivered at the Royal Academy of Fine Arts by Henry Howard, Esq. R.A.*, ed. F. Howard, London 1848.
Jeffrey, F., Review of A. Alison, *Essays on Taste, Edinburgh Review*, vol. 18, no. 37, May 1811.
Contributions to the Edinburgh Review, 4 vols., London 1844.
Kent, N., *Some Particulars of the King's Farm at Windsor*, Oxford 1798.
Knight, R. P., *The Landscape, A Didactic Poem in Three Books* (1794), London 1795.
The Progress of Civil Society, A Didactic Poem in Six Books, London 1796.
A Monody on the Death of the Right Honourable Charles James Fox, London 1806–7.
Analytical Inquiry into the Principles of Taste (1805), London 1808.
Review of *The Works of James Barry, Edinburgh Review*, vol. 17, August 1810.
Review of Northcote's *Life of Sir Joshua Reynolds, Edinburgh Review*, vol. 23, September 1814.
Knowles, J., *The Life and Writings of Henry Fuseli*, 3 vols., London 1831.
Landseer, J., *Lectures on the Art of Engraving delivered at the Royal Institution of Great Britain*, London 1807.
Lawrence, T., *Address to the Students of the Royal Academy ... 10th December 1823*, London 1824.
Lewis, J., *A Topographical Dictionary of England ... with Historical and Statistical Descriptions*, 7th edn, 4 vols., London 1849.
Mackay, C., *The Thames and its Tributaries*, 2 vols., London 1840.
Mannings, J. S., *Cromer, A Descriptive Poem*, London 1806.
Manship, H., *The History of Great Yarmouth*, ed. C. J. Palmer, Yarmouth 1854.
Moss, W. G., *The History and Antiquities of the Town and Port of Hastings*, London 1824.
Paley, W., *Natural Theology: or, Evidences of the Existence and Attributes of the Deity, Collected from the Appearance of Nature* (1802), London 1803.
Palmer, C. J., *The Perlustration of Great Yarmouth*, 3 vols., Great Yarmouth 1874.
Pasquin, A., *The New Brighton Guide*, 4th edn, London 1796.
Peacock, T. L., *The Genius of the Thames, Palmrya, and other Poems*, London 1812.
Phillips, T., *Lectures on the History and Principles of Painting*, London 1833.
Piles, R. de, *The Art of Painting, with the Lives and Characters of above 300 of the most Eminent Painters*, tr. B. Buckeridge, London n.d.
Pott, J. H., *An Essay on Landscape Painting*, London 1782.
Preston, J., *The Picture of Yarmouth*, Yarmouth 1819.

Price, U., *Thoughts on the Defense of Property, Addressed to the County of Hereford*, Hereford 1797.
Essays on the Picturesque, 3 vols., London 1810.

Priestley, J., *An Historical Account of the Navigable Rivers, Canals, and Railways, throughout Great Britain* (1831) reprint, Newton Abbott 1969.

Pye, J., *The Patronage of British Art, An Historical Sketch*, London 1845.

Repton, H., *The Landscape Gardening and Landscape Architecture of the Late Humphry Repton, Esq.*, ed. J. C. Loudon, London 1840.

Reynolds, J., *The Works of Sir Joshua Reynolds*, ed. E. Malone, 3 vols., London 1809.

Richardson, J., *The Works of Mr Jonathan Richardson*, ed. J. Richardson, Jr, London 1772.

Richter, H., *Daylight; A Recent Discovery in the Art of Painting*, London 1817.

Robberds, J. W., *Scenery of the Rivers of Norfolk, from Pictures painted by James Stark*, Norwich and London 1834.
A Memoir of the Life and Writings of the Late William Taylor of Norwich, 2 vols., London 1843.

Robertson, A., *A Topographical Survey of the Great Road from London to Bath and Bristol*, London 1792.

Robertson, E., ed., *Letters and Papers of Andrew Robertson 1777–1845*, London 1897.

Rowlandson, T., *An Excursion to Brighthelmstone, made in the year 1789, by Henry Wigstead and Thomas Rowlandson*, London 1790.
Poetical Sketches of Scarborough: Illustrated by Twenty-One Engravings of Humorous Subjects, London 1813.

Rymer, J., *A Sketch of Great Yarmouth . . . with Some Reflections on Cold Bathing*, London 1777.

Sayers, F., *Collective Works of the late Dr Sayers*, ed. W. Taylor, Norwich 1823.

Shee, M. A., *Rhymes on Art; or, the Remonstrance of a Painter*, London 1805.
Elements of Art, London 1809.
A Letter to the President and Directors of the British Institution, London 1809.

Skrine, H., *A General Account of all the Rivers of Note in Great Britain*, London 1801.

Smith, J. T., *Remarks on Rural Scenery*, London 1797.

Soligny, V. de (P. G. Patmore), *Letters on England*, 2 vols., London 1823.

Stacy, J., *A Topographical Study and Historical Account of the City and County of Norfolk*, Norwich 1819.

Stewart, D., *Philosophical Essays*, Edinburgh and London 1816.

Story, A. T., *The Life of John Linnell*, 2 vols., London 1893.

Taylor, W., 'Outlines of a Discourse on the History and Theory of Prospect Painting', *Monthly Magazine*, vol. 37, 405–9, vol. 38, 211–15, 499–503, 1814.

Uwins, S., *A Memoir of Thomas Uwins, R.A.*, 2 vols., London 1858.

Varley, J., *A Treatise on the Principles of Landscape Design*, London 1816–17.

Wainewright, T. G., *Essays and Criticisms by Thomas Griffiths Wainewright*, ed. W. C. Hazlitt, London 1880.

Westall, W. & Owen, S., *A Picturesque Tour of the River Thames*, London 1828.

Wodderspoon, J., *John Crome and his Works*, Norwich 1858.

Wood, J. G., *The Principal Rivers of Wales Illustrated*, London 1813.

Wornum, R., ed., *Lectures on Painting by the Royal Academicians: Barry, Opie, Fuseli*, London 1848.

Young, E., *Conjectures on Original Composition*, London 1759.

Literature published after 1900

Abbey, J. R., *Scenery of Great Britain and Ireland in Aquatint and Lithography 1770–1860 from the Library of J. R. Abbey*, London 1952.

Abercrombie, N., Hill, B., & Turner, S., *The Dominant Ideology Thesis*, London 1980.

Abrams, M. H., *The Mirror and the Lamp: Romantic Theory and the Critical Tradition*, Oxford 1971.

Aers, D., Cook, J., & Punter, D., *Romanticism and Ideology: Studies in English Writing 1765–1830*, London, Boston and Henley 1981.

Allthorpe-Guyton, M., *John Thirtle 1777–1839, Drawings in Norwich Castle Museum*, Norwich 1977.

Anderson, P., 'Origins of the Present Crisis', *New Left Review*, no. 23, January/February 1964.

'Components of the National Culture', in A. Cockburn and R. Blackburn, ed., *Student Power/Problems, Diagnosis, Action*, Harmondsworth 1969.

Aspinall, A., *Politics and the Press c. 1750–1850*, London 1949.

Asquith, I., 'The Whig Party and the Press in the early Nineteenth Century', *Bulletin of the Institute of Historical Research*, vol. 49, 1976.

Bagwell, P. S., *The Transport Revolution from 1770*, London 1974.

Barbier, C. P., *William Gilpin: His Drawings, Teachings, and Theory of the Picturesque*, Oxford 1963.

Barrell, J., *The Idea of Landscape and the Sense of Place 1730–1840*, Cambridge 1972.

The Dark Side of the Landscape: The Rural Poor in English Painting 1730–1840, Cambridge 1980.

English Literature 1730–80: An Equal Wide Survey, London 1983.

The Political Theory of Painting from Reynolds to Hazlitt, 'The Body of the Public', New Haven and London 1986.

Barthes, R., 'L'Effet de Réel', *Communications*, no. 11, 1968.

Image–Music–Text, New York 1977.

Bauer, J., *The London Magazine 1820–29*, *Anglistica*, vol. 1, Copenhagen 1953.

Beckett, R. B., ed., *John Constable's Correspondence*, 6 vols., Ipswich 1962–8.

John Constable's Discourses, Ipswich 1970.

Bermingham, A., *Landscape and Ideology: The English Rustic Tradition, 1740–1860*, London 1987.

Bourdieu, P., 'Intellectual Field and Creative Project' in M. F. D. Young, ed., *Knowledge and Control*, London 1971.

The Cultural Field and the Economic Field, tr. R. Nice, CCCS Stencilled Paper No. 46, University of Birmingham 1977.

Outline of a Theory of Practice, Cambridge 1977.

Distinction: A Social Critique of the Judgement of Taste, tr. R. Nice, London & New York 1984.

Briggs, A., 'Middle-Class Consciousness in English Politics, 1780–1846', *Past and Present*, no. 9, April 1956.

The Age of Improvement 1783–1867, London 1959.

Bristol, City Art Gallery, *The Bristol School of Artists, Francis Danby and Painting in Bristol 1810–1840*, text by F. Greenacre, Bristol 1973.

Burke, E., *Reflections on the French Revolution*, ed. A. J. Grieve, London and New York 1910 (Everyman edn).

Butler, M., *Romantics, Rebels and Reactionaries: English Literature and its Background 1760–1830*, Oxford 1981.

Butlin, M., & Joll, E., *The Paintings of J. M. W. Turner*, 2 vols., New Haven and London 1977.

Chitnis, A. C., *The Scottish Enlightenment: A Social History*, London 1976.

Christie, I. R., 'British Newspapers in the Later Georgian Age', in *Myth and Reality in Late-Eighteenth-Century British Politics and Other Papers*, London 1970.

Clarke, M., *The Tempting Prospect: A Social History of English Watercolours*, London 1981.

Clarke, M., & Penny, N., *The Arrogant Connoisseur: Richard Payne Knight 1751–1824*, Manchester 1982.

Clifford, D. & T., *John Crome*, London 1968.

Cohen, G., *Karl Marx's Theory of History: A Defence*, Oxford 1979.

Coleridge, S. T., *Biographia Literaria* (1817), ed. G. Watson, London and New York 1956 (Everyman edn).

Colley, L., 'Whose Nation? Class and National Consciousness in Britain 1750–1830', *Past and Present*, no. 113, November 1986.

Cookson, J. E., *The Friends of Peace: Anti-War Liberalism in England 1793–1815*, Cambridge 1982.

Corfield, P. J., 'The Social and Economic History of Norwich 1650–1850: A Study in Urban Growth', unpublished Ph.D. thesis, University of London 1976.

The Impact of English Towns 1700–1800, Oxford 1982.

Corrigan, P., & Sayer, D., *The Great Arch: English State Formation as Cultural Revolution*, Oxford 1985.

Cosgrove, D., & Daniels, S., ed., *The Iconography of Landscape: Essays on the Symbolic Representation, Design and Use of Past Environments*, Cambridge 1988.

Daniels, S., 'The Political Landscape', in G. Carter, P. Goode, & K. Laurie, ed., *Humphry Repton, Landscape Gardener 1752–1818*, catalogue to an exhibition at the University of East Anglia, Norwich 1982.

Davidoff, L., & Hall, C., *Family Fortunes: Men and Women of the English Middle Class, 1780–1850*, London 1987.

Davidoff, L., L'Esperence, J., & Newby, H., 'Landscape with Figures: Home and Community in English Society', in Mitchell, J., and Oakley, A., eds., *The Rights and Wrongs of Women*, Harmondsworth 1976.

Dickes, W. F., *The Norwich School of Painting*, London and Norwich 1905.

Dickinson, H. T., *Liberty and Property: Political Ideology in Eighteenth-Century Britain*, London 1977.

Dobai, J., *Die Kunstliteratur des Klassizismus und der Romantik in England 1700–1840*, 3 vols., Bern 1974–7.

Edwards, J. K., 'The Economic Development of Norwich, 1750–1850, with Reference to the Worsted Industry', unpublished Ph.D. thesis, University of Leeds 1963.

'The Decline of the Norwich Textiles Industry', *Yorkshire Bulletin of Economic and Social Research*, vol. 16, no. 1, May 1964.

'Communications and the Economic Development of Norwich 1750–1850', *Journal of Transport History*, vol. 7, no. 2, November 1965.

'Norwich in the Eighteenth Century: A Study in Social and Economic Organisation', 1972, Manuscript in Local Studies Library, Norwich.

Emsley, C. J., *English Society and the French Wars 1793–1815*, London and Basingstoke 1979.

Everett, N. H., 'Country Justice: The Literature of Landscape Improvement and English Conservatism with Particular Reference to the 1790's', unpublished Ph.D. thesis, University of Cambridge 1977.

Farington, J., *The Diary of Joseph Farington*, ed. K. Garlick and A. Macintyre; K. Cave, 16 vols., New Haven and London 1978–84.

Fawcett, T., 'The Culture of later Georgian Norwich: a Conflict of Evidence', *UEA Bulletin*, vol. 4, no. 4, March 1972.

The Rise of English Provincial Art: Artists, Patrons, and Institutions outside London, 1800–1830, Oxford 1974.

'Thorpe Water Frolic', *Norfolk Archaeology*, vol. 36, Part 4, 1977.

Finberg, A. J., *The Life of J. M. W. Turner, R.A.*, Oxford 1961.

Finberg, H. F., 'Turner's Gallery in 1810', *Burlington Magazine*, vol. 93, December 1951.

Fitzwilliam Museum, Cambridge, *John Linnell: A Centennial Exhibition*, text by K. Crouan, Cambridge 1982.

Ford, J., *ACKERMANN 1783–1983 the Business of Art*, London 1983.

Ford, J. & G., *Images of Brighton*, Richmond-upon-Thames 1981.

Foucault, M., *The Archaeology of Knowledge*, London 1974.

Fullerton, P., 'Patronage and Pedagogy: The British Institution in the Early Nineteenth Century', *Art History*, vol. 5, no. 1, March 1982.

Gage, J., *Colour in Turner: Poetry and Truth*, London 1969

J. M. W. Turner, 'A Wonderful Range of Mind', New Haven and London 1987.

'An Early Exhibition and the Politics of British Printmaking, 1800–1812', *Print Quarterly*, vol. 6, no. 2, June 1989.

ed., *Collected Correspondence of J. M. W. Turner*, Oxford 1980.

Gear, J., *Masters or Servants ? A Study of Selected English Painters and Their Patrons of the Late Eighteenth and Early Nineteenth Centuries*, New York and London 1977.

Gilbert, A. D., *Religion and Society in Industrial England: Church, Chapel, and Social Change, 1740–1914*, London and New York 1976.

Golt, J., 'Beauty and Meaning on Richmond Hill: New Light on Turner's Masterpiece of 1819', *Turner Studies*, vol. 7, no. 2, Winter 1987.

Gombrich, E., *Art and Illusion*, London 1972.

Goodman, N., *Languages of Art*, Brighton 1981.

'The Status of Style', *Critical Inquiry*, no. 1, 1975.

Habermas, J., 'The Public Sphere: An Encyclopedia Article', *New German Critique*, vol. 1, no. 3, Fall 1974.

Halévy, E., *The Growth of Philosophic Radicalism*, London 1972.

Hall, D., 'The Tabley House Papers', *Walpole Society*, vol. 38, 1960–2.

Hawcroft, F., 'John Crome and the Yarmouth Water-Frolic', *Burlington Magazine*, vol. 150, July/August 1959.

'Crome and his Patron; Thomas Harvey of Catton', *Connoisseur*, vol. 144, December 1959.

Review of D. & T. Clifford, *John Crome*, *Burlington Magazine*, vol. 111, December 1969.

Hawes, L., *John Constable's Writings on Art*, Ph.D. thesis, Princeton University 1963, Ann Arbor University Microfilms 1964.

Hayden, J. O., *The Romantic Reviewers 1802–24*, London 1969.

Haydon, B. R., *The Diary of Benjamin Robert Haydon*, ed. W. B. Pope, 5 vols., Cambridge, Mass. 1960–3.

Hazlitt, W., *The Complete Works of William Hazlitt in Twenty-One Volumes*, ed. P. P. Howe, London and Toronto 1930–4.

Hemingway, A. F., 'Meaning in Cotman's Norfolk Subjects', *Art History*, vol. 7, no. 1, March 1984.

'Academic Theory versus Association Aesthetics: The Ideological Forms of a Conflict of Interests in the Early Nineteenth Century', *Ideas and Production*, Issue 5, 1986.

'The Political Theory of Painting without the Politics', review of John Barrell's *The Political Theory of Painting from Reynolds to Hazlitt*, *Art History*, vol. 10, no. 3, September 1987.

'Cultural Philanthropy and the Invention of the Norwich School', *Oxford Art Journal*, vol. 11, no. 3, 1988.

'The Sociology of Taste in the Scottish Enlightenment', *Oxford Art Journal*, vol. 12, no. 2, 1989.

Hill, C., 'The Norman Yoke', in J. Saville, ed., *Democracy and the Labour Movement: Essays in Honour of Dona Torr*, London 1954.

Hilles, ed., *Portraits by Sir Joshua Reynolds*, London 1952.

Hipple, W. J., *The Beautiful, the Sublime, & the Picturesque in Eighteenth-Century British Aesthetic Theory*, Carbondale, Ill. 1957.

Hont, I., & Ignatieff, M., ed., *Wealth and Virtue: The Shaping of Political Economy in the Scottish Enlightenment*, Cambridge 1983.

Horn, P., *The Rural World 1780–1850: Social Change in the English Countryside*, London 1980.

Jewson, C. B., *The Jacobin City, A Portrait of Norwich in its Reaction to the French Revolution 1788–1802*, Glasgow and London 1975.

Kallich, M., *The Association of Ideas and Critical Theory in Eighteenth-Century England*, The Hague and Paris 1970.

Kauffmann, C. M., *John Varley 1778–1842*, London 1984.

Kitson, S. D., *The Life of John Sell Cotman*, London 1937.

Koss, S., *The Rise and Fall of the Political Press in Britain*, vol. 1, London 1981.

Kristeller, P. O., 'The Modern System of the Arts', in *Renaissance Thought II, Papers on Humanism and the Arts*, New York 1965.

Laqueur, T. W., 'The Queen Caroline Affair: Politics as Art in the Reign of George IV', *Journal of Modern History*, no. 54, September 1982.

Larrain, J., *The Concept of Ideology*, London 1979.

Marxism and Ideology, London 1983.

Lee, R. W., *'Ut pictura poesis': The Humanistic Theory of Painting*, New York 1970.

Lehmann, W. C., *John Millar of Glasgow 1735–1801: His Life and Thought and his Contributions to Sociological Analysis*, Cambridge 1960.

Leslie, C. R., *Handbook for Young Painters* (1855), London 1887.

Lindsay, J., *J. M. W. Turner: A Critical Biography*, London 1966.

The Sunset Ship: The Poems of J. M. W. Turner, London 1966.

Lovejoy, A. O., *Essays in the History of Ideas*, Baltimore 1948.

McKendrick, N., Brewer, J., & Plumb, J. H., *The Birth of a Consumer Society: The Commercialisation of Eighteenth-Century England*, London 1983.

Meek, R. L., *Social Science and the Ignoble Savage*, Cambridge 1976.

Messmann, F. J., *Richard Payne Knight: The Twilight of Virtuosity*, The Hague 1974.

Mitchell, W. J. T., *Iconology: Image, Text, Ideology*, Chicago and London 1986.

Moir, E., *The Discovery of Britain – The English Tourists 1540–1840*, London 1964.

Monk, S. H., *The Sublime: A Study of Critical Theories in XVIII-Century England*, Ann Arbor 1960.

Moore, A., *The Norwich School of Artists*, Norwich 1985.

Mosley, P., 'Much Ado about Norwich?', *UEA Bulletin*, vol. 5, no. 5, June 1973.

Nesbitt, G., *Benthamite Reviewing: The First Twelve Years of the Westminster Review 1824–1836*, New York 1934.

Nicolson, M. H., *Mountain Gloom and Mountain Glory: The Development of the Aesthetics of the Infinite*, Ithaca, NY 1959.

Norwich Castle Museum, *A Decade of English Naturalism 1810–1820*, text by J. Gage, Norwich 1969.

Park, R., *Hazlitt and the Spirit of the Age: Abstraction and Critical Theory*, Oxford 1971.

Parker, R., & Pollock, G., *Old Mistresses: Women, Art and Ideology*, London and Henley 1981.

Pears, I., *The Discovery of Painting: The Growth of Interest in the Arts in England 1680–1768*, New Haven and London 1988.

Pimlott, J. A. R., *The Englishman's Holiday: A Social History* (1947), Brighton 1976.

Plumb, J. H., 'The Public, Literature and the Arts in the Eighteenth Century', in M. R. Marrus, ed., *The Emergence of Leisure*, New York 1974.

Pocock, J. G. A., 'Civic Humanism and its Role in Anglo-American Thought', in *Politics, Language and Time: Essays on Political Thought and History*, London 1972.

Pointon, M., 'Portrait-painting as a Business Enterprise in London in the 1780s', *Art History*, vol. 7, no. 2, June 1984.

Mulready, catalogue to an exhibition at the Victoria & Albert Museum, London 1986.

Pope, A., *The Poems of Alexander Pope*, ed. E. Audra & A. Williams, London 1961.

Potts, A., 'Picturing the Modern Metropolis: Images of London in the Nineteenth Century', *History Workshop Journal*, issue 26, Autumn 1988.

Prothero, I., *Artisans and Politics in Early Nineteenth-century London: John Gast and his Times*, London 1981.

Rajnai, M., with Stevens, M., *The Norwich Society of Artists 1805–1833, A Dictionary of Contributors and their Work*, Norwich 1976.

Reading Museum & Art Gallery, *William Havell 1732–1857*, text by F. Owen and E. Stanford, Reading 1981.

Reynolds, G., *Victoria and Albert Museum, Catalogue of the Constable Collection*, London 1973.

The Late Paintings and Drawings of John Constable, 2 vols., New Haven and London 1984.

Rogers, N., 'Money, Land and Lineage: the Big Bourgeoisie of Hanoverian London', *Social History*, vol. 4, no. 3, October 1979.

Rorty, R., *Philosophy and the Mirror of Nature*, Princeton, NJ, 1980.

Rosenthal, M., *Constable: The Painter and His Landscape*, New Haven and London 1983.

Ross, I. S., *Lord Kames and the Scotland of his Day*, Oxford 1972.

Rudé, G., *Hanoverian London 1714–1808*, London 1971.

Schapiro, M., 'Style', in A. L. Kroeber, ed., *Anthropology Today*, Chicago and London 1953.

'On Some Problems in the Semiotics of Visual Art: Field and Vehicle in Image-Signs', *Semiotica*, vol. 1, no. 3, 1969.

Shearer, E. A., 'Wordsworth and Coleridge Marginalia in a Copy of Richard Payne Knight's *Analytical Inquiry into the Principles of Taste*', *Huntington Library Quarterly*, vol. I, October 1937.

Smith, H., *Peter De Wint 1784–1849*, London 1982.

Solkin, D., *Richard Wilson: The Landscape of Reaction*, catalogue to an exhibition at the Tate Gallery, London 1982.

Solly, N. N., *Memoir of the Life of David Cox* (1873), London 1973.

Southey, R., *Letters from England* (1807), ed. J. Simmons, London 1951.

Stafford, W., *Socialism, Radicalism and Nostalgia: Social Criticism in Britain, 1775–1830*, Cambridge 1987.

Stolnitz, J., 'On the Origins of Aesthetic Disinterestedness', *Journal of Aesthetics and Art Criticism*, vol. 20, Winter 1961.

'"Beauty", Some Stages in the History of an Idea', *Journal of the History of Ideas*, vol. 22, no. 2, 1961.

'Locke and the Categories of Value in Eighteenth-Century British Aesthetic Theory', *Philosophy*, vol. 38, January 1963.

'"The Aesthetic Attitude" in the Rise of Modern Aesthetics', *Journal of Aesthetics and Art Criticism*, vol. 36, Summer 1978.

Stout, G. D., *The Political History of Leigh Hunt's Examiner*, Washington University Studies, n.s., Language and Literature, no. 19, Saint Louis, Mo. 1949.

Stuckey, C. F., 'Turner's Birthdays', *Turner Society News*, no. 21, April 1981.

Tate Gallery, London, *Turner 1775–1851*, text by M. Butlin, J. Gage & A. Wilton, London 1974.

Constable Paintings, Watercolours and Drawings, text by L. Parris, I. Fleming-Williams & C. Shields, London 1976.

Augustus Wall Callcott, text by D. B. Brown, London 1981.

Taylor, B., *Eve and the New Jerusalem: Socialism and Feminism in the Nineteenth Century*, London 1983.

Therborn, G., *The Ideology of Power and the Power of Ideology*, London 1980.

Thomas, W., *The Philosophic Radicals: Nine Studies in Theory and Practice 1817–1841*, Oxford 1979.

Thompson, E. P., 'Patrician Society, Plebian Culture', *Journal of Social History*, vol. 7, 1973–4.

'The Peculiarities of the English' (1965), in *The Poverty of Theory*, London 1978.

'Eighteenth-century English Society: Class Struggle without Class?', *Social History*, vol. 3, no. 2, May 1978.

The Making of the English Working Class (1963), Harmondsworth 1980.

Thomson, J., *The Complete Poetical Works of James Thomson*, Oxford 1908.

Tuveson, E., *The Imagination as a Means of Grace*, Berkeley and Los Angeles 1960.

Victoria & Albert Museum, London, *Joshua Cristall 1768–1847*, text by B. Taylor, London 1975.

V. Vološinov, *Marxism and the Philosophy of Language*, New York 1973.

Walvin, J., *Beside the Seaside: A Social History of the Popular Seaside Holiday*, London 1978.

Wark, R. R., ed., *Sir Joshua Reynolds, Discourses on Art*, New Haven and London 1975.

Whitley, W. T., *Thomas Heaphy (1775–1835), First President of the Society of British Artists*, London 1933.

Whyman, J., 'A Hanoverian Watering Place: Margate before the Railway', in A. Everitt, ed., *Perspectives in English Urban History*, London 1973.

Williams, R., *Culture and Society 1780–1950*, Harmondsworth 1961.

The Country and the City, St Albans 1973.

Culture, Glasgow 1981.

Wordsworth, W., & Coleridge, S. T., *Lyrical Ballads* (1789, 1800), ed. R. L. Brett and A. R. Jones, London and New York 1965.

Wright, E. O., *Classes*, London 1985.

Yarrington, A., 'Nelson the Citizen Hero: State and Public Patronage of Monumental Sculpture 1805–18', *Art History*, vol. 6, no. 3, September 1983.

Ziff, J., '"Backgrounds: Introduction of Architecture and Landscape": A Lecture by J. M. W. Turner', *Journal of the Warburg and Courtauld Institutes*, vol. 26, 1963.

Index